Nathalie Prézeau

Fifth Edition

TORONTO
FUN
PLACES
... for families

The family-tested guide to
year-round fun in and around
the GTA and Southern Ontario

Word
— of —
Mouth
Production

This book is dedicated
to Laurent and Roxane for having always been
so kindly oblivious to my camera.

Published by Word-of-Mouth Production
299 Booth Avenue
Toronto, Ontario M4M 2M7, Canada
Tel.: (416) 462-0670
mail@torontofunplaces.com

www.torontofunplaces.com

Writing and photos: **Nathalie Prézeau**
Illustrations: **Johanne Pepin**
Research assistants: **Claudette Gravel, Claire Marier, Julie Sabourin**
Proofreading: **Kerstin McCutcheon**
Design and layout: **Publisher Friendly** (416) 465-2107
Printing: **Marquis Book Printing Inc.** (418) 246-5666

Library and Archives Canada Cataloguing in Publication

Prézeau, Nathalie, 1960 –
        Toronto fun places ... for families/Nathalie Prézeau – 5th ed.

Includes index.
ISBN 978-0-9684432-5-5
Fourth edition published in 2008
Third edition published in 2004
Second edition published in 2001
First edition published in 1999 under title:
Toronto: the family-tested guide to fun places

1. Family recreation – Ontario – Toronto Region – Guidebooks.
2. Toronto Region (Ont.) – Guidebooks. I. Title.

FC3097.18.P74 2011   917.13'541045   C2011-901757-1

A word from the author

Kids grow fast! I started the research for Toronto Fun Places in 1995 with my 2-year-old and here I am, 16 years later, with a fifth edition.

My little blond guy is now a 6-foot musician and my baby girl has turned into a mini version of myself at 14 (but much cuter). And you know what? It will happen to you too!

Fortunately, some things never change, such as my great friendships with the funny women who undertook the big adventure of motherhood with me.

Together, we've shared tips, tears and laughter throughout the different phases of development. (As they say, it takes a village to raise a child.)

My wish is for this guide to inspire you to steal some time now and then from your busy schedule to enjoy the ride with your friends and family. Believe me, those are the moments that will stick with you for years to come.

It is always a pleasure to search, find and share the excitement with you.

Sincerely,

Nathalie Prézeau
mail@torontofunplaces.com

TABLE OF CONTENTS

PLAYGROUNDS

SPORTS

CALL FIRST!
All the information was accurate at the time of print (March 2011). Before going to an attraction, I recommend you call first (sometimes, even the websites don't reflect the latest changes):
• To make sure that it still exists.
• That it's open on the day you go, and not closed for private functions
• That the one thing your child really wants to see in this attraction is still offered.
• Most places are closed on December 25 and January 1.

About the TTC

• FUN PLACES bearing the bus symbol offer **TTC** (Toronto Transit Commission) public transportation (subway, bus or streetcar) in their vicinity. Those without might still be reached by another local public transportation system.

• To find out about the **TTC** route to an attraction, go to www.ttc.ca to their *Trip Planner* section. Type the name of a major intersection or landmark (ex. Queen @ Logan, or Jimmie Simson Park) at your starting and arriving points. You will get the name of the route suggested, details of the trip as well as time estimate (including walking time).

• You can also call **TTC Infoline** (416) 393-4636 (press "0" to reach someone in person from 8 am to 6 pm, 7 days a week except during Holidays).

ABOUT CALENDARS OF EVENTS

Feeling up to it?

My favourite kind of outing used to involve a latte in a nice café, with a great book and a sleeping baby in a stroller. When they're older, this just won't do. They need to explore the world. You need to save your furniture. So off you go, but where? That is the question.

A good calendar of events is a wonderful tool to find out about seasonal activities, Holiday outings and P.D. day and March Break specials, or simply to avoid cabin fever on the weekend.

Many websites for parents have worked very hard for years to create and maintain exhaustive calendars of local family events. So I thought, why reinvent the wheel in my guide? Here are the ones with the most ambitious calendars, incidentally, all managed by local moms. (You go girls!)

Once you've found the calendar of events with the format that best suits you, I recommend you subscribe to their mailing list to get regular news on the latest happenings.

www.kidsaroundcanada.com
(Click *Events Calendar*.)

You can click *Today*, *Tomorrow*, or any day on the monthly calendar on the right hand side for a list of activities to browse through for that specific date.

The info page you access when clicking on the link for an activity offers a clean and easy-to-read layout with a great time-saving feature: the listing of all the other dates for this event.

Check their *E*Magazine* (in which I've contributed a few articles, I must add). It includes many regular columnists.

www.toronto4kids.com
(Click *Events*.)

You can choose a category and/or a date. You can also select *Free Events Only* to zero in right away on free activities.

If you're a dog owner, go to their *Dog Zone*. It includes information on all kinds of resources, products and services (dog walkers, dog sitters), and a selection of interesting dog related articles.

www.helpwevegotkids.com
(Click *Event Calendar*.)

You'll get a list of events by dates, in three columns with a clear layout (for the current month and the following two).

They're the ones who started it all in 1994 (before Internet), with their book *Help We've got kids*, offering a printed version of GTA's complete family resources. You can order their yearly directory from their website (through Amazon).

www.littlepaper.com

(Choose a category under their *Find it fast* section to get a listing of activities for this category.)

Check their *Latest tipsheet*. I've often found funky little local suggestions in there such as Bike Courier's Races on ice at Dufferin Grove Park, an Uberswap Clothing and Toy Swap at Lil' Bean n' Green Café.

Other useful references

www.torontopubliclibrary.ca

(Click on *Programs, Classes & Exhibits*.)

Check the featured programs or browse programs by branch for schedules. The **Toronto Public Library** offers a line-up of free drop-in shows, storytelling and other family activities in its different branches.

www.cinemaclock.com

(Click on *Theatres*, then select a theatre in the city of your choice to get its listing.)

When you click on a movie on the list, you get a great page with description, preview, links to all the actors involved and, most importantly, access to the public's reviews for that movie.

www.familyfun.com

(Click on *Crafts*, then *All Holiday and Seasonal Crafts*.)

OK, I'm cheating here. This one is for when you don't feel like leaving the house. Their Holiday section covers all possible occasions.

I also really like their *Crafts by Material* section. (Very handy, because you don't feel like leaving the house, remember? And the last thing you want to do is to choose a craft activity for which you lack the material!)

www.meetup.com

(Click on *Find a Meetup Group*.)

Meetup's mission: "to help the world's people to self-organize into local groups". Search by postal code and interest (family), then select a distance (within 3 kms) to find an existing group you might want to join in your neighbourhood. Or better yet, create a new one!

How to use this guide

In **Toronto Fun Places**, you'll find seasonal symbols indicating when an attraction offers specific activities for **March Break**, **Easter**, **Halloween** or **Christmas**.

When an outing suggestion in your favourite calendar of events catches your attention, I encourage you to check **Toronto Fun Places**' index to see if this event (or the attraction in which it is taking place) is featured in the guide.

I have personally visited all the places described in this book, so you will get a better idea of what to expect. This should hopefully help you decide if the outing would be fun for your child.

My descriptions always include **TIPS** from a mother's point of view and suggestions of **Nearby Attractions** for a full day trip.

General tips about
Amusement Corner:

- Always check height requirements before waiting in line! Most amusement parks are really strict about these. And no! Fluffing your kid's hair over her head won't do!
- Be ready to spend a lot on all the extra costs in most amusement parks: higher cost for snack bar food and bottled water, special activity with an extra cost on top of the admission fee, parking.
- In most cases, if you intend on visiting a specific attraction more than twice during the season, consider investing in a season pass. It will be approximately the same cost but will take out the stress of feeling that you're not getting your money's worth if you don't stay until closing time! You can come back when you want when you have a few hours.
- Note that prices are to be considered as a reference. Some places include tax in the fees they advertise, others don't.

AMUSEMENT
CORNER

See **Lucky Strike Lanes** on p. 23.

ABOUT PARTIES

Bring it on!

I really enjoy throwing parties. (I've done most of my kids' birthday parties at home.) And for years, I was the end-of-school party planner at their elementary school. So, of course I'm hooked on Party Packagers.

I've bought a few birthday party packages at attractions and loved them. They're perfect for moms who don't have the inclination nor the time, but usually end up being quite expensive.

I figured out that one money-saving advantage to planning a kid's party at home was that it allowed me to make sure the loot bag would include things that could be used during the party, which the kids would take home after. (Just make sure you throw in a few candies and you're good to go!)

I've never decided on a theme for a party before going to **Party Packagers** to check out what they had in stock. I'd find the item that gave the most bang for the buck and would work around it.

One year, I bought cheap fishing gear with plastic fish included. It became a fishing party. I made the guests fish in a huge bucket. We had a fish cake, Golden Fish crackers, etc. The kids couldn't believe their luck when I handed them the rod and fish in a loot bag at the end of the party. (Did I say not to forget the candies?)

Another year, there were little guns and bandanas. We did a cowboy party with a cactus cake and Wanted posters featuring two of the dads. (They were caught and tied up to a tree by the little sheriffs.)

When my daughter turned 12, we got plenty of fuzzy balls which light up and suspended them from the trees in our backyard. I invested in sparklers and silly string for the preteens to go crazy in the park. The guests left with the balls.

Party Packagers also sells $15 rolls of large plastic fabric in many colours. Meant to be cut into table covers, I've cut them into fringes to create rivers, stripes to weave into ugly wire fences, costumes for school parties, flowers for decoration.

For more tips about parties, go to *Party Centre* on their website.

TIPS (to plan a birthday party)

• Every attraction in this guide featuring the **Birthday** symbol offers birthday packages.

• Some birthday packages don't leave much time. You don't want your child to waste it unwrapping gifts, she can do it at home. Make sure you're clear on the time allowed in the birthday room and in the attraction.

• A childhood friend of mine has created a website which might interest you: **www.birthdaysongbox.com**. He's a professional singer who's done jingles for the best TV commercials in Quebec and has lent his voice for the French version of songs in Disney's most popular animated movies. From his website, you can download for free an original birthday song personalized for over 100 names, each in five different musical styles.

Party Packagers
www.partypackagers.com

 Schedule: The stores are open Monday to Friday, 10 am to 9 pm, Saturday, 9:30 am to 6 pm and Sunday, 11 am to 5 pm.
Directions: Go to their website and click on their *Store Locator* for a list of over 20 stores in Ontario, with maps.

POLSON PIER

O Boy!

There's lots of action to observe from Toronto's largest waterfront patio: police boats, tall ships, ferries, with Toronto's Islands as a backdrop on one side and the CN Tower by the lakeshore on the other. And it just got better, thanks to a partnership with O Boy! Burger Market (declared by some as the best burger and onion rings joint in Toronto).

The administration that took over a few years ago tried many things, including offering a skatepark and a snowboarding slope by the water (both of which they dropped).

They now seem to have found their stride. In the last years, they've improved their patio experience and maintained the activities which have always worked well at that location: the drive-in, the driving range and the mini golf. They've focused on their rental services (indoor soccer dome, outdoor beach volleyball courts, event venue), added a line-up of concerts in their venue **Sound Academy** and created a new go-kart track.

What really does the trick for me is the 40,000 square foot waterfront patio. It is the best place to sip a drink by the water (with or without alcohol... or kids).

TIPS (fun for 8 years +)
• Bring a sweater for evenings on the patio.
• Parking is free by go-karts and mini golf.
• Some concerts presented at the Sound Academy can be attended by all ages (the shows' rating are stated on their website).

NEARBY ATTRACTIONS
Cherry Beach (2-min.) .... p. 395

It even offers a few games such as ping pong (for a fee), which could help keep the kids busy while you admire Lake Ontario and the city's lights.

Last time we visited during the summer, my kids wanted to swim in the octagonal pool in the middle of the patio. Denied! (Me? Paying to parade in a bathing suit, in a 4-foot- deep fenced pool surrounded by customers leisurely watching?)

The driving range is open year-round. It turns into a drive-in theatre on weekends during the warmer nights, screening a double-feature of the latest movies. (In 2011, they've added a second screen on the southwest side of the drive-in space.)

When weather allows, they open the mini golf behind the driving range and the adjacent go-kart track. (They have some Rookie Karts for kids 11 to 15 years old; younger kids can ride with drivers 18 years and over in the double seaters.)

Polson Pier
(416) 461-3625
www.polsonpier.com
www.gokartsatpolson
pier.com

D-3
Downtown
Toronto
5-min.

Schedule: The driving range is open year-round (they use orange balls and heated tees in the winter). Weather permitting, the other outdoor activities open from Victoria Day to Labour Day. The drive-in theatre opens Friday to Sunday (screening starting at 9:30-10 pm). The patio opens at 12 noon (kids not allowed after 9 pm).

Admission: Swimming Pool: $10/ adults, $6/12 years and under. **Mini golf**: $6/adults, $4/12 years and under ($2 more on the weekends). **Drive-in theatre**'s double feature is $13/adults, $4/3-12 years old. **Go-kart**: $2.50 per lap or $20 for 20 minutes. (Parking is $10, $15 if you arrive after 6 pm.)

Directions: 11 Polson St., Toronto. Take Cherry St. southbound (note that you can't turn left on Cherry St. when driving westbound on Lake Shore Blvd.), turn west on Polson.

ONTARIO PLACE

In the first place

Ontario Place is an excellent water park as well as theme park. The numerous rides offer adrenaline rushes for young and old. It is also entertaining, with Imax movies and numerous musical shows on different stages. Finally, it is like a conservation area, with paddle boats, large green spaces and the surrounding lake.

For those who have never visited it, **Ontario Place**'s architecture is an attraction in itself. Children enjoy watching people from the bridges linking the huge white pods built atop the water in the western part of the park. You'll find the **Imax** theatre in the sphere attached to the white structure.

West Island

Riding one of the paddle boats from **Bob's Boatyard** (included with the Play-All-Day pass) is a great way to admire it all. It is located in the **GoZone** in the western part of the park.

In the GoZone, we really were excited by the **Atom Blaster**. There, parents become the favourite targets for foam balls launched by air cannons. The less combative kids prefer to feed the balls into a huge cannon which eventually will blow them to the ceiling in a spectacular blast.

Nearby **H₂O Generation Station** is an impressive structure composed of towers linked by tunnels. Some transparent ones are way up high!

In **Adventure Island**, further west, is the infamous **Wilderness Adventure Ride** (42"+): A raft ride

through canyons that features animated characters with a final 50-foot drop. Bring a garbage bag to cover yourself if you want to stay dry!

The **F/X Adventure Theatre** in that area includes a 30-seat motion simulator taking you on a ride. The **Megamaze** was replaced in 2009 by the **Wild World of Weather** where I'm told you can feel the shake of an earthquake as well as fog, rain and snow.

In the **Marina Village**, closer to the big white Cinesphere, you'll find the **O.P. Driving School** (for drivers 40" to 60"). It comes with real traffic lights! The smile on their faces... The older kids will want to ride on the **Bumper Boats** (48"+).

Cinesphere

Cinesphere is the biggest Imax theatre in the GTA. The experience can be somewhat hard on young eardrums but it is impressive for those who've never been into an Imax theatre. And it can cool the kids on a very hot summer day. In early 2011, it has undergone major renovations (3D screen, new seats, new floors).

Walk east past the Cinesphere and you'll get to the water park section.

West Island

By the water park section, in the **Market Square**, is the **Treehouse Live! Stage** with free live shows and the mini golf. Further north in that section, younger children will love the **Mini Bumper Boats** and the **Power Wheels Cars** (both 36" min. to 48" max.),

but expect a long line-up. Fly down the **Super Slide** with your kids 36" and over. Bigger kids will be happy with the **Free Fall** ride (42" min.).

In the summer, we now can watch dynamic wakeboard and waterski shows in the body of water next to what they call the **South Beach**.

TIPS (fun for 2 years +)

• Ground admission is the cheapest way to visit if you just intend on accompanying a young child to the water park and to the kiddie rides. It allows you to watch shows on outdoor stages or special events such as the **Canadian International Air Show** and the fireworks.

• You can always upgrade your ground admission to an all-day pass or buy Pay-as-you-play tickets for some of the rides on the site if you change your mind.

• There is usually a water shuttle linking both islands but I recommend you try to end your visit in the part of the park that is the closest to your parking spot. Kids will be exhausted after all this fun.

• Ontario Place usually offers some major **firework** displays. Expect at least one on **Canada Day**.

• Cinesphere continues to offer screenings until the end of December. During the **March Break**, you can also see movies at the **Cinesphere** and maybe, like us, see swans on the icy lake! Check the schedule on their website. Parking is $5 off season. (Fees for movies at the newly renovated Cinesphere were not available at the time of print.)

• There's a free shuttle bus running from **Union Subway Station** during **Ontario Place**'s operating hours (except for weekdays in June).

• More about **Soak City**, Ontario Place's water park, on p. 425.

Ontario Place
(416) 314-9900
www.ontarioplace.com

D-3
Downtown
Toronto
10-min.

Schedule: Open weekends in May and on Victoria Day. Open daily from the first weekend in June until Labour Day, then weekends in September. Attractions open 10 am to 8 pm in July and August. ATTENTION: Shorter hours in June and in the fall!

Admission: (tax not included) **Play-All-Day** with the ground admission is around $32/6-64 years, $17/seniors and 4-5 years, FREE for children 3 and under and $100/family of 4. **Ground admission** alone is around $17/6-64 years, $11/seniors and 4-5 years. Call to confirm. **Parking:** $12 (reaches $20 during special events and CNE).

Directions: 955 Lake Shore Blvd., Toronto (turn south at the set of lights at the corner of Lake Shore and Newfoundland Rd., west of Strachan Ave.).

CANADA'S WONDERLAND

In Planet Snoopy, young kids will have the chance to get a hug from Snoopy and his gang.

More rides

In the **Medieval Faire** is the **Speed City Raceway** (where cars run on 9 hp engines), for older riders (58", or 40"+ with an adult).

We love the gorgeous animals on the large **Antique Carousel** (46"+, or any age with an adult) in the **Action Zone**. On our way there from the main entrance, we watched with fascination the "crazies" who leap from the top of the **Xtreme Sky Flyer** tower (48"+), the one you jump off with a bungee cord; a show in itself!

Then, it was my own son with his life hanging by one thread! "You have to try it!" he exclaimed after his jump. Yeah, sure!

Do your kids measure up?

I figure children measuring less than 40 inches tall can access about 40% of the rides and attractions. When they reach 44", two rides out of three become accessible to them. As soon as they're 48" tall, they're allowed on over 80% of Wonderland's attractions and roller coasters.

Children's rides

The **Candy Factory** is a great playground where kids can use up lots of energy. Near it are two areas for children: **Kidzville** and **Planet Snoopy**.

If your children are comfortable with the **Taxi Jam** roller coaster (40", or 36" with adult) you might want them to try the **Ghoster Coaster** (46"+, or 40"+ with adult).

Our other favourite rides in these sections include the **Frequent Flyers'** hot air balloons, the turning cups of the **Flavourator** and the bumper cars (**Joe Cool's Dodgem School**, 36"+).

Kidzville features more exciting rides for young thrill-seekers. There's **Silver Streak**, the long suspended coaster, **Blast Off** where kids rise and drop on a rocket ship, and **Jumpin' Jet**, flying riders through looping spins.

Shows

Aquatic shows are available at **Arthur's Baye** and professionals dive daily from atop the mountain waterfall.

There's the **Action Theatre** (46"+), a motion simulator with seats that move in sync with the action on the screen. (There's motionless seating for kids 44" and under.) In 2010, they added a **Snoopy Rocks** ice show (google *snoopy ice show* to get an idea).

More big rides

When my son hit 54", all of a sudden he could go on all the gut-wrenching rides: **Drop Zone**, **Psyclone**, **Cliffhanger** and the likes.

My first choice is the **Thunder Run**, going through the mountain (46"+, or 40" with adult). It puts you in good spirits for the day!

Photo: Courtesy of R.Giddings

Further on, you're sure to get wet (if you haven't covered yourself with a garbage bag) at the **White Water Canyon** and the **Timberwolf Falls** (both 46"+)!

From the water park section, we can hear the cries of thrill-seekers riding at full speed on the **Mighty Canadian Minebuster** (48"+) and those (of horror, I suspect) of the **SkyRider** passengers, tracing loops with their feet hanging in the air. For roller coaster fans, there are many other options including the **Time Warp** in which you are hung under a hang- glider-like structure. A few thrill rides are accessible to children of 44 inches and over.

In 2008, they added the **Behemoth** (Canada's tallest, fastest roller coaster). In 2011, it's the **Windseeker**, a 30-storey (yes, 30) high swing ride running at up to 50 kms per hour. Where will this end?

TIPS (fun for 3 years +)
• More about **Splash Works**, Canada's Wonderland's water park, on p. 427.
• Canada's Wonderland will please children of all ages but for children measuring under 44", I recommend sticking to **Ontario Place** (see p. 16).
• Consult the *Ride Guidelines* for a table with height requirement on their website (under *Rides & Attractions*). I saw several children crying their hearts out after a long wait for a ride, as they were finding out they weren't tall enough.
• The best way to enjoy the Wonderland experience is to arrive at opening time and go straight to your favourite ride! Then, spend some time studying the map and schedule of shows, available at the entrance, to plan your day.
• There usually is a **fireworks** display on Sunday of **Victoria Day** weekend and maybe on **Canada Day**. Check their website for confirmation.
• They offer a **Halloween Haunt** in October when the park is converted into a "dark playground" with several mazes, lots of monsters and many regular rides. NOT recommended for kids under 13 and NO costumes, for security reasons. Costs around $35.
• They've also created **Camp Spooky** for the younger kids (Halloween action in Planet Snoopy), included with day activities during October weekends.
• Closest campground is **Yogi Bear's Jellystone Park**, (905) 775-1377, www.jellystonetoronto.com.

NEARBY ATTRACTIONS
Reptilia (5-min.) .... p. 72

Canada's Wonderland
• Vaughan

C-3
North
of Toronto
40-min.

(905) 832-8131
www.canadaswonderland.com

Schedule: Open on weekends starting the first Sunday in May right through to Thanksgiving and daily from Victoria Day to Labour Day. Open from 10 am to 10 pm in the summer (closes at 8 pm in Spring and Fall). Also open in October, Friday to Sunday + October 31, 7 pm to midnight for Halloween. Check their website closer to opening day for confirmation.

Admission: (taxes not included) around $56/adults, $33/3 years old to kids up to 48 inches tall and seniors, FREE for 2 years and under. Parking is around $10.

Directions: 9580 Jane St., Vaughan. Take Hwy 401, then Hwy 400 North. Take exit Rutherford Rd. (#33) eastbound.

PLAYDIUM MISSISSAUGA

Jump-start into adolescence

In awe, my son proceeds into a cold-coloured corridor which leads him under an interstellar-like canopy with noisy machines scattered around. Then, his eye is caught by sculptures reaching towards a black ceiling with coloured dots; luminous floor drawings dance to background music.

I am so terrible at the video games that I keep "dying" within 60 seconds. It's another story for my son and his buddies! They spend a long time competing against each other in the **Indy 500** race cars.

The place includes over 200 games. Many are physically fun to ride (and the demos shown on their screens are often entertaining enough for little ones so you won't have to spend a penny): motorcycle, surf, seadoo, cross-country biking, flight simulator.

Last time I visited, my 10-year-old companions were really interested in a soccer game (with ball attached) and basketball.

In the summer, there is a mini golf and a 1.2 km go-kart track awaiting outside. We opted for the latter. Go-kart riders need to be 52"+ and 11 years old (they'll ask you your date of birth!). They also offer seasonal rides such as bungee trampoline, rock climbing and **Water Wars**. (Yes, you can pay for water balloons and use a catapult to attack your opponent behind a trench!)

Last but not least, there's a whole section of redemption games dispensing tickets which can be exchanged for trinkets. Don't grind your teeth, it comes with the territory. I think kids enjoy the machines counting the tickets as much as the games themselves.

There's an indoor **Baseball Dome** (accessible from a corridor near the food area). This section offers many batting cages where you can use your Play Card.

TIPS (fun for 5 years +)
• Call before you go to avoid disappointment. All or part of the Playdium may be closed for a private function.
• Beware, the noise level is very high!
• Don't hesitate to ask the attendants how a game works. If you have had troubles, they might even credit games for you.
• There's decent fast food sold on site.
• **Coliseum Mississauga Cinemas** is a 1-min. drive west of the Playdium.

NEARBY ATTRACTIONS
Square One (2-min.) .... p. 181
Pearson Int'l Airport (15-min.) ...... p. 190

Playdium Mississauga • Mississauga (905) 273-9000 www.playdium.com	D-3 West of Toronto 30-min.

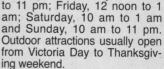

Schedule: Open year-round, Monday to Thursday, 12 noon to 11 pm; Friday, 12 noon to 1 am; Saturday, 10 am to 1 am and Sunday, 10 am to 11 pm. Outdoor attractions usually open from Victoria Day to Thanksgiving weekend.

Admission: On a pay-as-you-play basis debited from your **Play Card**. Family Power Pack offers 160 credits for $25 (min. 2 family members). The average game costs 4-6 credits. Go-kart is $4/lap, $22/9 laps; $4/mini golf; $4-$8/seasonal ride; $3/bucket of 6 water balloons.

Directions: 99 Rathburn Rd., Mississauga (just south of Hwy 403 and west of Hurontario).

DAVE & BUSTER'S

For big... and small kids

What is this place exactly? Isn't it for adults? Can kids go? Is it big? Is it fun? Is it a restaurant? All of the above, and a little bit more.

Some of you might have heard about this entertainment complex... at the office. It is actually a popular corporate outing and primarily an adult establishment. But their arcade section is such a "natural" fit for kids that they have come up with a house policy to suit all ages.

Basically, guests under 19 years old (the legal drinking age) must be accompanied by a parent or a guardian 25 years or older. One guardian can accompany up to six young guests.

Entering this establishment feels like entering a casino. A large portion of the complex hosts a posh restaurant with bars and pool tables (as well as an amazing indoor golf simulator you can rent by the hour). All the action for kids (small and big) takes place in what they call the midway section.

From your children's perspective, passing its threshold will be like entering Alibaba's cave. There are some 250 games, all competing for your attention so expect noise!

A huge counter bar greets you at the entrance. Around the bar area are retro black-lacquered booths lined with red vinyl. We grabbed one and it became our meeting point for the next three hours.

A third of the floor, to the left, is covered with games rewarding players with coupons they can exchange for trinkets or something fancy (remember, it's an adult place).

To the right, one finds all the virtual games technology can exploit. There were riding games (race cars, 18-wheelers, motorcycles, planes, tanks, helicopters), sports games (surfing, snowboarding, skiing, skating, football, basketball, hockey, golf, bowling, horse racing), hunting games (alien, dinosaurs... even turkeys!). The works!

TIPS (fun for 5 years +)

• When we visited, it was not busy at all so we had the chance to play on the funny horse-race track (against a wall to the left) where the winner gets 50 coupons. Since it was only our family playing, one of us was sure to win!

• The midway section offers an affordable kids' menu and edible adult food.

NEARBY ATTRACTIONS

Dave & Buster's • Vaughan (905) 760-7600 www.daveandbusters.com	**C-3** **North** of Toronto **30-min.**

  Schedule: Open from 11:30 am to midnight minimum. Kids can stay until 9 pm if with an adult 25 years and over.
Admission: The **Power Card** is $2 and you load the amount of money you want to spend on it.
Directions: 120 Interchange Way, Vaughan. Take Hwy 400 North. Turn east on Rutherford, then south on Jane St. and west on Interchange Way.

BOWLERAMA

Little kingpin

His young hands drop the balls more often than they manage to throw them. The tiny bowler stamps his feet, jumps up and down and huddles with anticipation. Adults' mute prayers and crossed fingers change to cries of joy, as the ball miraculously knocks down one of the five pins! A young champion is born, amidst the excitement of Bowlerama.

The day we visited, our group consisted of seven adults, three preschoolers and two babies. It was our first family bowling experience. Excitement was in the air as pins and balls rolled down 60 shining lanes, knocking noisily against one another.

It's a challenge to have little busy bodies try on bowling shoes! The ones my little lad put on didn't close properly, while his friend's were simply too large. Not to worry, it didn't hold anyone back from the game.

We registered. Up to six players can play on one lane. After a somewhat chaotic first round, we finally understood the key procedures, and were better able to focus on our delighted kids. They understood the idea: With three balls, you try to knock down five pins.

Of course, many other aspects of the game will elude them, such as respecting the line between two alleys, not running after the ball, waiting their turn... etc. Besides, little kingpins are different from adults. It was great to see their faces as they watched their ball roll towards its goal. Will it hit… or not? Well, it's hard to miss when you're bumper bowling!

TIPS (fun for 5 years +)

• When calling to reserve, mention you'll be bowling with younger children in order to get an alley lined with bumpers.

• Make sure you reserve a 5-pin lane, with the smaller and lighter balls. (They also have 10-pin lanes with big, heavy balls.)

• If you are in a Bowlerama which charges by the hour, accompany children to the washroom before registering! If you play beyond your allotted time, you'll be charged an additional hour.

• All Bowleramas offer glow-in-the-dark bowling, called **Cosmic Bowling**.

• As a souvenir, you can ask for a printout of your scores.

• In Toronto, **Thorncliffe Bowlerama** (www.thorncliffebowlerama.com, 45 Overlea Bldv., (416) 421-2211) and **Bathurst Bowlerama** (www.bathurstbowlerama.com, 2788 Bathurst St., (416) 782-1841) don't belong to the same owners. The online coupon doesn't apply.

• For a fancier experience, see **Lucky Strike Lanes** at Vaughan Mills on p. 23.

LUCKY STRIKE LANES & LOUNGE

Striking!

Stick to less expensive Bowlerama if your kids are young or if your family is new to bowling. Once you've upped your game, it will be fun to treat yourself with a visit to fancier Lucky Strike. Think lounge decor, food service at the 10-pin lanes and electronic game cards.

I was with a friend and three pre-teens when I visited this alley. We were all thrilled by the look of the place with the brightly lit red pool tables and the leather booths in blond wood stalls with their own lamp.

TIPS (fun for 8 years +)

• This bowling alley has 10-pin lanes with heavy large balls. The balls available at the lanes have different weights, the lightest being 6 pounds. You can ask for a bowling ramp (a device holding the ball for you, from which you push the ball) as well as bumper pads (to prevent the ball from running off the lane).

• More about **Vaughan Mills** on p. 71 and 183.

• At the time of print, a similar fancy bowling alley has opened in downtown Toronto, at Richmond and John: **The Ballroom**. It has 9 lanes for 10-pin bowling and costs around $25/8 people for 30 minutes, all ages accepted until 9 pm (www.theballroom.ca).

We ate in a booth, not realizing that they served food at the lanes. The pizza took a little while to arrive and the kids were impatient to play. Eating at the lane would have been the best scenario. We later ordered virgin drinks while we played.

The 22 polished lanes looked amazing, each of them reflecting the light of large screens lining the whole back wall. The screens were airing different sports shows all at once. Maybe not a good thing for those suffering from attention deficit but quite cool visually.

I have never played enough to remember how to calculate bowling scores from one time to the next. No problem! Here, the electronic board calculates everyone's score automatically at each lane. We had to get a little coaching to learn how to enter the info into the game but afterward, we were OK.

After each strike, the board would suggest how to play next time for maximum effect. As if I could control where my ball was going.

Lucky Strike Lanes & Lounge

• Vaughan
(905) 760-9931
www.bowlluckystrike.com

C-3
North
of Toronto
35-min.

Schedule: Open from 11 am to 11 pm, Sunday to Thursday (closes at 2 am, Fridays and Saturdays. (Kids can stay until 10 pm.)

Admission: Around $6/person per game; $4/shoes rental.

Directions: 1 Bass Pro Mills Dr., Vaughan. Take Hwy 400 North. Exit at Bass Pro Mills, turn north on Edgeley Blvd. and park near Entry 4 at **Vaughan Mills**.

NEARBY ATTRACTIONS

HARBOURFRONT CENTRE

Harbour fun

Harbourfront Centre sits on the edge of the water. Its waterfront terrace with panoramic views of Lake Ontario on one side and CN Tower on the other, the long promenade along the pier with its many choices of harbour cruises, and most of all, the large and small events taking place year-round, explain the site's huge popularity.

For the inquisitive mind, the **Craft Studio** allows visitors to watch artists in residence in action as they are crafting glass, metal, ceramics or textiles. Children are generally impressed by the glassblower's prowess with the large red ball coming out of the oven's belly, and its patient transformation into a shapely vase with handles.

There is the Harbourfront Centre for adults, with its ambitious roster of dance, music and theatre festivals, conferences and visual arts exhibits. At all times you can view at no cost an eclectic selection of art works in the **Main Gallery**, along the main building's corridors and at nearby **Power Plant**.

Then there is the Harbourfront Centre for children with **Music with Bites** (see p. 106) and **HarbourKids** which offers great activities three times a year: over Victoria Day weekend (see **Toronto International Circus Festival** on p. 27), during Thanksgiving weekend, and in December. HarbourKids also offers free kids activities on Sunday afternoons during the World Routes festivals.

During the summer weekends, the lively **World Routes** festivals allow visitors to sample different cultures with a marketplace, the World Cafe for an exotic bite and world music as a bonus.

In the winter, Harbourfront's pond turns into the **Natrel Rink**, Toronto's prettiest rink (see p. 352).

Around Harbourfront

Harbourfront Centre is at the heart of the waterfront action. Walk 10 minutes east and west of it along Queen's Quay and you'll find plenty enough to spend the whole day.

Just west of Harbourfront, you'll see the **Simcoe WaveDeck** along Queens Quay. Kids love to explore the different levels of this elegant wavy wooden deck.

Less than 10 minutes further west, you'll notice the umbrellas of **Ht0 Park**, the large sand patch coined an "urban beach". It feels like a beach, which is cool because of the **CN Tower** in the background but you won't be able to swim in the lake at this level.

The next block, at the foot of Lower Spadina, hosts the lovely **Toronto Music Garden** (see p. 259). A few blocks more, and there's **Little Norway Park** (see p. 324) facing the Western Channel and the airport.

You'll see it all from the lake if you catch a ride in one of the boats anchored at Harbourfront, such as the **Tall Ship Kajama** (see p. 209).

Queens Quay Terminal is the gorgeous shopping centre just east of Harbourfront (www.queensquay.sites.toronto.com). It includes a big toy store and a good ice cream shop.

At the southwest corner of York and Queens Quay, look carefully at your feet. You'll see a school of brass fish set in the cement.

Further east, the whale mural on the **Red-path** building is a waterfront landmark not to be missed.

Look east and you'll see the pink umbrellas of the new **Canada's Sugar Beach** (see p. 420).

The new **Sherbourne Common** park has opened just east of this beach, with a lovely rink doubling as a pond with water jets in the summer.

Finally, a good way to end the stroll is to grab snacks at **Loblaws** market on the other side of the street and go upstairs to eat it by the windows.

If you walk towards the lake from that corner, you'll see the intriguing 6-metre ball-shaped sculpture *Sundial Folly* facing the lake by the boardwalk, with nooks and crannies to explore.

Keep going east to reach **Harbourfront Square Park**, adjacent to the ferry terminal serving **Toronto Islands** (see p. 392).

Captain John's seafood restaurant in a boat is quite impressive when you look up at it, standing at the foot of Yonge Street. When you look down, you see metal letters on the sidewalk running to the west, listing names of cities and distances reminding us it is the "longest street in the world".

TIPS (fun for 5 years +)

• More about the underground streetcar you can take from **Union Station** to get to Harbourfront on p. 474.
• They usually offer a **Swedish Christmas Festival** in November.
• Check **www.paddletoronto.com** for information about canoe and kayak rentals to paddle on Lake Ontario.
• The **Lakeside EATS** terrace is great during the warmer days and on cold days after skating. The restaurant's menu at the counter is affordable. During the summer, there's also the **Splash** patio between the pond and the lake, serving food and alcohol.
• If you want to have a bite by the water, walk across the passageway linking Harbourfront to the western pier and around the building towards the lake and you'll find the outdoor snack bar of the **Pier 4 Storehouse**. Beware of the seagulls, they love their French fries!

NEARBY ATTRACTIONS
PawsWay Toronto (2 min. walk) .... p. 70
Roundhouse Park (5 min. walk) ... p.199

Harbourfront Centre
(416) 973-4000
www.
harbourfrontcentre.com

D-3
Downtown
Toronto
5-min.

Schedule: Open year-round with variable opening and closing hours depending on the events. Go to *What's On* on their website for listing of events. **Admission:** FREE ground admission. **Directions:** 235 Queen's Quay West (west of York St.), Toronto. There's a municipal parking lot across the street.

TODAY'S PARENT KIDSUMMER

One treat a day

On a Kidsummer day, one might get the "inside scoop" on how ice cream is really made, create a clay-mation short film or have a behind-the-scenes look in television or radio studios.

For the past 24 years, **Kidsummer**'s mission has been to give children access to fun events during the summer months.

Under the auspices of Canadian magazine *Today's Parent*, the yearly summer-long event provides a myriad of activities all across the Greater Toronto Area and beyond.

Its biggest focus is on offering free children's admission to specific attractions. Accompanying adults usually pay regular admission fees, yet it can represent great savings for a family, especially with big league attractions such as the Toronto Zoo.

Of course, the roster of activities varies from one year to the next but they always rely on sure values. Over 75%

of the attractions offered in Kidsummer are usually described in this guide. In order to choose a Kidsummer activity, check their calendar, then look up the attraction right here!

Kidsummer also offers the opportunity for exceptional activities you might not have the chance to do normally. Some years, kids could become restoration experts at the Elgin and Winter Garden Theatres, they could watch the sun through the large telescope of Night Sky Tours, they could watch a live firefighting demonstration at the Toronto Fire Services training station.

The year I participated with my family, drop in activities were offered at the Orthopaedic and Arthritic Hospital. It turned out to be interactive, fun and educational. My son ended up with a cast!

TIPS (fun for 3 to 12 years)

• Kidsummer is under *Today's Parent* administration. You will find the Kidsummer calendar and pre-registration information in the July issue of *Today's Parent* and *Chatelaine* magazines.

• Approximately one third of the activities require pre-registration due to a limited capacity. Pre-registration costs are involved (not determined at the time of print, check their website). In the past, registration gave access to a wacky show from Dufflebag Theatre, a dog & bird show with the Wonderful World of Circus, cooking classes at Loblaws, a tour of the Rogers Centre, to name a few.

Today's Parent Kidsummer
1-866-363-5437 (hotline)
www.kidsummer.com

 Schedule: July 1 to August 31 (hours vary for different events). Pre-registration starts mid-June.

  Admission: Most events are FREE for children 12 years and under but some adult fees might apply. Pre-registration fee to specific activities applies. See

 details on their website.
Directions: All over the Greater Toronto Area and beyond.

TORONTO CIRCUS FESTIVAL

Don't try this at home

The Toronto Circus Festival is the best time to visit Harbourfront Centre. It is a perfect match for the location and it fills the void left by our beloved and gone Milk Festival. During the event, clowns, buskers and acrobats take over and their cheerful mood is contagious.

The festival is as interactive as can be. Our kids just could not stay away from the padded path with trampoline allowing them to jump as high as they could. The daredevils tried the low tra-peze. Many activities were offered throughout the site: juggling demos, clowning workshops, mask and clown hat creation.

Some outdoor busker performances were presented east and west of the central building, and more shows were offered in the different rooms and stages throughout the site but the main show was taking place under the covered **Sirius Stage**.

When we visited, it was hosted by the most hilarious clowns posing as a couple of official (but goofy) ambassadors from an imaginary East European country. The full show lasted one hour and featured a roster of skilled acrobats and dancers with many numbers starring children.

TIPS (fun for 4 years +)
• If you buy the 3-day passport for this event, it is worth attending the main show on two different days. First, kids really enjoy seeing again a number they've liked the day before. Second, some numbers are replaced by new ones, depending on the availability of the artists.
• Many food options are sold on the premises.
• More about **Harboufront Centre** on p. 24.

NEARBY ATTRACTIONS
PawsWay Toronto (2 min. walk) .... p. 70
Roundhouse Park (5 min. walk) ... p.199

Toronto International Circus Festival
(416) 973-4000
www.tocircusfestival.com

D-3
Downtown
Toronto
5-min. walk

Schedule: On **Victoria Day** weekend, Saturday to Monday, 11 am to 5 pm.

Admission: FREE.
Directions: Harbourfront Centre, 235 Queens Quay West,

Toronto (at the foot of Lower Simcoe Street).

PORT PERRY FAIR

Family rodeo

Where else could your child try "mutton" rodeo, pig catching, egg throwing or wheelbarrow racing?

After watching the whole **Family Rodeo** with excitement, my daughter promised to participate next year. This fair was in its 154th year when we attended the event so it is fair to assume it will keep going.

"Sophie needs her mom right now!" announces the caller as a little girl is quickly thrown off her sheep. An eager boy climbs on a new sheep, determined to beat the 57-foot record achieved by the previous participant. He's dismounted in the flash of an eye. (This activity is for kids under 60 pounds.)

Two lines form for the **Egg Throwing Contest** and (raw) eggs start flying. They keep bouncing, a testimony to their healthy shells.

Moms and dads line up for the **Wheelbarrow Race**. Their young partners have to ride in the wheelbarrow to and from a post where a heavy sandbag has to be loaded. The trick is for the child to be young enough to be light, and old enough not to be traumatized by the speed!

There was even a **Ladies Frying Pan Toss** for the moms.

Later, we learned how ropes and hay bails are made during demonstrations, and how cars are destroyed during a demolition derby!

There are shows, tap dancing and music in the barn, a big midway, food, horse rides, bull rodeo and more.

The **Junior Fair** building showcased the best "anything" made by local kids: best "rock concert" (with characters made out of rocks), best "ugly cupcake", best "odd-shaped veggie", etc.

TIPS (fun for 5 years +)

• We took a break from the fair in the middle of the day, hoping for a swim. When we visited, **Palmer Park**'s beach by Water Street in Port Perry was declared unfit for swimming so we opted for the heated outdoor pool at **Birdseye Aquatic Facility** (by the water, past the **Port Perry Marina**, (905) 982-0830). Note that in 2010, they've added a splash pad to Palmer Park. Good move! And there's an ice cream shop nearby.

• The **Boardwalk Café** by the marina offers a nice view of **Scugog Lake**. Queen and Water Streets in Port Perry are lovely, with lots of restaurants and gift shops.

NEARBY ATTRACTIONS
Northwood Zoo (10 min.) .... p. 66

Port Perry Fair
• Port Perry
(905) 985-0962
www.portperryfair.ca

B-4
N-E
of Toronto
75-min.

 Schedule: Labour Day weekend, event opens Saturday evening until 11 pm (but midway starts Friday evening), then Sunday, 9:30 am to 11 pm and Monday, 9:30 am to 4 pm.

Admission: $10/14 years +, $4/5-13 years, FREE for 4 years and under. Parking is $3. Weekend pass: $15.

Directions: From Hwy 401, take exit #412 (Thickson Rd) North then turn east on Winchester, north on Simcoe Street (Road #2), then west on Reach Street.

KINGSTON SHEEP DOG TRIALS

That'll do!

Remember the movie *Babe*, about the little pig who wanted to become a sheep dog? His master congratulates him at the end with a discreet "That'll do, pig. That'll do." Little did I know that it was an actual command used at sheep dog trials.

This and a few other things about sheep dogs I learned by reading the event's program they handed to us at the door such as: the dogs don't know "personally" the flock they're managing and sheep dogs are silent working dogs.

The trials are a test of a dog's ability to move sheep through a specific course. I can't say we understood what was taking place on the vast field where we could observe the tiny pinpoint of a Border Collie handling a small group of sheep far far away, in front of an attentive audience. I must add we did not have the patience to stay around to better understand. We were too distracted by all the other activities we did not want to miss.

There were dog training demos, flyball games for dogs, sheep shearing, birds of prey and, our favourite, the agility course where keeners followed their masters through a circuit.

My dog lover was as thrilled by the sight of all the dogs around us. It seemed like half the visitors were dog owners.

TIPS (fun for 5 years +)

• There was lots of comfort food sold on the premises. We indulged in yummy spiral potatoes on a stick and cupcakes decorated with a miniature sheep made of icing sugar.
• A visit to the small **MacLachlan Woodworking Museum** located at the entrance of the park is included with the admission fee to the trials.
• Bring your bathing suits in case the weather is nice enough to take advantage of **Grass Creek Park**'s wide beach by the playground.

Kingston Sheep Dog Trials
• Kingston
(613) 546-4291
www.cityofkingston.ca/
sheepdogtrials

Off the map
East
of Toronto
3 1/4 hrs

Schedule: Always on Friday, Saturday and Sunday after Simcoe Day in August. Most activities from 9 am to 5 pm.
Admission: $10/person, FREE for 10 years and under. FREE parking.
Directions: From Hwy 401, take exit #632 (Joyceville Road/ON-16 S), go south on Joyceville Rd. to Hwy 2, then turn east. **Grass Creek Park** is located by Lake Ontario.

LASER QUEST

Gotcha!

On our way back in the car from Laser Quest, my friend and I can't get a word in edgewise. Our three boys aged 7 to 9 are still beaming from their first experience with the laser game that even their mothers thoroughly enjoyed. Aerobic exercise has never been more fun!

Our little warriors are rehashing the game to its last detail, score cards in hand. It lists who they tagged, who tagged them, how many shots they fired and how they ranked in the group of sixteen.

At the front desk, each player was invited to choose a nickname. Being a pacifist at heart, I went for Positive. The kids chose (what else!) Pokemon names. On our second tour, the names get funnier. One of the fathers becomes Save Me and my friend, at other times a refined woman with excellent manners, picks the misleading name of Tralala and turns into an aggressive amazon ranking third at the end of the game.

In the science-fiction airlock where we put on our equipment, our ranger briefs us on the few rules and we enter the vast two-level maze of walls riddled with large holes. Except for splats of paint

lit by black light, we're in the dark and the fog, with loud music matching the pounding of our hearts! I lose the kids in a flash and find them afterwards, teaming up against the adults, from the highest lookout in the room.

The laser beams reach as far as we want them to, amazingly bright and precise. Whenever one hits the flashing lights on our equipment, we are neutralized for 5 long seconds, preventing us from tagging our adversaries.

After 25 minutes of playing, our laser device indicates "Game over" and we follow the arrows on the floor to find our way out of the maze.

Laser Quest is exactly what it claims to be: a 21st century combination of two old-fashioned games, tag and hide & seek.

TIPS (fun for 6 years +)

• You may call ahead to reserve. Most players play twice, but there should be half an hour between the two games. The kids will be red-faced and thirsty after the first one.

• We played solo (each on our own). Larger groups play in teams, in which case each team's equipment bears a different colour of lights, and players can't neutralize a player on their own team.

Laser Quest
www.laserquest.com

Schedule: In general, they are at least open Tuesday to Thursday, 5 to 9 pm; Friday, 5 to 11 pm; Saturday, 10 am to 11 pm; Sunday, 10 am to 8 pm. Many are open on Mondays and several have longer hours. They offer extended hours during March Break. Call to confirm.

Admission: $9/per game.

Directions:

Brampton: 241 Clarence St., (905) 456-9999.

Kitchener: 1381 Victoria St. North, (519) 579-9999.

London: 149 Carling St., (519) 660-6000.

Mississauga: 1224 Dundas St. East, (905) 272-8000.

Richmond Hill: 9625 Yonge St., (905) 883-6000.

Scarborough: 1980 Eglinton Ave. East, (416) 285-1333.

CENTREVILLE AMUSEMENT PARK

Old fashioned way

Did you know that an amusement park existed in 1894 at the very same place today's airport sits?

Maybe it's not by chance that **Centreville** has the charm of a turn-of-the-century village. It is a small-scale amusement park. With over 20 rides, Centreville is perfect for young families!

Our group really loved the beautiful carousel, a feast for the eyes! It includes ostriches, zebras, lions, pigs, cats, giraffes, as well as the traditional horses. The animals are laid out in three rows and turn rapidly as they go up and down to the sound of lively music.

The little ones are fascinated by the train that travels through a long tunnel, by the antique cars set on tracks which they drive "themselves" and by the swan ride on the pond. They're also pretty excited by the **Bumble Bees** ride at the entrance.

Older children appreciate the bumper boats and cars, the **Monster Coaster** and the train of the **Haunted Barrel Works**.

Those who like heights will want to try the **Sky Ride** cable car or the Ferris wheel. Don't hesitate to try the **Saugeen Lumber Co. Log Flume Ride**, even with the smaller kamikazes.

There's a small farm in the far end of the site and a wading pool right in the middle. Note that there is a bigger wading pool (and a great splash pad) a few minutes from the amusement park, on the other side of the bridge leading to the south shore. A perfect spot for a picnic.

Bring the bathing suits!

TIPS (fun for 2 to 10 years)

• A reader wrote to me with a good tip! If you arrive at opening time and there's a line-up at the entrance, don't buy your tickets there. Enter the park (there's no admission fee), there are more ticket booths inside with no line-ups.
• Both **Shopsey Café**, near the ferry, and the **Carousel Café** in the amusement park overlooking the Long Pond have a kids' menu.
• More on **Toronto Islands** on p. 392.

More on **Toronto Islands** on p. 392.

NEARBY ATTRACTIONS
Harbourfront Centre (15-min.walk) p. 24

Centreville Amusement Park
(416) 203-0405
www.centreisland.ca

D-3
Toronto Islands
15-min.

Schedule: Open weekends in May and September and daily from early June to Labour Day, weather permitting. Opens at 10:30 am. Closes at 8 pm during July and August and between 5 pm and 7 pm the rest of the season.
Admission: All-Day-Ride Pass is $29/visitors over 48", $21/48" and under, FREE for baby in arms, $90/family of 4 (good discounts if you book online). Individual ride tickets can be bought. Ferry is $6.50/adult, $3/kids, FREE under 3.
Directions: In **Toronto Islands**, directly accessible by Centreville Ferry line (a 10-min. walk from Centre Island dock).

THE CNE... AND BEYOND

Midway stop

With the big rides located close to the Princes Gate, and the younger children's section, located by Dufferin Gates, CNE is indeed a children's paradise and the perfect finale to a great summer!

There is a great variety of rides at the **Kids' Midway**: merry-go-round, Ferris wheel, small and medium-sized roller coasters, bumble bee, flying helicopter and planes, jeeps and construction trucks that go round and round, tossing submarines, shaking strawberries and more.

Parents can accompany their young kids on more than half of those rides. In this area, there are also games of dexterity for an additional cost, where children are guaranteed a prize. That's all they ask for!

The midway closer to the **Princes Gate** is for bigger kids and adults. Many require a minimum height of 48".

Activities at **Kids' World**, located by the Kids' Midway, are of another kind, but equally entertaining. Among them, expect a great petting zoo. If it is offered this year, don't miss the original **Backyard Circus Show**, very interactive for young children. When we visited, it ended with a parade of huge puppets held by the parents themselves!

Included with ground admission, there's the **Super Dogs** performances, a big favourite, where dogs compete on an obstacle course.

The **Farm** exhibits feature more animals and antique farm equipment along with interactive displays. They have daily demonstrations such as goat milking, rope making or sheep shearing.

I recommend you download the *CNE Map* on their website under the *Plan your visit* section. It clearly lists all the activities, shows and exhibits included with the admission throughout the site.

In 2010, among the main attractions, they had acrobats on an 80-foot pole, a Mardi Gras parade, **Rock On Ice** (an aerial and ice skating show) and the **Flowrider Splash Zone** (with flowridering demos).

You can also watch the **Canadian International Air Show** (which always takes place on the **Labour Day** weekend) from the grounds of Exhibition Place (www.cias.org, 416-263-3650).

Photo: Courtesy of the CNE

Other events at Exhibition Place

More events take place at Exhibition Place throughout the year starting with the **Medieval Times** show mixing dinner with chivalry (see p. 370).

Every Halloween brings back **Screemers** (www.screemers.ca, 416-979-3327). Expect a haunted house and a haunted castle with monsters in every corner, a 3-D maze, a black hole, a maniac maze and an executioner theatre... Not recommended for visitors under 10 years old. It usually costs around $30 and runs for 13 consecutive nights ending October 31, from 7 to 11 pm, closing at midnight on Fridays and Saturdays.

The same people who are responsible for Screemers have created a March Break event for the whole family called **Wizard World** (see p. 186). This one is intended for children 2 to 12 years old.

The **CHIN Picnic** returns every year during **Canada Day** weekend (www.chin-radio.com. 416-531-9991). Organized by the multicultural radio broadcaster, this free event includes non-stop multicultural community shows, rides, circus, petting zoo, exotic food and Bazaar booths.

The **Masala! Mehndi! Masti! South Asian Festival** is also held in the Exhibition Place in late July (www.masalamehndimasti.com, 416-MMM-9494). I have not attended it but it seems a fun opportunity to get a Bollywood immersion. They feature various children's dance showcases.

Photo: Courtesy of the CNE

TIPS (fun for 3 years +)

• It could cost you approximately $15-$25 to park your car on the Exhibition Place site during main events. Try private parkings on Fleet St., east of Strachan Avenue.

• From **Union Subway Station**, you can take the 509 streetcar to The Ex.

• During the CNE, express trains transport you free of charge across the site. Take advantage of this service as it easily takes 20 minutes to walk from one side to the other.

NEARBY ATTRACTIONS	
Ontario Place (15-min. walk)	.... p. 16
Fort York (5-min.)	.... p. 372

Canadian National Exhibition (CNE) (416) 393-6300 www.theex.com	**D-3** **Downtown** Toronto 10-min.

Schedule: Open daily from mid-August to Labour Day Monday, 10 am to 10 pm (gates close at 10 pm but the big midway closes at midnight on weekends). Closes earlier on Labour Day.
Admission: Admission only is $16/ adults, $12/seniors and children 3-13 years old, $48/family of 4. FREE under 3 years. Ride pass is $36 (or pay-per-unit). Check the website for specials.
Directions: Exhibition Place, Toronto. Take Lake Shore Blvd. and turn north on Strachan Avenue. Princes Gate entrance is on the west side.

FANTASY FAIR

Photo: Courtesy of K.McCutcheon

Footloose at the Fair

On the verge of panic, I alerted the Woodbine Centre security guards. I was searching for my young fugitive, lost in Fantasy Fair. I eventually saw him as he was getting expelled from the little train he had illegally hopped on without a passport bracelet on his wrist.

The **Woodbine Centre** includes two levels linked by several escalators. It is connected to a huge parking area by large, easily opened doors so I recommend being careful if you go there on a busy day.

Having said this, the place is very pleasant. Thanks to skylights and bay windows, **Fantasy Fair** is bathed in natural light. The fair offers nine rides and a giant playground over three storeys high and an arcade section. It doesn't sound like much, but it is plenty for children 8 years and under.

Among other things, there's a magnificent antique carousel, bumper boats (must be under 54"), red and white airplanes that give young pilots a surprisingly realistic feeling (36" to under 54"), two spinning rides and a bumper car ride for drivers min. 54" and passengers min. 36".

The train running through the park is a youngster's favourite attraction. Avoid the Ferris wheel if the waiting line is long (the ride is very slow). The **Dreamer's Play Village** is 5,500 sq. ft. with climber, long slides and a dynamic section with interactive foam shooters! This attraction is for kids 60" and under but parents can accompany their kids, free of charge.

TIPS (fun for 2 to 10 years)
• You can visit Santa too when visiting before Christmas. See **Woodbine Centre** on page 183.
• On busy days, bring snacks to pass the time while waiting, instead of planning a sit-down meal. The wait for each ride can be as long as 20 minutes. (A reader told me there were no line-ups on a PA day in December!)
• There's a **Rainbow movie theatre** in the lower level of the mall, (416-213-9048, www.rainbowcinemas.ca).

NEARBY ATTRACTIONS
Playdium Mississauga (20-min.) ... p. 20
Pearson Int'l Airport (15-min.) ..... p. 190

Fantasy Fair
• Etobicoke
(416) 674-5437
www.fantasyfair.ca

D-3
N-W
of downtown
25-min.

Schedule: Open Monday to Thursday, 12 noon to 7 pm; Friday to Sunday, 11 am to 7 pm. Open from 12 noon to 6 pm on Holidays.

Admission: Around $14.50/for child under 36", $16.75/36" to under 54", $15.50/visitor over 54", $56/pass for a family of 4, $3.75/ride or 10 rides for $35.50.

Directions: Woodbine Centre, Etobicoke. Take Hwy 427 North, exit at Rexdale Ave. East, turn left on Queen's Place Drive. At Woodbine Centre, park between **The Bay** and **Sears**.

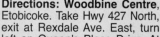

BEACH FAIRWAY GOLF RANGE

In a hole...

There aren't that many places where one can play mini golf east of downtown Toronto! Actually, this is the one.

Beach Fairway mini golf is really cute with its 18 holes layered along a gentle slope.

Mini golf places are often designed with a theme but very seldom do they simply focus on offering a lovely setting amidst the trees, (like a miniature golf course, come to think of it).

I visited the place on the occasion of a birthday party my daughter was invited to. The small gazebo was put to good use for the gifts and cake. After the game, the kids were introduced to the pleasure of driving with a club, with the help of a few parents. They had a blast cheering for each other.

I saw some parents practising their shots while their kids played a game of mini golf. Everybody was winning!

TIPS (fun for 5 years +)
• There's a **McDonald**'s restaurant just south of the golf range.
• The other mini golfs I have seen outside an amusement park are **Polson Pier**, located downtown Toronto (see p. 15), **Bathgate Golf Centre** in Mississauga including a driving range (600 Eglinton Avenue, off Cawthra, 905-890-0156) and the very pretty **Timber Creek Golf** on 9th Line in Stouffville, including 37 holes with waterfall, jumping castle, slides, gemstone mining area and more (www.timbercreekgolf.ca).

NEARBY ATTRACTIONS

Beach Fairway Golf Range
(416) 686-4101
www.beachfairway.com

D-3
East
of downtown
20-min.

Schedule: Open mid-March to early November, weather permitting, from 8 am until dusk.

Admission: $7.50/adults, $6.50/13-17 years and seniors, $4.50/12 years and under. Second round is half price. Small basket of 45 balls costs $8.

Directions: 411 Victoria Park Ave., south of Danforth, Toronto (less than 10-min. walk from **Victoria Park Station**).

PUTTING EDGE

Glowing with joy!

Walking through the dark place is like being on the set of a children's production. Tall houses in funny shapes seem to lean over the players. Every detail covered with glow-in-the-dark paint contrasts with the darkness of all that wasn't painted. The greens are... black and we are golfing in the dark. Rocks are bright red and yellow. Trees are green and turquoise, with a whole forest glowing in the background.

On the first green, when one of my enthusiastic 7-year-old partners hits his ball and made it fly to the third hole (bouncing on its way off four different vertical props), I realized that watching over them would be quite a challenge!

As we left the forest, we entered an aquatic zone where a whole green takes the shape of a shark. The colour theme switched to blues and pinks. Fish shapes were cut out in the walls and schools of fish were painted on the murals. There was even a treasure glimmering in the middle of a green.

We eventually climbed stairs and reached a level with a space theme and a nice twist, taking the ball back to the first floor through a vertical labyrinth against the wall. My little sportsman insisted on doing it repeatedly when nobody else was playing.

From the flowers painted on the ground and the psychedelic whale hanging from the ceiling to the fluorescent balls and clubs, the attention to detail made this outing a real success.

TIPS (fun for 5 years +)

• Each Putting Edge offers different murals and themes so it is fun visiting different ones.
• You don't have to pay if you just prefer to accompany your children, keeping an eye on them so they won't step into other people's games.
• A maximum of four players per group is permitted. It is suggested you allow faster groups to play through.
• The whole game took us forty minutes to play.

Putting Edge
www.puttingedge.com

Schedule: In general, they are at least open Monday to Thursday, 2 to 9 pm; Friday, 3 pm to midnight; Saturday, 10 am to midnight; Sunday, 11 am to 8 pm. Some have longer hours.
Admission: $10.50/adults, $8.50/4-12 years, FREE for children 3 years and under with a paying adult.

Directions:
Barrie: 34 Commerce Park Dr., (705) 737-2229.
Burlington: 1250 Brant St., (905) 315-9155.
Mississauga: 90 Courtneypark Dr., (905) 564-1888.
Oakville: 2085 Winston Park Dr., (905) 829-8833.
Richmond Hill: 9625 Yonge St., (905) 508-8222.
Vaughan: 60 Interchange Way, (905) 761-3343.
Whitby: 75 Consumer Dr., Unit 4, (905) 430-3206.

ST. PATRICK'S DAY PARADE

Green power

This has to be the easiest parade a family could attend, near subway stations, and with enough room on the sidewalk all along its circuit.

The appeal of any parade is the anticipation. What surprise is awaiting us around the corner?

Bands can be majestic (especially the bagpipers playing and walking in perfect sync). Floats can be interesting and often funny with original details.

At the **St. Patrick's Day Parade**, we saw a "castle" with beautifully costumed lords. There was another one with barbarians feasting at the king's court. This float was followed by peasants pushing their wheelbarrows filled with straw. The parade ended with St. Patrick "himself" waving at us from inside a glass box, not unlike… the Pope himself.

The real appeal of the parade for children is the music from bands and floats. They create ambiance and are a reason to wave flags and shake it!

The interaction with the parade's marchers also contributes a lot to the fun of the experience. We saw a clown on a wacky bicycle, two walkers on stilts and a teasing leprechaun, dressed in green with the trademark hat, throwing chocolate coins to the crowd.

Right after the parade, marchers usually reunite in a venue in the vicinity, for a beer and some dynamic Celtic music. (You'll have to check their website closer to St. Patrick's Day for the exact address.) Anyone can attend; it gives you a chance to have a closer look at Miss St. Patrick and some of the costumed marchers.

When we left, children were starting to flood the dance floor to skillfully try a few Celtic dance steps.

TIPS (fun for 5 years +)

• This is no Santa Claus Parade. Don't go expecting many elaborate floats.
• When we attended, the parade started at noon, at the corner of Bloor and St. George Streets. When we got to the intersection of Yonge and Queen Streets at 1:45 pm, the parade was already there, and went on until 3 pm.

NEARBY ATTRACTIONS

St. Patrick's Day Parade (416) 487-1566 www.topatrick.com	**D-3** **Dowtown** **Toronto** **10-min.**

 Schedule: If March 17 falls on a Friday, Saturday or Sunday, the parade takes place the Sunday of that weekend, from noon to 3 pm. Otherwise, the parade is on the preceding Sunday.

Admission: FREE.

Directions: Goes from Bloor (at St. George) eastbound, southbound on Yonge then west on Queen. The parade ends at **Nathan Phillips Square**, Toronto.

BEACHES EASTER PARADE

Yummy parade

There could hardly be a better setting for a successful Easter parade: The Beach, with its quaint, pleasant architecture, discreet storefront signs and wide sidewalks. With the support of costumed volunteers, pastel-coloured balloons, vehicles decorated by enthusiastic amateurs, and with the participation of clubs and organizations of all kinds, all takes on the atmosphere of a joyous celebration.

Of course, we're not talking about Stations of the Cross and resurrection… but rather about the Easter Bunny and coloured eggs. The **Beaches Lions Club** chapter has been organizing this parade for over thirty-three years. More modest than the Santa Claus Parade, it features majorettes, small marching bands, amateur gymnasts from the area, as well as Mounties and fire trucks.

Certain store owners and organizations create ambitious mini-floats. When we were there, we saw a pick-up truck topped by a giant Easter hat, a "steamboat", a travelling garden, a tractor pulling a multicoloured cart full of clowns, and even a tractor-trailer with costumed children.

Among those parading, there are children on decorated bicycles, boy scouts, preschoolers from local daycare centres riding in decorated wagons, clowns and mascots (Star Wars characters, when we were visiting!).

To sum up, it appeals to the community because the whole community participates! Encouraged by the Lions, a few people wear beautiful hats they made themselves, and some children hold on to their stuffed bunnies.

Don't be scared off by the small crowds gathering at either end of the course. In between, I found lots of room on Queen Street East, even close to Kew Gardens. I recommend that you stay close the park located close to Glen Manor Drive. (Check **The Pie Shack** just across the street while you're there, 2305 Queen East, www.thepieshack.com).

TIPS (fun for 3 years +)

• More than one hour before the parade, a long stretch of Queen Street is closed to motor vehicles and the Queen streetcar line ends at Woodbine.
• For a religious event, look for the **Good Friday Procession** organized by the parish of St. Francis of Assisi. It's an Easter Friday march that involves the re-enactment of the fourteen Stations of the Cross, starting at **St. Francis of Assisis Church**. See the pictures on their website (www.stfrancis.ca, 416-536-8195).
• More about the **Beach Neighbourhood** and restaurants on p. 404.

Beaches Lions Club Easter Parade
(416) 693-5466
www.beacheslions.com

D-3
East
of downtown
20-min.

Schedule: Easter Sunday at 2 pm, rain or shine.
Admission: FREE.
Directions: On Queen St. East, Toronto (begins near Victoria Park and ends at Woodbine).

PORTUGAL DAY PARADE

Portuguese immersion

Strolling along Dundas Street during the Portugal Day Parade, we can see how strong and alive the Portuguese community is in the area. There were 114,000 Torontonians claiming Portuguese as their mother tongue in 2006. I think they all showed up. Wear red if you want to blend in!

The parade runs from Lansdowne to **Trinity-Bellwoods Park** along Dundas West and the street is closed to vehicles for the occasion. You could stick to one viewing point but I recommend you take advantage of the sidewalk's action by doing the 25-minute stroll along the parade's route.

You'll see the street adorned with garlands and balloons, three-generation Portuguese families greeting their

friends in the parade, tight t-shirt clad young men strutting about to impress the pretty girls, people admiring the parade from their balcony decorated with giant Portuguese flag.

Along the way, we came across bakeries selling the great little Portuguese custard pies, a sports bar treating passersby with grilled sardines (in front of funky Lula Lounge), colourful murals (by Sheridan Ave.) and a wedding inside gorgeous **St. Helen Church** (1680 Dundas).

The parade itself was a display of local folk attires from different regions of Portugal

(flamboyant ones alternating with modest or very sober ones) worn by people of all ages. There were musicians, soccer players and dancers.

One ambitious float featured a piece of cliff with a real goat and a beach segment with real kids playing in the sand; another one a church on a hill with old ladies clad in black.

TIPS (fun for 5 years +)

• The parade ends at **Trinity-Bellwoods Park** (see p. 268). In 2010, it was followed by shows of folk dances and Portuguese music going on until 11 pm.
• At Gladstone's height, you'll find the nice specialty shop with seating area **Grain, Curd and Bean** (1414 Dundas) selling great coffee. Just north of Trinity-Bellwoods Park is a good espresso bar selling snacks, **The Communal Mule** (984 Dundas).

Portugal Day Parade (416) 536-5961 www.portuguesealliance.com	D-3 **Downtown** Toronto 10-min.

 Schedule: The parade is usually on the first Saturday of June starting at 11 am.
Admission: FREE.
Directions: The parade starts at Dundas St. West and Lansdowne Ave., goes eastbound along Dundas to end at **Trinity-Bellwoods Park**.

PRIDE PARADE

What did you expect?

The least we can say is that this is not your typical family event. But the Pride Week has included a Family Corner in its line-up of activities for a few years now so I had to check it out!

OK, I'll admit this is not for everyone, but the event certainly has come a long way since the days when floats and streets were overflowing with participants dressed in drag or S & M outfits and Church Street was infused with a riotous celebration.

Some lament this evolution. Others consider it a statement to the efficiency of the gay lobbying to forward their cause. You can explain as much, or as little, as you want about the colourful drag queens, kids won't be traumatized. Remember they all know it's John Travolta dressed as a woman in *Hairspray*.

The "Men-who-like-to-be-naked" float is a bit trickier, depending on your take on nudity. And you have to know that chances are you'll see a few... eh, members of this association walking naked.

Otherwise, a great ambiance rules on Yonge Street while the crowd awaits. Some have brought huge balls that we push over our heads, like at a concert. Many carry water guns to spray the people on the street and on the floats. Most participants on the floats will respond in kind or throw freebies at us.

Anybody with access to rooftops is out, throwing confetti at us. Some of the floats are really colourful, with a Caribana feel to them. I was moved by the floats of support groups created over the years to address the gay issue: kids for their gay parents, parents for their gay kids. So many stories behind it all.

Later, go to Church Street to get a free rainbow flag. Amidst the merchants' booths (selling anything in the colour of rainbows, funky wings or crowns with ribbons), expect scantily-clad painted guys promoting big corporations exploiting the hype. A Kodak moment for many passersby!

TIPS (fun for 5 years +)

• The **Family Pride** is on the last weekend of Pride Week in the schoolyard of **Church Street Junior Public School** at Church and Alexander. It features free activities, interactive little shows, playground and is a great source of information.

• The younger the child, the more likely they are to see it just as any other fun parade. Still, I was told by some parents that their pre-teens were really uncomfortable with the whole thing.

NEARBY ATTRACTIONS

Allan Gardens (10-min. walk) ...... p. 260
Around Bay Subway Station .... p. 459

Pride Parade
(416) 927-7433
www.pridetoronto.com

**D-3
Downtown**
Toronto
10-min.

 Schedule: The parade is on the last Sunday of Pride Week (usually the last Sunday in June) at 2 pm.
Admission: FREE.
Directions: The parade starts at Church and Bloor, Toronto (goes west on Bloor, southbound on Yonge, then east on Gerrard). It ends at Church Street.

EAST YORK CANADA DAY PARADE

The one and only

If you're looking for a parade on Canada Day, look East, as in East York. This parade ends its route at Stan Wadlow Park, which has a lot to offer in addition to the day's events especially planned for the occasion: outdoor public pool, large playground, funky skatepark and access to Taylor Creek Park with its kilometres of paved trails east and west of Stan Wadlow Park.

East York Canada Day celebrations have been going on for over 50 years. They've got it all. There's a large midway section in the northern part of the park, food vendors and tents in the middle, shows on two stages and a fireworks display at 10 pm to top it off.

I recommend you try to find a parking spot in the big parking lot in front of the outdoor pool just north of **Stan Wadlow Park** (near the end of Cedarvale Ave.). It will take you 15 minutes to walk down

Woodbine and west on Sammon to get a nice viewing spot in the tree-shaded residential area. When we visited, there were clusters of red-attired people here and there, fully equipped with chairs, parasol, water and Canadian flags. The parade included the usual suspects: good-spirited Shriners, bands, marching groups, dancers, floats, decorated cars and bikes, veterans and sports groups.

The crowd was ready to be amused by any funny detail. Our favourite participant was the **Rameses Hillbilly Shrine Club**. For the occasion, the club had brought hillbillies in a rolling loo, on antique cars with teddy bears and in a shack. There even was a man and his skunk (faux) in a hot tub (real) on wheels.

With older kids, you will prefer to arrive later (be prepared to look around a bit for a parking space) to enjoy the midway, the shows and the fireworks.

TIPS (fun for 5 years +)

• In 2010, most of the participants met at **Dieppe Park** on Cosburn Ave., joined by the motorcade from East York Town Centre. They all proceeded along Coxwell, east on Sammon Ave., then north on Woodbine Ave. to Stan Wadlow Park.

• There's another Canada Day event with large parade, activities and fireworks in Port Credit (Mississauga by the Lake, see www.paintthetownred.ca).

• More on **East York Skatepark** in Stan Wadlow Park on p. 349.

NEARBY ATTRACTIONS

East York Canada Day Parade (647) 345-7303 www.julyfirstparade.com www.eastyorkcanadaday.com	D-3 **East** of downtown 20-min.

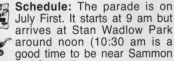
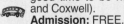

Schedule: The parade is on July First. It starts at 9 am but arrives at Stan Wadlow Park around noon (10:30 am is a good time to be near Sammon and Coxwell).

Admission: FREE.

Directions: The parade ends at **Stan Wadlow Park**, 373 Cedarvale Ave., Toronto (east of Woodbine Ave., south of O'Connor Drive).

CARIBANA PARADE

Irresistible!

We are mesmerized by the explosion of colourful spandex, tulle, lace, sparkles, fringes and pompoms, in what has to be Toronto's hottest street celebration and North America's largest such festival.

When the large float finally reaches us (we heard its loud music from blocks away)

everybody is consumed by an irresistible euphoria. Lost in the engaging rhythms of calypso, the crowd joins the contagious lead of tireless street dancers. A baby claps enthusiastically while a young girl throws in the occasional whistle blow, perched atop her father's shoulders.

Adorable little girls walk in the procession, adjusting accessories and pink leotards too big for them, while some kids catch their breath on a float before jumping again. When we reach the parade's finish point (at Dowling Avenue and Lake Shore Boulevard), some 3.5 km away from Exhibition Place, at around 1:30 pm, we are right on time to see it arriving.

The north side of Lake Shore Boulevard was not crowded as most spectators favour the south side and its line-up of food stands. At no time did we feel overwhelmed by large crowds.

Many pedestrian access points open up during the parade to allow passage across the boulevard.

TIPS (fun for 5 years +)

• Rain or shine, Caribana takes place. I've attended the celebrations under a torrential downpour and admired participants' determination to continue.
• Bring the fun up a notch and equip your youngsters with their own whistle.
• Remember to bring bottles of water, hats and sunscreen on sunny days.
• Be warned, music from the floats can be deafeningly loud to young ears.
• Caribana is notorious for starting later than scheduled, and there can be up to 30 minutes between floats.
• The best way to catch sight of the many fabulous costumes (and snap a few pictures), is at **Exhibition Place**. At 3 pm, dancers are still there waiting for their turn in the procession.
• There is a **Junior Caribana** celebration for children 4 to 16 years old. It usually happens two Saturdays prior to Caribana at 12 noon at Jane/Finch corner.

NEARBY ATTRACTIONS

Caribana Parade
www.caribanatoronto.com

D-3
Downtown
Toronto
10-min.

Schedule: Usually the Saturday of the first weekend in August, from 10 am. Check their website closer to August.

Admission: FREE (around $20 for premium seating at Exhibition Place's Stadium).

Directions: Starting point at **Exhibition Place**, Toronto. Runs westbound along Lake Shore Boulevard up around Dowling Avenue.

OKTOBERFEST PARADE

Yodoheleeetee!

There is a great ambiance on the street as we wait for the Oktoberfest Parade to start. The crowd is keen; everyone likely got up at the crack of dawn so as not to miss a minute of what must be Canada's earliest parade!

The event, also known as the **Thanksgiving Parade**, begins in Waterloo at 8:30 am and runs a five-kilometre stretch along King Street. It ends in Kitchener at approximately 10 am. Coming from Toronto, we decide to catch the parade at the end of its journey in Kitchener.

We easily find affordable parking on a public lot. It is 9 am and the crowd keeps pouring in. East of St. Francis Street (where King Street narrows and becomes prettier), there is still plenty of room on the sidewalks. By the **Kitchener City Hall**, kids burn off some energy jumping on an inflatable structure, while others warm up inside.

By 9:30 am, we find a spot at the corner of Ontario Street next to a family clad in the traditional feathered Bavarian hats. A few minutes later, forty policemen on motorcycles appear in a roar, blasting

sirens and all, followed by the first band, from Michigan.

Composed of around 20 bands and 30 floats (varies from one year to the next), the hour-and-a-half parade boasts a line-up of public officials: mayors, judges, Miss Oktoberfest, the mascot Onkel Hans, as well as members of various German clubs, outfitted in Tyrolian shorts and low-cut dresses. Some really catch children's attention as they flip their whips in the air and yodel. So do the dancers, holding their partners by the waist, feet up in the air and spinning fast.

The floats, although modest, were fun to watch. There was a huge bear drumming on a turtle, a 2-storey-high inflated clown, a 40-foot inflated lion and a big turkey. Shoppers Drug Mart's trademark giant bear was so huge it had to be pulled down to slip under traffic lights.

After the parade, we take in a number of street entertainers at the **Wilkommen Platz**, downtown Kitchener.

TIPS (fun for 5 years +)

• No wonder Oktoberfest is so strong in that region. In 1873, Kitchener, with a population of 3,000, was still called Berlin!
• The Oktoberfest-Thanksgiving Parade is broadcast live on CTV.
• Call or check the website to find out more about the Oktoberfest program.

Oktoberfest Thanksgiving Day Parade	D-1 West of Toronto 75-min.

• **Kitchener/Waterloo**
1-888-294-4267
www.oktoberfest.ca

 Schedule: Held on the Thanksgiving Monday, usually starting at 8:30 am and ending at 1 pm.
Admission: FREE.
Directions: From Hwy 401 West, exit #278/Hwy 8 northbound. Follow King St. to downtown. The parade runs southeast from Waterloo to Kitchener along King Street.

NEARBY ATTRACTIONS
Children's Museum (same place) p. 216

PUMPKIN FESTIVAL PARADE

from the local paintball company. The local music store's float was a big hit with its impersonators of famous singers.

On the cute side: llamas, a dog kennel parading puppies, a clown on tractor with a beaver puppet...

The rest of the day was not enough time to explore everything. There was the 12-row-tall pumpkin tower to admire, not too far from the giant pumpkin display. Further, a small midway and a great 2-storey-high antique shop filled with enough small trinkets to interest my 10-year-old.

The Pumpkin Express tractors could take us to the other attractions along a circuit: "scary" haunted house, indoor inflated bouncing structures, outdoor stage with food court and the **Van-Go Adventure Farm**.

Party line

Families and friends line up their lawn chairs on their front yards in anticipation of the parade. Kids drink hot chocolate from little stands here and there. All these local private parties going on make you want to live in this town.

Waterford takes great pride in its festival. After the parade, we strolled around and admired the Victorian beauties on Main Street and pretty houses on the side streets, many of them decorated for the occasion.

The parade itself is a charming collective effort of the residents and the local business community.

We saw horses, fire trucks complete with their Dalmatian mascot, tractors with the biggest wheels ever and a funky float

TIPS (fun for 5 years +)

• There are admission fees to the **Van-Go Adventure Farm**. More on this farm on p. 153.

• The countryside around Waterford is lovely but leave early to get there, the event is popular and you don't want to get caught in local traffic while the parade goes on. There might be lots of walking from the parking lots. Bring a stroller.

• On our way back, we stopped for ribs at **Moose Winooski's** in Brantford (30 mins. from Waterford). We loved the self-serve peanut barrels with peanut shells all over the stool section's floor, and all the fun objects to look at. (In Waterford, take Thomson West, follow RR-9, turn right on Hwy 24, leading onto Rest Acres Rd/CR-24, take Hwy 403 towards Hamilton, then exit at Hwy 24/Cambridge/King George Rd.) The restaurant is at 45 King George, www.moosewinooskis.com.

Waterford Pumpkin Festival Parade
• Waterford
(519) 443-4944
www.pumpkinfest.com

Off the map S-W of Toronto 1 3/4 hr

Schedule: The parade usually starts at 12:30 pm on the Saturday after Thanksgiving (2011: October 15).

Admission: Parade is FREE, small fees apply to some activities in Waterford and parking.

Directions: From Hwy 403 southbound, take exit Rest Acres Road (Hwy 24 South), go southbound then turn east on Thompson St., and follow signs for parking. (I recommend you check their website for the latest news regarding parking location.)

TORONTO SANTA CLAUS PARADE

For over 100 years

Kids are on grown-ups' laps, shoulders or in their arms, on stairways, windowsills or walls. Kids are everywhere, in small clusters in the foreground or packed 2 or 3 rows deep. Among this gigantic brood, brave adults tackle this event with a smile, initiating their little ones to the Santa Claus Parade.

1:30 pm – We settle at the corner of Yonge and Front. At the other end, the parade had begun an hour earlier. We've arrived in time to find a small but comfortable patch of sidewalk, but the rows are filling in all around us. We recognize seasoned members of the crowd by their gear: They're fully equipped with snacks, drinks, blankets, chairs, strollers, backpacks, toys and stuffed animals.

1:45 pm – Mothers distribute Smarties to occupy their little elves. The number of grown-ups returning to their stations with coffee in hand is multiplying. Security guards are starting to push feet back on the sidewalk. Are these drums we're hearing? The excitement is rising...

2:30 pm – Children squirm on their parent's shoulders. On the other side of the street, I see two grandparents grinning widely, warmly clothed and seated on their lawn chairs, delighted to mingle with the youngsters.

2:15 pm – The growing clamour is announcing the arrival of the parade. For an hour, we'll be seeing wonders: two dozen marching bands with majorettes, more than 1000 costumed volunteers and about twenty floats, with Santa's sleigh as the highlight.

In the past years, we've admired Captain Hook's huge crocodile leaping towards the crowd, a rabbit-magician that pulled a man out of his hat, a dog-robot, a teddy bear picnic, a king with his dragon... and it's been going on for over 100 years!

TIPS (fun for 3 years +)

• To obtain a vantage point suitable for children, it's best to arrive at a chosen spot at least an hour before the parade passes by.

• During the parade, postmen normally collect children's letters to Santa. Write to: Santa Claus, North Pole, H0H 0H0, and bring it to the parade just in case!

• If you don't want to brave the traffic, the lack of parking and the cold, you'd better stay home and watch the parade (usually on Global TV at around 4 pm) on the day of the parade.

• If you'd like to see a less-crowded parade, you can turn to Peterborough's (see p. 48), Oakville's (since 1948, normally on the third Saturday of November at 9 am, check **www.oakvillesantaclausparade.ca**) or Etobicoke's (since 1991, usually on the first Saturday of December at 10 am, check **www.lakeshoresantaclausparade.com**).

• See pages 457-460 and 472-474 for suggestions of attractions and restaurants near the subway stations.

NEARBY ATTRACTIONS
ROM (1-min. walk) .... p. 222
Bata Shoe Museum (1-min. walk) p. 225

Toronto Santa Claus Parade

www. thesantaclausparade.com

D-3 Downtown Toronto 10 to 30-min.

Schedule: The parade is held on the 3rd Sunday of November and now begins at 12:30 pm.

Admission: FREE.

Directions: Starts at Christie and Bloor West and ends at Front and Church (the route usually runs along Queen's Park, University Ave., Queen, Yonge and Front St. but it is better to check the route on the website).

KINSMEN SANTA CLAUS PARADE

Santa goes local

For most kids, the highlight of these parades is getting to see Santa at the end so basically, any Santa Claus parade in any town will do the trick. Combine your attendance to such a parade with another local attraction and you get a great day trip. Last year, we opted for Peterborough's parade, then in its 36th year.

They say approximately 15,000 people line up to see the **Kinsmen Santa Claus Parade**. We're far from the crowd of hundreds of thousands attending Toronto's parade, and this comes with its advantage. No problem to find a viewing spot along the road.

Some corporate floats were ambitious. Among others, there was a school bus dressed up as a dog (or was it a rabbit?), a Christmas tree forest covering a float and a 16-wheel truck filled with wrapped gifts (what a tease!).

Many small displays were cute and funny, nicely adorned with lights. We even saw guys riding motorcycles covered with lights. The decorated monster truck was a hit with our 10-year-old companions.

The local marching bands were dynamic and the crowd, eager to be pleased. Many businesses were giving away goodies and Santa's handlers were distributing Christmas carol booklets.

I don't know if these are a tradition but they came in very handy keeping the kids busy as we drove towards the next attraction on our schedule.

TIPS (fun for 5 years +)

• We had dinner before the parade at whimsical **Wimpy's Diner**, a few minutes walk from St. George where the parade starts (228 Charlotte St., www.wimpysdiner.net). From the Parkway to Peterborough, we turned right at Clonsilla Ave. and continued into Charlotte.

• We combined this outing with a visit to **Lang Pioneer Village** to see their **Christmas by Candlelight** (see p. 175), which required that we go after the parade, when it's dark, a 30-min. drive from Peterborough. It was a bit crazy but it gave us an hour to enjoy the village. Don't try this if the weather conditions are not great. (Call to make sure it is offered on the day of the parade.)

• Another interesting combo, you could go see a movie and an early dinner before the parade. **Galaxy Cinemas Peterborough** is conveniently located at the corner of Charlotte and Water Street, a few minutes walk from the starting point of the parade and from Wimpy's Diner mentioned above (see www.cinemaclock.com for listings).

Kinsmen Santa Claus Parade www.kinsmenclub peterborough.ca	B-5 N-E of Toronto 1 3/4 hr

Schedule: The parade is always on the first Saturday of December, starting at around at 4:45 pm.
Admission: FREE.
Directions: Take Hwy 401 eastbound, then exit at Hwy 115/35 and follow north. Exit at The Parkway (read TIPS). The parade starts at **Peterborough City Hall** at Murray St. and runs southbound along St. George to **Morrow Park** at Lansdowne Street.

Photo: Courtesy of K.McCutcheon

Photo: Courtesy of Santa's Village

Sportsland

Sportsland is beside Santa's Village and is managed by the same organization. It is an area designed with older kids in mind. The place has less character than the Village, but is well adapted to its clientele. Expect noisy arcade games, a laser tag

TIPS (fun for 2 years +)
• I know Santa's Village is far from Toronto, but it's so well designed that I never regretted driving back and forth on the same day. To create excitement, ask your little copilots to watch for Santa signs lining the road. Don't worry about the way back. They'll have played so hard all day they'll be sleeping like logs in no time.
• Santa's Village itself is fun for children 10 years and under. Sportsworld is fine for kids 5 years and over.
• Even during busy weekends, there's hardly a 10-minute wait for attractions. On weekdays, you rarely wait!
• If it's not windy, bring insect repellent. The Muskoka region is paradise for mosquitoes!
• There are many snack bars on the premises.
• Since my last visit, they've annexed **Eaglecrest Aerial Park** to Sportsland (www.aerialparks.ca, 705-640-4040, $46-$56 for 3 hrs). This treetop adventure for kids 9 years and older includes ziplines, monkey walks, wobbly bridges and more!
• **Santa's Whispering Pines Campground** is located across the road from Santa's Village. It usually offers an attractive package (including 2 nights camping and 2 days family admission to Santa's Village) for approx. $189. You can reach the campground at (705) 645-5682, **www.muskokacamping.com**.

room, a go-kart track, a mini golf course and a batting cage.

My pre-preteen tremendously enjoyed a go-kart ride along with his Dad (no minimum height for the passenger). Two laser-gun fights helped reinforce their male bonding even more.

Santa's Village & Sportsland
· Bracebridge
(705) 645-2512
www.santasvillage.ca

Off the map North of Toronto 2 1/4 hrs

Schedule: Open daily mid-June to Labour Day, plus the following weekend, from 10 am to 6 pm. Sportsland closes at 9 pm (except on Sundays when it closes at 6 pm).

Admission: (taxes not included) The Village: around $27/5 years and up, $22/ children 2 to 4 years old and seniors, FREE for children under 2. Sportsland is a pay-as-you-play zone.

Directions: Take Hwy 400 North, continue on Hwy 11. Take exit #4 (Muskoka Rd./Hwy 118 West). Turn left on Santa's Village Rd., at the first light after the bridge in Bracebridge.

NEARBY ATTRACTIONS

STORYBOOK GARDENS

The whole story

Millions have been injected into the place. Ambitious new playgrounds, gorgeous spray pad, different characters, more vegetation. Add a path which turns into an ice skating trail in the winter and you get a clue to another major change: the attraction is now open year-round.

For more than 40 years now, the **StoryBook Gardens** have been one of London's feature attractions. With a collection of farm and exotic animals, living in cages and paddocks, it could almost qualify as a small zoo but as its name indicates, its primary mission is to display within gardens, various decorative sets inspired by children's fairy tales.

A Cheshire Cat greeted us at the entrance, smiling through a screen of smoke coming from a well. Humpty Dumpty awaited us to our left. To our right, we entered through the mouth of a large whale to see the treasure she had swallowed.

Many animals were miss-

ing when we visited, due to the renovations. It gave us more time to admire the five harbour seals playing in the large pool. We got pretty close to them so we could enjoy their frolicking.

A bit further, an otter was swimming to and fro her small pond.

Deeper into the park, the kids tried the climbing rocks but the immense red spider web was even more challenging. It connected three poles, each offering anchorage for children to climb up. Don't try this barefoot! There was a 3-storey-high slide, a large wooden structure and an impressive pirate ship and a maze.

After all that playing, the **Slippery's Lagoon** was most welcome. It is a large colourful spray pad with water cannons, bucket dumps and sprays of all sorts. Kids all ages had a blast.

After they'd cooled down, we watched a little show put together by the young staff, a (free and funny) interactive adaptation of *Hansel & Gretel*.

Kids always like to watch the large carp and ducks from the covered bridge overlooking the pond. This pond was being rejuvenated when we visited. It will be the cutest little nook.

They've added a few rides (elephant carousel, Ferris wheel, super slide, inflatable bounce, swings). Outside of the attraction's gate, a miniature steam train with its railroad track stretching over one kilometre, adds to the fun. So does the carousel by the water (both for an extra fee).

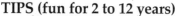

TIPS (fun for 2 to 12 years)

• The attraction's snack bars are conveniently located by the water games.

• Check their *Calendar* under *Plan your visit* on their website for details on Easter, Halloween and Christmas activities.

• In the winter, the refrigerated path can hold ice for a fun skating experience through the gardens, decked with Christmas lights. Animal exhibits are open.

• You can catch the bicycle trail bordering the **Thames River** directly from StoryBook Gardens' parking lot. It runs amidst pretty scenery.

• Check **www.londontourism.ca** for their section *Places to stay*. We took a room at the **Hilton** to spend one night in the area. It allowed us to wind down completely. What a perfect little getaway!

• The **Fanshawe Conservation Area** on the northeast edge of London includes a campground. Call 1-866-668-2267.

• The cute restaurants and cafés in London are found along Richmond Street by **Victoria Park** in downtown London.

• **Victoria Park** also hosts the major musical event **Sunfest**, a four-day festival usually held around the second weekend in July (www.sunfest.on.ca).

• You could combine your outing with a visit to the local water park **Wally World** in **East Park**, east of Highbury Avenue, on Hamilton Road. Admission cost is reduced after 4 pm. For information, call (519) 451-2950, www.eastparkgolf.com. East Park also includes go-karts, batting, 36 holes of mini golf, indoor rock climbing, bumper cars and a kids' jungle gym.

NEARBY ATTRACTIONS

StoryBook Gardens
• London
(519) 661-5770
www.storybook.london.ca

Off the map
S-W
of Toronto
2 1/2 hrs

 Schedule: Open year-round, at least on weekends. May, June and after Labour Day until April, open Friday to Sunday from 10 am (closing time varies). From late May to Labour Day, open daily 10 am to 6 pm.

 Admission: $7.50/adults, $6.50/2-17 years, $25/family of 4, FREE under 2. (Around $3 less per person in winter.) Other attractions are $2/ride.

 Directions: Take Hwy 401 West, exit # 183 to Hwy 402 westbound. Turn north at Colonel Talbot Rd. Stay on that road until it ends at the entrance to **Springbank Park**.

HALIBURTON FOREST & RESERVE

Walk in the clouds

"Wow! Hooking on to the web takes on a new meaning!" comments a guy in the group as he literally hooks himself to the lifeline some twenty metres above the ground.

As I carefully walk on the 12-inch wide boardwalk suspended in the air by an elaborate series of ropes knotted into a handrail, I realize I would be very nervous doing the same with my son, had he met the required minimum age of 10.

Our guide assures me he's never had to turn back because of a scared child, adding he remembers some kids who got bored by the experience! Bored?! If my children got bored by such an experience, it would be time to lock up the video games and throw away the key!

The 4-hour round-trip starts with a 15-minute van ride through the reserve, catching a glimpse of some of the campsites located in semi-wilderness along beautiful lakes. We then take a 10-minute walk along scenic **Pelaw River** before canoeing for 15 more minutes to a large stand of old growth White Pine. It would not surprise us to see a moose in such a landscape.

Our guide demonstrates how to put on our harness (to be hooked to a lifeline, a short walk from there). And we're off to the canopy trail.

It consists of half a kilometre of suspended boardwalk, painstakingly installed to ensure no harm comes to the tall White Pines. "The owner wanted to spruce up the forest trail" jokes the guide. We are each assigned a buddy before we hook ourselves and climb the ladder to our first section of boardwalk.

We walk from one tree to the next. Every time we change direction, we have to hook ourselves to a new lifeline while our extra hook remains attached to the line under which we stand. Taller buddies often have to lower the lines to allow shorter partners to hook themselves (that would be the tricky part for parents).

A large platform surrounds a very tall and straight pine, suspended from the tree top. We stop for a snack and to take in the amazing panorama while our guide tells us more about the crazy adventure in the building of this one-of-a-kind canopy boardwalk.

The Wolf Centre

The **Wolf Centre**, also located in Haliburton Forest, is only a few minutes drive from Base Camp.

A big line-up of visitors stood by the large bay windows overlooking a tiny part of the 15-acre enclosure, anxious to catch a glimpse of the wolves. Through loud speakers we could hear the animals' growls.

The clan has reduced its size over the years. Last time I visited, it was down to just a few wolves. It still is truly interesting to observe them interacting and listen to the expert explain the hierarchy and the personality of each member of the clan.

Inside the Wolf Centre, there are many exhibits and some interactive displays, as well as a book section and an art gallery featuring works on wolves.

TIPS (fun for 10 years +)

• Bring bug repellent in the spring.
• In July and August, if you attend the afternoon excursion, try to book it on a Thursday, when they offer a **Wolf Howl** session at around 8 pm (donations accepted). You might be lucky enough to hear the wolves howl back at the guide.
• 17 of the 50 lakes in this privately owned 50,000-acre forest are accessible by car. It is possible to buy a day pass ($15/adult, free for 17 years and under) to hike in the park and swim in the lakes). This is a great family outing for children under 10 years old and their parents, while older siblings tackle the canopy trail. A detailed map is available on site.
• Haliburton Forest is renowned for its mountain bike trails (over 300 kms). Trail pass is $15/day. Bike rental is $35/day or $25 after 1 pm (15" frames and up).
• They have a small wooden observatory the roof of which can roll off, equipped with three Meade LX200 telescopes. Presentations (pre-registration required) are offered Saturday and Sunday at 9:30 pm in July and 9 pm in August ($20/adults, $15/17 years and under).
• These lakes host great campsites but most are leased annually, except for 20 designated sites available for short term use ($15 plus the cost of day use permit). They also rent 2- or 3-bedroom housekeeping units and log cabins for 6-10 people for $65 per night, per person ($89 in the winter). It includes the day use permit. BEWARE! These are popular among the snowmobile amateurs. The roaring motors will trouble the quietness of the natural setting. Better rent during the fall to enjoy the colours.
• Ask about their dog sledding excursions starting at $115/person for 2 hours.
• Haliburton Forest was the first to offer a canopy trail attraction in Ontario. There are now more of such trails within 2 hours of Toronto. Check the **Treetop Walk** of **Eco Adventure Tours** in Collingwood (www.sceniccaves.com), the trails of **Arbraska Treetop Trekking** in Barrie (www.horseshoeresort.com) and the **Eaglecrest Aerial Park** in Bracebridge (www.aerialparks.ca).

Haliburton Forest & Wildlife Reserve • Haliburton (705) 754-2198	**Off the map N-E of Toronto 3 hrs**

www.haliburtonforest.com

 Schedule: Open year-round with extended office hours in July and August and during the winter. The **Canopy Trail** runs at least two times daily from early May to late October. The **Wolf Centre** is open from 10 am to 5 pm, daily from Victoria Day to Thanksgiving, Saturday and Sunday only the rest of the year.

Admission: The **Canopy Tour** is $95/adults and $75/10-17 years old (includes daily use permit and admission to Wolf Centre). The **Wolf Centre** is $9/adults, $6/under 18 years old, $20/family. The daily use permit is $15/adult ($39 during the winter).

Directions: R. R. #1, Haliburton. From Hwy 404 North, take exit #51/Davis Rd. eastbound. Follow Hwy 48 North to Coboconk. Take Hwy 35 North and drive past Minden to Carnarvon. Take Hwy 118 East to West Guilford. Cross the bridge and take County Rd. 7 (Kennisis Lake Road) for approximately 20 kms to the Base Camp.

General tips about
Animals:

- A great free outing to do with kids is a visit to a big box pet store. Don't underestimate these! Some are amazing, with rabbits, snakes, hamsters, fish, dogs, cats, ferrets, parrots and so on.
- **Big Al's Aquarium Supercentres** are great places to observe fish. When we visited the one in Scarborough , we loved the line-up of turquoise rectangles against a dark background... and the (small) shark feeding! The **Shark Feeding Frenzy** is offered on Tuesdays at 7 pm in most of their locations (but not all). Check www.bigalscanada.com for details and addresses.

ANIMALS

See **Reptilia** on p. 72.

WOOFSTOCK

Humans allowed

They come in all kinds, with assorted masters: pocket dogs with funny hairdos, fabulous royal poodles, good old golden retrievers with kids attached. Dog owners really are in their element at this festival.

This event has grown so much over the last years, it now includes hundreds of exhibitors and vendors competing at every corner for the attention of dog owners. Dogs (not kids!) get free cookies, samples, and gifts.

The event is obviously for dog owners but frustrated dog lovers like me (who can't have one because of an allergic family member) will enjoy the display of breeds… and masters' reactions.

Last summer, I thought it was hilarious to observe the disapproving looks of the masters of "better behaved" dogs as they watched other owners let their "bad" dogs frolic in the large fountain. (The weather was so hot we personally envied the canines ourselves!)

Who knew there were so many products catering to dogs: summer camps, "neckties" for dogs, organic cookies, pet cuisine express, exclusive pet photographers, pet plan insurance, posh pet furniture, dog paddling adventure… the list goes on.

With my dog-lover of a daughter, we camped by the catwalk (is that what you call it when it is for dogs?) across the park by the **Flatiron** building's mural, to see great dogs parade with their masters and to watch funny costume contests.

TIPS (fun for 5 years +)
• All dogs must be on a leash.
• This event is the perfect place to go if you'd like to get a dog and are wondering what breed to choose. I think you'll see them all amongst the visitors!
• For 2011, they've created their first **Winter Woofstock** on November 26-27 (indoor, right next to the **One of a Kind Show**). See www.winterwoofstock.com for details and to buy a discounted ticket.

NEARBY ATTRACTIONS
St. James Cathedral (2-min. walk) p. 132
Hockey Hall of Fame (5-min. walk) p. 340

Woofstock
(416) 410-1310
www.woofstock.ca

**D-3
Downtown
Toronto
10-min.**

Schedule: Usually the first weekend in June, from 10 am to 6 pm.
Admission: FREE.
Directions: Around **St. Lawrence Market**, Toronto. Runs along Front and Wellington Streets, from Jarvis to Scott, overflowing on Church and Market Streets, south of Front.

TORONTO ZOO

Kid-friendly all year long

Sometimes, we adults tackle an itinerary through the zoo as if it were a shopping list. We just have to see all 5000 animals between lunch and naptime. Orangutan? Been there! Giraffes? Done that! Hippo?... "Darn! We missed the hippo!" And while we stand there, confounded in the midst of such a tragedy, we miss the sounds of our young explorers laughing in front of a small otter's cage.

It would take more than eight hours to tour all the trails shown on the zoo's map. How many of us have ever reached the Grizzly Bear den located more than a one-hour walk from the admission gate? (Their trackless train is the way to go!)

The zoo fascinates each child in a different way. It seems logical to adapt the visit according to their interest of the moment. The visitor's guide handed out at the admission gate is packed with useful information and includes a map, which will help you locate your child's favourite animals.

Discovery Zone

Splash Island is so much fun that it could become the main reason we go to the **Toronto Zoo**, with the animals as a bonus! It is located within the **Discovery Zone**.

The spray pad is simply gorgeous. The giant animals seem to be popping out of the water. Kids run from the lake to the wetlands, the river (with water slides), and back to the ocean with whales and polar bear. All of these generously sprayed us when we least expected it.

The section located near the water games is jam-packed with things to do and animals to see. There's a two-storey "tree" from which you'll get a view of all the action: the cute prairie dogs we can observe from viewing domes, many small animals to look at, digging for dinosaur bones, giant egg or turtle shells to get into...

Another favourite: the **Waterside Theatre** with daily encounters with animals. We've seen birds of prey, skunks, wild cats, and fun ferrets running through tunnels held by the kids.

a carousel ride at $4 (daily May to October and weekends), all located near the **Zootique Gift Shop**).

Past the Australasia Pavilion is a neat attraction: the **Aussie Walkabout**. It is a fenced section where we're allowed to walk on a path, amidst dozens of kangaroos (don't expect them to come really close and it is closed during the off-season).

Interactive zoo

There's more to the Toronto Zoo than just walking and spying on animals. At the entrance, take a few seconds to check out the day's schedule for feedings and encounters with animal keepers.

Over 70 keepers take care of the animals; many of them meet visitors daily. From them, you'll learn the animals' names, what and how much they eat and the answers to any other questions the children might have.

Kesho Park (a 15-minute walk from the admission gate) is beautiful. Large bay windows allow you to watch the animals through rock walls. Along the trail, kids can go right inside a large Baobab tree, peek inside a termite mound, look at footprints, spy zebras and touch elephant tusks.

You can catch a pony ride in the Discovery Zone ($5), a camel ride for $6 or

Indoor zoo

The zoo's five pavilions make it possible to spend most of your visit indoors. With their jungles and tropical surroundings, they offer a great outing during winter's cold days and they're perfect on rainy days.

Personally, I really like these pavilions because they're enclosed spaces. Animals are within arm's reach … and so are the kids!

In the **Indo-Malaya Pavilion**, have a close look into the amazingly intelligent eyes of the orangutan. We always spend a long time admiring them interacting with their babies in their beautiful environment. In the **Americas Pavilion**, children are fascinated by the incessant moves of the lively otters.

Inside the **Africa Rainforest Pavilion** awaits the huge gorilla. Don't miss the intriguing (and very ugly) naked mole rats in their cross-sectioned maze of tunnels.

In the **Australasia Pavilion** is a great barrier reef with jelly fish, sea horses and more.

I have not had the chance to visit the **Tundra Trek** completed in 2009. It seems amazing, with a state-of-the-art habitat for the polar bears and arctic wolves, arctic foxes, snow geese and reindeer nearby. Seems like a must when visiting the zoo during the winter.

Note that the fur seal pool is still there but at the time of print, it was empty and getting renovated for penguins!

TIPS (fun for 2 years +)

• Fall colours are great at the zoo when the trails are covered with leaves.

• Halloween time brings **Boo at the Zoo**, usually a two-weekend event with special activities, when costumed children receive treats.

• During the **Christmas Treat Walk** organized every Boxing Day (December 26), starting at 10 am, visitors walk with the keepers from one den to the next to watch them offering certain animals their favourite treat (half-price admission with a food bank donation). When we attended this event, 300 people were gathering around the dens, leaving not much space for children to see anything. We stayed behind to have a good look at the tiger while everybody was following the keeper to the next animal. The beast slowly walked to its treat, had a sniff at its red steak ... and went back to sleep. Not exactly what we expected. Good time to visit the heated pavilions. By the way, the keepers swear elephants, lions and tigers love to play in the snow.

• Usually on Easter Sunday, children get a passport to stamp and get treats at the exit. Call to confirm.

• During March Break, there are more daily feedings and meetings with the keepers.

• The zoo's gift shop is huge and filled with animal-related items.

• The **Zoomobile** (a trackless train) runs through the zoo in 40 minutes. You hop on and off of it all day long when you buy the $8 pass for anyone 4 years and older. BEWARE! Only collapsible strollers can get on. It runs daily from Victoria Day until Thanksgiving and usually on weekends in April and October. Call to confirm.

• Find out about their family **sleepover** nights in the **Bush Camp** (6 years old minimum, around $80-$90).

• **Glen Rouge Campground** is the closest campground to the zoo. It is located at 7450 Kingston Road in Scarborough. Call (416) 338-2267.

• On their website, the zoo advertises a package with the hotel **Delta Toronto East**. Look under *Explore the Zoo*, click *Visitor Information*, then *Accommodations*.

• There are several snack bars throughout the site.

NEARBY ATTRACTIONS	
Whittamore Farm (10-min.)	p. 138
Rouge Park (5-min.)	p. 304

Toronto Zoo
• Scarborough
(416) 392-5900
www.torontozoo.com

D-3
N-E
of downtown
35-min.

Schedule: Open year-round except December 25 minimum from 9:30 am to 4:30 pm, extended hours in the summer (last admission one hour before closing time). **Splash Island** (weather permitting) open weekends end of May to June and daily from end of June to end of August; then, weekends only until mid-September. **Kids Zoo** and **Splash Island** open at 10 am. **Admission:** $23/13-64 years, $17/65 years +, $13/4-12 years, FREE for 3 years and under. Parking is $10 (cash only). If you plan to go more than once in the year, ask about membership! **Directions:** Take Hwy 401 East. ATTENTION! Follow the signs to Morningside exit and stay in the collector lanes (you can't exit at Meadowvale directly from the express lanes).Then follow Meadowvale Rd. (#389) northbound to the main zoo parking.

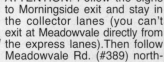

OSHAWA ZOO

Farm animals?

A cute lemur with fluffy white ears holds out his little paw to delicately pick the popcorn off my daughter's hand. He quietly starts to eat it while staring at her with interest. We are in the peaceful little Oshawa Zoo and enjoy every minute of it.

Despite its small size, the **Oshawa Zoo** holds a few surprises, the most awkward being the sight of a camel in the shade of a mature tree with lazy black and white cows grazing in the background! Thankfully, most enclosures are set in the middle of green pastures, adding to the quaint atmosphere of the place.

Further, we notice colourful pheasants on a grassy outcrop. The zoo counts an interesting variety of animals, including donkeys, llamas, goats, antelope and even a breed of rabbits from Argentina that look like kangaroos. The zoo is apparently home of Canada's only albino Wallaby (born in Oshawa Zoo).

While it doesn't take long to complete your visit, children can take as much time as they want to feed the animals (popcorn is sold at the entrance for this purpose).

TIPS (fun for 2 years +)

• You'll find picnic tables on site. We chose, however, to go back on pretty Columbus Road, westbound and down to Simcoe Street where we found a chip truck selling decadent fries and hamburgers by a gas station. We took our lunch to the playground beside the adjacent church.

NEARBY ATTRACTIONS
Automotive Museum (15-min.) .... p. 198
Cedar Park Resort (15-min.) .... p. 430

Oshawa Zoo
• Oshawa
(905) 655-5236
www.oshawazoo.ca

**C-4
East
of Toronto
45-min.**

Schedule: Open daily in July and August, 10 am to 5 pm. Open on weekends from the time grass is green to the time there's snow, 10:30 am to 4 pm. Call to confirm.

Admission: (cash or Interac) $10/adults, $9/seniors and students, $7/3 years and up, FREE for children 2 years and under, $34/family of 2 adults and kids under 16. Around $2/popcorn bags.

Directions: 3377 Grandview St. North. From Hwy 401 East, take exit #419/ Harmony Rd. northbound. Turn right on Winchester Rd., then left on Grandview St. North, right on Columbus Rd. The zoo is on the left hand side.

BOWMANVILLE ZOO

Please feed the animals

"Not in your mouth!" For the umpteenth time, my friend catches her little one as he is about to eat an animal treat. True, the Monkey chow in the greasy brown

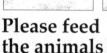

paper bag does look very appetizing.

Unlike the Toronto Zoo, **Bowmanville Zoo** (the oldest private zoo in North America) gives visitors the opportunity to feed most of the animals, much to the delight of children. In fact, without supervision, kids would likely give their entire feed bag to the greedy and plump little goats that await them in the first compound located across the bridge.

The Bowmanville Zoo also contrasts with its big brother by its smaller size (42 acres compared to 710 acres at Toronto Zoo), and a more modest sampling of animals (a little over 200 animals). The upswing is the convenience of touring the zoo in a single visit and interacting with the animals.

The broad paths that criss-cross the zoo are generally well shaded by the bordering mature trees; a real plus on hot summer days. There is a lovely country feel to the site.

We began our tour with the parrots, reptiles, cuddly lemurs and llamas. We then crossed a bridge over a small stream, that brought us to the elephants, lions and zebras' area. That's where you'll do the **Expedition Predator,** a short trolley ride in an enclosed space where a handler interacts with a large animal, included with admission. There's also a raised catwalk to look down on the enclosure.

There were also various kinds of horned animals, large birds and intriguing Capybaras, the world's largest rodents.

Daily summer performances involving lions, elephants or the many other kinds of animals, are presented in the impressive 400-seat indoor **Animatheatre** at 12 noon, 2 pm and 4 pm, also included with admission.

TIPS (fun for 2 years +)

• They have a **Splash Bash** (included with admission). Bring the bathing suits!

• I recommend you buy one animal feed bag per child (sold at the entrance for $2.50).

• Camel rides in the summer and elephant rides in the fall are offered for $6. Small vintage mechanical rides are located near the entrance in July and August. They are included with the admission fee.

• We had a picnic under the trees, but there is an air-conditioned snack bar near the entrance, with washrooms, tables and an aquarium to entertain visitors. Their gift shop is well stocked.

NEARBY ATTRACTIONS
Petticoat Creek (15-min.) .... p. 419
Cedar Park Resort (15-min.) .... p. 430

Bowmanville Zoo
• Bowmanville
(905) 623-5655
www.bowmanvillezoo.com

C-4
East
of Toronto
50-min.

Schedule: Open daily from May to end of September, and weekends only in October until Thanksgiving, weather permitting. Open minimum from 10 am to 4 pm (closes at 6 pm on May and June weekends and daily in July and August).

Admission: Around $19/adults, $16/ seniors and students, $13.50/3-12 years, FREE under 3 years.

Directions: 340 King St. E. (Hwy 2), Bowmanville. From Hwy 401 East, exit #432/Liberty St. northbound. Turn east on King St.

ELMVALE JUNGLE ZOO

I spy...

If your child swears she is seeing a zebra in the woods as you drive along Hwy 27, she speaks the truth!

Elmvale Jungle Zoo houses more than 300 zoo-reared animals that have known no life in the wild: lemurs, tigers, snakes, flamingos, kangaroos, giraffes and more.

I really enjoyed the design of this small zoo. Trees everywhere make it the perfect place to hang out on a very hot day. Some cages are very nicely set along shaded trails in the woods.

The trout pond has a small island inhabited by ducks and has a fountain that throws water way up in the air. We could feed the fish to generate some action. Parrots were fun to watch as they tried to grab the shells with their beaks.

There's a petting zoo, a snack bar and a playground.

Elmvale Jungle Zoo • Elmvale (705) 322-1112 www.elmvalejunglezoo.com	A-2 **North** of Toronto 75-min.

 Schedule: Open daily late May to Thanksgiving, from 9:30 am to 5 pm minimum. (Closes at 5 pm until June, at 7 pm in July, and at 6 pm until Labour Day. Then open daily until Thanksgiving, 10 am to 5 pm, weather permitting. Last admission one hour before closing time.

Admission: $14.50/adults, $12.50/seniors and students, $7.50/3-12 years, FREE for 2 years and under.

Directions: 14191 County Rd. #27. From Hwy 400 North, take exit #98/Hwy 26, turn left at Bayfield Street. Follow Hwy 26 into Hwy 27 (zoo is before Elmvale).

NORTHWOOD ZOO

Nose to nose

Northwood Zoo is a great place to look straight in the eyes of a tiger, and to see its teeth from up close.

The zoo includes many large felines but there's more to it. After observing the monkeys, we headed towards the huge buffalo den at the top of a small hill.

I loved the feeling by the wolves habitat which boasted plenty of trees. There were eagles and goats. But our favourite were the Grizzly bears.

When we visited, they were so playful, wrestling for fun, strolling all around their den, that we enjoyed them for more than 30 minutes.

Northwood Zoo and **Animal Sanctuary** • Seagrave (905) 985-2738 www.northwoodzoo.com	B-4 N-E of Toronto 75-min.

 Schedule: Open May long weekend to mid-October, 10:30 am to 6 pm.

Admission: (cash only) $17/adult, $14/senior, $12/3-11 years, FREE 2 years and under.

Directions: 2192 Cookston Lane, Seagrave. From Hwy 401, take exit #412 (Thickson Road) northbound. Turn east on Winchester Rd. and north on Simcoe St./Hwy 2. Turn left on River St. and watch for signs.

BIG APPLE

The Big Apple, well, is big. It stands more than 10 metres (35 feet) high and you can climb to the top from inside while reading a few apple-theme displays. (It is open from end of May to Thanksgiving.) Children want to reach the tiny balcony at the top of the apple. The scenery offers nothing outstanding, but you can see far away.

For a small fee, you may rent clubs in the gift shop to play mini golf, or take a ride in the small train.

Small dens are inhabited by deer, sheep and llamas. They can be fed with grains from vending machines. Behind them, you will find a few small trails, one of them quite pretty with wild flowers. Perfect to stretch small legs before continuing your journey.

Have a bite

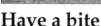

While I'm busy taking a picture of my children having fun at the Big Apple, I felt something applying pressure on my feet. Looking down, I discover a cute bunny chewing calmly on my straw handbag!

The **Big Apple** located on the south side of Hwy 401 is worth the stop when driving in the corridor between Montreal and Toronto, or to end a day trip to one of the nearby provincial parks with a sweet touch. The apple desserts counter inside the main building will make your mouth water: cookies, tarts, dumplings...

Large windows allow visitors to look inside the kitchen, where the bakers are in action, all dressed in white.

The outdoor playground is fun and the bunny rabbits are adorable. Last we checked, there were more than twenty roaming freely on the site.

TIPS (fun for 2 years +)

• Bring some change for the vending machines to feed the animals (and baby carrots for a real treat for the rabbits).
• Their store is huge and filled with trinkets, souvenirs, funny gadgets and more.
• You can buy fast food at the large restaurant but the tasty apple pies are the main reason to stop for a bite at the Big Apple.
• It you sit by the large windows of the restaurant, you can watch your kids play in the playground while you finish your meal.

The Big Apple
· Colborne
(905) 355-2574

C-6
East
of Toronto
1 hr 40

Schedule: Open year-round, 7:30 am to 8 pm (closes at 10 pm from April 1 to October 31).

Admission: FREE admission to the park and Big Apple, small extra fee for little train ride, mini golf and other seasonal rides available.

Directions: On Big Apple Drive, Colborne. From Hwy 401, take exit #497 (C. R. 25, Percy St./Big Apple Dr.) going south. Turn west (right) on Dudley Rd. (Big Apple Dr.), then right again.

MUSKOKA WILDLIFE CENTRE

Wild for animals

My young wolf lover and her friend are so thrilled by the promise of seeing three great specimens that they can't resist running wildly up and down the large trails until they reach their favourite animal's den.

This animal haven is like no other I have visited. (Have you ever been face to face with a moose? Now is your chance.) In true Muskoka fashion, it is set on uneven beds of rock. This makes for a lovely stroll through the forest with a new habitat to discover at every turn.

Signage by each den offers personal information on each tenant and once you've read one, you're hooked and have to read them all.

Here, we learn that Kootenay, the orphaned black bear, was raised by a B.C. family and now lives with his friend the cougar (they are separated only during feeding time!).

There, we read that Rufus was de-clawed with human nail clippers by a woman who wanted to keep him as a pet. Further, we meet the beaver. Its teeth were broken when it got to the centre. They healed him and have run all his food through the blender ever since.

During one of the **Meet the creatures** sessions offered indoors near the reception, we could pet a skunk, an opossum and a snapping turtle. Check the animal gallery on their website to see pictures of all their animals.

TIPS (fun for 5 years +)

• Their Meet the Creatures shows feature different animals at different time of the day.
• The centre's gift shop has a great collection of nature books with local content such as *Animal Tracks of Ontario*.
• Your admission is good for the day. You can go and have lunch outside the premises and come back for more fun.
• The picnic area near the beaver den is gorgeous and adjacent to the wolf space. They open a snack bar during the summer.
• A few minutes south of the centre on Hwy 11 you'll find a great burger place **Webers** by the overpass, with parkings lot on both sides of Hwy 11. They have a train theme going on. (You'll eat in a wagon.) By Hwy 11 South near the parking, there are large beds of rock to explore. To top off this outing, stop at the **Candy Shoppe**. It has two locations on each side of Hwy 11, a 2-min. walk north and 2-min. drive south of Webers (www.candyshoppe.ca).

Muskoka Wildlife Centre
• Severn Bridge
(705) 689-0222
www.muskokawildlifecentre.com

Off the map North of Toronto 1 3/4 hr

Schedule: Open daily from Victoria Day to Thanksgiving, 10 am to 6 pm. Open on weekends the rest of the year, 12 noon to 5 pm, weather permitting.
Admission: Around $12.75/adult, $10.75/senior & student, $9.75/3-12 years, $45/family of 5, FREE 2 years and under.
Directions: 1266 Hwy 11. Take Hwy 400 northbound, follow Hwy 11 North, 20 min. past Orillia, it's by the highway.

RIVERVIEW PARK & ZOO

On the right track

What a unique combination: a great outdoor playground and a beautiful little zoo with a small train ride along Otanabee River as a bonus. This is a definite must if you are in the Peterborough area.

The exhibits (over 27) offer a habitat well-adapted to the animals. Some are quite lovely! I am not the only one to think so, since the Peterborough Zoo was declared one of the two most ethical zoos in Canada by Zoocheck, a Toronto-based organization.

Yaks, various monkeys, snakes, camels, parrots, reindeer, ducks in a huge pond, pot-bellied pigs and other farm animals are nice. But if you ask my children, the playground is even nicer! Kids are attracted like magnets to the long flume slide that stretches amongst wild flowers, many climbing structures and a spray pad. (I got all excited when I saw the picture of the Dolphin Fountain on their website but I checked it out and it is not a wading pool!)

We walked past the duck pond towards the train track, passing by a real plane jacked up on a post. We unfortunately missed the last train. The ride seemed like fun; it crosses over **Otanabee River**, goes through a tunnel, takes a loop and returns.

We reached the Monkey House and strolled on the trail along the river, back to the playground for more zip line rides.They have an otter exhibit with waterfall and underwater viewing and daily feeding time at 1:30 pm.

TIPS (fun for 2 years +)

• Their splash pad includes dumping buckets, water cannons and sprays! Don't forget the bathing suits.

• Bring insect repellent if you want to go on the trails. It took us approximately 20 minutes to walk from the parking lot to the train stop at the other end of the park.

• During the summer, there are open-air **Sunday Afternoon Concerts** at 1:30 pm in the park's gazebo.

• There's a snack bar and a gorgeous picnic spot down from the playground by the river, where we can walk to a tiny island across a small bridge.

NEARBY ATTRACTIONS
Wild Water & Wheels (10-min.) ... p. 430

Riverview Park & Zoo • Peterborough (705) 748-9300 (ask Zoo line) www.puc.org/zoo	**B-5** **N-E** **of Toronto** **2 hrs**

 Schedule: Open daily year-round, 8:30 am to dusk. The train operates daily from Victoria Day to Labour Day, 10 am to 6 pm (then on weekends 12 noon to 5 pm until Thanksgiving).

 Admission: FREE admission to the park, $2/train ride and FREE under 2 years old.

Directions: 1230 Water St. North, Peterborough. From Hwy 401 East, take exit #436/Hwy 35/115. Near Peterborough, exit at The Parkway, turn right on Lansdowne St. West, turn left on George Street South, turn right on Water Street.

PAWSWAY TORONTO

Aaaaaaw!

First thing that caught my attention as we got in were the dogs. Many people had brought along their dogs inside the premises. Because they can! Then we saw the lower water fountain near the regular one, and sets of mop and bucket here and there with the sign Woops Station. Purina has indeed created the ultimate place for pet lovers.

Our favourite part of **PawsWay** was the **Purina Animal Hall of Fame** section. Attracted by a display showcasing the model of a dark lake with a tiny boat, we realized it included a miniature dog pulling it by a rope. We then learned that when their boat's oars were swept away by unexpected rough weather, Pat, a

black Labrador Retriever from Kingston, plunged into the frigid waters and pulled it for three hours, bow line in his jaws to save his master. We were hooked and proceeded to read all the true stories of pets who saved people's lives (many cats among them).

The centre includes a movie viewing corner, a large resource section filled with books and many educational displays regarding the health of our pets, how they see, how they talk and more.

When we were visiting, there was a small pet fair going on in the large room and mezzanine in the back of the building with an exhibition of pets' portraits and an adoption zone from the **Toronto Animal Services**. Sometimes, they organize **Ask the vet** free consultations.

The place also has an agility playground, with small obstacles, where free drop-in sessions are offered. PawsWay has become a meeting place for dog associations. Last time I checked, there were socials planned for Chihuahuas and Dobermans during the month.

TIPS (fun for 6 years +)
•   The place is not that interactive but there's lots of interesting reading to do, hence my recommendation for 6 years and older.
•   Pets are allowed in a large section of the snack bar within the centre.
•   Many indoor off-leash sessions are offered throughout the month for $5/session (or 5 sessions for $20), for large breeds and for small ones. First time visitors must take a $10/family off-leash safety course to be allowed to participate in these sessions. Check the calendar on their website.
•   Halloween is a fun time to come and watch pets in cute costumes.
•   You can consult the *Purina Animal Hall of Fame* on their website!

NEARBY ATTRACTIONS

PawsWay Toronto
(416) 360-7297
www.pawsway.ca

D-3
Downtown
Toronto
5-min.

Schedule: Open year-round, 11 am to 8 pm (closes at 6 pm on weekends). Closed on Tuesdays.
Admission: FREE.
Directions: 245 Queens Quay West, Toronto. Just west of Harbourfront Centre (east of Reese Street).

BASS PRO AT VAUGHAN MILLS

It's a zoo out there!

OK, maybe I'm stretching it a little bit here by including Bass Pro in this chapter. Yes, it is filled with animals, but most of them dead. Yet, certain displays of the real stuffed animals are so well executed, they could be featured at the ROM. And there are live fish in a gigantic tank.

The first time I visited **Bass Pro**, I was with my 11-year-old daughter and her cousins. I thought they'd like to see the waterfalls by the entrance, the real floatplane over our head and the huge fish tank where we might catch a fly fishing demonstration by a pro.

I didn't expect we would spend the next hour exploring the store. So, let me share with you what a few preteens with some imagination will do in such a store (if you're a store manager, you'll weep).

TIPS (fun for 6 years +)

• They put up a **Santa's Village** in the month before Christmas. But don't forget that Bass Pro is a hunters store! They shoot deer in this village and promote shooting games. (BEWARE! **Vaughan Mills** also has a Santa just around the corner, to your left when you exit Bass Pro into the mall (see p. 183). You don't want to have to explain about the two Santas!)

• You can play an *I Spy a Plane* game with the kids as you stroll around the mall. In addition to the float plane in Bass Pro, there's one painted on the mural outside of Bass Pro (going towards **Disney Store**); and a third, crashed on the facade of pet shop **Safari** (near **Speedpark**).

They'll do a fish contest with the huge fish-shaped pillows. They'll put on camouflage gear and hide in the hunting gear section. They'll practise shooting on interactive targets in a real campsite in a realistic forest in the far right of the store (for a small fee). They'll catch each other with fish nets. They'll grab a fishing line and will fish from one of the motor boats (in the far left of the shop).

The place is huge, with a very high ceiling. Look carefully, the attention to detail in the displays throughout the store is amazing. There are life-size wolves circling bisons, others attacking a deer, bears looking for fish in the water, totems, murals, guys on the mountain, raccoons...

The spread of merchandise is incredible. From weird camouflage gear, life-size decoys, riffles and bows, to very large boats, all-terrain vehicles and shiny fishing equipment, with clothing, decoration items and toys, all related to fishing or hunting, in between.

Think Disney-World-meets-Sarah-Palin and you get the picture!

Bass Pro	**C-3**
• Vaughan	**North**
(905) 761-4000	**of Toronto**
www.basspro.com	**35-min.**

 Schedule: Monday to Saturday, 9 am to 9 pm; Sunday, 10 am to 7 pm.

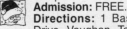 **Admission:** FREE.

Directions: 1 Bass Pro Mills Drive, Vaughan. Take Hwy 400 northbound, exit at Bass Pro Mills Dr. and look for the huge lodge attached to **Vaughan Mills** to your right.

NEARBY ATTRACTIONS

REPTILIA

Hungry anyone?

On the week we visited, *Newsweek* magazine had featured the best shots of the year and they included that of a zoo handler's arm coming out of the mouth of a crocodile. It was hard not to think about it as we watched Reptilia's staff poke at their biggest crocodile so it would come out of its slump to eat its weekly feed.

Reptilia used to be a retail store and breeding facility with an education centre on the side. In 2006, it moved into a much bigger facility and became Canada's biggest reptile zoo, with animal handlers initiating encounters, special feeding sessions, larger displays, hatcheries ... and a huge store on the side. They got me from the start, with the large waterfall by the entrance and the washrooms' water streams from which to wash our hands.

Then you access the wide and sinuous corridor lined with reptile habitats, some of them simply beautiful. We mothers were enthralled by the beauty of the green iguana. Not that the kids would notice, they were way too excited to see the small "crocodiles" (actually, they're caimans).

Most of the large snakes were quite lively, the Burmese pythons raising vertically four feet off the ground, as if under the influence of a flute charmer. Even the turtles moved a lot! (We saw turtle eggs under lamps in one of the hatcheries.)

In the next hours, we attended an interactive reptile show (to be followed later by a snake show) hosted by a handler with an appropriate Australian accent in the amphitheatre.

The crocodile feeding (with raw chicken) took place near the theatre. We later saw the viper swallowing a whole (dead) mouse. It is really impressive to see up close how they use their fangs to take in the body. Kids were fascinated. As a bonus, we even saw the handler walking with a gigantic snake wrapped around his body. What a sight!

TIPS (fun for 4 years +)

• To get the feeding schedules, go to their website in the *Visit our Zoo* section, then select *Feedings*.
• Their store sells reptiles along with everything to take care of them, as well as toys, posters, gadgets and t-shirts for the reptile fan.
• There's a snack bar selling pizza, burgers, fries, slushes and more. There's also a **Chuck E. Cheese** west of Reptilia, on the south side (3255 Rutherford, www.chuckecheese.com, see p. 316).

NEARBY ATTRACTIONS
Putting Edge (10-min.) .... p. 36
Bass Pro (5-min.) .... p. 71

Reptilia
• Vaughan
(905) 761-6223
www.reptilia.org

C-3
North
of Toronto
35-min.

Schedule: Opens at 10 am, closes at 8 pm Monday to Friday, at 6 pm Saturday and Sunday, and at 5 pm on holidays. The shows are offered on the weekends, during Holidays and all summer long.
Admission: $15/adults, $12/seniors, $10/4-12 years, FREE for 3 years and under.
Directions: 2501 Rutherford Rd., Vaughan. Take Hwy 400 northbound, exit at Rutherford eastbound. Reptilia is on the south side.

JUNGLE CAT WORLD

Mommy's there!!!

"What's she doing?" a girl is cooing to a couple of tame tigers in a back cage, as her friend the keeper cleans their main cage. The big "kitties" brush their backs against the wired fence, allowing the girl to touch their beautiful fur. Then they engage in a friendly fight. Intimacy is the operative word in this privately owned accredited zoo.

My daughter, the animal lover, who's been going to their summer camp for the last few years, has seen from up close how well treated the animals are by the attentive staff .

A cage, located close to the zoo entrance, often temporarily houses the "baby" of the moment. When I visited for the

first time in 1996, I was surprised to discover a German Shepherd pup and a baby lion cohabiting like the best of friends. During my most recent visit, there was a young leopard gnawing a stuffed teddy.

We particularly enjoy the otters and the small rabbit enclosures.

Generally, the cages are relatively small, except those of the Siberian tigers with its large pond and of the white wolves. (You can better see them from a tower nearby.)

Amongst the zoo's many tenants, you'll also find lions, bobcats, leopards, cougars, lynx, a black jaguar, lively gibbons and fun lemurs; many of them born on site.

The zoo also features a small playground with free-roaming deer, goats and peacocks. You can purchase grain to feed the animals. Those goats are greedy!

TIPS (fun for 2 years +)

• Count on daily feeding sessions at 1:30 pm to see the felines in action.
• Ask about their **Night Safari sleepover** experience allowing groups (20 people min., $40/person) to sleep over. It will allow you to see the animals once the general public is gone! Could be your chance to pet a baby tiger or a cute ... tarantula. (I held one and you can actually feel the weight of their legs on your hand as they crawl!)
• The zoo has a snack bar but there's a family restaurant, the **New Dutch Oven**, located just across from the zoo, (905) 983-5001.

NEARBY ATTRACTIONS
Automotive Museum (30-min.) .... p. 198
Cedar Park Resort (20-min.) .... p. 430

Jungle Cat World	**C-5**
• Orono	**East**
(905) 983-5016	**of Toronto**
www.junglecatworld.com	**60-min.**

 Schedule: Open year-round, 7 days, 10 am to 5 pm.
 Admission: $15/adults, $10/ seniors and students, $7.50/2-12 years, FREE under 2 years old.
 Directions: 3667 Concession Rd. 6, Orono. Take Hwy 401 East to Hwy 35/115 (exit #436) northbound. Take exit Concession Road 6/Taunton Road. Turn right on Concession Rd. 6.

WHITE ROCK OSTRICH FARM

Now, that's interesting!

What has three pairs of eyelids, two toes and one toenail? An ostrich! Want to see for yourself? Go to this ostrich farm!

It seems that health-conscious North Americans are turning to low-cholesterol protein sources. In that light, ostrich meat is gaining in reputation. This could explain the ostrich farms that are popping up here and there. But not all are open to the public.

The owners of this farm housing some 75-130 big birds obviously have fun with their unusual herd. In the gift shop, you can admire carved ostrich eggs (watch the kids, as these are an expensive item to break!).

Visitors are not allowed to roam freely on the site. They are invited on a bumpy hay-wagon ride to the fields.

As the ostriches are called, the children can feed the huge birds with corn (at $2/cup). When the bravest bird sneaks its head through the wire fence, we can appreciate the flexibility of that long, muscled neck.

TIPS (fun for 3 years +)
• The visit is not very long (approximately half an hour). It's a good stop to combine with an outing to another regional attraction.
• Usually the last three Fridays and Saturdays before October 31, the farm hosts a Screamfest. It seems to have gotten quite ambitious over the years with actors, intense sound and light effects, computers and pneumatic props. Suitable for 8 years and over, $12/12 years and older, $10/8-11 years (cash only). Check www.screamfest.info for more details.
• Ostrich burgers are sold on site. Frozen ostrich meat can be bought on the premises. If you wish to take some home, it would be a good idea to bring a cooler. Cash only.

NEARBY ATTRACTIONS

White Rock Ostrich Farm
• Rockwood
(519) 856-2629
www.whiterockostrichfarm.com

D-2
West
of Toronto
60-min.

Schedule: From June to October, open Saturdays, 10 am to 5 pm and Sundays, 12 noon to 5 pm. In July and August, also open Thursday and Friday, 10 am to 5 pm. Open for meat sales only on weekends in November and December, noon to 4 pm.

Admission: Hay-wagon tours: $5/adults, $3/3 to 17 years, FREE under 3. Cash only.

Directions: 13085 4th Line, Rockwood. From Hwy 401 West, take exit #320/Hwy 25 northbound. Turn west on Regional Rd. 12, then north on 4th Line.

CAMBRIDGE BUTTERFLY

The butterfly effect

We had just spent fifteen minutes focusing on the impressive hatchery inhabited by dozens of still cocoons so it was quite a contrast to return to the path with free-flying butterflies where we were literally cut off by reckless flyers zooming by. It felt like this was the highway and we had to be careful.

There's action in the butterfly conservatory: babbling brooks, small cascading waterfalls and, at times, close to 3,000 butterflies, many of them frolicking about.

It is fascinating to observe the chrysalis set in different hatching stages in the hatchery. The cocoons come from Costa Rica and Malaysia. Nearby are resting specimens of the amazing Atlas Moth, a nocturnal insect wider than the face of a ten-year-old.

We have to watch where we walk to avoid crushing butterflies on the floor. A

staff member explains it's a sign they are getting weaker and closer to the end of their life cycle.

The weak beauties accept our hand as a perch when laid in front of them. The children understand intuitively how to behave with the fragile butterflies.

The vegetation surrounding us is tropical. The humid air smells of flowers and fruit (butterfly meals on plates). The controlled weather under the glassed roof ranges from 24 to 28 degrees Celsius. After a while, a visit to the cooler galleries is most welcome.

A large number of butterflies are framed in one of the galleries; some are endangered species. The adjacent gallery includes intriguing displays of dead insects. A few live specimens are sometimes displayed on the site (such as a humongous millipede, when we were visiting. Yuk!).

A great time to visit the conservatory is during the **Monarch Days**, always the second weekend in September, when there's Monarch tagging and releasing, and migration exhibits.

TIPS (fun for 4 years +)

• They've added over 80 species of flowering plants around the site, creating an outdoor butterfly garden.
• They offer the drop-in **Bugfeast** event during the March Break: A lifetime opportunity to taste chocolate-dipped crickets!
• Ask about their **Brunch with Santa** and **Mystery in Paradise** events during Christmas time.
• The gift shop is well stocked with butterfly-themed toys, books, clothes and trinkets. My kids went crazy for chocolate butterfly lollypops.
• The **Paradise Café** serves light lunches and snacks.

NEARBY ATTRACTIONS
Shades' Mills C.A. (20-min.) .... p. 401

Cambridge Butterfly Conservatory • Cambridge (519) 653-1234	E-1 West of Toronto 85-min.

www.cambridgebutterfly.com

Schedule: Open daily from March to mid-October, 10 am to 5 pm. Closed on Mondays the rest of the year except on most major Holidays.

Admission: $11/adults, $9.75/seniors & students, $5.75/3-12 years, FREE under 3 years.

Directions: 2500 Kossuth Road, Cambridge. From Hwy 401 West, take exit #282/Hespeler Rd. North-Hwy 24. Turn west on Kossuth Road. The conservatory is on the left side.

AFRICAN LION SAFARI

Close encounters of the animal kind

Go figure why children are so attracted to animals! They're happy visiting a traditional zoo, but become literally ecstatic when encountering the fantastic opportunities offered by African Lion Safari. The park is huge and offers the unique opportunity to drive through the animals' living quarters, with your car windows as the only screen between your children and the animals.

African Lion Safari houses over 1000 exotic animals and birds of 132 species. When we drove through the seven large game reserves, we first encountered big birds such as emus.

We then watched sleeping lions that didn't lift an eyebrow. The tigers were just as lethargic. The whole scenery lacked action... then a crowd of baboons started to jump on our car!

If you're able to live with the idea of a monkey's "little present" decorating the hood of your car, I strongly recommend using your own vehicle instead of the zoo's bus. Children become delirious with joy with baboons perched on the windshield.

Having tried both, I see some disadvantages to the bus option. First, you don't control the amount of time spent watching each animal (the **Safari Tour Bus** ride takes

approximately one hour). In your own vehicle, it lasts as long as you please.

Second, the bus offers little grip for the monkeys, while cars make comfortable perches. Note that they sometimes succeed in detaching little parts of cars...

Bears were strolling amongst the monkeys. Quite a mixed company!

You'll meet amongst others: a few tall giraffes (rather impressive from up close), some rhinoceros, zebras and antelopes. My kids went wild when the tall giraffe licked our windshield with her black tongue.

Further on, you can witness the elephants swimming, pet the animals at the **Pets Corner**, watch shows by parrots and birds of prey and see other trained animal performances.

You can cross the pond on board the small boat named **African Queen** and ride the small train.

In the summer, children will enjoy playing in interactive water games at the **Misumu Bay Wet Play** area, located close to the restaurant's terrace. So don't forget the bathing suits!

TIPS (fun for 3 years +)

• Check their website for a list of hotels offering a package.

• The park's restaurant and gift shop are well stocked and affordable. In the gift shop, look at the t-shirts. When we visited, some of them were painted by the elephants! Now, that's a unique souvenir.

NEARBY ATTRACTIONS
Mount Nemo (30-min.) .... p. 238
Emerald Lake (25-min.) .... p. 412

Photo: Courtesy of African Lion Safari

African Lion Safari
• Cambridge
1-800-461-9453
www.lionsafari.com

E-2
S-W
of Toronto
75-min.

Schedule: Open May to mid-October, 10 am to 4 pm. Closes at 5 pm during weekends until end of June, then at 5:30 pm daily until Labour Day. Ground remains open for 2 hours after game reserves close.

Admission: (taxes not included) $30/13-54 years, $28/seniors, $25/3-12 years, FREE for children 2 years and under ($5 less during Spring and Fall). Tour bus costs approx. $5 extra per person.

Directions: From Hwy 401 West, take exit #299/Hwy 6 southbound for 14 kms and turn west (right) on Safari Rd.

NIAGARA PARKS BUTTERFLY

Butterfly-friendly attraction

The visit begins with the viewing of a short film. It is followed by a leisurely walk around the greenhouse for as long as we want. The conservatory layout includes trees, bushes and flower clumps, as well as a waterfall. The hot and humid air contributes to the overall exotic feel of the place. Would be perfect on a cold day!

Between 40 to 50 butterfly species live freely at the **Niagara Butterfly Conservatory** (over 2,000 specimens). I couldn't tell most of them apart, yet I saw at close range all sorts of exotic kinds including blue, black, red, yellow and orange ones. Here and there, fruit plates are left for the hungry butterflies, so that we may admire them while they feed. We can also observe their cocoons in each phase of development, suspended from the shelving in front of a large window with openings.

The beautiful winged insects are quite tame. In truth, they were born in this environment and have grown accustomed to the crowds that regularly and respectfully visit the hothouse.

My little naturalist miraculously stops moving for a minute, hoping that one of the two thousand butterflies in the greenhouse will mistake him for a flower and land on him. A woman, looking through her camera, waits for the perfect moment to snap a picture, unaware that a wonderful specimen is resting on her head. I take my time to capture (on film) a superb green and black butterfly standing 10 centimetres away from me.

Don't miss the interactive stations in the lobby. And check the *Teacher's Guide* on their website.

TIPS (fun for 4 years +)
• Purchase your tickets as soon as you arrive at the conservatory, as only then will the time of your visit be assigned (often one hour later, in the high season).
• If you arrive at opening time, chances are there will be many butterflies on the floor.
• Washrooms at the conservatory are less busy than those at the snack bar.
• You can end your outing with a visit to the adjacent outdoor gardens (the conservatory sits at the centre of **Niagara Parks Botanical Gardens**), have a bite at the snack bar or browse in the large gift shop.
• More on **Niagara Falls** on p. 253.

NEARBY ATTRACTIONS

Niagara Parks Butterfly Conservatory • Niagara Falls	E-4 Niagara Region 90-min.

www.niagaraparks.com
(go to *Things to Do*, then *Attractions*)

Schedule: Open year-round from 10 am (opens at 9 am in the summer). Closes at 6 pm from mid-June to early September, earlier during other seasons (last admission 30 mins. prior to closing time).

Admission: $12.25/adults, $8/6-12 years, FREE 5 years and under.

Directions: 2405 Niagara Pkwy., Niagara Falls. Take QEW towards Niagara, Fort Erie. Past St. Catharines, keep left to take Hwy 405 (Queenston). Take Stanley Ave. exit on the right (at the top of the ramp, turn left onto Stanley). Turn right on Portage Rd., then turn right on Niagara Parkway. The conservatory will be on your right.

BIRD KINGDOM

Indonesian experience

If you find there's an Indonesian feeling to the site, it is because the main aviary is in fact the showcase for a pièce de résistance: a gorgeous original Javanese house circa 1875, richly carved out of solid teak. Add to this the "Indiana Jones" feel of the Nocturnal Zone with bats, scorpions and crashed plane.

The noise takes you in as you enter the **Main Aviary**, with the birds' songs laced with the sound of the 40-foot waterfall. Then, your eyes are filled with the sight of the tall palm trees and the carved ruins amidst the walls of plants.

With all this distraction, we did not notice the birds right away. Then, we started an *I Spy* game, discovering the inhabitants one after the other (80 species!).

There's a great story behind the beautiful house! It was discovered by the owner of the aviary 30 kms from Niagara, laying in pieces, forgotten in some farm's barn. It took over two years to figure out how to assemble the numbered pieces back into the house we now see in the Main Aviary. Instructions had been lost. Talk about a puzzle!

We arrived too late to feed the Lorikeets ourselves (with a $2 portion of nectar, a big favourite here). But the kids had a blast with the parrot by the gift shop.

The dark **Nocturnal Zone** on the 3rd floor is truly beautiful, with crashed plane and stars on the ceiling. That's where they feed the bats. They've reversed the internal clock of the animals by turning the lights on at night and off during the day. That's why we can see them in active mode!

Over 40 species of smaller birds live in the **Small Aviary** on the 2nd floor.

TIPS (fun for 3 years +)

• In 2011, they're adding a **Discovery Zone**, **Kids Archeology Dig** and a scavenger hunt, among other things.
• The attraction's store is filled with great merchandise. The **Java House** sells food daily in the summer and on weekends the rest of the time.
• Your ticket is a day pass so you can show up early and return later in the day after visiting other Niagara attractions. More on **Niagara Falls** on p. 253.

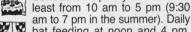

Bird Kingdom
• Niagara Falls
1-866-994-0090
www.birdkingdom.ca

E-4
Niagara Region
90-min.

Schedule: Open year-round at least from 10 am to 5 pm (9:30 am to 7 pm in the summer). Daily bat feeding at noon and 4 pm. Several daily Lorikeet feedings.
Admission: Around $17/16 years and older, $15/seniors, $12/4-15 years old, FREE 3 years and under. Save $5 per ticket when booking online!
Directions: 5651 River Rd., Niagara Falls. From QEW towards Niagara, take Hwy 420 (The Falls), continue on Falls Ave., turn left at Clifton Hill, then left at River Rd., then left at Hiram for parking.

MARINELAND

Not just another fish story...

As soon as kids try to feed one of the deer Marineland is swarming with, they're swept away amidst a sea of white spots with dozens of wet noses and velvety antlers tickling their faces.

When you think of **Marineland**, the first thought that comes to mind is the sight of killer whales splashing the crowd or a dolphin show. Yet this attraction offers plenty of other activities as well: a huge fish-feeding pond, a bear pit, a deer park, rides, a roller coaster and of course, coves allowing a closer view of the killer whales and belugas.

Performances

As soon as you arrive, head for the theatre where the next performance will be held. Schedules for the shows are posted at the site's entrance. It's better to get there 15 minutes before performances begin.

Dolphin, walrus and sea lion shows (which last approximately 30 minutes) are presented in the **King Waldorf Theatre**, left of the entrance. We walked along the amphitheatre's edge and reached a ramp that lead to the top of the auditorium and found seats in one of the last rows (where we had a good view of the show).

The **Aquarium Dome** with underwater viewing windows located in the basement allows us to watch sea lions and seals in action. There are freshwater aquariums located on this level as well.

The best way to watch the killer whales is through the fabulous underwa-

ter viewing windows of **Friendship Cove** (located a 15-minute walk away from the admission gate). The first sight I had of them left me standing open-mouthed. It is incredible to watch these impressive forces of nature.

Friendship Cove is surrounded by walkways for above-water viewing. You might even get a chance to touch the whales. Camera holders, beware! You really can get wet when the beasts suddenly jump out of the water.

There are feeding and touching sessions with the beluga whales in a separate habitat called the **Arctic Cove,** further down the park. It used to be free but you now have to pay around $8.50 for this.

One, two, three, GO!

There are three other points of interest not to be missed by animal lovers: the fish pond, the bear pit and the deer park. For the best effect, visit them in that order. A detailed map is given to visitors at the entrance.

You'll be surprised by the number of deer greeting you at the back of the deer park. Most of the animals (over 100) stay close to the stand where deer food is for sale. Don't expect your corn cup to last long and make sure to hold younger kids in your arms when they feed the deer.

When heading towards these attractions, you'll pass by the kiddie rides area. It includes a small roller coaster, especially designed for the younger crowd, that we really enjoyed. There's a **Viking Boat** carousel for the whole family and popular

TIPS (fun for 3 years +)

• During the summer, try to arrive no later than 10 am to avoid long line-ups, especially if you want to try the rides.
• Marineland's parking lot is set up lengthwise. If you're parked at one of the extremities, you'll have to walk more than 5 minutes before reaching the park entrance. Furthermore, the attraction is vast. You'll require a stroller for young children. Dolphin-shaped strollers can be rented on site for around $9.
• There's barely any shade on the Marineland site. Don't forget water bottles, hats and sunscreen!
• Don't do what my friend and I tried: to prop our children's caps up on their heads in order to make them reach the required height for a certain ride! The employee took a good 30 seconds to measure them carefully, then refused them access without batting an eye.
• The gift shop is huge and filled with small souvenirs. And by the entrance, there's a noisy (but air-conditioned) video arcade, with games galore.
• The closest campground, **King Waldorf's Tent & Trailer Park** is located behind Marineland by **Welland River** at 9015 Stanley Avenue, (905) 295-8191.
• For lunch, expect to pay about $7 for a hamburger with fries at the Marineland cafeteria. You'll find large indoor and outdoor areas with tables by a playground, perfect for picnics.

Wave Swinger (42" min.).

Beyond Friendship Cove, you can find the more elaborate rides, some way too testing for me but all included with the admission.

Dragon Mountain, going through a fake mountain amidst the trees is the world's longest steel roller coaster. It includes lots of tunnel travelling (48" min.). Even the entrance through a tunnel to access it is cool.

My daredevil went three times in a row on the **Sky Screamers**, a 450-foot triple tower (48"). It takes stamina to walk up the hill to the tower but you're rewarded by a great view from the lookout. The perfect place to stop for an ice cream cone.

Marineland | E-4
• Niagara Falls | **Niagara**
(905) 356-9565 | **Region**
www.marinelandcanada.com | **90-min.**

Schedule: Open from Victoria Day until Thanksgiving, weather permitting. From Victoria Day to late June, open from 10 am to 5 pm. In July and August, open daily from 9 am to 6 pm. Then, open from 10 am to 5 pm until Thanksgiving. All park activities remain in operation until dusk, after the admission gate closes.

Admission: (taxes not included) From the end of June until beginning of September: around $42/10-59 years, $35/5 to 9 years and seniors, FREE 4 years and under.

Directions: 7657 Portage Rd., Niagara Falls. Take QEW west towards Niagara and Fort Erie (don't follow Hwy 420!), take McLeod Rd. exit and follow signs.

NEARBY ATTRACTIONS

General tips about
Arts & Culture:

- BEWARE! If you buy tickets through services such as **Ticket Master** (www.ticketmaster.ca), there could be an extra charge of $5 per ticket or more! And they won't deliver if you buy at the last minute. You can usually buy tickets directly from the venue's box office to save the extra cost.
- Check **www.totix.ca** for discounted tickets sold at 5:30 pm for 8 pm shows (5 pm for 7:30 shows). Matinees are sold the day before the performance. They have a permanent booth at **Yonge-Dundas Square** (see p. 112).

ARTS
& CULTURE

See **AGO** on p. 88.

DUSK DANCE

Dance to another tune

Going to the park takes on new meaning when the Dusk Dance event is on. Kids are in for a surprise! They might see white-clad people hiding in the forest under the spell of strange music, graceful women running around the field with flowing scarves, acrobat dancers jumping from trees...

Dusk Dance provides quite a refreshing approach to modern dance and clearly is an original way to expose our kids to contemporary dance.

The concept is clever. The public is led from one station to the next through a public park, to enjoy a series of five 10-minute choreographies inspired by the natural surroundings.

The choreographers love to make good use of the environment. One year, we saw an amazing tap dance routine which integrated the park's picnic tables.

Some pieces are more traditional; others are quite experimental or even hilarious. The dancers are often within arms reach of the wide-eyed kids. You can see many children impulsively mimicking the movements of the artists.

Even the presentation between choreographies is funny. As we walked to the next performance, following our host, he suggested, tongue in cheek, that we do a collective sound: "Lets all say bahhhhh!" Hundreds of us did... Picture that!

Dusk Dance
(416) 504-6429, ext. 41
www.duskdances.ca

Schedule: Usually several evenings in a row. In 2010, it went from end of July to early August (the dates depend on the dance companies' schedules). A band starts at 7 pm, first dance follows at 7:30 pm.

Admission: Pay-what-you-can.

Directions: In Toronto, held in different parks every year but you can always count on performances at **Withrow Park** (south of Danforth Avenue, between Carlaw and Logan). Check their website for locations selected for the current year in and outside of Toronto.

TIPS (fun for 5 years +)

• Don't install yourself too comfortably before the event because you will keep changing places to watch the next choreography somewhere else in the park. A thick blanket could be useful.

• If with young kids, don't stand close to the speakers. It can be quite loud.

• More on **Withrow Park** on p. 462.

FAMOUS PEOPLE PLAYERS

In the dark

Taking your child to Famous People Players' dinner theatre is as close as you'll get to a grown-up outing without incurring the cost of a sitter.

Your only concern here may be to maintain children's appropriate behaviour during the elaborate hour-long dinner. After the show, all guests come back to the dining room for a tasty dessert.

It is likely the white-gloved waiter serving your meal in the dining room will also perform on stage

that evening. This you won't find out though until all performers remove their black hoods for the closing salute.

All productions are presented in black light, that is with performers who remain unseen to the public because they are dressed in black against a black backdrop. They manipulate various fluorescent props that seemingly "float" around with a life of their own.

TIPS (fun for 6 years +)
• Stars' photos you'll see on the walls aren't there just for decorating purposes. These famous actors and singers have actually made financial contributions to Famous People Players.

Lighthearted, the shows often include tall puppet characters (controlled by three performers), lip-syncing to original musical scores, and humourously designed objects miming scenes in a lively choreography.

Various musical productions are presented throughout the year, with some involving a story, while others simply present a series of great songs. All use the same concept.

I attended a Christmas show with two boys aged 7 and 9, and both loved it. Musicals are appropriate for any child who likes lively songs.

Parents will be moved when they learn this company's mandate is to present world class stage productions and integrate, through training, people who are developmentally challenged. Between the reception, the restaurant, and the performance, these people run the whole show!

They've changed their location in 2010 but we are told to expect the same ambiance.

Famous People Players
· Etobicoke
(416) 532-1137
www.fpp.org

D-3
West
of downtown
15-min.

 Schedule: Open year-round from Tuesday to Saturday. Dinner shows: arrival at 6 pm, dinner at 6:45 pm, show at 8 pm, dessert at 9 pm. Lunch shows: arrival at 11:30 am, lunch at 12 noon, show at 1 pm, dessert at 2 pm.
Admission: (tax not included) $59.50/adults, $52.50/seniors, $40/12 years and under.
Directions: 343 Evans Ave., Etobicoke. From the Gardiner Expy., take Kipling exit south, turn east on Evans.

NEARBY ATTRACTIONS

MYSTERIOUSLY YOURS

Guess what?

Around dessert time, the extroverted members of a noisy family pour into the restaurant from every angle, entering into individual conversations with diners, in a joyous cacophony. A piano player swiftly replaces the taped music in the background and all of a sudden, we are in the midst of the Godfather's retirement party.

A nervous black-eyed man with unbuttoned tuxedo shirt asks my wide-eyed son if he has seen a little plastic bag somewhere while the Godfather, his dad, graciously welcomes "dear friends" at the next table. In the vicinity, his sister is fishing for compliments on her Versace party dress while a pink satin-clad woman is kissing an "old boyfriend" she had just "recognized" amongst the guests.

TIPS (fun for 10 years +)

• The restaurant opens at 6:30 pm but action only starts at around 8 pm. The mystery is solved before 10:30 pm.
• Drinks and soft drinks are not included in the fixed price of the meal.
• Most items offered on the menu won't appeal to the average child. You may arrive a bit before 8 pm and pay only for the play. Note there's a **Mandarin** at 2200 Yonge Street, in **Canada Square**, four blocks north of the theatre (with well-priced parking at the top of Canada Square). Reservations are a must, as you don't want to be late for the show; call (416) 486-2222.
• Matinee presentations are offered at least two Wednesdays each month at the Toronto Historic **Old Mill Restaurant** (lunch at 11:30 am, mystery at 1 pm); around $55/lunch and show, around $37/show only, plus tax.

People of all ages attend the show. The nice (and young) grandparents at our table are quick to offer repartees to the actors who come to visit us. The more we improvise, the funnier it gets. My companion is thrilled to watch adults play make-believe!

It doesn't take long for a murder to occur (the Godfather's son) and for Lieutenant Carumbo to appear, bearing an unmistakable resemblance to Peter Falk's Colombo. The subsequent interrogation launches into quick and witty dialogue between the comedians evenly spread throughout the restaurant.

Many of us end up acting a small staged part, adding to the interactive nature of the attraction (my 10-year-old was turned into a mobster offering his condolences to the Godfather, cigar in mouth). Throughout the play, clues are given away; little details that will help those who listen carefully solve the mystery. We are too busy laughing to pay attention.

The murders staged by **Mysteriously Yours** keep changing. Over thirty plays were created over the years. You can expect a different mystery roughly every six months, investigated by the likes of Hercule Poirot, Miss Marple or Sherlock Holmes.

STAGE WEST

Go West!

A buffet instead of a fixed menu makes a big difference, especially with young children. It allows them to stretch their legs, returning again and again to explore the exciting display of food. Then, they're ready to settle down to watch the show.

We remain at our table in the elegant theatre restaurant to enjoy the performance. Many seats in the large multi-level room are horseshoe-shaped booths. I love the cozy feeling of these and they were a great hit with my daughter. Covered with a long tablecloth, it made for a nice little fort to hide under with her little friend after dessert, before the play.

If you can't book a booth, don't worry. Conveniently, you'll have a good view of the stage from any of the well-padded seats.

The children's productions are lunch shows presented during the March Break and Christmas time. I've seen three different ones; they all lasted a bit less than one hour. While I found some better than others, my kids were equally thrilled by the whole experience on all three occasions.

All year round, they also produce dinner musicals and concerts, many suit-

Photo: Courtesy of Stage West

able for families such as tributes to the Beatles, Abba and other legendary singers. They look like the real thing! I suspect these would be fun for preteens.

To give you an idea of the kind of plays they produce: In 2011, they present among other things *Joseph and the Amazing Technicolour Dreamcoat* Broadway musical and *Happy Days*.

Stage West is also a hotel! Their family packages are popular among local families who just want a change of scene. Must be the hotel's pool with a 3-storey-high water slide!

TIPS (fun for 4 years +)

• Their **Christmas Getaway Package** for a family of 4 includes: 2 nights in a suite, 4 tickets to kids' lunch show, buffet breakfast for 4 (2 mornings), use of pool and water slide (around $400 plus tax).
• Their **March Getaway Package** for a family of 4 includes the same and more: craft room, games room, bingo, fun classes, Children's Museum on the Go exhibit and free shuttle to **Square One** (around $350 plus tax).

Stage West Theatre Restaurant
D-3 N-W of Toronto 30-min.
• Mississauga
(905) 238-0042
1-800-263-0684
www.stagewest.com

Schedule: Lunch normally from 12:30 pm, show at 1:45 pm. Call to confirm. **Christmas** shows on Saturdays, usually mid-November to first week of January. **March Break** shows on some Saturdays in March/April and during the March Break weekdays (except Wednesday). Check their website or call for the year-round program of concerts or plays.
Admission: Kids lunch shows around $30/person + tax. Other dinner shows around $60 + tax.
Directions: 5400 Dixie Rd., Mississauga (south of Hwy 401, turn west on Matheson Blvd. to access entrance).

ART GALLERY OF ONTARIO

Wow!

The 600-foot-long glass and wood facade was truly impressive, standing like a huge Noah's ark along Dundas.

The first time I visited the AGO after the completion of its ambitious renovations, I was with two 11-year-old girls.

We walked through **Walker Court** to see if **The Grange** house was still open (it is), and were stunned by the permanent installation *The Index* by Canadian David Altmejd in the Atrium by the historic building.

A large angular grotto made of mirrors awaited, with real stuffed animals in its

reflecting nooks and crannies and slick man-birds overlooking werewolves torn into pieces by sharp fragments of mirrors. (I don't recommend this section for kids under 8 but my preteens were fascinated. You can avoid this section by using the central staircase.)

We chose to take the elevators to go directly to **Level 5** to see the contemporary art (saving the gorgeous wooden staircase to access the lower floors afterwards).

There were three spectacular totems made out of golf bags, a camping tent

complete with bathroom (all done in see-through screen) and a giant hunk of pink chewed bubble gum. They change the displays regularly, but this gives you an idea.

On **Level 4** we found some modern art that truly pushed the limits in the 60's such as five squares painted white with visible masking tape marks, giant stamps with ink to print activist posters, a pile of rocks on a mirror (try to explain that one to a 4-year-old!).

Something you won't have to explain to a young child is the **Thomson Collection of Ship Models** in the **Concourse Level**. Don't miss the magnificent **Galleria Italia** (see p. 83) by the Canadian art on **Level 2**. It features fascinating woodwork from Giuseppe Penone, blending perfectly with the architecture.

If the goal of contemporary art is to give us a fresh take on the world around us, it's mission accomplished for the AGO! When we reached one of the rooms featuring classic European artwork, my exhausted young companions prudently checked with me while pointing at a well-designed bench: "Is it art or can we sit on it?".

The **Grange Park** in the back of the AGO offers a playground, a wading pool, a small painted labyrinth and a good view of the funky **OCAD** building.

TIPS (fun for 3 years +)

• At the time of print, the Hands On Centre for children was closed, to be relocated into the exciting **Weston Family Learning Centre** opening in fall 2011. Until then, AGO is more fun for 8 years +.
• They offer free tours daily at 1 pm (beginning in **Walker Court**).
• The **AGOKids** section of their wonderful store includes an amazing selection of art activity books and fun items.
• You can always count of a great line-up of activities during the March Break.
• The **Café**, at the **Concourse Level**, serves tasty light meals and snacks.

NEARBY ATTRACTIONS

Art Gallery of Ontario (AGO)
(416) 979-6615 (family)
or **(416) 979-6648**
www.ago.net

D-3
**Downtown
Toronto
10-min.**

Schedule: Tuesday to Sunday, 10 am to 5:30 pm. Closed on Mondays. Open until 8:30 pm on Wednesdays.

Admission: $19.50/adults, $16/seniors, $11/6-17 years, $49/family of 7, FREE/5 years and under, FREE Wednesdays after

6 pm. Extra for special exhibits.
Directions: 317 Dundas St. West, Toronto (between McCaul and Beverley), a 5-min. walk from **St. Patrick Subway Station.**

MOCCA

Queen buzz

Knitted muffins, Chiyogami paper, blue trees, antique brass elevator, funky characters... and you've not even entered the MOCCA yet!

Start your Queen West journey with the **Museum of Contemporary Canadian Art (MOCCA)** as an anchor. Then, take it from there and see what comes along. There are enough funky things to discover between **Trinity-Bellwoods Park** (see p. 268) and Gladstone Avenue to spend a nice afternoon with older kids with artistic sensibility.

You'll recognize MOCCA's building by the huge art by its entrance. One year is was tall blue trees. The next year, a mind-blowing mural by David LaChapelle was displayed for our enjoyment.

Once, we were greeted at the door by cheers and flashes. This art installation recreated for us the feeling of being rich and famous on the red carpet. That put us in a playful mood!

A pile of posters ornate with intricate drawings seemed to invite us to help ourselves... each of them warned us that it was printed with poison ivy. The adult in me played mental games, trying to figure

out if an artist would dare punish me in such a way for touching her art. The youth accompanying me didn't even think and grabbed one (with no harm).

In the rest of the large room, different exhibitions were calling for our attention: a movie on a wall, a sports circuit, collages, etc. Exhibits change but you'll always find art to fuel interesting conversations with young art buffs.

Walking eastbound from the museum, you'll reach Trinity-Bellwoods Park where the Queen West Art Crawl is held every September (one of the best times to visit the area). Across the street is **The Paper Place** (887 Queen), offering an amazing selection of papers and related products, and the hip **Chippy's Fish & Chips** (893 Queen).

Go westbound and you'll see **The Knit Cafe** (1050 Queen), where you can buy unique yarn and simple patterns, knit and have a cappuccino. Check www.theknitcafetoronto.com (click on the door) to see how funky they are! First time I saw their shop, their window was filled with knitted muffins on plates.

You might want to check the bargains at **Woolfitt's Art Supplies** (1153 Queen). You'll definitely want to see the **Gladstone Hotel** (1214 Queen, 15-min. walk from the MOCCA) to feel the real buzz of Queen West.

Show your young companions the room photos in the hotel's scrapbook at the reception. Each one was decorated by a different artist. Then, ride up the antique elevator to the upper floors where you'll find art exhibitions in the corridors.

TIPS (fun for 10 years +)
• The **Queen West Art Crawl** is organized by **Toronto Artscape**, an organization dedicated to unlocking "the creative potential of people and places". For details on their lively event (including an interactive kids zone), visit www.toronto-artscape.on.ca and click *Programs*.

NEARBY ATTRACTIONS
Trinity-Bellwoods (5-min. walk) ... p. 268
Canoe Landing Park (5-min.) ...... p. 421

Museum of Contemporary Canadian Art (MOCCA)	D-3 Downtown Toronto 10-min.

(416) 395-0067
www.mocca.toronto.ca

Schedule: Tuesday to Sunday, 11 am to 6 pm. Closed on Mondays and during change of exhibitions. Better call ahead.
Admission: Pay-what-you-can.
Directions: 952 Queen St. W., Toronto (between Ossington Ave. and **Trinity-Bellwoods Park**).

GARDINER MUSEUM

Great on all levels!

Hard to imagine a ceramic museum could be of much interest for the kids but put yourself in the *I-Spy* game state of mind and you'll find something to catch their imagination on all four levels of the Gardiner Museum.

Start your visit with a look at the original pieces in the **Modern and Contemporary Ceramics** section at the ground level.

Not only will you be able to admire a Picasso vase and Chagall art but kids will be amazed to see that ceramic can be made to look like leather, metal, cement, glass, fabric or wood in the skilled hands of modern artists.

In the **Ancient Americas** gallery, you'll see fascinating artefacts dating from A.D. 200-850 (A.D. meaning Anno Domini, Latin for "in the year of our Lord" or after the birth of Jesus).

The colourful art in the adjacent **Italian Renaissance Maiolica** gallery was detailed and beautiful. Don't miss the *Fiery Furnace* scene on a 1550's dish by Urbino (for an old-fashioned view of Hell).

On the second level, there are battle scenes on the plates of the **Chinese Porcelain** section to your right, bathed with sunlight from the large windows.

In case you were wondering what exactly is Chinese porcelain, it is a mixture of kaolin (a pure white clay that forms when certain minerals break down) and petuntse (or China stone, ground to a fine powder), fired at a very high temperature.

The most whimsical pieces are found in the **European Porcelain** gallery and date from mid-18th century. Among our favourites: the **Monkey Orchestra** figurines and the Pug dogs from Germany, the porcelain dog house and the scene of a wolf eating a deer on a plate from Austria, the life-size rabbit from England and the wall displaying one hundred tiny scent bottles.

The third level hosts a vast **Special Exhibition Gallery** where changing exhibitions are displayed, with plenty of space to circulate between the masterpieces.

This is the level where you'll find the stylish **Gardiner Café** (managed by chef Jamie Kennedy) and the two terraces from which you get a gorgeous view of Queen's Park and the ROM. Note that the restaurant, which used to be quite expensive, now offers more affordable light lunches daily, from 11 am to 3 pm. (Try their fancy fries!)

When the **Open Clay Studio** is open for drop-in sessions in the lower level, there's a professional ceramist on hand to help.

TIPS (fun for 8 years +)

• Tickets for the drop-in Open Clay Studio sessions go on sale 30 minutes prior to each session (does not include the admission cost).
• More about the **Twelve Trees of Christmas** on p. 177.

NEARBY ATTRACTIONS
ROM (1-min. walk) .... p. 222
Around Bay Subway Station .... p. 459

Gardiner Museum	D-3
(416) 586-8080	**Downtown**
(416) 362-1957 (Café)	**Toronto**
www.gardinermuseum.	**10-min.**
on.ca	

Schedule: Open daily at 10 am. Closes at 6 pm, Monday to Thursday, at 9 pm on Fridays, and at 5 pm on weekends. **Open Clay Studio** drop-in: Wednesdays and Fridays, 6 to 8 pm, and Sundays, 1 to 3 pm.
Admission: $12/adult, $8/senior, $6/student, FREE 12 years and under. FREE on Fridays, 4 to 9 pm and all day on first Friday of every month. **Open Clay Studio** drop-in: $15/adults, $12/seniors, $5/12 years and under, $5/firing fee per piece.
Directions: 111 Queen's Park, Toronto (just south of Bloor Street).

McMichael Art Collection

Inspired hands-on

There is no better way to introduce kids to art appreciation than by taking them to a drop-in studio activity in the heart of the McMichael gallery on a Family Sunday. Who knows what awaits them? They might create their own sketch book or cut and layer coloured tissue paper into a landscape.

When we were visiting, one hands-on workshop was held in the little studio located in front of the gallery. Our youngster got to choose from a mountain of socks adorned with glass eyes and rubber noses and made her own animal puppet.

No other painters have better depicted nature than Tom Thompson and the Group of Seven. The museum holds more than 2000 of their masterpieces.

Seeing Group of Seven reproductions on placemats and stamps has never given me the feeling of being overexposed to their art. Each time, I rediscover them with the eyes of a child. But seeing these paintings with a child is another story, I must admit.

An easy way to do it is to select a theme and have them look for it in the paintings. This treasure hunt may lead to cries of excitement when they spot their theme but galleries are not churches after all!

We criss-crossed all the rooms, looking for autumn leaves (our theme) on the canvases. The gallery's walls seemed to my son like storybook pages on which he was looking for coloured trees.

Meanwhile, he was noticing that certain landscapes were covered in snow and that people were drawn on others. It became a great observation exercise on the sly.

Wide windows, framing the same nature painters seek to capture, are another reason to appreciate the gallery. Just looking through them makes us want to go outside and play. That's exactly what we did after our tour. A wide path, lined with little trails, undulates through the site. On our way to the parking lot, we stopped to pet a few bronze wolves resting by the path. I hope they're still there!

TIPS (fun for 4 years +)

• For a great March Break off the beaten track, the gallery offers special drop-in craft activities, hands-on activities and entertainment in the lobby and in different galleries.
• The **Discovery Space** on the upper level is more interactive than the other galleries.
• The **McMichael Café** sells light lunches.

NEARBY ATTRACTIONS

McMichael Canadian Art Collection • Kleinburg (905) 893-1121 www.mcmichael.com	C-3 N-W of Toronto 45-min.

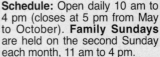

Schedule: Open daily 10 am to 4 pm (closes at 5 pm from May to October). **Family Sundays** are held on the second Sunday each month, 11 am to 4 pm. **Admission:** $15/adults, $12/6-18 years and seniors, $30/family of 5, FREE for 5 years and under. Parking is around $5. **Directions:** 10365 Islington Ave., Kleinburg. From Hwy 400 North, take exit #35/Major Mackenzie Dr. westbound, then turn north on Islington to Kleinburg.

TORONTO PUBLIC LIBRARY

Kids will flip... the pages

Through the Toronto Public Library, over 12 million items are put at our disposal: books, videos, CDs, DVDs, cassettes, magazines and newspapers, in more than 100 languages. All for free.

To obtain a library card, go to any branch and bring identification on which your name and address appear.

We can borrow up to 50 items for a 21-day period, a manageable time limit for busy parents. Videos can be borrowed at no charge for a 7-day period.

Thanks to a computerized system, most books (except the current Best Bets) can be borrowed from and returned to any branch (which can be useful when visiting another part of the city). You can also request books to be shipped to your local branch from any of the 99 branches.

Library activities

Books are just the tip of the iceberg. You need to flip through a copy of the **Toronto Public Library** publication *What's On* to grasp the extent and variety of the free activities that take place at the different branches, many of which are drop-in activities. Most programs are less than one hour long.

Many branches offer programs for children: **Babytime** (for babies 0-18 months) or **Toddler Time** (19-35 months). **Preschool Storytime** is for those who are ready to be on their own in a group. **Family Preschool Storytime** is for children 1 to 5 with their caregivers.

I have attended many activities with my children. Each time, we stayed afterwards and brought back piles of books.

Lillian H. Smith Library

The **Lillian H. Smith** branch (located at 239 College Street, east of Spadina, (416) 393-7746) offers thousands of illustrated books, hundreds of books for toddlers. Younger children love to go there to see the spiral staircase and to sit in the pleasant reading corner for kids.

TIPS (fun for 2 years +)

• Obtain a library card under your child's name. The late fine is much lower for children than for adults! Take a sturdy bag to the library to bring back all the books your children want.

• Your child can hear a story on the phone 24 hours a day with the **Dial-A-Story** service! Stories for different age groups are told in over 12 languages: (416) 395-5400.

• Toronto Public Library pays special attention to the March Break. In the *What's On* issue of January to March, you may consult the March Break Highlight pages or check the programs scheduled for each branch to find out about entertainment and free activities involving Reptilia, Stylamanders, Mad Science or clowns, to name a few cool options.

• Many branches also offer activities during Halloween.

Toronto Public Library

(416) 393-7131
www.torontopubliclibrary.ca

 Schedule: Varies. Check online.
Admission: The late fine is 30¢ per day per item up to a maximum of $12 per item for adults; 15¢ per day up to a maximum of $6 per item for teenagers and 10¢ per day up to a maximum of $4 per item for children 12 years and under. To replace a lost card, it is $2/adults and $1/children (cash or cheque only).

 Directions: 99 locations around the GTA. See those located near a subway station on pp. 452-477.

WORD ON THE STREET

Street smart

In the large Kidstreet section, you may see favourite children's hosts on the stage, hug Caillou, Franklin the Turtle or other popular characters. (You will definitely see me in my Toronto Fun Places booth!) But more importantly, savvy young readers can see in the flesh Canadian Children's authors and browse through all the important children's book publishers and bookstores' booths.

For one day, book lovers of all ages take over the street. Some 185,000 visitors take advantage of this great cultural event every fall. They have done so for over 20 years. They know they can always rely on over 260 exhibitors under tents: book and magazine publishers, bookstores and more offering bargains or freebies.

The event's setting in and around **Queen's Park** is perfect. It is common to see visitors sitting on the grass, already involved in the reading of a new book.

There is a large food vendors' section offering a wide variety of take out options to eat at the picnic tables.

For a site map and exhibitors listing check the *Toronto Star* the day before the event (Saturday).

Got kids in immersion?

Indoor book fairs have been a tradition for years in Quebec so it was natural for Toronto Francophones to import the concept.

Le Salon du livre de Toronto (Toronto French Book Fair) provides a space where you can buy French books and meet with authors from Quebec, Ontario, France and other francophone countries, with a great emphasis on children's books.

Thousands of students flock from the French and immersion schools all around the GTA to attend workshops put together for them.

The event is usually scheduled over 3-4 days, Wednesday to Saturday. In the last years, it had been offered in December, in different locations. In 2010, admission was $6/adults, $5/students and FREE for 12 years and under. Check their website around October to get more details (www.salondulivrede toronto.org).

NEARBY ATTRACTIONS

| **Word On The Street** (416) 504-7241 www. thewordonthestreet.ca | **D-3 Downtown Toronto 15-min.** |

Schedule: Rain or shine. Usually on the last Sunday of September, from 11 am to 6 pm. **Admission:** FREE.
Directions: The Toronto event runs on both sides of Queen's Park Circle, from Wellesley to Charles St., just south of the **Royal Ontario Museum** as well as in the park. The Kidstreet section is usually located on the west side of Queen's Park Circle. Closest subway access is **Museum Station**. (Note that the event also runs in Kitchener's **Victoria Park**, on the same day!)

NFB MEDIATHEQUE

Photo: Courtesy of NFB

Culture doesn't get cooler than this!

My young movie buff casually slides behind a console in the cozy parlour, as if he had lived in this kind of futuristic environment all his life. Down goes the headrest with enclosed speakers, up goes the volume, tap-tap knock the fingers on the touch screen and off he boldly goes, in the universe of Canadian cinematic culture.

You can use the digital viewing stations for free. The staff member gives you an access code to enter into the console and it's all yours.

The fact is, our tax dollars have allowed Canadian creators to explore their art for decades and the free **Mediatheque** is **National Film Board**'s way of giving something in return while celebrating Canadian productions. (Over 5,500 animated, documentary, short and feature films are available!)

The NFB went even further to stimulate the young visitors by offering $5 animation workshops where grateful parents watch their kids absorbed in the production of a real segment in claymation (remember *Wallace and Gromit*?) or other types of animation.

On the first weekend of every month, **Animate This** workshops for 6-13 years old are offered Saturdays and Sundays, from 12:30 pm to 2:30 pm. Kids 3 to 5 years can rely on similar workshops (**Can't Sit Still**) on Saturdays, from 10:30 am to 12 noon (followed by a special movie screening). Screening of shorts related to the workshop's theme are shown in their cinema, Saturdays and Sundays at 12 noon ($2 for those who didn't do the workshop).

We attended the workshop. Every time a child finished his animation, the friendly and patient professional staff would play it on the two monitors and large screen for the benefit of everybody. And each time it never failed, every one in the room would cheerfully applaud the new production and its proud creator.

You can also rent or buy NFB productions at the Mediatheque.

TIPS (fun for 3 years +)

• When viewing shorts with children at the consoles, it is better to select the *Children's Material* category under the *Film Genre* section. It will direct you to all productions appropriate for children.
• The animation workshop is a drop-in activity but it is very popular. It is better to reserve in advance and to arrive at the beginning of the workshop to ensure that your child will have enough time to complete his animation. An adult must accompany children.
• They email your child's animation file at the end of the workshop. Kids get to take home their clay creation.
• No food is allowed on the premises. Finish with a snack at neighbour **Indigo**.
• Neighbour **TIFF Bell Lightbox** has followed in NFB's footsteps by offering free workshops as well. See p. 95.

NEARBY ATTRACTIONS

CN Tower (5-min. walk) .... p. 124
CBC Museum (3-min. walk) .... p. 220

National Film Board (NFB) Mediatheque
(416) 973-3012 (general)
www.nfb.ca
(search *Mediatheque*)

D-3 Dowtown Toronto 5-min. walk

 Schedule: Open Tuesday and Wednesday, 12 noon to 7 pm; Thursday to Saturday, 12 noon to 10 pm; Sundays, 12 noon to 5 pm. Closed on Mondays.
 Admission: FREE viewing. Workshops are $5 per child, adults take part for free.
 Directions: 150 John Street, Toronto (at the corner of Richmond, just south of Queen Street).

SPROCKETS FILM FESTIVAL

Reel fun

"Didn't we get the ticket already?" inquires a four-year-old girl standing in line in front of us at the Festival. "Yes sweetheart", replies her dad, "but that was the parking ticket".

First held in 1998, **Sprockets (Toronto International Film Festival for Children and Youth)** is the TIFF's little brother. It aims to present the best films from around the world, made for children of all ages. In 2011, it featured over 100 films, a mix of features, animation, shorts and documentaries from 28 countries.

I am not one to think that big commercial successes are automatically lacking depth and meaningful messages, but it is a great opportunity to take a break from Hollywood! In many of the films for children 8 years and older, young viewers can relate to the way the young characters learn to overcome their difficulties.

Looking for the next Atom Egoyan? **Jump Cuts** is another original event under the TIFF umbrella, showcasing short films made by Ontarians in Grade 3 to 12.

Sprockets now has a permanent home in the new magnificent **TIFF Bell Lightbox** with five cinemas, two restaurants and a wonderful lounge on the second floor overlooking King Street. (Look for the two halves of a cow on the Kit Kat building!)

The new Bell Lightbox learning studios are be the perfect setting for the activities the Sprockets offers on the weekends of the event. In 2011, we could have fun with a green screen, make buttons, watch special effects makeup demonstrations and more.

TIPS (fun for 3 years +)

* It is better to reserve tickets online or by calling. They start selling public tickets a few weeks prior to the event. You can order on the same day if there's availability. They'll give you a confirmation number to present at the theatre with your ID and Visa card used (the only credit card accepted).
* Note that the general public can buy tickets to the weekday screenings if they're not sold out to schools.
* English subtitles for many foreign language films are read aloud by a narrator.
* They try to program the shorts, most appealing to younger kids, earlier in the day. Look for their **Reel Rascals** program (usually for 3-6 years old).
* The new TIFF building includes **O & B Canteen** at the ground level, where you can have light meals and snacks. There's also a concession on the second floor.

NEARBY ATTRACTIONS

Sprockets (416) 599-8433 www.tiff.net/sprockets	**D-3 Downtown Toronto** 5-min. walk

 Schedule: Now runs for 13 consecutive days in April. (Call to confirm exact dates.) Opens from 9:45 am to 7 pm on the weekends (on the weekdays, it is open to schools from 9:45 am). They usually have a special opening night on the first Friday but in 2011, it was sold out to TIFF members (who have the privilege to buy earlier.)

Admission: Around $12/adults, $9.50/ seniors and students, $8.50/12 years and under.

Directions: TIFF Bell Lightbox, 350 King St. West, Toronto (at the corner of John and King Streets).

BABY-FRIENDLY THEATRES

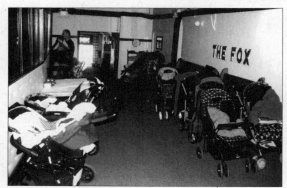

No more cabin fever

When I was on maternity leave, I sneaked into matinee screenings with my baby. Sometimes, I was lucky and he would sleep through the whole presentation. Other times, I had to promptly leave the theatre with a screaming baby. But that was before a trend that would fulfill the needs of a forever-grateful niche: movie buffs with babies.

The first to understand this craving new mothers have to just get out and see the latest movie was **Movies for Mommies**, which showed its first Toronto screening in 2001. From the beginning, this film event producer has favoured small independent cinemas, more suitable for moms networking, with their intimate environment.

On the day I attended one of their presentations in **Fox Cinema** at The Beach, there was a line-up of moms with strollers waiting to get in. The back of the theatre was packed with strollers. A table offered free diapers, baby wipes, bottle warmer and free welcome packs were given by sponsors to first-time attendees.

During the screening, we could hear the babies cooing because there was no Dolby sound to bury their noise. When a baby cried, his mom would walk up and down the aisle and he would usually settle down. Of course, when they don't, the civil thing to do is to step out into the lobby, guilt-free, until the little one has quieted down.

I could see little heads sticking out behind the arms of nursing mothers. Some infants were jumping on their parent's knees (some dads were in the audience). Five moms stood in the aisles, rocking their babies to sleep as they watched the movie. One mom was even sitting in the aisle with her young toddler. All sorts of things mothers would not dare to try during regular presentations.

Of course, the major movie theatre chains joined in. Cineplex (which now includes the formerly Famous Players theatres) offers **Stars & Stroller**. Empire Theatres has jumped on the bandwagon with **Reel Babies** in Ontario.

Whatever the location, always count on reduced sound. New locations are added periodically. Bring on the popcorn!

TIPS (fun for moms with babies)

• Check moviesformommies.com for tips on how to make the most of the experience. They should know, they started it all!
• You can bring toddler siblings if you feel they can sit through an adult movie (but bear in mind that most films screened are meant for adults; it's your "me" time, remember?).
• Food concessions are not necessarily open for these special screenings in the independent cinemas (in which case they will allow you in with your own coffee and popcorn).
• Check www.cinemaclock.com for current movie descriptions, theatre listings and more.

Movies for Mommies
(905) 707-8866
www.moviesformommies.com
(click *Locations* for independent theatres and listings)

Cineplex
www.cineplex.com
(search *Stars & Strollers* for chain theatres and listings)

Empire Reel Babies
www.empiretheatres.com
(click *Reel Babies* for chain theatres and listings)

DRIVE-IN THEATRES

Don't remain seated

Some families are real pros at making themselves at home at the drive-in. One of them has parked its mini-van with open hatchback facing the screen, allowing two teenagers to lay down on their bellies to watch the movie. Their parents are comfortably seated wrapped in blankets on foldable chairs, beside the vehicle, feet up on a footstool and small dog on their lap.

Where else can your kids leave their seats to stretch their legs while watching a movie? At home, watching a video?... That's true. But here, you get

TIPS (fun for 5 years +)

• You will catch the movie sound track on your car radio, through a local radio frequency, motor off. Don't worry, it won't drain your battery.
• You can play volleyball while you wait for the movie to start.
• There is a snack bar with the narrow look of diners from the 50's in the **Starlite** section. During the summer, it includes a BBQ pit from which you can get corn on the cob, sausages, chicken...
• See p. 15 for information on the only drive-in in Toronto at **Polson Pier**. Read about the new drive-in at **Wild Water Kingdom** on p. 426.
• The **North York Drive-in Theatre**, in Newmarket/East Gwillimbury, is located at 1025 Mount Albert Rd., (905) 836-4444, www.northyorkdrivein.com.

NEARBY ATTRACTIONS
Shell Skate Park (15-min.) .... p. 351
Coronation Park (15-min.) .... p. 424

to see the latest movies and you have a chance to socialize. Plus, smokers find an obvious advantage to the outdoor drive-ins.

To get to the **5 Drive-In** in Oakville, we drive through farmland (maybe not for long considering the way developments are catching up).

A big 5 Drive-In neon sign glows in the twilight. "Why do you call it 5 Drive-In if you have only three screens?" enquires my son. The man at the booth laughs and explains: "Cause we're located near Dundas, still called Hwy 5 by some!"

The three screens are placed back to back in a triangle. The biggest, **Starlite** (#1), can park 520 cars while the **Sunset** (#2) and **Cosmic** (#3) theatres respectively accommodate 330 and 150 cars with smaller screens.

It's 7:40 pm. We have to wait until the sun sets, at around 8:30 pm (we attended on a night in September). Kids play ball under the Sunset screen. My son is engaged in a game with new friends.

We admire a magnificent sunset, another advantage to a drive-in, and the double feature begins. Oops! I realize I should have brought Windex to clean my windshield!

---

5 Drive-In
• Oakville
(905) 257-8272
www.5drivein.com

**D-2
West
of Toronto
35-min.**

Schedule: Opens 3 days/week from late winter, daily during the summer, then 5 days until early winter, first feature starting at sundown. Go online for details.
Admission: $11/adult, $2/6-12 years, FREE for 5 years and under, $5/adults on Tuesdays, $15/car on Thursdays.
Directions: 2332, 9th Line in Oakville. Take QEW, exit at Ford Dr. North. It becomes the 9th Line, check east side.

KENSINGTON MARKET

Truly eclectic

I find it hard to put a label on a place where an "Urban Herbivores" sits next to a "Fat Burrito"; a sushi bar stands by an espresso bar, not too far from a "Hungary Thaï" (real name) and "Jumbo Empanadas".

The **Kensington Market** is located west of Spadina and south of College. It includes **Bellevue Square Park**, a small park with playground, by Augusta.

On Balwin Street (in the heart of the Market), **Roach Rama** brags they've served potheads since ah... they forget. It's located near the **Chocolate Addict** (185 Baldwin) where I read the sign "I could give up chocolate but I'm not a quitter". There's a theme right here, isn't there?

Make sure you check the masks and costumes normally on display in the windows of the **Red Pepper Spectacle Arts Studio** (160 Baldwin). They are the people responsible for the great **Kensington Winter Solstice** (formerly known as the Festival of Lights).

Kensington Café (73 Kensington, at Baldwin) used to have a couple of real swing chairs, popular with my son. They've changed the decor but they still have some version of a swing chair.

Most of the stretch on Kensington Ave., south of St. Andrews, is chock-full of funky vintage stores which are a hit with many teenagers. If you were a teen in the 70's, chances are you'll recognize some of the stuff in those shops! You don't need to be a fan of vintage clothing to be charmed by the candy coloured facades on that street.

Another big hit with the preteens and older kids is **Blue Banana Market** (250 Augusta, north of Baldwin). It feels like a souk. The marketplace offers a truly eclectic mix of merchandise on two floors.

Further north past Oxford St., for the last year, I've seen a really odd thing: the **Community Vehicular Reclamation Project**. It is a real car on cement blocks, filled with soil and live plants, taking over a parking spot. This is a signature action from the cool local organization responsible for the funky feel of Kensington Market (see **www.streetsareforpeople.org** and go to their *Action!* section). I hope it's still there!

Last summer, we tried and loved **The Grilled Cheese** restaurant, just west of Augusta (66 1/2 Nassau), serving (what else) all kinds of yummy grilled cheese sandwiches. We also enjoyed browsing through the cool stuff at the gift shop **Good Egg** (267 Augusta).

The best of the rest includes bakeries, cheese store, nut importer, fruit and vegetable stalls, bargain stores and other choices to discover as you stroll around.

Chinatown is at the edge of Kensington Market, along Spadina and Dundas. The restaurants, stalls and stores are of a different nature and offer a nice complement to a stroll around Kensington's funky blocks.

TIPS (fun for 8 years +)

• There's a municipal parking lot east of Kensington Ave. on the south side of Baldwin.
• Street celebrations are really this neighbourhood's forte. Check their *Market Calendar* (and the *Patio Guide*) on their website www.kensington-market.ca.
• Also see www.pskensington.ca for information about their **Pedestrian Sundays**. On the last Sunday in October, you can expect some Halloween activities in the streets.
• More about the **Kensington Market Winter Solstice** on p. 49, which always takes place on December 21. This participatory lantern parade is a great way to put ourselves in the spirit of Christmas.

NEARBY ATTRACTIONS
AGO (5-min. walk) .... p. 88
Trinity-Bellwoods (5-min.) .... p. 268

Kensington Market | D-3
www.
kensington-market.ca | **Downtown Toronto**
www.pskensington.ca | **10-min.**

Schedule: Most of the Market's shops are open 7 days a week, year-round, usually at least from 11 am to 7 pm. **Pedestrian Sundays** are on the last Sunday of the month from May to October, usually from 12 noon to 7 pm.

Admission: FREE.

Directions: Between Spadina and Augusta Av. (between Dundas and College St.) in Toronto.

CHINATOWN

Sticks to you!

My son digs into his plate of noodles after my crash course on how to handle the sticks. Then he slurps the tapioca balls from the bottom of his bubble tea. The outing is already a success.

Later, we hit **Furama Cake & Des-**

TIPS (fun for 6 years +)

• It adds to the fun if you allow a small budget for your child to spend. Many shops offer cheap trinkets you would not find in a regular dollar store.

• For a great panorama of Chinatown, take the elevator to reach the **Sky Dragon Restaurant** (on the 4th floor of Dragon City at 280 Spadina). It is flanked with a long balcony overlooking Spadina and Dundas, with a view of the **CN Tower** to the south and the table-top like structure of the **OCAD** building on the east side.

• Want to see a real karaoke place with private rooms and all (like the ones in the movie *Lost in Translation*? See **Echo** on the 2nd floor of Dragon City.

• For a description of the adjacent **Kensington Market**, see p. 98.

NEARBY ATTRACTIONS
AGO (5-min. walk) .... p. 88
Trinity-Bellwoods (5-min.) .... p. 268

sert Garden (248-50 Spadina) where we stack a decadent pile of inexpensive pastries on our tray (you know, to get "energy" for the stroll up and down Spadina).

Densely aligned signage is mainly in Chinese or Vietnamese (I think...). Most passersby are of Asian descent. From the sidewalk, you can see the chefs at work through the restaurants' windows and the exotic offerings on the outdoor stalls.

In a glance, I spot $1 glass eggs in a bowl of water, $1 tokens that look straight out of a treasure chest and $2 ornate metal nails to put on your fingertips.

My favourite places for great finds (bargains or merchandise I don't see anywhere else) are: **Pashmina Group** for its $10 pashminas in all colours (Unit 23B in the basement of **Chinatown Centre** at 222 Spadina), **Tap Phong Trading Co.** (360), **B & J Trading** (376) and **Harvest Int'l Trading** (406).

Flags International (422 Spadina) is a great place to find flags from every country in all sizes. (There's are now three other flag stores nearby.)

When I checked the small **Gwartzman's Art Supplies** (448 Spadina), they had the biggest (affordable) collection of wood manikins I have ever seen: horses, robot, dinosaurs, hand, etc.

Bright Pearl Seafood Restaurant (a large room with wide windows on the 2nd floor of 346 Spadina) is famous for its wide selection of dim sum. (Check their menu on www.brightpearlseafood.com.)

Chinatown	D-3
(416) 260-9800	**Downtown**
www.chinatownbia.com	Toronto
	10-min.

 Schedule: Open year-round. Most shops open at least from 11 am to 7 pm.

Admission: FREE. Many stores or restaurants accept only cash.

Directions: Along Spadina Avenue, Toronto (between Queen and College).

LITTLE INDIA

What a feast!

Glittering wedding saris in the bright windows, tiny stores stocked with spark-ling gods and god-desses, wood carvings and jewels, steaming roasted corn on the cob, colourful posters of the latest Bolly-wood movies. Little India is quite a feast for the eyes.

There's nothing like walking along the strip of Gerard Street east of Coxwell on a warm summer evening. Indian music bursts from welcom-ing open-door shops, women are lovely in their saris, men look sharp in their crisp shirts and the whole street is lit in a fes-tive way.

Street vendors offer exotic food: sugar cane juice mixed with lime, coconut milk directly from a freshly cut shell and fried pastries.

We don't try these yet because we're on our way to **Lahore Tikka**, my abso-lute favourite restaurant on the strip. If you've not visited the place lately, you're in for a sur-prise! The little covered patio, draped with silky fabrics in the summer, is gone but don't be sad! It's gone bigger, with the same owner. The restau-rant, still unfinished after all these years, is always busy with customers amidst the renovations. There's a cheerful chaotic feeling to the place.

Kids will enjoy climbing up the huge wooden wagon straight from India, adorned with the typical pompoms and flowers. Who knows, we might be able to ride on one of these some day on Gerrard.

After a great meal, we admire the exquisite **Rang Home Decor** (1413 Gerrard Street East, www.ranghomede-cor.com). My little princess chooses pretty 10¢ metal brace-lets from a bin in one of the small shops and I find myself a gorgeous gold and teal sari ($25 for a 5-yard piece) that I turned into exotic curtains that I can admire in my office as I write these lines!

TIPS (fun for 6 years +)
• For even more ambiance, visit this neighbourhood during one of their cel-ebrations. Expect a **Festival of South Asia** in the middle of July (2011: July 15-17) when there's music, dance, more vendors and lights. It's usually the best time to get a henna temporary tattoo!
• Indian food is spicy. Let the kids gorge on white rice, warm naans and ice cream while you enjoy the attack on your taste buds.

NEARBY ATTRACTIONS
The Beach (5-min.) .... p. 404

Little India
(416) 465-8513
www.
gerrardindiabazaar.com

D-3
East of
downtown
15-min.

Schedule: Open year-round. Most shops open at least between 12 noon and 9 pm.
Admission: FREE. Many stores accept only cash.
Directions: Located on Gerrard Street East, Toronto (between Greenwood and Coxwell Avenues).

PACIFIC MALL

Ticket to Hong Kong

I have heard from several friends of Chinese friends, who've actually lived in Hong Kong, that going to Pacific Mall would be the closest to experiencing the real thing without catching a plane. Good enough for me! So I grabbed my 10-year-old and took him on a trip... to Markham.

I'm surprised by how small most stores are in the mall (self-proclaimed as the largest Pacific Mall in North America). It includes some 300 indoor outlets plus 100 more outdoor stores and restaurants surrounding the building.

We can't understand one word anybody says and most signs are not in English. It is all really exotic to us! But the truth is, we feel quite at ease being the visible minority in this environment.

My son thinks he's in heaven when he spots a store selling the collector cards in fashion at the moment, with a dozen guys challenging each other at tables (**Pacific Gifts**, first floor, number E61). Then, on the second floor, is **Playscape**, also named **Orbit Entertainment Centre** (F83), a cool arcade where the teenage crowd plays on electronic guitar, keyboard and drums.

I can't resist buying the cutest outfit for my niece, pink and gold with the Chinese buttons and collar ($35, tax included in the price, cash only; many stores carry these). Adorable toddlers are actually wearing these clothes in the mall.

We try bubble tea. Our pastel drinks are topped with huge straws and stocked with tapioca spheres at the bottom. We buy tons of nicely packaged snacks never seen before at **Ding Dong** (a large con-

venience store located at C70/C72). I make a mental note to come back to stock up for my daughter's next party!

The second floor is where we find the most exotic section of the mall. Shops are even smaller. The entrance is adorned with dark wood and dragons greet us on large murals. In the small foodcourt, we eat a Japanese meal served in gorgeous bento boxes where everything has its own little compartment. Not your usual cafeteria tray. Let's hope they keep serving food in those!

My personal biggest find in this mall is the **MHQ Karaoke Box** (F33)! Behind a spectacular wall of brushed metal with portholes, are corridors with a series of doors leading to small rooms. Movie buffs will remember such rooms from the film *Lost in Translation* with Bill Murray! It does not get more exotic than that on this side of the planet!

Pacific Mall
· Markham
(905) 470-8785
www.pacificmalltoronto.com

C-3
N-E
of Toronto
35-min.

 Schedule: Sunday to Thursday, 11 am to 8 pm; Friday and Saturday, 11 am to 9 pm.
Admission: FREE.
Directions: 4300 Steeles, Markham. Take Hwy 404 north, turn east on Steeles. The mall is at the northeast corner of Steeles and Kennedy Roads.

TIPS (fun for 6 years +)
• Some stores only take cash.

CARABRAM

Remember Caravan?

It all started with Caravan, the first real multicultural festival launched in Toronto in the 70's. Then came Carabram in 1982, followed by Carassauga in 1985.

Carabram, Brampton; **Carassauga**, Mississauga. Get it? If they did one in Markham, they could call it Caraham! Or the City of Vaughan, Caravaughan. That would work. (OK, I'll stop here.)

The last Toronto event **Caravan** unfortunately took place many years ago. But if you feel like a trip around the World in one day with your kids, you can turn to Brampton and Mississauga, where the two annual three-day festivals are going strong.

We visited Carabram, but judging from the info on Carassauga's website, you can pretty much expect the same experience in Mississauga.

Both events last three days and include between 15 to 20 pavilions. Both cities offer free transportation and special

shuttle buses for the occasion. Most importantly, at both events, you get a passport to stamp at each "country" you visit. Kids just love that! The countries represented are not necessarily the same in both multicultural festivals.

At Carabram, most pavilions were less than a 10-minute drive apart. In "Hawaii", we were reminded that there is nothing cuter than a tiny hawaiian dancer. The market was very lively in "Philippines", where we saw a funny tease game (a bit like a mexican pinata). Displays were colourful in the pavilions of Pakistan and Caribbean.

TIPS (fun for 6 years +)

• **Carassauga** normally takes place on the last weekend of May or first of June (June 3-5 in 2011). Check www.carassauga.com or call (905) 615-3010 to confirm.

• There's a wading pool with water sprays in **Gage Park** on the southwest corner of Queen and Main Streets, downtown Brampton.

Carabram	D-2
• Brampton	N-W
(416) 452-4917	of Toronto
www.carabram.org	35-min.

Schedule: Normally on the weekend after Canada Day, call to confirm.

Admission: Passports are $10 in advance and $12 at the door. FREE for children 12 years and under.

Directions: From Hwy 401, take Hwy 427 northbound to the end, then turn west to reach Brampton. Check their website for a map of the pavilions.

NEARBY ATTRACTIONS

CANADIAN ABORIGINAL FESTIVAL

Dance competitions are the heart of the festival, usually attracting over 800 dancers competing in different categories.

They are accompanied by the rhythm of several live drummers and singers who perform around what is known as a "dance circle".

The **Women's Jingle Dress Dance** is a high point with the clattering sounds of dresses covered with over 300 tin cones. Similarly, men move around with tiny bells attached around their ankles.

Regalia of sound and colours

Strolling the open space during this festival reminds me of the activity and excitement backstage of a show. Whether standing in a food line-up, checking out the market's many stalls or tidying fringes and feathers, dancers clad in beautiful traditional regalia are everywhere and mingle informally with visitors before the competitions.

Most visitors prefer to stand near the "circle of dance". This allowed my 3-year-old great freedom to roam around without annoying spectators. In fact, children can stroll easily all over the grounds. But most of all, it was playing with newfound friends inside the large teepee that captivated my little papoose most.

Since my last visit, the festival has moved its location from Toronto to Hamilton but the experience remains the same.

TIPS (fun for 5 years +)

• Toronto is an aboriginal word meaning "the gathering place" (it used to be relevant but the festival is now in Hamilton).

• You'll find interesting things at the marketplace. We bought a nice wooden set of bow and arrows as well as a leather quiver (each around $10), on which an artist burned my daughter's name along with drawings of rabbits and beavers.

• Most activities are adult-oriented: traditional teachings, art exhibition and fashion show. Check the schedule at the entrance to find out more about the children's activities such as storytelling and games.

• See the **Six Nations Fall Festival** on p. 105.

NEARBY ATTRACTIONS
Children's Museum (10-min.) ...... p. 218
Football Hall of Fame (5-min.) ...... p. 339

Canadian Aboriginal Festival
• Hamilton
(519) 751-0040
www.canab.com

E-2
S-W
of Toronto
60-min.

Schedule: Usually starts last Friday in November, to Sunday.
Admission: $14/adults, $6/12 years and under, $30/family of 4. Many municipal parking lots around.
Directions: Copps Coliseum, 101 York Blvd., Hamilton. From QEW westbound, take exit # 73 for York Boulevard.

SIX NATIONS FALL FAIR

Teenagers and grandparents, preschoolers and adults, male and female alike, all participate in the dance competitions.

I am really pleased that my daughter sees how great the kids are doing. She actually becomes so enthused that I have to restrain her from joining the Powwow (which should never be confused with a dance party). I tell her she could dance outside of the stadium instead.

After enjoying the dance competition, we spent a full hour alternating between the midway (offering some fifteen rides on a pay as you play basis) and the food lane.

The event may include birds of prey demonstration, rodeo or even a demolition derby. It changes every year.

Light feet in action

We hear the live singers and musicians as soon as we arrive at the fairground. In order to reach the dance circle, we have to cross a gravel road that has been blocked. With other visitors, we patiently wait (wondering why exactly). All of a sudden, a four-horse wagon flashes by, leaving a huge cloud of dust behind. Now I get it. Crossing the road in the middle of the chuck wagon race of the Six Nations Fall Fair would be a perilous affair!

Once the race is over, the gate is opened and we walk to the baseball diamond turned into the perfect spot for a great **Powwow**.

The dance circle is surrounded by sets of bleachers where all visitors can get a good look at participants, dressed in colourful regalia. We are close enough to appreciate the intricate steps performed with such light feet that the dancers seem to never rest their full weight on the ground.

TIPS (fun for 5 years +)

• The event actually starts on the Thursday following Labour Day. Expect **fireworks** on the Friday night. The powwow takes place during the weekend.
• Check the **Canadian Aboriginal Festival** on p. 104.

NEARBY ATTRACTIONS
Warplane Museum (20-min.) ...... p. 194

Six Nations Fall Fair	E-2
• Ohsweken	S-W
(519) 445-0783	of Toronto
www.sntourism.com	90-min.

Schedule: Always the weekend following Labour Day weekend.
Admission: (cash only) Around $8/adults, $6/seniors, $4/6-12 years, FREE for 5 years and under. Pay-per-ride midway.
Directions: Take QEW then follow Hwy 403 towards Hamilton. Exit Hwy 18 southbound, follow Hwy 54 past Onondaga. Turn right on Chiefswood Rd. to 4th Line.

MUSIC WITH BITE

Have a bite

"Perfect setting for a pillow fight, isn't it? I'll join you... but after the concert." insisted the smiling pianist to the bunch of kids slumped on the cushions by the stage. He then proceeded to give a taste of his medicine for the next 45 minutes, with as much cool interaction with the young public as will allow a piano concert.

This was our first experience with **Music with Bite.** I observed my then 6-year-old daughter with her friends. They carved themselves a comfortable nest in the cushions. (Maybe too comfortable, I wondered?) They seemed ready for a sleepover. A quick look at the other kids reassured me. They all did the same.

As the musician created magic right under our nose, I saw very young kids fidgeting their little fingers along with him. One toddler was mimicking the pianist's way of lifting the hands between musical phrases.

He explained how to appreciate moments of silence in Chopin's *Mazurka*: "They hold you in the clouds." He helped them discern the spring wheel in a Schubert's piece, and the rhythmic waves

supporting the melody by Liszt.

During the question session, young pianists ask funny questions: "Don't your fingers get really tired?" and "How many minutes do you practice every day?" (Every adult in the room who has to fight for 10-minute piano practice sessions was roaring with laughs hearing that one.) How about five hours!

A treat of cookies and milk was offered in the back of the room.

In 2010, we were treated with TorQ, a passionate group of percussionists with a twinkle in their eyes. Opera and harp were introduced to the young audience through story-telling.

This is Music with Bite's way to make kids hungry for more.

TIPS (fun for 5 years +)

• Parents don't have to sit on cushions. There are tables and chairs in the room.
• More about **Harbourfront Centre** and what's around on p. 24.

NEARBY ATTRACTIONS
Roundhouse Park (10-min. walk) p. 199
Canada's Sugar Beach (5-min.)   p. 420

Music with Bite
(416) 964-9095
www.
harbourfrontcentre.com

D-3
Downtown
Toronto
10-min. walk

Schedule: On selected weekends (or holiday) throughout the year, at 1 pm. Go to *What's On* on their website for listing of events.

Admission: FREE.

Directions: Harbourfront Centre, 235 Queen's Quay West (west of York St.), Toronto. There's a municipal parking lot across the street.

TORONTO SYMPHONY ORCHESTRA

A classic outing

A dark-clad man is testing his tuba, casually sitting on the edge of the stage and beating the tempo with his legs. Musicians and spectators alike are slowly reaching their respective seats and the joyous cacophony of a full orchestra tuning before the show fills the air.

I tease the two mature women in front of us who did not feel they needed to be accompanied by a child as an excuse to attend the **Young People's Concert** which is about to delight us. We came to see the animated movie based on Raymond Briggs' touching book *The Snowman*, with live music from the **TSO**!

On the program are printed *Jingle Bells* and *Frosty the Snowman* songs, for the sing-along part of the show. Among other things, we will also be treated to excerpts from a full orchestra version of the theme song of (what used to be) *Hockey Night in Canada* and Vivaldi's *Winter* enriched by the conductor's reading of Vivaldi's comments on the original score.

Storytelling, theatrical situations, dramatic conductors or even puppets, nothing is ruled out by the Young People's Concerts series in order to initiate children to the world of classical music.

TSO's roster varies from one year to the next but it always includes a Christmas show (2011, *Twelve Days of Christmas* on December 11). Another TSO Christmas tradition is their Handel's *Messiah*, performed with the **Toronto Mendelssohn Choir** (this choir usually performs a great **Festival of Carols** in December at the **Roy Thomson Hall** but sometimes, it takes place in another venue, check www.tmchoir.org). The younger body of TSO, the **Toronto Symphony Youth Orchestra,** involves musicians 22 years and under; a great model for young spectators! (See their website to see when they perform.)

TIPS (fun for 5 years +)

- Children 5 years and older with purchased tickets are welcome to any TSO performance.
- TSO offers the **tsoundcheck** price of $12 on certain performances for spectators 15-29 years old. Check www.tso.ca/tsoundcheck on Mondays to find out what tickets are currently available.
- Also performing at Roy Thomson Hall is the **Toronto Children's Chorus.** We saw their Christmas show. Most memorable was the 300 children's passionate expressions as they sang carols. And what parent wouldn't wish for the level of attention these children so easily give their conductor!
- Fancy frozen desserts and refreshments are usually sold during intermission.
- More on **Roy Thomson Hall** on p. 126.

NEARBY ATTRACTIONS

NFB Mediatheque (5-min. walk) ... p. 94
CN Tower (5-min. walk) .... p. 124

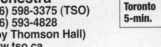

Toronto Symphony Orchestra (416) 598-3375 (TSO) (416) 593-4828 **(Roy Thomson Hall)** www.tso.ca	**D-3 Downtown** Toronto 5-min.

Schedule: Young People's Concerts run 5 times between October and May, at 1:30 and 3:30 pm on Saturdays.

Admission: $20-$31.50/person (with the Desjardins Family Pack deal, pay $15/person when you buy 3 or more. This offer is also valid for the Sunday Light Classics performances.

Directions: 60 Simcoe St., **Roy Thomson Hall**, Toronto (southwest corner at King Street).

IRELAND PARK

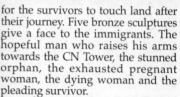

Out of sight

Lots of people I know who went looking for this park, missed it. I had noticed the tiny sign in front of an old building but had thought what I saw was the extent of it: A small patch of grass by the water. Not at all! It is just the entranceway to the quay where you'll find a ship sculpture and life-size statues of emaciated Irish people overlooking Lake Ontario's open water and downtown Toronto.

It is hard to imagine that the city's population was just 20,000 when over 38,000 Irish immigrants reached it by boat in 1847. **Ireland Park** commemorates the Great Famine which made them flee their country, with a focus on the 1,100 unlucky who died almost upon arrival.

Look between the cracks of the limestone structure which looks like a shipwreck to read the names of the people who died (675 of them listed here).

The waterfront location helps us understand what it must have felt like

for the survivors to touch land after their journey. Five bronze sculptures give a face to the immigrants. The hopeful man who raises his arms towards the CN Tower, the stunned orphan, the exhausted pregnant woman, the dying woman and the pleading survivor.

When visiting, we had the chance to observe the tall ship **Kajama** (see p. 209) glide by, all sails out, into the narrow canal between the shore and **Toronto Islands**.

Between this and the surprising monument of Ireland Park, it was a surreal experience.

TIPS (fun for 6 years +)

• This outing is more interesting if the kids can read the name on the ship-like structure. It is less stressful with kids 6 years and over since the park has no fence to separate it from the open water.
• Parking is super expensive near this park due to the airport. Try to find parking along the streets west of **Little Norway Park** (see p. 324), west of Bathurst.

NEARBY ATTRACTIONS

Ireland Park
Dial 311 (new service)
www.toronto.ca

D-3
Downtown
Toronto
5-min.

Schedule: Open year-round.
Admission: FREE.
Directions: South of Queens Quay West, Bathurst Street becomes Eireann Quay which leads to the ferry ramp in front of the airport. **Ireland Park**'s entrance is on the last patch of land on the east side of Eireann Quay, Toronto. Most of the park is hidden and by the water.

VILLAGE OF ISLINGTON MURALS

Artist's touch

These murals are like chips, you can't stop at one! I came across one of them by chance, I had to see them all. They're absolute gems of urban art.

It takes less than 15 minutes to walk from the first to the last mural of the **Village of Islington**.

The first art work was created in 2004 but they seriously started in 2007 and have added murals ever since.

Twelve of them are from amazing Toronto-based artist John Kuna (who graduated from OCAD in 1997).

It is a real pleasure to walk and dis-

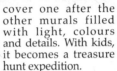

cover one after the other murals filled with light, colours and details. With kids, it becomes a treasure hunt expedition.

Don't tell them where they are so your kids have to pay attention, but here's a list of the Dundas Street West addresses of the buildings around which you'll see the murals. Let them find 4879, 4884, 4901, 4937, 4946, 4959, 4968, 4972, 4984, 4986, 4988, 4994, 5110 and 5126.

TIPS (fun for 6 years +)

• There's a **Second Cup** just west of Islington Avenue. The first mural at 4879 Dundas W. is just a 2-min. walk further west.

• The last mural to the west is a somewhat boring "Welcome" mural on the west wall of **Alex Family Restaurant** that doesn't look like much but has nice staff and a huge menu selection (5164 Dundas).

• You'll find municipal parking space in the back alley one street north of Dundas West, between Royalavon Crescent and Renown Road. Try to park closer to Royalavon Crescent, you'll be closer to the **Michael Power Park** with playground and you will find a cluster of murals starting one block east of the park (after Avonhurst Rd., on the north side).

NEARBY ATTRACTIONS
Montgomery Inn (5-min. walk) .... p. 376
Around Islington Station .... p. 452

Village of Islington Murals
· Etobicoke
www.villageofislington.com

D-3
N-W
of downtown
20-min.

Schedule: Accessible year-round.
Admission: FREE.
Directions: The murals are found on both sides of Dundas St. West, between Islington and Kipling Avenues. The first mural near Islington is a 10-min. walk from **Islington Subway Station**.

ART WALK OF TREE SCULPTURES

Back to life

Ever since the first old maple tree died on my street, I've dreaded the inevitable day when the quiet giant gracing my front yard will have to go too. When I heard about the great project Art Walk of Tree Sculptures initiated in Orangeville, I had to check for myself how that town succeeded in giving a second life to some of their cherished trees.

We stopped in Orangeville on the day we went to visit **Belfountain Conservation Area**. It turned out to be a great combo on a sunny day in October. The colourful trees (many of them still standing, don't worry) nicely framed the great Victorian houses in the old part of the town.

You've got to download the map of the **Art Walk of Tree Sculptures** ahead of time to get the full treasure hunt feeling that is the appeal of this attraction. (Also, there's the fact that the sculptures are spread over a vast area. You could easily miss most of them without the map.) They've just updated it.

The map showed a cluster of sculptures along First Street so we parked on Broadview near that street (which allowed us to admire the lovely main street).

We could see First Street stretching a long way in front of us. It offered one of our favourite sculptures: the *Tree Spirit* allowing us to stand inside a silhouette carved into the trunk. We then turned left onto McCarthy Street (where my daughter sympathized with a moose), and left again on Faulkner Street, to reach Zina Street (a truly beautiful street with splendid houses).

We walked west (right) on Zina, then turned left on Louisa Street to continue west on Broadway where we admired a tree painted and carved all around with different moon phases.

The energy was winding down so we hopped in our car to look for a few sculptures south of Broadway that caught our attention on the map. The Hobbit house, located at 30 Margaret Street, was a hit with us.

TIPS (fun for 6 years +)

• To download a PDF map of the walk, go to their website, click *Tourism* on the menu, then go to the *Tourist Attractions* section.

• We had a hot chocolate complete with real whipped cream at **Mochaberry Coffee & Co** (www.mochaberry.ca, 177B Broadview) before starting our tour. I also tried their grilled cheese and thought it was delicious.

• To go to **Belfountain** after this, I thought it prettier to take a country-road instead of Hwy 10. I took John Street southbound from Broadway. It becomes the country road Willoughby Road. I then turned west (right) on Charleston Side Road and south (left) on Mississauga Road, which runs into Belfountain.

NEARBY ATTRACTIONS

Orangeville Art Walk of Tree Sculptures	C-2 N-W of Toronto 60-min.

• Orangeville
(519) 941-0440
www.orangeville.org

 Schedule: Open year-round.
Admission: FREE.
 Directions: Take Hwy 410 north-bound, it becomes Hwy 10. Turn west at the lights on Hwy 10 to get to Broadway, which runs through old Orangeville. Try to park near First Street.

HARVEST MOON BAKERY & GARDENS

A pie in the sky

What made the artist bakers choose to set foot there, I'll never know but I'm truly grateful for the treats and the trails they offer off Hwy 6. This is the best way to end an outing in the region.

A friend of mine who regularly rents a cottage at Lion's Head had mentioned the place to me. Her family has made it a tradition to end their summer vacation with a scrumptious pie from **Harvest Moon**, which they would savour back home in Toronto.

She was so enthralled by the memory of the tasty pies that she forgot to mention what a funky little place Harvest Moon is.

The bakery looks like it's standing on stilts, cute and whimsical. Nearby, the bakers' house is fit for Tolkien's *The Hobbit*. And the sculpture walks and gardens were created in the same spirit.

Look carefully as you stroll along the path of the **Wildflower Way** and you'll notice carved trees, unnaturally large nests, chiseled wine glasses hanging from branches, painted rocks blending with the greenery... A real treasure hunt.

The rain started pouring before we could explore the **Froggy Walk** but it was as promising, starting with a giant bug made out of sticks and wires.

TIPS (fun for 4 years +)

• There's more than pies on their menu. Check the menu on their website (and look at the pictures under *Bakery*) for an idea of what could await when you go: cookies, brownies, breads, pasties, etc.

• I always spot their sign too late along Hwy 6 (you can't see the bakery from the road). If going northbound on Hwy 6, they're approx. 10 kms past Ferndale, on your left. Going southbound on Hwy 6, they're approx. 5 kms south of Lindsay Rd. 20, on your right.

NEARBY ATTRACTIONS
Bruce Peninsula Park (30-min.) ... p. 276
Sandy Beach (20 min.) .... p. 402

Harvest Moon Organic Bakery & Sculpture Gardens
· Lion's Head
(519) 592-5742
www.harvestmoonbakery.ca

Off the map N-W of Toronto 3 1/2 hrs

Schedule: Open 9 am to 4:30 pm; in the Summer, Wednesday to Sunday and Holiday Mondays); in Spring and Fall, Thursday to Sunday.
Admission: FREE, donation box.
Directions: 3927 Hwy 6, Lion's Head. Look for sign on the west side of Hwy 6, between the town of Ferndale and Lindsay Rd. 20.

YONGE-DUNDAS SQUARE

Our own little Times Square

The first time I took my nephews from Montreal to Yonge-Dundas Square, they thought they had arrived in New York! There's indeed a buzz to the place, with the line-up of activities at the square, the numerous billboards and the huge crowd gathering at the crosswalk of Yonge and Dundas.

Yonge and Dundas intersection was the first in Toronto to offer scramble crossing, where pedestrians can cross in any direction including diagonally on the green light (Bloor and Yonge is the second one).

It gives a very liberating feeling the first time you try it. For a few minutes, the street belongs to the people.

Weather permitting, when there's room left by the other activities going on (multicultural markets, free shows, outdoor movies, etc), you can see up to twenty water fountains spurting from the ground, surrounded by tables and chairs. Kids find them very hard to resist!

In turn, we've seen chalk artists undertake ambitious drawings, duos of drummers performing in unison, and hip-hop dancers compete for our attention. The place is brightly lit during Christmas time.

TIPS (fun for 6 years +)

• Check the calendar of events on their website for a list of the various events taking place at Yonge-Dundas Square year-round (including outdoor cinema!).

• The square also hosts the **T. O. Tix** box office where you can buy discounted tickets at 12 noon for same-day shows. See www.totix.ca.

• With our visitors, we visited the **Hard Rock Café**, just south of the square (you can't miss that giant guitar). It features a large collection of electric guitars on the ceiling by the entrance and showcases genuine rock stars' clothing or instruments on every wall. There was so much to look at, we decided to stay for a bite, there's something for everyone on their menu.

• Other times, we've enjoyed great burgers at **Johnny Rocket**, right across Dundas Street, before or after a movie at the **AMC Yonge & Dundas 24** next door.

• Just east of Johnny Rocket (north on Victoria St.), see the surprising pond at **Devonian Square**, which turns into a rink in the winter. A dead-end was made out of Victoria and tables and chairs are often installed in the middle of the street. This is turning into a lovely little hideaway.

NEARBY ATTRACTIONS

Yonge-Dundas Square
(416) 979-9960
www.ydsquare.ca

D-3
Downtown
Toronto
10-min.

Schedule: Open year-round.
Admission: FREE.

Directions: Located right across from the **Eaton Centre** in Toronto, at the corner of (what else?) Yonge and Dundas Streets. There's a parking lot with reduced prices after 6 pm just north of Dundas on Victoria Street.

SCOTIABANK BUSKERFEST

Real urban fun

A menacing gladiator slowly walks towards my son and stops one foot short of his face. My son bravely sustains the look, at the same time shy and amused by the attention while people start to gather around us. Little did he know that he was about to be held hostage, serving as a shield between the heartless warrior and his enemy.

Now, we know first hand the **BuskerFest** qualifies as an interactive event! In the next two hours as we walked from one attraction to the next, my 9-year-old keener took part in a sword fight, he

shook hands with an extra-terrestrial, he was involved in a balloon sculpture contest and he passed the hat for a wacky cowgirl. I think his blond hair had something to do with being selected at every corner.

Among other skits, we saw a wacky black-belt performer from New York, the most interactive Men in Tights from Toronto and a Californian cowgirl who claimed she would "milk us for all our worth".

The following year, we saw a naughty Australian contortionist covered with tattoos, amazing break-dancers from New York, out-of-control acrobat dancers from the UK and a local favourite, Mark Cmor, who will grab your cell phone if it rings during his performance and engage in a conversation with your unsuspecting friend.

Shy people beware! Expect great interaction and lots of jokes and teasing from these free-spirited street performers.

It is quite interesting to see how humour differs from one country to the next. Over the years, I have noticed that Australians are the most provocative, UK performers play with the absurd, Americans are more politically correct and Canadians have a tendency to downplay their act to better surprise you with something bold when you're off guard.

TIPS (fun for 5 years +)

• Make sure you bring a handful of loonies to the event. The shows are free but hats circulate at the end of every performance. Kids like to contribute their share. Buskers are not paid to perform during the event. Our donation is their bread and butter.

• The donations you make at the entrance to the car-free zone goes to **Epilepsy Toronto**. Scotiabank BuskerFest is actually an awareness event organized by this not-for-profit charity.

• The event includes free little workshops under the Scotiabank tent, allowing kids to learn more about the art of mime, drama, magic, etc. More children's activities are offered in other sections.

• Read about what's around **King Subway Station** on p. 473.

NEARBY ATTRACTIONS
St. James Cathedral (1-min. walk) p. 132
Hockey Hall (10-min. walk) .... p. 340

Scotiabank BuskerFest (416) 964-9095 www. torontobuskerfest.com	D-3 Downtown Toronto 10-min.

  Schedule: The organizers want to stick to the weekend before Labour Day, in August (including the Thursday and the Friday preceding this weekend), from 12 noon to 10 pm minimum (closes at 8 pm on Sunday). Check their website to confirm.
Admission: Donations for **Epilepsy Toronto** at the entrance. Pay-what-you-can for individual busker performances.
Directions: Front St., between Church and Jarvis, Toronto. There's a public parking lot at the foot of Church, south of Front.

SCOTIABANK NUIT BLANCHE

Sleepless in Toronto

Here's an urban phenomenon you can show to your kids... except when stated otherwise in their fat brochure!

Your **Nuit Blanche** probably won't be sleepless if you're with kids (those days are over!) but you can start as early as 7 pm, before the crowds kick in, and enjoy as many eclectic activities as your gang can bear. Warning, my friend's four kids were still going strong at midnight!

After attending different venues for the last four Nuit Blanche, I can tell you it is very hard to predict what awaits you.

Activities created for the event can last anywhere from two minutes to half an hour. There can be a massive crowd attending, or hardly anyone. They can be extremely creative or very disappointing.

The unknown is actually part of the fun. Control freaks will want to avoid this experience.

There were over 130 options to choose from when we attended the event in 2010. We started with the pièce de résistance, the sound and light installation which took over **Nathan Phillips Square**. Then we went through the dense crowd at the corner of Queen and Yonge to admire a splendid minivan laced with an intricate pattern of little dots. Further south, immense clowns' heads could be seen, peeking between the austere buildings.

On the plaza of **Commerce Court**, sixty young dancers forming a circle were dancing around the clock... literally! Each one represented one minute, and offered a 1-minute improvised dance when their time came.

On our way to **The Distillery**, in **Berczy Park**, we visited a chapel entirely made of camping gear, with a cross made out of canoes, sections plastered with chiseled oars, Jesus on the Cross, made out of life jackets.

TIPS (fun for 8 years +)

• Call them to learn where to find the event's brochure ahead of time (hard to find during the event). It offers tons of information (including age recommendations) and is very useful to generate the treasure hunt feeling when strolling the city with kids. They also help to identify where the clusters of attractions are located so you get the most out of your stroll.

• Expect bigger crowds (and waiting lines) near Bloor and Avenue Road.

• Take advantage of the **TTC**'s extended services during the event, including special shuttle buses.

Scotiabank Nuit Blanche
(416) 338-0338 (Access Toronto)
www.scotiabanknuitblanche.ca

Schedule: Usually last Saturday of September or first Saturday in October, from 7 pm to sunrise (2011: Oct. 1, 2012: Sept. 29).
Admission: FREE.
Directions: Check their website for the directions to the different venues.

OUTDOOR SUMMER THEATRE

Smooth theatre

I watch a little boy strolling along the park's path, unaware that a Shakespearean play is taking place right next to it. I laugh as I observe his astonished look when two big men engage in a fight. It caught the attention of other passersby who decide to join in the crowd already following the play.

Withrow Park offers a perfect setting for an outdoor theatre. Two mature tress frame the stage, small pickets with lines mark imaginary aisles and spectators sit on the small slope, ensuring a good view.

When we attend, *Othello* is playing. The fact that we could see him coming from the grass field added a realistic touch impossible to recreate in an indoor theatre. Later on, as the scenes unfold,

we can still watch a naughty Casio running after a playful Bianca in the distant background.

Open-air plays also mean we can observe the actors "behind the scene". What I mistook for a flea market clothing sale was actually the actors' costume rack!

Some spectators come fully equipped to enjoy the show. The man in front of me brought his folding chair and coffee in a thermos. A mother of three offers an endless supply of snacks to her kids. Babies are quietly sleeping in their parent's arms. There's even a master petting a happy dog by his side.

The actors' voices are strong, which is a good thing with all those cicadas singing in the background!

When I attended, the play was performed by the Shakespeare in the Rough (SiTR) company until 2006 (**Driftwood Theatre** took over in 2007). The artistic director of SiTR recently started **Humber River Shakespeare Co.** which aims at performing in the Humber River area (www.humberrivershakespeare.ca).

TIPS (fun for 8 years +)

• **Withrow Park** includes a gorgeous playground with wading pool much appreciated by local families. Danforth Avenue offers a wide choice of restaurants east and west of Logan. Read about what's around nearby **Pape** and **Chester Subway Stations** on pages 461-463.

• See **Bradley Museum** on p. 158 (another location in the GTA where **Driftwood Theatre** is usually performing).

• **Dream in High Park** offers a Shakespeare play from the end of June to Labour Day at 8 pm, at the **Amphitheatre** in **High Park** (416-367-8243, www.canadianstage.com). Costumes and sets are more ambitious and the stage allows for dramatic lighting effects but it runs later and it is harder to leave the premises if your younger child loses interest. (Pay-what-you-can, they strongly suggest $20/person, FREE for 14 years and under).

Driftwood Theatre
(905) 576-2396
www.driftwoodtheatre.com

Schedule: Check **Driftwood's** website for dates and locations of their **Outdoor Summer Theatre** program.

Admission: Pay-what-you-can, suggested price $15 per adult.

Directions: Withrow Park, south of Danforth (between Carlaw Ave. and Logan Ave.); **Todmorden Mills**, 67 Pottery Rd. (from Bayview, turn east on Pottery Rd.); **Bradley Museum**, Mississauga (see p. 160). They perform in many more places (2011: Ajax, Bowmanville, Burlington, Cobourg, Oshawa, Peterborough, Pickering, Port Colborne, Port Perry, Waterloo, Whitby and more).

THEATRE VENUES

Live it up!

What a treat it is to watch children engaging with something other than a screen for a change. The palpable energy that comes from good live performances is simply irreplaceable.

For years, events such as the Milk Festival at Harbourfront or the Mississauga Festival were like a smorgasboard of high quality children's productions. They unfortunately don't exist anymore but you can count on other options to get your fix.

Note it is sometimes difficult from simple descriptions to know if performances involve actors or puppetry, if it's a musical or a simple storytelling. Better call the theatre beforehand to avoid any disappointment.

Photo: Courtesy of LKTYP

Lorraine Kimsa Theatre for Young People

Lorraine Kimsa Theatre for Young People (LKTYP) can be seen as the next level up in theatre initiation as it can also serve an older audience. The bigger stage allows for more ambitious productions. While their season is intended primarily for children 8 years and older, some productions, usually presented on a smaller stage, will interest younger audiences.

Here, my young designer has discovered wondrous theatre sets and props; my little animal lover has seen giant butterflies magically flying in the air. Both have been captivated by harmless villains, introduced to the magic of elegant puppetry and to the mystery of ancient tales (with a little help from pyrotechnic and sound effects).

Solar Stage

Most plays at Solar Stage are intended for children aged 3 to 8; some are meant for children up to 10 years old.

The younger crowd gathers in front of Solar Stage's intimate stage, comfortably seated on floor cushions.

Parents of young children attending for the first time shouldn't worry about letting their child sit by themselves. Sooner or later most little ones join their parents during the performance; it's part of the deal and performers know it.

TIPS (fun for 3 to 10 years)

• The **Madison Centre**'s shops are closed on Mondays. You'll find a **Second Cup** on Yonge St., south of the building.

Solar Stage
(416) 368-8031
www.solarstage.on.ca
Concourse Level of **Madison Centre**, 4950 Yonge St., North York (a 5-min. walk north of **Sheppard Station**).
Admission: $14 + tax.

TIPS (fun for 3 years +)

• When attending with younger children, I suggest you avoid the front rows of the balcony section as the railing sits at their eye level.

• To ensure LKTYP is accessible to all audiences, at least one performance of each production is Pay-what-you-can. These tickets can be purchased in person (cash only) and they go on sale at 9 am on the day of the show. Call the box office for more information.

• There's a snack bar with tables at the lower level.

LKTYP (416) 862-2222 www.lktyp.ca 165 Front St. East, Toronto.	**D-3** **Downtown** **Toronto** **5-min.**

Admission: $15-$20.

Family series

Many performing arts centres are committed to affordable and quality family shows at a cost starting at $25 per show.

Popular productions, musicals or children's shows are often booked in more than one venue during the same season. If you've missed a favourite show at your local theatre, call other performing arts centres on the listing to see if it is being presented at any of them. They will mail their season's program upon request.

Performing Arts Centres:
- **The Sony Centre**
  (416) 872-2262
  www.sonycentre.ca
  1 Front Street East, Toronto
- **St. Lawrence Centre for the Arts**
  (Bluma Appel Theatre)
  (416) 366-7723
  www.stlc.com
  27 Front Street East, Toronto
- **Rose Theatre Brampton**
  (905) 874-2800
  www.myrosetheatre.ca
  1 Theatre Lane, Brampton
- **Living Arts Centre**
  (905) 306-6000
  www.livingartscentre.ca
  4141 Living Arts Dr., Mississauga
  (west of Square One)
- **Meadowvale Theatre**
  (905) 615-4720
  www.meadowvaletheatre.ca
  6315 Montevideo Rd., Mississauga
- **Markham Theatre**
  (905) 305-7469
  www.markhamtheatre.ca
  171 Town Centre Blvd., Markham
  (north of Hwy 7, west of Warden Ave.)
- **Oakville Centre**
  (905) 815-2021
  www.oc4pa.com
  130 Navy St., Oakville

TIPS (fun for 3 years +)

- www.ticketmaster.ca is very useful to get information regarding the venues and current shows, even if you don't intend to book through them (and pay the extra cost per ticket). You can view the seating chart of a venue by typing its name in the search box.
- The **Sony Centre** sometimes features ice skating shows!
- The **Fringe** is Toronto's theatre festival including **FringeKids**, a selection of family theatre. Usually held for 12 days including the first week in July. For details, call (416) 966-1062 or check www.fringetoronto.com.

Photo: Courtesy of National Ballet

Prologue

Did you know that as a parent, you can help to bring a production to your school via its school council (the parents association)?

I've been a member of the board of **Prologue to the Performing Arts** for years and I know first hand that this non-profit organization is often the only way to ensure kids have access to performing arts. For over 40 years, it has been assisting professional artists in creating and touring shows suitable for the schools.

Performances are presented on their website under different categories such as dance, music, puppet shows, theatre, storytelling, etc. Schools can book shows for an average cost of $3 or less per student. Some school councils book as many as ten shows every year! Many share the costs with their school's administration.

The benefits are obvious. The school presentations give a break from the routine. They enhance the curriculum, injecting arts into the programs and exposes many kids to performing arts they might not experience otherwise, for lack of money or time! Prologue even offers shows for French Immersion.

Prologue to the Performing Arts
(416) 591-9092
www.prologue.org

55 Mill St., **The Case Goods Building**, Suite 201, Toronto, ON, M5A 3C4.

STRATFORD SHAKESPEARE FESTIVAL

Much ado!

Use Stratford as an excuse for a family getaway. Enjoy the town and theatre with your kids. (Then, come back with the girlfriends.)

I went twice to Stratford. Once with four girlfriends, once with a 12-year-old. No need to mention they were two totally different getaways, one of them involving much more shopping and dining but both revolving around great plays.

Every season, you can expect at least four productions of Shakespeare plays but you can also count on at least one musical, always very popular with families. (For 2011, they're producing *Camelot* (for 8 years and over) and *Jesus Christ Superstar* from Lloyd Weber (12 years and over).

When you click on the name of a play on their website, in their *Content Advisory* section, you'll find their age recommendation. They might say "not likely to be of interest to young children" or "nudity and strong language". Most of the programming is accessible to children 12 years and older but don't forget: "accessible" doesn't mean "interesting for children"!

The two great venues where the more ambitious plays and musicals are presented are the **Festival Theatre**, by the river (seating 1,824) and the **Avon Theatre** (seating 1,093). The other two venues seat less than 500 people.

We found **Festival Theatre** quite impressive when attending the musical *Oliver!* and everyone in that theatre could obviously get a good view of the stage.

The best thing about staying over-night in Stratford is that it gives you time to do one of their **Festival Tours** such as the **Costume and Props Warehouse Tour** where you get to visit the amazing costume warehouse to dress up at the end of the tour. They show you props, clothes, hats, wigs, shoes and more while giving you interesting details. "This head is anatomically correct" mentions the guide while holding a bloody prop used in a theatrical combat.

They also offer backstage tours of the **Festival Theatre**, and **Theatre Explorer** workshops. For 2011, I noticed the $29 workshop **Camelot: Song and Dance** (suitable for children), in which you learn first hand what it's like to be in a musical.

These activities really add to the experience.

Other things to do

If you go during the summertime, you could rent a paddle boat (around $15/hour), a canoe or a kayak, or take a tour on a boat to explore the **Avon River** (around $8/adult, $4/12 years and under) by the **Riverside Patio** on York Street. That's where you could also buy a bag of corn to feed the swans.

TIPS (fun for 8 years +)

• An older child might better appreciate a Shakespeare play if he has seen a movie adaptation prior to the show.

• We enjoyed a generous breakfast at an all-day breakfast place **Features Restaurant** (159 Ontario St.), and finished with better coffee at nearby **Balzac's** (same one you find at The Distillery). We had a delicious lunch at the colourful **York Street Kitchen** (41 York St., www.yorkstreetkitchen.com) and the whole family was more than satisfied with the dinner in one of the dark booths at **Bentley's**, where we played darts while waiting (99 Ontario St., www.bentleys-annex.com).

• I recommend staying at the **Festival Inn** (1144 Ontario St., 1-800-463-3581, www.festivalinnstratford.com). It is at the edge of the action, modern, with a great indoor pool and a fabulous Sunday Brunch in their sunny dining room. We stayed at the Victoria Inn because it had an indoor pool... and I didn't know about the Festival Inn. It has since been renovated and renamed the **River Garden Inn** (10 Romeo St. North, 1-800-741-2135, www.therivergardeninn.com).

• On our way to Stratford, we stopped at **The Best Little Pork Shoppe**, a funny little farm market selling lots of animal-related trinkets (2146 Hwy 7&8, Shakespeare, www.porkshoppe.com).

Or you could walk to the outdoor **Lions Pool** right across the bridge. It offers a waterplay area including a water umbrella, spraying palm trees, shooting streams, arch spray and small dumping buckets ($4.75/adults, $3/2-15 years old, $14/family). Check www.stratfordrecreation.ca for photos.

Make sure you take in the view of the bridge and surrounding stone buildings for a glimpse of England.

Then stroll around the prettiest block in town (York and Ontario Streets), and stop at the very cool toy store **Family and Company** (6 Ontario St., www.familyandcompany.com) for a big finish.

Stratford Shakespeare Festival · Stratford 1-800-576-1600 www.stratfordfestival.ca	**Off the map West of Toronto 2 hrs**

  Schedule: Most plays open end of May; most activities and plays go on from early June to early November. Most performances are presented at 2 pm or 8 pm. Check their calendar for dates and availability.

Admission: Musicals cost more than plays. Expect around $70 to $110/adult (depending on the seating). Children 18 years and under pay around $36. Tours cost $8/person ($6/students or seniors).

Directions: From Hwy 401 westbound, take exit #278 at Kitchener, follow Hwy 8 West onto Hwy 7 & 8 to Stratford. It becomes Ontario Street, which runs through Stratford.

General tips about
Buildings:

- See **Doors Open Toronto** on p. 130 for an interesting way to discover architecture with kids.
- Read about the **Canada Life** building (with the flashing weather beacon on top) and miniature model inside in the **Osgoode Subway Station** section on p. 475.
- The modern architecture of the **AGO** on p. 88 and the **ROM** on p. 222 is impressive enough to catch any kids' attention.

BUILDINGS

See **City Hall Podium Green Roof** on p. 127.

CN TOWER

Broaden their horizons

With kids, you have to think big and tall... as tall as the CN Tower! It's great to see them looking up over and over again, attempting to make out the top of the 550-metre-high tower! It's well worth stopping at the base, just to see the great view from down there.

Arriving from Front Street, we walk over several railroad tracks via an enclosed bridge. This location is an excellent vantage point to see the sculptures of giant characters in their **Rogers Centre** balconies. Inside, before getting to the elevators, we walk across a spacious mezzanine housing displays and interactive computers.

You'll find visual displays throughout the building with many fascinating stories about the engineering involved in the building of the tower.

Up! Up! And away!

Then comes the famous ride up the elevator: It's a one-minute climb on a fair day (over an hour if you climb the 1760 stairs), but it can take up to four minutes in high wind. Only those who got close to the glass door used to have a view to the outside. Not anymore, now that they've added glass panels... on the floor! The view will blow you away.

The elevator leads to the interior observation deck, 346 metres (1136 feet) from ground level, from where we can admire Lake Ontario and the four corners of the city. Children are allowed inside the **Horizons Restaurant** located at this level.

One floor down is the fascinating glass floor surrounded by a beautiful mural depicting a construction site in the sky. When he was five, my little one didn't show any fear while walking on the glass floor. At six, he joined the rank of grown-ups cautiously remaining on the edge of the glass.

If you're wondering how such a surface can support visitors, a sign states that this glass floor can hold the weight of 14 large hippos!

We can read lots of interesting and fun information on large panels around the room, such as the fact that the **CN Tower** holds the world record for longest egg fall (it lost the tallest standing structure record to Burj Dubai Tower in 2007).

At this level, you can also access the exterior observation deck, to better feed your vertigo. We didn't feel the need to pay extra to go up to the **Sky Pod**. I suggest you do it only if there's no line-up. I must admit 100 metres more make a difference. The Rogers Centre really looks smaller from up there!

Special effect

That day, we completed the visit with a stop at the FX Shop where my teenager companions had their picture added to the background of their choice. The shop was replaced with **Sharpshooter** souvenir photo booth (also offering special effects, but maybe not the same). It costs $20 for a 6 X 8 photo ($30 with magnetic frame).

Other activities are offered at the base of the CN Tower for an extra fee. There's a new 3D surf movie experience and a motion theatre ride. There's also an arcade. Very few games are suitable for smaller children, but when we were there, my little one had a great time driving the motorcycles, and he and I teamed up, frantically rowing on a rubber dinghy, while attempting to avoid danger. I sweated up a storm and we laughed the whole time. The games keep changing but you get the idea.

... and out!

For a better viewpoint of the tower in all its loftiness, stand on the outside terrace located between the tower and the Rogers Centre. You'll have to lay down on the ground to take a picture!

The CN Tower is adorned with a 1,330-fixture programmable lighting system and treats us with myriads of colours and effects adapted to every special occasion (including New Year's Eve countdown).

TIPS (fun for 5 years +)
• Avoid foggy days, otherwise you'll be paying a lot just to have your head in the clouds...
• Try to visit the tower before or after the summer rush. We had a perfect visit during the March Break when it was not crowded by tourists (they offered special activities for the occasion).
• You can see the new 23-minute-long **Ultimate Wave Tahiti 3D** movie. You can also do the **Himalamazon** motion theatre ride (with wind and water effects, must be 42 " and taller). Both are $10/person each, and both are located at the concourse level.
• **Horizons Restaurant** is not the expensive revolving restaurant but a fixed one underneath, with affordable menu, really worth the stop for the view!
• Read about what's to see in nearby courtyards on p. 126.

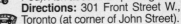

CN Tower
(416) 868-6937
www.cntower.ca

D-3
Downtown
Toronto

Schedule: Open year-round, 9 am to 10 pm, closes at 10:30 pm on Fridays and Saturdays (extended hours during the summer).

Admission: (taxes not included) $23/adults, $21/seniors, $15/4-12 years, FREE for children 3 years and under (extra fees for Sky Pod). Ask about their packages.

Directions: 301 Front Street W., Toronto (at corner of John Street).

DOWNTOWN COURTYARDS

Think big!

Whether you have a child enthralled with anything huge (they all get to that phase) or visitors who want to feel how big and bold Toronto really is, this stroll is for you.

The adventure starts at the edge of the round and shiny structure of **Roy Thomson Hall**. At the underground level, you'll discover the large pond simulating a Canadian lake with evergreens and boulders.

Then, walk west through the vast paved courtyard between Roy Thomson Hall and **Metro Hall** to admire the buildings' architecture and water flowing from a modern sculpture.

Show the giant shiny arrow pointing down by the broken pillar inside Metro Hall (by King Street).

Going south of the courtyard, across Wellington, you'll see the **CBC** building, easy to recognize with the red window frames. Make sure you enter both Metro Hall and CBC buildings and look up. Their glassed ceilings are quite impressive.

TIPS (fun for 6 years +)

• There's a **Tim Hortons** in **Metro Hall Concourse** accessible from 200 Wellington St. West, just south of Roy Thomson Hall. For a fancier snack, go to the **Canteen** in the **TIFF Bell Lightbox** at the northwest corner of John and King. Yum!

On the courtyard east of CBC, closer to Front Street, you'll see a 25-foot aluminum structure shaped like the Scarborough Bluffs.

On the south facade of CBC, along Front Street, you'll notice a very long slab of granite. The first time my then 10-year-old boy saw this monument, commemorating the workers of Ontario who died in the workplace, he had to read all the engraved "say-it-as-it-is" descriptions of fatal accidents.

If you walk west across from Front, you'll be able to see more big things: the **CN Tower** (quite a sight when you're at its foot) and the gigantic sculptures of playful fans east and west of the **Rogers Centre**.

Downtown courtyards
D-3 Downtown Toronto

Schedule: The courtyards are accessible year-round.
Admission: FREE access.
Directions: Roy Thomson Hall is at the southwest corner of King and Simcoe Streets, Toronto. **Metro Hall** is just west of Roy Thomson Hall, they share the same courtyard. **CN Tower** and **Rogers Centre** are both at the foot of John, across from **CBC** (at the corner of Front Street).

CITY HALL PODIUM GREEN ROOF

An oasis above it all

"Look at that fescue! It goes so nicely with the amsonia and the sedum here!" exclaims my friend the hardcore gardener as we walk around City Hall's new green roof. I'm no gardener myself and my Latin is nonexistent, but I know a thing of beauty when I see one and this is the real thing.

There were not many flowers out when we visited during the fall, but the gardens still looked amazing and elegant, with an emphasis on textures as opposed to colours. It will be fun to follow the changes throughout the seasons in this year-round garden made of both perennial and seasonal plants and tall grasses.

We got up to the podium roof (that's the part of **City Hall** which looks like a spaceship) from the large ramp in **Nathan Phillips Square**, which used to be closed. I always found it sad when visiting the square with my son that I could not take him to see the "spaceship". Now, kids won't have this frustration anymore.

They say the concrete path which

runs around the green roof is half a kilometre long. You know what it means? It's got to be the best beginners' ride for rollerbladers! (I read somewhere that they would not discourage bikers and joggers from using the path but that could change...)

We saw that squirrels had already adopted the place. Many benches with built-in roofs were installed, for the benefit of those who will want to eat their lunch in this oasis.

TIPS (fun for 2 years +)

• There are plans for a food kiosk on the southeast corner of the roof for 2011 but you can always count on the good old chip trucks along Queen and **The Café on the Square** on the street level of City Hall.
• While you're at **City Hall**, go inside on the ground level to see the model of the city and the mural made out of nails.
• More on **Nathan Phillips Square**'s rink on p. 352.

City Hall Podium Green Roof
Dial 311 (new service)
www.toronto.ca/greenroofs

D-3
Downtown
Toronto
10-min.

Schedule: Open year-round, Monday to Friday, 7:30 am to 9:30 pm; Saturday and Sunday, 8 am to 6 pm.
Admission: FREE.
Directions: Nathan Phillips Square, Toronto (northwest corner of Bay and Queen Street West). Take the exterior ramp up **City Hall** (on the east side).

CASA LOMA

ecstatic little girl in her arms. Further in the room, Cinderella's cruel sisters, seemingly not as mean as their reputation and splendid in their period dress, were flirtatious with visitors.

On the three occasions I saw a show at Casa Loma, actors were always very nice with the little ones who were looking at them lost in wonder. And they never stepped out of character. So far, we've seen Snow White, Robin Hood and Cinderella spread their magic.

I didn't expect such high-quality musicals (presented several times daily in the castle library during the special events).

"I'm the king of the castle..."

Glancing at Casa Loma from the outside is enough to excite young minds. No mistake, we're about to enter a "real" castle. Inside, it seems like the fairy godmother waved her magic wand to transform the whole castle. It has regained the splendour of its younger days and a magical look

worthy of Cinderella's Christmas. Those who visit Casa Loma at other times don't get to appreciate how great it is during the Christmas period and March Break.

During the Christmas holidays, the grandeur of Casa Loma awaited us. A 15-metre-high fir tree didn't quite reach the main hall ceiling. Illuminated chandeliers and tinsel garlands contributed to the ambiance of opulence, absent at other times of the year.

Between two performances, characters in the brief musical, produced for the occasion, mingled throughout the impressive decor.

One year, Christmas was celebrated with Cinderella as a theme. We could see the handsome prince dressed in royal velvet answer a child's question in a gentlemanly fashion. The fairy godmother, in a cloud of pink tulle, held an

Even if we were off-off-Broadway, voices were quite strong and well modulated, the actors expressive and smart, the songs original and the musical arrangements harmonious. There were amusing, interactive dialogues aimed at the parents. The sets (often mounted on curtains) compensated for the stage's limited size.

TIPS (fun for 4 years +)

• Parking is available on site. After 11:30 am, it is sometimes full, but spots free up rapidly at any hour.
• In the room where the musical performances are presented, the audience sits on the floor (there are a few chairs for adults). It is better to arrive fifteen minutes before a performance. Shows only last half an hour.
• The admission counter is inside a portico too small to contain the whole waiting line. Dress warmly!
• In the winter, the long tunnel is definitely cold. It's better to put on your coat before walking through there.
• Santa Claus arrives on the first day the castle presents its Christmas performances, and stays until December 24th. Ask about their **Breakfast with Santa** on Sundays in December!
• It is less interesting to visit Casa Loma when children's shows are not scheduled (the admission fee remains the same and the castle isn't decorated). On the plus side, the place is not as crowded.
• March Break is as much fun as Christmas. The same concept applies. And they now have added a similar Halloween-themed concept! They're the best (and most crowded) time to visit.
• A cafeteria located in the castle's basement offers an affordable menu with little variety. At the same level, the unfinished pool lies inside an enclosure. Decorations pertaining to the current theme are often displayed in it.
• Check the *Seasonal Events* section on their website for details about very original events taking advantage of the castle's set-up and ambiance (such as interactive **Dracula** plays, **Ghost Tracking** and **Knighting Ceremonies**).

NEARBY ATTRACTIONS
Winston Churchill Park (5-min.) .... p. 362
Spadina House (2-min. walk) ...... p. 374

In the beautiful marble-floor conservatory, a second good clown or magic show is usually performed several times daily during the special events.

Walking up the imposing grand staircase, we arrived in a wide, richly decorated corridor lined with costumes or cut-out props. Kids could step behind them to have their pictures taken. Little adventurers were thrilled when they found out they could also use the secret staircase hidden behind the wood panelling in Sir Henry's office!

From there, we visited the former rooms of Sir Henry Mill Pellatt (the romantic Toronto financier who had the castle built in 1911) and his wife. These were also decorated along the year's theme.

During Christmas time, Santa awaits visitors in the billiard room on the ground floor, filled with multicoloured gifts and stuffed animals. You have time to take a picture of your little elves... if they cooperate.

Staircases located on the top floor lead to the castle's two towers, where you can enjoy a great view of the city.

A 250-metre tunnel links the castle with the stables. The tunnel's entrance faces the gift shop located on the lower level of the castle. (Frankly, this level isn't more exotic than any basement, but nevertheless, it intrigues children.)

Furthermore, it leads to impressive stables. Their mahogany stalls and Spanish tile floors attest to Sir Henry's taste for luxury.

Casa Loma
(416) 923-1171
www.casaloma.org
D-3
North
of downtown
20-min.

 Schedule: The **Christmas** show is presented daily from end of November to early January, from 9:30 am to 5 pm, excluding December 25th and January 1. On December 24, the Castle closes at 1 pm. During March Break, the show is performed everyday, from 9:30 am as well. (Last admission always at 4 pm.) **Admission:** At all times, even during events with kids' shows, around $20/adults, $15/ seniors and students, $11/ 4-13 years. FREE for children 3 and under. Parking max. is $9. **Directions:** 1 Austin Terrace, Toronto. (southbound from St.Clair Ave., Spadina Rd. becomes Austin Terrace).

DOORS OPEN TORONTO

out to be a great choice, especially with animal lovers! Low relief sculptured horses on the top of the Art Deco façade and horseshoe imprints in the concrete at our feet reminded us that we were indeed at the Horse Palace. There were lots of activities going on and no line-ups to be suffered.

We had a close look at the horses of many officers of the Toronto Mounted Unit casually riding

Feel free to come in

To some, the event's appeal is the opportunity it gives to visit free of charge buildings usually accessible for a fee. To others, it's the thrill of being allowed to explore buildings normally closed to the public. Whatever the reason, this is the occasion to appreciate our heritage.

Doors Open began in France in 1984, Ontario Heritage Trust joined in in 2002, and the event has been going strong ever since.

You can browse through their website to see which buildings are part of their roster this year. (Not all buildings return every year.)

We first wanted to check out the **Flatiron** building. We've always loved the unique triangular building with amazing trompe-l'oeil on its flat façade but never had a chance to visit it inside. We showed up at 2 pm but the line-up was at least one hour long (worth it for adults but too long for adults with kids). I decided that we should stick to larger attractions, less appealing to a mature public.

So we headed to the **Horse Palace** within **Exhibition Place**. It turned

around the site. We saw young acrobats performing on their horses. We observed a horse-drawn wagon speed up near the tiniest horse carriage. We admired riders jumping around the arena. Many beautiful horses were resting in the stalls.

A big hit with the kids was the fake horseback to climb on without fear of being thrown off.

TIPS (fun for 6 years +)

• If you go to the **Horse Palace**, don't be afraid to ask about the activities going on. Once back home, I looked at the programming on the website and there are many things I did not see: the Horse Palace's green roof and the **Toronto Animal Services'** two-storey tall shelter with dogs' play area, rabbit and rodent room.

• Go to the section *For kids* on their website to download the *Kid's Guide*. Last time I checked, we could download the guides from the last five years. I thought they were quite nicely done.

Doors Open Toronto
(416) 364-7865
www.toronto.ca/doorsopen

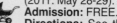

Schedule: Usually the last weekend in May, 10 am to 5 pm (2011: May 28-29).
Admission: FREE.
Directions: See the link *Buildings to visit* on their website.

DUNDURN CASTLE

Yes, Sir!

Outside the 1832 building, a woman in a long dress is plowing the garden. To go inside, we have to walk through an interior courtyard. At the entrance, children play with antique toys while waiting for the guided tour to begin.
Dundurn Castle is in fact a superb manor that once belonged to one of Ontario's first Premiers, Sir Allan MacNab. The building has been preserved with much of its initial splendour, with magnificent furniture, trompe-l'oeil walls and original artwork.

The guided tour, which lasts a bit more than an hour, allows us to admire the manor's three floors. Not interactive

enough for my then 5-year-old son, he made us leave after 30 minutes. It's a shame! During the last third of the visit his patience would have been rewarded when visitors get to the Castle's basement (looking like an underground passage to a 3-year-old.

These stone-floor corridors are the part of the manor that younger children will readily relate to a true castle. At the end of the visit, they're expected in the kitchen for a treat served by employees in period dress.

Back outside, children inevitably stop to look at the large cannon sitting by the **Hamilton Military Museum**. Small but efficient, this museum traces military history from the War of 1812 until World War I, using many photos, military uniforms and artillery pieces. Inside the museum, in a small, dark corridor, a trench has been reconstructed. The sound effects are very effective; you will have the uneasy feeling of really being at war!

The Military Museum includes a **Discovery Gallery** for children, with hands-on activities allowing them to wear costumes, load a cannon, build a fort and more.

They traditionally host a **Scottish Celebration** in late August (2011: Aug. 28).

TIPS (fun for 4 years +)
• The gift shop is usually well stocked with children's books on castles.
• During March Break, expect an activity centre with a dress-up area, puzzles and games and maybe a puppet show.
• From the end of November until the beginning of January, Dundurn Castle puts on its Christmas finery: cedar garlands, red ribbons and flowers add to the Castle's rich Victorian ambiance. They offer special tours and workshop for an extra fee (pre-registration needed).
• The gift shop sells snacks.

NEARBY ATTRACTIONS

Albion Falls (15-min.) .... p. 252
Football Hall of Fame (10-min.) ... p. 339

Dundurn Castle & Hamilton Military Museum
E-2
S-W
of Toronto
60-min.
• Hamilton
(905) 546-2872
www.hamilton.ca
(Click on *Culture & Recreation*, go to *Hamilton Civic Museums* under *Culture*)

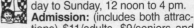
Schedule: Open daily from July 1 to Labour Day, 10 am to 4 pm. The rest of the year, open Tuesday to Sunday, 12 noon to 4 pm.
Admission: (includes both attractions) $11/adults, $9/seniors and students, $5.50/6-12 years, $27/family (around $3.50/person for museum admission only).
Directions: 610 York Blvd., Hamilton. Take QEW West, then Hwy 403 towards Hamilton, exit York Blvd. and follow the signs.

ST. JAMES CATHEDRAL

The sound of music

I glance sideways at my little lad, amused by his reaction as music from the 87 ranks and 5000 pipes of the St. James Cathedral's grand organ surrounds us.

Short concerts to broaden children's musical horizons, a lovely church to show them things of beauty grown-ups sometimes create and a cute little garden to stretch their legs; **St. James Anglican Cathedral** is one of those best kept secrets I'm glad to share with you.

TIPS (fun for 5 years +)

• See the **Crèche Exhibition** (p. 171) organized by **St. James Archives and Museum**.

• Check the **Sculpture Garden** right across King Street. It usually displays eye-catching outdoor installations!

• We really like **Le Petit Déjeuner**, a Belgium place near the cathedral, offering delicious all-day breakfast, waffles, mussels and French fries, and much more (191 King East, www.petitdejeuner.ca).

NEARBY ATTRACTIONS

With its huge and gorgeous stained glass artwork framing the pulpit, and twelve colourful triptychs adorning the side walls, St. James is a beautiful cathedral of gothic architecture and proportions.

It is topped by a set of twelve ringing bells (the only such ring of 12 in North America). These are heavy bells, ranging from 631 lbs to 2418 lbs! Bell ringing practices take place every Monday at 6:30 pm. Free recitals are held Tuesdays at 1 pm, September to June, and year-round at 4 pm on Sundays (donations welcome).

During **Christmas** time, we are sometimes treated to a concert from the **Toronto Mendelssohn Youth Choir** (admission fees apply).

Got a cherished pet? St. James offers the **Blessing of the Animals** near St. Francis Day, end of September or early October! The special service usually gathers over 300 people with their pets (outside of the church of course), plus the Toronto Police on horseback, working dogs and exotic animals from Bowmanville Zoo. Check the *Events & Cathedral Community* section on their website!

St. James Cathedral (416) 364-7865 www. stjamescathedral.on.ca	D-3 Downtown Toronto 5-min.

Schedule: The cathedral is open Monday to Friday and Sundays, 7:30 am to 5:30 pm; Saturday, 9 am to 5 pm.
Admission: FREE.
Directions: 65 Church Street, Toronto (at the corner of King and Church Streets).

SWAMINARAYAN MANDIR

A vision

That's what you'll think you're having the first time you notice the creamy limestone towers of the Hindu temple by Hwy 427.

A building made out of 24,000 stones beautifully carved in India by over 1,800 craftsmen and assembled here with the help of hundreds of volunteers: kids get it!

More numbers for them? There are 132 archways and 101 ceilings, just on the first floor and 340 pillars, some of them so intricately carved it takes one artisan almost a year to create.

You could spend some time playing an *I Spy* game with the breathtaking outer wall of the temple, sculpted in teak.

Inside, each sex leaves their shoes in their respective section and meet again by the prayer hall.

The most breathtaking part of the temple is the 16-sided Mandir, hosting five sacred deities on the second floor. We counted no less than 100 different musicians carved in white marble in one of the twelve circles inside its dome.

We really stood out amongst the worshippers. It was like wearing a "Tourist" sign on our foreheads but I felt the members of this community were more than open to sharing their culture.

TIPS (fun for 8 years +)

• The temple is open to the public but remains a place of worship where knees and shoulders must be covered. They graciously supply visitors with saris if need be. No photographs are allowed inside.

• The centre includes a **Canadian Museum of Cultural Heritage of Indo-Canadians**. It is small but nicely put together. Note that it focuses more on the Indian heritage than on the Indo-Canadian reality and that there is lots of reading involved.

• In the centre's gift shop, I noticed inexpensive comic books telling Sanskrit classic tales in English, and workbooks for kids to learn Gujarāti (spoken by about 46 million worldwide), an interesting way to expose kids to different writing systems created by mankind.

• We continued our immersion with Indian snacks from a nearby food store (**Shayona**, 46 Claireville Dr.). They sold colourful pastries, samosas and drinks we don't find in the major supermarkets.

Swaminarayan Mandir	D-3 North
• Etobicoke	of downtown
(416) 798-2277	25-min.
www.baps.org	

(click *Toronto* at the bottom of the home page)

Schedule: Open year-round, from 9 am to 6 pm.
Admission: FREE, donations appreciated. The suggested donation is $5/adult and $3/child to access the Museum.
Directions: 61 Claireville Drive, Etobicoke. From Hwy 427, take the eastbound exit at Finch, then turn north on Humberline Drive and west on Claireville Drive.

NEARBY ATTRACTIONS

Humber Arboretum (5-min.) .... p. 271
Wild Water Kingdom (10-min.) .... p. 426

THE BLUFFER'S ROGUE SHACK

The more we look, the more we marvel at the details: heart shaped out of a wire, small medal nailed to the wall, little plastic bee by the entrance. There are benches built into the walls of this two-room roofless shack with a backyard mostly made out of driftwood from Lake Ontario. The whole structure seemed solid enough to withstand time. Hopefully, it will have been maintained by whoever initiated this wonderful rogue construction so you can enjoy it too. Look for it on the farthest half of the beach, where you notice more driftwood.

More about **Bluffer's Park** on p. 406.

Nice chilling spot

Carved on the driftwood forming the wall of this shack we found by the beach, is this invitation to chill. It feels like we're in this fabulous tree house built by very resourceful (big) kids.

Bluffer's Park • Scarborough Dial 311 (new service) www.toronto.ca/parks	**D-3** **East** **of downtown** **30-min.**

Open year-round, FREE, see p. 406 for directions.

YELLOWSTONE CAVE IN BELFOUNTAIN

two more arches with openings. We can see the base of some man-made stalactites that were created initially to simulate a cave. I assume the place was closed to the public because these were falling off. There's nothing left to fall now. If you look carefully, you'll see some interesting details carved in the stone. More about **Belfountain Conservation Area** on p. 306.

I spy a face

For years, the Yellowstone Cave was closed to the public. For the first time last summer, we could enter its intriguing arch down the stairs to have a look.

It is cold, dark and damp inside, contrasting with the bright sunny day shining through the door. Light rays also pierce in through holes in the ceiling and

Belfountain **Conservation Area** • Belfountain (519) 927-5838 1-800-668-5557 www.creditvalleycons.com	**D-2** **N-W** **of Toronto** **45-min.**

 See p. 306 for schedule, admission and directions.

CASTLE VILLAGE

Take a peek!

Slightly off the beaten track in the Georgian Bay area, the Castle is an intriguing sight in itself. But the little village hidden in its backyard was an even bigger surprise to us when we stopped there on our way back from a great weekend by the beach.

Delightful little houses awaited us in the **Enchanted Kingdom Park**, with inviting windows to peek through. Inside, we could see the **Teddy Bears' Tea Party**, **Goldilocks and the Three Bears**, **Little Red Riding Hood** and her grandmother and **Mother Goose** at reading time.

Since our last visit, **Snow White** with the Seven Dwarfs' house and **Merlin the Magical Wizard's Tower** were added. All the beautiful small interiors are skillfully decorated with painstaking attention to original detail.

There is also the old mill and dwarf village to climb and slide, the **Hansel & Gretel** real snack bar with tiny tables and chairs, a 222-foot-deep well to taste crystal clear water (we were invited to fill our jugs) and a small educational trail.

TIPS (fun for 3 years +)

• The Castle houses a large gift shop and two indoor attractions: a series of small prisons inhabited by a few horror characters ($2) and a section showcasing medieval arms ($3). I was personally more impressed by the craft involved in the creation of the Enchanted Kingdom.

NEARBY ATTRACTIONS

Castle Village
• Midland
(705) 526-9683
www.castlevillage.ca

A-2
North
of Toronto
90-min.

Schedule: The park is open May to Thanksgiving (weather permitting) Tuesday to Saturday, 10 am to 5:30 pm (12 noon to 5 pm on Sundays). Open on Mondays as well in July, August and long weekends.

Admission: Enchanted Kingdom access is $3/person, FREE under 2.

Directions: 701 Balm Beach Rd., Midland. From Hwy 400 North, take exit #147/Hwy 12 westbound. Turn north on Hwy 93 and west on Balm Beach Road.

General tips about
Farms:

- Pets are not allowed on the farms!
- Most of the extra activities offered during the farm festivals are available on the weekends only.
- A good website to find a pick-your-own farm in your area is: www.harvestontario.com (click *What's in season*, then browse by *Urban Centre*).
- Always call to check the current crop report of the farms you want to visit. Mother Nature sometimes plays tricks on us! (I remember picking a pumpkin as it snowed!)

CROP CALENDAR	May	June	July	Aug.	Sept	Oct.
Asparagus	■	■				
Rhubard	■					
Strawberries		■				
Raspberries			■	■		
Flowers	■	■	■	■	■	■
Sweet Corn				■	■	
Squash & Gourds					■	■
Apples					■	■
Indian Corn						■
Pumpkins						■

FARMS

See **Yeehaw Adventure Farm** on p. 151.

WHITTAMORE'S FARM

Photos: Courtesy of Whittamore's Farm

Aaah, strawberry fields

The first time we stopped at this farm, we were on our way home from a nearby attraction, and the ice cream sign caught my ever-hungry son's attention.

I was really glad we made that impromptu stop. Not only was the ice cream cone delicious, but the farm's market was well stocked with preserves and baked food. It had an entertaining playground, complete with chickens and goats.

When the berry season came, we went back to pick our own strawberries in **Whittamore's** huge fields. My friend's baby could not believe his eyes when he squished his first juicy strawberry.

When we last visited, children were playing with small trucks inside two giant tires turned into a sandbox and a gravel pit. There was also a hay maze and a hay pile to climb on.

TIPS (fun for 3 years +)
• Pick your own strawberries, raspberries, peas, beans, beets, potatoes, tomatoes, eggplants, melons and pepper.
• Don't wear white clothes!
• There's a snack bar on site. If I remember well, the fries were good!

NEARBY ATTRACTIONS

They've kept adding activities every year. Now, Whittamore's Farm boasts a **Fun Farm Yard** with all kinds of original structures: the **Strawberry Mountain** with long slide, the 2-storey tree fort, the **Tractor Tire Climb** and a funny computerized **Singing Chicken Show**.

On the weekends, they add a **Barn Bouncer** and a pedal tractor track.

During **Pumpkinland** time, they also offer a corn maze, a **Friendly Haunted Forest** and, on the weekends, a pumpkin cannon show and the **Balloon Typhoon**.

Whittamore's Farm • Markham (905) 294-3275 www.whittamoresfarm.com	C-3 N-E of Toronto 35-min.

 Schedule: The **Fun Farm Yard** and market are open early May to mid-September, 9 am to 6 pm, then 10 am to 5 pm until October 31. **Pumpkinland** runs on weekends and Holiday Monday from mid-September to October 31, 10 am to 5 pm.

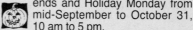 **Admission: Fun Farm Yard**: $6/2 years and older. **Pumpkinland** (on the weekends): $10/2 years and over, $36/family of 4.

Directions: 8100 Steeles Ave. East, Markham. From Hwy 401 eastbound, take exit #389/Meadowvale Rd. northbound and follow signs.

FORSYTHE FAMILY FARMS

Come to your senses

Multicoloured flower baskets, delicious warm pies, smooth stacks of hay, apple turnovers fresh out of the oven, candied apples and children's laughter in the playground. You're at Forsythe Family Farms.

When we arrived at **Forsythe Farms**, we were struck by the beauty of the large, rustic market. Then, I appreciated all the cute playful touches, thanks to well-drawn cut-outs. (I have seen them change over the years but the spirit remains.)

The kids could play in the straw and pet the animals in the barn. Then they went to enjoy the slide, rocking horses made from recycled tires and the tricycle track for the little ones.

A 10-minute wagon ride brought us to the entrance of a tiny forest, where we were greeted by a funny face painted on a tree. Lovely paths carpeted with twigs criss-crossed the woods. From time to time they revealed scenes from several popular fairy tales.

TIPS (fun for 2 years +)

• Pick-your-own peas, beans and pumpkins.
• Each weekend in October is **Harvest Festival** with Halloween activities (inflated pumpkin for jumping, wagon rides, $5 pony rides and more).
• During Christmas time, free hot cider is offered at the farm's market and the farm sells Christmas trees. Their store includes gift items and seasonal decorations.
• You may buy snacks at the market. Their outdoor snack bar is open only during the fall weekends.

For little ones, the simple act of taking a stroll in the woods is impressive in itself. Ask the older kids to identify the depicted fairy tales.

After the ride back, there's more to be seen: the **Barnyard Adventure** with a **Bunnyville**, a rope maze following the *Little Red Hen* theme (harder than it looks many parents have commented) and beehives.

They now have a pedal cart track for older kids... and the adults.

Forsythe Family Farms • Unionville (905) 887-1087 www.forsythefamilyfarms.com	C-3 N-E of Toronto 35-min.

Schedule: Usually open on the weekends in May, then daily from early June to October 31. Variable hours depending on crops. Open Thursday to Sunday in November then daily again until December 24. (Check their website closer to the date of your planned visit to confirm exact hours.) **Enchanted Forest** is open weekends only May to October (closed all August). The corn maze opens on Labour Day weekend. The **Harvest Festival** runs each weekend in October, 9 am to 5 pm.

Admission: Admission to the Fun Area varies with the spread of activities offered. FREE in December.

Directions: 10539 Kennedy Road, Unionville. From Hwy 404 North, take exit #31/Major Mackenzie eastbound, turn north on Kennedy Road.

NEARBY ATTRACTIONS
Bruce's Mill (10-min.) .... p. 243

SOUTHBROOK PUMPKIN PATCH

Attention shoppers!

We're on the last patch of country road in an area which has experienced major residential expansion in the last few years. And Southbrook's working farm is flooded by city dwellers starving for fresh and locally grown produce and a little piece of natural setting.

On the weekend we visited, the drive along Major Mackenzie was busy with cars lining up to enter the farm's parking lot or by passersby who are wondering what's going on.

This is a place where you'll want to spend money: at the bakery filled with scrumptious goodies, at the farm's country store, at the Halloween store, and at the **Kid's Carnival** with rides, inflatables and games on the weekends.

I must say I found that their Halloween store alone was worth the stop. It took us half an hour to explore all its content. When we visited, it offered an extensive selection of costumes and accessories at all prices. It was the perfect setting for some ambitious decorations. We saw a large graveyard turned into a picnic spot for witches.

The market smelled of fresh pies and fudge. It displayed an abundance of produce, baked products, preserves as well as herbs, flowers, decorative items and snacks.

On the weekends, they have a snack bar and all kinds of fair food. (Those caramel apples were hard to resist!). You also can catch a wagon ride.

On weekdays, there's still the playground for the kids to enjoy (while parents are sipping a coffee), a corn maze and a long walk to the forest.

TIPS (fun for 3 years +)
- You can pick your own pumpkin.
- I visited this farm years ago when it was on the south side of the street. In the fall, you could not miss the tall silo with an orange pumpkin face. It's gone. I heard that the owner gave the land to the city who will probably have a school built at this location. Southbrook Farm & Winery relocated to the north side of Major Mackenzie. It has become **Southbrook Pumpkin Patch** and keeps on offering all its activities, on a bigger lot.

NEARBY ATTRACTIONS

Southbrook Pumpkin Patch
· Richmond Hill
(905) 832-2548
www.southbrookpumpkinpatch.com

C-3 North of Toronto 35-min.

Schedule: The **Kids Play Area** and the stores are open to the public from September 1 to November 1, 10 am to 6 pm. The **Family Fun Fall Festival** runs on weekends and Holiday Monday.
Admission: FREE admission to Kids Play Area, Pay-as-you-play for the activities in the Kid's Carnival.
Directions: 1150 Major Mackenzie Drive West, Richmond Hill. The farm is west of Bathurst Street.

DOWNEY'S FARM MARKET

Mountain goats, sea of pumpkins

Navigating in an orange ocean, my tiny adventurer thinks he's dreaming. Then, we get into the action: jumping on hay-covered mattresses, visiting the haunted barn and the destabilizing black hole, racing on huge balloons, exploring the big corn field maze and sending feed to the mountain goats perched high above our heads.

When we visited during the **Pumpkinfest**, the **Black Hole** barn was a great attraction. Completely dark inside, it included a trip through a turning black cylinder, studded with stars, with sound effects to boot. We literally lost our balance. (My little one also lost her boot and it was hard finding it in the dark!)

TIPS (fun for 2 years +)
• Pick-your-own strawberries, raspberries (wagon ride to the berry patch) and apples in August and September).
• Their **Easterfest** includes (plastic) egg hunts to exchange for treat basket, egg decorating, puppet shows and children's entertainers.
• They celebrate **Canada Day** with a **Strawberry Festival** (free admission) with live music, dog show, antique cars, pony rides (for a fee).
• **Christmas** trees are sold in December. Ask about their **Lunch with Santa**!
• The farm's market is brimming with goodies. We indulged ourselves with cheese bread and pumpkin doughnuts. There's ice cream in the summer and a snack bar truck on the weekends.

NEARBY ATTRACTIONS
Heart Lake (10-min.) .... p. 397
Professor's Lake (20-min.) .... p. 410

The Pumpkinfest also features a dump truck slide, a **Balloon Typhoon** (inflated structure filled with balloons) and a **Boo Barn** for young kids.

For an additional fee, you could make a big scarecrow, which seemed like a great project for the whole family to create together!

Their corn maze (included with admission) opens in mid-August and offers around 7 kms of trails.

The regular **Play Area** (also open during the events) includes the tractor tire sandbox, a trike track, wooden play train, monster truck and ship, wagon rides and **Kritter Korral**. This petting farm section is safe for children of all ages and filled with pretty animals. We particularly enjoyed petting a small white goat with a soft coat.

Other farms have climbing goats but no other place has such an ambitious setting for them. At the crossing of four wooden corridors mounted on stilts, hungry goats bleat at us. The intelligent animals started to move only when I had filled a dish fastened to a rope and my little engineer had enthusiastically hauled it up using the pulley system.

Downey's Farm Market
• Caledon
(905) 838-2990
www.downeysfarm.on.ca

C-2
N-W
of Toronto
45-min.

 Schedule: Play Area: Mid-May to October 31, 10 am to 5 pm. **Easterfest** usually on Easter weekend (Friday to Sunday) and weekend prior to that, 10 am to 5 pm. **Pumpkinfest** with full line-up is during October weekends (plus the last weekend in September or first weekend in November, see website to confirm). **Admission: Play Area**: $5.50/person. **Pumpkinfest weekends**: $11/person, FREE under 2 years. **Easterfest**: $10/person. Cash only.

Directions: 13682 Heart Lake Rd., north of Brampton. Take Hwy 401 West, then Hwy 410 northbound until the end, where it becomes Heart Lake Road.

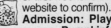

BROOKS FARMS

You'll have a blast!

Most of the farms around Toronto are strongly feeling the pressure of residential development. Not this one. It still stands in the middle of farmland, which is a good thing. You wouldn't want those pumpkin cannons disturbing a baby's nap!

Once you walk past the entrance, you can assess in a glimpse the wide range of activities going on here during the **Fall Festival**: pig races, pumpkin cannon demonstrations (they were one of the first to offer this), "train" ride to the pumpkin field, straw jumps, corn maze, farm animals, and my kid's favourite, the zip lines. The announcement of the cannon blast about to take place could not lure many young acrobats away from this activity!

Wondering how pumpkin cannons work? With propane gas and some crazy guys loading wet newspapers and pumpkins into the cannons, which are aimed at some target, far away. The anticipation before each blast is just too much for the very excited kids. The strange muffled explosion doesn't disappoint them.

For the pig races, the same crazy

guys encourage the crowd to cheer the pigs with resounding "Sue Wee" combined with a ridiculous dance step they demonstrate.

We went on Thanksgiving. We could only stay for 3 hours and it went by in a flash at this most dynamic farm. Allow plenty of time to enjoy all the activities.

Since my last visit, the owners have gone even crazier. They've created a line-up of alien characters called the **Barnyard Bumpkins** (with a whole line of t-shirts and hoodies featuring those) and put on the **Alien Mystery Show** presented during the Fall Festival. Check the video on their website (under *Farm Fun*, click *Fall Fun Festival*).

TIPS (fun for 3 years +)

• Pick-your-own strawberries, raspberries, currants, apples, pumpkins and more.
• They've added bouncing ponies and a pirate ship structure since my last visit.
• In the summer, they have a wacky **Alien Sprinkler** kids can activate. Bring the bathing suits!
• They have a small snack bar which makes hot dogs and tasty small doughnuts and a chip wagon. Bring a blanket to sit on the ground to eat lunch (not many tables around).

NEARBY ATTRACTIONS
North York Drive-in (15-min.) .... p. 97

Brooks Farms
• Mount Albert
(905) 473-3920
www.brooksfarms.com

C-3
N-E
of Toronto
45-min.

Schedule: The **Fall Festival** is on weekends from mid-September to October 30 and Thanksgiving Monday, 10 am to 5 pm. The **Summer Festival** is on weekends, mid-May to end of June, then daily until Labour Day Monday, 9 am to 3 pm.

Admission: $11.50/person for the Fall Festival. FREE under 2 years. (Summer Festival and Fall Festival on weekdays are $6/person.)

Directions: 122 Ashworth Rd., Mount Albert. Take Hwy 404 North, exit at Vivian/Mulock eastbound. Turn north on Hwy 48, then Mount Albert Rd. East. Drive to Durham 30 and Ashworth Rd.

ANDREWS' SCENIC ACRES

Your pick

The first time we visited this farm, we picked strawberries. The ten-minute wagon ride led to the row assigned to us.

I must say my then 2-year-old son wasn't that fascinated by the picking itself. However, children 4 years and over seemed to be captivated by this activity. Furthermore, the rows of fruit were well spaced out, allowing little ones to run and explore easily.

After half an hour, our basket was full and my son's patience was coming to an end. Time to go back to the farm's big playground equipped with swings, a giant tire, an old tractor to explore and

an animal corral inhabited by rabbits, goats and chickens.

From mid-September to end of October, they set up a straw jump, a corn maze and a small haunted forest near the playground. Don't expect a spooky trail but the winding trail created in the narrow forest made for a nice stroll.

The mountain of straw erected for the fall was a hit with my family. There's real free play going on here. Try it! You'll be impressed by the straw's softness.

TIPS (fun for 3 years +)

• Pick-your-own rhubarb, asparagus, strawberries, raspberries, black currants, cherries, blueberries, flowers, gooseberries, apple, Indian corn and pumpkins.

• Wear comfortable, stain-resistant clothes. Don't forget hats and sunscreen. You can bring your own containers or buy them on site. As for the price of the fruit itself, it's about equivalent to what you would pay at your local store.

• They don't have a maze but they offer an Indian Corn field walk where we can also pick our own Indian Corn for decoration (mid-September to October 31).

• Several picnic tables are located close to the playground. The farm market fills a large Mennonite barn with baked goods, delicious frozen yogurt and ice cream, and produce as well as snacks. (BBQ food on weekends).

NEARBY ATTRACTIONS
Halton Railway (20-min.) .... p. 207

Andrews' Scenic Acres
· Milton
(905) 878-5807
www.andrewsscenicacres.com

D-2
West
of Toronto
45-min.

Schedule: Open 7 days from early May to October 31, 8 am to 6 pm (usually longer during summer) and weekends until December 31, plus the week before Christmas.

Admission: FREE ($3/person mid-September to October).

Directions: From Hwy 401, exit at #328/Trafalgar Rd. northbound. In Ashgrove, turn west on 10th Sideroad, to #9365.

SPRINGRIDGE FARM

Happy ending

Less than a 15-minute drive from other attractions in the region, you will find Springridge Farm on the way back to Toronto. It is ideal to loosen little legs, grab a snack and finish off your outing nicely.

Springridge's farm market far exceeds what you would expect from an average farm market. Inside the pleasantly decorated market you'll find a broad selection of seasonal decorative garden accessories, small toys, preserves and, best of all: excellent pies, tarts, cookies, muffins, cakes, breads, hot soups and delicious sandwiches. (Ask about their fun $6 **Sandbox Lunch** served in a pail with shovel!)

In the **Fun Farm Yard**, kids get to

play with the trucks in the giant sandbox, climb up the antique tractor and fly down the new pipe slide and spider climber. They can "milk" a cut-out cow.

There's also the corn trail you enter into through the mouth of a witch (the **Tricky Trail**). And on weekdays they can use pedal tractors.

Daily wagon rides are included with the regular admission fee. (Try it! It will lead you to a section of the farmland which is elevated, giving you a postcard perfect panoramic view.)

In the fall, the Fun Farm Yard offers more: the straw bale jumping and pyramids. Kids can't to that at home!

TIPS (fun for 2 years +)

• Pick-your-own strawberries.
• During the **Easter Festival** weekend, kids participate in an egg hunt with the Easter Bunny. The festival usually includes a puppet show and the activities vary from one year to the next. (If Easter falls in March, call to confirm if they will offer their festival.)
• The **Fall Harvest Festival** includes a visit to the **Boo Barn** (cute rather than scary) and a puppet show. We can catch a wagon ride to go through the 5-acre corn trail which is open during this festival.
• Every weekend from mid-November to mid-December, gingerbread making or glass ball painting are offered for $5 and you get to visit Santa on the first weekend.

NEARBY ATTRACTIONS

Springridge Farm
• Milton
(905) 878-4908
www.springridgefarm.com

D-2
West of Toronto
45-min.

Schedule: Open daily from early April until Christmas, 9 am to 5 pm. The **Easter Festival** is on Easter weekend (Friday to Sunday). The **Harvest Festival** is on weekends from end of September through October, 10 am to 4 pm.

Admission: FREE to get into the market. **Fun Farm Yard:** $4/2 years and over. Costs $10/person during Easter and Fall festivals.

Directions: 7256 Bell School Line, Milton. From Hwy 401, take exit #324/James Snow Pkwy southbound. Turn west on Derry Road and north on Bell School Line.

CHUDLEIGH'S FARM

Their two giant slides offer an exciting sliding experience. When we visited, it was surrounded by a thick carpet of straw, topped by bales of hay that children climbed as if they were mountain goats (hence the straw!). The petting zoo is fun and includes climbing goats.

Afterwards, my kids were thrilled to ride to the orchard in a wagon drawn by a mighty tractor. My 3-year-old apple picker was quite satisfied by a half-hour harvest coming from a few trees, an operation made easier by the small size of the apple trees. From the beginning of their season to the end, there's a wide maze built with bales of hay.

You can usually take a 3-minute pony ride around a small orchard (for a fee). They've added a trail behind the bush with signs (to let your child guide you through the hardwood forest).

Chudleigh's Farm also grows pumpkins in a large patch by the orchard. After Thanksgiving, you can enjoy a wagon ride through the pumpkin patch to select your pumpkin.

Hay! You!

"Something's bothering me!" my farm boy insists. For the third time, I stop the car at the side of the road to look for small pieces of straw slyly lodged in his clothes. This time, I extract the last intruders... from inside his underpants! That's what happens when you spend an afternoon running, jumping, sprawling and rolling in the play area at Chudleigh's Farm.

The site is huge, but the layout of the attractions gives it the charming and intimate character of a village fair. I doubt that your kids will let you begin by apple picking, as there are so many other tempting activities on site. I prefer to allow them to let off steam first in the **Children's Area**. (It is actually worth going to the farm for the sole reason of having your children enjoy it.)

TIPS (fun for 2 years +)

• Pick-your-own apples starting mid-August to late October depending on the variety (they grow over 20 varieties) and pumpkins.

• Giant hot dogs, European sausages and corn barbecued in its husk are sold during the fall weekends. At the tempting outdoor market you can buy delicious homemade soup and eat it while observing the golden fish in the pond.

NEARBY ATTRACTIONS

Chudleigh's Farm
· Milton
(905) 878-2725
www.chudleighs.com

| D-2 |
| West |
| of Toronto |
| 45-min. |

 Schedule: Open daily July 1 to October 31, from 10 am to 5 pm. (It's extremely busy on Thanksgiving weekend and the two weekends prior to that. Try to go other times.)

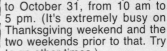 **Admission:** FREE to get to the market. To use the fun area in July and August: around $6/adults, $3/seniors and children, FREE/3 years and under. Rates are higher in the fall. Check their website for details.

 Directions: 9528 Hwy 25, Milton. From Hwy 401 West, take exit #320/Hwy 25 northbound.

PUCK'S FARM

My little pony

Puck's Farm is a site where you can wander freely while giving children the opportunity to experience a real day at the farm.

The farm's pony ride is unquestionably the best I've seen. It delighted my young cowboy.

Here, no sorry lads turning endlessly around a minuscule carousel. Ponies travel along a path bordering a pond inhabited by ducks.

You will find a large barn with famil-iar animals (a few lucky ones will even experience cow milking). Outside, you can pet lambs, cows and goats. You can take a ride on a horse-drawn wagon that takes you through a picture-perfect country-side.

The admission fee includes unlimited access to the activities such as the pony rides.

It was corn-picking season when we visited and ears of corn, picked by the visitors, were cook-ing in huge bubbling cauldrons and were to be eaten on the premises. We thought it was quite exotic to roam inside a 2-metre-high cornfield!

I was told that we can walk 15 min-utes through the fields to reach the edge of the farm, where a ladder awaits to help us go over the fence (and back, of course). Beyond that is a marsh area with board-walk to explore. Ask them to point you in the right direction.

TIPS (fun for 3 years +)

- Pick-your-own pumpkins.
- After rainy days, it is difficult to manoeuvre strollers on the muddy ter-rain. The sticky mud can suck boots in and may curb your appreciation of Puck's Farm's activities.
- Show up early on Easter weekend! We went on Easter Sunday. It seemed the whole city came along with us, we had to park far away from the farm. Easter Egg Hunts take place, rain or shine. Chocolate eggs are hidden all over the place by the Easter Bunny. And he does it all day long. You get unlimited access to a few Carni-val rides with the admission.
- Ask about their **Pumpkinfest** on the weekends in October. (Here also, you get unlimited access to a few Carnival rides with the admission.)
- You can purchase hot dogs, pizza, hamburgers, fries and beverages from a snack bar in a Western wagon.
- Watch out for the hens as they'll keep an eye on your food. It's part of the fun!

NEARBY ATTRACTIONS
South Simcoe Railway (15-min.) p. 206
Albion Hills (20-min.) .... p. 398

Puck's Farm • Schomberg 1-800-621-9177 www.pucksfarm.com	C-2 N-W of Toronto 45-min.

 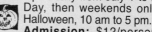 **Schedule:** Open two weekends prior to Easter and on Easter weekend (Friday to Monday), then weekends until end of June. Open daily from July 1 to Labour Day, then weekends only until Halloween, 10 am to 5 pm.

 Admission: $12/person, $6/ seniors, FREE for kids under 2 years old. Get their free admis-sion coupon online.

Directions: #16540 Concession Rd. 11, Schomberg. From Hwy 400 North, take exit #55/Hwy 9 westbound. Turn south on Con-cession Rd. 11.

PINGLE'S FARM MARKET

Big field trip

At Pingle's Farm Market, the pumpkins are mighty impressive! There must be 10,000 of them, sitting in an amazing patch. We enter armed with a wheelbarrow, and pass through a winding corridor of lovely pumpkins standing at attention. It's well worth the trip, if only to take a look.

The farm's setting was nicely decorated for the season when we visited in the fall. An old wooden witch eyed my little one, and friendly scarecrows stared at us mischievously.

We visited the farm on a weekend during the **Fun Fall Weekends** when the outdoor playground was transformed into a **Fun Farm Area**.

Kids bounced in the inflated struc-ture, they rode on an amusing tricycle race track (they since added a pedal cart track), they jumped into the straw and saw a cute puppet show.

The farm has a **Bunnyville** (with rabbits inhabiting little holes in a small fenced space). Then there's the elevated goats walk and mini-maze. They offer pumpkin cannon shows (they're a blast!).

For an additional fee, you could carve or paint a small pumpkin or get your child's face painted.

TIPS (fun for 3 years +)

• Pick your own strawberries, fall raspberries, apples and pumpkins.
• During the Easter weekend (Friday to Sunday) Pingle's Farm offers Easter egg hunts (around $9/adults, $5/children): Kids decorate their basket then fetch plastic eggs hidden by the Easter Bunny, which they trade for chocolate eggs and pot and seed to plant, earth provided on site.
• Pingle's creates a different wide corn maze every year, which opens mid-August ($7/person). The maze usually gets haunted in October (when you can also stroll through their **Spooky Orchard**).
• You can buy snacks and their own baked goods in the large market or fast food under a large tent.

NEARBY ATTRACTIONS	
Bowmanville Zoo (15-min.)	p. 65
Automotive Museum (20-min.)	p. 198

Pingle's Farm Market	C-4
• Hampton	**East**
(905) 725-6089	**of Toronto**
www.pinglesfarmmarket.com	**50-min.**

 Schedule: Opens for Easter (10 am to 5 pm), then daily, May 1 to Christmas Eve, at least from 10 am to 5 pm. **Fun Fall Weekends** is offered mid-September to October 31 and Thanksgiving Monday.

 Admission: Fun Fall Weekends is $6/person ($3 on weekdays).

 Directions: 1805 Taunton Rd. East, Hampton. From Hwy 401 East, take exit #425/Courtice Rd. northbound. Turn east on Taunton Road.

CHAPPELL FARMS

Did you see that?

I'm sure we looked like a bunch of hens in a red cage while riding a wagon through Chappell Farms' fields. Soon, our kids were competing to see who could spot the many surprises hidden in the cornstalks: pumpkin heads, old witches, a headless horseman and scarecrows who seemed to wave at us from their lawn chairs. This was no traditional wagon ride!

We arrived in the middle of the **Pumpkin Festival**. This means that in addition to the animal petting, playground, trike track, maze, cut-out characters and **Boo Barn** the farm offers on weekdays during the festival, we were also treated to a **Haunted Barn**, an inflatable structure and a magic show. (Now, they offer a dog show as well!)

I inadvertently entered the Haunted Barn with my 3-year-old, intending on the more suitable Boo Barn. Big mistake! Dimmed in light barely sufficient to appreciate the special effects, the place was so dark I could barely see my own hand, let alone the scary actors breathing down my neck o the progressivel narrowing fur covered walls with their unpre dictable shar turns.

The whol ex-perience, suc cessfully disori enting, left m younger on completely pan icked, while m 7-year-old lovec every minut of it. (The Boc Barn, on th other hand, i lined with sma friendly ghost and funny char acters.)

The farm als includes nanny mountain goat climbing aroun a silo.

This farm ha been in the Chap pell family fo over 175 years!

TIPS (fun for 3 years +)
• Pick your own pumpkins.
• For Easter, they organize egg hunts (no more than 250 children at a time, scattered in a large area; kids are almost guaranteed to find candy), magic shows and wagon rides. Of course, there's always the **Bunny Village**, with its own school, church, windmill and all.
• The big shop in a barn is packed with seasonal goodies and crafts.

NEARBY ATTRACTIONS
Simcoe Museum (10-min.) p.386

Chappell Farms
• Barrie
(705) 721-1547
www.chappellfarms.ca

**B-2
North
of Toronto
60-min.**

Schedule: Open the weekend prior to Easter and on Easter weekend (Friday to Sunday, 10 am to 4 pm). The **Pumpkin Festival** runs daily from last week in September to October 31, 9 am to 5 pm. (Magic shows and inflated castle on weekends only.) Haunted Adventure daily on last week of October, 5 pm to 8 pm.
Admission: Around $10/visitor on weekends and holidays, $6 on weekdays, FREE under 2 years old.
Directions: 617 Penetanguishene Rd., County Rd. 93, Barrie. Take Hwy 400 northbound, stay on centre lane onto Hwy 11, exit County Rd. 93/Penetanguishene Rd. westbound.

DYMENT'S FARM

Simply awesome!

Dyment's keeps you so busy you tend to forget you came to pick a pumpkin in the first place!

Every year, **Dyment's** celebrates the ritual of pumpkin picking by opening its doors to the public on the weekends of October.

I strongly recommend this unique and delightful farm located in the Hamilton area. This outing is also a wonderful opportunity to view the colourful landscapes of fall as you head towards the Niagara escarpment where Dyment's is nestled.

A traditional playground including a "retired tractor" and "tired horse swings" greets us by the entrance. I was taken by the fun tricycle track, located close to the barn. It is outfitted with a small bridge, a tunnel and a traffic light which my young driver enjoyed obeying. Unfortunately, children older than 5 years old are often too big to fit the small tricycles.

Our kids were reluctant to leave the table filled with replicas (to scale) of farm machines in the **Machinery Shed** to visit the other attractions: the **Spook Hut** with cute light and sound effects, the **Corn Bin** with 10,000 yellow balls into which kids can plunge, the bouncing ball track where we can race. There are also animals to pet

and the straw fort filled with clean straw in which to frolic. Since our last visit, they've added a mini golf, a tall climber made out of rope and a zip line!

En route to the hilly pumpkin fields, the tractor trail borders the Niagara escarpment, offering a lovely view through the trees and providing one of the most enjoyable farm rides I can remember.

An interactive exhibit called **Agri-Maze**, where you can learn about the daily life of a farmer named Jim, is one of the farm's most interesting features. It's full of amusing touches and usually includes Jim with a television set as a head that speaks to the viewing public (unfortunately under renovation for 2011). He'll be back.

TIPS (fun for 2 years +)
• They have a chip wagon for fast food and their bakery and dairy bar is filled with yummy treats and meals to go.

NEARBY ATTRACTIONS
Warplane Museum (20-min.) p.194
Westfield Village (15-min.) p.385

Dyment's Farm
• Dundas
(905) 628-5270
www.dyments.com

E-2
S-W
of Toronto
60-min.

Schedule: Their market and bakery are open year-round from 10 am to 7 pm. The **Pumpkin Patch** activities are open to the public on the weekends in October, 10 am to 5 pm. (More options for birthay parties and school tours)

Admission: Around $8/adults, $7/children, FREE under 2 years.

Directions: 416 Fallsview Rd. East, Dundas. Take QEW, follow Hwy 403 towards Hamilton. Exit Hwy 6 northbound, turn west on Hwy 5, then south on Sydenham Rd. After the curve, turn right onto Fallsview Road.

HANES CORN MAZE

Fun at every corner

We had to think in three dimensions in order to figure out our position in the maze. "We're in the letter O!" understands my son, looking at the map. It turns out the framed letters on top of the map, which I mistook for a mere title, have actually been carved in the corn field. Amazing!

The corn stood ten feet high. The two 9-year-old boys I brought along couldn't get inside the (then)10-acre maze fast enough. They were armed with a map showing the contours of the five continents. Seven bullets on the map marked the places where they would find

a box with codes: a series of letters and numbers plus interesting information about the continent on which it "sat".

This elaborate activity took them over an hour, after which they found the keys to the codes on a board, obtaining seven syllables to sort into a message. How clever! They had to spin a wheel to claim their prize.

The design and concept varies every year but it's been over 20 acres for a few years now! (Depending on your maths and reading skills, it takes 45 min. to 2 hours to complete.)

My 6-year-old daughter never wanted to get near the maze (afraid of getting lost and scared of potential spiders). Fortunately, **Farmland**, the other section of the farm was just perfect for her and we could explore it while the older kids finished touring the maze. She was excited to pet animals. She could play house in a tiny bungalow. She could even "milk" a wooden cow by pulling its rubber udders, filling a bucket with the water spitting out of them. There's a mini maze in the play area.

TIPS (fun for 3 years +)

• Pick your own pumpkins.
• The maze experience can be fun for younger school-age kids if with older children but 9 years and over seems more appropriate. Your kid has to have the energy to walk for over an hour in the maze. (I know dads who have found out it's a long time to hold a kid on their shoulders.)
• They also open in the evenings during the **Moonlight Mazes** (Fridays and Saturdays in September, they close at 9 pm). Every night in October, they add to the fun with spooky music. Bring a flashlight! (It closes at 5 pm on Sundays.)
• In their **Tiny Shop Bakery**, they sell all kinds of pies, cookies and squares. (They're quite proud of their Belgium cookies.)
• I checked the **Dutch Mill Country Market**, a 10-min. drive on our way back (see their photos on www.dutchmill.on.ca). This quaint place includes a bakery, a lovely tea room, an amazing store and many farm animals (533 Millgrove Side Road; go east on Hwy 5, north on Millgrove Sdrd., look to your left).

NEARBY ATTRACTIONS
Christie Lake C.A. (5-min.) .... p. 401

Hanes Corn Maze Farmland
• Dundas
(905) 628-5280
www.hanescornmaze.com

E-2
S-W
of Toronto
60-min.

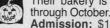

Schedule: Farmland and maze open late August to October 31, 11 am to 5 pm in August and September and later in October (check their website for details). Their bakery is open from May through October.
Admission: $11/13 years and over, $9/5-12 years old, $2/2-4 years old, FREE under 2 years old.
Directions: 1001, Hwy 5, Dundas. Take QEW, then Hwy 403/Hamilton. Exit at Hwy 6 North. Turn west on Hwy 5 (located across from **Christie Lake C.A.**).

YEEHAW ADVENTURE FARM

Fun family

How can it not be pure family fun when the members of the family involved in the creation of this great attraction are obviously enjoying themselves so much!

OK, not to sound like a groupie but last time I admired the attention to detail of an attraction this much, it was at Disney World.

The Walker family, three generations of them all costumed and staying in character, push the Hillbilly theme of their **Annual Fall Halloween Harvest Hillbilly Hoedown** as much as could be.

From the toothless girl welcoming

us in her little shack with rugged roof to the hilarious gang awaiting to entertain us with music during the pig races down the hill, the whole adventure is a hoot.

Flo Gently, the host of an "educational" show going on in one of the barns, strangely resembles Robin Williams in his famous role as the nanny Mrs. Doubtfire. Parents laugh out loud at the double meaning of Flo's jokes while kids are thrilled by the animals "she" brings in with the help of a funny ranger with his own agenda.

The place is jam packed with everything you normally see in a good fall festival but presented with a twist (I saw the "menacing" burning furnace of my childhood in their **Boo Barn**).

Many more features, I have never seen in a farm: silo climbing, working outhouse, rope climbing to go down the 30-foot slide, hillbilly music fusing through speakers all over the place... The list goes on.

TIPS (fun for 3 years +)
- Certain activities you'll be allowed to do just once, by submitting a passport handed to you at the entrance.
- They have a great snack bar on the premises.
- On your way to or back from the farm, stop at **Dee's Bakery** on R.R. 97 just east of Hwy 52, for their self-proclaimed "to die for" butter tarts (1817 R.R. 97, Valens, www.buttertartstodiefor.ca).

NEARBY ATTRACTIONS
African Lion Safari (10-min.) p.76
Shade's Mill C.A. (15-min.) p.401

Yeehaw Adventure Farm · Cambridge (519) 624-0085 www. yeehawadventurefarm.com	E-1 West of Toronto 75-min.

 Schedule: Open to the public every weekend in October and Thanksgiving Monday, usually from 11 am to 5:30 pm.
 Admission: Around $16/3 years and older, $60/family of 4.
 Directions: 1817 Concession 8 West, Cambridge. From Hwy 401, take exit to Hwy 6 southbound, turn west on R.R. 97. Past Valens, you'll eventually see signs for **Yeehaw Farm**, turn south on that road (Hwy 52), then east on Concession 8. The entrance will be up the hill, to your left.

ROUNDS RANCH

Photos: Courtesy of Rounds Ranch

Doing the rounds...

At this farm, you might find a special catapult that throws apples at a scarecrow and see free-roaming rabbits and hens. Kids will ride on large pedal carts and families will be challenged with a well-planned maze adventure.

My dentist is a big fan of labyrinths. So when I mentioned this one, he had to check it out with his three children in tow. His family enjoyed it so much that I decided to include it even though I did not personally see it.

When they visited, a pirate theme was going on. The next year, the theme was to be Australian Outback. They have decided to stick to a Western theme for a while and build on it, only changing the design of the maze every year.

When he visited, it took my dentist and his boys over two hours to get out of the giant labyrinth. (Since then, they've reduced the maze to a more manageable size which should take no longer than one hour to complete.)

The maze is usually open on certain nights for a "moonlight" experience. (Bring your flashlight!)

Ranchland is the play area normally open to the public. It includes a roster of fun activities. The ones that caught my

attention are the **Bucking Bronco**, a saddle on bungee cords over mattresses (for a safe rodeo session) and the corn box where you can immerse yourself in corn kernels.

My friend's daughter thought she was in heaven, petting the cute rabbits and other animals. The boys loved the pedal cart racetrack. There are also wagon rides and 5-min. pony rides for an extra fee.

Their **Pumpkin Mania** event includes all kinds of original activities in addition to the regular spread of Ranchland fun: seed spitting, pie eating contest, pumpkin hockey, pumpkin slam dunk, pumpkin catapult and a pumpkin hunt. In addition, visitors during the Pumpkin Mania get a free pumpkin.

Photo: Courtesy of G. Servinis

TIPS (fun for 3 years +)
• Pick-your-own pumpkins.
• If Easter doesn't come too early, they organize fancy egg hunts, offering three different trails everyone can do.
• There's a snack bar selling hot dogs, burgers, fries, corn on the cob and more.

NEARBY ATTRACTIONS

Rounds Ranch • Elmvale (705) 322-6293 www.roundsranch.com	**B-2 N-W of Toronto 90-min.**

 Schedule: Ranchland opens July long weekend to end of October, 11 am to 5 pm (the corn maze opens end of July). The **Pumpkin Mania** is offered on weekends and Holiday Monday from end of September to end of October.

 Admission: Access to **Ranchland** when no festival is going on: Around $10/10 years and older, $8/2-9 years; **Pumpkin Mania** is around $10/person; $4/pony rides.

Directions: 1922 County Rd. 92, 4 kms west of Elmvale. Take Hwy 400 North. Exit at Hwy 26/27 North to Elmvale. In Elmvale, turn west at the second set of lights, to County Rd. 92.

VAN-GO ADVENTURE FARM

It's a go!

Oblivious to the whole line-up of activities, my animal-lover and her new friends couldn't stay away from the animals and kept feeding them with grass from the surrounding lawn until dusk.

We visited **Van-Go Farm** after a day of activities at the **Waterford Pumpkinfest**. There was so much to do in this attraction in itself that we couldn't see it all.

The farm was at the end of the circuit of the Pumpkin Express tractors offering free rides during the Pumpkinfest. It included a huge parking lot easily accessible once the **Pumpkinfest Parade** was over.

By a vast field, the pumpkin cannon awaited its master. The farmer really loves his toy! I have seen such cannons fed by a regular BBQ gas tank but this baby was attached to the kind of tank you normally see on a train wagon! He was aiming at the old car way up in the field and reached his target, to cheers from the crowd.

In the heart of the farm, awaited the

climbing goats, alpacas, pigs (involved in pig races during the day), peacocks and pheasants. Nearby, were a bunny village, funny rubber duck races, sand pit, straw pile and jump castle, live music in the pavilion. The works!

We tried the pumpkin slingshot. Loaded it, pulled the bucket and ... saw it come back full speed right at us with the pumpkin still inside. That was close!

They now have a little **Water Gun Park**, a **Storyland** and they've added a section with life-size animated characters.

TIPS (fun for 2 years +)

• For an extra fee, you can use their **Paintball Barn** and you can do some panning for gold.

• They usually open their corn maze mid-August and turn it into a haunted maze at nights in September and October.

• During the warm season, bring the bathing suits! They offer a splash pad and they have a water gun park with hay bales for hiding.

• There's a snack bar on site as well as a market store.

• More on the **Pumpkinfest Parade** and a themed restaurant on the way back on p. 44.

Van-Go Adventure Farm · Waterford (519) 443-0001 www. vangoadventurefarm.com	Off the map S-W of Toronto 90 min.

 Schedule: Open daily from late May to October 31, 10 am to last admission at 6 pm. Check their website for November and December hours.

 Admission: $6/person, FREE 2 years and under.

 Directions: 710 Old Hwy 24, Waterford. From Hwy 403 southbound, take exit Rest Acres Road (Hwy 24 South), go south then turn east on Thompson St., and south at the stoplight.

ROYAL WINTER FAIR

Fair enough!

If you think this nearly 90-year-old fair is all about livestock and show-jumping competitions, you're in for a surprise when you first visit this huge event!

Strolling around watching farm animals lined up in preparation for competitions is not particularly stimulating for younger children, yet, they are impressed when they meet large furry cows nose to nose. Here, you'll find the obvious dairy cattle section (where we saw young beasts being lead by 10-year-old farmers), the large beef cattle stalls, along with the swine (there are cute piglets to see), rabbits and poultry sections.

There's also the **Royal Horse Palace** to the extreme west side of the site, with its imposing stalls, some heavily decorated with champions' medals; a world in itself.

Other animals can be touched at the petting farm. There are more paddocks where goats and sheep are competing for titles.

When visiting, we saw interesting demonstrations in one of the rings, such as the large animal Vet check-ups, which allowed young aspiring veterinarians to listen to a huge horse's heartbeat with a stethoscope. We also saw live auction simulations and sheep-shearing sessions. Activities and floor plan change every year but you get the picture.

The horse shows in the **Ricoh Coliseum** are ticketed and not included with general admission. (But Monday night Horse Show is free with general admission.) During our visit, we saw a jumping competition.

Some of the ticketed attractions of the **Horse Show** seem quite fun, such as the Rodeo event featuring Ladies Barrel Racing (!), Bull riding and Saddle Bronco riding.

Throughout the fair there are several educational displays, such as maple syrup-making, egg grading, honey production and animal and sheep wool care.

Not to be missed are the sculptures carved out of a 25 kg block of butter! When we visited, over 12 creations were kept in a refrigerated room.

Of course, the **Royal Fair** is about seeing animals in action. Superdog shows are included with admission. You can often see a keen dog barking enthusiastically at its master, begging her to start the routine through a series of obstacles. They seem to live for that kind of action.

Check the schedule for the day as soon as you get to the fair.

TIPS (fun for 4 years +)
• Not all activities are presented daily. Check their website to select the day offering your favourite activity.
• We found the giant vegetables, which were part of a competition during the fair, a bit "deflated" by the end of the fair, but still impressive.
• In the **Ricoh Coliseum**, you will have to leave your stroller at the foot of the bleachers.
• Snack bars are found on site.

NEARBY ATTRACTIONS
Jamie Bell Adventure Park (10-min.) p. 326

Royal Agricultural Winter Fair
(416) 263-3400
www.royalfair.org

D-3 Downtown
Toronto
10-min.

 Schedule: 10 days long, usually starts around first week of November, 9 am to 9 pm (usually closes at 6 pm on last day).

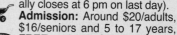 **Admission:** Around $20/adults, $16/seniors and 5 to 17 years, FREE under 5, $46/family of 4. Parking around $15.

Directions: Direct Energy Centre in **Exhibition Place**. Take Lake Shore Blvd., go north on Strachan Ave. The entrance is to your left.

ALBION ORCHARDS

Climb up the ladder!

A few things distinguish this orchard from others: many tall apple trees, ladders to reach the upper branches, and a long winding road running down the beautiful scenery of Caledon.

There's something about climbing a ladder that adds to the pleasure of apple picking. The orchard closest to the entrance included taller trees than the ones I'm used to seeing in the region. My little picker was thrilled to climb hers and grab the red apples that seemed inaccessible from the ground.

We stopped to buy a treat at the farm store and then off we went. The biggest part of the orchard is located much farther, hidden from our sight by a hill. Up the hill, we observed an intriguing little graveyard under the shadow of a very large tree, where the likes of A. Lawyer, I.M. Gone and Lou Zer were buried...

Going downhill, we could take in the panorama of the white gravel sinu-ous road contrasting with the greenery of the apple trees and pumpkin field, with a tiny touch of orange in the background. As we got closer, the orange spot turned into a giant pumpkin decoration sitting next to the remains of an old orchard, creating a picture perfect Halloween scene. (The big pumpkin has been "retired" since but they'll eventually find something to replace it.)

We reached the entrance to the orchard where small red wagons to carry the apples (or the kids) were waiting.

The tricky part here is to leave before the kids run out of energy. (You still have to walk back up and down the hill to the starting point.) Note on the weekends, a wagon ride can take you to the orchards.

By the main building, there's a play area where tires and hay were put to good use when we visited. They now have a few animals as well.

TIPS (fun for 3 years +)
• Pick your own apples and pumpkins and Christmas trees (on weekends).
• They sell fudge in their store and gift baskets. They also sell Christmas trees and advise you to call to find out when Santa is visiting.
• I recommend you drive along Old Church Road, just north of Albion Orchards. It is as gorgeous a little country road as can be.

NEARBY ATTRACTIONS
Cheltenham Badlands (15-min) ... p. 232

Albion Orchards · Caledon East (905) 584-0354 www.albionorchards.com	C-2 N-W of Toronto 55-min.

  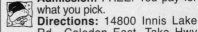

Schedule: Pick your own on weekends only from mid-August to October 31, 10 am to 6 pm (wagon rides on weekends only late September to October 31). Store open daily until December 23, (closes at 5 pm on weekends in November and December).

Admission: FREE. You pay for what you pick.

Directions: 14800 Innis Lake Rd., Caledon East. Take Hwy 400, exit on Hwy 7 going west. Turn north on Goreway Dr., it becomes Innis Lake Road. The farm is 15 km away, on the west side of the road.

MAPLE MAGIC AT BRADLEY MUSEUM

Condensed sweetness

The sugar bush may be the smallest I have seen but nothing's missing: maple trees with spouts, sweet maple water smell around the fire pit, maple sugar molding demonstration in the pioneer house, horse-drawn wagon and a craft activity.

Maple syrup time is probably the best time to visit this heritage attraction. It is located in a residential area but nestled among trees and charming.

Bradley House itself is not big. We used the maple sugar molding demonstration as an excuse to visit it but we spent most of our time outside.

Our kids were just happy hiding in the teepee the museum had built the year we visited (not guaranteed every year) in the **First Nation Campsite** section and checking out the maple sap level in the buckets on the trees.

We waited in line to catch a $2 wagon ride (offered every day during the March Break). Exploring Bradley House had been a bit like time travelling but the ride took us amidst modern houses and cars. This reminded us that we are indeed in a residential area!

Then we did some small crafts in the big barn in the middle of the place. All in all, this was a short and sweet outing.

TIPS (fun for 4 years +)
• They serve pancake breakfasts in the Log Cabin during March Break.
• Ask about their **Shakespeare Under the Stars** event presented by the **Driftwood Outdoor Theatre Group**, usually on the mid-July Friday and Saturday, around 7:30 pm (call to confirm). Suggested donation of $15. Come early, it is very popular.
• In mid-September, there's usually a **Fall Fair** (call for exact dates and fees). It includes musical entertainment, bake sale, children's area, wagon rides and contests.
• Call closer to December to find out about their official opening of the Log Cabin with Santa, with music and crafts.

NEARBY ATTRACTIONS

Bradley Museum
· Mississauga
(905) 615-4860
www.museumof
mississauga.com

D-3
West
of Toronto
30-min.

Schedule: Maple Magic: open during March Break and weekends before and after, at least 12 noon to 4 pm. **Museum**: open year-round on Wednesdays and Sundays, 1 to 5 pm (Wednesday to Sunday in July and August).

Admission: Around $17/family during **Maple Magic**, $14/family when there are no events.

Directions: 1620 Orr Road, Mississauga. From QEW, take exit # 126/Southdown Rd. (Erin Mills Pkwy becomes Southdown Rd. south of the QEW). Turn east on Orr Road (south of Lakeshore).

BRUCE'S MILL SUGARBUSH FESTIVAL

Hop on the wagon!

My little lumberjack is dying to put a log on the huge bonfire all by himself. Not far away, white smoke escapes from the sugar shack's chimney. The fire gives off an odour that blends beautifully with the pancakes' sweet smell. It's the busiest time of the year at Bruce's Mill.

At other times, **Bruce's Mill Conservation Area** is a rather modest attraction, its main asset being its proximity to Toronto. So I was really surprised to discover how well it was set up during maple syrup season.

Bruce's Mill Sugarbush Trail is the most manicured of all those that I visited. The trees are scattered, the areas where the self-guided trail signs are located are bare. It takes about 15 minutes to do the trail, nonstop, but you'll want to take your time.

The course is lined with some characters cut out of wood, illustrating the different methods of maple syrup production. When we visited, "Buddy" (a maple leaf bud character) was teaching us, among other things, that the maple syrup season ends once he and other buds appear.

TIPS (fun for 3 years +)
• This sugar bush is my favourite when visiting with younger children. They can handle the short trail, and the wagon ride through the forest adds a feeling of adventure to the outing.
• The trails can be really muddy. Don't wear your best boots!
• They serve all-day pancake breakfasts during the festival (extra fee).
• More about **Bruce's Mill Conservation Area** on page 243.

The children particularly enjoyed going in the tall teepee (not there every year), which reminded us that the natives discovered the maple sap's properties. The kids also liked to pet the real horse in its pen, a reminder of the time when sap was collected in large barrels pulled by such horses. A jolly fellow, clad in overalls and checkered shirt, offered us a taste of syrup, prepared in a huge pot the old-fashioned way.

You can count on a horse-drawn wagon ride, a petting zoo and strolling entertainment. In 2011, there were also pony rides for a fee.

Bruce's Mill Sugarbush Maple Syrup Festival
• Stouffville
(416) 667-6295
www.trca.on.ca

C-3
N-E
of Toronto
35-min.

Schedule: The season may start early March and last to mid-April. (Call to check the exact dates.)

Open Wednesday to Sunday, 9:30 am to 4 pm.
Admission: $9/adults, $6.50/ seniors and children, FREE under 5 years, FREE parking.
Directions: Between Warden and Kennedy, Stouffville. From Hwy 404 North, take exit #37/Stouffville Road eastbound.

KORTRIGHT SUGARBUSH FESTIVAL

Mouth-watering

The sugar content of maple sap is between 2 and 3%, while maple syrup has at least 66%. It takes up to 40 buckets of the former to produce one bucket of the latter. It's not surprising that the cost of syrup is so high. It's only made in North America and 80% of the world production comes from Canada. No wonder maple syrup is so precious to us.

Kortright Centre moves heaven and earth to educate us on the subject.

You can cover the path crossing the sugar bush in half an hour. It begins with

a steep downward slope that seems difficult to tackle, but the secret is to go slowly. Kids won't resist the call of gravity and will go down at full speed. However, they'll surely stop before the big turn if tools were left to drill tap holes the old-fashioned way, using a brace and bit!

On the path, buckets have been installed lower than usual, allowing children a peek at the dripping sap. Pioneers are cooking maple sap inside huge pots. (When visiting, we could try the shoulder yokes.)

Modern maple syrup production techniques are presented inside the sugar cabin. It's easy to see the modern maple sap collecting system and to explain its functioning to kids. My little engineer was fascinated by this gravity-fed system that moves the sap from the trees directly to storage tanks inside the cabin.

Kortright's version of the festival includes magic and music shows, storytelling, and strolling entertainment. In 2011, there were also pony rides for a fee.

TIPS (fun for 4 years +)

• Staff members told me that the first weekends of the festival are the quietest. Saturdays are quieter than Sundays. On weekdays during March Break, arrive after 2 pm when the school buses leave.

• During the **Maple Syrup Festival**, pancakes with syrup are sold at the centre's cafeteria. Tasty snacks made with maple syrup are sold in the shops.

• The admission includes a horse-drawn wagon ride. I was disappointed by the ride as the course was uninteresting. On the bright side, the succulent maple popcorn we had bought kept my little companions' boredom at bay as we waited in the long line-up and the pleasant cart driver was very talkative. She taught us a lot about her horses and invited children to pet them.

• More about **Kortright Centre** on p. 241.

NEARBY ATTRACTIONS
McMichael Collection (10-min.) ..... p. 91
The Wave Pool (20-min.) .... p. 417

Kortright Sugarbush Maple Syrup Festival
· Woodbridge
(416) 667-6295
www.trca.on.ca

C-2
N-W
of Toronto
40-min.

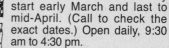

Schedule: The season may start early March and last to mid-April. (Call to check the exact dates.) Open daily, 9:30 am to 4:30 pm.

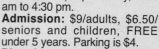

Admission: $9/adults, $6.50/seniors and children, FREE under 5 years. Parking is $4.

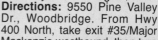

Directions: 9550 Pine Valley Dr., Woodbridge. From Hwy 400 North, take exit #35/Major Mackenzie westbound, then turn south on Pine Valley Drive.

HORTON'S HOME FARM

It's personal

No bells and whistles at this farm. So why bother coming here? For the timeless charm of the place, I would say. For the "monkey tree" would claim my children!

Everything about this place is laid-back. Your kids really want to climb up the tall "monkey tree"? "Be our guest." The 450-year-old dying maple tree still standing is actually the best climbing tree I have seen in ages!

The maple sugar bush has been family-run since 1963. The guide who walks us through the short trail around the sugar bush is the son of the founders.

A lady clad in old-fashioned dress and cap serves us nice warm pancakes. They also sell hot chocolate and maple products.

The sun shining through the windowpanes inside the shack accentuates the warmth of the wooden walls and tables. Outside, it gives a dazzling glow to the snow. Later, as I sit by a tree, I hear water dripping from the melting icicles and the laughter of the children involved in a snowball fight. It was so relaxing.

Note that you'll have to go through 500 metres of mud by foot or be pulled behind a tractor to reach the sugar bush.

Horton's Home Farm · Stouffville (905) 888-1738 www.hortontreefarms.com	C-3 N-E of Toronto 40-min.

 Schedule: Saturdays and Sundays from 9 am to 4 pm, usually from mid-March to early April.
Admission: $6.50/adults, $5.50/seniors & students, $4.50/5-12 years old. Cash!
Directions: 5924 Slater Road, Stouffville. Take Hwy 404 North. Turn east on Aurora Road, then south on Warden Avenue, and west on Slater Road.

SILOAM ORCHARDS

Off the beaten track

I was concerned there wasn't much of the white stuff left on the ground. But I had called to check if they still could offer taffy on the snow and they had confirmed it. I found out later that they've learned to store snow in the freezer after a fresh fall. Clever.

The maple taffy on the snow in itself was reason enough for this outing! Call before you go.

Before reaching their 2,500-tree maple forest, we walked by the farm's orchards. The self-guided walk was as simple as can be (and muddy) but it explained well how the sap was collected from the green pipelines we saw emerging from the holes drilled into the maple trees. We could sample the sap in the buckets along the trail. The **Cider Café** serves pancakes with maple syrup, breakfast sausage, coffee, apple cider, hot dogs and homemade apple pie.

Siloam Orchards · Uxbridge (905) 852-9418 www.siloamorchards.com	C-3 North of Toronto 50-min.

 Schedule: Open in March and early April on the weekends, from 9 am to 3 pm.
Admission: $4/person (includes maple taffy on the snow and access to self-guided walking tour to the bush).
Directions: 7300-3rd Concession, Uxbridge. From Hwy 404 North, take exit #41 (Bloomington RR 40), follow to Goodwood, then turn left on Front Street (it becomes 3rd Concession).

MOUNTSBERG MAPLE SYRUP TIME

Maple syrup time, with animals to boot

When you visit, if you are lucky, the hatchery in the Discovery Room might be bursting with little chirping chicks who undulate as one big yellow wave when children get close to them. What a great bonus!

The **Mountsberg Conservation Area** has a lot to offer during **Maple Syrup Time**.

Past the **Visitors' Centre**, there's a railroad crossing (it may be the first time your child walks over some tracks!) It gets us to a field from which you can walk to **MapleTowne** or wait for the horse-drawn wagon ($3/adults, $2/kids). It will take you on a good ride through the sugar bush.

MapleTowne, a series of small, rustic houses, is in the heart of the action. In one of them, syrup is produced. In the next one, maple sugar is made (yes, everybody can have a taste). Another one is a country shop.

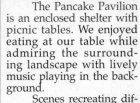

The Pancake Pavilion is an enclosed shelter with picnic tables. We enjoyed eating at our table while admiring the surrounding landscape with lively music playing in the background.

Scenes recreating different maple syrup production techniques through the ages are displayed around the pavilion.

On a Sunday before March Break, they hold a **Flapjack Olympics** (they've done this for the last ten years). It involves pancake-related events (such as frozen pancakes stacking) and fun torch run with snow shoes or some other wacky activity. Check their website for the date.

TIPS (fun for 4 years +)

• During the Maple Syrup Time, live raptor demonstrations, normally offered only on weekends and holidays at that time of the year, are shown at 12 noon, 1 pm, 2 pm and 3 pm.

• Friday to Sunday on **Easter** weekend, expect an Easter Egg Hunt, Scavenger Hunt (for 10 years and over), crafts and more (11 am to 3 pm).

• More on the **Mountsberg Wildlife Centre** on page 244.

NEARBY ATTRACTIONS
Hilton Falls (15-min.) .... p. 250

Mountsberg Maple Syrup Time
• Milton
(905) 854-2276
www.conservationhalton.on.ca

**D-2
West
of Toronto
55-min.**

 Schedule: The season may start early March and last to mid-April (depends when Easter falls). Activities are offerred on weekends, Holiday and daily during the March Break, 10 am to 4 pm.

 Admission: $7.25/adults, $6.25/seniors, $5/5-14 years, FREE under 5 (extra for pancakes, kids' meal under $5).

 Directions: From Hwy 401 West, exit #312/Guelph Line southbound. Turn west on Campbellville Rd., then north on Milborough Line to the park entrance.

WARKWORTH MAPLE FESTIVAL

The real stuff!

Thanks to the Warkworth Maple Syrup Festival, my son had a taste of his first warm, amber-coloured ribbon, rolled around a wooden spoon.

When we parked in a field close to the **Sandy Flat Sugar Bush**, the snow was melting in the bright sunshine and getting mixed with the path's dirt. Better wear those rubber boots to appreciate the event!

We'd just driven an hour and a half, leaving behind grey Toronto to go taste taffy poured on to white snow. (This activity isn't generally offered in sugar shacks neighbouring the city, as they suffer from a lack of snow.) The country road we had been driving on for the last half an hour was charming and put us all in good spirits.

The place is very popular; there was a short line-up at the entrance booth. The warm and friendly ambiance reigning over the site is contagious. By observing closely, one understands why. Retired people from the area serve breakfast, boy scouts clean tables and local musicians play the violin. It seems that the whole Warkworth community is present!

All of the festival's activities revolve around a square, worthy of a postcard, where a happy crowd is gathered. There's spontaneous dancers moving to a jig. Here, two kids can't believe how lucky they are to be allowed to cut a slice off a log with a double-handled saw. There, contestants being timed run in the snow, wearing snowshoes and holding a pail of maple sap. Pretty funny to watch!

The excitement rises each time a new pail of delicious taffy is ready. Grown-ups and kids alike line up eagerly in front of troughs full of snow where they can have a taste of the delicious treat.

TIPS (fun for 4 years +)
• Bring a change of clothes for the kids ... just in case. (It could save your car seats!)
• There are two walking trails allowing visitors to burn off some of those maple syrup pancakes! The short one takes 20 minutes to complete, the other is one mile long. They include little bridges and signs.
• During the **Maple Syrup Festival** weekend, activities are held in Warkworth Village: craft show, antique show, art show, pony rides and petting farm (check www.maplesyrupfestival.com).
• Every weekend after the festival, you can also visit Sandy Flat Sugar Bush to taste taffy, go on a sleigh ride (weather permitting).
• They sell many maple sugar treats.

Warkworth Maple Syrup Festival	B-6 East of Toronto 1 3/4 hr
• Warkworth (705) 924-2057 www.sandyflatsugarbush.com	

 Schedule: The annual festival is held the second weekend in March, 9 am to 4 pm. The sugar bush is open year-round but call ahead during the weekdays.
Admission: FREE taffy sampling. Small fees apply for the sleigh ride. Breakfast of pancakes and sausages with syrup costs around $6/adults, $3/children.
Directions: Sandy Flat Sugar Bush, Warkworth. From Hwy 401 East, take exit #474/Hwy 45 northbound, then take County Rd. 29 eastbound towards Warkworth. Go to Burnley then turn left onto Noonan Road and follow the Sandy Flat Sugar Bush signs.

General tips about
Holiday outings:

- This chapter describes unique seasonal attractions, mostly **Christmas** activities.
- For a quick reference **Halloween**, **Christmas**, **March Break** and **Easter** activities, look for the following seasonal symbols in the information boxes of the attractions throughout the guide.

- Read pages 10 and 11 for my review of the best **Calendars of Events** for family events.
- You'll find a description of the seasonal parades in the **Parades** section under the **Amusement Corner** chapter.

HOLIDAY
OUTINGS

See **Santa at the mall (Square One)** on p. 181.

THE NUTCRACKER

Magical in all points

A ballet that involves a rat, horse, ram, rooster, fox, bee, sheep, unicorns, mice, bears, cats and dogs will get their attention, believe me!

The **National Ballet** first performed the **Nutcracker** in 1964. The current choreography was created by James Kudelka in 1995.

Whether or not you intend to get tickets to the **National Ballet of Canada**'s lavish **Nutcracker** accompanied by the **National Ballet Orchestra**, you must visit their Nutcracker's website.

The video excerpt which opens on the home page is worth a thousand words

Photos: Bruce Zinger

to describe the dazzling magic of their performance in a Russian setting.

Click on *Skip* and go to *Videos* for the clip on the make-up session to become Uncle Nikolai, the one on costume design and, my favourite, the fascinating explanation on the making of a tutu (they cost thousands of dollars!). Note that all these website references were valid at the time of print.

The **Nutcracker Story Time** is a 45-minute bonus event offered prior to the show to introduce kids to the storyline. To download their activity book, go to the *Learn More* section on their Nutcracker home page.

The seating plan of the **Four Seasons Centre** includes **Orchestra**, **Grand Ring**, **Ring 3**, **Ring 4** and **Ring 5** (the latter being the least expensive). We sat in Ring 5 to test it and found we had a very nice view of the whole ensemble of dancers from there.

We did not realize that we were missing the upper part of the spectacular set until we toured the lower levels after the show! Note that Ring 3 tickets would cost around $40 more per person. Your call.

TIPS (fun for 5 years +)

• A few years ago, I wanted to test the (then $30) **Rush Tickets** option (which you can buy on the same day as the show) so I went to the box office on a Wednesday at noon. They had tickets available in the Ring 3 (then normally worth $70-$78!). At 6 pm, they still had many Ring 5 tickets (then worth $31-$41).

• For the first time in December 2007, a matinee performance of the **Nutcracker** was presented, live from the **Four Seasons Centre**, in **Cineplex** theatres across Canada. Let's hope they bring it back! In 2010, they presented the Bolshoi Ballet's version.

• If this is your child's first **Nutcracker**, why not initiate her first with a more modest version? The following companies have created their own Nutcracker, look them up to see if they're offering it this year: **www.balletjorgen.ca**, **www.ontarioballettheatre.com**, **www.piaboumanschool.org**, and **Toronto International Ballet Theatre** at www.starsofthe21stcentury.com. Rule of thumb, expect their best tickets to cost near the price of National Ballet of Canada's cheapest ones.

NEARBY ATTRACTIONS
The Bay's windows (4-min. walk) p. 171
Cavalcade of Lights (2-min. walk) p. 176

The National Ballet of Canada

D-3
Dowtown
Toronto
5-min.

(416) 345-9595
www.thenutcracker.ca
www.national.ballet.ca

Schedule: The Nutcracker is normally offered throughout December (but not daily).

Admission: Around $44-$116/adult, $32-$101/15 years and under, $142-$380/4 people. Ask about their $35 Rush Tickets.

Directions: Four Seasons Centre, 145 Queen Street W., Toronto (at University Avenue).

SING-ALONG MESSIAH

Photo: Courtesy of Tafelmusik

Hallelujah!

As he's talking to us, Maestro Handel is interrupted by... a bawling baby. Tongue-in-cheek, he comments on the great potential of the future singer (while the mother sheepishly reaches the exit) and goes on introducing the great masterpiece we've all come to sing.

When we handed in our ticket at the entrance, we were asked in what register we sang. I used to contribute a thin soprano voice to a choir in my life b.c. (before children) but I was accompanying a friend of mine with his two young daughters so we opted for the mixed section selected by many families.

TIPS (fun for 8 years +)
• Arrive early if you want to buy the $10 Messiah score. Consult the Sing-Along program to find out which portion of the score will be performed. (You can also get it at **Remenyi** stores, www.remenyi.com).
• Handel interacts with us again after the intermission. Remember it is only in the second part that you will be able to belt the famous "Hallelujah! Hallelujah! Halleeluujaaah!"
• The **Tafelmusik Baroque Orchestra and Chamber Choir** also present their *Messiah* (although not in the sing-along version). They usually offer a few performances mid-December. (In 2011, they will perform it at the **Royal Conservatory**.)
• See what's around **Dundas Station** on p. 472.

NEARBY ATTRACTIONS
St. James Crèches (5-min. walk) p. 171
Eaton Centre (1-min. walk) .... p. 182

To reach it we had to climb way up through the narrow backstairs of the old 1804 **Massey Hall**.

From our seats, we could get quite a view of the happy crowd, most spectators eagerly holding on to their score. Later on, I realized that most of them had been there before and just could not wait for the magic to start.

The maestro, quite handsome in his overcoat and wig, encouraged us to "zing along" with his strong German accent, and helped us warm up. **The Tafelmusik Baroque Orchestra and Chamber Choir** and special soloists were accompanying us.

Listening to thousands of voices joining in to present Handel's *Messiah* is an amazing experience. You literally become the music. One has to know that Handel composed his masterpiece in 21 days, partially paralyzed from a stroke!

At one point, I was totally lost and frantically flipping through the complicated score when I felt a gentle tap on my shoulder. Alia and Alex, aged 10 and 11, earnestly wanting to help, quietly pointed out to me the right spot on the right page. Hallelujah! (It makes one wonder what do they teach these kids in whatever school they attend?)

Sing-Along Messiah (416) 872-4255 (box office) www.masseyhall.com (416) 964-6337 (company) www.tafelmusik.org	D-3 Downtown Toronto 10-min.

Schedule: Usually at 2 pm on the Sunday right before Christmas (2011: December 18).
Admission: $43/person (tickets are on sale by mid-August, they sell out quickly).
Directions: Massey Hall, on Shuter St., Toronto (just east of Yonge Street by the **Eaton Centre**'s parking lot entrance).

SOULPEPPER'S *CHRISTMAS CAROL*

Extreme make-over... of the soul

What better way to end the year than to see the infamous and selfish Scrooge morph before our eyes into an exalted man determined to dedicate the rest of his life to become the best he humanly can.

Dynamic and proactive **Soulpepper Theatre Company** was involved in the creation of the **Young Centre for the Performing Arts** at **The Distillery** from the beginning.

For some years now (twice every three years), the company has presented its own theatrical version of *A Christmas Carol* on a central stage surrounded by the audience.

As we sat, we could appreciate the intimate feeling created by the original layout of the venue. As soon as the play began, we could see how well it served

Dickens' beloved story. Actors could arrive from four different places. This greatly helped to recreate the ambiance of a busy crowd in the town's public place on Christmas Eve.

Special effects were few, not to distract us from the storytelling, but quite efficient: a tablecloth would fly in the air, people would disappear into the stage, the arms of a giant clock would run like crazy on the floor.

Props were as ingenious. A ladder on wheels would allow us to imagine Scrooge overlooking the whole city in the night. Actors would quietly install garlands without interrupting their delivery to turn a working space into the cutest ballroom.

We then were treated with the most engaging dance by the full cast, initiated by Scrooge's boss from the past Christmas, with the help of live violin fiddling. Even grumpy Scrooge couldn't resist the impulse to emulate the dancers (that's when we all started to feel for the old guy).

Can't imagine a better inspiration to start on our New Year's resolutions.

Photos: Courtesy of Soulpepper Theatre Company

TIPS (fun for 6 years +)

• This performance will feel like great storytelling to younger school-aged kids. If you think your child is mature enough to sit for two hours, including a 20-min. intermission, go for it!

• The venue includes a gorgeous atrium with café/bar and fireplace. They allow bottles of water inside the theatre.

• Ask about their **Rush** tickets. Most performances prior to December 25 usually sell out quickly but you can try your luck with performances after December 26 by showing up one hour before presentations. In the worst scenario, you still get to enjoy strolling about The Distillery.

• See p. 380 for more info about **The Distillery** (such as nearby **Soma Chocolatemaker**). It offers the perfect Victorian feeling for a Dickens' outing.

Soulpepper's *Christmas Carol* (416) 866-8666 (box office) www.soulpepper.ca	**D-3** **Downtown** Toronto **10-min.**

 Schedule: Call to confirm if offered this year. Usually over a few weeks prior to Christmas until end of December.

 Admission: In 2010, was $40/adults, $31/students.

 Directions: Young Centre for the Performing Arts, 55 Mill St., Building 49, Toronto (between Cherry and Parliament Streets).

ROSS PETTY PRODUCTIONS

Photos: Courtesy of Ross Petty Productions

Silly, very silly

For years, Ross Petty Productions has presented panto-mime versions of fairy tales such as Robin Hood, Aladdin, Snow White and Beauty and the Beast at the beautiful Elgin Theatre. These presentations are pure entertainment for the whole family.

Traditionally, the **Ross Petty Productions** involve a villain impersonated by Ross Petty himself, who everyone loves to hate. I always find it hilarious to watch first time adult spectators trying to prevent their kids from booing at the villain when it is exactly what he wants them to do. (He would be so disappointed if they didn't!)

For the fun of it, performers take liberties from the original tale and talk directly to children as if they were part of the action, adding as many modern references as they can.

From songs complete with dances that are choreographed in a hilarious cartoon-like fashion, to elaborate costumes and decor, all contribute to the success of this goofy entertainment!

They always choose a funny way to acknowledge their sponsors and they're totally unapologetic about this (and all the other non-politically correct faux-pas they make on purpose). Throughout the show, parents will find double-meaning to the jokes.

In every production, expect a star from another discipline. In the past years, we've seen a ballet dancer, a TV star, a Canadian Idol, an ice skater and even a wrestler. Most of the time, you can also count on a male actor playing a female role, the trademark of a good pantomime.

TIPS (fun for 5 years +)
• To avoid the extra charge of around $5 per ticket from **Ticket Master**, buy your tickets directly at the **Elgin Theatre**'s box office (on a day when you're visiting the Eaton Centre). The box office is open Monday to Saturday from 11 am to 5 pm and prior to the shows.
• For a description of things to see around the Eaton Centre, see what's around **Queen** and **Dundas Stations** on p. 472.

NEARBY ATTRACTIONS
The Bay's windows (2-min walk) p. 171
Crèche Exhibition (5-min. walk) ... p. 171

Ross Petty Productions (416) 872-5555 www.rosspetty.com	**D-3 Downtown Toronto 10-min.**

 Schedule: From late November to early January at around 7 pm, with matinees at around 1 or 2 pm. Call for exact schedule. **Admission:** Around $64-$85/ adults, $59/12 years and under, $235/4 people.
Directions: Elgin Theatre, 189 Yonge Street, Toronto (across from **Eaton Centre**.

MOTUS O'S CHRISTMAS CAROL

Dancing Scrooge

Wacky cartoon-like scenes alternate with emotionally charged choreographies in this original take on the classic Dickens, rendered by dance company Motus O. Expect crooner angels, Irish dancers, disco studs, tap-dancing toast (really) and a few spirits of Christmas to play along with a dancing Scrooge.

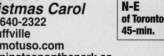

Stouffville is home to **Motus O**, an internationally acclaimed company. Quietly, they have carved the local tradition of producing a yearly production of *A Christmas Carol*, well worth sharing with the rest of the GTA.

Nineteen on the Park, featuring the show we're about to see, is located in old Stouffville. We are greeted by a Victorian lad from the outdoor balcony of the small theatre as we enter. Inside, a 15-member choir treats us with Christmas songs from the mezzanine while we wait.

The show opens with the joyful chaos of a village scene featuring over twenty extras selected from the Stouffville community. They've practiced for weeks to be able to share the stage with the professionals and have seamlessly been integrated into the show. We see, among other things: carolers, a hockey game, bullies, a thief, bakers, cross-country skiers, and families carrying mountains of gifts. The whole production is a mix of theatre, musical and dance show, sustained by an energetic and versatile cast capable of great comic timing.

A few choreographies remind us that Motus O is indeed a company of serious dancers. The way they express how Scrooge forgot about life and got swallowed by his work is truly creative. (As he dances with the love of his life, one after the other, three women undertake to distract him like seductive mistresses, bearing a quill pen, a register, and... a telephone.) Tiny Tim's parents dancing their sadness over his grave offers a very poignant moment.

Kids will certainly appreciate how a structure on wheels becomes in turn Scrooge's office, his bed, a front door, a window, a disco dance floor and a grave. Everyone will love Scrooge's inevitable redemption to prove that humans indeed can change for the better.

TIPS (fun for 5 years +)
• **Fickle Pickle Dining Lounge** is an unassuming family restaurant with decent food located right in front of the theatre (6302 Main St.). The **Corner House Restaurant**, one block east, is quaint and pretty and serves fancier food (6403 Main St., www.thecornerhouse.ca). A few blocks west, there's a great café, **Red Bulb** (6148 Main St., www.redbulb.ca).

NEARBY ATTRACTIONS
York-Durham Railway (30-min.)   p. 204

Motus O's *Christmas Carol* (905) 640-2322 • Stouffville www.motuso.com www.nineteenonthepark.ca	C-3 N-E of Toronto 45-min.

Schedule: On at least three consecutive days in early to mid-December, at 2 pm and/or 7 pm. (Call to confirm and to reserve.)
Admission: Around $35/adults, $18/students.
Directions: In the **Nineteen on the Park (Lebovic Centre for Arts)**, 19 Civic Ave., Stouffville (across from 6302 Main Street).

St. James & Crèche Exhibit

I spy...

Find the crèche made out of walnut. Which crèche figures are actually flutes? Where's the one with a pinecone roof? Can you see the shepherd feeding his sheep from a basket? These are a few of the items children were asked to find throughout the exhibition when we visited.

St. James Cathedral's annual crèche exhibit has grown to include over two hundred Nativity scenes. Most of them are quite modest in size. This actually adds to the pleasure of the hunt!

They come from over 40 countries and are made with every possible material: gingerbread, straw, clay, wool, stone, shells, tin cans... They were knit, modeled, painted, baked... No need to be Christian to appreciate the lovely figures.

More on **St. James** on p. 132.

St. James Cathedral & Crèche Exhibit (416) 364-7865 www.stjamescathedral.on.ca	D-3 Downtown Toronto 10-min.

 Schedule: Due to ongoing renovations of the **Parish House**, it was uncertain at the time of print if the exhibit could take place there in 2011. Check their website in November for confirmation of dates and location.
Admission: FREE.
 Directions: The **Parish House's** entrance is on Church Street, Toronto (north of King Street).

The Bay's Christmas windows

You're not alone!

Wish you could join your extended family on the day of Christmas but can't make it happen this year? This could help chase away the blues.

One year, we happened to be in Toronto on December 25. We went downtown to admire the gorgeous scenes in **The Bay**'s windows as well as the lovely decorations inside the **Eaton Centre** (kept open for those using the subway).

We then joined the action at **Nathan Phillips Square**. The place was busy with families skating around the rink (bring your own skates because the rental shop is closed). They would then head off to **Timothy's**, across the street, for a hot chocolate. We chose to walk down Yonge to the **Marché** for yummy desserts (at Yonge & Front in Brookfield Place).

The Bay (416) 861-9111 www.hbc.com	D-3 Downtown Toronto 10-min.

 Schedule: From mid-November to December 31.
Admission: FREE.
 Directions: 176 Yonge Street, Toronto, at the corner of Queen Street.

THE CHRISTMAS STORY

A time for rituals

A tiny house of worship dating from 1847 is caught in a stranglehold by the buildings that have sprung up since then. For over 73 years, it has been telling the story of Christmas to Torontonians, with the assistance of its great organ, accompanied by a singing quartet and amateur actors of all ages miming the narrators' words.

The **Christmas Story** performances held at the **Church of the Holy Trinity** are certainly the most concrete way to explain to children the story of the nativity scene displayed at Christmas time. The Anglican church is modest but gorgeous. The great organ plays softly while we wait for the show to begin. The first two rows of pews, as well as two large carpets at the front, are reserved for young spectators.

Children hold their breath when all the lights go out, emphasizing the large stained-glass windows at the back of the altar, before a spotlight shines on the two narrators. For the remainder of the performance, the actors perform within islands of light standing out against the darkness. The amateur production offers studied and harmonious scenes, and the costumes are very nice. The Annunciation angel has majestic wings, the shepherds' clothing is meticulously draped, and the Three Wise Men are dressed in rich fabrics.

The actors are all volunteers, generous with their time and enthusiasm, but they're confined in a relatively static formula (you don't attend "Christmas Story" for acting performances).

I was charmed by many of the child actors: a pageboy with the giggles, a little angel forgetting to leave the stage, baby Jesus happily babbling as the myrrh is shown to him and quivering with joy during the offering of the third Wise Man, with the audience laughing. When I visited, Jesus was played by... eight-month-old twins, sharing the role according to their mood of the moment!

TIPS (fun for 5 years +)
• The performance lasts about an hour and combines perfectly with a short visit to admire **Eaton Centre**'s Christmas decorations (p. 182) and **Nathan Phillips Square**'s Cavalcade of lights and skating rink (p. 176).
• In the summertime, you can enjoy this lovely church by attending the free concerts of the **Music Mondays** (from late May to early September, at 12 noon, www.musicmondays.ca). A $5 donation is suggested.

NEARBY ATTRACTIONS
Cavalcade of Lights (5-min. walk)   p. 176

The Christmas Story
(416) 598-4521
www.holytrinitytoronto.org
(click *Music and Arts*)

D-3
**Downtown
Toronto
10-min.**

 Schedule: Usually on the three weekends before Christmas: Friday and Saturday evenings, 7:30 pm. Saturdays and Sundays, 4:30 pm. (Call to confirm and to reserve.)

 Admission: Suggested donation: $10/adults, $5/children.

Directions: Church of the Holy Trinity, 10 Trinity Square, Toronto (west of **Eaton Centre**).

CHRISTMAS FLOWER SHOW

Allan Gardens' most interactive day

The opening day of the Christmas Flower Show is the only time of the year when activities are planned for children.

For the occasion, the greenhouses have donned reds, pinks, greens and whites (which they will keep until the New Year).

Under the big glass dome, we admire a few Christmas shapes covered with plants (in the past, we've seen a toy soldier, a rocking horse and a fireplace).

During the opening day, singers in Victorian costumes perform Christmas carols under that same beautiful dome.

A "make-and-take" activity takes place in one of the greenhouses and more activities are held outside the conservatories.

When visiting, we could grab free Christmas cookies and hot cider and enjoy them as we caught a glimpse of a Victorian Santa (St. Nicholas).

We also took a horse-drawn wagon ride around the site.

TIPS (fun for 4 years +)

• A craft activity is usually offered every year. In 2010, there was a polar bear theme and the kids learned to build a small polar bear topiary frame.

• **Centennial Park Greenhouse** also hosts a **Christmas Flower Show** with an open house offering similar activities (usually one week later). Call 416-394-8543 for details.

• In 2010, they offered extra **Candlelight Hours** on some evenings from 5 pm to 7 pm. Call to see if they're still offering it this year.

• More about **Allan Gardens Conservatory** on page 260.

NEARBY ATTRACTIONS
Riverdale Farm (5-min.) .... p. 60
Riverdale Park (5-min.) .... p. 360

Allan Gardens
(416) 392-7288
www.toronto.ca/parks

**D-3
Downtown
Toronto
15-min.**

Schedule: Christmas Flower Show: Daily from first Sunday of December to first weekend in January, 12 noon to 5 pm. **Opening day:** On first Sunday of December, 12 noon to 5 pm. **Admission:** FREE. **Directions:** 19 Horticultural Ave., Toronto (between Jarvis and Sherbourne, south of Carlton).

CHRISTMAS AT BLACK CREEK

Victorian Christmas

During the Victorian Christmas, the village is adorned with decorations. Don't go expecting glittering frills and colours however, as decorations were humble and homemade. The village's old houses are quite bare and pioneers certainly did not waste money on candles. As a result, it is likely your children won't even notice they are decorated!

When we last visited, we got to craft homemade presents and taste some treats. We toured the village muffled by the white snow.

One of the most popular events at Black Creek Pioneer Village is **Christmas By Lamplight** for which you need advance reservations. For the occasion, candles and lanterns lend a magical feel to the village. Singers dressed in costumes of the times present Christmas carols in the streets.

When we attended this event, chestnuts were cooked on a bonfire and hot cider was served. Kids could do make-and-take Christmas crafts, and have old-fashioned wagon rides in the dark.

TIPS (fun for 5 years +)

• The **Christmas By Lamplight** event is so popular, try to reserve as early as October. They give priority to people booking the **Christmas Dinner** as well (which I prefer not to attend with kids) but you can ask to be put on the waiting list!

• More on **Black Creek Pioneer Village** on p. 381.

NEARBY ATTRACTIONS

Black Creek Pioneer Village
• North York
(416) 736-1733
www.blackcreek.ca

**D-3
North
of downtown
35-min.**

Schedule: The **Victorian Country Christmas** runs from mid-November to December 31 from 9:30 am to 4 pm on weekdays and from 11 am to 4:30 pm during the weekends (more activities offered on the weekends in December before Christmas). **Christmas by Lamplight** is offered at least three Saturday evenings in December.

Admission: Regular activities: $15/adults, $14/seniors, $11/5-14 years, FREE 4 years and under, tax not included. Parking is around $7. **Christmas by Lamplight** is $30/person (dinner extra).

Directions: 1000 Murry Ross Pkwy, North York (at the southeast corner of Steeles Avenue and Jane Street. The entrance is east of Jane Street.

CHRISTMAS BY CANDLELIGHT

Candles, lamps and lanterns

Everything is so lovely under the warm yellow glow of candlelight. Everything that we can see, that is. We're so used to our electricity that we don't realize how dark things can be without it. Our stroll through the village really feels like an adventure as we walk in the cold black night in search of the next welcoming building.

After paying our admission, we saw Santa next door (a good-looking vintage Santa in long robe with a kind face). We then dragged the kids out of the visitor centre's gift shop (keep this for the end, they carry many small old-fashioned toys) and walked towards the barns, the darkest section of the village.

Don't worry, there's nothing creepy about **Lang Pioneer Village** by night. We heard the bells of the horse-drawn wagon and kids laughing around a crackling fire.

Past the shingle mill and the cheese factory, we entered into the small school house where awaited a patient schoolmistress under a large Union Jack flag.

We visited the blacksmith shop, the lumbering display, the general store and the little church.

I was accompanied by 10-year-old musicians who couldn't resist the call of the carolers strolling in the park so we joined the singers who kindly shared their music score with us.

We then hopped on the wagon as it was passing by and stopped a bit further to warm up around the fire. Our young urbanites don't get to sit by a fire too often so it was a big attraction in itself. It was near the tinsmith shop, where we could admire beautiful lanterns.

We checked a few more houses, loved the print shop, heard live music in the **Douro Town Hall** and bought snacks at the **Keene Hotel** that we ate on our way back home.

TIPS (fun for 6 years +)

• In the past, they've offered a live Nativity scene with real farm animals on the Sunday at 7:30 pm. Check with them.
• If you want to combine this with Peterborough's **Kinsmen Santa Claus Parade**, I recommend you watch the parade near its starting point so you can leave earlier to spend more time at the pioneer village (see p. 48).

Lang Pioneer Village • Keene (705) 295-6694 www.langpioneervillage.ca	B-5 N-E of Toronto 1 3/4 hr

 Schedule: Usually on the first weekend of December, 5 pm to 9 pm.

 Admission: $10/adults, $8 seniors & students, $6/5-14 years, $30/family of 6, FREE under 5.

 Directions: 104 Lang Rd., Keene. Take Hwy 401 eastbound, then exit at Hwy 115/35 and follow north. Past Peterborough, it becomes Hwy 7. Turn south on County Rd. 34 (Heritage Line). Turn east on Lang Road.

CAVALCADE OF LIGHTS

High-spirited countdown

Our eyes are riveted on the lighted skating rink, shining in the frigid darkness. In less than one minute, the event we've all been expecting will take place. The 300,000 lights adorning the square and the tall Christmas tree will light up at once. Anticipation is building among the excited crowd.

Children delight in excited expectation and they, like us, marvel at the magical effect of this illumination. It's not surprising the City has been organizing this event for decades!

You can arrive as late as a half-hour prior to the illumination, and easily find space in **Nathan Phillips Square**'s large underground parking lot, and a viewing spot (providing you perch your little one on your shoulders).

The **Cavalcade of Lights** usually includes a skating party with DJ, free concert and fireworks on the opening night (4th Saturday prior to Christmas) and more parties and concerts in the following Saturdays, but not in 2011 (due to Nathan Phillips Square renovations).

The opening night offers a holiday concert so most of the performers sing holiday songs for the delight of the crowd.

Don't forget to visit inside **City Hall** while you're there to view a model of the city sure to amaze the kids.

On Cavalcade's page on the City's website, you'll find a link to the different lighting displays throughout the city (such as Yorkville Park on Cumberland).

TIPS (fun for 5 years +)

• **Nathan Phillips Square** usually hosts a **CityTV New Year's Bash** that begins at 10 pm on December 31 and ends with **fireworks**.
• The **CN Tower** also presents a **New Year's Countdown** with special effects on its programmable lighting system.
• More on the **Nathan Phillips Square**'s rink on p. 352.

Cavalcade of Lights Dial 311 (new service) www. toronto.ca/special_events	**D-3 Dowtown Toronto 10-min.**

Schedule: The event opens with a lighting celebration usually on the 4th Saturday before Christmas, at around 7 pm (with fireworks display at 8 pm). Check exact hour closer to the event (2011: November 26). The lights will be brought down on January 1st. (Expect more activities and dates for 2012, after the Square's renovation.)
Admission: FREE.
Directions: Nathan Phillips Square, Toronto (at the corner of Queen West and Bay Streets).

TWELVE TREES OF CHRISTMAS

Gardiner's trees

Every year, designers are given "carte blanche" to their wildest fantasies with the decorating of twelve Christmas trees, which are then displayed throughout the museum. The result is lavish, if somewhat loaded, with a myriad of lovely details that small eyes enjoy discovering.

While this is one of those places where the "do not touch" prevails, I mention it nevertheless for those who get swept away by glittering Christmas trees.

As an example of how they exploit a theme, one year we visited when it was *Christmas through the decades*, an exhibit where each designer created a tree evocative of a decade between 1888 and 2008. It included a tree reminiscent of 1938, decorated as a Monopoly game.

I enjoyed the tree of 1908 with its dolls and "Anne of Green Gables" memorabilia. Children preferred the 1968 "Space Race" tree with its rockets, or the moving disco balls and plastic jewelry of the 1978 "Groovy Christmas", or again, the dozens of Beanie Babies on the 1998 tree. The trees are auctioned to raise funds, which explains why they're taken away so early in December.

Read p. 90 for a description of the many ceramic pieces of interest for children at the **Gardiner Museum**.

TIPS (fun for 5 years +)
• While you are in this neighbourhood, you might want to see the Christmas lights in the **Yorkville Park** on Cumberland and finish the outing with a movie at the **Cumberland** (159 Cumberland St.) or the **Varsity** (55 Bloor St. West).
• After seeing all this porcelain, why not push it to **Ashley's** (5-min. walk east on Bloor) for a look at their trademark "Great Wall of China".

Gardiner Museum	D-3
(416) 586-8080	**Downtown**
www.	**Toronto**
gardinermuseum.com	**10-min.**

 Schedule: Usually from mid-November to early December. The museum is open daily at 10 am; closes at 6 pm, Monday to Thursday, at 9 pm on Fridays, and at 5 pm on weekends.

 Admission: $12/adult, $8/senior, $6/student, FREE 12 years and under. Half-price admission on Fridays, 4 to 9 pm.

 Directions: 111 Queen's Park, Toronto (just south of Bloor St.).

NEARBY ATTRACTIONS

DRYSDALE'S TREE FARM

That's the spirit!

It's the beginning of December and a snowfall has yet to happen. It is actually raining as my husband tucks under low branches on all fours, deep in mud, to cut our Christmas tree. He is on the verge of losing his spirits when the kids reward him with ecstatic exclamations as the tree finally falls.

Drysdale's Tree Farm is beautiful and very popular. The owner's house is picture perfect, all dressed up in decorative lighting. The parking lot is almost full when we arrive shortly after 3 pm. We catch a ride on a horse-drawn wagon (for a small fee), expecting it will lead us to the cutting

zone, only to find ourselves back to departure point some 20 minutes later. The kids enjoy the ride nonetheless, and we hop out to warm up by a bonfire. We will eventually get to the cutting area (in the back of the farmyard) on a large wagon fit to hold everybody's trees.

Back at the farm, we drag our designer tree to a counter, where we pay while a machine wraps our tree so it will fit on top of our vehicle. Mr. and Mrs. Claus have their

own little hut where families enter one at a time. They look like the "real" thing so bring your camera!

Afterwards, we reach the farm's **Christmas Store** where we are greeted by an impressive herd of wooden deer and moose (for sale). It was redesigned since my last visit and offers an even wider selection of housewares, gifts and seasonal novelties as well as treats such as homemade chocolate and fudge.

TIPS (fun for 4 years +)

• If you intend to bring toddlers, remember it is difficult to cut a tree and care for highly mobile little ones.
• The farm could lend us a saw when we attended but it is always better to bring your own tools.
• There's a food concession on site and they sell snacks in the store.
• During Easter time they do **Easter Egg Hunts** and wagon rides. Kids look for plastic eggs to trade for generous loot bags (hence the admission price of $18/children, $3.50/adults). Call to pre-register.
• During October weekends, Halloween activities include: pick-your-own-pumpkins, wagon rides and the one-acre-large hay maze (approx. $7/family).
• For more cut-your-own Christmas-tree places, check **www.harvestontario.com**.

NEARBY ATTRACTIONS
Albion Hills (25-min.) .... p. 367

Drysdale's Tree Farm
· Alliston
(705) 424-9719
www.drysdales.ca

B-2
N-W
of Toronto
75-min.

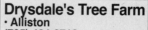
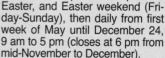
Schedule: Open week prior to Easter, and Easter weekend (Friday-Sunday), then daily from first week of May until December 24, 9 am to 5 pm (closes at 6 pm from mid-November to December).

Costs: FREE admission. Trees cost from $40-$60.

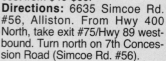
Directions: 6635 Simcoe Rd. #56, Alliston. From Hwy 400 North, take exit #75/Hwy 89 westbound. Turn north on 7th Concession Road (Simcoe Rd. #56).

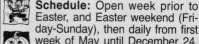

WINTER FESTIVAL OF LIGHTS

Photo: Courtesy of E. Ritson

Lighten up!

It's ironic that Niagara Falls should be a viable family destination given all the jokes that refer to it as the honeymooners' haven. Yet, this is what you get with the **Winter Festival of Lights**.

Created over twenty years ago, the **Niagara Winter Festival of Lights** comes to life at dusk. When I visited, years ago, it featured some twenty lighted animated scenes (many representing Walt Disney characters), all at **Dufferin Islands**, located south of the Niagara Parkway.

They say the **Winter Wonderland** now includes over 120 displays all along Niagara Parkway and leading into Duf-

ferin Islands! Most visitors observe the displays from their cars, and traffic is understandably slow, especially on the small road that travels the islands.

The waterfalls themselves are lit by a powerful system, with sweeping colour spots that change throughout the evening. The light reflects nicely on the surrounding ice-laden trees.

Add to this the new outdoor roofless **Rink on the Brink** (across from Table Rock Centre, overlooking the falls) and **Santa's Village** (along Queen Street, including a **Candle Light Stroll**) and Friday night fireworks displays... Next time I'm staying overnight.

Photo: Courtesy of Winter Festival

TIPS (fun for 4 years +)
• I strongly recommend you arrive in **Niagara Falls** at the beginning of the afternoon to enjoy the wealth of family attractions available in the area.
• You have to check the *Events* section on the festival's website. The line-up of activities is too long to list here.
• Winter time could be the best time to stay overnight and enjoy the indoor **Fallsview Waterpark** packages (see p. 431).
• More on attractions around **Niagara Falls** on p. 253.

NEARBY ATTRACTIONS
Bird Kingdom (5-min.) .... p. 79
Fallsview Waterpark (5-min.) .... p. 431

Niagara Falls Winter Festival of Lights
· Niagara Falls
(905) 374-1616
www.wfol.com

E-4
Niagara Region
90-min.

Schedule: From early November until January 31, 5 pm to midnight.
Admission: FREE. Suggested donation of $5/car.
Directions: From QEW towards Niagara, take Hwy 420 (The Falls), continue on Falls Avenue. It becomes Niagara Pkwy. Drive past the falls, **Dufferin Islands** are on your right. After the tour, drive back on Niagara Pkwy to the Falls Parking lot across from **Table Rock Centre**.

BREAKFAST WITH SANTA

See you in Court

It feels so weird to enter into deserted The Bay store at 9 am that it makes me doubt we are in the right building. Yet, when the elevator's doors open on the eighth floor, the Arcadian Court is already buzzing with the excitement of families gathering around their tables.

Even though there has been a restaurant on The Bay's eighth floor since 1889, I had never been to the Arcadian Court restaurant open daily to the public. The large white and cream room with high ceiling, suspended chandelier and marble floors offers the perfect setting for a breakfast with Santa.

Most girls did not want to miss a chance to dress up so we see a parade of pretty dresses and the colour red reigns. People are still arriving at 9:30 am when the breakfast buffet opens. Don't go expecting fancy eggs Benedict or French toast soaked in maple syrup. Nevertheless, the buffet concept is enough to excite most kids and mine at the sight of the scrambled eggs, sausage, bacon, small potatoes, pancakes, small muffins, fruit, yogurt and juice. Parents are content with the bottomless cups of coffee and tea.

As we eat at our table covered in fine linen, an interactive singer warms the place with his Christmas songs. Meanwhile, clowns are creating shapes with balloons and offering face paint to the kids between bites.

When Santa arrives, a stampede is contained by the promise that each table would be called in its turn to visit the jolly man waiting in his large chair (all tables were previously assigned a colour). By 10:30 am, all food is removed.

The Breakfast with Santa has become a tradition for many extended families to launch the festive season.

TIPS (fun for 3 to 10 years)
• At this kind of event, kids will have more fun if they come with cousins or friends to dance and sing with.
• You can access the Eaton Centre from the overpass on The Bay's second floor to admire their Christmas decorations (no need to put the coats back on). BEWARE! "Santa" is also there! Be prepared with a good explanation.
• Arcadian Court is open for fancy lunches Monday to Saturday, 11:30 am to 2:30 pm (might be closed for private functions, call to confirm).
• Casa Loma also organizes popular breakfasts with Santa, normally from 8:30 to 9:30 am on the three Sundays prior to Christmas (p. 128). It includes the visit of the castle after breakfast and costs around $23/per person, plus tax. To confirm check www.casaloma.org/seasonal.

NEARBY ATTRACTIONS
Nathan Phillips Rink (1-min.walk) p. 352

Breakfast with Santa
(416) 861-4517
www.arcadiancourt.ca

D-3
Dowtown
Toronto
10-min.

Schedule: They try to offer it on Saturdays and Sundays of the three weekends prior to Christmas, from 9 am to 10:30 am. Call to confirm. (Reservations are a must.)

Admission: Around $30/adults, $22/12 years and under. Call to confirm.

Directions: In the Arcadian Court, on the 8th floor of The Bay, Toronto (at the corner of Bay and Queen Streets).

SANTA AT THE MALL

Spotted in shopping malls: He really exists!

Does your neighbourhood mall host the real Santa in a magical setting? Does it house your favourite shops? Does it offer a drop-in child-care service? Some malls do but… which ones?

Starting mid to late November until December 24th (inclusive), you can visit Santa Claus in several shopping malls. It is an adventure that requires some determination. Line-ups can be long and impatient children, who have waited for an hour, may decide to opt out at the last minute. But most kids don't, and that's why a visit to Santa has become a tradition in many families.

Sherway Gardens

The Santa Claus display is always enchanting and colourful at **Sherway Gardens**, and it is the only one I know which incorporates distractions into the line-up, year after year.

For a few years now, they've offered a great concept. They gave timed-tickets allowing groups of kids to meet Santa for 30 minutes at once, for some interactive storytelling and song. No official photo sessions. Parents could take all the pictures they wanted of their kids in action. They are continuing to offer the interactive experience in 2011.

Sherway Gardens houses over 200 stores, including **Holt Renfrew**, **The Bay**, **Sporting Life**, **Sears**, and many children's clothing stores.

Square One

This mall used to host Santa in a wonderful and huge castle under the dome in Centre Court.

In 2008, they went in a totally different direction. They've heard the call of the techno sirens, have dismantled the castle, and have replaced it with a **Magical Video Christmas Tree** (which is kind of cool actually, when we visited, they would project the pictures taken with Santa on the huge tree, for an extra fee).

Starting at around 5 pm, every half-hour, they offer the **Melody & Magic** show, a beautiful 4-min. long light and sound show where the small lights are lit at the sound of lively music through the trees and large ornaments suspended from the ceiling, Wow! (Note that their opening night is too crowded for young children.)

Square One houses over 350 stores including **The Bay**, **Sears**, **Walmart**, **Zellers**, **Toys, Toys, Toys**, **Disney Store**, **Build-a-Bear Workshop**, **P.J's Pet Centre**, many children's clothing stores and **Empire Studio 10**, (905) 275-2640. **Coliseum Mississauga** sits across Rathburn, (905) 275-3456.

Eaton Centre

I recommend a ride in the glass elevator near the large water fountain in the **Eaton Centre**. It usually gives you a good view of the overall Christmas display.

There used to be a large reindeer-pulled sleigh, traveling through a multitude of lights, suspended amidst giant Christmas trees and the 4-storey-high water spray that spurts out at regular intervals. In 2010, it was down to the large **Swarovski Crystal Wish Tree** covered with crystal.

The centre is undergoing its biggest upgrade since 1977. The renovations should be done by summer 2011.

They promise a new sculpture with lights from the glass ceiling above the fountain, spreading 100 feet in either direction (expect something modern), which won't affect our beloved geese suspended near the Queen Street end. (They're also changing both food courts.) At the time of print it was too early to see how they will use these new features at Christmas time.

This downtown mall is home to some 300 stores including **Disney Store**, **Toys, Toys, Toys**, and many children's clothing stores. (See what's around **Queen** and **Dundas Subway Stations** on p. 472.)

An overpass links the Eaton Centre to **The Bay** (read about their gorgeous Christmas windows on p. 171).

A good place to eat is the **Bon Appetit Café** along the window side on the 8th floor of The Bay, with breakfasts and affordable cafeteria-like meals (Monday-Wednesday, 10 am to 4:30 pm; Thursday-Friday closes at 5 pm; Saturday, 11 am to 5 pm; Sunday, 12 noon to 5 pm).

Yorkdale Centre

Yorkdale Centre also features trees lit with a special system (smaller than Square One's), where you can meet Santa.

You have to walk to another section of the mall, near the **Indigo**, to see the **Starlight Spectacular**, their own light and sound show.

Here, instead of playing with height, the lights run along the length of the corridor to create a great visual effect, with the help of over 75 large stars in the air. When we visited, it was 8 minutes long and presented every hour after 5 pm.

You will find over 240 stores in Yordale Centre, including the **Rainforest Café**, **Holt Renfrew**, **The Bay**, **Sears**, many children's clothing boutiques, as well as **Silvercity Yorkdale**, (416) 787-2052. Read about what's around **Yorkdale Subway Station** on p. 477.

Woodbine Centre

Located close to Pearson Airport, with some 150 stores, it includes **The Bay**, **Sears**, **Zellers** and some children's clothing stores, as well as the movie theatres **Rainbow Cinemas Woodbine**, (416) 213-9048. It also houses the large indoor amusement park **Fantasy Fair** (p. 35), which adds to the fun (or torture) of seeing Santa.

Scarborough Town Centre

When we visited, Santa was awaiting in a Victorian living room. This mall is the only one with a daycare offering a drop-off service. This can be a life saver during the trying Christmas shopping spree (**Kornelia's Korner**, (416) 296-0901). If your child is toilet-trained and independent, you could leave her with them for up to 3 hours at $5/hour (leaving time for you to beeline to pre-located stores to buy those gifts and drop them in the trunk of your car).

The mall is home to more than 200 stores, including **The Bay**, **Sears**, **Walmart**, **P.J's Pet Centre**, **Toys, Toys, Toys** and many children's clothing stores. It also hosts the **Coliseum Scarborough**, (416) 290-5217.

Vaughan Mills

Here, the kids will be able to fish with Santa in Santa's cabin near Bass Pro shop!

This is the cutest setup for the big man. You can take your own photos of your kids as they fish (a magnetic fish) from a water hole in the "frozen lake", from Santa's boat by his cottage, encouraged by Santa himself.

ATTENTION! In the back of **Bass Pro** shop's boat section is another Santa in his village! You don't want to enter the mall through this store directly from the parking lot unless you don't mind having to explain why there are two Santas at **Vaughan Mills**. (Bass Pro itself is fun to visit, read about it on p. 71.)

Happy Hull-i-days

In addition to over 250 stores including **Toys "R" Us, Build-a-Bear Workshop, Safari** pet shop and **Winners**, it hosts **Lucky Strike Lanes & Lounge** (p. 23) and **NASCAR Speedpark**, with go-kart track and arcade.

Shopping centres

• **Eaton Centre/Toronto**
(416) 598-8560
www.torontoeatoncentre.com
(Yonge St. and Queen St.)
• **Sherway Gardens/Etobicoke**
(416) 621-1070
www.sherwaygardens.ca
(QEW, exit Browns Line, take Evans Ave.)
• **Yorkdale Centre/North York**
(416) 789-3261
www.yorkdale.com (Hwy 401, Allen Rd. exit, take Yorkdale Ave. southbound)
• **Woodbine Centre/Etobicoke**
(416) 674-5200
www.woodbinecentre.ca
(Hwy 427 North, exit Rexdale East)
• **Scarborough Town Centre**
(416) 296-0296
www.scarboroughtowncentre.com
(Hwy 401, McCowan exit southbound)
• **Square One/Mississauga**
(905) 279-7467
www.shopsquareone.com
(Hwy 403, exit Hurontario southbound)
• **Vaughan Mills/Vaughan**
(905) 879-2110
www.vaughanmills.com
(1 Bass Pro Mills Dr., east of Hwy 400)

HALLOWEEN IN THE COMMUNITY

At a house near you

The event started seven years ago with arts industry professionals turned parents, who gradually got the help of more talented volunteers with kids.

When we attended, the street ambiance was fantastic. Many of us could not even see the stage encompassing two front lawns, but we could see the special lighting, hear the music, feel the vibe. (Sorry for the bad picture, it's all I could do in a dark setting at the time.)

The production in **Riverdale** (on Langley Ave., west of Logan) is exceptional but many other keeners go the extra mile to surpass themselves year after year.

You normally hear about these local events through word-of-mouth. In my neighbourhood, we all know about the little house overloaded with seasonal decorations at 37 Bertmount Ave. (the street across from scrumptious bakery **Bobette & Belle** at 1120 Queen St. East).

I heard about a guy in a new development in **The Beach** neighbourhood who is now in his 10th edition of the **Halloween Haunted Graveyard** he created on his street to raise funds for the Juvenile Diabetes Foundation (Joseph Duggan Rd., south of Queen East, west of Woodbine). Another guy in The Beach puts up an ambitious display to raise funds for the Sick Kids Hospital (on Silver Birch Ave., north of Queen East, near **Fox Theatre**).

Then, check the website **www.thornhillwoodshauntedhouse.com** to see to what extent someone deadly serious about having fun will go. This Thornhill guy has accumulated over $50,000 worth of decorations over the years (on Thornhill Woods Drive, south of Rutherford, west of Bathurst). His event fortunately runs for a week to October 31.

There's also the **Powerhouse of Terror** displays, which started in a guy's backyard and was moved into the Power House of the old Lakeshore Psychiatric Centre in **Colonel Samuel Smith Park**, in Etobicoke (www.charityhaunt.ca).

Cadbury Chocolate Factory

A popular community event which has become a tradition on October 31 (starting at around 5:30 pm) is the **Cadbury Gladstone Chocolate Factory Halloween Celebration.** I observed the people in the long line-up running along Gladstone Ave. north of Bloor Street. They waited for over an hour, then disappeared inside the decorated building amidst loud music, to exit under the carport, one minute later!

The parents I interviewed were thrilled. Their kids got a full bag of free chocolate and they had fun in the line-up. If you do that, I recommend you take the kids afterwards to pass Halloween south of Bloor on Gladstone and adjacent streets. There was a lovely intimate feeling to that part of Little Italy.

TIPS (fun for 6 years +)

• The private initiatives usually take place in residential areas and they're offered for one night only. Expect the area to be packed. The mingling is part of the fun but that's why I don't recommend going with younger kids.

Halloween in the community

 Schedule: Private initiatives of haunted houses tend to take place on October 31.

Admission: Usually FREE, donations accepted.

Directions: Check your local newspaper (or local blogs) on the weekend prior to Halloween. They're usually the ones to cover that kind of local happening.

HAUNTED ADVENTURE

Scary news!

This WAS the best attraction of its kind in and around the GTA. Located in the perfect setting of dark countryside, in woods and fields, and created by people who've shown a real passion for entertainment in the last 17 years.

I'm talking here about **Magic Hill Haunted Adventure** in Stouffville. As I was updating my page about this great attraction, I learned that it was closed for good.

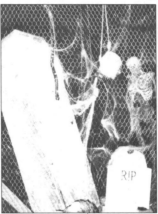

I still wanted to describe to you our experience. There are other farms offering haunted adventures. It will give you a taste of what to expect when this kind of event takes place at a farm (the best kind of set-up for it).

We visited on a Friday, arriving shortly before 7 pm. We found parking in the field right next to the entrance. Only 70 people were waiting ahead of us. When the doors opened at 7 pm, it was almost dark.

As we waited our turn to enter the **Haunted Barn**, we read one of the signs on the barn wall: "Rub the rock or you'll never see daylight again." My 9-year-old son kept bragging that he was not scared but I saw him rubbing the stone more than once! The tour of the barn lasts less

TIPS (fun for 8 years +)
• You can expect fewer people when arriving at around 7 pm to that kind of event. Shortly after that, the line-ups can be scary! It is more crowded closer to October 31 and less crowded on Sundays.

than 15 minutes. Among other things, we saw the kitchen from hell, a smoking electrical chair and sophisticated special effects. It ended with us being chased by a crazy man armed with a noisy chainsaw!

Before heading in a wagon for the **Howling Hayride** through the **Field of Screams**, we were invited to shout at the top of our lungs, to practice for what awaited us: A morbid car accident, chains raking the metal roof of our wagon, and UFOs, to name a few.

My favourite was the **Terror Trail Trek**. The trail was beautiful, on top of a hill, with red spots in the bushes and the city lights in the background. "Monsters" jumped out of the woods at every turn, quicksand effects, a hung dead man, a tricky labyrinth and more made for a stimulating walk.

The **Black Cavern** had narrower walls, scarier situations. My 9-year-old was not enjoying it anymore even though the staff toned it down when they saw his reaction. I was so busy protecting him from the "danger" that I hardly remember what I saw. We had a good scare!

Magic Hill's Haunted Adventure	C-3
• Stouffville (13953 9th Line)	N-E of Toronto 50-min.

Schedule & Admission: They closed their attraction and website in 2010 but google them again closer to October to see if they are back on track.

Other night-at-the-farm options:
• **Screamfest** at **White Rock Ostrich Farm**, Rockwood, for kids 8 years and older, see p. 74.
• **Moonlight Mazing:** Many farms with giant corn mazes offer evening maze strolls with some effort to make it scary. Bring your flashlight for good old-fashioned fun!

WIZARD WORLD

Full of tricks

Wizard World has become a tradition during the March Break. At this colourful event, you'll find a bit of everything for everyone 12 years and under (usually not a good idea, but here it works!).

Photo: Courtesy of Wizard World

With the admission cost, you have access to all their shows, the petting zoo (an addition in 2010) and the **Wizard's Fun in 3D** (a fun maze you walk through wearing special glasses to see a few things pop up at you).

The good magic show we saw when we attended years ago was still going on in 2010. It is performed by the **Magic Family** (a mom and a dad with their two daughters). It was obvious that the kids in the audience could really relate to these two kids, which added to the fun.

Expect **Birds of Prey** shows and music shows as well. At the petting zoo, you can buy food to give to the animals (a big favourite, according to the producers). Mascots stroll around the site, inter-

acting with the young visitors. If you buy the all-day wrist band in addition to the admission, you get unlimited access to some twenty carnival rides. In 2010, two of them where outside (the go-kart track and the Ferris wheel).

Their rides include a laser game inside a spaceship, **Turtle Racers** (fun ride-on toys). Check their website for photos of all the rides.

There are vendors selling gadgets (potato shooters, anyone?) and carnival games you can play for a fee to win little prizes.

There's also a **Little Tykes Play Area** where smaller kids can have their share of the fun. Since kids two years and under get free admission, you can take your little one with you and let the older siblings enjoy the rest of the attractions, knowing where to find you when they're ready to cool down with some refreshments.

TIPS (fun for 3 to 12 years)
• They sell food on the premises.
• In 2010, they organized the exact same event (same concept, same time) in the **Careport Centre** in Hamilton. Check their website for details.
• Their Wizard World is not to be confused with the Wizard World pop culture company catering to an older crowd and behind the Toronto Comic Con event (in 2010, their event also took place during the March Break in the Exhibition Place).

NEARBY ATTRACTIONS
Cinesphere (5-min.) ...... p. 16

Wizard World
(416) 585-9263
www.wizardworld.ca

D-3
Downtown
Toronto
5-min.

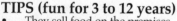 **Schedule:** Daily during the March Break. Usually starts on the Sunday before the March Break and on the weekend after, 10 am to 5 pm.

 Admission: Ground admission: around $9/person, FREE for 2 years and under. **Rides:** around $15/All-Day wrist band; individual tickets also available. Parking is around $10.

 Directions: In the **Better Living Centre** by Ontario Drive (in the western part of **Exhibition Place**), Toronto.

ABOUT NEW YEAR'S EVE

Ontario, it is midnight in Dakar (Senegal) and London (England). When it is 8 pm here, it is midnight in the Azores (Portugal) in the Atlantic Sea; 9 pm here, midnight in Rio de Janeiro (Brazil); 10 pm here, midnight in Santiago (Chile); 11 pm here, midnight in Halifax (Nova Scotia) and Saint John (New Brunswick) in Canada. Perfect time for a geography lesson!

Celebrations

Of course, there's the **Nathan Phillips Square** party with music on the outdoor stage, culminating with an exciting countdown. It is not really suited for children (too loud, too long, too late) but it is broadcast live on City TV and CP 24. In the past, we've watched the last minute of it to do our own countdown.

Toronto Zoo has been offering for a few years now, its own version of a New Year's Eve party for families, with countdown at around 9 pm (see p. 63.)

Bronte Creek Provincial Park offers an early countdown by the skating rink, which stays open past midnight for the occasion (read tips on p. 288). **Mountsberg Wildlife Centre** also does activities with an early countdown (see p. 245).

At **Niagara Falls**, Canadian music superstars start warming up the crowd in **Queen Victoria Park** at 6:30 pm, with fireworks displays at 9 pm and midnight (see p. 179).

In the (time) zone

New Year's Eve is all about the build-up to the countdown. It's so much fun, why stick to celebrating only once when there's a countdown going on at every hour somewhere around the world.

If you don't think the kids will be able to stay up late (or for the mere fun of doing more countdowns), you can always celebrate the New Year's countdown happening earlier in other time zones.

For your information, on New Year's Eve, when it is 7 pm sharp in

TIPS (fun for 4 years +)

• A fun website to find out about how New Year's is celebrated throughout the world is: www.newyearfestival.com. That's where we learned that Julius Caesar officially declared January 1 to be the beginning of a new year in 46 B.C., but we had to wait until the Gregorian calendar in 1582 for it to become a sure thing.
• If you want to know the current local time in cities and countries in all the time zones around the world, go to the **World Clock** on www.timeanddate.com. (Note that the time on the screen will be frozen to the time at which you logged in.)
• We really love the rolls filled with metallic confetti that pop out when you twist the base. They're user-friendly. **Party Packagers** always carries different sizes (p. 14).

Family fun

If you want to make it memorable, here's an idea we tried a few years ago, which was a true success! In a room, we individually filmed ten family members, each shouting a number in the countdown. We plugged the result into the television (in front of an eager audience) and played it for the real countdown. It was hilarious!

In order to make noise to welcome the New Year, we bought bubble wrap from an office supplier (the kind with one-inch bubbles is the best) and lined it on the floor for everyone to step on. It was a blast.

Whichever kind of confetti you use, don't clean it up right away! The kids will love playing with it in the morning (this could buy you an extra 30 minutes of sleep... Think about it).

General tips about
Machines:

- In this chapter, you'll find attractions, events or places to observe things that roll, float, fly or work.
- I've enjoyed exposing my son to the vehicles that were fascinating him at the moment. After singing *The Wheels on the Bus Go Round and Round* for the 100th time, I realized it would be fun to take him on his first bus ride.
- When we read Robert Munch's *Jonathan Cleaned Up and Then He Heard a Sound*, about a boy whose house turns into a subway station, the momentum was perfect for a first subway ride.
- Want to turn your subway ride into an adventure? Check my chapter **AROUND THE SUBWAY** (pages 449 to 477) on all things to do or see around each subway station in Toronto. Tell the kids you're all going on a subway ride, just for the fun of it, and surprise them with one of the fun destinations within a 10-min. walk described in the chapter.

MACHINES

See **Fall Colours at Kelso** on p. 193.

PEARSON INTERNATIONAL AIRPORT

took me a little while to even find the viewing spots outside of the airport. And these have kept changing due to construction. So here's what I found.

Two east-west runways share the bulk of flights. A good way to view the planes flying over Hwy 427 is from Carlingview Street, a parallel street east of Hwy 427. You can see the planes at closer range from outside the **Coffee Time** at 215 Carlingview Street. (Between two planes, you can treat the kids to a snack.)

The planes that circulate on the north-south runway fly just above Airport Road. There used to be serious observers with cameras standing there by their cars along the side road. That viewing spot is gone. But all is not lost. I recommend parking at the **Wendy's** (6585 Airport Rd.) almost across the street from the runway. There's still enough space by the fence for passersby to stand and you can cross at the lights at Orlando Drive.

You can watch them land on the ground from Airport Road, a bit east of the **International Centre** located at 6900 Airport Road.

There!

"You're serious? You mean there is not one single viewing window in the entire airport?" I asked baffled. I squeezed my little guy's hand, glancing at him sideways checking for his reaction. Since morning I had been promising him beautiful planes.

The sad truth is that when you're accompanying travellers, you don't get to see the planes. It

TIPS (fun for 5 years +)

• Have you ever noticed the monorail running over the highway near the airport? It is the **LINK Train** taking travelers between Terminals 1 and 3. A mom reader told me her young kids love it! The cheapest way to enjoy this free shuttle is to park (for a fee) at the outdoor **Value Park Lot** located on 6135 Airport Road (from Hwy 427 northbound, exit at Dixon, turn left, it becomes Airport Road). This parking lot is across from the Sheraton. The airport's parking fee of $3 per 20 minutes applies but instead of the hefty $28 maximum charge of the other parking lots, the daily maximum is $15. The ride feels like a futuristic subway tour. The view is interesting but we still don't get to see the planes from up close!

NEARBY ATTRACTIONS

Pearson International Airport	D-3 N-W of Toronto 30-min.
· Mississauga (416) 247-7678	

Schedule: Heavy air traffic peaks daily between 3 and 7 pm, with most impressive sightings on weekends.
Admission: FREE parking at the restaurants.
Directions: From Hwy 427 northbound, take Dixon Road exit. **To Coffee Time**: turn east at Dixon, then south to 215 Carlingview. **To Wendy's**: turn west on Dixon Rd., it becomes Airport Road. Stop at 6585 Airport Rd., on your right.

CANADIAN AIR & SPACE MUSEUM

This one takes off!

The museum is located in the original factory of the manufacturer De Havilland Aircraft of Canada Ltd (currently Bombardier). Bombardier continues to use the adjacent runway for testing and delivery of aircraft, and planes continue to be restored on the premises.

Some of the things displayed among the eclectic collection of this jam-packed museum: the **Ornithopter** (an experimental craft designed by researchers from U of T to fly by flapping its wings), one of the aircrafts used by the Canadian **Snowbirds** Aerobatic Team and a simulator from the 40's. In the mezzanine, you can see a model of **Alouette**, Canada's first satellite (assembled in the museum in the 60's!) and a half-size model of the **Canadarm**.

Volunteer staff involved with the museum are obviously passionate about restoration of artifacts from the aviation heritage of the GTA.

If a staff member proudly shows you the full-scale replica of the Avro Arrow, learn why he's so enthusiastic about it. It turns out the Arrow has quite an intriguing story. Built around 1958, it was capable of going at twice the speed of sound, still accelerating at over 1,000mph while climbing 50,000 feet. Experts agreed that it was 20 years ahead of its time. Yet, the government of the day ordered the production stopped and destroyed all aircrafts and plans! (An order that wasn't followed through apparently!)

You can also watch work-in-progress restoration projects, see the cockpit simulator from up close, sit in a jet cockpit and watch a clip inside the belly of a plane.

TIPS (fun for 6 years +)
• Their shop offers a wide selection of original trinkets (lovely plane pins for $4 and mini dye cast planes for $2.50), videos, books, posters and models related to airplanes.
• Check their **Wings & Wheels Heritage Festival** on the last weekend of May (www.wingsandwheelsfestival.com). It features the flying of dozens of aircraft, various displays, a vintage automobile parade, kids activities and the possibility to fly in a light aircraft, a helicopter or a war trainer for an extra fee. Order online to save a lot on their admission price (which includes access to the museum). The online fees: $12/adults, $8/seniors and kids, $25/family of 4 (it will be $3 to $5 more per person at the door).
• They offer special Halloween activities on October 31 (with aviation ghost story, design of paper airplane and more).

NEARBY ATTRACTIONS
Downsview Park (2-min.) .... p. 272

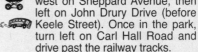

FOUR WINDS KITE FESTIVAL

The few times we attended the festival held at the **Kortright Centre** (but organized by the **Toronto Kite Flyers**), the wind was rather timid! As a result, only the skilled participants managed to raise their flying apparatus into the air. The smaller amateurs' kites only went up slightly, thanks to air drafts generated by laughing children pulling on their toys' tight cords. We had a lot of fun, regardless.

Most young children remain within the small valleys surrounding the **Visitor Centre**. Farther, past a vast field, is the site where real pros compete for two days.

These artists, solo or as part of a team, create impressive ballets with their splendid kites, to the sound of music. The public can get a close look at their kites before they fly. There are individual precision and ballet disciplines, as well as "quad-line" kites (pulled by four strings), and team competitions.

Flying high

Need to get out for some air (with the kids in tow)? During this spring weekend, if Mother Nature bestows good winds upon us, you'll want to take advantage of the Four Winds Kite Festival. When decent wind is part of the picture, loads of large, graceful kites colour the sky.

TIPS (fun for 4 years +)

• If it has rained for a few days prior to the festival, rubber boots are a must.

• During the festival, don't miss the **Teddy Bear Drop** during which a couple of furry creatures, equipped with parachutes, are dropped from flying kites and gently fall before young spectators' eyes. You can see them being launched in the competition field on Saturday and Sunday. Check the exact time of launching at the entrance.

• Around Kortright Centre's main building, kids pull small kites that they build themselves. The centre supplies little builders with the instructions, paper, balsam sticks, glue and string. This craft is suitable for children aged 4 years and up and usually costs about $5.

• The gift shop also sells kites for the occasion.

• More about **Kortright Centre** on pages 160 and 241.

NEARBY ATTRACTIONS
Putting Edge (15-min.) .... p. 36
McMichael Collection (10-min.) .... p. 91

Kortright Centre
• Woodridge
(905) 832-2289
www.kortright.org

C-2
N-W
of Toronto
40-min.

Schedule: On a weekend, usually late April or early May (2011: May 7-8) from 10 am to 4 pm. **Admission:** $8/adults, $6/children, FREE for children 4 years and under. Parking $4.

Directions: 9550 Pine Valley Drive, Woodridge. From Hwy 400 North, take exit #35/Major Mackenzie Drive westbound. Turn south on Pine Valley Drive, follow signs.

FALL COLOURS CHAIRLIFT RIDE

This outing passes with flying colours

It is so much fun to catch a chairlift ride when it's not freezing. (No need to stress when it is time to get off: we are free of gear.) And what about the view!

This activity had been offered on and off at **Kelso C.A.** around **Thanksgiving**. It's been going strong for the last few years so I'm including it in this edition. (Let's hope they maintain it. Make sure you check their website to see if it is currently offered.)

The chairlift ticket resembles a regular ski ticket printed on a large sticker. None of us has zippers to attach it to. The weather is superb and no one is wearing a coat.

I see guys riding the chair-

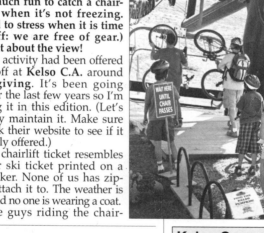

lift with their bikes! Kelso is famous for its mountain bike trails for all levels but not having to ride up the mountain is a real bonus (otherwise, they either ride up the hill or drive up Steeles Ave. off Regional Rd. 25 to the **Summit Gatehouse**'s parking lot at Old Bell School Line).

Some families are slowly walking up the grassy hill. They will truly deserve their ride back. Others choose to take the ride up but to walk down the winding path to the right of the chairlift, along the escarpment.

We opt to explore the trails into the trees at the top. They were ok but next time, I'd rather try the **Escarpment Trail** which takes advantage of the view.

TIPS (fun for 5 years +)

• There might be a bit of a wait going down. I recommend you bring bottles of water and snacks and take them out while you wait.
• Our son was two years old when he first rode a chairlift. My husband and I held him firmly between the two of us (there are no safety belts on these things). I found that he was too young to be impressed by the height.
• Go to their website to download a map of the trails. (Select *Parks & Recreation*, then *Conservation Halton Parks*, click on *Kelso*, then on *Hiking* or *Biking* icons.)

NEARBY ATTRACTIONS
Springridge Farm (10-min.) .... p. 144

Kelso Conservation Area
• Milton
(905) 878-5011
www.conservationhalton.on.ca

D-2
West
of Toronto
50-min.

Schedule: On two consecutive weekends (including Thanksgiving long weekend).
Admission: Park admission: around $6.25/adults, $4.50/5-14, FREE under 5 years. Chairlift: $3/adults, $2/kids.
Directions: 5234 Kelso Road, Milton. From Hwy 401, take exit #320/Hwy 25 northbound. Turn west on Campbellville Road, then south on Tremaine. Turn right on Kelso Road.

CANADIAN WARPLANE MUSEUM

Down-to-Earth airplanes

When we arrive, children's imaginations are fired up by a real Starfighter jet, its nose pointing towards the sky like a church steeple in front of the building. More than forty, genuine, functioning specimens now await in the museum's immense hangar. Add cabins, cockpits, switches and buttons to explore and you get a great family outing!

Before entering the hangar, we saw a display on the use of planes in Canadian military history. Budding pilots enjoyed operating the model airplanes. (Note that the displays change regularly.) Then, we circulated amongst the impressive hangar's fleet bathed in natural light.

The wheels of certain planes were as tall as my future pilot. Part of the site is dedicated to the restoration of a few vintage models. It's an excellent opportunity to appreciate aeronautical engineering while examining airplanes from every angle.

We were not allowed to touch most of the gleaming aircraft, but don't worry,

we could still access two specimens and their engaging cockpits and they've added two more since my last visit: **WWII trainer**, **CF-100** jet aircraft, **Vampire** and **Sabre** jet fighters.

Our kids loved the two-seat **Flying Boxcar** simulator, with its wall-to-wall switches and dials. They've now traded this for four modern flight simulators which you can try for around $5 (a big success with video gamers).

Stairs at the back of the hangar lead to an observation deck, from which we have an overview of the museum's squadron.

Higher up the stairs, we can access the exterior terrace, from which other planes can be seen. Most aircraft are maintained in flying condition. Between May and November (weather permitting), you might have the chance to observe a vintage aircraft in flight on the weekends. (Paved roads connect with the **Hamilton International Airport**'s runways, located 1 km away.)

TIPS (fun for 4 years +)

• They're re-establishing the **Hamilton Airshow** in 2011 (June 18-19, opens at 9 am, flights start at 2 pm). The entire show will feature over 40 vintage aircraft. Expect an even bigger one in 2012 to celebrate the museum's 40th Anniversary ($25/adults, $20/seniors & students, $15/6-12 years, FREE under 6, free shuttle service from the parking lot).

• The museum includes a big gift shop and a cafeteria-style restaurant in a vast room and, best of all, a panoramic view of the outside.

NEARBY ATTRACTIONS

Canadian Warplane Heritage Museum
• Mount Hope
1-877-347-3359
www.warplane.com

E-2
S-W
of Toronto
70-min.

Schedule: Open year-round, 9 am to 5 pm.

Admission: $11/adults, $10/seniors and students, $7/6-12 years, FREE for children 5 years and under.

Directions: Hamilton International Airport, 9280 Airport Road, Mount Hope. Take QEW West, follow Hwy 403 towards Hamilton, exit at Hwy 6 South and follow the museum's signs.

DOUBLE-DECKER RIDES

On top of things

"I have not had a good hair day since I started this job" claims the tour operator. I believe her. As we drive under the Gardiner, we feel quite a draft!

There are a few things you can experience only if you've taken a ride on the open top of a double-decker. You get to see the top of the TTC buses, your head is at times only a metre away from the traffic lights, and branches get close enough to brush your hair.

My daughter also enjoyed having a closer look at the CN Tower. For the first time, she saw the huge fans fooling around on Rogers Centre's balcony and the Flatiron's mural looking like a painting peeling off its facade.

Your ticket gives you the right to step on and off as you wish, throughout the day, at any of the stops during seven consecutive days.

Most importantly, when touring with **City Sightseeing Toronto**, you get one free 45-minute boat cruise around **Toronto Islands**! (Note that you can use your boat voucher any other time during the year of purchase, weather permitting.)

You could do the 2-hour loop double-decker tour from **Harbourfront Centre**, catch a boat ride, and hop on again on their bus to visit one of the attractions along their route. (Make sure you know the time of their last departure from that attraction!)

TIPS (fun for 4 years +)

• As a local, I think too many stops take place in front of hotels in uninteresting areas. But it is worth it if your child has shown a fascination for double-deckers, and a trip to London, England is not in the plans... The free boat cruise of **City Sightseeing Toronto** greatly adds to the fun.
• You can bring a stroller on the bus and the boat rides. They'll store it for you.
• The operator told me that their 9 am bus departure always leave fairly empty. (Good to know if you want to make sure to sit on the top of the double-decker.)
• The competitors offer very similar tours, but no free boat ride. If you don't mind about that, see www.sightseeing-toronto.com about the **ShopDine Tour Toronto** tours in yellow double-deckers (hop on in front of Hard Rock Café on Yonge for maximum fun) or **Gray Line**'s slightly cheaper tour at www.grayline.ca.

NEARBY ATTRACTIONS
Harbourfront Centre (2-min. walk)   p. 24

City Sightseeing Toronto (416) 410-0536 www. citysightseeingtoronto.com	D-3 **Downtown** **Toronto**

 Schedule: From May through October, runs every hour from 9 am to 5 pm (from 9 am to around 3 pm the rest of the year).
Admission: Around $35/adults, $31/seniors and students, $18/4-12 years old, FREE for 3 years and under on lap, $102/family of 4 (around $3 cheaper per person when ordering online).
Directions: You can hop on at any of their stops (see the exhaustive list on their website). Their Stop #1 is at 249 Queens Quay West, on the east side of **Radisson Hotel**. It is a 2-min. walk from their boat **Harbour Star**, at **Harbourfront Centre's West Pier**.

CENTENNIAL PARK MINI-INDY

Step on it!

According to my young co-pilot, I drive my go-kart like a grandma on a Sunday outing. Since everybody is passing us, I must admit he has a point, so I step on it!

To drive on the .75 km recreational track, one has to be at least 54 inches tall or 10 years of age and older. However, they have double-riders where kids 4-9 can ride for free as a passenger.

The place used to have a kiddie track but they've closed it. Instead, they've opened a track especially for the members of the Canadian Karting League (CKL), who use more powerful karts.

After a couple of rides, we bought tokens to play with some 30 machines in the 3,000-sq.-ft. arcade (where they sell snacks).

TIPS (fun for 5 years +)

•   It is advisable to call or check the *Event Calendar* on their website ahead as the attractions are sometimes closed for private or corporate functions.

•   At the south end of the park, you will find a big wading pool with spray pads, and a greenhouse you can visit for free (fun alternatives for little ones who can't accompany their older siblings on the go-kart rides).

•   **Centennial Park Golf Centre** (a 10-min. walk south of the Mini-Indy) includes a large mini golf (www.centennialparkgolfcentre.com, around $9/adults, $6/6-15 years, $3/under 6).

•   More on **Centennial Park** during the winter on p. 363.

NEARBY ATTRACTIONS
Playdium Mississauga (20-min.) ... p. 20
Pearson Int'l Airport (5-min.) .... p. 190

Centennial Park Mini-Indy

**D-3
N-W
of downtown
30-min.**

• Etobicoke
(647) 724-7357 (go-kart)
(416) 394-8750 (park)
www.centennialmini-indy.com

Schedule: Open daily at least mid-June to mid-September, 11 am to 10 pm. Check their website for hours in May, September and October.

Admission: $15/10 minutes. They don't sell by the lap but say you can do 12 laps in 10 minutes (young passengers don't pay in the double-riders).

Directions: 575 Centennial Park Blvd, Toronto. From Hwy 427 North, take exit Rathburn Road westbound, turn north on Centennial Park. FREE on-site parking.

GRANDPRIX SLOT CAR RACEWAY

Eat my dust!

There's something mesmerizing about watching cars (big or small) on a racetrack.

This is the only place I know where you can race slot cars. Their long 6-lane road course is colour coded. You can rent colour matching slot

cars or bring your own to compete against fellow racers... or within your own family.

TIPS (fun for 5 years +)

• Their **Slot Car Birthday Party** package seems quite fun and affordable. For $60, you get exclusive access to the six slot car racing tracks for 30 minutes (cars are supplied), plus a private party room for 45 minutes. You can bring your own cake.

• BEWARE! The minimum height to drive a go-kart at **GrandPrix Kartways** is 52 inches (despite what they say on their website www.gpkartways.com). They don't have double karts. The young (min. 52-inch tall) drivers will be given a junior go-kart. They offer **Junior** race sessions, when no more than 4 junior go-karts will compete. Up to 8 cars can compete during the **Senior** races with the bigger karts. Arrive early if there are more than 2 drivers in your group! They don't take individual reservations. Count around $22/race.

• They sell slot cars and tracks, and also do repairs. There's a snack bar open during go-kart times and an arcade with some 20 games on site.

• More about **Downsview Park** on p. 272.

Most cars fit the tracks, except for the Hot Wheels type of small cars. I saw a savvy young racer buy tiny magnets to install underneath his car. (I learned it helps to prevent it from flying off the track).

The manager told me that 5-6 year-old kids enjoy playing with the hand controller to race the cars around the 75 foot circuit. But it's usually by age 8 that they have enough patience to learn how to speed on the straight sections and slow down in the sharp curves. He's always there to help the racers with technical problems. Racers' scores appear on a screen.

The attraction is located within the **GrandPrix Kartways**, which adds to the fun. You can watch the big go-karts race before or after your time with the slot cars.

GrandPrix Slot Car Raceway	D-3 North of downtown 35-min.
• Etobicoke (416) 638-5277	
www.raceworldcanada.com	

Schedule: Tuesday to Friday, 2 pm to 9 pm; Saturday and Sunday, 12 noon to 6 pm. Call for hours during Holidays. (Note that the go-karts section opens at 6 pm, Tuesday-Thursday, and at 5 pm on Fridays.)

Admission: $5.50/15 minutes using their slot cars ($4.50 if you bring your own), $22.50/full day.

Directions: Downsview Park, 75 Carl Hall Road, Bay 3, Unit #9, North York. From Hwy 401, take Allen Road North and turn west on Sheppard Avenue. Turn left on John Drury Drive to enter the park. Turn left on Carl Hall Road and drive past the railway tracks.

NEARBY ATTRACTIONS

Air & Space Museum (1-min.) ..... p. 191
Around Wilson Station .... p. 477

CANADIAN AUTOMOTIVE MUSEUM

Hot wheels

It is probably the least interactive museum I've visited with children. But I couldn't resist including it in this guide. It is filled with over 60 vehicles from 1898 to 1980 displayed in an authentic car dealership.

Don't forget to raise your head at the entrance. You wouldn't want to miss the vintage red racing car pinned to the ceiling!

The first floor of the **Canadian Automotive Museum** is made of cement, pipes run on the low ceilings and there's not much room for all the beautiful cars. However, memorabilia related to the different periods of vehicles make it fun to explore.

The children who know the movie *Chitty Chitty Bang Bang* will think they recognize it in many of the cars displayed. But the classy 1926 **Bentley**, sassy 1931 **Alfa Romeo**, gorgeous 1939 **Rolls Royce**, and all the other shiny cars are not to be touched, a rule which can be extremely frustrating for a young child.

On the second floor it's easy to observe the progression from horse carriages to cars. We can see wooden vehicles that were made by a carriage builder from Oshawa named McLaughlin. When increasing speed made the windshield a necessity, roofs were added and the look of cars changed dramatically from carriages (although it's funny we're still talking about horse power!).

TIPS (fun for 5 years +)

• If you've come this far, pay a visit to the **Oshawa Aeronautical, Military and Industrial Museum**. This museum involves passionate volunteers. They have organized the space around the time line of the origin and evolution of the militia (King Louis X1V ordered Frontenac to create the first "milice" in Canada in 1669), with a focus on all the generals up to today, and displays of uniforms and weapons. The museum owns dozens of restored and working war vehicles (including a missile launcher), of which we can see some 15 inside the building and more around the site.

NEARBY ATTRACTIONS

Kids Zone (15-min.) .... p. 317

Canadian Automotive Museum
· Oshawa
(905) 576-1222

C-4
East of Toronto
40-min.

Schedule: Open year-round Monday to Friday, 9 am to 5 pm; Saturday and Sunday, 10 am to 6 pm.
Admission: $5/adults, $4.50/seniors and students, $3.50/6-11 years, $13.50/family of 4, FREE for 5 years and under.
Directions: 99 Simcoe Street South, Oshawa. From Hwy 401 East, take exit #417/Simcoe Street northbound; the museum is on the east side.

Oshawa Military & Industrial Museum
(905) 728-6199
Schedule: Friday, Saturday and Sunday, 1 pm to 5 pm, Easter to November 1 (call for tours rest of year).
Admission: Around $4/adults, $3/seniors, FREE 12 years and under.
Directions: 1000 Stevenson Road North, Oshawa. From the **Automotive Museum**, take Simcoe Street northbound, turn west on Rossland Road, then turn north on Stevenson Road.

For both museums:
www.oshawa.ca
(click *Things to do*, then *Attractions and Events*)

ROUNDHOUSE PARK

A round of applause!

I had checked once, years ago, to see if there was anything of interest to kids about the roundhouse housing the Steam Whistle Brewing Company at the foot of the CN Tower. Nope, it smelled of beer and that was it. That was then. Now, the whole area has been landscaped following an obvious railway theme, with the formidable 120-foot turntable able to face each of the 32 bay doors making up the inner rounded facade of the locomotive roundhouse.

The first phase of the fully restored railway village opened in May 2010, closed for the winter and opened again in Spring 2011. When I came across the place by chance in late fall of 2010, the installations were closed but we could stroll around the park located just across from the **CN Tower** and admire full-sized locomotives, the turntable, a lovely train mural, nicely restored **Cabin D** interlocking tower and the **Don Station**, both from 1896 and a 1914 gatehouse.

TIPS (fun for 3 years +)

• In the southwest side of **Roundhouse Park**, you'll find a train-shaped structure in the little playground overlooking the highway. If you walk down the path adjacent to the playground, you'll reach Lower Simcoe St. leading directly to **Harbourfront Centre** in five minutes.

• In spring 2011, the 1,000-seat **Roundhouse Theatre** was being built to present the perfect production for such a place: *The Railway Children* from England (involving a real steam train!), during summer 2011. Consult www.railwaychildren.ca for more information.

I saw that the large building housing the brewery is now also home to a **Leon's Furniture** store! It seems an awkward choice for the site but I must say they did a very good job with the building's architecture.

The **Toronto Railway Heritage Centre (TRHA)** is a new kid on the block as well. It is responsible for the outdoor exhibitions and manages a railway museum on the premises with interpretive exhibitions, including the original switching system of Cabin D.

The TRHA is entirely volunteer driven, so the additional activities offered on any given day will depend on how many of them show up to operate the attractions.

When possible, they will offer historical tours. They'll run a miniature train holding 24 people for a half-kilometre ride (hence the small tracks throughout the park). We will be able to hop on board one engineer's cab and watch a computer simulated ride set in the 50's in an actual diesel locomotive by **John Street Roundhouse**.

Roundhouse Park www.trha.ca	D-3 **Downtwon** Toronto **2-min. walk**

Schedule: Park open year-round. **TRHA** activities from May to October, at least on weekends from 12 noon to 5 pm.
Admission: Donations accepted. Train rides: $3/adults, $2/kids.
Directions: 255 Bremner Boulevard, Toronto (just south of the **CN Tower**).

NEARBY ATTRACTIONS
Harbourfront (5-min. walk) .... p. 24

GO TRANSIT TRAIN RIDE

One, two, three... GO!

For children fascinated by anything on wheels, the GO Train offers the ultimate experience of real train travel. Most importantly, it costs a fraction of the price of a regular train ride and you don't end up far from home. Let's not forget the journey is as important as the destination!

Union Station, on Front Street, is a great starting point for a child's first ride on the GO Train. Suburban and intercity trains are next to one another and children get the chance to see imposing locomotives from up close.

Green and white signs lead us to the GO Train's ticket office and customer service department. When we stopped there to ask for information, we got lucky, they gave my son a few gadgets to celebrate his initiation. (Ask if they have some handy!)

After admiring a large mural decorating the outside of a railcar, we sat on the train's second level in order to see further. We were facing south to take in the view of Lake Ontario. Seats are very com-

fortable and each car is equipped with restrooms... Like in a real train.

After analyzing GO destinations, I decided the most interesting was Pickering with the varied panorama of its itinerary: downtown skyscrapers, residential neighbourhoods, countryside and most of all, long stretches alongside Lake Ontario (and in our case, this line passes right in front of our house!). The ride to Pickering lasts 40 minutes and doesn't require a transfer (easier with younger kids).

There's another reason to choose this destination. By the end of summer 2011, Go Transit should have completed the construction of a very modern looking pedestrian bridge over Hwy 401 to link Pickering Go Station to Pickering Town Centre (which includes a Mastermind Toys store, www.pickeringtowncentre).

TIPS (fun for 4 years +)

• I recommend that you avoid the stress of rush hour, favouring departures between 9:30 am and 2:30 pm. You'll be sure to get a window seat, as there are fewer passengers on board outside peak times. Little ones can be rambunctious without disturbing too much.

• A day pass is sold at the cost of two single fares and allows one person unlimited rides between two specified zones throughout the day of the purchase. This is perfect if you want to get off at different stations and catch the following train.

NEARBY ATTRACTIONS
Hockey Hall (5-min. walk) .... p. 340
Union Station (same place) .... p. 474

GO Transit
(416) 869-3200
www.gotransit.com

D-3
Downtown
Toronto
5-min.

Schedule: Daily, from early in the morning to late at night.
Admission: An adult day pass for Union-Pickering-Union costs $12.40. (There's a fare calculator on their website.) It is half price for children 6-12 years old, FREE for one child 5 years and under for each paying adult.
Directions to Union Station: On Front Street, Toronto (between Bay and York Streets).

MODEL RAILROAD CLUB

Give then an inch...

Fascinated children of all ages are perched on steps running alongside the huge raised table. They watch small locomotives pulling long strings of railcars through villages, mountains and a harbour. Behind them, impressed adults admire the genius of miniaturization. This is the result of 180,000 hours of work by passionate people!

You can forget the metric system as everything displayed here is built to a 1:48 scale (or Õ scale)! Railcars that measure 40 feet in reality barely make 10 inches. The entire set, inspired by the styles of the 1955-62 period, comprises the equivalent of 10 miles of track.

The installation sits approximately a metre and a half off the floor. One has to actually walk around it to truly measure the magnitude of this ambitious set.

All the children in our small group easily found an observation point, changing places frequently so as to capture every angle of the fourteen moving trains. It took them more than an hour to get their visual fill!

Cargo and passenger trains, even circus trains, move along cliffs taken on by mountain climbers. They border a little harbour with its busy docks, construction sites, villages, factories and warehouses. Here, a fisherman indulges in his sport. There, a tow truck is pulling a car out of the ditch. Together, these contribute to making the installation incredibly realistic along with tunnels, huge bridge, aqueducts, turntable, overpasses with real light signals and even a soundtrack of moving trains!

Installed at the centre of the set with remote controls in hand, switchmen are directing railway traffic. They are members of the **Model Railroad Club of Toronto**, the over 70-year-old association responsible for this wondrous display.

TIPS (fun for 3 years +)

• As visitors circulate within a two-metre-wide corridor around the set, manoeuvering strollers is impossible. Comfortably nestled in my arms, my little one did not mind and was perfectly positioned to view the railway activity.
• If your kids are truly hooked and ask for more, make sure to read the association's posted notices advertising other similar events and activities held regularly by other regional associations.
• The club is now surrounded by trendy **Liberty Village**. There's a **Balzac's Coffee** shop at the corner of East Liberty and Hanna. The **Liberty Village Market & Café** is a cafeteria-like restaurant with a nice vintage feel in the back (further west, at Jefferson). I recommend you stop at the truly funky **School Bakery & Café** for some scrumptious scones, cookies or cupcakes (at Fraser, west of the **Stadium Park**, www.sbcto.com). Check the mural on the building north of the restaurant!

Model Railroad Club of Toronto (416) 536-8927 www. modelrailroadclub.com	D-3 Downtown Toronto 15-min.

Schedule: Usually on the last three Sundays (and Family Day) in February, 12 noon to 4:30 pm, call for exact dates.
Admission: $8/adults, $5/seniors, $4/children (cash only)
Directions: 171 East Liberty St., Suite B1, Toronto. (Note that the building has a different civic address, it was formerly 37 Hanna Ave.). From King St. West, take Atlantic Ave. southbound, then Liberty St. eastbound. The club is in the basement below the **Casalife** store.

CHRISTMAS TRAIN SHOW

Adults play too!

My action-driven son is fascinated by the small trains riding full speed on parallel tracks. His friend, the observant type, is absorbed in the examination of detailed small-scale landscapes. My young daughter is delighted by every display featuring a cow in a field. Whatever their personality, a child's attention is sure to be caught at a train show.

The model train shows I have visited never had a unified look to them. But each model railway association represented there was a small world in itself.

One association tested children's observation skills by providing a list of funny details to spot on the landscape and allowed them to pick chocolate balls

from the display. Another was quite interactive, allowing visitors to play with remote controls moving lifts up and down, handle baggage, control the saw mills and more.

One long train track was set on the floor. We saw a couple of miniature circuses by the railway in small towns.

Some buildings along the track in some exhibits were real pieces of art. We could even observe some exhibitors in the process of building copper trains from scratch.

Such shows could easily become more interactive but let's not forget that their main purpose is not to amuse small kids. It is to delight the child within big people…

TIPS (fun for 4 years +)

• There was nothing really "festive" about the Toronto Christmas Train Show (except for a few small Santas here and there) but it offered enough train displays to make it worth the visit.
• I saw a dad carrying a little stool for his 4-year-old. It is a great idea since many displays are 48" high, preventing the younger ones from seeing without help.
• Not all exhibitors have the same attitude towards children. Some get really nervous with them. Make sure you are in control of your little ones' hands unless you want to see a grown man cry!
• There are tables and a snack bar on the premises.

NEARBY ATTRACTIONS

Toronto Christmas Train Show
• Mississauga
(905) 945-2775
www.antiquetoys.ca

D-3
N-W
of Toronto
30-min.

Schedule: Usually on a weekend around the end of November, at least from 11 am to 4 pm. Call for exact schedule.
Admission: Around $12/adults, $10/seniors, $4/6-12 years, FREE for 5 years and under.
Directions: International Centre, 6900 Airport Rd., Mississauga. Take Hwy 427 North. Exit Dixon Rd., turn west on Dixon, it becomes Airport Road.

RICHMOND HILL LIVE STEAMERS

I found the (rail) way!

The track site lies in a beautiful woodland setting, in harmony with the trees. From the road, we can barely see it, but can hear the whistles' wet hissing, as the small steam engines rustle along the 7 1/4-inch wide tracks.

On location, you see marvels of miniature trains, their steam puffing high; those little guys use real coal to produce their steam! At close range, you can even feel droplets coming down on your shoulders as they quickly condense (a refreshing mist on a hot summer day).

In addition to the miniature track, there are two larger tracks that cover the entire site. Many trains circulate on them, and they are conducted for the most part by enthusiasts, outfitted with overalls and caps. Some of these hand-built steam engines range in cost up to $40,000. This is the achievement of passionate members of the **Richmond Hill Live Steamers**, dedicated to the craft for more than twenty years.

TIPS (fun for 3 years +)
•   I recommend you arrive before noon to avoid long line-ups leading to the individual rides. Otherwise, we waited no more than 10 minutes for a ride on the larger train with wagons.
•   You can buy snacks, burgers and hot dogs on site during the Open House events. Washrooms are also available.

NEARBY ATTRACTIONS
Whitchurch C.A. (5-min.) .... p. 242
Burd's Family Fishing (15-min.) .... p. 336

On the central track, the shortest, the steam engines carry one passenger at a time. Conductor and passenger are literally straddling the small but solid locomotives. They go past a water tower and over a bridge. As for the track that surrounds the site, it boasts larger and stronger trains that can carry up to 16 passengers on their small cars, and travel through the forest site.

Richmond Hill Live Steamers
· Stouffville
(416) 261-9789
http://richmond-hill-live-steamers.tripod.com

C-3
N-E
of Toronto
40-min.

Schedule: They hold two **Open House** events, usually on the weekend after Canada Day and after Labour Day, 10:30 am to 4 pm (2011: July 9-10, September 10-11). Gates are also open to casual visitors June to September on most Sundays, 1 pm to 3 pm, weather permitting.
Admission: Donations appreciated.
Directions: 15922 McCowan Road, Stouffville. From Hwy 404 North, take exit #45/Aurora Sideroad eastbound, turn north on McCowan Rd. The site is on the southwest corner of St. John's Sideroad and McCowan.

YORK-DURHAM RAILWAY

Choo-choo!

A two-hour ride for the return trip on a 1900's diesel train. That's enough "choo-choos" to fill young railroad men's (and women's) ears for quite a while, believe me!

The railroad crosses many rural roads and the train has to blow its whistle each time. My two-month old daughter was stressed by the "CHOO... CHOO's" that delighted her brother!

If you can, visit the railcars before choosing one, as there are different types. I opted for one with wine-red upholstery. Its windows didn't open very wide, but the car was comfortable and, above all, there was a space between the seats big

enough for children to hide in.

There, my young Captain Kirk imagined a spaceship, while others saw it as a tent or a little house. At that age, it's impossible to look at the scenery for two hours!

Conductors are attentive to children and answer all their questions. I also recommend you take your children for a walk through the moving train. They'll love to watch the tracks from the last car on the northbound trip.

The railroad passes through fields and woods. We only got off to stretch our legs at the last train station, in Uxbridge, and chose to catch our train back right away.

TIPS (fun for 4 years +)

• Watch the children while they walk through the train. They could pinch their fingers in the joints between cars, as it moves with each bump.
• Check the calendar of events on their website. They offer **Teddy Bear Specials** when kids with their plush friend get in for free, Halloween rides (no need to reserve) and very popular rides with **Santa** (reserve early).
• They offer $8 rides from the **Stouffville Station** on the Saturday of Canada Day weekend during **Stouffville Strawberry Festival** (www.strawberryfestival.ca).
• See the tips on p. 170 for restaurants and café in Stouffville.
• A 2-min. walk from the **Uxbridge Station** is the really cute **Tin Cup Caffe**, great for coffee, lunch and desserts (86 Brock St., Uxbridge).
• You could finish the outing with a movie at **The Roxy** in Uxbridge (46 Brock St., www.roxietheatre.com).

York-Durham Heritage Railway • Stouffville and Uxbridge (905) 852-3696 www.ydhr.on.ca	**C-3** **N-E** **of Toronto** **40-min.**

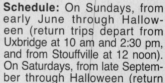 **Schedule:** On Sundays, from early June through Halloween (return trips depart from Uxbridge at 10 am and 2:30 pm, and from Stouffville at 12 noon). On Saturdays, from late September through Halloween (return trips from Uxbridge to Goodwood at 11 am and 2:30 pm).

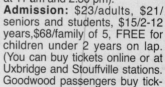 **Admission:** $23/adults, $21/seniors and students, $15/2-12 years, $68/family of 5, FREE for children under 2 years on lap. (You can buy tickets online or at Uxbridge and Stouffville stations. Goodwood passengers buy tickets on the train.)

Directions: Uxbridge: From Hwy 404 North, take exit #41/Bloomington Rd. East (it becomes County Road 47), then Toronto Street downtown Uxbridge. Turn west on King Street. **Stouffville:** From Hwy 404 North, take exit #37/Stouffville Rd.eastbound (it becomes Main Street). The Stouffville Go Station is on the north side of Main Street, east of 9th Line.

ABERFOYLE JUNCTION

A labour of love

So many details, such a beautiful layout recreating the Southern Ontario of the 50's, so many little stories going on... There's no doubt this attraction is a labour of love undertaken by very keen-eyed and patient artisans.

Most of what you see was hand built with only basic parts rearranged according to the artists imagination. Amazing!

One of the most original features of this miniature world is the night fall (a 10-minute dusk to dawn sequence every 40 minutes or so).

At one point during your visit, the light will gradually fade until all that's left to see is the little bright rectangles of the windows lit from within the small buildings and miniature trains.

Then, you start to distinguish details you hadn't noticed before: passengers in the wagons, customers inside the tiny restaurants and shops, and street lights.

If you look closely, you could see: campers on the verge of being bothered

by a bear, a mother petting a cat and waving at her kids in the water, a fisherman and his dog, a musician playing the banjo and kids selling lemonade. You'll even see someone escaping from a hotel's window with the help of good old sheets tied together, and a life model posing in the nude for a painter. High rises are being raised, houses are being built and streets are being repaired. It's a busy town.

When you notice a restaurant called **Sam & Ella's** (get it?), you realize the creators had fun with the signage too.

A few families were visiting when we went. "Duck!" shouted a mother to her husband holding their son on his shoulders. They were so taken by all the action that they had not seen the floor of the control tower running the trains, two metres above the ground.

TIPS (fun for 3 years +)
• A dad brought in a rubber stool for his son, the best thing to make sure kids can see (without touching).
• In the tiny gift shop they sell, among other things, a die-cast set of trains for $9, posters for $15 and a DVD of the attraction for $30 (which you can watch while sitting at the tables in the snack bar).
• There's a cozy little snack bar selling hot dogs and snacks.

Aberfoyle Junction
• Aberfoyle
(519) 836-2720
(905) 527-5474
www.
aberfoylejunction.com

D-2
N-W
of Toronto
50-min.

Schedule: Spring show, usually first two weekends in May (2011: April 30, May 1, 7-8 and 14-15); Fall Show, usually the three weekends following Thanksgiving (2011: October 15-16, 22-23, 29-30); from 10 am to 4:30 pm.
Admission: $8/adults, $6/seniors and students, $5/children.
Directions: From Hwy 401, take exit #299, go northbound on Brock Road for 1.5 km (it is on the east side).

SOUTH SIMCOE RAILWAY

Full steam ahead !

Here we are, my son and I, in the middle of nowhere. Fortunately, the return trip is included in the 50-minute ride. We'll come back to our starting point after our charming ride in a vintage 1920's railcar pulled by a steam engine dating back to 1883.

You have to see the children's eyes when they watch the small train in the distance get closer and finally appear as the colossus it really is, with its whistle and its plume of steam.

Because there's only one track, the locomotive has no other choice but to move forward and then to back up. Mind you, it makes no difference from a passenger's point of view. For part of the ride, we see backyards full of flowers and a few commercial plots of land.

Then comes the countryside with farms, cows, cornfields and trees. Most trees along the track are deciduous and must take on beautiful colours during the fall.

When you're riding, try to make your children listen to what the conductor says, especially if he is telling the story of the train that disappeared into the river on a foggy night, a long time ago. (To put us in the mood, the conductor stopped the train and blew the whistle three times, hoping that the ghost of the missing train will answer back…)

At the end of the line, we wait a few minutes before heading back. "We're waiting, because all the wheels must be reinstalled for us before we head in the other direction" the conductor seriously explains. It takes kids a few seconds to wrap their minds around that one!

TIPS (fun for 4 years +)
• Arrive at least 30 minutes before departure time. After you've paid for your ticket, you'll be able to wait for the train to arrive (and hear it coming).
• Inside the railcars, don't expect luxury. Giving some of the seats a good knock could release a 50-year-old cloud of dust! (Just in case, don't wear white pants.) No washroom in the cars, no food allowed.
• There's a small gift shop.
• See the calendar of events on their website for their special rides during Easter and Halloween and for their **Santa Claus Express** (must reserve in advance.)
• On hot summer days, you'll be happy to take advantage of the **Tottenham Conservation Area**'s beach and playground, located less than 5 minutes from the train station on Mill Street.

NEARBY ATTRACTIONS

South Simcoe Railway
• Tottenham
(905) 936-5815
www.southsimcoerailway.ca

C-2
N-W
of Toronto
60-min.

Schedule: Open every Sunday and Holiday Monday, from Victoria Day weekend to one week after Thanksgiving (plus Mondays and Tuesdays in July and August as well as Saturdays in October). There are usually departures at 10:30 am, 12 noon, 1:30 pm and 3 pm.
Admission: Return fare is $13/adults, $11/seniors, $8/children 3-15 years, FREE for children 2 years and under, on lap.
Directions: From Hwy 400 North, take exit #55/Hwy 9 westbound. Turn north on Simcoe Road #10/Tottenham then west on Mill Street (first set of lights in the town).

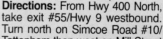

HALTON COUNTY RAILWAY

On the right track

We climb into the first vehicle ready to leave. It is a superbly renovated passenger train car from the 1915 – 1960 period. It has elegant woodwork, velvet upholstery and copper tin ceiling decorations. Before long, the car heads towards a lavish green forest.

The streetcar museum differs from other railway attractions in the region. First, because its primary activity is the collection and renovation of trains, electric tramways and buses. Second, its track system is short (2km). Instead of offering long rides, the museum offers as many short ones as you wish, on any of the different vehicles available that day.

Their collection is large and vehicles are primed for service according to drivers' availability. When we visited, we took a ride aboard the elegant "#8-Steel Car passenger", as well as an open-roof car replica of the 1890s, reminiscent of ancient carriages, in which we enjoyed a ride in nature.

Ten minutes later, our train reached the end of the line, not far from a lovely pond. The kids looked at some old abandoned railcars (most likely future renovation projects), including a run down, but amusing caboose that entertained children. Young visitors also enjoyed the opportunity to walk along the tracks.

Upon your return, you may jump into another train ready to leave, or hang around to admire those displayed in the barns or in the yards.

TIPS (fun for 4 years +)
• Make sure to pack some insect repellent; the little bugs are overtly present in the many bushes around the station.
• Check their website for details about their **Halloween Spooktackular** evenings (with haunted car barn and streetcars) and **Christmas on the Rails** (with Christmas carols).
• They have a gift shop, and an ice cream shop (the **East End Café**) in a vintage streetcar!

NEARBY ATTRACTIONS
Springridge Farm (20-min.) .... p. 144
Hilton Falls (15-min.) .... p. 250

Halton County Radial Railway
· Milton
(519) 856-9802
www.hcry.org

D-2
West
of Toronto
60-min.

Schedule: Open weekends early May to late October, 11 am to 5 pm, plus weekdays in July and August, 11 am to 4:30 pm.
Admission: Return fare is Around $11.50/adults, $10.25/seniors, $8.75/4 to 17 years, $33/family of 5, FREE for children 3 years and under.
Directions: 13629 Guelph Line, Milton. From Hwy 401 West, take exit #312/Guelph Line northbound (railway is on east side).

TORONTO HIPPO TOURS

It's a bus! It's a boat! No, it's a Hippo!

We notice something peculiar underneath the vehicle... Long wet weeds! You know, like the ones that can be observed at the bottom of Lake Ontario. The fact is, Hippo's drivers have to be licensed marine captains as well to be allowed to pilot the intriguing Canadian-made amphibious buses.

The kids are already excited by the overall look of the vehicle, adorned with colourful depictions of hippos in the water. Accessing the bus from a rear entrance just adds to the novelty. The windows are large and part of the ceiling is glass so we know we'll get a good view of Toronto's tall buildings throughout the tour. (Some of their buses have such glass ceilings, others have canvas.)

My young companions feel like royalty when they see the reactions our hippo gets from the people along the sidewalks. Kids are laughing and pointing at us. The **Hippo** rides along Beverley Street (to see a bit of Chinatown), then McCaul Street by the impressive AGO and the intriguing table-like architecture of the Ontario College of Art and Design.

TIPS (fun for 5 years +)
• You can reserve by calling or book online (no extra charge).
• They can store strollers in the Toronto Hippo Tours office.

NEARBY ATTRACTIONS
Roundhouse Park (5-min. walk) ... p. 199

Next, it's hip Queen Street to Bathurst and down to **Ontario Place**, our launching point.

It makes one feel uneasy to watch one's vehicle get nearer to the water than reason would dictate, then definitely too close... Then it's too late, we're in it with a splash, floating! We undertake our smooth ride on the lake amidst the elegant structures of Ontario Place. Our captain leads us up to the end of the channel opening into **Lake Ontario**.

Our guide, who's been commenting all along on Toronto's landmarks as we drove by, now cedes her front seat and

microphone to a few young riders who pretend for a while they've got the job.

We leave the water with regret and drive towards Harbourfront Centre, by Air Canada Centre and around the Rogers Centre before reaching the finish line on Front Street.

Toronto Hippo Tours

D-3
Downtown
Toronto
5-min. walk

(416) 703-4476
1-877-635-5510
www.torontohippotours.com

Schedule: Runs daily May 1 to October 31, from 11 am to 5 pm (also a departure at 6 pm in July and August).

Admission: Around $43/adults, $38/ seniors and students, $28/3-12 years, $125/family of 4, $5/1-3 years, FREE under 1, if sitting on lap.

Directions: Departs from 151 Front Street West (near Simcoe Street), Toronto.

Tall Ship Kajama

As they came in, guests rearranged the chairs to their liking all over the large and unobstructed deck. Half an hour later, the Kajama left its mooring spot, motors on. The wind was blowing very gently. We headed towards Ontario Place.

Everything looked different from that angle: the amusement park, Toronto Islands, the CN Tower. My daughter undertook a thorough exploration of the 165-foot deck.

After a while, I noticed people were more cheerful and relaxed. Each small group seemed involved in its own little private party. Only then, did I realize the captain had shut down the engine and we were actually sailing!

Don't expect the soothing sound of the wind against the sails and the waves brushing the hull. We are in Toronto and it's noisy with hoards of motor boats in the harbour and planes landing and taking off at the Toronto City Airport, when it is not helicopters flying over our heads.

Still, as my small crew member played hide-and-seek with her dad in the lower deck, I admired the sparkling blue water dotted with dozens of tiny boats right under the nose of the Kajama for the next hour. Now, that's my kind of outing!

Merrily, merrily...

My 5-year-old was not excited by the promise of the 7000-square-feet of sail we could potentially put up if the wind allowed, but she was thrilled when the captain summoned us with mock authority to help his crew pull the ropes to set sails. She would have loved the fact that they now fire their own black powder canon on every cruise. It is loud!

We climbed aboard the **Kajama**, in the midst of a colourful and lively event at **Harbourfront**, accompanied by a whimsical chaos of music and vendors teasing the crowd, under a blazing sun. The illusion of playing tourists on some exotic cruise in the Islands was perfect.

TIPS (fun for 5 years +)
• Don't spend too much time trying to figure out the best spot to stay away from the sun. The boat keeps moving and so do the shadows. Bring hats!
• The return sail trip takes around two hours, boarding included.
• You can order from a menu on board.
• There are many other boat tours offered in the harbour that are less ambitious, and don't require pre-booking. And there's always the ferry! (See **Toronto Islands** on p. 392.)

Tall Ship Kajama (416) 203-2322 www.tallship cruisestoronto.com	**D-3 Downtown Toronto 5-min.**

Schedule: Daily from July to Labour Day (check website for June's schedule). Boardings at 11:30 am, 1:30 pm and 3:30 pm (departure half an hour later, sailing time is 90 minutes).
Admission: Around $22/adults, $20/seniors, $12/5 to 15 years old, FREE under 5.
Directions: Harbourfront Centre, Toronto (at Queen's Quay and Lower Simcoe Street behind the **Power Plant**).

YOUR FANNY DOWN THE GANNY

Among others, we admire a crew of eight rowers in their rail-car-boat, the Flintstones in their prehistoric craft and an airplane-shaped raft. But the golfers on a floating green, who'll reach the shore without getting wet, definitely take the cake!

More than 20 years ago, the **Ganaraska River** burst its banks; Port Hope was officially declared a disaster area. Since then, during

That sinking feeling

A brave pooch barks frantically, running along the banks of the Ganaraska River. A small boat has just capsized in the current... to the audience's great delight! The good dog doesn't realize he's in the middle of Port Hope's annual event. He tries to rescue the laughing crew, who clumsily attempt to reach their home-made craft to finish the race.

To my little landlubber, a grown-up reluctantly immersed in cold water is the funniest sight he's ever seen! Most crews take the plunge. Their craft is usually precarious: pieces of Styrofoam, wood, metal or plastic barrels piled or tied together, sometimes quite artistically.

TIPS (fun for 4 years +)

• Along Cavan Street, close to where it crosses Barrett Street, the banks are lined with flat stones and slope down gently. It forms a natural amphitheatre, stroller accessible with a great view.
• Many people bring blankets to sit on the ground, which can sometimes be muddy at this time of year.
• It's best to get to your observation point before 10:30 am. At 11 am, the first boats can be seen from downtown.
• Temporary toilets are available. Stands sell hot dogs and coffee.
• Port Hope hosts the only "atmospheric theatre" in Canada. Built in 1930, the **Capitol Theatre**'s interior was painted like a medieval castle, with clouds projected on the ceiling. Check their website for up-coming plays, films, and concerts at www.capitoltheatre.com or call 1-800-434-5092.

the sudden spring rise in the water level, the city has been organizing this race for canoes, kayaks and floating creations.

Each year, participants create their boat. Usually, about fifty crazy crafts are expected, but they don't all finish the race. A technical error happens so fast!

The ten-kilometre course followed by the boats ends downtown, where the crowd gathers to applaud the participants. The ambiance is great; it shows that people know each other.

Float Your Fanny Down the Ganny River Race	C-5 East of Toronto 60-min.

· Port Hope
1-888-767-8467
www.floatyourfanny.ca

 Schedule: Usually the first Saturday in April or the Saturday following Easter. Starts at 10 am. Participants race downtown between 11 am and 2 pm.
Admission: FREE.
Directions: From Hwy 401 East, take exit #464/Port Hope/Hwy 28 southbound (it becomes Mill Street). Turn right on Walton Street, then left on Queen to find parking. On foot, go back to Walton. Cavan Street, where the action is, is located west of the river, north of Walton.

NEARBY ATTRACTIONS

HMCS Haida

Afloat and well

Ontario Place visitors remember the huge destroyer that used to greet them by the entrance of the amusement park. We visited it in its current setting in Hamilton, better looking than ever.

HMCS Haida is the last survivor of 27 **Tribal destroyers** having served in three Commonwealth navies. Many rooms were restored so we could get a feeling of what the life on the warship must have been like.

At arrival, grab a self-guided tour brochure and start what will feel to kids like a treasure hunt.

They'll be oblivious to shiny brass and varnished woods but torpedo tubes, all kinds of big guns, mortar barrels and catwalks will do the trick.

Reading the signs really adds to the visit, putting things into perspective. On the mess deck, we learn that 40 men lived there, with an 18-inch space to hook their hammock, lockers doubling as seats.

We all agreed that the highlight of our visit was the engine room. So many nooks and crannies between boilers and turbines! Pipes, instruments, and throttles were everywhere. It was easy to imagine the noise, smell and heat in that section when the destroyer was in action.

From the main deck, we could see the **QEW Skyway Bridge** far away and cormorants fishing nearby.

TIPS (fun for 4 years +)

• You could get to Haida from Hwy 403 but I prefer driving over the QEW bridge, then along the industrial complex (read directions). Kids don't get to see that kind of panorama (and smell) very often!
• You'll have to do lots of contortions to cross through the numerous hatchways. Not recommended with a baby in arms or in a backpack!
• Interesting items noticed in their small gift shop: a $2 old-fashioned comic book *HMCS Haida Rescue at Sea* which brings Haida back to life, all kinds of badges for 50¢, $1 ribbons printed with HMCS and name of a city, to decorate a hat.
• Note that the Parks Canada Discovery Centre we used to visit in combo with Haida is now closed.

NEARBY ATTRACTIONS
Dundarn Castle (5-min.) .... p. 131
Football Hall of Fame (15-min.) ... p. 339

HMCS Haida | E-2
• Hamilton | S-W
(905) 523-0682 | of Toronto
www.hmcshaida.ca | 60-min.

Schedule: Usually open daily, 10 am to 5 pm, from Victoria Day weekend until Labour Day weekend, then fewer days in the week until Thanksgiving (call to confirm). Closed during the winter.
Admission: Around $4/adults, $2/youth and children, $10/family of 5, FREE for 5 years and under, FREE for all on Canada Day.
Directions: Pier 9, 658 Catherine Street North, Hamilton. Take Q.E.W. towards Niagara, go over the bridge, then take exit #89 (Burlington Street). Drive past the industrial complex, keeping left, turn right at John St. (past Wellington Street), right at Guise, then left at Catherine. Haida's entrance is to the right.

WELLAND CANALS CENTRE

The ups and downs of a canal

A drawbridge lets the freighter go by with its iron ore cargo. The gigantic lock gates shut heavily behind the 225-metre-long ship finishing its course through the canal. Tons of water lift the boat. It gets even better when sailors working on the main deck wave at the children. The kids, confined to the observation platform, look at them with envy. Here in St. Catharines, at Welland Canals' Lock number 3, we're amidst a world of *Mighty Machines*.

The **Welland Canals'** eight locks allow ships from thirty countries to cross the **Niagara Escarpment**, which brings about a 100-metre level difference between Lakes Ontario and Erie. Because of its ideal set-up for visitors, **Lock 3** is the best place to initiate children to the science of locks. It boasts an interactive centre, a souvenir shop and the great little **St. Catharines Museum**. And best of all, the lock's observation platform offers a breathtaking view.

A bulletin board by the entrance to the museum lists the boats that will pass through the lock during the day. It mentions each boat's name, port of registry, length, destination, type of cargo it carries and its approximate time of arrival at the lock. This helps to put young minds to work...

A question of time

During our visit, a good half hour went by between the moment we saw the arriving freighter passing under the drawbridge and the time it entered the lock. The kids weren't expecting it to be so gigantic!

To help them pass the time while waiting for a ship, we went to the snack bar and explored the playground. We also visited the St. Catharines Museum. Don't hesitate to go there at any time, as speakers inside the museum will announce the arrival of each ship. You can then return to the lock and when the ship has finished passing through, resume your visit to the museum.

It took 15 minutes for the Canadian cargo, called the *Jean Parisien*, to station itself inside the lock. This allowed us time to admire it from every angle. The little sailors accompanying me had many questions: "Why is the bridge watered by those hoses? Why are there only a few life boats?"

It takes about 10 minutes for the lock to fill with water. The freighter was rising before our very eyes and the kids enjoyed identifying the objects that were getting closer. "Wow, look at the lifebuoy! Can you see the white stairs? And the blue basket?"

Finally, the lock opened on the other side.

St. Catharines Museum

The museum includes various activities around the naval theme and several time-travel exhibits. The **Lacrosse Hall of Fame** comes with a shooting gallery, where kids can throw balls into a net. There are more hands-on pioneer artefacts to play with.

My little inspectors fell for the captain's wheel with a landscape seen through portholes in the background. We watched a 15-minute video presentation to learn more about the four Welland Canals (there were three previous versions).

The freighter's engines restarted and caused the water to swirl around. The ship continued its slow course upstream. It was about time, as my little sailors' level of interest was beginning to sink dangerously low! We improved the situation by returning to the museum.

TIPS (fun for 5 years +)

• The lock can remain empty for more than 5 consecutive hours. For a successful visit, it is best to call the centre before you leave home. They will be able to give you the dayly schedule, with the approximate arrival time of each ship. (It is best to go to the site when three or four ships are scheduled to pass through the lock within a 3-hour period.)

• The perspective is best when you watch a ship rising from "upbound", that is when it goes upstream from **Lake Ontario** towards **Lake Erie**.

• At the museum entrance, get your copy of the very interesting booklet *ABC's of the Seaway*, free with admission. Using simple terms, it describes the functioning of the locks that the kids have just seen live.

• There's a snack bar on site open at least from April to October.

NEARBY ATTRACTIONS	
Niagara Falls (15-min.)	p. 253
Wild Waterworks (15-min.)	p. 428

St. Catharines Museum & Welland Canals Centre • St. Catharines 1-800-305-5134	E-3 **Niagara Region** **75-min.**

www.stcatharines.ca (go to *Experience in*, then *Things to do & see*)

 Schedule: Ship viewing between April up to shortly before Christmas. Centre open 9 am to 5 pm from May through November (closes at 5:30 pm in July and August). From December through April, 9 am to 5 pm on weekdays and 11 am to 4 pm on weekends.
Admission: FREE admission to the centre. Museum: around $4.25/ adults, $4/seniors, $3.25/students, $2.50/6-13 years, FREE for children under 6.
Directions: Lock 3, 1932 Welland Canals Pkwy., St. Catharines. Take QEW Niagara to St. Catharines, exit at Glendale Ave. West, cross the lift-bridge and turn right on Welland Canals Pkwy.

General tips about
Museums:

- Museums change their exhibits on a regular basis. Points of interest described in this guide were accurate at the time of print. Based on my experience, they rarely change for the worse!

- In most cases, if you intend to visit a specific museum more than once during the year, it is worth considering a membership (normally no more than the price of two admissions). It will give you privileges and most importantly, it will give you the liberty to come for a quick visit whenever you have a chance, without being concerned about not getting your money's worth!

- All museums are closed on December 25 and January 1st.

MUSEUMS

See **the Royal Ontario Museum** on p. 222.

THE (CHILDREN'S) MUSEUM

Charge!

The yellow Swiss cheese slice covering the whole wall in the four-storey atrium certainly got our attention! It went perfectly with the two-storey moon-like projection on the round screen. The giant kaleidoscope of **Shadow Play** was throwing its ever-moving light on it, while enlarged shadows of kids danced on the screen. My companions could not get through the gate fast enough.

Since my last edition, the Children's Museum has renamed itself **The Museum** (probably to better represent special exhibitions appealing to the general public) but it still feels like a bigger version of the whimsical Kid-Spark section in the Ontario Science Centre.

Don't be fooled by the stiff facade of the building. It used to be a department store, which sat vacant for 15 years. To see its inner beauty, enter through the child-size doors (next to the full-size ones), even 10-year-olds find it amusing.

Go past the huge round reception counter and admire natural light pouring from skylights and the glass front, three mezzanines and a gorgeous tempered glass staircase bordered with glass guardrails, wooden floors and a line-up of creative activities.

On the **Street Level**, the **Atrium** area by the giant kaleidoscope is quite popular with kids. Several building systems are usually at their disposal in that section.

Another hit is the enclosed and carpeted area **TotSpot** in a corner of the vast floor. Meant for preschoolers and babies, the cocoon-like room is mesmerizing for anyone, with five bubbling water tubes lit in the dark and a ceiling covered with wavy mesh.

The **Second Level** focuses on mechanics and hydraulics. We loved the **Construction Alley** with its sails of stretch-fabric panels we could hook with the help of fasteners on poles to create labyrinths. The two-sided **Pin Walls** next to it were a blast. Kids could leave a life-size impression on it. (Beware, make sure no other explorer is simultaneously pushing pins on the other side while you're pushing on yours.)

The water section used to include a 15-metre-long stream when the museum opened but it has been downsized to a 4-metre water table, still fun enough for my two 10-year-old companions to spend 30 minutes steering boats between sections.

This floor also offers a craft section and a large magnetic board.

On the **Third Level** was an infrared pod with a screen registering our body temperatures (the more layers of clothing, the colder it registers!). There was a sec-

tion with a few vibrating seats reacting to the projection of a space launch.

It offers interesting scientific activities as long as you have the patience to figure them out (tip: you have to wait for buttons to light-up before pushing them and wait a few seconds to leave time for the experiment to start).

The highlight of this floor was the opportunity to lay down on a bed of nails which would come out of a plexiglass sheet under your body with the help of a control button.

The **Fourth Level** hosts travelling exhibitions. Expect something interactive. When visiting, we saw displays on the chimpanzees in Jane Goodall's world. They've featured exhibitions on the Titanic, space travel, the human body...

TIPS (fun for 2 years +)

• Make sure there's an exhibition on the 4th floor when you visit. There can be a few weeks between exhibitions.
• The **Museum Café** sells light lunches.
• If you walk a few blocks to your right when exiting the museum, you'll find **Kitchener's City Hall** with a nice fountain in the summer, which turns into a rink in the winter. Bring the skates! (There's a **Williams Fresh Cafe** right next to it).
• Check the calendar of shows presented at the **Registry Theatre** (122 Frederick, a few minutes from the museum, (519) 745-6565, www.registrytheatre.com). Their summer production would be a nice complement to the museum visit. In 2011, their company JM Drama presents the musical *25th Annual Putnam County Spelling Bee*. In previous years, they've produced *Cabaret, Sweeney Todd, Urinetown, The Importance of Being Earnest.*
• More on the **Oktoberfest Parade** taking place on King Street on p. 43.

The Museum
• Kitchener
(519) 749-9387
www.themuseum.ca

D-1
West
of Toronto
1 1/2 hr

Schedule: Wednesday to Friday, 10 am to 4 pm; Saturday, 10 am to 5 pm; Sunday, 12 noon to 5 pm. Open Mondays and Tuesdays early July to Labour Day, 10 am to 4 pm. Closed for two weeks after Labour Day.
Admission: $10/person, FREE for children 3 and under (additional fee when there's a visiting exhibition).
Directions: 10 King Street West, Kitchener. From Hwy 401 West, take exit#278/ Hwy #8 West towards Kitchener-Waterloo. Keep right, it becomes King Street. The museum is past Queen. There's a parking lot on Duke Street, just north of King Street and west of the museum.

NEARBY ATTRACTIONS

HAMILTON CHILDREN'S MUSEUM

Hamilton for kids

Don't be disappointed by the building's small size. The philosophy behind this museum is to maximize the use of space and make it as interactive as can be.

The museum is constantly reinventing itself (whenever new funds are available!). For every new edition of my guide, I have had to rewrite this page.

Last time I visited it (in December 2010), I fell in love again with the place. This time, past the **Brain Room** with the wall of pipes, the bins of blocks, the weaving board and the reading nook was the ingenious **Doo Wop Diner** room.

A couple of booths and a counter to sit at, a checkered black and white dance floor complete with a working jukebox (three songs for $1) and a working kitchen to get busy. Staff members told me kids

are crazy about this room. Make sure to encourage the kids to admire the "artwork" on the wall (a real diner's table, with all the chewing gum accumulated over the years)!

The third section is the **Media Room** featuring a green screen in front of which kids can dress-up and act while watching themselves on a television. Costumes and the background appearing on television are regularly changed. Following a castle theme when I was visiting, it was soon to be changed into an underwater theme.

There's also a craft room (featuring a funky faux-fur fridge) open to the public when there's not a birthday party going on.

I walked through the adjacent **Gage Park**. It is huge! Its great outdoor playground with dragon-shaped spray pad is located just a two-minute walk away from the museum, in the western part of the park, and sits near an amazing grove of huge ancient trees.

TIPS (fun for 2 to 10 years)
• During the winter, you'll find a short hill for tobogganing a couple of minutes into the eastern part of **Gage Park**.
• Just west of Gage Park you'll find the really retro **Connaught Fish & Chips** restaurant by the train track (at 976 Main Street East), with a gorgeous mural on its side. It is the real thing! The fries are yummy. They offer kids portions and in case you were wondering, for the *Sheena's DFB Delight* offer on the menu, DFB stands for Deep Fried Brownies! Can't get more decadent than this!

NEARBY ATTRACTIONS
Dundurn Castle (5-min.) .... p. 131
Warplane Museum (15-min.) .... p. 194

Hamilton Children's Museum
• Hamilton
(905) 546-4848
www.myhamilton.ca
(click on *Arts*, *Sports & Recreation*)

E-2
S-W
of Toronto
60-min.

 Schedule: Open Tuesday to Saturday, 9:30 am to 3:30 pm (from April to September). Closed on Tuesdays but open on Sundays, 11 am to 4 pm, from October to March, plus the whole week of **March Break** and the **Christmas Break** from Boxing Day to before school starts again. Closes between new exhibits, better call ahead to confirm it is open.
 Admission: $3/1-13 years old, $1/adults, $7/family of 4.
 Directions: 1072 Main Street East, Hamilton. Take QEW West, then Hwy 403 towards Hamilton, exit Main Street East.

LONDON CHILDREN'S MUSEUM

Fun space

The museum's large dimensions and its lovely setting inside a former three-storey school, enchanted me. My son loved its child-sized village, then it was the Space gallery that thrilled him.

It took us more than two hours to explore the **London Regional Children's Museum**.

On one side, the prehistoric room boasts two complete dinosaur skeletons and a deep cave, with its dark and realistic nooks and crannies, prehistoric drawings and cleverly designed sandbox, in which children can dig for stones with genuine fossils. On the other side, you will find the new **Arctic Discovery** gallery (opening in May 2011).

TIPS (fun for 2 to 12 years)

• Hot food service is available (but not weekdays in the off season). There is an interesting outdoor playground.
• The museum offers many special activities during their Summer Carnival. They also offer special fun during Easter, **Canada Day**, Halloween, Christmas and March Break.
• The **London International Children's Festival** is the only such festival left (Milk and Mississauga Children's Festivals have been cancelled). It usually runs for 5 consecutive days including the first or second weekend in June. It takes place in and around **Victoria Park** in London. Check www.londonchildfest.com. Good time for a getaway!

NEARBY ATTRACTIONS
London StoryBook (10-min.) .... p. 52
Fanshawe Village (15-min.) .... p. 389

In the mezzanine on the second floor is the cool **Jellyfish Junction** with underwater theme and sand floor. The miniature rendition of a village is also located on the second floor. Its small buildings depict the decor, accessories and costumes of various businesses you'd find in any town.

On the third floor, there's a room where kids can enjoy a huge tree that houses a slide and hiding places. There were a few other displays on the science in our life but we did not explore them, the **My Place in Space** gallery nearby was way too attractive!

Wow! What a beautiful gallery to look at and to explore too! You're inside a space station with a central control module with large bay windows and monitors allowing you to see the visitors in all the other sections of the station. Cargo, docking, experiment module and habitation module complete the gallery, along with projected constellations in the dark on the dome ceiling of the planetarium.

My kids looked like astronauts when they wore the silver costumes at their disposal. My daughter felt like a real one when she heard the noise after she had pushed the launch button in her space shuttle. Clever!

London Children's Museum
· London
(519) 434-5726
www.londonchildrensmuseum.ca

Off the map S-W of Toronto 2 hrs

Schedule: Open Tuesday to Sunday, 10 am to 5 pm (closes at 8 pm on Fridays). Open Mondays also, from Victoria Day to Labour Day and during holidays.

Admission: $6/2 years an older, $2/under 2 years.

Directions: 21 Wharncliffe Road South, London. From Hwy 401 West, take exit at Wellington Road northbound, turn west on Commisionner's Road, then north on Wharncliffe Road. (past Horton Street and railway bridge). The museum is located on the left side.

CBC MUSEUM

CBC Museum on the west side of the building. Kids shows' props can be seen in the little museum (*Sesame Street, Mr. Dressup*). A large selection of clips from CBC programs for adults or kids can be watched.

In the back of the little museum are a series of displays explaining how they did the sound effects for the radio, with computer clip demonstrations. Kids can even listen to the sound they create by manipulating different objects.

Look up!

When looking at the building from the outside, you'd never guess how breathtaking the ceiling of the CBC building is. Use the little museum as an excuse to admire some amazing architecture.

From the main hall at the centre of the building, by the indoor café where many CBC staff have their meals, you can admire the **Atrium**'s grandiose architecture and the spectacular skylight.

You can then carry on to visit the

CBC Museum	D-3
(416) 205-5574	**Downtown**
www.cbc.ca/museum/	Toronto
index.html	2-min. walk

 Schedule: The CBC building is open daily. The museum is open Monday to Friday from 9 am to 5 pm.
Admission: FREE.
Directions: 250 Front St. West (across from the **CN Tower**), Toronto.

TORONTO POLICE MUSEUM

Good guys, bad guys

At the entrance, officers in uniform impressed my little citizen, but not as much as the gleaming police edition Harley-Davidson posted nearby. He happily (and legally!) hopped on the motorcycle.

Mannequins display uniforms dating from the 1850's to the present. There's even a Toronto Police mounted officer on a life-size horse and a genuine police car with live feed on its radio.

Initiate your miniature CSI investigator to the display with several pieces of evidence: a drinking glass covered with fingerprints, nails stuck in garden hoses

used by robbers to slow down the police during a chase.

There's a prison cell, (unfortunately closed). Further on, my son saw his first real car wreck. It faces a 1950's road sign encouraging us to drive safely. The sign compares the number of automobile accident deaths from the current and previous year.

The billboard is old, but the statistics are current and updated weekly! They have a **Cop Shop** in the lobby.

Toronto	D-3
Police Museum	**Downtown**
(416) 808-7020	Toronto
www.torontopolice.on.ca	15-min.

 Schedule: All visits must be booked ahead. Open Monday to Friday, 8:30 am to 4 pm.
Admission: Suggested donation (nominal fee).
Directions: 40 College Street, Toronto (one block west of Yonge Street).

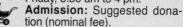

TEXTILE MUSEUM

Strong artistic fibre

In the Discover Fibre section, there's a discovery drawer to learn about the living things producing fibres. I really enjoyed the exercise but my five-year-old couldn't care less. She's too distracted by the alignment of colourful threads inside a large cage in the Discover Colour section.

It doesn't take long for her to rearrange the threads into an artful display. Then, she makes patterns using a wide choice of pre-cut shapes.

While she's busy, I can't believe I finally get to see what a silkworm looks like and touch real cocoons, so white and soft between my fingers. The Fibrespace education gallery within the Textile Museum is filled with such things to discover.

TIPS (fun for 5 years +)
• The March Break is usually a great time to drop in with artsy kids who would like to create textile art! Special craft activities are then adapted to the current exhibitions.
• Their store is filled with original works of some 50 artisans. It carries a great selection of textile-related books, for adults and children (even some storybooks involving fabrics). Kids' stuff also includes textile-related kits, learning activity books and craft projects.
• There's no restaurant on the site but the museum is only a 10-minute walk from the Yonge and Dundas intersection.

NEARBY ATTRACTIONS

There's also the **Discover Textiles** corner with a "knitted zoo", hooked rugs and lace making trials, and the **Discover Meaning** section where activities constantly change to coincide with specific exhibitions.

You can expect up to six exhibitions going on in the three exhibition spaces throughout the year. They're always intriguing and interesting for adults, like the one on geotextiles, or the one on the molecular structure of fabrics.

You can usually count on artistic installations involving fabric in some way. Once, a dramatic organza curtain pinned with thousands of rose petals by the artist stunned me. And the installation "I've got balls" was quite a sight, with over twenty nylon legs suspended from clothes lines, heavy with baseballs in their feet. Even my daughter reacted to that one.

Our favourite was the one where real bugs were pinned on the walls to recreate the intricate pattern of a Victorian tapestry...

Textile Museum of Canada (416) 599-5321 www.textilemuseum.ca	**D-3 Downtown Toronto 5-min.**

 Schedule: Open daily, 11 am to 5 pm, (closes at 8 pm on Wednesday).

 Admission: $15/adults, $10/seniors, $6/5-14, $30/family of 5, FREE under 5 years old, Pay-what-you-can on Wednesdays, 5 to 8 pm.

 Directions: 55 Centre Avenue, Toronto (south of Dundas, one block east of University Avenue).

ROYAL ONTARIO MUSEUM

Crystal clear

When you stand on Bloor and look up at the windows on the second floor of the ROM, you see the full length of the largest dinosaur featured in the Crystal. I can't think of a better way to tease families into the museum.

From the kids' point of view, the highlight of the **ROM** has to be the **Temerty Galleries of the Age of Dinosaurs**.

Level 2

Don't take the elevators to get there or you'll miss the amazing staircases built in the **Michael Lee-Chin Crystal**. They are breathtaking, an attraction in themselves, and include a few collections encased like gems in a cave.

The first room in the **Dinosaurs Gallery** is interesting, with the largest fossils I have ever seen and the longest skeleton of the collection: the Barosaurus.

In the next room, across the corridor, huge marine specimens hung over our heads. Tyranosaurus Rex and the Tryceratops skull awaited in all their splendour.

But what blew us away was the adjacent **Gallery of the Age of Mammals**. It displayed contemporary skeletons next to those of their prehistoric ancestors, and a mammoth from... Welland, Ontario!

From there, you can access the most interactive part of the ROM, starting with the **Discovery Gallery** (with costumes, exploration boxes, bone digging and more), followed by the **Birds Gallery** (where you've got to invite the kids to explore the series of discovery drawers under the glass displays). Then you head to the **Bat Cave**. It was renovated in 2010 and I was told it is even better and bigger, with 800 bats (some mechanized).

Past the Bat Cave, the **Gallery of Hands-On Biodiversity** is a whole little museum in itself. Its stuffed forest mammals and realistic displays give us the impression of being on a field trip in Canada's lake and cottage regions. This section includes guessing games, hands-on tables, costumes, a tunnel to explore and an active beehive linked to the outside world.

You'll pass through the **Life in Crisis Gallery** on your way to the east side of the museum. Showcasing sharks over our heads and all kinds of animals (can't miss that huge rhino). What you could miss, on the other hand, is the **Earth Rangers Studio**. Look at the door of the studio for the schedule of the presentations offered in that space from Tuesday to Saturday. When we attended, there were live animals involved, and nice rangers to tell us more about specific animals.

Further, you'll reach the spectacular golden rotunda all covered in mosaic. Look to your right, and there it is: the amazing **Teck Suite of Galleries: Earth's Treasures**.

The first time I entered into the **Minerals Gallery**, I was speechless. They come in all shapes and colours. The displays are so interesting and beautiful, I felt all the privilege of having access to such an extensive collection.

There are projections on two screens on both sides of the entrance, to add to the experience. You'll see real meteorites, minerals grouped by shapes, by colours, by hardness (showing the molecular structure of diamonds). In the back, huge mineral rocks are displayed, offering a nice contrast with the exquisite gem carvings from Idar-Oberstein: a delicate skating mouse, a chubby toad carved into ruby, graceful weasels and butterflies.

Levels 3 and 4

With so much to see on Level 2, we hardly ever get to visit the other galleries. Among the best of the rest to see with the kids, you might want to pay a visit to the mummies in the **Africa: Egypt Gallery** on Level 3. You'll find displays of Islamic arms and armour in adjacent **Middle East Gallery**, also on Level 3, in the Crystal.

There are more shiny armours in the **Samuel European Galleries**. I personally really enjoy walking through the **Weston Family Wing** in that section. It consists of a string of period rooms furnished and decorated in different styles in a chronological order, offering a real time travel experience.

If you have a young fashion aficionado, you'll want to see the **Textile & Costumes Gallery** on the Level 4 of the Crystal.

Level 1

If you still have energy on your way back to Level 1, there's the Samurai warrior armour to see in the **Japan Gallery**, and the full-scale replica of the corner of an imperial palace hall in the **Gallery of Chinese Architecture,** both on the west side of the museum.

On the opposite side, near the rotun- da, are the **Canada** and **First People Galleries**. The showcases could hardly be more enticing. The art mixed with the artefacts brings them back to life. Small details add warmth to the displays, such as Inuit dolls in their little sealskin garments next to the life-size ones.

Finally those of your little group who are not shopping at the museum store should sit on the crystal-like chairs in the **Spirit House** by the entrance. You'll feel like you're in the abdominal cavity of an organic spaceship... And you'll hear voices.

TIPS (fun for 3 years +)

• There's a **Toronto Parking Authority** affordable parking lot on Bedford Street, north of Bloor Street, west of Avenue Rd.

• Every weekend is **ROM Family Weekend** with more activities, solo artists strolling through the museum, live music or presentation in the Earth Rangers Studio.

• The ROM offers even more activities during the March Break, Halloween and around Christmas time. Find out about their **sleepover** nights on their website (around $75/person).

• The large **ROM Museum Store** by the entrance offers an amazing selection, from trinkets to jewelry, from gorgeous books to quality games and toys. There's also a small **ROMkids Store** on Level 2, beside the Discovery Gallery.

• The fancy cafeteria-style **Food Studio** on Level B1 offers great choices for all tastes.

NEARBY ATTRACTIONS
Bata Shoe Museum (15-min. walk) p. 225
Around Bay Subway Station .... p. 459

Royal Ontario Museum (ROM)
(416) 586-8000
www.rom.on.ca

**D-3
Downtown
Toronto
20-min.**

 Schedule: Open daily, 10 am to 5:30 pm, closes at 8:30 pm on Fridays.

 Admission: $24/adults, $21/seniors and students, $16/4 to 14 years, FREE for 3 years and under. Half-price admission on Fridays, 4:30 to 8:30 pm. FREE on Wednesdays from 3:30 pm to 5:30 pm.

 Directions: 100 Queen's Park, Toronto. The entrance is on Bloor Street.

THE BATA SHOE MUSEUM

The shoe fits!

Since the company has always focused on low-end shoes, I was quite curious to see what the Bata Shoe Museum had to offer. Well, I was impressed! The museum is gorgeous and Bata has shown great skill in putting itself into its young visitors' shoes to get their attention.

The **All About Shoes** semi-permanent exhibition reviews the history of shoes, from prehistoric times until the present, using many props: art reproductions, informative text, mannequins, lighting effects and fascinating artefacts. They change the displays from time to time to feature different shows from their vast collection.

TIPS (fun for 5 years +)

• March Break activities are original. Last time I was there during this period, visitors could play with Brio-like tracks and "shoe" trains. They could create socks and shoes for a multi-legged dragon. They could decorate a clog shoe for an extra fee. The activities vary but you can usually count on crafts and dress-up sessions ($9/adults, $8/kids).

• Check out their website to find out about special family activities on Saturdays, Easter, Halloween, Christmas and more.

Once, when visiting, we saw the oldest closed shoe dating from the 1400's! Among other things, I learned that in 14th Century England, length of the shoe tip was related to social status and regulated by law. That explains the disproportionately long shoes seen in some medieval paintings!

Children can't appreciate the historic value of ancient shoes. But they'll be impressed by the variety of footwear displayed here, especially if you explain the use of certain shoes to them. At the time of print, we could see astronaut training boots, chestnut crushing clogs, Dutch smugglers' clogs designed to create a footprint! And what can we say about the ancient Chinese shoes used to reduce the foot size of women victims of their time?

We then move on to the Star Turns display, showcasing some famous footwear: one of the Beatles' ankle boots, Marilyn Monroe's red pumps, Picasso's pony-skin boots. Kids will favour the size 20 EEE shoe of basketball player Shaquille O'Neil and... Justin Bieber's sneakers.

Three other galleries feature temporary exhibitions with interesting themes. We've seen dancing shoes, athletic footwear, art in shoes, native footwear, etc.

NEARBY ATTRACTIONS
ROM (15-min. walk) .... p. 222

The Bata Shoe Museum
(416) 979-7799
www.batashoemuseum.ca

D-3
Downtown
Toronto
20-min.

Schedule: Open on weekdays and Saturdays, 10 am to 5 pm (closes at 8 pm on Thursdays). Open Sunday, 12 noon to 5 pm.
Admission: $14/adults, $12/seniors, $8/students, $5/5-17 years, $24/one adult + 4 kids, $35/two adults + 3 kids, FREE for children 4 years and under. FREE on Thursdays, 5 pm to 8 pm.
Directions: 327 Bloor Street West, Toronto (at the corner of St. George Street, in front of **St. George Subway Station**).

ONTARIO SCIENCE CENTRE

The science of fun

What a unique playground! Cave, 5-metre-high tornado, rocket chair, interactive floors, magnetic liquid, wall of bubbles; the list goes on. Mind you, nobody has to see it all in just one visit!

The visit starts with the **Teluscape** space created outdoors in front of the Centre. Since my last visit, they've added a very cool water maze, with sprays creating imaginary walls. (Try to keep this for the end of the visit so the kids have time to see all the attractions inside.)

On your way to the escalators, you'll cross the **Great Hall** adorned with the *Cloud*, the permanent art work that now hangs from its ceiling. It con-

sists of 100 shafts, each one rotating at a slightly different speed, catching the light at a changing angle over a 20-minute cycle. What we have here is the best example of science meeting the arts!

Also check the *Lotic Meander* on the outdoor terrace overlooking the valley (use the door from the Great Hall). The overall effect of this artistic representation of a meandering river is simply whimsical. It includes a 300-foot-long sinuous path adorned with 860 discs, glass eggs and polished stone boulders.

I recommend starting the indoor visit with **The Living Earth**, three escalators down to Level 6 and to your far right. For younger kids, this ride is an adventure in itself!

Take your time in the tropical rain forest, to feel the climate, see the waterfall and watch the colony of leaf-cutting ants circulating through transparent pipes. Then, get your kids excited with the 5-metre-high tornado. It vanishes when you blow on it! The large cave includes a TV monitor showing the visitors inside.

Up the stairs in that room, you can lay on your belly and watch a short movie of a flight from the perspective of the flying eagle!

At the end of Level 6 is the **Science Arcade**. This is where you'll find the hair-raising ball (a Van der Graaf generator) used during daily electrical demonstrations. Then, it's shadow tunnel, pedal power, jiggling sculpture, steel drums, optical effects, exhibits testing friction, resonance, vibration and more exhibits for bigger kids to pump and pull.

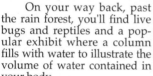

On your way back, past the rain forest, you'll find live bugs and reptiles and a popular exhibit where a column fills with water to illustrate the volume of water contained in your body.

Older kids will appreciate the confinement chamber in the adjacent **A Question of Truth** or the exhibit on the 256 symbols learned by chimpanzees to communicate with humans in **Communication**.

Returning to the centre of Level 6, try the interactive floor! Can you figure out how it works? Every time I introduce visitors to this floor, they go wild (whatever the age).

Temporary exhibitions are featured in that area of the centre. (At the time of print, they were featuring **Nature Unleashed: Inside Natural Disasters**.)

After this, we normally split our group: younger kids and a few adults going to **KidSpark** (Level 4, two escalators up) while teenagers head to the fantastic **Weston Family Innovation Centre**.

This addition was a stroke of genius, kind of like finding the missing link. It was created with teenagers and young adults in mind.

They can create stop-motion animations, record and replay weird sounds they make on special DJ's tables, make a ferro liquid react to sound, have their pic-

ture taken and reproduced 5 minutes later on a wall of small air bubbles moving along thin water pipes, play music by touching lights, create shoes, play in a paper plane testing zone with targets...

With all of these options, it is easy to miss the **Human Body** on Level 5 (check their map). The modules you will find there are quite daring, covering the reproductive system and birth control.

Ask your little explorers to stand in front of a smiling little girl's picture. Then, open the "window" around her face. Behind this opening, her face contracts and a hidden water spray system reproduces a generous sneeze. It's quite funny when you don't expect it. Don't give it away!

On Level 4, the **Space** section is a good place for older kids to hang around while the younger ones are still playing in nearby **KidSpark** (we were never able to play less than an hour in this section, parents just need to go with the flow!)

The airlifted rocket chair is worth trying! We were also fascinated by the room focusing on cosmic rays, with the amazing table allowing us to "see" the passage of particles using a condensation process. You've got to see this for yourself.

Thanks to Hubble's telescope, the universe gets all the attention it deserves. The pictures will give the kids a sense of the vastness of it all, from our solar system to the confines of the universe.

As for KidSpark, it is located in two adjacent rooms and simply lovely. It was designed for kids 8 years and under, but my son really enjoyed it beyond that age (they would allow older siblings to play if the place is not too busy).

Hard to say what my kids preferred: the mesmerizing interactive **Rhodes Sculpture** by the entrance, the stage where you lip-sync while playing fake instruments and creating light effects, the construction site with lifts and blocks and the floating balls in the first room, or the water table and the tree house in the other room with large windows overlooking the pond. (Yes, there's a pond at the Science Centre! It is accessible from the path outside the Great Hall.)

TIPS (fun for 2 years +)

• Don't be afraid to take young kids to this museum. They will be elated to be allowed to touch everything.

• The gift shop on Level 1 is a **Mastermind Educational Toys** store. It is a fabulous place to buy educational toys, books, posters and $10 science gadgets. It offers a huge selection of activity books.

• On Fridays and Saturdays at 7 pm, you can see two consecutive **Imax® Dome** films ($20/adults, $18/seniors & students and 4-12 years, FREE for 3 years and under). The exhibits close at 5 pm but the snack bar by the entrance remains open.

• There's even more activities during the March Break. Beware! It's their busiest time of the year.

• Find out about their **sleepover** nights on their website (only a few nights in the year, around $55/person, book in advance!).

• The big **Valley Market Place** on Level 6 sells pasta, stir fry and many more food options. You can eat outside and enjoy the natural surroundings of the ravine (along with the raccoons).

NEARBY ATTRACTIONS
Shops at Don Mills (5-min.) .... p. 422

Ontario Science Centre	D-3
Ontario Science Centre · North York (416) 696-3127 www.ontariosciencecentre.ca	**North** of downtown 25-min.

Schedule: Open year-round, 10 am to 5 pm (extended hours during the March Break, July and August).

Admission: $20/adults, $16/seniors and students, $13/4-12 years, FREE for 3 years and under. Parking costs $10. (With one Imax® Dome film, it is $28/adults, $22/seniors and students, $19/children). Ask about their membership rates if you intend to visit more than twice in a year!

Directions: 770 Don Mills Road, North York. Take Don Valley Pkwy, exit Don Mills North.

HAMILTON MUSEUM OF STEAM

19th century techies

Our guide puts an oily paper hat on my nephew's head, turning him into one of the kids hired in the 19th century to keep the pumps well oiled. We all laugh at his funny "oiler" look until we are told this was the only protection those working children had when working in that environment. What about their little fingers?

The steam engines before us are quite impressive, at 70 tons each and 45 feet high. We're actually too close to see them in one shot as we look at them from the mezzanine. Canadian made, they're the oldest surviving examples in the nation and we can see them in operation under our noses.

Before we were allowed to see this phenomenon, our guide took great pains to explain to us the "beauty" of the technology involved by means of an interactive demonstration perfectly adapted for children. During the tour (which lasted 40 minutes), kids were allowed to use a lever to make the huge wheel turn.

We could also admire a model of the pump house, in a large barn-like display room filled with charts explaining the system. Each of the 12,000 parts of this model were handmade by a Hamilton resident in the 80's and it is functioning.

In addition, there's always a temporary exhibit in the main building.

TIPS (fun for 6 years +)
• Every now and then during a **Golden Horseshoe Live Steamer Day**, you can catch a ride on a miniature steam-powered locomotive. Check their website for specific dates.
• During March Break, including the weekends before and after (and opening at 10 am) they offer more drop-in special demonstrations and craft activities.
• During Christmas break, they offer a special activity including two crafts and a craft bag to take home (for an extra fee).
• They offer some nice trinkets in their small gift shop. We bought a train whistle and a cute little tin boat moving with the heat of a candle!
• Read about nearby restaurants in the tips section of **Wild Waterworks**, p. 428.

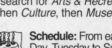

Hamilton Museum of Steam & Technology
· Hamilton
(905) 546-4797
www.myhamilton.ca
(search for *Arts & Recreation*, then *Culture*, then *Museums*)

E-2
S-W
of Toronto
65-min.

Schedule: From early July to Labour Day, Tuesday to Sunday, 11 am to 4 pm (opens at 12 noon the rest of the year). Closed on Mondays.
Admission: $6.50/adults, $5.50/seniors and students, $4.50/children, $16.50/family, FREE for 5 years and under.
Directions: 900 Woodward Avenue, Hamilton. Take QEW towards Niagara, exit at Woodward Avenue and follow signs.

General tips about
Nature's call:

• Did you know **poison ivy** often climbs up larger trees? Me neither! In case you were wondering, here's what poison ivy looks like.

Look for shrubs with distinctive three-part pointed leaves, the central of which has a longer stem than the two side leaflets. The edges of the leaves can be smooth or very jagged. It loves sunny areas along trails, roads and beaches.

The rash appears 24-48 hours after contact. Beware! You can get it from touching your pet if it has brushed itself against it in the woods.

We can complain about it but let's not forget it is a good source of food for fall and winter animals!

• In the summer, have bathing suits handy! You never know when you'll find a swimming hole.

• In the spring and the fall, it is a good idea to have a change of clothes in case young kids fall in the mud!

NATURE'S CALL

See **Cheltenham Badlands** on p. 232.

CHELTENHAM BADLANDS

lands. It runs up and down through patches of trees but you can still see the pink and white clay-rich soil amidst the bushes. We just walked 10 minutes into it so I don't know where it leads but it was a lovely stretch.

Both times we visited, there was a rope hanging from a bush by the side road, offering a more adventurous way to ease ourselves into the badlands. A big hit with kids!

A rare sight!

You might have seen glimpses of them in ads and wondered where on earth is this? You've got to map Cheltenham Badlands Ontario on Google Satellite to believe it! You'll see a strange wrinkled patch of pink dirt lined with white stripes. It looks even more out of this world when you see it for real.

A picture is always worth a thousand words but it is even more true with this geologic phenomena so I'll keep my text short to make room for more photos.

The badlands are managed by the **Bruce Trail Association**. Most people stick to the section devoid of vegetation but it is worth walking past it and following the path on the edge of the bad-

TIPS (fun for 5 years +)

• The first time I explored the Cheltenham Badlands was on a bright fall day early October. The experience was amazing and surreal. When we returned during the Thanksgiving long weekend, the place was so crowded, we had to park far from it along the road. Our contact with nature did not have the same feeling under those conditions.

• I did not see washrooms on the premises.

NEARBY ATTRACTIONS
Belfountain C.A. (10-min.) .... p. 306

Cheltenham Badlands
• Cheltenham
www.ontariotrails.on.ca

C-2
N-W
of Toronto
50-min.

 Schedule: Open year-round (but no evening parking along sideroad from 9 pm to 7 am).

Admission: FREE.

Directions: Take Hwy 410 northbound (it becomes Hwy 10). Turn west at Olde Base Line Road. The badlands are on your left. If you reach Mississauga Road, you've gone too far.

WARSAW CAVES

Underground experience

A while ago, I visited Warsaw Caves at the end of a cold afternoon, on a wet fall day, with a two-year-old and no flashlight. You might as well say I did not see them. Still, we were there long enough to assess what a unique underground adventure it offers to any explorer.

Some of the seven biggest caves marked along the trails are up to 100 metres (300 feet) long. Some go as deep as 15 metres into the ground. Ice may be found in one of them all year round. The average temperature in the other caves is approximately 15°C.

The trail to the caves is indicated on a map by the parking lot. It starts out smoothly but is soon covered by large plates of rock (at times slippery), which offer a unique scene. We easily lose track of the trail but the caves are not too far apart.

Bright green touches of moss cover the stones, and straight tall trees have popped up wherever they can. Some have actually managed to grow from the bottom of 2-metre-deep crevices. Everywhere, there are natural nooks and crannies to explore.

Approximately 20 minutes further, another trail leads to a lookout. Off the path, you will observe kettles, which are holes created by the movement of melting glaciers. They can be quite small but the biggest in the conservation area measures over 5 feet wide.

TIPS (fun for 5 years +)

• It is a must to bring flashlights and good shoes for everyone!
• You can print a great *Caves Guide* from their website (go to *Maps* and look under the Other Downloads section).
• Our pint-size paleontologist never wanted to go deeper than one metre into the caves. The guide I talked to told me she recommends exploring the caves with children 7 years or older. They need to be a certain height to stroll more at ease in the underground corridors.
• During the summer, visitors can swim in a calm river only three feet deep, accessible from a beach where canoes and kayaks can be rented. There are 52 campsites in the conservation area.
• The staff sells snacks and drinks during the summer. I was told there is a great chip truck in the town of Warsaw, five minutes away from the **Warsaw Caves**.

NEARBY ATTRACTIONS
Jungle Cat World (70-min.) .... p. 73

Warsaw Caves Conservation Area
• Warsaw
(705) 652-3161
Campground
1-877-816-7604
www.warsawcaves.com

B-5
N-E
of Toronto
2 hrs

Schedule: Open to vehicles from Victoria Day to Thanksgiving, from 8 am to sunset.

Admission: (cash only) around $10/vehicle. Canoe rental is $17/2 hours or $34/day. (Headlamp rental for around $3.)

Directions: From Hwy 401 East, take exit #436/Hwy 35/115 northbound. It becomes Hwy 7, follow it east of Peterborough. Turn north on Regional Rd. 38 (2nd Line Road), then take County Rd. 4 to Caves Road.

SCENIC CAVES ADVENTURES

Get to the bottom of it!

At the beginning of the path, you cross the Ice Cave, a natural fridge which maintains a cool 4 degrees Celsius in summertime. Even its exterior walls are cold. Hugging my small baby, I remain in the cave's narrow and cool vestibule, while father and son explore further down a corridor that descends into the even cooler part.

TIPS (fun for 5 years +)

• The trail system is accessible for the entire family but not stroller accessible!

• Running or hiking shoes are a must, and take extra care when ground is wet.

• Equip your children with flashlights, it will enhance their explorations.

• The self-guided visit and the suspension bridge experience take about two hours.

• There is a large pond filled with enormous trout you can feed, a great playground, and small train rides. For an extra fee, you can enjoy mini golf or **Gemstone Mining**, a great "panning" structure allowing kids to find semi-precious gems from bags of mine rough.

• The treetop canopy walk experience of their **Eco Adventure Tour** includes zip lines (one of them 1,000 feet long) you slide down, hanging 40 feet above the ground. Check their website for details or to make reservations. The 2 1/2 hr tour is $95/adults, $85/seniors and 10-17 years old, plus tax.

NEARBY ATTRACTIONS
Wasaga Beach (30-min.) .... p. 408

At the top of a path in the forest, iron railings sit at the opening of a large crevice, leading us some 20 metres below amidst magnificent rock formations and tender green foliage against the dark mossy rock face.

On a sunny day the sight is breathtaking. An information plaque tells us that some 300 years ago, Hurons used the natural fortress of the **Scenic Caves** to protect themselves from the enemy. That sparks the imaginations of young visitors!

The trail is filled with spots to explore and includes a few benches. You can easily recognize **George Washington**'s profile, naturally sculpted by the shapes in the wall above our heads. While we didn't see any bears in the **Bear's Cave**, a small bat escaped. My young speleologist just loved the **Fat Man's Misery** passage. Its 36-centimetre width, at its narrowest, is not for everyone. Fortunately, there is an alternative path that circumnavigates the rock.

The crossing of a 126-metre-long suspension bridge is included with the admission to the caves. It is a 10-min. walk away or a wagon ride takes you there on weekends (daily during the summer). It is 4 feet wide and offers lots of exciting sway in the middle, 25 metres above the valley and the stream. Wow!

Scenic Caves Nature Adventures	B-1 N-W of Toronto 2 hrs
· Collingwood (705) 446-0256 www.sceniccaves.com	

Schedule: Open daily from early May to end of October, at least 9 am to 5 pm (closes at 8pm in July and August).Last admission two hours prior to closing.

Admission: (including bridge) around $21/adults, $18/ seniors, $17/3-17 years, FREE 2 years and under. Extra for mini golf and gemstone mining (save money with their combos).

Directions: From Hwy 400 North, take exit #98/Hwy 26/27, then follow Hwy 26. At Collingwood, take Blue Mountain Rd., which will cross the Scenic Caves Road.

SCARBOROUGH BLUFFS PARK

No bluffing!

The stunning Scarborough Bluffs can reach 60 metres in height. In some places, the sandstone cliffs are beautifully carved in such a way to have inspired the name The Cathedrals.

Don't be put off by the simple look of the **Scarborough Bluffs Park**, as you can't readily see the many benches sitting at the back. Nothing announces the breathtakingly beautiful panoramic view you'll get from each one. Try them all!

Facing us, the lake spreads endlessly.

On the west side, we discover cliffs covered with trees, while the east side reveals the park's 400 acres, with its marina and the cliffs with their rocky peaks.

On the park's eastern side, there is a lovely path that borders the cliffs. There, I noticed, just before it heads north, another steeper path going down towards **Bluffers Park** (don't try this with young kids).

TIPS (fun for 5 years +)

• As you drive along Kingston Road, between Warden and Midland Roads, ask your young companions to spot the ten murals along the road. See if they can find the race car, ladies in gowns, a row boat and some tubas and drums. I particularly enjoyed the one with a row boat approaching the cliffs, while my young arts critic loved the military band.

• There is a good playground with big splash pad by the tennis courts on the eastern part of Scarborough Bluffs Park.

• There's a **Lick's Homeburgers** a couple of blocks west of Midland Ave. on the south side of Kingston (2383 Kingston Rd., (416) 267-3249).

• More about **Bluffer's Park** on p. 406.

Scarborough Bluffs Park	**D-3 East of downtown 35-min.**
• Scarborough Dial 311 (new service) www.toronto.ca/parks	

Schedule: Open year-round.
Admission: FREE.

Directions: From Midland Ave., just south of Kingston Rd., turn east on Kelsonia, then south on Scarboro Crescent. It ends by

the park. You'll find street parking nearby. (Check the hours!)

NEARBY ATTRACTIONS
Rosetta Gardens (5-min.) .... p. 264

SCARBOROUGH HEIGHTS PARK

Top to bottom

I was delighted when we discovered another way to explore the Bluffs from top to bottom: Scarborough Heights Park, just east of Rosetta Gardens!

The park doesn't look too appealing but as you get closer to the edge the gorgeous view of the lake emerges.

We took one of the makeshift trails leading down to the beach. (Boy! It was steep!) We loved it, but I suspected there was a safer way down. There is!

Between **Scarborough Heights Park** and **Rosetta Gardens** is a closed road accessible from a small opening to the

TIPS (fun for 4 years +)
• Keep some energy to go up the slope on your way back!
• Last time I did this stroll, I was with a friend and her dog. We wanted to combine this with a visit to nearby **Rosetta Gardens** but dogs are not allowed in the gardens. The locals are quite adamant that it stays that way.
• To get to this park, we choose to drive through The Beach on Queen Street and make a stop at **Remarkable Bean** (2242 Queen East) to grab a cup of coffee and some of their amazing salty muffins. The park is a 12-min. drive further east.

NEARBY ATTRACTIONS
Rosetta Gardens (5-min. walk)   p. 264

left of the gate. The paved road fades into a hard pressed dirt road following the shore.

When we visited it years ago, the path was bordered by huge boulders. Last summer, I saw that they had been used to create a few breakwalls and had been replaced by lovely tall grass.

We walked for 10 minutes and got a breathtaking view of the white cliffs, the best I have seen so far, completely surreal so close to Toronto.

Scarborough Heights Park
• Scarborough
Dial 311 (new service)
www.toronto.ca/parks

D-3
East
of downtown
35-min.

Schedule: Open year-round.
Admission: FREE.

Directions: From Kingston Road, turn right at Glen Everest Road southbound (just past **Rosetta Gardens**), then

right again on Fishleigh Drive. Look for the pumping station.

DORIS MCCARTHY TRAIL

Passage

The turquoise shade of Lake Ontario I saw, walking down the trail, was mesmerizing with the sun lighting thousands of gems on the water. Powerful waves were brushing the shore. Everything seemed so exotic. Then, it revealed itself at the foot of the trail, blending so lovingly with the surroundings: *Passage*, a work of art to celebrate a great artist.

The **Doris McCarthy Trail** started predictably, enclosed by tall thin trees blocking the view. But very soon it widened and cleared to reveal the sky. Then, I heard the whimsical sound of a small stream. Its bed eventually got two metres lower than the level of the trail, forming an irresistible corridor with large rock plates.

I returned later with the kids. We jumped into the bed of the small brook and started to hop from one plate to another over pockets of water. Down stream, the water pockets were getting larger and the plates fewer so we climbed back onto the trail. There's a beach, east of the trail.

By the shore, the *Passage* stands like the remnants of an ancient canoe or the rib cage of a strange aquatic mammal, overlooking the cliffs along the shore. It seems the perfect testimony to McCarthy, a renowned painter who has spent her life capturing the beauty of the light on Canadian landscapes and passing on that passion to students.

The trail was officially named after Doris in May 2001 and the sculpture by Marlene Hilton-Moore, was unveiled in October 2002 in her honour. She died at the ripe age of 100 in 2010.

This inspiring woman wrote a biography titled *A Fool's Paradise* (the name of the property she had on the Scarborough Bluffs). In it, she relates her journey from childhood, in the Beaches neighbourhood, to a mature painter on top of the bluffs.

TIPS (fun for 5 years +)

• It takes less than 15 minutes to go down the trail; more if you go the harder way, along the bed of the stream. BEWARE! There are thorns on the bushes bordering it. It takes longer to climb your way back up the trail, especially with tired children (not for under 8 years).

• It is better to keep dogs on leash. Coyotes have been seen in the area. Experts say they're not dangerous to humans if left alone but they can attack a dog if caught by surprise.

NEARBY ATTRACTIONS

Doris McCarthy Trail · Scarborough Dial 311 (new service) www.toronto.ca www.dorismccarthy.com	D-3 East of downtown 35-min.

Schedule: The trail is open year-round.
Admission: FREE.
Directions: Take Kingston Road eastward, turn south on Ravine Drive (which is named Bellamy Rd. on the north side of Kingston). You can park on the street past the sign marking the entrance to the trail off Ravine Drive.

MOUNT NEMO C.A.

Don't worry

From here, catch the most breathtaking views of the Niagara escarpment. Between the fragrant cedars, you can even admire the turkey vultures' wingspans while they silently glide at eye level, against a backdrop of checkered fields. Don't worry, there's very little chance that your little ones will fall from this 85-metre cliff without rails. The crevices will prevent this from happening!

Seriously, I was enthralled by the **Mount Nemo Conservation Area** when I realized that here, children could disco-ver the natural phenomena of cliffs and crevices. During our last visit, we accompanied two mountain climbers, aged four and five, who thoroughly enjoyed these famous crevices.

For little ones on foot or in strollers, there's a wide gravel path (**Bruce Side Trail**), a shortcut leading to the **Brock Harris** observation point in 10 minutes. From behind a solid, safe low wall, this belvedere offers a superb panorama. On a clear day, we can even make out the CN Tower, 60 kilometres away.

The crevices most accessible to young adventurers are located just left of the belvedere. The two we explored were about 30 metres from the cliff. Their narrow openings slope gently. Five metres down, their bottoms are lined with large stones. Natural footbridges cross over the crevices and give access to the edge of the cliff.

Beyond the first two crevices, the path sometimes gets as close as two metres from the escarpment, and crevices abound. Incredibly tortuous, criss-crossed by roots, lined with moss-covered rocks, with spots of light piercing through the trees, this trail is beautiful. Its course is clearly marked by white paint on tree trunks. It leads you back to the parking lot in an hour.

TIPS (fun for 4 years +)

• With children 7 years and older, I recommend you take the 2.3 km **North Loop** (the first one to the left when you walk on the gravel path by the parking lot, with orange markers). Kids will love to spot the **Bruce Trail**'s white marks (two marks on a tree means that there's a turn). The **South Loop** is less interesting. To download a map of the trails, go to Halton's website, select *Parks & Recreation* and click on *Maps and Trail Guides*.

• Accompanying adults who fear for their children's safety may want to stick to the first two crevices along the trail.

• Good walking shoes are a must; increased attention is required on certain slippery patches.

• You may use a stroller only on the gravel road leading to the belvedere.

NEARBY ATTRACTIONS
Crawford Lake C.A. (10-min.) .... p. 384
Kelso Beach (10-min.) .... p. 399

Mount Nemo Conservation Area
· Mount Nemo
(905) 336-1158
www.conservationhalton.on.ca

D-2 West of Toronto 45-min.

Schedule: Open year-round, 8:30 am to dusk.

Admission: $6.25/adults, $5.25/seniors, $4.50/5-14 years, FREE under 5 (around $5/vehicle in self-serve fee box when

no attendant on duty) or show same-day receipt from another conservation area in Halton area.

Directions: From QEW West, take exit #102/Guelph Line northbound. From Hwy 401 West, take exit #312/Guelph Line southbound. Turn east on Colling Road (north of Sideroad 2).

RATTLESNAKE POINT C.A.

Shortcut

I first visited Rattlesnake Point with an energetic mom carrying her chubby baby on her back. I didn't dare bring my five-year-old explorer close to 25-metre cliffs before having inspected the surroundings first. What's the verdict? Well... With a firm hand and a strong heart, you can take children along to see the panorama from Rattlesnake, extending as far as the eye can see. The area's many natural assets are worth it.

The cliffs are a five-minute walk away from the first parking lot, giving children instant gratification!

The first parking lot is accessible via a small, one-way loop road to the left.

TIPS (fun for 5 years +)

• To download a map of the trails, go to Halton's website, select *Parks & Recreation* and click on *Maps and Trail Guides*.
• You need good walking shoes. As soon as a child is less than ten metres away from the escarpment, you should hold his hand. A ratio of one adult per young child is advisable.
• Some readers told me they found small caves along the rock walls, barely noticeable through shady cracks.
• Depending on which way the wind blows, your nose may be bothered by a smell emanating from a nearby mushroom-growing farm. Had to mention it.
• A most moving detail seen on the course: a 40-cm-wide flat stone with a plaque mentioning *Baby Nina Anna Glinny Copas, June 23, 1996*. I was assured this child didn't fall off the cliff. It should still be there.
• Keep your Rattlesnake Point entrance ticket. During the same day, it gives you free access to **Crawford Lake** (see p. 384), ten minutes away.

The **Vista** trail which begins in that area leads you directly to an observation point and to the stairway.

The stairs lead down to the foot of the cliff. This gives visitors a totally different perspective of the rock. Furthermore, the rock formations in this area allow sturdy little explorers to climb enthusiastically, emulating the rock climbers who are most likely on the premises.

Rattlesnake Point is indeed a great spot for rock climbing (a waiver form must be signed). While walking along the path, you might spot seemingly abandoned backpacks, but look closely. You'll eventually notice brightly coloured ropes wrapped around trees, with climbers silently perched at their ends.

Before reaching the stairs, you'll notice a small path leading left to the nearby **Trafalgar** observation point. You'll find another viewing point overlooking **Nassagaweya Canyon**, a 15-min. walk away to the right (also accessible from the second parking lot).

You'd have to walk another half-hour beyond that to reach **Buffalo Crag** lookout, lengthening the return trek by about an hour. When you're accompanying kids, that's a serious consideration to ponder.

Rattlesnake Point Conservation Area • Milton **(905) 878-1147** www.conservationhalton.on.ca	**D-2** **West** **of Toronto** **50-min.**

 Schedule: Open year-round, from 8:30 am to dusk.
Admission: $6.25/adults, $5.25/seniors, $4.50/5-14 years, FREE under 5, (around $5/vehicle in self-serve fee box when no attendant on duty).
Directions: From Hwy 401 West, take exit #320/Hwy 25 northbound. Turn west on Campbellville Rd., south on Tremaine Road, west again on Steeles Avenue, then turn south on Appleby Line.

BOYD CONSERVATION AREA

Look Mom! Toads!

Some of the mature trees look impressive in these woods where the sun can't reach through the thick canopy of leaves. Many toads can be spotted on the dirt ground, as well as intriguing little man-made constructions from dead wood. The adventure begins!

A small playground greets us close to the parking lot at the end of the park's only road.

We walk back onto the road to the first entrance in the woods, and soon reach a fork. We opt for the left trail where our kids run wildly, until they are slowed down by a steep section with stairs made of running roots.

Soon, our little scouts are inspired by strange lean-tos made out of branches.

Building our own becomes our family project for a good half hour.

Back on this trail, we soon reach a picnic shelter. From there, we headed right onto the first little road along the river (no swimming!) and discovered a great picnic spot. (You can also walk back to the gravel road, towards the parking lot.)

While the trail is a bit confusing, there's no fear of getting lost! Simply stand still, and the sounds of traffic on Islington Avenue will remind you this oasis still sits in the middle of civilization.

TIPS (fun for 4 years +)

• We went with a couple of 3-year-olds, one of whom was scared by the darkness of the woods (made darker by cloudy skies). They both had a tough time managing the steeper sections of the trail, but really enjoyed the toads!

• Bug repellent is a must, especially after a rain fall.

• When in this area, we like to drop by **Humber Nurseries** (15-minute drive). This is the largest garden centre I have ever seen. They used to have a small butterfly conservatory but they closed it. It's still fun to see the life-size bronze statues and the aquatic section with some 40 little pools. Take Hwy 427 northbound, turn west on Hwy 7, then south on Hwy 50 (8386 Hwy 50, Brampton, (416) 798-8733, www.humbernurseries.com).

NEARBY ATTRACTIONS

Boyd Conservation Area
· Vaughan
(905) 851-0575
www.trca.on.ca

C-3
North of Toronto
30-min.

Schedule: Open end of April to early October, 9 am until dusk.
Admission: $6.50/adults, $5.50/seniors, FREE/15 years and under with accompanying adult.
Directions: On Islington Avenue, Vaughan. Take Hwy 427 North, exit Hwy 7 eastbound. Turn north on Islington Avenue.

KORTRIGHT CENTRE

Busy bees

As the kids get older, one visit after another, families discover new aspects of this dynamic centre with the help of over one hundred events staged throughout the year.

There are enough trails throughout **Kortright Centre** to overwhelm newcomers. Fortunately, the centre puts great effort into the design of relatively short, self-guided trails (such as the **Power Trip Trail** to admire the wind turbines).

You can download the trail maps from their website or ask the staff to point you in the right direction.

From December to February, greedy birds of all kinds visit the numerous feeders on certain trails.

In May, some trails offer the advantage of blossoming wild flowers. From June until September, a trail leads us in 15 minutes to the bee house on the site. (Kortright is home to a **Bee Space** which hosts over 2 million bees.) During some summer weekends, children can taste fresh honey and learn the bee dance.

There's also the trail to admire the fall colours in October. On occasion, we've also wandered on the wooden trails surrounding the centre (where nature gets a little more imposing) and other paths running through the fields to a pond.

In addition, kids can look at the interactive displays in the centre's exhibit section. Last time we visited, my small naturalist really appreciated the display challenging him to spy on more than 30 insects and animals camouflaged in a recreated microenvironment.

TIPS (fun for 4 years +)

• I prefer to visit the centre on weekends, when more volunteers are present and chances are the visitor centre will offer guided walks, demonstrations or crafts.
• Make sure you consult Kortright's section *What's On* on their website. It points out events of special interest to children. From dog sled races (end of January) to Halloween night hikes, activities vary from one year to the next.
• The March Break takes place during the **Kortright Maple Syrup Festival**. More about it on page 160.
• See **Four Winds Kite Festival** on page 192.

Kortright Centre for Conservation
• Woodridge
(905) 832-2289
or (416) 661-6600 ext. 5602
www.kortright.org

C-2
North
of Toronto
40-min.

 Schedule: Open year-round, 10 am to 4:30 pm.
 Admission: $6.50/adults, $5.50/seniors, FREE/15 years and under (extra fees during special events). Parking is $4.
 Directions: 9550 Pine Valley Drive, Woodridge. Take Hwy 400 North, exit Major Mackenzie Drive (exit # 35) westbound and follow the signs.

WHITCHURCH C.A.

Memories

When was the last time you saw a real frog? And a school of tiny fish? The intimate Whitchurch Conservation Area is a beautiful spot to enjoy the small joys of nature.

We stroll for five minutes on a trail before we reach a clearing. The pond is located down a small hill and we have to get closer to take it all in; it is beautiful! Tall trees and bushes on the other side of the water are reflected on the still pond's mirror-like surface. Everything is so quiet that we can hear the living creatures that surround us: the song of birds, the humming of insects and the funny "Daow!"

sound of a loud frog.

As we get even closer, the kids jump on a thin strip of sandy shore behind a wild flower bush. They are not a big threat to the small quicksilver fish they try to catch with their bare hands. BEWARE! The water is not tested.

Whitchurch Conservation Area
• Stouffville
(905) 895-1281
www.lsrca.on.ca

C-3
N-E
of Toronto
35-min.

Schedule: Open year-round.
Admission: FREE.
Directions: Aurora Road, Stouffville. From Hwy 404 North, take exit #45/Aurora Road eastbound. The park is on the south side, between Warden Avenue and Kennedy Road.

SCANLON CREEK C.A.

Nice boardwalk!

Swimming is not allowed anymore in the reservoir. Now, we go there for the lovely trail around the marsh, the boardwalk, the wildlife and the fall colours.

We prefer to park in the farthest parking lot, closer to **Scanlon Reservoir** and the boardwalk at the western end of what used to be the beach. The main trail runs over the reservoir on a boardwalk across marshland.

A side trail climbs up a forested hill and goes east towards a bridge crossing the creek, leading us back to the beach at its other end in less than 45 minutes. To download a trail map, go to *Maps* on their website, select *Explore our conservation areas* and click on **Scanlon Creek**.

Scanlon Creek Conservation Area
• Caledon
1-800-465-0437
www.lsrca.on.ca

C-2
N-W
of Toronto
45-min.

Schedule: Open year-round from 9 am to dusk.
Admission: FREE (donation box).
Directions: From Hwy 400 North, take exit #64/Simcoe Rd. 88 eastbound, turn north on County Rd. 4 (formerly Hwy 11), then east on 9th Concession.

BRUCE'S MILL C.A.

Conservation 101

The recreational pond created by the dam was affecting the natural watershed system, an important component of the Rouge River. So goodbye beach. Native grasses are overtaking the place.

When I did my third edition in 2004, we had lost the beach. As I went to print for the fourth edition in 2008, I learned that we'd lost the pond as well.

The good news was that we'd gained a private pool available for rental in this conservation area. It is near the **Beech Tree** area and is not open to the public but we can reserve it for $385 for 4 hours for parties of up to 50 people; the rental price includes the services of a lifeguard. (To rent, call 416-667-6295.)

The pond has been dried up to undertake a renaturalization project. Meanwhile, the conservation area continues to include trails which fork into several paths covered with boardwalks in their most spongy areas. They are regularly maintained but still, should you take the stroller along, be prepared for a few portages.

There's also a playground on the premises, between the **Spruce Tree** and the **Beech Tree** areas.

The park now hosts a driving range, past the gate on the left hand side. It is managed by a different administration (905-887-1072). If you're only going to the driving range, mention it at the gate so they don't charge you the admission cost.

TIPS (fun for 4 years +)

• Nearby, we visited **Lionel's Pony Farm and Petting Zoo** at 11714 McCowan Rd., north of 19th Ave. It costs $5 for a pony ride (only on Sundays, 12 noon to 5 pm, May to November 1st). It is free to visit their petting zoo from May to December, 9 am to dusk (10 am on Sundays) (905) 640-7669, www.lionelsfarm.com.

• More about **Bruce's Mill Maple Syrup Festival** on page 159.

Bruce's Mill Conservation Area
· Stouffville
(905) 887-5531
www.trca.on.ca

C-3
N-E
of Toronto
35-min.

 Schedule: Open late April to early October, 9 am to dusk (earlier in April and October). Also open during maple syrup time (see. 158).

 Admission: $6.50/adults, $5.50/seniors, FREE/15 years and under with accompanying adult.

Directions: On Stouffville Road, Stouffville. From Hwy 404 North, take exit #37/Stouffville Road eastbound (drive past Warden Avenue).

NEARBY ATTRACTIONS
Applewood Farm (10-min.) .... p. 156
Burd's Family Fishing (15-min.) .... p. 336

MOUNTSBERG WILDLIFE CENTRE

Wild!

I see a free-roaming rabbit by the trees and more farm animals at the base of Cameron Barn. Geese are flocking by the reservoir. After we've strolled through the Raptors Walkway including several cages with hawks and owls, we spot frogs by the reservoir. This conservation area is almost a zoo!

Many birds of prey are injured every year. Some fly through power lines or step in traps. Others are struck by vehicles or their nest is accidentally cut down by landowners. On signs, we could read about some birds' misfortunes: wing tip lost in wolf snare, permanent wing muscle deformity, etc.

The **Raptor Centre** at the **Mountsberg Wildlife Centre** site offers them a hospital with treatment and recovery areas. The birds we saw in the **Raptor Walkway** were non-releasable residents due to permanent injuries.

Weather permitting, the centre holds live raptor presentations in a 6000-square-foot netted outdoor enclosure. Check out the round windows on the curved wall surrounding the enclosure. They allow you to peek into more bird cages. Otherwise, presentations are held in the indoor theatre. We can also peek into the Raptors' hospital through a one-way viewing window. The exhibit gallery artistically displays many mounted specimens.

Another time we went, we were lucky enough to see the bisons staring at us impassively at the end of the **Wildlife Walkway**, usually far away in the fields. They now offer **bison rides** on the weekends in September and October, to allow us to see them better. (No, you won't be riding a bison, but you'll enter their enclosure on the back of a tractor, $3/adults, $2/kids.)

On our way back from the end of

the trail, we watched the ducks from the lookout blind by the reservoir (a good spot to see frogs).

The **Lookout Trail** is 6 kms long but the first observation tower overlooking the reservoir is less than 15 minutes away from the Visitor Centre. On our way, we notice **Swallowville**: a "village" of 25 birdhouses standing on poles. We walked 15 minutes more and could observe a flock of geese from a quiet spot by the shore.

Ten minutes further, we caught a trail to our right, going up a hill and back to our starting point. It offered a wide view of the area.

TIPS (fun for 3 years +)
• To download their map of trails, go to their website, click *Parks & Recreation*, then choose *Maps and Trail Guides*.
• The Visitor Centre includes displays and a gift shop (selling snacks, hot and cold beverages.
• During their **Fall Harvest** event (some time in the fall around Thanksgiving, check their website to confirm), there are horse-drawn wagon rides ($3/adults, $2/kids), craft activities for kids, a 5-acre maze, pumpkin carving, straw piles and more.
• You can pre-book as early as beginning of September for the very popular event **ChristmasTown.** On the weekends from the end of November to right before Christmas, the **MapleTowne** section is transformed into Santa's village. Includes Santa's visit, special wagon ride, crafts, cookies, etc., around $19/adults, $13/16 years and under. Note that the rest of the site is open to the public during that time.
• Ask about their **New Year's Eve Hoopla** on December 31, 6 pm to 9 pm (you'll need to pre-register). It includes scavenger hunt, bonfire and countdown.
• See **Mountsberg Maple Syrup Time** for **March Break** and **Easter** activities on page 162.

NEARBY ATTRACTIONS
Mount Nemo (15-min.) .... p. 238
Kelso Beach (15-min.) .... p. 399

Back to the Visitor Centre, we checked out their wonderful **Cameron Barn** which includes a play barn. It has a zip line, ladders, slides, climbing ropes and tons of wood shavings to soften the landings. This was heaven for the kids! I enjoyed the rays of sunlight shooting through the cracks of the wooden walls, like some laser beams.

Raptor Encounters are the new thing at Mounstberg. They're private 45-minute tours with special interaction with the birds of prey, offered three times a day on the weekends, year-round. It is better to call to reserve. The tours cost $35 plus tax, for a maximum of 3 persons.

The wagon rides ($3/adults, $2/ kids) are offered in the winter, from early January to Family Day in February, and during Christmas and March Break.

Mountsberg Wildlife Centre
• Milton
(905) 854-2276
www.conservationhalton.on.ca

D-2
West
of Toronto
45-min.

 Schedule: Open year-round, 8:30 am to at least 5 pm. Closes at 9 pm in the summer, varying earlier times the rest of the year.
Birds of Prey presentations: on weekends at 12 noon and 2 pm.
 Admission: $7.25/adults, $6.25/ seniors, $5/5-14 years, FREE under 5.
 Directions: From Hwy 401 West, take exit #312/Guelph Line southbound. Turn west on Campbellville Road, then north on Milborough Line, to the park's entrance.

ROCKWOOD C.A.

Stunning!

Rockwood Park Conservation Area is a stunningly beautiful place that offers a complete change of scenery, with ruins, caves and natural reservoirs.

I still can't get over it: so much beauty, so close to Toronto and open to everyone. We're lucky…

As you arrive, take the first path on your left after **Rockwood**'s entrance and

you will reach large ruins; the site's first attraction. It was under renovations in 2010 but is now accessible to the public again.

This old windmill stopped functioning in 1925. It burned down in 1967 and only a few pieces of the stone walls remain today as my aspiring historian discovered. He was captivated by these explanations while he pursued his explorations of the site.

Another road, accessible by stroller, borders the ruins. It leads to two large caves a half-kilometre further, which I found fascinating.

Daylight enters the grottos and children find them amusing to explore. Outside the caves, along the rock walls, make them shout and listen to the echo. It is amazing.

There's actually more to it than meets the eye! The conservation area has a network of twelve caves. It is one of the most extensive in Ontario and includes stalactites and stalagmites (but I don't think we can access these).

On the other side of the parking lot, you will discover a path that travels around over 200 potholes: Some kind of natural tanks of all sizes created by the abrasive whirlpools from glaciers that melted over 15,000 years ago.

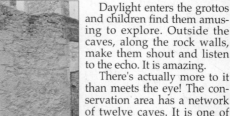

While you can't access the path with a stroller, it is nevertheless safe and inviting as it turns into small wooden bridges here and there. It borders the **Eramosa River**, a narrow brook that runs lazily amidst a fabulous landscape of rock and trees. Visitors explore it with canoes, kayaks and paddle

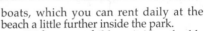

boats, which you can rent daily at the beach a little further inside the park.

With young children, it is preferable to take your car to reach this beach. There, you will also find a small snack bar and washrooms. The beach is really nice with pleasantly smooth sand.

TIPS (fun for 4 years +)
• The park includes 110 campsites.
• Bring a flashlight for the children to explore the small cave.
• There's a mini golf course on the site by the entrance ($5/adults, $2.50/kids, weather permitting).

NEARBY ATTRACTIONS
Ostrich Farm (10-min.) .... p. 74
Halton Railway (5-min.) .... p. 207

**Rockwood
Conservation Area**
· Rockwood
(519) 856-9543
1-877-558-4722
(camp reservation)
www.grandriver.ca

**D-2
West
of Toronto
60-min.**

Schedule: Open from end of April to mid-October, 8 am to 9 pm.

Admission: $5.50/adults, $2.75/6-14, FREE 5 years and under. Kayak, canoe and paddle boat rental is around $18 an hour.

Directions: From Hwy 401 West, take exit #312/Guelph Line northbound. Turn east on Hwy 7, then right on Falls Street.

SANDBANKS PROVINCIAL PARK

Three beaches, three worlds

As soon as my son and his friends reached the top of the golden dunes overlooking the lake 30 metres below, they playfully fell on their knees, thanking Heaven like grateful desert survivors who just realized they're saved.

The first time I visited **Sandbanks Park**, I literally missed **Dunes Beach**. We went straight to **Outlet Beach** and stayed there for the whole day. Upon returning later, I was better able to appreciate the uniqueness of **Sandbanks Beach** and Dunes Beach which remained to be explored.

Dunes Beach

Dunes Beach is definitely unique. As you observe the tall dunes bordering the left side of the beach adjacent to the parking lot, you realize that your eyes are not accustomed to this kind of panorama. You must get closer to the lake shore to better gauge the size of this natural playground.

You must then hike the highest peak of the dunes. The scenery is grandiose and conducive to daydreaming. Then, gravity calls and kids can't resist sliding down the silky slope all the way to the water. Others, of all ages, run wildly or simply tumble

down with glee. The water with sandy lake bottom is calling them.

Because of its location, the water of the beach at the foot of the dunes is the quietest of the Sandbanks. Located close to **West Lake**, it doesn't face **Lake Ontario** like the others (one has to consult a map to figure that one out). Well isolated, its water is warmer! The school of small fish moving at our feet and the tiny frogs in the reeds added to the kids' enjoyment.

You can walk a lot farther through the dunes along the lake. The further you go, the less crowded it gets, naturally. Don't forget bottles of water!

Outlet Beach

Outlet Beach's wonderfully fine and pebble-free sand is outstanding for building castles or digging a maze of interconnected waterways. Also, the very large area of shallow water along its shores is ideal for swimming toddlers, and great for parents' peace of mind.

The beach stretches along three kilometres, reaching depths of 30 metres in some places, which the surrounding tall trees can't completely shade.

Its name changes to **Camper's Beach** where it meets the **River Outlet** (which you can cross by foot). There's a specially designated off-leash pet area nearby!

TIPS (fun for all ages)

• Last time I checked, those who wanted to go to **Dunes Beach** didn't follow the signs leading to the park's main gate. Instead, they stayed on Road 12 to reach Dunes Beach's day-use parking lot and payed the admission at the automatic machine (accepts coins and credit cards). I hope this is still true. It saved us time!

• The beautiful semi-wild **Outlet River Campground** has 270 campsites. **Cedars Campground**, set further back from Outlet Beach has 190 more sites. **Richardson's Campground** sits in a young and sparse forest near Sandbanks Beach, and offers less privacy than the two other sites.

• A visitor centre and a nature shop are located at the entrance of **Outlet Beach**, close to Parking lots #1 and #2. This beach is well outfitted with picnic tables; you can easily get a hold of one before 11 am. A well-stocked snack bar is also located near Parking lot #7. There's another one at **Dunes Beach**.

• We overnighted at the **Bloomfield Inn**, a motel located in Bloomfield. A room with two double beds costs $115/double occupancy in summertime with a cost of $20 per person for additional guests (children under 10 years old stay for free). The motel belongs to the owners of **Angeline**, a French gastronomic restaurant located on the same property. We also booked babysitting services to fully enjoy a great meal. See www.angelines-restaurantinn.com or call 1-877-391-3301.

• The first time we were in the area, we visited Picton's **Birdhouse City**. It is actually a vast park with a few trees here and there and over 100 birdhouses mounted on poles. Most are miniature reproductions of historic buildings. The **Friends of Birdhouse City** have built, and tried to maintain the houses (they are currently actively seeking volunteers to restore the little houses in real need of a make-over).

From Main St. in Picton, take Union Street, it becomes County Rd. 8; the park is on the right hand side.

Sandbanks Beach

Sandbanks Beach offers 8 kilometres of sand; an obvious favourite for hikers. Lovely trails surround the slopes on these shores.

Here, the beach is not as wide as that of Outlet Beach. With a few pebbles here and there, its water is a bit deeper and nice waves usually form, greatly pleasing the young swimmers.

Last time we went, end of June, early

July, hundreds of small silver fish were washed up on the shore, a natural phenomena I was told occurs often at this time of the year. (If you think it would gross you out, call the park to see if it is currently going on.)

NEARBY ATTRACTIONS
The Big Apple (80-min.) .... p. 67

HILTON FALLS C.A.

Falls 101

We're on the way back. I'm puffing like an old locomotive while I pull my precious load, comfortably seated in the red wagon. I then hear his voice, somewhat concealed by the noise of wheels crunching on the gravel, chanting: "I think I can, I think I can." I burst out laughing when I recognize the chant from *The Little Engine that Could*. Those who know the classic tale will smile as I did when faced with my son's empathy. This goes to show how our children never miss a beat when we take them on outings!

The falls are a 30-minute walk away from the parking lot (follow the **Hilton Falls Trail**). With good shoes, you can easily get close to the falls (there may be a cold shower included!). Here and there, makeshift bridges are made of tree trunks. If little explorers are able to cross

the river on these, they're big enough to romp about in this natural playground: a cave, rock climbing and the discovery of a "secret" passage inside the ruins (even so, tell them to be careful on the sawmill wall).

Go for a short walk on the trail downstream from the falls. A huge round pothole was formed 12,000 years ago by the movement of rocks on the riverbed. It's quite safe for children to go down into it. However, they (and you) should be vigilant in areas closer to the cliff's edge.

From the belvedere in front of the falls, an unexpected view reveals the ruins of a 19th century sawmill. Further ahead, along the **Bruce Trail**, stairs lead to the riverbank.

To return, I recommend you find your way to the trail with red circles (**Red Oak Trail**). It will lead you to the parking lot, crossing a small river that flows down into a wide reservoir along the way. To download a map of the trails, go to their website, select *Parks & Recreation* and click on *Maps and Trail Guides*.

TIPS (fun for 4 years +)

• During spring and summer, blackflies might swoop down on visitors as soon as they stop on bare trails, bring insect repellent. They're nearly absent close to the falls and in the woods.

• The gravel paths are wide and stroller-accessible except for the first hundred metres of the yellow trail going up hill.

• There are single tracks for mountain bikes (helmet mandatory).

• In wintertime, the falls surrounded by ice make for an original family outing. There's also cross-country skiing.

NEARBY ATTRACTIONS

Hilton Falls Conservation Area
• Campbellville
(905) 854-0262
www.conservationhalton.on.ca

D-2
West
of Toronto
50-min.

Schedule: Open year-round from 8:30 am until dusk.

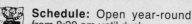
Admission: $6.25/adults, $5.25/ seniors, $4.50/5-14 years (around $7 for mountain bikes).

Directions: From Hwy 401 West, take exit #312/Guelph Line northbound. Turn east on Campbellville Road. The park is on the north side.

WEBSTER'S FALLS C.A.

Double feature

A majestic gorge and powerful falls, plus the rainbow effect, the mist on our face and the gorgeous trail: I did not expect such a wholesome program! I'll just have to go by the usual cliché: This is the best-kept secret in the region.

Let your ears guide you to the water from the parking lot (but don't miss the tiny cemetery nearby to find out who the falls are named after).

You'll need to cross the cobblestone bridge to get a good view from the top and then to get to the trail leading down the falls. The adventure starts with the stairs. They were steep and slippery when we visited but will be refurbished soon.

I just love the thundering noise of falls, and this is a good 79-foot one, with the bonus of a full rainbow when you look at the right place at the right time. The beauty of the trail bordering the river is that it is at the water level and the river cascades and dances all along.

We walked for 30 minutes before heading back (to maintain the children's momentum to the end).

A small sign from the parking lot indicated a trail leading to **Tew's Falls**. We were told it would take approximately 20 minutes to reach it but the kid had had it by that time so we drove to get there.

Many written sources described it as towering 41 metres, "only a few metres short of Niagara Falls"... So I went back a week later. It was tall indeed but only a metre wide! It's probably better in the spring.

TIPS (fun for 4 years +)

• The trail to **Tew's Falls** runs along the escarpment. To download a map of the trails, go to **www.waterfalls.hamilton.ca** (a website on Hamilton's best falls) and select *Self Guided Walks*.

• We were told the site is beautiful in the winter when part of the waterfalls are frozen and sparkling.

NEARBY ATTRACTIONS	
Dyment's Farm (15-min.)	p. 149
Christie Lake (5-min.)	p. 401

Spencer Gorge/ Webster's Falls C.A.
• Dundas
(905) 628-3060
www.conservationhamilton.ca

E-2
S-W
of Toronto
60-min.

Schedule: Open year-round.
Admission: $6 per vehicle.
Directions: From QEW/Hwy 403, exit at Hwy 6 North then turn west on Hwy 5. Turn south on Brock Road, and east on Harvest Road. Turn south on Short Road (it becomes Fallsview Road) to get to **Webster's Falls**, or drive a bit further on Harvest Road to reach **Tew's Falls**.

ALBION FALLS

Rock and roll!

You could go the easy way and use the stairs for instant gratification... or build your kids' anticipation (and their muscles) by taking a 30-minute upstream trail to reach the impressive falls.

The 10-minute trail by the parking lot took us down to the **Red Hill Creek**. We could have walked across the creek to explore the large boulders but started instead to walk upstream into a luscious ravine. Previous visitors had cut trails along the stream, some of them steep.

As I was wondering what age recommendations I would make for this attraction, we came across a

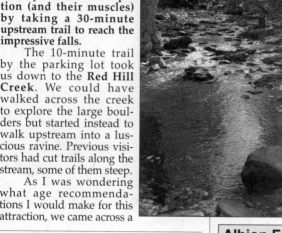

brave father and his three young "entomologists" hopping across the creek, taking advantage of the rocks revealed by the lower level of the water during the fall season.

After a 20-minute walk in the gorgeous forest, accompanied by the whimsical sound of the water, we finally saw the falls through the trees. Only once we reached past those trees could we appreciate the 18-metre-wide body of water cascading down the 19 metres of natural stairs. Wow!

You realize how impressive the scale is when you actually see someone walking on the humongous boulders at the foot of the falls.

We noticed a young man rummaging through some rusting metal junk unfortunately gathered by the boulders. I assumed he was one of those artists using recycled material for weird installations. Turns out he was just a nature lover understanding the value of small gestures, picking up one piece of junk every time he goes on a trail. Inspiring, isn't it?

Stairs took us to the top of the falls where we followed a small trail along the road leading back to the parking lot in 5 minutes.

TIPS (fun for 6 years +)
• Want to do it the easy way? There's a parking lot in **Upper King's Forest Park** by Mountain Brow Blvd., on the west side of the falls. It's just a few minutes walk from the stairs located by Albion Falls.
• Good shoes are a must.
• To download a map of the trails, go to **www.waterfalls.hamilton.ca** (a website on Hamilton's best falls) and select *Self Guided Walks*.

NEARBY ATTRACTIONS
Canadian Warplane (15-min.) ..... p. 194
Children's Museum (15-min.) ...... p. 218

Albion Falls
• Hamilton
(905) 525-2181
www.
conservationhamilton.ca

E-2
S-W
of Toronto
60-min.

Schedule: Open year-round.
Admission: FREE.

Directions: From Hwy 403 towards Hamilton, take Lincoln Alexander Pkwy east (for about 9 kms), exit at Gage Street, go northbound, then east on Mohawk Road until you reach Mountain Brow Blvd. The parking lot is past Pritchard Road.

NIAGARA FALLS

Fall for them

A couple of kilometres upstream along the Niagara Parkway, we observe the large cascades as they roar into the falls. Through the car's open window, we can hear their thundering sound and feel a mist blowing towards us.

Even though it is midweek on the summer afternoon we visit, we are caught in the long line-ups, and the closest available parking space, **Rapidsview Parking**, is located on Upper Rapids Drive, two kilometres away from the **Niagara Falls**.

Don't worry if it happens to you, it does not mean you will have to walk that distance or watch it all from your car! From the Rapidsview Parking ($10/day), a free shuttle will take you to the falls.

If you buy the **Peoplemovers** all-day pass, it will allow you to travel all day long in the air-conditioned buses going up and down the Niagara Parkway. They are simply the best way to enjoy the area if you don't find parking right away and kids love to ride them.

Upstream

Upstream from the falls is the **Floral Showhouse**. Its admission is free, with free-flying exotic birds. It is a good observation game for the children to spot them among the colourful plants. (They put together eight annual flower shows.)

A five-min. walk away upstream leads you to the **Dufferin Islands** (eleven little islands linked by small bridges).

We got close enough to touch the dozens of wild ducks swimming around the bridges in the fall season.

At the Falls

The **Table Rock** (which was fully renovated a few years ago) is located right at the falls, and so is the attraction **Journey Behind the Falls**.

My children's favourite part of this attraction is the ride in the elevator down to the tunnels. You may observe the white wall of water falling from a terrace or through the viewing portals.

The Fury is the latest big attraction in the area. I have not had the chance yet to visit it but I expect a lot from this 360° theatre experience reproducing the creation of the falls, where the temperature drops and we feel the mist and snow fall (See www.niagarasfury.com for details, around $15/adult.)

Elements on the Falls, the new restaurant at Table Rock, still offers the best view of the falls from panoramic windows. The price range is a bit higher than before ($8/dessert, $5/cappuccino) and the menu less interesting for the kids (no fast food). Fortunately, they've built a two-level viewing gallery within Table Rock so eveyone can still admire the view.

A ride on the **Maid of the Mist**, a bit further down the river, is your surest bet to get in the middle of the real action.

"Maid of the Shower" would be a more accurate name for this boat. Don't go expecting not to get wet! After my ride, I started to notice all the visitors with wet pant legs (where the ponchos end).

You don't get to see much of the falls as the boat approaches them (because your eyes are shut to avoid the water spray). But you get to hear them pretty well. Our greatest surprise was the beautiful rainbow above our heads. Later on, as we took the 15-minute walk back to the Table Rock, we could again admire a rainbow. It was also the best spot to admire the evening lights on the falls.

The **Incline Railway** ride linking the Table Rock to upper Fallsview area costs $2.50. It is a big hit with the children! The Peoplemover Buses all-day pass also gives access to the Incline Railway for the entire day. Note that this ride and the Peoplemovers buses are not wheelchair accessible.

Downstream

I think the visit to the **White Water Walk** (also called the **Great Gorge Adventure**) a few kms down the river is under-rated. It is usually less busy than the other attractions and shows you the river from a different but equally powerful point of view.

The elevator ride down to the dark and cool tunnel is as much fun for the kids as the one at Journey Behind the Falls.

It leads us to a board-walk by the spectacular rapids. The river, being 38 metres (125 feet) deep at this level, makes the water gush down in large impressive swirls at the speed of over 60 km/h. Our 15-minute walk on the boardwalk was beautiful, safe and refreshing (in mid-summer), without soaking us, and the kids enjoyed climbing up the giant boulders.

The **Whirlpool Aero Car** is a 10-minute walk further north from the gorge. This car hangs 76 metres (250 feet) above the river. The track cable system that moves the car was invented by a Spanish engineer also responsible for the world's first computer (Leonardo Torres Quevedo). I have not tried it, but from what I saw, young kids will only have an obstructed view through the railing.

Last year, I explored the **Niagara Glen** (see p. 307) which leads us down 60 metres (200 feet).

Bikers and hikers can admire the gorge from the bike trail running along the road. My husband has often cycled from **Niagara-on-the-Lake** to Niagara Falls and back with his friends. They all agree the 4-hour ride is beautiful (even better when topped with a drink on a patio in Niagara-on-the-Lake.)

Dry fun

The area is chock-a-block with attractions of all kinds in and around Clifton Hill Centre Street. **Guinness World of Records** (www.guinnessniagarafalls.com) and the **Ripley's Believe It or Not Museum** (www.ripleysniagara.com), despite some displays of question-able taste, are likely to strike children's imaginations, whether with "the biggest man in the world" or a sculpture made with one grain of rice. One! (Some displays of nature's anomaly can disturb kids under seven.)

Visits to the non-interactive wax and horror museums are too short for their cost.

Last time we went, the kids enjoyed **BrickCity** (4943 Clifton) featuring impressive constructions all made by one single guy out of the kids' favourite blocks, including a model of the falls!

Don't miss the huge marble ball and the giant chair by the entrance of the Guinness World of Records.

TIPS (fun for 4 years +)

• The first time we went to the falls, we visited the **Niagara Falls Imax Theatre**, at the end of the day, to watch the movie *Legends and Daredevils*. I wish we had started our outing with it. The legends, accidents and stories of daredevils, which were re-enacted on the huge screen, shed a new light on the falls. The daredevil artefacts shown in the lobby and the museum are fascinating when seen after the movie (6170 Fallsview Blvd., 1-866-405-4629, www.imaxniagara.com).

• Wondering how the falls generate electricity? Tons of water are channelled through underground tunnels on each side of the river, into huge reservoirs behind the power plants downstream from the whirlpool. **Sir Adam Beck 2 Generating Station** is open for tours to explain it all ($9.50/adults, $6.25/6-12 years old).

• No need to wait in line-ups. You can buy timed tickets in advance at the attractions' ticket booths and show up 15 minutes before the booked time slot.

• My 3-year-old was a bit distressed by the showers of water falling over her on the **Maid of the Mist**. Kids normally scared by thunderstorms will probably not enjoy this noisy attraction. I don't recommend you go on with a stroller either.

• There usually are some **firework** displays between mid-May and early October, including **Victoria Day**, **Memorial Day**, **Canada Day**, **Independance Day** and **Simcoe Day** but they could not confirm what the schedule will look like for 2011. The falls are illuminated at night year-round. Check their website under *Things To Do* and click *Attractions* for the fireworks and illumination schedules.

• The **Rainforest Café** and the **Hard Rock Café** are both in the middle of the action and great restaurants that the kids will enjoy. Check *Restaurants* under **www.cliftonhill.com**.

• For the best value in the summer, go to the all-you-can-eat breakfast/lunch/dinner buffet at **Almacs Buffet** (5435 Ferry Street, 905-357-6227 (seasonal number), go up on Clifton Hill, then left on Victoria., it becomes Ferry St.). With a 200-seat patio, kids rates and a really wide selection, everyone in our gang of 10 was happy (not for foodies though). It is just on the way out of Niagara, west of Stanley Ave. leading to Hwy 420.

NEARBY ATTRACTIONS
Bird Kingdom (2-min.) .... p. 79
Marineland (10-min.) .... p. 80

• Find out about their **Niagara Falls & Great Gorge Package** including admission to Journey Behind the Falls, White Water Walk, Maid of the Mist and The Fury (you don't have to see them all in one day) with Peoplemovers all-day pass for two days. On their website, go to *Things To Do* and click *Experience* for details.

• Read about our stay at the **Skyline Inn** on p. 431, to take advantage of the amazing indoor **Fallsview Waterpark**.

• See **Butterfly Conservatory** on p. 78.

• See **Niagara's Winter Festival of Lights** on p. 179.

Niagara Parks Commission
· Niagara Falls
1-877-642-7275 (info line)
www.niagaraparks.com

E-4
Niagara
Region
90-min.

Niagara Parks Attractions Schedule: Journey Behind the Falls is open year-round. Most other main attractions are open at least from early April to late October. All are at least open from 10 am to 5 pm. **Peoplemovers:** From mid April to late October. See website for exact dates and times. **Rapidsview Parking Lot:** Open weekends only mid-May to June, then daily until Labour Day, and back to weekends only until late October.

Admission: All attractions are FREE for children 5 years and under. **Journey Behind the Falls** is $13.25/adults, $8.65/6-12 years; **Maid of the Mist** is around $15/adults, $9/6 to 12 years; **White Water Walk** is $9.50/adults, $6.25/6-12 years; **Whirlpool Aero Car** is $12.25/adults, $7.95/6-12 years; **Sir Adam Beck 2 Generating Station** is $9.50/adults, $6.25/6-12 years; **Peoplemovers** all-day pass is around $7/adults, $5/6 to 12 years.

Directions: From QEW towards Niagara, take Hwy 420 (The Falls), continue on Falls Avenue. Keep going to get to the falls or turn right at Clifton Hill, to be in the middle of the dry action.

To Rapidsview Parking Lot: Take QEW west towards Niagara and Fort Erie (but don't follow Hwy 420!). Then take McLeod Road exit (it becomes Marineland Pkwy). Turn left at Upper Rapids Boulevard and follow the All Day Park signs.

HIGH FALLS

Small adventure

My son just loves exploring natural wonders full of nooks and crannies. High Falls is filled with these.

First, we tried to get as close as we could to the thundering **High Falls**. The powerful white body of water was fascinating to my then 5-year-old. In some spots, we had to jump more than one metre down onto lower rocks, to get closer.

All around the park, the ground is covered with big slabs of rock. Vegetation has tried to grow over and hold on to as much as it could with the help of really long running roots.

We slid down a steep hill filled with roots and followed a natural trail towards the water. We walked over a couple of miniature, natural bridges and small strips of rock with water on each side. It added to the feeling of adventure.

We explored the surroundings of a stream running into the woods. Part of the stream had enough water for it to expand into a nice wading pool among the trees. I wanted to stop for a while to listen to the musical sound of the water flowing over the stones, but my son felt like a pioneer, stick in hand and wanted to keep going.

TIPS (fun for 5 years +)

• The rocks and ground can be quite slippery. Bring rubber boots or shoes to better explore the stream.

• Bring insect repellent if you want to explore the stream.

• The **Trans-Canada Trail** reaches High Falls. There is now a bridge running over High Falls offering a great panorama.

NEARBY ATTRACTIONS
Santa's Village (20-min.) .... p. 50

High Falls
· Bracebridge
(705) 645-5264

**Off the map
North**
of Toronto
2 1/4 hrs.

 Schedule: Open year-round.
Admission: FREE.
Directions: North of Bracebridge. Take Hwy 400 North then follow Hwy 11 northbound. Take exit #193 and drive westbound over Hwy 11, enter **High Falls Resort** to your right, then drive up the hill.

WONDERS OF THE EARTH

A real gem

This gem show has been organized by the Gem & Mineral Club of Scarborough for the last 35 years. It is a great starting point for young geologists.

My kids were thrilled by the **Kids Quarry** where we could get a sandbag of minerals for a small fee. They would dump its content into a sifter and discover at least 6 specimens. A little plastic pouch included contained labels to identify the rocks. There were also hands-on soapstone carving and fossil preparation.

The show is held in a large gym. Many members exhibit their collections. You can watch lapidary work and jewelry making, gem cutting, soapstone carving and fossil preparation.

There's also a **Mineral Identification Table** where your child can take the "precious" stone he found for the experts to identify. But maybe he doesn't really want to know...

There were many 50¢ to $1 minerals to choose from. My daughter went for a $2 fabric surprise bag holding three stones. We could buy strands of fresh water pearls for $5.

TIPS (fun for 6 years +)

• To find a local gem club, go to the website of the **Central Canadian Federation of Mineralogical Societies** (www.ccfms.ca) and click on *Member Clubs*.

NEARBY ATTRACTIONS
Scarborough Bluffs (15-min.) ...... p. 235
Warden Woods Park (15-min.) .... p. 464

Wonders of the Earth
• Scarborough
(905) 396-4043
(community centre)
www.scarbgemclub.ca

D-3
N-E
of downtown
25-min.

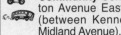

Schedule: On the second weekend after Labour Day, Saturday, 10 am to 6 pm, Sunday, 11 am to 5 pm.
Admission: $5/adult, $1/child.
Directions: Don Montgomery Community Centre, 2467 Eglinton Avenue East, Scarborough (between Kennedy Road and Midland Avenue).

ROCK POINT PROVINCIAL PARK

On this rock, I will build... a park

Photo: Courtesy of E. Ritson

Romantic picnic lovers and those longing for Cuban sand, stay away from Rock Point Park. Make way for miniature paleontologists, ornithologists, pebble collectors... and arachnid enthusiasts.

When you arrive, ask at the gate for the trail leading to the fossils. On our visit, we parked not too far from a beaten dirt path which led us to **Lake Erie** (where we intended to picnic). What I saw was quite unexpected!

A rock floor covered the whole ribbon of "beach". The breaking waves were loaded with slimy moss and gave off a fishy smell. There was also the odour of the stagnant water evaporating from various natural basins carved in stone.

We had to choose between mosquito bites under shady trees and sunburn in open areas. At any rate, rock spiders heavily patrol the place.

Visitors who decide not to leave will be rewarded. From up close, we noticed that the fissures trapping the stagnant water were covered with fossils, dating back 350 million years!

Three-year-old tots aren't impressed by this discovery, but it will surely have an effect on older kids, especially if you do research before the outing. Personally, I was fascinated.

While I was examining the rocks, my two companions settled into a small, pebble-lined cove, fairly moss-free, where they "fished" with sticks for quite a while. Later, we walked to a viewing tower. We then drove to the beach on the other side of the park where beautifully rounded pebbles formed the lake bed.

TIPS (fun for 4 years +)

• There's a nicer sandy beach by the campgrounds.

• Beach shoes are helpful to deal with the pebbles rolling under your feet in the water at the day-use beach. The green space adjoining this beach by the parking lot is too bare for my liking; not what I would expect in a provincial park.

• There are 178 campsites. They are surrounded by quite a bit of greenery. Campers have a direct view of neighbours camping across the road, but it's far from the sardine can concept found in several campgrounds.

Rock Point Provincial Park
· Dunnville
(905) 774-6642
www.ontarioparks.com

Off the map
S-W
of Toronto
2 1/4 hrs

Schedule: Open mid-May until mid-October.
Admission: $10.75-$19.50/ vehicle pass.
Directions: Take QEW towards Niagara, exit Hwy 20/Centennial Park southbound (it becomes Hwy 56). Take Hwy 3 eastbound through Dunville, continue on Main Street, then follow the park signs.

TORONTO MUSIC GARDEN

On a fun note

It seems nobody thinks to walk west of the popular Harbourfront Centre so this part of the water's edge feels like an oasis in the midst of the city.

The garden is developed following a dance theme. Accessible from Spadina, we first encounter the **Minuet**, impressive with beautiful hand-made ornamental steel adorning its rotunda.

Walking down from the rotunda (kids will actually run), we reach a gentle slope of grass broken with grass stairs forming a sort of curved amphitheatre facing the water. At the foot stands a small stone stage. This whole section is called the **Gigue**. Both the Gigue and the Minuet are the chosen stages for dance and music shows during the summer.

The **Sarabande** offers a small spiraling trail surrounded by Evergreen trees, turning this corner into a nice little retreat.

TIPS (fun for 4 years +)

• The **Marina Quay West** located at 539 Queen's Quay, near the garden's western entrance, offers underground parking at $7-$10. It is the place to rent $7 audio wands for a 70-min. self-guided tour of the garden, (416) 203-1212.
• Harbourfront is producing the **Summer Music in the Garden** series. For a performance schedule, go to their website, select *The Waterfront*, click on *Parks*, then *Toronto Music Garden*.
• It takes less than 5 minutes to walk along the garden on Queen's Quay West. **Harbourfront Centre** is a 10-min. walk east of the garden's entrance. More about what's around Harbourfront on p. 24.

The **Courante** stands out with its tall Maypole spinning in the wind, competing with the CN Tower against the sky. It is surrounded by luscious borders of flowers and tall grass.

Numerous granite boulders greet us in the **Prelude** section. It is also a good spot to observe the planes taking off and landing at the airport across the water.

If you rent the audio wand for a self-guided tour, you'll hear candid comments from the kids of a neighbourhood school who were involved in the landscaping of the garden. You'll also be able to hear music segments associated with the different dances.

Just east of the **Toronto Music Garden** lies the **Spadina Quay Wetland**, an old parking lot transformed into a small marsh.

Toronto Music Garden
(416) 973-4000
www.harbourfrontcentre.com

D-3
Downtown Toronto
5-min.

Schedule: Open year-round. Guided, self-guided audio tours and shows offered from early June to late September.
Admission: FREE, $7/audio wand rental.
Directions: Runs along Queen's Quay between Lower Spadina Avenue and Bathurst Street, Toronto.

NEARBY ATTRACTIONS
Little Norway Park (10-min. walk) p. 324
Canoe Landing Park (5-min. walk) p. 421

ALLAN GARDENS CONSERVATORY

An oasis in the city

I tell my 3-year-old son we'll be visiting a greenhouse. "Is the house all painted in green?" he asks incredulously. "No, it's a house made out of glass and full of green plants that believe it's summer all year long!" I reply.

Talk about a greenhouse effect! Five buildings with large windows, covering over 16,000 sq. feet are filled with plants for all occasions. Some are filled with exhibits which gradually change into new ones according to the plants' life cycles.

Enter through the building with the high palm tree filled dome. Go right to enter a tropical hothouse with hibiscus set amidst a tapestry-like leafy backdrop. Beyond it, a large selection of hairy, prick-ly, and fluffy cactuses await (you will want to touch them).

Retracing your steps to the other side of the dome, you'll find a cooler space with a small waterfall and a gold fish pond, with its penny-carpeted bottom, at the foot of a statuette.

The tropical mood is definitely on with its hot and humid climate in the next room. Here, orchids bloom against the roar of water going through a paddle wheel attached to a small house. In winter, you can admire shapes covered with flowers installed amidst hundreds of poinsettias and palm trees.

During the **Spring Flower Show** (mid-February to end of April), a new selection of flowers adds its sweet perfume to the conservatory. We visited on an early Easter and we were struck by the sweet bouquet and the visual richness of the settings. What a contrast with those of wintertime! The **Summer Flower Show** goes from early June to end of September, followed by the **Mums Show** (starts one week before Thanksgiving for 4-6 weeks).

TIPS (fun for 4 years +)

• We played at guessing from which plant the fallen leaves belonged. A fun initiation to botany and observation game.
• The park includes two **off-leash** enclosed areas for big and small dogs, overlooked by two giant watchdogs.
• More on their **Christmas Flower Show** on p. 173.
• **Chew Chew's Diner** is a good all-day breakfast joint with a fun train theme, a 2-min. walk east (186 Carlton, www.chewchewsdiner.com).

Allan Gardens Conservatory (416) 392-7288 www.toronto.ca/parks	D-3 Downtown Toronto 15-min.

 Schedule: Open daily, year-round, 10 am to 5 pm.
 Admission: FREE.
Directions: 19 Horticultural Avenue, Toronto (south of Carlton, between Jarvis and Sherbourne Streets).

NEARBY ATTRACTIONS

MOUNT PLEASANT CEMETERY

The circle of life

A smart girl had just concluded the dispute she had been having with my son by striking with an ultimate, irrefutable argument, that had nothing to do with their quarrel: "Oh yeah? Well, girls live longer than boys!"

"Is it true?" asked my anguished son, who was shattered when I confirmed this dire statistic. He was ready for a visit to the cemetery to help us approach this delicate but very natural topic in a more realistic (but non creepy) fashion.

Few people realize that the **Mount Pleasant Cemetery** is far from being sinister. The setting is so pretty, it attracts walkers, joggers and cyclists.

Sculptures adorning numerous graves give the visit an interesting cultural quality.

The cemetery is located between Yonge and Bayview, north of Moore Avenue. Paved roads criss-cross the site and

cars can stop wherever they please. A tunnel allows vehicles to circulate under Mt. Pleasant Road, which separates the cemetery into two sections.

After reading for my son a few dates written on gravestones, I was able to discuss with him the random nature of death. Here, parents bid farewell to their child; there, a woman said good-bye to her husband; farther away, an entire family was buried a long time ago.

Many tombstones even show a picture of the deceased. This confers a more concrete image to the experience. The cemetery really is a fertile ground for discussion.

TIPS (fun for 6 years +)

• **Davisville Subway Station** is just a 5-min. walk from the cemetery's northern entrance at Yonge (see p. 471).

• There's an intriguing stone garden east of the Moore Street pedestrian entrance.

• A great variety of trees can be found in this cemetery. During the fall, it becomes a great harvesting ground for young leaf collectors.

Mount Pleasant Cemetery

D-3
North
of downtown
20-min.

Schedule: Open daily, year-round from 8 am to 8 pm.
Admission: FREE.

Directions: 375 Mount Pleasant Road, Toronto. You can drive through the entrance off Yonge and the two entrances east and west of Mount Pleasant Road, south of Davisville Avenue.

TORONTO BOTANICAL GARDEN

It has blossomed!

A 5,000-square-foot glass pavilion and a 4-acre garden near Edwards Gardens have turned the place into a real botanical garden. What an elegant setting!

The building gracefully mingles with the landscaped surroundings, the architectural form of the plants blending with the natural texture of the walls.

A wall of water welcomes us by the main entrance of the building. We explore it on both sides which leads us to the **Floral Hall Courtyard**. We can see the shadow of the trees through the acid-etched glass. It is like being in our own little Japanese world.

A stone bridge runs over a small canal by a waterfall in the **Garden Halls Terrace**. From there, we can see the plants on the sloping green roof and the **Spiral Mound**, a viewing platform three metres above the ground.

This section of the garden is so popular with kids (it allows a 360-degree perspective of the site and a view of the whimsical **Knot Garden**) that it was under renovations during my last visit, to make it sturdier. (It's OK now.)

Five minutes down the west side of **Edwards Gardens**, past the weeping willow and the small valley, you'll find a **Teaching Garden** open to the public when not in use for the programs. It includes a giant butterfly sundial.

Behind the **Carpet Bed Garden** by the parking lot, you can access the **Wilket Creek** ravine.

TIPS (fun for 5 years +)

• Grab a visitor's map inside the main building to better enjoy the stroll.

• You'll need to register in advance for their programs or family events but they offer drop-in storytime in their library on Mondays at 11 am for toddlers.

• **Wilket Creek**'s wide paved trail starts at the southern edge of Edwards Gardens. Along its course, you'll find a few benches, a singing river flowing underneath several small bridges, beautiful undergrowth facing the river as well as 30-metre-tall maple trees and several other species of deciduous trees that take on magnificent hues in autumn. Beware, cyclists sometimes rush through the trail. Within 30 minutes, you'll reach the road going through **Sunnybrook Park** (where you can find washrooms). You can continue your stroll on **Serena Gundy Park** trail located across Sunnybrook Road.

• Their store offers a gorgeous selection of home & garden accessories, books and more (closed on Mondays).

• The **TGB Café** is open daily from May to October from 11 am to 4 pm (closes at 5 pm on weekends).

Toronto Botanical Garden
• North York
(416) 397-1340
www.torontobotanicalgarden.ca

D-3
North
of downtown
25-min.

 Schedule: Open year-round.
Admission: FREE.
 Directions: Edwards Gardens, North York (at the corner of Lawrence Avenue and Leslie Street). There are a few pedestrian entrances to **Wilket Creek Park** on Leslie, south of Lawrence.

NEARBY ATTRACTIONS
Ontario Science Centre (5-min.) p. 226

JAMES GARDENS

has been designed parallel to an asphalt one along the **Humber River**. It is reserved for pedestrians, so as to avoid collisions with cyclists and roller blade enthusiasts.

Heading towards the small forest of **Lambton Woods**, my aspiring botanist noticed

Cool picnic!

The flowerbeds full of tulips and other spring blooms don't impress my little thrill-seeker. However, he really falls for James Gardens after he discovers the stairs. They climb 30 metres up towards the panoramic viewpoint overlooking the Humber River. To add to the picturesque character of this surprising city outing, we walk the trails through Lambton Woods and we head for a picnic on a bridge over the river.

The **James Gardens** are not particularly imposing, yet they have lovely symmetrical flower displays as well as several small ponds straddled by footbridges where ducks and chipmunks cavort here and there.

Small paths require the odd portage for those visiting with strollers, while a gentle slope offers a convenient alternative to the stairs leading to a terrace with a great viewpoint. A small pebble trail

curiously shaped and knotted trees and many tame birds with red wings. We observed with great interest a female duck in her nest ... perched atop the chopped trunk of what would have been a mature tree. After a 15-minute walk, the path turns onto a long footbridge leading to a bridge with benches. We stopped there and enjoyed our picnic. Below, the river cascaded down, glistening in the sun. Some 40 metres above, trains rolled down tracks set on high pillars. The overall effect was stunning!

TIPS (fun for 4 years +)
• **Lambton Woods** is well-known for spring wildflowers and the area is a favourite for birders.
• If you picnic on the bridge, make sure to sit on the sidewalk stretching along its railing to avoid cyclists travelling in the middle on the bike trail.

NEARBY ATTRACTIONS

James Gardens	D-3
• Etobicoke Dial 311 (new service) www.toronto.ca/parks	N-W of downtown 30-min.

Schedule: Open year-round.
Admission: FREE.
Directions: From Royal York Road (halfway between Dundas Street West and Eglinton Avenue), take Edenbridge Street eastbound.

ROSETTA MCCLAIN GARDENS

Perched garden

If you're in Scarborough to admire the Bluffs, don't forget to stop by the Rosetta McClain Gardens, perched atop the cliffs. You'll catch a breathtaking view of Lake Ontario, 60 metres below.

You can go round the gardens' paved trails in about twenty minutes. In the centre, there are symmetrical raised planter beds adorned with a few large stones. A scent garden filled with fragrant plants will titillate little noses. Numerous benches allow visitors a chance to admire the landscaping.

Young visitors like to take refuge underneath a large bandshell located at one end of the gardens.

I went with my family on a beautiful autumn day. The sun was shining on Lake Ontario and the ground was littered with large leaves in bright yellow and red hues.

On the eastern part of Rosetta, you'll find a mature and luscious forest and an elegant vine covered trellis.

TIPS (fun for 4 years +)

• No dogs allowed.

• During my first visit, on a rainy day, fog created a white screen that completely hid the lake from my view! The atmosphere was magical; I felt cut off from the rest of the world… but I did not get to see Lake Ontario.

• Read about adjacent **Scarborough Heights Park** on p. 236.

NEARBY ATTRACTIONS
Scarborough Bluffs (5-min.) .... p. 235
Birchmount Pool (5-min.) .... p. 415

Rosetta McClain Gardens
• Scarborough
Dial 311 (new service)
www.toronto.ca

**D-3
East
of downtown
30-min.**

Schedule: Open year-round.
Admission: FREE.
Directions: From Kingston Road, access the gardens' parking lot, just before Glen Everest Road.

THE GUILD INN GARDENS

Art comes naturally

We usually walk by the architectural details of downtown Toronto's buildings without giving it a thought, but here, in the natural setting, they regain all their beauty.

It is almost poetic, these wall fragments amidst the forest. One could imagine the ruins of an ancient civilization.

In the 50's, when Toronto began to tear down the downtown area to make room for the new, there was not much concern about preserving historical buildings. The owners of the Guild, already offering an outdoor sculpture garden, decided to collect the pieces of historical sites they came across.

Nowadays, among other things,

you can admire fragments of the Imperial Bank of Canada, built in 1928, and the Toronto Star Building, erected in 1929. You can see animal bas-relief panels, angel panels, lion's head keystone, column fragments, archways, bear sculpture and more, spread all around the site.

But the pièce de résistance is the central entrance to the Bank of Toronto, built in 1912 and turned into the impressive Greek Theatre.

There used to be a theatre company that would produce a play every summer in this setting but not lately. We loved the plays but exploring the architectural fragments all around was as much fun. And we would top it off with a stroll along the westbound trail bordering the cliff.

TIPS (fun for 5 years +)

• There has been an **Art Naturally Festival** for years, normally on the weekend following Simcoe Day. Check www.scarborougharts.com or call (416) 698-7322 to find out about events organized by the **Scarborough Arts Council**.

• The place has belonged to the City of Toronto for a while now and the City, which used to manage the Guild Inn hotel for weddings and conferences, has closed down the venue. For years, there's been talks to build a hotel and arts gardens, looking great on paper. Nothing has happened yet. At the time of print, you could still download a 2-page *Guild Sculpture Walking Tour* at the bottom of their web page.

NEARBY ATTRACTIONS	
Scarborough Bluffs (5-min.) .... p. 235	
Rosetta Gardens (5-min.) .... p. 264	

The Guild Inn Gardens	J-11
• Scarborough	**East**
Dial 311 (new service)	**of downtown**
http://www.toronto.ca/culture/	**30-min.**
the_guild.htm	

Schedule: Open year-round.
Admission: FREE.
Directions: 201 Guildwood Parkway, Scarborough. Take Kingston Road East to Guildwood Pkwy, then turn south.

ROYAL BOTANICAL GARDENS

Royal treat!

As we walk down towards the lilacs, the vivid greens among the tall trees of the luscious valley catch my breath. To top it off, a live jazz tune is filling the air along with the sweet fragrance of the lilacs. This is what I call a well-cultivated event!

The lilac season is my favourite time of the year to visit the **Royal Botanical Gardens** (RBG). The weather is mild and the event takes us to the **Arboretum**, a large section 3 km from the **RBG Centre**, home to lilacs and magnolias and surrounded by fun nature trails to explore with the kids. One needs to explore the Arboretum to begin to grasp how vast and wild the RBG really is.

The RBG is comprised of 30 kms of nature trails, four separate gardens and four nature sanctuaries, one of which is the **Cootes Paradise Marsh**, right at the edge of the Arboretum.

You want to stop at the Arboretum's **Nature Interpretive Centre**, by the Arboretum's parking lot, to get trail maps and check out their interactive displays (with stuffed animals, microscope, live turtles and more) and their little shop, well stocked with trinkets.

During the **Lilac Celebration**, we were handed a map of the lilac dell. Everywhere, nature was splendid, especially the section with gorgeous yellow, pink and white magnolia trees. Bring your camera, the contrast between the dark branches and the delicate magnolia petals when the sun is shining through is simply beautiful!

You can access the **North Shore** trail from that section. It runs along the Cootes Paradise Marsh. It was amazing to stop on the boardwalk just to listen to the birds and quite captivating to watch dozens of Cormorants hanging over their nests on the trees on a small island.

As a bonus for children, at different times and in different gardens throughout the year, the RBG displays interactive **Discovery Carts** filled with things to touch. During the Lilac Celebration, kids could compare the odours of different lilacs. Some really stink! They were invited to draw a lilac flower, choosing from the numerous characteristics: single, double, small, medium or large with lobes cupped, flat or curled down. Then, they could check on a chart if it already existed and where they could find it in the lilac dell. Activities vary from one year to the next but you can always expect something as interesting.

The **Rock Garden**, much appreciated by the children, offered a different kind of fun. Built in 1929, it was the first major display at the RBG. The huge mature trees are a testimony to that. Tulips and rocks take over the show in that garden. Rock stairs leading to secret corners, rocks becoming small bridges over the pond, huge rocks to climb on. This is a great spot for little explorers!

The fish in the pond of the indoor **Mediterranean Garden**, inside the RBG Centre, were a hit, along with some huge flowers. The outdoor **Discovery Garden** was fun with its giant leaves and hollow tree trunk (both accessible from the centre).

TIPS (fun for 5 years +)

• The **Lilac Celebration** is usually held on the last two weekends of May but call before going to make sure the lilacs have bloomed. The same goes for all the other blooms. Call closer to the planned time to confirm the state of bloom and the exact date of the celebrations.

• Here's a calendar of some blooms to expect: **tulips** (early May in the Rock Garden), **lilacs** (late May in the Arboretum), **iris and peonies** (early June in the Laking Garden), **roses** (late June in Hendrie Park). In September and October, you still can see annual flowers, roses, dahlias and chrysanthemums, (although not at their best!). From November to March, there's the indoor **Mediterranean Garden** in the **RBG Centre**.

• **Rock Garden**, **RBG Centre** and **Hendrie Park** are stroller accessible. I would dare to push a stroller across the **Arboretum** and part of the adjacent **South Shore** when it is not too muddy. Expect to lift it over stairs here and there.

• They don't have the double-deckers shuttles anymore. They might offer a school bus shuttle service on the weekends of the bloom festivals. Call to confirm.

• As a reference, it took us 30 minutes to walk from the Rock Garden to the Arboretum's nature centre, following an unofficial narrow trail along the road. Not good with younger kids; better take the car from one garden to the next.

• There's no food service at the **Arboretum**. Bring your own water and snacks (beware of the little chipmunks!). If you are planning a picnic during the Lilac Festival, bring a thick blanket and some plastic garbage bags to line it! The ground might still be a bit wet.

• The **Rock Garden Tea House** (open early spring to Labour Day) is very nice with its elevated terrace (in the Rock Garden). We also enjoyed locally famous **Easterbrook's Foot Long Hot Dog** snack bar (at 694 Spring Garden Rd. near the parking lot of RBG, 905-527-9679).

We have not had a chance to visit the other sanctuaries. There is the **Hendrie Valley** with 5 kms of trails starting at the **Hendrie Park** parking lot. The Berry Tract is connected to **Cootes Paradise Marsh** and **Rock Chapel** by the **Bruce Trail**. (I have to see Rock Chapel next time. It boasts a 25-m waterfall and 3.5 kms of trails along the **Niagara Escarpment**, coinciding with the Bruce Trail.)

I was told the **Fishway** is quite interesting. It was created to prevent non-native carp from entering into Cootes Paradise in order to bring back other species. It operates mostly on weekdays at 8:30 am and 3 pm. It's a 10-min. walk from the closest parking lot by Princess Point. Ask at the RBG how to get there.

Royal Botanical Gardens • Burlington (905) 527-1158 www.rbg.ca	E-2 S-W of Toronto 50-min.

 Schedule: The outdoor garden areas are open from 10 am to 8 pm (until dusk in fall and winter). The **Nature Interpretive Centre** opens from 10 am to 4 pm. The **RBG Centre** and the **Mediterranean Gardens** (the greenhouse inside the RBG Centre) are open from 10 am to 5 pm. Hendrie Park, Laking Garden and Rock Garden are closed from Thanksgiving to early May.

Admission: $10/adults, $7.75/seniors & students, $5.75/5-12 years old, $25/family of 4, FREE under 5.

Directions: 680 Plains Road West, Burlington. Take the QEW to Hwy 403 West (East Hamilton/Niagara). Exit at Waterdown Rd. (new since 2010), turn right on Plains West. RBG is on left side.

TRINITY-BELLWOODS PARK

Artsy Trinity

I just love the vibe around Trinity-Bellwoods Park. On one side, you've got Queen West and a profusion of funky shops, restaurants and cafés, not to forget the always intriguing MOCCA art gallery nearby. On the other, there's upcoming (and less busy) Dundas West where good cafés are starting to pop up.

The solemn stone and iron gates fronting **Trinity-Bellwoods Park** along Queen West are the remnants of Trinity College

built in 1852. When you pass through those gates and see the whimsical playground, it is hard to imagine it once was the site of a serious private school with strong Anglican ties.

The original playground includes a wading pool. A bit further north, you'll find a large sand pit with logs to sit on. There are many trees, which makes for a great stroll in the fall. On the **Friends of Trinity Bellwoods**' website, it is mentioned that from the end of August to early October at sunset, there's a fantastic gathering of birds all chattering at once near the playground. They say Trinity-Bellwoods Park becomes the "Bird Transit Lounge".

If it's your first time at this park, walk north along the path and you're in for a surprise. There's a huge natural pit, or bowl, that we can't see from the street. When you stand at the bottom, you see the tip of the **CN Tower** pop out of the horizon on the east side.

This is the off-leash dog section of the park (one of the biggest in Toronto) and it seems the perfect setting for some fantastic tobogganing with various inclines to choose from. There's also a skating rink and tennis courts.

TIPS (fun for 2 years +)

• The modern building of the **Trinity Community Recreation Centre** hosting an indoor pool is located near the playground. Go to www. toronto.ca (search *Trinity Pool*, then select *Trinity CRC*) for pool schedules.
• From May to end of October, there's the **Trinity Bellwoods Farmers Market** on Tuesdays from 3 to 7 pm (www.tbfm.ca).
• For great fries, stop at **Chippy's Fish & Chips** (893 Queen West). For good coffee and most probably hot chocolate in the winter, there's the **White Squirrel Coffee Shop** (907 Queen West) and **The Communal Mule**, also serving great treats (984 Dundas West).
• More about **Toronto Zombie Walk** starting from this park on p. 45.

More about **Toronto Zombie Walk** starting from this park on p. 45.

NEARBY ATTRACTIONS
Kensington Market (5-min.) .... p. 98

Trinity-Bellwoods Park Dial 311 (new service) www.toronto.ca	D-3 **Downtown** Toronto 10-min.

  Schedule: Open year-round.
Admission: FREE.
Directions: The park is set on Queen Street West, Toronto (between Queen and Dundas Streets, west of Bathurst Street).

HUMBER BAY PARK

Etobicoke's gem

We explored Humber Bay Park over three visits and I still feel I've missed a few spots. The park is huge and has many interesting angles to it, from the gazebo overlooking the lake at its far west part to the little turtles carved on Humber Bridge at its eastern border, with butterfly garden, Mimico Creek and sculptures in between.

From the public parking lot off Humber Bay Park Road West (south of Lake Shore Blvd), walk west across the road to reach **Humber Bay Promenade Park**, the small extension of the park along the luxurious condos.

This promenade truly makes us feel like we're in a small village by the ocean. It will lead you in 10 minutes to the gazebo, near a tall (seasonal) fountain, past a large sculpture of sails by reflecting pools.

Back to the parking lot, you'll notice the white pedestrian bridge crossing over **Mimico Creek**. If you cross it and walk straight for 10 minutes, along Waterfront Drive, you'll find the lovely **Humber Butterfly Habitat**.

Its paths are lined with flowers and tall grasses, with an elaborate bird house and beautiful metal crows on top of poles. Last time I visited, real birds had chosen to build their nests in the hallow bodies of these crows!

If you walk 20 minutes further east, you'll reach the 139-metre **Humber Bay Arch Bridge**. (We noticed twenty turtles and 4 snakes carved on its structure.)

Just around the butterfly habitat, you can walk along decks crossing the basins serving to filter storm water. When we visited, it was inhabited by cranes, cormorants and ducks and there were big fish in the water.

If you follow the path going towards the lake from the butterfly habitat, you'll come across the surprising **Air India Memorial**, a sundial erected for the 329 victims of the Air India terrorist bombing in 1985. Keep walking less than 10 minutes (towards the lake, then west) and you'll find a pretty oasis where a small stream runs into the lake from an adjacent pond.

TIPS (fun for 5 years +)
• Note that the parking lot off Humber Bay Park Road East is closer to the butterfly habitat.
• The whole park is a great place to bike with kids. All the paths are flat and paved and there's lots to see along the way. If you ride east past Humber Bridge, you'll quickly reach **Sunnyside Beach** (see p. 403).

NEARBY ATTRACTIONS
Sunnyside Beach (10-min.) .... p. 403
Sunnyside Pool (10-min.) .... p. 418

Humber Bay Park · Etobicoke Dial 311 (new service) www.toronto.ca/parks	D-3 West of Downtown 10-min.

 Schedule: Open year-round.
Admission: FREE.

 Directions: From Lake Shore Boulevard (west of Park Lawn Road), take Humber Park Road towards the lake.

WOODBINE PARK

Downhill from there

Forget the 30-foot-high fountain, the bulrushes, the big frog, the giant gazebo or the little climbing wall. If you ask my kids, they'll tell you the park's best feature is the hill.

Woodbine Park popped out along with the new developments by Lake Shore in **The Beach** neighbourhood. It will show a very different face depending where you access it.

If you want to go directly to the spray pad with giant frog and fun playground, access the park on its east side off Northern Dancer Blvd.

When with first time visitors, I prefer to access it at the corner of Eastern Avenue, and Coxwell. It's the least pretty entrance, which allows for a more dramatic effect when we get to the steep hill, past the giant gazebo.

Up the hill, you'll get a vantage point to admire Toronto's skyline with its trademark CN Tower on one side and the vast pond and 30-foot-high fountain on the other. Then, you can roll down the hill.

On the south part of the park is a lovely winding path through tall grass leading to the fountain.

TIPS (fun for 2 years +)

• The parking lot on the south side of Eastern Avenue costs only $2. I would not be surprised if they eventually raise the price for those who don't attend the cinema. But so far, so good.

• **Beach Cinemas**, across the parking lot on Eastern, is one of the best movie theatres in town: perfect seats, adjacent parking lot, great coffee, often with live jazz on summer weekends. For a movie listing, look for *Beach Cinemas* on **www. cinemaclock.com**.

• More on biking in **Ashbridge's Bay Park** on p. 333 and **Ashbridges Bay Skatepark** on p. 348, both activities located by Woodbine Park.

NEARBY ATTRACTIONS
Cherry Beach (5-min.) .... p. 395
Beach neighbourhood (2-min.) ... p. 404

Woodbine Park
Dial 311 (new service)
www.toronto.ca

D-3
East
of downtown
20-min.

Schedule: Open year-round.
Admission: FREE.
Directions: Located east of Coxwell Avenue, between Eastern Avenue and Lake Shore Blvd. East, Toronto. You can park in the $2 parking lot on Eastern, east of Coxwell.

HUMBER ARBORETUM

Urban ecology

On the day we visited, right after Halloween, some tall trees looked beautiful, adorned with long flowing stripes of... toilet paper. I did not know then that Humber is home to a very special kind of wildlife: college students.

After this special introduction to the attraction, we headed towards the nature trail. Leading to the woods by the **Arboretum**'s gardens, it began nicely with rustic stairs.

We spent some time in a small ravine near a curiously shaped old tree, then followed a path down to the meadow. We discovered many nests in the high bushes and played with velvety cocoons from which seeds lazily escaped, carried by their shiny umbrellas in the fall breeze.

The path took us by a large garden section. Its educational value seems most appropriate for a school trip.

We preferred to return to wander informally in the gardens by the Arboretum entrance, with its pond, small pergola and little bridges.

The **West Humber River** runs at the south edge of the woodland. There's a paved path beside it that leads to the main **Humber River Trail**.

Their **Centre for Urban Ecology**, in the heart of the site has a really cool architecture. It is open for drop-in most weekends and offers display cases, touch tables, stuffed animals and live reptiles.

TIPS (fun for 4 years +)

• From their website, you can download a *Discovery Walk* brochure to explore the surroundings.

• Most of the Arboretum activities are programs you need to pre-register for and camps. One of their few drop-in events, the **Winter Festival**, usually takes place the first Saturday in December from 10 am to 3 pm (check their calendar for exact date and fees). In the past, it has included hay rides, a visit from Santa Claus, Christmas tree sale and children's crafts.

• They offer Halloween activities involving a haunted house for younger kids. It is preferable to pre-register.

NEARBY ATTRACTIONS

Humber Arboretum
· Etobicoke
(416) 675-6622, ext. 4467
www.humberarboretum.on.ca

D-3
N-W
of downtown
30-min.

Schedule: Open year-round.
Admission: FREE.
Directions: 205 Humber College Blvd., Etobicoke. Take Hwy 427 North, exit at Finch Avenue eastbound. Turn south on Humber College Blvd. Obtain an Arboretum pass at the College's parking kiosk, go to Lot #1.

DOWNSVIEW PARK

The missing link

The former military base was a bit of a no man's land for a while. It is slowly turning into an urban park. Planned transformations of Downsview Park intend to integrate it into the system of wooded river valleys, ravines, parks and public paths already in existence in adjacent areas. Apparently, back in 1857, Central Park in New York did not look better than Downsview does now.

The development project will be a very long time in the making. As of January 2007, 30,000 trees had been planted in the Canada Forest. In 2008, the park still didn't look too appealing but in late summer 2010, things were shaping up and trails were running through the small forest by the parking lot in the middle of the park.

I noticed the promising shape of an artificial lake in the southwest part of the park.

Since the land is owned by the Government of Canada, **Canada Day** is an obvious time to visit the park. In the past, the event has offered children's activities (petting zoo, buskers, dog shows, etc, during daytime) and they've presented a roster of stage performers and a large midway topped with an ambitious fireworks show. At the time of print, they foresaw something different for 2011 but still promised a fireworks display.

For a few years now, they've put up the **Trail of Lights**, a series of drive-through light displays around the park from late November to early January ($25/vehicle, see details on their website).

TIPS (fun for 5 years +)

• The park has offered many events and activities throughout the year. Check their website for dates and description of current events. For two years, they've offered a **WinterFest** day in February with ice maze, snow painting, and dog sledding! They've also done **Family Day Fest** activities and indoor **Springfest** with midway.

• The park is a haven for teens. Off Carl Hall Rd., you'll find **The Rail**, a huge indoor skatepark with no age minimum (www.therailskatepark.com), equally huge **GrandPrix Kartways**, a go-kart place including slot car tracks(!), see p. 196, and outdoor **Defcon Paintball**, recommended for 12 years and over (www.defconpaintball.ca).

• Now, people play soccer or volleyball in the **Hangar** (formerly used for aircraft assembly, 75 Carl Hall Rd.). It also hosts the **Hangar Grill**, serves burgers, fries and more.

• On weekends, 10 am to 6 pm, there is the very big **Downsview Park Merchants Market** at the entrance of the park, with 600 vendors (www.dpmarket.com).

NEARBY ATTRACTIONS
Air & Space Museum (2-min.) ..... p. 191

Downsview Park
• North York
(416) 952-2222
www.downsviewpark.ca

D-3
North
of downtown
35-min.

Schedule: Open year-round.
Admission: FREE.

Directions: Take Allen Road northbound (north of Hwy 401). Turn west on Sheppard Avenue,

then turn left on John Drury Drive (before Keele Street).

EVERGREEN BRICK WORKS

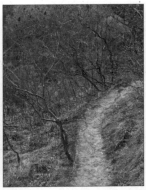

Surprise, surprise

A couple of years ago, we needed to see the bricks mingle with the sand and pebbles on the paths to remind us there was a brick factory for a whole century on this site! Not anymore! Thanks to the massive development project managed by Evergreen, all deteriorating heritage buildings have been salvaged and integrated into an exciting showcase of urban green design.

As a result, there's three times more parking spaces and the place is buzzing with activities (especially on Saturdays) around the now so cool industrial buildings.

But **Brick Works** still feels like a precious enclave hidden in the big mega city as soon as you go past the complex. We could mistake the walls of the old quarry for a small natural escarpment shielding us from the urban noise.

Following the pleasure of observing the fish in the large pond amidst the water lilies, we had the chance to see a crane. With bulrushes, frogs, wildflower meadows, small creek with rocks to jump,

small trails climbing up slopes, the place is perfect for young explorers.

Moore Ravine (see p. 300) is accessible from a staircase on the western part of the site before your reach the pond.

There's one of the best dog off-leash area (small but in a fenced area with trees and trail) near the western parking lot.

In 2010, they added an outdoor garden within walls which turns into a cute skating rink in the winter (see p. 353). Check *What's On* on their website to see their growing list of year-round activities.

TIPS (fun for 4 years +)

• An outdoor covered space hosts the year-round **Farmer's Market** on Saturdays, 9 am to 1pm. Expect booths with great coffee and fancy breakfasts to go, best fries in town, and other goodies.

• At the time of print, they announced, coming soon: **Café Belong** (all-day foodie restaurant in the middle of the action) and an elevated tree-house made of salvaged material.

NEARBY ATTRACTIONS

Evergreen Brick Works
(416) 392-1111
www.evergreenbrickworks.ca

D-3
North
of downtown
20-min.

Schedule: Open year-round.
Admission: FREE. Paid parking.

Directions: 550 Bayview Avenue, Toronto. It is on the west side of Bayview, at the light (south of Pottery Road). There's a free **Evergreen Shuttle** leaving every 30-45 minutes just north of **Broadview Subway Station**.

RATTRAY MARSH C.A.

A real enclave

A marsh is an unusual site in a residential neighbourhood, yet Rattray Marsh sits, sheltered deep within the conservation area sandwiched between Mississauga and Oakville.

Rattray Marsh, with its many viewpoints along tree-bordered walkways, attracts young explorers and bird watchers.

On our first visit, to reach it, we parked in the farthest parking lot we saw in **Jack Darling Park**. Then, we walked west for 20

Photo: Courtesy of Peter & Jean Flemington

minutes (through several beaches and another interesting playground) until we reached a footpath to Rattray Marsh.

Near the entrance off Jack Darling Park is a wide pebble beach.

It will take you a good half-hour to cross the conservation area from east to west through trails and boardwalk. In some parts, you get quite close to the local residences' backyards. In others, near the eastern part of the boardwalk, it feels like you're by the ocean. There are tall grasses, marsh, forest, flowers... and deer!

This little patch of nature is a gem.

TIPS (fun for 4 years +)

• There are no washrooms at Rattray Marsh. The closest is located in **Jack Darling Park** and is closed in the winter.
• The marsh's boardwalk has too many stairs to be fully stroller accessible but there's another trail you can use to enjoy the site.
• When I returned to the marsh in 2010, I saw that they have rebuilt the boardwalk. It is prettier, sturdier and more secure with younger children.
• Rubber boots are recommended after a rainfall (especially if kids want to explore the forest).
• Make sure to stop from time to time and invite children to listen to, and locate, the many birds. Ornithologists have identified some 277 species here! There is a wide range of wildflowers as well.

NEARBY ATTRACTIONS

Rattray Marsh Conservation Area

D-3 West of Toronto 30-min.

• Mississauga
(905) 670-1615
www.creditvalleycons.com

Schedule: Open year-round.
Admission: FREE (donation).
Directions: To **Jack Darling Park**: Take QEW West, exit Mississauga Rd. southbound. Turn west on Lakeshore Rd. Enter into Jack Darling Park (on the south side) and drive to the last parking lot on the south side. **Or:** Stay on Lakeshore past the park. Turn south on Meadow Wood Rd. Turn left at Bob-O-Link Rd. and left on Old Poplar Rd. The marsh is at the end. You can normally find legal parking along the streets nearby.

WYE MARSH WILDLIFE CENTRE

Water lily land

How about a canoe excursion amidst water lilies and turtles, paddling through corridors of tall grass and cattails? Interested? Then, Wye Marsh may be just what you need!

On the weekends from the end of May to the end of September (and daily in July and August), you can reserve a seat on one of the long canoes that traverse the water of **Wye Marsh**. (These canoes can hold 7 to 9 people.)

As father and son embarked on this one-hour guided tour, I took off for a stroll with my younger one towards the beautiful boardwalk that spans the marsh.

As we approached the wooden trail, we could hear trumpet sounds blowing high and strong. As we moved closer to the large water hole, we discovered that, yes indeed, the noise came from spectacular white Trumpeter Swans, dozens of them, swimming through the channels. A three-storey-high tower afforded us a better view of the colony.

On the boardwalk, we found a sheltered section with long landing nets to explore the marsh's bed. Quite a hands-on experience!

In two places, the trail turns into a bridge and from there, my happy girl greeted her canoeist dad and big brother as they paddled underneath us. My boy could not contain his excitement when he caught a glimpse of some turtles between the water lilies and rocked the boat in a manner none of the other passengers appreciated.

In the **Visitor Centre**, you'll find live animals (snakes, turtles, frogs, toads). Included with the visit are **Wet and Scaly** live animal shows and guided walks. See their calendar for times.

Since my last visit, they've added 25 kms of bike trails and two wind turbines.

TIPS (fun for 4 years +)

• Six years is the required minimum age for canoe trips with an adult.
• The swan eggs hatch in mid-June. Right after the school year would be a lovely time to visit the place.
• In the winter, there are cross country and snowshoe trails with rental services. We then get a good look at the swan who all gather around the open water section.
• They offer a wide variety of programs, workshops and eco tours throughout the year. Check their website for seasonal activities. (You'll need to pre-register.)

NEARBY ATTRACTIONS

Wye Marsh Wildlife Centre
· Midland
(705) 526-7809
www.wyemarsh.com

A-2
North
of Toronto
90-min.

Schedule: Open year-round, 9 am to 5 pm.

Admission: Around $12/adults, $8.50/seniors and students, $8/6-12 years, $30/family of 4, FREE under 6 years. **Canoe tours** under $10 /person (call to confirm).

Directions: Same entrance as **Sainte-Marie among the Hurons**, Midland. Take Hwy 400 North, exit Hwy 12 westbound. Wye Marsh is just east of Midland.

BRUCE PENINSULA PARK

Breathtaking!

When I first came across a picture of the turquoise waters of Indian Head Cove on flickr.com, I just couldn't believe that it was located in Ontario. It could have been straight from the Bahamas but there it was, a mere 4-hour-drive north of Toronto. So we packed the car on the last week of the summer and headed towards that little piece of refreshing paradise.

The first day we went, we took the road to the left of the park office to reach what we thought was the only parking lot for the daytime users. It took us 40 minutes to walk along the easy **Cyprus Lake Trail** and the steeper **Georgian Bay Trail** to get to **Indian Head Cove**. (Grab a map when you pay your admission. The trails are well indicated.)

When we returned a few days later, we learned that we were allowed to use the road to the right of the park office to drive to the **Head of Trails** parking lot, only 20 minutes from the cove (a shorter walk for the younger kids).

Nothing beats the moment when, after a good walk up a trail in a shady forest, you suddenly spot the glittering turquoise panorama against dark waters and pale dolomite through the clearings by the edge of the cliff.

Indian Head Cove

You'll find changing rooms and washrooms by the cliff. Then, you'll have to carefully negotiate your way to get closer to the shore through the stairs naturally formed by the layers of rock.

As I took in the scene, I chuckled. We were all wobbling amidst the rocks and looking like bundles of penguins on the different plateaus.

But penguins we are not. The pure water is pretty cold out there! We were lucky enough to visit during a heat wave so I didn't mind taking a dip with my daughter in the 18-degree-or-less water (for the best part of a full 10 minutes). She and many of the other kids on the premises seemed oblivious to the cold after the first few minutes into the swim.

The Grotto

Once you've explored the cove, you might want to climb back to continue on the **Bruce Trail** past the changing rooms. (Following the trail's white marks painted on trees and rocks is the best way to play an *I Spy* game.)

Within a couple of minutes, you'll find the **Grotto**. You'll have to walk left, around the horseshoe-shaped edge, to see from above the impressive cave carved into the dolomite cliff.

Most visitors were climbing down the rock wall like mountain goats to access the grotto. I spent some time observing how they did it before attempting it myself. (I must say watching a guy lightly stepping down the cliff with a baby in his back carrier shamed me into trying it.)

It was not too hard after all but it is easier if you have someone to tell you where to step for the last two metres. It was totally worth it! My husband and daughter joined me later.

When you walk into the deep and dark space, you get to see a turquoise patch of light under the water. Sun shining through a hole in the underwater wall of the grotto is responsible for this cool phenomenon. That's where many choose to jump off a natural platform above the water.

Overhanging Point

Most people don't go past this point, so those who feel the Indian Head Cove is too crowded will appreciate the more secluded spots on the lower cliff a few minutes beyond the grotto.

We chose to follow the shore further west. In 15 minutes, we reached large boulders that offered a totally different kind of panorama. We then walked back to take the Bruce Trail to access the top of the cliff. It offered a challenging climb we all really enjoyed, which led in 15 minutes to **Overhanging Point**, a famous rock plateau hanging over the lake.

It took us 30 minutes to walk back to the Head of Trails parking lot following the **Marr Trail**. A few minutes further, the trail runs along **Lake Cyprus**. The shallow water of this lake is notably warmer than **Georgian Bay**'s. We stopped there on our second visit for a last dip before returning to the Head of Trails parking lot.

Tobermory's best spots

We stayed in Tobermory at the end of Hwy

6 (just a 30-minute drive from the Bruce Park). It is the port from which the **Chi-Cheemaun Ferry** takes visitors to Manitoulin Island. We really enjoyed returning to its lovely harbour, good grocery store and nice selection of restaurants after a day in the wild.

Tobermory is blessed with one of those whimsical places with a soul we usually find in vacation spots in the South: **A Mermaid's Secret** (7433 Hwy 6, to your left, just one block before Bay Street with the cluster of shops leading to the little harbour).

Think delicious organic food, decent coffee, great salads, quesadillas, waffles, desserts, super smoothies and cocktails.

(Loved their mojitos made from scratch!)

Here's an idea for you moms (which I tested a few times). Wake up before everyone, grab a book, leave a note to tell your gang to meet you there, and head to the Mermaid's Secret (which opens quite early) for some "me-time" in a cool surrounding.

We had a ball at the equally cool joint **Shipwreck** (at the corner of Bay Street and Hwy 6) where a cute pirate with his beard split into three small braids served us "all you can eat" delicious fish and chips (the Georgian Bay Whitefish is the best). Kids paid only $2 for a generous portion.

We had a true greasy spoon breakfast at **Craigie's Harbourview Restaurant** (which hasn't changed since the 50's) at the foot of the harbour. We ordered yummy thin-crust pizzas from **Della Rocca Pizzeria** (30 Bay Street) and sweet treats at **The Sweet Shop** nearby.

TIPS (fun for 5 years +)

• Throughout the summer until mid-October is the best time to visit the area. After that, many shops and restaurants close for the season.

• I have seen people of all ages exploring the **Indian Head Cove** and surroundings in the Bruce Peninsula Park but the older your kids, the farther you'll go. Parents of young children will need free hands to help them walk along the Bruce Trail left of Indian Head Cove (some of the natural steps are over 2-feet high). Those with weaker eyes and legs will need the hand of a sturdy companion and probably should not go past the cove. Good shoes are recommended.

• Bring some rubber shoes for your young swimmers. The rock shore is slippery and it hurts to walk barefoot on the pebbles. I also recommend bringing a mask for your little divers to enjoy the fish in the clear water.

• **Bruce Peninsula National Park** holds 242 semi-wild campsites. You can make online reservation at www.pccamping.ca.

• We chose to sleep at the **Bruce Anchor Motel** (around $100 for a room with two double beds) because it provided access to a deck across the street by the lake, the perfect spot to admire sunsets. Plus, it was just a 5-minute walk from the action of Little Tub Harbour. (We got to see a few magnificent sunsets but note that anyone can reach the shore near that deck to enjoy the view. Bring bug repellent and wear long sleeves and legs!)

• Check www.tobermory.org for suggestions on where to stay. Note that the accommodations at 34 Bay Street and lower are the closest to the water (Not all their rooms offer a clear view to the harbour.) I noticed easy-to-miss **Peacock Villa Motel** on Legion Street across Hwy 6 from Bay Street. It offers some cute separate one-room cabins that you don't see from Hwy 6.

• Combine this with a day trip to **Fathom Five National Marine Park**. It involves a boat ride with the **Blue Heron Company** from Tobermory. See p. 279.

• A nice way to end your outing is to stop at **Harvest Moon Bakery** to buy some pies and visit their sculpture trails. See p. 111.

• On your drive to Tobermory on Hwy 10, there's an exciting sight to be seen north of the town of Shelburne along Hwy 10 (approx. 1 hour 1/2 from Toronto): a "wind farm" including 51 windmills called **Melancthon EcoPower Centre**.

We really enjoyed browsing through **Marco Polo Cargo** shop (16 Bay Street). It was much bigger than it seemed from the outside and filled with an eclectic assortment of merchandise. Another surprise was the vast books selection in the **Marine Chart Shop** (17 Bay Street South, near the cruise boats).

Tobermory is a famous divers' haven (masochist divers, if you ask me, considering the water temperature). There are at least three places by the harbour where you can rent snorkeling and scuba diving equipment and book charter boats to diving spots.

Finally, the **Visitor Centre** to the **Bruce Peninsula National Park** is a 10-min. walk from **Little Tub Harbour** (at the end of Head Street). It is worth the visit, to enjoy the view from the viewing tower and to admire the elaborate displays. Don't miss the "boots" tree.

Bruce Peninsula National Park
• **Tobermory**
(519) 596-2233
www.pc.gc.ca/bruce

**Off the map
North
of Toronto
4 1/4 hrs**

Schedule: The park is open year-round. The **Visitor Centre** is open early June to early September, 8 am to 8 pm (closes at 9 pm on Fridays); then, open 10 am to 6 pm until mid-October (open at 8 am on Saturdays). It is open 10 am to 4 pm from Thursday to Sunday, the rest of the year.

Admission: Around $12 per vehicle.

Directions: Take Hwy 410 northbound (it becomes Hwy 10). Stay on Hwy 10 through Owen Sound. Turn right at Hwy 6 (signs to Tobermory). Follow Hwy 6, turn right at Cyprus Lake Road, it will lead you to the office. (Take the road on your right, past the office, if you want to get closer to **Indian Head Cove**. (Tobermory is 15 min. further on Hwy 6.)

FATHOM FIVE MARINE PARK

Reaching rock bottom

We knew shipwreck sightings were included in the fare we booked with Blue Heron Cruise, but I didn't expect the tour to start a stone's throw from our motel. As we scanned the clear water of Big Tub Harbour, which is part of the national marine park, I suddenly realized that we were right above the 36-meter vessel which sank in 1885!

They promote the glass bottom of the **Great Blue Heron** but don't get too excited. It only consists of a couple of small windows at the bottom of a well-like opening. Better to watch the panorama from the upper deck as you head to **Flowerpot Island** after a good look at the wrecks.

We chose to reach the famous flowerpots from the shore as soon as we hopped on the island. It turned out to be trickier then it seemed. I don't recommend it if you're carrying big bags or if you're with young children.

Don't worry, you can use the easy trail through the trees. It will get you to a belvedere in 12 minutes, followed by a staircase leading to the shore between the two flowerpots. A great spot to have a picnic and swim (if you dare, bring rubber shoes).

Five minutes further along the trail (where we left the rocks to enter the domain of ferns and green moss), we saw the sign to a cave which we could observe from a viewing deck. Another 10-minute walk and we got to the lighthouse and the keeper's house we could visit.

We loved the rest of the **Loop Trail** which got us back to our starting point in 30 minutes. It was more challenging than the first part leading to the lighthouse. We saw the six decks serving as campsites by the water. Now, that would be quite the camping experience!

TIPS (fun for 5 years +)

• For a cheaper family option to observe some wrecks, rent a canoe, kayak or paddleboat at $30/hour at the **Big Tub Harbour Resort**. You'll be two minutes away from the two shipwrecks we saw from the Great Blue Heron. Afterwards, you can stay for dinner at rustic **Bootlegger's Cove Pub**, the resort's restaurant with view of **Big Tub Harbour** and then check the lighthouse (less than a 5-minute walk from the resort). Check www.bigtubresort.ca for more info.

• There's no food outlet on **Flowerpot Island** but they sell drinks and snacks at the lighthouse. (You could buy food and beverages for a picnic at **Peacock's Foodland**, the local grocery store by Tobermory's marina before catching your ride.)

• At the height of the season, it's better to show up early in the morning and reserve a timed ticket for the same day. I don't recommend taking less than three hours to explore the site. We stayed four.

• For more info regarding the campsites on the island, call (519) 596-2233.

• More on **Bruce Peninsula National Park** on p. 276.

Fathom Five National Marine Park • Tobermory (519) 596-2233 www.pc.gc.ca/fathomfive www.blueheronco.com	Off the map **North** of Toronto 4 1/4 hrs

 Schedule: Boat rides from early May to mid-October (several daily departures).

 Admission: Boat ride: Around $38/adults, $36/seniors, $29/4-12 years, FREE under 4 (around $10 less if not stopping at marine park). Add the park's admission if stopping: around $15/family.

Directions: Take Hwy 410 northbound (it becomes Hwy 10). Stay on Hwy 10 through Owen Sound. Turn right at Hwy 6 (signs to Tobermory). Follow Hwy 6 to Tobermory. Turn right on Carlton Street (in Little Tub Harbour). The **Blue Heron Company**'s booth is by the water.

GRAIGLEIGH GARDENS

Doorway to the ravine

The park feels like it is from another time. Truly out of the way, it lies quiet and quite classy with its black iron gate, surrounded by majestic stone houses. Yet, despite its manicured look of a proper lady, Graigleigh Gardens is actually a doorway into the adventure of Toronto's wilderness.

My favourite way to access this park is from the private-looking corridor at the junction of Castle Frank Road and Hawthorn Gardens (a lovely dead-end branch north of Hawthorn Avenue). It opens into the wide clearing of the park.

Halfway along the northern length of **Graigleigh Gardens**, you'll find an opening to access the trail going down to the ravine.

Keep going down to your right and you'll reach the wider trail indicating **Moore Park** and **David A. Balfour Park**.

I followed the trail to my right and had the surprise to find myself nose-to-nose with drivers on the Bayview access road arriving from the Don Valley.

Ten minutes further, and one would arrive at **Evergreen Brick Works** (see p. 273).

TIPS (fun for 5 years +)
• Watch out for the mud patches on your way into the ravine. The trail can get slippery.

NEARBY ATTRACTIONS
Around Bloor/Yonge Station .... p. 460
Around Broadview Station .... p. 460

Graigleigh Gardens
D-3
North of downtown 15-min.

Dial 311 (new service)
www.toronto.ca/parks

 Schedule: Open year-round.
Admission: FREE.

 Directions: From Bloor Street East, turn north at the light on Castle Frank Road, Toronto. Look for street parking along Dale Avenue, the second street to your left off Castle Frank, or Hawthorm Avenue, the first to your right off Dale. A narrow entrance to **Graigleigh Gardens** is right at the first turn left of winding Castle Frank Road. Continue on Castle Frank, then take Elm and turn right on South Drive to see the park's main entrance. The park is a 10-min. walk north of **Castle Frank Station**.

CEDARVALE PARK

All in one park

Cedarvale Park spreads its wings through Toronto in a north-south paved corridor almost 2 kms long. For this reason, it has a lot to offer. Its natural features are changing at every turn, from steep hills to marshland and ravine. Plan for a lovely bike ride!

If you start your stroll from the south part of the park, there's the advantage that your kids will still be "fresh" for the walk when they have to go uphill. It will take you approximately 30 minutes to walk to the northern end of **Cedarvale Park**. Running down the hill will be a breeze on their way back.

I like to stop in **Forest Hill Village** (parking in the public lot at the corner of Spadina Rd. and Thelma Ave.). A short walk north of Thelma, on the west side of Spadina, you'll see **Suydam Park**. Go through that park, you'll reach **Relmar Gardens** (the loveliest setting for a small playground). It is lined with beautiful houses whose front yards blend directly into a path leading to Cedarvale Park.

The tall trees are majestic in that part of the park, especially during the fall. Keep to your right, the path eventually leads through a pretty marsh filled with wildlife. Further, you'll pass under Bathurst's bridge, then you'll come across the bridge of Glen Cedar Road. It is sided by a great staircase. Time for a workout! It is worth climbing all the way up for a great view of the trail below.

The trail goes up and opens into a valley with a long steep hill to the left and a fenced off-leash park for dogs to the right. I saw many people rolling down that hill. It must be amazing for tobogganing! You'll also find a small educational garden along the winding path past the dog park.

TIPS (fun for 4 years +)

• I recommend you include a stop in **Forest Hill Village** (just a 5-min. walk from Suydam Park) to get a feeling of this quaint neighbourhood. There's the popular **Hope Street Café** (324 Lonsdale Rd., www.hopest.ca) serving generous all-day breakfast and many other food options. I used to love its narrow patio aside the steep street. They were renovating at the time of print (to be finished later in 2011) but I suspect they'll find a way to maintain its charming assets. Just across the street is a good ice cream counter.

NEARBY ATTRACTIONS
Casa Loma (5-min.) .... p. 128
Around St. Clair West Station ..... p. 476

Cedarvale Park
Dial 311 (new service)
www.toronto.ca/parks

D-3
N-W
of downtown
20-min.

Schedule: Open year-round.
Admission: FREE (donation).
Directions: 443 Arlington, Toronto. Two blocks south of Eglinton, between Arlington and Strathearn Road (where you'll find street parking). The north part of the park is a 10-min. walk from **Eglinton West Station**. The south part is just at **St. Clair West Station** (Heath Street exit).

BAYVIEW VILLAGE PARK

It takes a village

With my mothers' group, we've often visited the playground of Bayview Village Park. The convenient parking lot, the spray pad, the swings, the climbing structures. Good times, good times.

It has not changed much in the last 10 years. Last time I checked, there was still the spray pad. Most of the structures were still standing.

One feature of the park we never got to check with the kids (they were having too much fun in the playground) is the lovely paved trail.

It is perfect for young kids, leading in 15 minutes to a street at the other end, with a small bridge going over a (very) thin stream along the way. The trail is cute and winding, lined with pine trees and a few tall weeping willows.

I noticed a large old tree, near the beginning of the path, which must have seen its share of little monkeys, judging by the worn bark near the lower branches.

TIPS (fun for 2 years +)
• The park is a 10-minute walk from the shopping centre **Bayview Village**, which includes a **Chapters**.

NEARBY ATTRACTIONS

Bayview Village Park
• North York
Dial 311 (new service)
www.toronto.ca/parks

D-3
North
of downtown
25-min.

Schedule: Open year-round.
Admission: FREE (donation).

Directions: 2945 Bayview Avenue, North York. From Sheppard Avenue East, walk north on Bayview (on the east side). The park

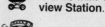
is a 10-min. walk north of **Bayview Station**.

DEMPSEY PARK

I Spy a great design

The whole park feels like a playground for little explorers, thanks to a very original design.

Play structures are usually confined into a specific area in municipal parks. Not in this one. They're spread all over the place.

Here, a little sandpit with a small barn, next to an upraised tunnel to sneak into. There, a climbing wall made out of logs. In the middle, a small hill with a long slide on one side and a spider web for young adventurers on the other. A winding paved path links it all (perfect for small bikes and rollerblades).

I noticed some squash cast in bronze, imbedded in the grass. Then, reading the

sign on the large boulder by the western entrance, I learned that there are more bronze casts around the place. A map invites us to play an *I Spy* game to spot animal tracks.

The historic building by the entrance off Beecroft is the **Dempsey Store**, an old hardware store which was built in 1860 at the northwest corner of Yonge and Sheppard. It was relocated in 1997 to this park.

TIPS (fun for 3 to 10 years)
• You won't find street parking along the park. Go to the municipal parking lot on Beecroft.
• There's a food court with washrooms off the **North York Subway Station**.
• Read about what's around **North York Station** on p. 467.

Dempsey Park • North York Dial 311 (new service) www.toronto.ca/parks	D-3 North of downtown 30-min.

 Schedule: Open year-round.
Admission: FREE.
 Directions: 250 Beecroft Road, North York. From Yonge Street, turn west on North York Blvd., then north on Beecroft. (Park at the municipal parking lot on the west side of Beecroft. **Dempsey Park** is a 5-min. walk further north.) The park is a 5-min. walk northwest of **North York Station**.

BIRKDALE & THOMSON PARKS

Paved with good intentions

While on a quest for stroller- and wagon-friendly paved trails, my wheels brought me to Scarborough. There I found great little asphalt paths in two adjoining parks: Birkdale and Thomson Memorial. Bathed in sunlight, the lush, leafy woods were abundantly laden with the autumn hues and shadows I enjoy so much. In addition, both parks offered a playground.

Usually, I'm not crazy about manicured parks. Nevertheless, I really enjoyed the intimate aspect of **Birkdale Ravine**. It is narrow, with plenty of curves and small valleys. The views are so diverse that you never know what awaits you around the next bend. It may be a small river, a pastoral valley, maple trees, either gigantically tall or short and stubby, or majestic weeping willows.

After a 20-min. fun stroll, we got to a

playground alongside Brimley Street. Last stop! Everybody off the wagon to move a bit!

If you wish to walk some more, you can cross Brimley Street and access **Thomson Memorial Park** further south, across the street. You'll need to walk another 15 minutes before reaching the heart of this park. It has large picnic areas and woods carpeted with leaves.

The picnic sites are pretty, and several are located under the trees. On the south side of the park, there's a small pond. It's a marvelously landscaped oasis located between two playgrounds with wading pool and close to the heritage buildings of the **Scarborough Historical Museum**.

When we were there, children were wading about in a brook emerging from the pond. Grandparents sitting on a bench under the weeping willows were observing children hidden inside flowering bushes along the creek. Simply lovely!

The trails along the border of the park are less interesting (on the east side, you pass under electrical towers).

TIPS (fun for 2 years +)
• Both parks offer free parking.
• Thomson Memorial Park hosts the **Scarborough Historical Museum** (416-338-8807), right next to its playground. During the summer weekends, costumed staff greet us in the four small buildings. On **Canada Day**, they offer a **Strawberry Social** with different activities from 10 am to 5 pm. Expect a **Victorian Extravaganza** at the end of July.

Thomson Memorial Park & Birkdale Ravine
• Scarborough
Dial 311 (new service)
www.toronto.ca/parks

D-3
N-E
of downtown
30-min.

Schedule: Open year-round.
Admission: FREE.
Directions: Birkdale Ravine's entrance is on Ellesmere Road, between Midland Avenue and Brimley Road. **Thomson Park**'s entrance is on Brimley Road, between Lawrence Avenue and Ellesmere. The ravine is a 12-min. walk from **Midland Station**.

L'Amoreaux & Milliken Parks

Ponds in the "hood"

For those short on time to explore the countryside, you can find a small oasis of nature in the suburbs.

Milliken Park offers paved trails, a large pond and a small island of trees. Those trees are mature and the variety of trails quite entertaining for young explorers. The forest sits next to the pond and a few picnic tables have been installed along the water under the trees.

The rest of the park is rather bare and offers little shade. We enjoyed, however, the nearby playground (with splash pad).

In the same region, you will find **L'Amoreaux Park North**, adjacent to the community centre of the same name. It holds a treasure of small paved trails that border a large pond. Interestingly, the cranes I saw resting along the edge seemed unaware they were in the middle of a residential neighbourhood!

Some of the paths lead to a small island of tall leafy trees that looks like some kind of a dense forest housing the neighbourhood's entire vegetation. It is circled by a woodchip covered trail (yet practical with a stroller), framed by trees. You can travel the entire trail in approximately 15 minutes, excluding the time to explore the selection of wild flowers.

TIPS (fun for 2 years +)

• The **Kitefest** traditionally held at Milliken Park was cancelled due to a new law that forbids kite flying at this park...
• Should you find yourself in the area during the fall however, take the time to enjoy the colourful foliage at these parks.
• There usually are **fireworks** at **Milliken Park** on **Canada Day**, at around 10 pm. Call to confirm.
• **Kidstown Water Park** is hosted in **L'Amoreaux Park South** (separated from the north part by **McNicoll Avenue**. More about this great water playground on page 423.

NEARBY ATTRACTIONS
Woodie Wood Chucks (5-min.) ... p. 312

L'Amoreaux & Milliken Parks
· Scarborough
Dial 311 (new service)
www.toronto.ca/parks

D-3 N-E
of downtown
35-min.

Schedule: Open year-round.
Admission: FREE.
Directions: Both parks are located north of Hwy 401. **L'Amoreaux Park** is north of McNicoll Avenue and west of Kennedy Road, **Milliken Park** is south of Steeles Avenue and east of McCowan Road.

CHINGUACOUSY PARK

Anything else?

This park has everything! Animals? Check. Splash pool? Got it. Mini golf? Skateboarding pipe? BMX course? Ski hill? Yes, yes and yes. Add a greenhouse, tennis courts, a playground, paddle boat rental on a large pond and you get a really dynamic municipal park indeed!

Last time I visited, many of the installations in the park were a bit outdated and tired, but it still was the perfect setting for a nice family outing. Well, they've gotten $24.5 million to improve the whole thing since then!

Chinguacousy Park is big but you can still walk from one attraction to the next. When visiting, we parked in the south lot off Central Park Drive and were seduced right away by the weeping wil-

lows throwing their shade over ducks on the sandy beach. A crane just happened to be standing there. It's always amazing to find spots like this in the middle of a city.

Right next to it, we visited the petting zoo ($1/person) including several pens with different farm animals: pigs, lambs, goats, horses, hens and more. (On the weekends, you can ride a pony for around $3.)

Further, we visited a large greenhouse amidst manicured gardens with a paved path leading to fields of grass.

Following the road back to the centre of the park, we found the snack bar, where you can rent the gear to play mini golf for around $4. It has just been replaced by one with a fresh new look (which they describe as a little escape within the city).

The old splash pad was also replaced by a bigger and better one, with free admission! By the pond, you can rent paddle boats to use on both sections of the pond.

Then, there are the spectacular skatepark with the small ski hill in the background (where we can ski and do snow tubing in the winter) and a fun dirt track for BMX bikes. Something for everyone!

TIPS (fun for 2 years +)
• More on **Chinguacousy Skatepark** on p. 350 and the small ski hill on p. 357.
• Due to the construction, some annual activities might not be offered in the summer 2011. Check their website to find out about potential events: **Canada Day** (with fireworks) or **Summer Festival** (a whole day of activities with fireworks during **Simcoe Day** in August).
• Along Queen Street (Hwy 7) just southeast of Chinguacousy Park, between Bramalea and Airport Road, you'll find a strip of fast food outlets and family restaurants: a good finish after an afternoon at the park.

Chinguacousy Park | D-2
• Brampton | N-W
(905) 458-6555 | of Toronto
www.brampton.ca | 45-min.

 Schedule: The park is open year-round. Most activities are available daily from late June to Labour Day weekend.

 Admission: FREE access to park, spray pad and skatepark. Paddle boat rental around $5/2-seater and $10/4-seater, for half an hour.

 Directions: Take Hwy 427 North to the end of the road, turn west on Hwy 7. Turn north on Central Park Drive. Go into the first parking lot (it is the closest to the pond and animal farm).

BRONTE CREEK PROVINCIAL PARK

Old MacDonald had a pool...

What a gorgeous summer day! Where can you go with children? To the farm? To the pool? There's no need to take a vote. Half an hour away from Toronto, Bronte Creek Park offers a great farm-pool combination, as well as many other sport and leisure activities.

Not only does **Bronte Creek Provincial Park** have the usual walks and nature centre, it also boasts farmyard animals, a Victorian-style farm where they work the

soil in the traditional way, and a barn transformed into an original playground. To complete this unique mixture of activities, it offers one of the largest pools in North America.

In this vast park, wanting to try every activity in a single day would be too ambitious. Hardy walkers can move from one attraction to the next by taking the trails and roads laid out on the site. However, young families would be better advised to travel by car between activity centres, in order to spare everyone's energy.

Around Spruce Lane Farm

I suggest you begin your Bronte Creek visit with a walk (while children are still full of energy!). Park at lot F to access the trails by the farm.

The **Half Moon Valley Trail** is an excellent starting point for the whole family. It offers a two-kilometre walk, and

is bordered by wildflowers and old trees of unusual shapes.

In certain locations, the wide path runs alongside the cliff bordering the wide **Bronte Creek**.

The two storeys of **Spruce Lane Farmhouse**, built in 1899, were laid out in accordance with the times. During July and August, costumed actors move about, showing visitors a glimpse of rural life in the early part of the last century.

In the kitchen, there's usually a little something for us to taste.

The play barn

Turtles, snakes and fish await us inside the small nature centre near parking lot C. Bees go in and out through a long pipe connected to the outside. Not far from there, various buildings house rabbits, hens, chicks, pigs and horses.

All that becomes less interesting when kids spot the great play barn with its hanging bridges, tunnels, large tires to climb on and its second storey platform from which children can jump into the big cushions, without breaking their necks. (It even has a heated section for parents who are waiting while their kids go wild, during the colder months!)

TIPS (fun for 3 years +)

•   Bring mosquito repellent if you intend to stroll on the trails. I've seen families fleeing from the woods because they weren't protected.

•   In 2010, they had special **Homestead Christmas** activities over many days, for an extra fee. Check their calendar of events for details!

•   The line-up of activities keeps changing from one year to the next. For a few years now, the park has offered an interesting **New Year's Eve** activity: **Howl'n Hikes** on December 31st. It includes a guided evening coyote howl hike to learn a few secrets about this mammal. Then there's a countdown by the fire at around 8:30 pm for the kids. The skating rink stays open till 12:30, weather permitting!

•   Bronte Creek's **Maple Syrup Festival** is usually offered on March weekends and daily during **March Break**. It includes a pancake house, candy making demonstrations, syrup trail and horse-drawn wagon rides around the farm.

•   The park's campground is located 5 minutes away, on another piece of land. Its 144 lots are relatively secluded. A Halloween event is organized for campers ONLY in October.

•   I've never had a chance to check this out but for a while, Bronte Creek has hosted the annual **British Car Day** drawing over 1,000 British cars (on the third Sunday in September, see www.britishcarday.com).

•   More on skating and tobogganing at **Bronte Creek** on p. 366.

Take the plunge

The Bronte Creek pool, located near parking lot D, holds 1.3 million gallons of water spread over a 1.8-acre area. An adult must walk 500 steps to go around it! It is fabulous for children: no more than two metres deep in the middle, more than half its area is like a gigantic wading pool where little swimmers can frolic without swallowing mouthfuls of water.

Naturally heated by the sun, the pool's shallow water is very comfortable during the afternoon. Those who seek shade can plant their umbrellas on the grass around it. Several picnic tables and a snack bar are located outside the pool grounds.

Bronte Creek Provincial Park
· Burlington
(905) 827-6911, ext. 234
www.brontecreek.org

E-2 West of Toronto 35-min.

Schedule: Park is open year-round, 8 am to dusk; playbarn and children's farm, year-round 9 am to 4 pm). **Spruce Farm** and **Nature Centre** open end of June to Labour Day, 11 am to 6 pm. Pool opens end of June to Labour Day, 11 am to 6 pm.

Admission: $16 fee per vehicle. Additional fees to access pool: $3/adults, $2/4-17 years, FREE for 3 years and under.

Directions: 1219 Burloak Drive, Burlington. From the QEW westbound, take exit #109/Burloak Drive northbound. To go to the campground, take exit #111/ Bronte Road northbound, turn west on Upper Middle Road.

SIBBALD POINT PROVINCIAL PARK

Swimming, sand & snacks

People who aren't inspired by Lake Ontario can turn to Lake Simcoe, the next closest large natural lake in the Greater Toronto vicinity.

The **Sibbald Point Provincial Park**, located on the shores of **Lake Simcoe**, is quite busy. One goes there to mingle with the crowd rather than to return to nature. The decibel level in the park doesn't exactly make it relaxing, as motor boats are allowed on the lake. On the other hand, adult swimmers can take advantage of great waves challenging those swimming beyond the buoys.

The beach is long. The sand is mixed with a few pebbles, but you can easily walk on it with bare feet. There's a very nice playground facing the beach. The children in our group spent their time visiting it, in between a swim and an ice cream cone.

TIPS (fun for all ages)

• Several picnic tables await under the shade of tall trees by the most crowded beach. I recommend getting there before 11 am if you wish to use one.
• There's a well-stocked store and a snack bar by the main beach. It seems their boat rental concession is back.
• Sibbald Point offers more than 600 campsites made private by tall, deciduous trees.

NEARBY ATTRACTIONS
North York Drive-In (40-min.) .... p. 97

Walking on the west side of Sibbald Point, across the farthest parking lot, you will find a tall pine and cedar forest where picnic tables are set up. Various natural clearings reveal a narrow pebble beach, much more isolated and not marked by buoys. The waves are stronger and more fun for big kids who can swim well.

Here, people settle in the patches of sun shining through the mature trees. You can hear the sound of the waves and the birds singing. This area of the park is perfect for little trappers and for those who are looking for a quieter location.

Sibbald Point Provincial Park
· Sutton
(905) 722-8061
www.ontarioparks.com

B-3 North of Toronto 60-min.

Schedule: Open mid-May to early October.
Admission: $10.75-$19.50/per vehicle for day use.
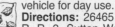
Directions: 26465 Hedge Road, R. R. 2, Sutton West. Take Hwy 404 North to the end, take exit #51 (Davis Dr./Hwy 31) eastbound. Turn north on Hwy 48, then follow Rd. 18/Park Road northbound.

McRae Point & Mara Parks

Best family picnic

Lake Couchiching and Lake Simcoe are separated by a shallow strip of land called the Narrows. Mara Provincial Park sits right by the Narrows. McRae Point Provincial Park lays further along the shores of Lake Simcoe.

TIPS (fun for all ages)
• You can fish in both parks. Both provincial parks include campgrounds.
• I recently revisited this area with girlfriends (to see a show at the Casino Rama). I noticed an ice cream stand **Sweet Dreams** by Hwy 12 on the way to the provincial parks. It sat by the small beach with playground of **JD Tudhope Memorial Park**. We followed the trail along **Lake Couchiching** (see upper right picture). It is a great place to bike. The 8-km trail reaches **Couchiching Beach** (p. 414).
• We stopped in Orillia to check out the main street and fell in love with the **Mariposa Market** (109 Mississauga St., 705-325-8885, www.mariposamarket.ca). This store with restaurant doesn't look huge from the outside but it is! It includes a clothing and accessories section, a gift shop, a counter restaurant with delicious and very affordable food, a kitchen store and shelves loaded with goodies. Stock up for the picnic!

We stopped for a swim at **Mara**'s wide beach with shallow water and great sand. Picnic tables were set in the shade of tall trees; unfortunately, they were too far from the water for my liking.

We preferred to spend the rest of the afternoon at **McRae Point** (10-min. drive further). We really fell for McRae's narrow beach bordered by grass, pretty trees and tables (as shown on the upper left picture).

As the day was fading away we had a great picnic, accompanied by the music of the lazy waves stroking the shore.

McRae Point P. Park	A-3
(705) 325-7290	**North**
Mara Provincial Park	of Toronto
(705) 326-4451 (seasonal)	**75-min.**

• Orillia
www.ontarioparks.com

 Schedule: Mara opens mid-May to Labour Day. McRae opens mid-May to Thanksgiving.

 Admission: $10.75-$19.50/per vehicle for day use.

Directions: Take Hwy 400 North, then follow Hwy 11. Take Hwy 12 eastbound and follow signs. Mara comes first.

EARL ROWE PROVINCIAL PARK

Some water holes!

Beaches offer everything pleasing to children: space to run, sand to build castles and water to float and swim. Add to this a pool the size of a football field, and you get a feel for Earl Rowe Provincial Park.

The two large beaches at **Earl Rowe Provincial Park** are not as busy as those located around **Lake Simcoe**. They are connected by small wooden bridges straddling the reservoir (the bottom of the lake is slightly muddy).

Children will enjoy crossing over the wooden bridge to reach the park store by the western beach. You may rent canoes and paddle boats, as well as bicycles, at the information centre.

Those who settle on the eastern beach will also enjoy the gigantic shallow pool (it took me 350 long strides to circumnavigate it), and a small playground.

When we visited, we missed the fish ladder in the dam across the **Boyne River**! It is only a few minutes from the two parking lots by the entrance.

TIPS (fun for all ages)
• There's a 5-km lookout trail at the northern part of the park. The main trail is 8 kms long. For a good description, go to **www.simcoecountytrails.net** and click on *Trails,* then *Loop Trails.*
• BEWARE! The beaches are closed on average twice through the summer due to high bacterial counts (lots of geese visit the park). Call before you go!
• Earl Rowe includes around 400 campsites.

NEARBY ATTRACTIONS
South Simcoe Railway (20-min.) p. 206

Earl Rowe Provincial Park
· Alliston
(705) 435-2498
www.ontarioparks.com

B-2
N-W
of Toronto
90-min.

Schedule: Open mid-May to Thanksgiving (pool opens end of June to Labour Day).

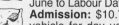
Admission: $10.75-$19.50/per vehicle for day use. The pool's entrance fee is $2.50/adults, $1.50/children, FREE 4 years and under. Canoe or paddle boat rental is around $10/hour.

Directions: From Hwy 400 North, take exit #75/Hwy 89 westbound. Turn north on Regional Rd. 15.

AWENDA PROVINCIAL PARK

A clear choice!

One of the best ways to enjoy Georgian Bay's clear water is to visit one of the four beaches in beautiful Awenda Provincial Park.

The first beach you encounter, a short walk from the first and second parking lots, is our favourite, with gulls resting on rocks sitting above the water, and small pebbles nestled in the fine sand.

From there, you can walk to the second beach (also a short walk from the second parking lot), crossing over a small rocky section in the water. Last time we visited, the water had receded so much that what used to be a narrow stretch of pebbles had turned into a sea of rocks, great for imaginative play!

A half-hour walk from the second parking lot, along the wide and well-groomed **Beach Trail** (time to get the bikes!), you'll find the third beach.

Located in a small tree-sheltered bay, this beach is everybody else's favourite because of its emerald water and perfect sand.

There are some serious bike trails throughout the park.

The two pictures below were taken five years apart. Notice how we did not see the sand strip by the trees in the top one! The water can really drop after a snowless winter.

A 10-minute walk farther brings you to the fourth beach, for a completely different panorama that embraces a wide view of **Georgian Bay**. Good news: Very few people choose to do the extra walking, and when we visited, we felt like we owned this sandy beach adorned with dunes and plants.

At last, on our most recent visit, we were able to pull the kids from the beach to explore Awenda's trails. We did the **Dunes Trail**, a 3-km trail which took us to a steep sandy slope. We actually walked to that slope and turned back, which was as much as my 6-year-old could bare; bring water!

We also enjoyed the 1-km trail strolling around **Beaver Pond** and walked a bit on **Wendat Trail** around **Kettle's Lake** (a 5-km trail). You can bring your own canoe.

TIPS (fun for all ages)
• Awenda Park's more than 320 campsites are really popular. Nicely set under tall trees, they offer great privacy. If you can't get a campsite there, you may try **Camping Lafontaine** on Lafontaine Rd., (705) 533-2961 or www.lafontaine-ent.on.ca. It offers very decent campsites amidst trees. From there, you can return to Awenda Park for day use.

NEARBY ATTRACTIONS
Discovery Harbour (20-min.) .... p. 387
Sainte-Marie (25-min.) .... p. 388

Awenda Provincial Park
• Penetanguishene
(705) 549-2231
www.ontarioparks.com

A-2
North of Toronto
90-min.

 Schedule: Open year-round (facilities available from mid-May to Thanksgiving).
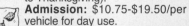 **Admission:** $10.75-$19.50/per vehicle for day use.
 Directions: Take Hwy 400 North, exit Hwy 26/27 (exit #98), then follow Hwy 27 northbound. After Elmvale, follow Simcoe Rd. 6 North. Turn east on Lafontaine Road (it becomes Concession Rd 16) and follow signs.

MONARCH & MIGRANTS WEEKEND

Tag!

You were wondering how one can possibly tag butterflies without seriously impairing their capacity to fly? Here's your chance to find out. Playing tag takes on a whole new meaning at Presqu'ile.

You will be relieved to learn that the kind of animal tagging we're talking about here is the gentle application of a very light sticker on the lower part of the butterfly's wing.

The wind was so strong on the day of our visit, we hardly saw birds while strolling on the 1.6-km-round trail of **Owen Point Trail**. Still, we enjoyed walking through very tall grasses and around the point overlooking the lake.

Butterflies were few in the bushes on that day. Yet, as we approached the tagging station near the lighthouse, we saw more monarchs than usual and there were enough around for everyone who wanted to tag their own butterfly, and for a chance to take great close-up photos of them as they rested on leaves.

The insects felt surprisingly sturdy as we held them between thumb and finger. Not at all as fragile as we expected. Note that those butterflies, born at the end of the summer, are biologically and behaviourally different from those we see earlier in the season. Only those are equipped to migrate to sites near Mexico City, some 3,400 kms away. They will eventually return to Canada. Only the children of their grandchildren will undertake the same trip.

We had our picnic by the water, walked around the lighthouse and returned to visit the interpretive centre with interesting displays and stories. Then, it was time to drive to the **Marsh Boardwalk**, a 1-km trail running through the marsh. Ask for trail maps when you enter the park.

TIPS (fun for 4 years +)

• You've got to check **www.monarchwatch.org** (especially the *Migration & Tagging* section). This website is a wonderful resource to consult before and after your visit.

• They sell snacks in the building near the lighthouse. In the **Lighthouse Gift Shop**, they sell a great booklet titled *Butterflies of Presqu'ile Provincial Park*.

• More about **Presqu'ile Provincial Park** on p. 295.

Monarch & Migrants Weekend
• Brighton
(613) 475-4324
www.ontarioparks.com

C-6
East
of Toronto
2 hrs

See **Presqu'ile Provincial Park** information box on p. 295.

NEARBY ATTRACTIONS

Big Apple (30-min.) .... p. 67

PRESQU'ILE PROVINCIAL PARK

A bit of everything

This provincial park is relatively small yet, it offers so many little worlds to discover that it makes for the perfect day trip with young explorers.

We decided to take advantage of the fact that our kids needed to stretch their legs after the long car ride to stroll through the Owen Point Trail.

We walked through corridors framed by 2-metre tall grass before reaching different lookout points into the open, where we faced the narrow **Gull Island**. We had the chance to observe many shorebirds foraging the sand. It takes about 30 minutes to complete the 1.6 km loop.

We then drove further to the lighthouse. The road includes a bike lane so we saw many cyclists as we went through the forest. The drive, which continued along the waterfront, was gorgeous. It truly felt like we were on a vacation far from home.

We enjoyed the little interpretive centre by the lighthouse. It included a small model of a shipwreck, a large one of the old lighthouse, and fun displays about rumrunners (bootleggers).

If you're visiting during a warm summer day, you'll then want to head towards the beach. You can access it from three entrances. (It's presented as three beaches but the three parking lots will lead you to different parts of the same 2-km beach.)

The fine blond sand of the long and wide beach has the tight and regular furrowed quality that resists under the foot. It extends like this for more than 100 metres under shallow and warm water; just heaven for kids.

On our last visit at the end of the summer, we preferred to enjoy the **Marsh Boardwalk** (with its own parking lot near Beach 3). It starts with a stop at the lookout platform, for a great view of the marsh.

On the boardwalk, we felt like we were gliding amidst the tall grass. Had it been early summer, we would have had a myriad of water lilies at our feet. The marsh is a mecca for birdwatchers every spring and fall, when you can listen to the birds' various and surprising calls. The 1- km loop ended in an intriguing old forest, with weird-shaped trees.

TIPS (fun for 4 years +)
• They sell snacks at the store of the Lighthouse Interpretive Centre.
• More about their **Monarch & Migrants Weekend** on p. 294.
• The park includes a small **Nature Centre** with a few animals on the way to the lighthouse and 394 campsites surrounded by beautiful trees (some facing a pebble beach).

NEARBY ATTRACTIONS
Big Apple (30-min.) .... p. 67

Presqu'ile Provincial Park
· Brighton
(613) 475-4324
www.ontarioparks.com

C-6
East
of Toronto
2 hrs

Schedule: Open year-round.
Admission: $10.75-$19.50/per vehicle.

Directions: R.R. 4, Brighton. From Hwy 401 East, take exit #497 to Hwy 25 (Big Apple Drive) southbound. Turn east (left) on King Street (Road #2), south on Ontario Street, then east again on Presqu'ile Pkwy (R.R. 66).

KILLBEAR PROVINCIAL PARK

were cooking their dinners and enjoying the final hours of daylight.

A few sailboats were slowly heading back home. Leaving this little piece of paradise was the hardest thing to do!

I totally missed the **Visitor Centre** offering 3,000 square feet of displays. Oops!

Life up there

As we're wondering if the park "bears" its name because it is actually inhabited by those animals, we see a sign that reads "Active bear in campground". Further, another sign begs us to "Please brake for snakes". This park is the real thing!

I only spent a few hours at **Killbear** on my way from the music camp where a friend and I had just dropped our sons. We thought a dip in **Georgian Bay** would be a nice treat for our trouble.

The site was so beautiful and our short visit so satisfying that I had to include it in this guide.

We did the **Lighthouse Point Trail**, a 1-km stroll. It emerged from the trees into a majestic rocky shoreline offering a breathtaking view of the bay (and the 30,000 Islands).

Most of the visitors seemed to gather on the beach located on the east side of **Lighthouse Point**. We chose to go to a more secluded one on the other side, accessible from a small trail on the north side of the parking lot. The water here was quite shallow. Any child could easily swim to reach a tiny rock island to "explore".

We also tried a section of the 2-km **Twin Point Trail** near the day-use beach on **Kilcoursie Bay**. Brochures describing the trail were available in a guide box.

A very soothing lap of gentle waves brushed a sand bar pushing into the bay. The families gathering along the beach

TIPS (fun for all ages)

• Killbear Park offers 881 campsites spread over 7 campgrounds. I've checked the "premium rate" campsites (indicated as such on the park's map) of **Kilcoursie Bay**, from 53 to 63, and **Beaver Dams**, 316 to 326 and 328 to 336, and they were truly fantastic, with an amazing view right on the beach. **Harold Point** and **Lighthouse Point** also offer such premium rate campsites.

• There's a 6-km bike trail parallel to the park's main road.

• Check **www.friendsofkillbear.com** to see their photo gallery of events taking place at Killbear: pancake breakfast on the 1st of July, **Bike Rodeos** in July and August, **Maple Syrup Festival** in March.

• Parry Sound's waterfront is worth the detour! (20-min. drive). Have a bite at the **Bay Street Café** (22 Bay Street, 705-746-2882); they have a kids menu and a wrap-around porch. Then stroll around the town dock.

• One annual event to check out in August: **The Georgian Bay Parry Sound Tugfest**, featuring tugboat races, Festival of Lights parade and more (www.tugfest.net).

NEARBY ATTRACTIONS
Bobby Orr Hall of Fame (45-min.) p. 342

Killbear Provincial Park
• Parry Sound
(705) 342-5492
www.ontarioparks.com

Off the map North of Toronto 3 1/4 hrs

Schedule: Visitor Centre open daily, 10 am to 5 pm during the summer, and 10 am to 3 pm in the spring and fall. Park open from 8 am to dusk.

Admission: $10.75-$19.50/per vehicle for day use.

Directions: Hwy 559, Parry Sound. From Hwy 400 North, follow Hwy 69/Parry Sound/Sudbury. Continue on Hwy 69/Trans Canada then turn west on Hwy 559.

OASTLER LAKE PROVINCIAL PARK

Point taken

I came across Oastler Lake Provincial Park on my way back from my son's summer camp. It was quite close to the road and small, but it was right on Oastler Lake so I knew it would be a great choice for first time campers. I did not expect to fall in love with the Point Campground. It was what you would call a case of love at first "site".

The campgrounds at **Oastler** are not very private. In addition, the main railway line runs nearby and you hear it loud and clear. It's hard to truly forget about civilization. But all this won't mean a thing to your young adventurers when they see the lake through the trees of **Point Campground**, the radio-free strip of land with a great Canadiana view to the bay.

As soon as they get there, they'll start to figure out a way to access the water below by exploring the natural

stairs along the edge. With younger kids, you might want to stay away from the campsites by the water since they don't offer an easy access to the lake, which could be too challenging for them (and their moms) but a major asset from older kids' points of view.

For all users, there's a 100-metre-long beach. You can rent a canoe. (**Oastler Lake**'s odd shape must be really fun to explore.) Fishing is permitted (bring your gear and permit). There's rainbow trout, pike and bass.

TIPS (fun for 4 years +)
• The park includes 148 campsites. My favourites for young explorers are located in **Point Campground** (numbers 132 to 140 and 200 to 209). Numbers 408 to 411 also look nice in **Hardwood Hill Campground**. I could see them from lot #136. Book early to reserve those spots.
• We loved the restaurant just west of the provincial park. **The Whitfield** (also a resort) has a great patio overlooking the lake and the burger, fries and club-sandwich we had there got an 8 out of 10 rating from my teenager (www.thewhitfield.net, 312 Oastler Park Drive). Parry Sound is less than 15 minutes away by car.

NEARBY ATTRACTIONS
Bobby Orr Hall of Fame (10-min.) p. 342

Oastler Lake Provincial Park
• Parry Sound
(705) 378-2401
www.ontarioparks.com

Off the map North of Toronto 2 3/4 hrs

Schedule: Open year-round.
Admission: $10.75-$19.50/per vehicle.

Directions: From Hwy 400 northbound, take exit # 217 (Barger Road towards Oastler Park Road). The park will be on your right, just before **The Whitfield** restaurant.

GLEN STEWART RAVINE

City trappers

As we happily complete our visit to the Glen Stewart Ravine, my son emerges from our expedition with muddy shoe soles, filthy elbows and knees, soiled pants and a sweater full of twigs, having climbed, slid, splashed about and crawled everywhere. We're perfect candidates for a detergent commercial!

TIPS (fun for 4 years +)

•   To avoid exhausting your kids, I recommend you park on Glen Manor Drive East near the ravine entry. You'll find a place, even on weekends.

•   Bring a small plastic or paper-made boat and follow its course down the stream. It won't be hard to retrieve when you are finished with the game.

•   Warning! If you plan on returning thereafter to civilization on Queen Street, bring a change of clothes for the kids.

•   Every year, locals enjoy **Carolling in the Park** by the rink at Glen Manor Drive, when 800 to 2,000 show up (depending on the weather) to hear Christmas music in a magical setting (on the second Tuesday before Christmas, 7:30 to 8:30 pm, 416-694-0617).

•   Nearby **Pie Shack** sells huge yummy pieces of pie that you could share (2305 Queens St. East, 647-351-1411).

•   See skating and tobogganing in the ravine at Glen Manor Drive on p. 360.

NEARBY ATTRACTIONS
The Beach (15-min. walk) .... p. 404

Past the boutiques of Queen Street East in **The Beach** and next to Glen Manor Drive, sits a gorgeous rock garden with many water fountains. From there, follow a path to a quaint and leafy park bordering the surrounding mansions.

Walk further, up the stairs and across Glen Manor Drive East, and you find yourself at the mouth of the **Glen Stewart Ravine**, a paradise worthy of any small Robin Hood! Its "unmanicured" qualities reminded me of the countryside forests of my childhood and won the interest of my young naturalist.

The small and narrow valley in the ravine is crossed by a log-straddled stream a few feet in width. Surrounded by steep tree-filled slopes, some paths and naturally-formed stairs are accessible and comfortably shaded by abundant undergrowth and sit desirably isolated from neighbouring houses.

Walking to the end of the main path bordering the ravine takes about fifteen minutes. Children love to climb the wooden stairs reaching the street, just for the sake of it. The rugged terrain is not recommended for strollers, and I recommend vigilance with young kids as they can easily slide down (more fright than harm).

Glen Stewart Ravine	D-3 East of downtown 20-min.
Dial 311 (new service) www.toronto.ca/parks	

 Schedule: Open year-round.
Admission: FREE.
 Directions: Located by Glen Manor Drive East, Toronto (accessible from Queen Street East).

MOORE PARK RAVINE

Darkest corners of the city

The sun beats down on our heads. Our sandals barely shield our feet from the hot asphalt. On the street, the heat bounces from one building facade to the next, their walls blocking a breeze that would otherwise clear away the heat. Not to complain about summer, but we can't wait to hit the shade of Moore Park Ravine.

Moore Park Ravine is undoubtedly a jewel of Toronto's natural crown. You enter the ravine through a steep little path, towards a forest of spectacularly high trees.

Here, you'll find a large and powerful stream with birds' songs playing against the ruffling of leaves. There, a pond potentially inhabited by frogs, and further, a large tree trunk inviting you to a moment of rest.

From this main path, many smaller trails depart, haphazardly fashioned by previous hikers. The main

path travels under a couple of imposing bridges, and continues towards a large opening we reach after a half-hour walk. It runs along **Evergreen Brick Works** and reaches **Mount Pleasant Cemetery** in the north.

TIPS (fun for 4 years +)
• Be cautious when visiting with young children as some slopes are exceedingly steep and there are no railings. However, strollers and bikes can manoeuvre without much difficulty.

NEARBY ATTRACTIONS
Mt. Pleasant Cemetery (1-min. walk) p. 261
Evergreen Brick Works (1-min. walk) p. 273

Moore Park Ravine **D-3**
Dial 311 (new service) **North**
www.toronto.ca/parks **of downtown**
 20-min.

 Schedule: Open year-round.
Admission: FREE.
 Directions: Located south of
Moore Avenue, Toronto (between
Mount Pleasant Road and Bay-
 view Avenue).

SHERWOOD PARK RAVINE

Diamond in the rough

As you walk down the path from Blythwood Road, you'll discover what has to be one of the prettiest playgrounds in the whole city! With interesting equipment, it sits like a jewel in the midst of tall trees, next to a beautiful wading pool adorned with giant water-spraying cattails.

It gets quite busy when summer camp children invade the place, but there is still plenty of room to comfortably roam the trails of this vast oasis.

The playground includes a small climbing wall much appreciated by the children. After a good play and nice picnic, we walked past the wading pool and reached long stairs leading up to a great off-leash dog trail.

Kids enjoyed the wooden stairs in the middle of the forest, and hopped from rock to rock over a shallow stream.

In all, it took us 40 minutes to complete the trail's return trip by foot.

TIPS (fun for 4 years +)
• The summer camps usually leave around 4 pm, perfect timing to enjoy the park for a couple of hours and a picnic dinner.
• Parts of the trails can be challenging for a 3-year-old. Hold on to their hand.
• With a stroller, it took us over twenty minutes to cross Blythwood Road from Sherwood Park, and walk through **Blythwood Ravine Park** (not particularly interesting) to the **Alexander Muir Memorial Gardens** (on Yonge Street, south of Lawrence Avenue). The gardens are very pretty but hard to stroll around because of stairs.

Sherwood Park Ravine
Dial 311 (new service)
www.toronto.ca/parks

D-3
North
of downtown
30-min.

Schedule: Open year-round.
Admission: FREE.

Directions: Sherwood Ravine Park's entrance is off Blythwood Road, Toronto (south of Lawrence Avenue between Mount Pleasant Road and Bayview Avenue).

PADDLE THE DON

It is the only time in the year when Toronto and Region Conservation allows people to paddle the Don River. For the occasion, they manage the water level to ensure there's enough for the participants to ride smoothly.

A cheerful crowd was already assembled on the patch of grass at the corner of Don Roadway (south of Lake Shore Blvd.) and Villiers Street when we arrived. This is where we waited for the participants to arrive. There was live music, BBQ stand, greeting committees and many sponsors distributing flyers related to canoes and kayaks.

We walked across the Lake Shore Boulevard to reach the pedestrian bridge, for a better look at the canoes as they went underneath.

When the Don comes to life

I was curious to check out this event, a good occasion to get a glimpse of the Don River in the middle of the downtown area. It was indeed special to see it, surrounded by concrete and highways. Then, canoes would appear, slowly gliding through the opaque waters of the urban river.

Paddle the Don is a free fundraising event aimed at collecting funds to regenerate the **Don River** watershed. The route starts at **Ernest Thompson Seton Park** and it ends at the **Keating Channel** (at the foot of the Don Valley Parkway). It is a 15-km paddle which usually takes paddlers 2 1/2 hours to complete.

TIPS (fun for 6 years +)

• If you keep walking west on the **Don Trail** across the little pedestrian bridge (just north of the Lake Shore Blvd.) you'll reach **The Distillery** in 15 minutes. If you go north after the bridge, in less than 5 minutes you'll find a track that deadends (an intriguing playground for young adventurers).

NEARBY ATTRACTIONS

Paddle the Don
(416) 661-6600, ext. 5397
www.paddlethedon.ca

**D-3
Downtown
Toronto
10-min.**

Schedule: Usually the first Sunday in May.
Admission: FREE to participate (but this is a fundraiser). You need to pre-register your canoe.
Directions: The finish point (where all the action, live music and suppliers are) is at 170 Villiers Street, Toronto (just south of Lake Shore Blvd.).

CREDIT RIVER

To Mississauga's credit

A friend of mine was anticipating the reaction of his sibling visiting from Quebec when he took him on a casual walk along the Credit River. It did not fail! His wide-eyed brother saw a man reel out of the water, right under his nose, the kind of salmon fishermen dream about. And this happened here, in the heart of the most urban part of Canada!

Credit River is a wild trout and salmon river where you can see huge fish swimming upstream into the shallow water. **Erindale Park** is the best spot from which to observe fishermen during the month of September.

The ride along Mississauga Road to get to **Erindale Park** is beautiful during the fall. The river is less than a 5-minute walk from the vast parking lot of the park. Downstream, right under **Dundas Street Bridge**, the shallow river joyfully cascades over the rock bed.

Upstream, the river is lined with high boulders overlooking deeper water. Many stone stairs offer lovely openings through the bushes leading to a large trail along the river, partly shaded by large trees. The trail is lovely and stretches past Hwy 403, approximately an hour walk away northbound.

Streetsville Memorial Park is the access point to a lovely stretch of the **Culham Trail** going upstream along the Credit River. Mature trees are found on both sides of the river. We loved the colourful carpet of leaves during our fall visit. It includes a playground and an outdoor pool. I encourage you to get closer to the cluster of huge trees in the wide field, across the bridge. One of them forms an intriguing figure that really looks like a hooded person sitting by the trunk. It will take you 15 minutes to reach the Main Street Bridge if you stay on the western shore. You'll get a great view of the Credit River from that bridge.

At the foot of Mississauga Road in Port Credit lies **J.C. Saddington Park**. Kids will enjoy exploring the large boulders along Lake Ontario's shore. I was impressed by the large area with picnic tables one can reserve for a large family gathering by the lake. The park includes a cute stream near a playground, a pond lively with ducks, a fountain and great willow trees almost brushing the water.

On Front Street, bordering the river, the boats of the companies offering fishing and cruises from spring to fall are located.

TIPS (fun for 5 years +)

• Stop at **Kate's Town Talk Bakery** at 206 Queen St. South in Streetsville near Streetville Park. It is closed on Sundays and Mondays but opens at 8 am every other day of the week.

• A **Fish & Chips** and a **Starbucks** are conveniently located at the corner of Front and Lakeshore Rd. near **J. C. Saddington Park**.

NEARBY ATTRACTIONS

River Grove Pool (5-min.) .... p. 416

Credit River	D-3
• Mississauga	**West**
(905) 896-5384	**of Toronto**
www.mississauga.ca	**30-min.**

 Schedule: Accessible year-round.
Admission: FREE.
 Directions: Erindale Park: Take Mississauga Road North, turn east on Dundas Street, the entrance is on the north side. **Streetville Memorial Park:** Take Mississauga Road North (it becomes Queen South), turn east on Beech Street. **J.C. Saddington Park:** from QEW, take exit # 130/Mississauga Road South to the end of the road.

ROUGE PARK

So long, civilization

The trail had led us to the river; we heard the clear sound of splashing water. Standing still, we heard it again, this time identifying the source of this noise: a 60-cm-long brown trout, jumping upstream! It is a shame my 3-year-old could not appreciate the wonder of such a scene. Mind you, everything she saw that day was a first for her.

You can't explore **Rouge Park** in a single day. It is huge, with the Toronto Zoo occupying only a tenth of its area. It offers a wide variety of natural settings accessible from different points.

Reesor Road access

I visited during the fall with my 3-year-old and I thought it was the perfect place to enjoy fall colours with a little one. A cascade of leaves would fall from the tall trees every time the wind blew, and the ground was covered with crisp leaves.

The easy trail runs along the river and, in many places, we had access to it over a wide band of pebbles. The river is very shallow. I was flabbergasted to discover a huge dead fish on the pebbles! Observing the fish's sharp teeth, my little one declared it was nothing less than a shark. Later on, I learned that trout and pike, even though they don't travel upstream to spawn like salmon, still like to roam up and down the river.

We laid out our picnic on a fallen tree by the river. Further on, the trail was narrower and bushier so we turned back. We were only twenty minutes away from the parking lot.

I was told there is a trail along the **Little Rouge River**

which would take us to **Pearse House** in approximately two hours.

Pearse House access

In the backyard of the pretty Victorian house that holds the **Rouge Valley Conservation Centre** (see www.rrcc.ca about their activities) we found a circle of intriguing and nicely painted rocks between a tent made out of cedar branches and the entrance to the trail. The beginning of this trail was steep and winding, and lead to an easier stretch.

Our first glimpse of the **Little Rouge River** off this path was simply gorgeous. The stream was shining like diamonds under the sun, framed by colourful leaves, with white cliffs and dark evergreens in the background.

Upstream, we explored the river banks. Large flat stones that popped through the shallow water allowed for a great hopping session. We reached the gravel road in twenty minutes, then walked along the road, back to the parking lot.

Twyn Rivers Drive access

During the fall, Twyn Rivers Drive is a real gem of a road in the midst of civilization! Breathtaking colourful leaves, white cliffs, a crossroad passing over two small bridges... and not a single house in sight!

Driving eastbound on Twyn Rivers, we found a large parking lot on our right. From there, we took the south trail along the river leading towards the bridge, which we crossed. Then we followed a trail off the road. It eventually started to run up a steep hill to our right.

For a little while, we explored the right-hand side of the fork up the hill. The path was really pretty, the dark trunks contrasting with a colourful patchwork of trees we could see on a hill in the far background.

We returned to take the left-hand side of the fork, which offered quite an interesting stroll. Roots were running across the path. We took the first downhill trail to our right, aiming at the river.

A strange vision of dark trees with peeling bark and tortuous branches among standing dead trunks awaited us. Soon after, following the sound of the river, we reached a postcard landscape of river and fall colours, complete with 50-cm trout

TIPS (fun for 5 years +)
• Exploring the shores would be even more fun with high rubber boots.
• The section of **Rouge Park** accessible from Twyn Rivers Drive is more fun to visit with energetic children 7 years and older with a taste for adventure.
• **Glen Rouge Campground** is located by the Kingston Road access. To reserve a campsite, call (416) 338-2267 or e-mail at camping@toronto.ca

NEARBY ATTRACTIONS

jumping against the current! I just could not believe we could observe such a phenomenon so close to Toronto!

We then walked back to the asphalt road and to the parking lot. The whole walk took us about one hour.

Kingston Road access

The path near the **Glen Rouge Campground** is the one that leads to the **Riverside Trail**, which has the biggest trees. The high canopy scarcely allows sunbeams to penetrate the forest. At the height of the summer, it is a great place to hide from the heat of the day.

When we were visiting, the riverside trail was closed to be rejuvenated. The path we took, steep at times, ran through the forest and reached a clearing in half an hour. We turned back while my little explorer still had energy left.

Rouge Park
• Scarborough
(416) 392-1111
www.rougepark.com
www.rvcc.ca

D-3
N-E
of downtown
30-min.

 Schedule: Open year-round.
Admission: FREE.
 Directions: Reesor Road access: Take Meadowvale northbound past the zoo, turn west on Old Finch, then north on Reesor Road. There is a small parking lot just south of Steeles. The park entrance lies at the end of a small clearing, not too far from the **Little Rouge River**.
Pearse House access: Go east on Zoo Road going over Meadowvale Road (in front of the **Toronto Zoo** entrance).
Twyn Rivers Drive access: Driving from Meadowvale, turn east on Sheppard Avenue and take the first fork to the left (The Twyn Rivers Drive). Pay attention, as this branch is easy to miss if you are coming from Sheppard eastbound.
Kingston Road access: From Hwy 401 East, take exit #392/Port Union northbound, turn east on Kingston Road, the entrance is on the north side.

BELFOUNTAIN C.A.

Small is beautiful

It's tiny. A short 1.5-km trail covers the whole park. However, it's so pretty! It boasts a fountain, a pond, a rumbling waterfall, a dam and a suspension bridge. No wonder so many people have their wedding pictures taken here.

I first stumbled upon **Belfountain C.A.** while driving on the beautiful Forks of the Credit Road, a small, tree-lined country road built over several sizeable hills. (It was closed for renovations in the fall 2010 so we arrived from Charleston Side Rd. and Mississauga Rd., not as spectacular but still offering a lovely ride.)

Nice picnic spots lie by the water. Swimming is not allowed but fishing in the cold, spring-fed water of the **West Credit River** is (with a licence).

The original owner, who put up all the other existing structures at the beginning of the last century, also built a mini "Yellowstone Cave" which fires up fertile imaginations. For the first time in years, it was open when we visited in 2010 (see p. 134).

The suspension bridge just down-

stream from the dam is long enough to impress children.

A path begins beside the fountain and disappears under the trees. It runs alongside the roaring river that lies 25 metres below. Now's the time to hold on to your little ones! At times, the path's incline is quite steep. It eventually leads to a small boardwalk that stands one metre above a large stream. The kids stopped and played a good while with the stream's running water.

If you cross on the other side, you'll head back to the suspension bridge through a demanding trail lined with roots and boulders.

Last fall, we chose to stay on the trail instead of crossing the bridge. It quickly led us into the **Bruce Trail**, where we could truly enjoy the fall colours. We walked for 20 minutes until we reached the Forks of the Credit Rd., which we took to our right. Just around the bend, we bought honey from a roadside stand and saw a historical train pass over our heads! (See **www.creditvalleyexplorer.com** for details about this 3-hour ride, around $45.)

TIPS (fun for 5 years +)

• Bringing a stroller along wasn't a great idea. When I did, I had to go down a long series of low steps leading to the river, then continue on rocky trails.
• At the park's exit, you will find a shop selling great ice cream.
• On a busy weekend, leave your car in the conservation area if you want to visit the village of Belfountain, a 15-min. walk away. It is small, but has a well stocked general store, a great coffee shop **Shed**, which also sells delicious soup and scones in the fall, near a snack bar selling hot dogs.

NEARBY ATTRACTIONS
Art Walk of Tree Sculptures (15-min.) p. 110
Cheltenham Badlands (15-min.)   p. 232

Belfountain Conservation Area	**C-2**
· Belfountain	**N-W**
(519) 927-5838	**of Toronto**
or 1-800-668-5557	**45-min.**
www.creditvalleycons.com	

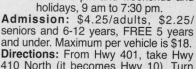

Schedule: From late April to late June, open on Fridays, weekends and holidays, 10 am to 5 pm. From late June to Labour Day, open daily 9 am to 9 pm. From early September to mid-October, Monday to Friday, 11 am to 6 pm and weekends and holidays, 9 am to 7:30 pm.

Admission: $4.25/adults, $2.25/seniors and 6-12 years, FREE 5 years and under. Maximum per vehicle is $18.

Directions: From Hwy 401, take Hwy 410 North (it becomes Hwy 10). Turn west at The Forks of the Credit Rd., the conservation is right before Belfountain.

NIAGARA GLEN & WHIRPOOL

This trail rocks!

The trail at Niagara Glen is packed with surprises at every turn over a short distance. The natural setting is so strong, with bold features, it is sure to melt any teenager's resentment over having been taken out of his little bubble. Guaranteed or your money back (but it's free).

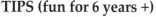

TIPS (fun for 6 years +)

• You can download the map from their website (go to *Things to do*, then *Nature Trails*, then *Niagara Glen & Whirlpool*). I should have done that. It would have made our lives easier!

• When looking at the online map, I realized that we missed a very interesting stretch along the red-marked **Terrace Path**. It seems we could have taken the light-blue **Trillium Path** (between the jet boat spot and the **Cobblestone Path**) to reach it, then turning left to see many points of interest. We could then have taken the white path up and back to the staircase.

• It would be stressful to go with a child who's not too sturdy on his legs. Some passages are too narrow to walk side by side, holding their hand. It may be slippery and you want to be extra careful by the river.

• Note that the **Totem Park** which was right by Niagara Glen, has unfortunately been permanently closed.

• For information about the jet boat rides, see **www.whirlpooljet.com**. They depart from Niagara-on-the-Lake.

NEARBY ATTRACTIONS
Butterfly Conservatory (1-min.) ..... p. 78
Niagara Falls (10-min.) .... p. 253

You can't see anything from the parking lot. Then, there it is, the 4-storey-high metal staircase that will take you down to the trail (a promising start for young explorers).

We chose to go to our right along the **Cliffside Path** (marked in white) and then to follow the green marks into the **Eddie Path**. It led us through our first set of stone stairs carved into the rock. Wow!

We kept walking towards the water, following the sound of... jet boats! It was very exciting to get a glimpse of them on the green water down from us. We followed the blue-marked **River Path** going downstream. A few minutes further, we saw a whole family going down a natural path to get closer to the water and the large boulders in the river.

We followed them and stayed for a while on the bedrock under the warm sun to admire the whirlpool jet boats trying to ride against the strong current. The perfect spot for a picnic!

We stayed on this path, where I saw a small spring spraying out of a green moss-lined hole on a wall of rock along the blue trail. We eventually reached the **Cobblestone Path** marked in lavender (another great rocky section) going up to the white path leading us back to the staircase on our left.

Niagara Glen & Whirlpool • Niagara Falls www.niagaraparks.com	E-4 Niagara Region 90-min.

 Schedule: Open year-round.
Admission: FREE.
 Directions: Take QEW towards Niagara and Fort Erie. Past St. Catharines, keep left to take Hwy 405 (Queenston). Take Stanley Avenue exit on the right (at the top of the ramp, turn left onto Stanley). Turn right on Portage Rd., then right on Niagara Parkway. Enter the **Niagara Glen** parking lot to your left.

General tips about
Playgrounds:

- Always have socks handy for your kids when visiting an indoor playground (even in the middle of the summer when they're wearing sandals). They're mandatory in all indoor playgrounds. Some sell them on the premises but many don't!

- Always call or check their online calendar before going to an indoor playground. Most playgrounds' bread & butter comes from birthday parties so it happens that they close earlier to accommodate such parties. In some cases, the playgrounds create special events for the benefit of their regular customers, with an extra fee involved. They often request people book in advance for these events.

- Many playgrounds offer extended hours on **P. D.** days, **Family Day** and **March Break**.

PLAYGROUNDS

See **Funnelz** on p. 313.

DROP-IN CENTRES

Just drop in!

My preschooler rushes to the sand box, thinking it's quite the treat, given that we are in the middle of winter! She then embarks on a creative game with her 3-year-old friend, involving a doll house, an army of plastic animals and a tow truck. Meanwhile, I sit in the baby section surrounded by age-appropriate toys and play with my friend's infant who lies on a floor cushion.

Drop-in centres vary in size, activities and members' involvement. Yet, all offer an opportunity for preschoolers and their parents or caregivers to meet other children and grown-ups and enjoy informal playtime.

Kids also really love the opportunity to play with toys different from those at home.

In most of the drop-ins I have visited, there was a kindergarten feeling to the place; from the layout of the room with their craft and snack tables, to an array of well categorized toys.

Most mornings, there is a circle time where adults and children are encouraged to sing or listen to a story. A healthy snack is usually provided in each of the morning and afternoon sessions.

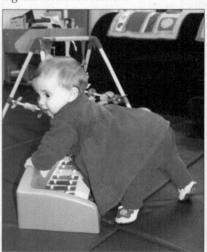

TIPS (fun for 5 years & under)
• Call them or check on their website (under *Locations*) to find the closest drop-in in your area. If it is not to your liking, try the next closest to you. Once you find a drop-in you like, adopt it! You and your child will eventually create a valuable network of friends.
• A mother told me about a very special drop-in centre catering to children (6 years and under) with hearing problems at the **Bob Rumball Family Resource Centre for the Deaf and Hard-of-Hearing** (2395 Bayview Ave., 416-449-9651, ext. 105, www. rumballfamilyresource.org). The staff is fluent in sign language. Call for exact schedule.

Ontario Early Years Centres
1-866-821-7770
www.ontarioearlyyears.ca

 Schedule: Most offer hours during school time. Schedules vary for each centre.
 Admission: FREE.
Directions: All around Ontario.
 Found by region on their website.

PLAYGROUND PARADISE

A divine mural

Playground Paradise's walls and ceiling are covered by a magnificent painted birch forest. The mural successfully gives an intimate feel to this vast area. This meadow-like atmosphere brightens up gloomy days.

Two-thirds of the space is occupied by a two-storey play structure designed to get muscles working. Children can circulate underneath it. Inside, there is an 8,000-ball pit with targets, as well as spiral and straight slides.

I was charmed by several of the place's original features: a zip line, a distorting mirror, big punching bags and more.

The rest of the space included a myriad of vinyl shapes used by children to build shelters. For preschoolers, there was a construction blocks table, a wide activity board and a few toys.

There are only a few benches for parents to sit on. Instead of sitting on the ground, you might as well... join the kids on the play structures!

Since my last visit, they've added a treehouse for the smaller kids.

TIPS (fun for 2 to 12 years)
• Socks are mandatory.
• They offer the cheapest birthday party package in town but you need to reserve way in advance.
• They have a small spray pad with a giant flower on the side of the building. Bring bathing suits... and sun screen (there's no shade).
• Kids can also play in the good outdoor playground in nearby **Flemingdon Park**, a few minutes walk away.
• The indoor playground offers an affordable snack bar and machines.

NEARBY ATTRACTIONS	
Ontario Science Centre (5-min.)	p. 226
Toronto Botanical (10-min.)	p. 262

Playground Paradise • North York (416) 395-6014	**D-3** **North** of downtown **20-min.**

Schedule: Normally open year-round on weekends, 12:30 to 5 pm. On weekdays, open Monday, Wednesday and Friday with varying hours through the year. (At the time of print, they opened 9:30 to 11:30 am, Monday and Wednesday; 1 pm to 3 pm, 4:30 pm to 8:30 pm, Monday, Wednesday and Friday.) Call before you go!

Admission: (cash only) $2.25/child on weekdays, $2.25/hour/child on weekends and holidays. FREE for accompanying grownup of 16 years and over.

Directions: 150 Grenoble Drive, North York. From Don Mills Rd. (south of Eglinton), turn east on Gateway Blvd.

WOODIE WOOD CHUCK'S

A kid-friendly interior

There's a major heat wave going on, and your house is not air-conditioned. The children are bursting with energy, but it's raining cats and dogs and the neighbourhood playground looks like a duck pond. So many good reasons to resort to the services of large playgrounds such as that of Woodie Wood Chuck's!

Neon lights, machine noises and children's screams bouncing off cement walls, all combine in a cacophony for the senses that makes me want to turn around as soon as we step in. A quick glance at my child's excited look convinces me we're here to stay... at least a couple of hours! Once I've come to terms with the idea, there are in fact several good surprises that await.

This indoor park is big. It includes a section of sixty "pay-as-you-play" token games, where you can test your throwing, pushing and hitting skills. **Woodie Wood Chuck's** main attraction, however, is its huge play area spread over two floors.

The imposing structure in itself is well worth the visit. Large modules are connected by transparent tunnels or suspended bridges. All abound with hidden corners to explore. Ropes, slides, an enclosure filled with colourful balls, boxing cushions, tunnels and ladders; everything has been planned for the enjoyment of young climbers.

A note of caution however: It is very easy to lose sight of a child in this maze of corridors, and while adults are allowed on the structure, they can only go on when the playground is not too busy. Younger ones should therefore be encouraged to stay in the smaller playing area.

The place includes a small stage with characters playing in a band.

TIPS (fun for 2 to 12 years)
• Socks are mandatory.
• Look carefully. You can't see the façade from Sheppard Avenue. It faces Brimley Road.
• They sell pizza and have a table section. There is also a large central area with tables, surrounded by bay windows. It is a great refuge for adults with sensitive hearing.

NEARBY ATTRACTIONS
Around Scarborough Station .... p. 465

Woodie Wood Chuck's
• Scarborough
(416) 298-3555
www.woodiewoodchucks.ca

D-3
N-E
of downtown
25-min.

Schedule: Monday to Thursday, 11 am to 9 pm, Friday, 11 am to 10 pm, Saturday, 10 am to 10 pm, Sunday 10 am to 9 pm.

Admission: $1.50/child, FREE for accompanying adult.

Scarborough: 4466 Sheppard Ave. East (from Hwy 401 West, take exit #379/ Kennedy northbound, turn east on Sheppard. It is east of Brimley Road.

FUNNELZ

Time to go ballistic

Seriously, your kids will go ballistic. The Ballistics Arena will make sure of that. Adults, beware. You'll be the target (of very soft foam balls mind you). And watch out for your rear when you go down the steep slides after your little one. Nobody said parenting was an easy job!

At the entrance, I see a mom in her winter coat flash by and return with her son who had fled towards the playground, boots still on, as soon as she had turned her back.

In the back of the room, closer to the snack bar section, is the area for the younger kids with balls section. Next is the popular **Ballistics Arena** providing unique features: three shooters facing each other in small raised booths and a large inverse funnel vacuuming the balls to then project them into the air. The older kids try to fill the huge funnel to create the biggest blast of colourful balls but younger kids who don't understand the concept keep pushing the button before it is time. Watching them blow into the air and rain down on the kids never gets tiring. (See photo on p. 309.)

You can jump into an inflatable structure, go through a corridor filled with punching bags, go over padded obstacles, ride the purple slide with bumps to slow you down or fly by the seat of your pants down the steep and large red slide. My young companions must have gone down twenty times in a row on that one. Me? Once.

TIPS (fun for 2 to 12 years)

• Parents are allowed on the structures. Socks are mandatory.
• When I visited, there were a few token machines to play with but none of those distributing tickets to exchange for trinkets.
• **Eglinton Town Centre** (part of Cineplex Odeon) is on the same block (see www.cinemaclock.com for listings) along with **Imperial Buffet**, a big all-you-can-eat buffet restaurant open for lunch and dinner (www.imperialbuffet.com).

NEARBY ATTRACTIONS
Botanical Garden (15-min.) ...... p. 262
Warden Woods (10-min.) .... p. 464

Funnelz Indoor Party & Play Center
• Scarborough
(416) 759-9555
www.funnelz.ca

D-3
N-E
of downtown
25-min.

Schedule: Tuesday to Saturday, 10 am to 9 pm; Sunday and Monday, 10 am to 7 pm.

Admission: Around $10/first child ($2 less on weekdays), $6/add. sibling (up to three), $5.50/1-3 years, FREE under 1.

Directions: 24 Lebovic Avenue, Unit C3, Scarborough. From Don Valley Parkway, exit at Eglinton and go eastbound. From Hwy 401, take Warden South, turn east on Eglinton. Lebovic is south of Eglinton.

KIDSPORTS

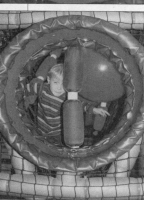

Fun network

Once again, a net partition separates us from our destination: a net corridor with deep holes filled with balls, located on the top level of the 3-storey-high structure. Finding the right entrance to get there is a real mind game and it's part of the fun.

Colourful houses dressed in turquoise, fuchsia, corals and blues mark the food area by **Kidsports'** entrance.

The apparent low height of the building from the outside is misleading because the interior is designed in split levels, with the play area actually nestled below ground level.

The impressive indoor climbing structure is topped with a bright papier mâché dragon. It is the best climber we have tried!

Adults and kids alike crouch to climb from one level of a net labyrinth to the next. It is the only way to reach the many slides, fire poles, tunnels, corridors outfitted with punching bags and ball rooms located in the vertical maze. (Grown-ups beware, the nets are hard on the feet.)

Some twenty token games are scattered around the structure, including an air hockey table which could make a few tokens go a long way!

There is a smaller structure for younger kids at the other end of the building, as well as a room filled with big toys and gym cushions ideal for toddlers.

TIPS (fun for 2 to 12 years)

• Socks are mandatory.
• Hundreds of happy kids and token machines in action creates high decibels. Be prepared.
• Most machines reward the players with tickets they can trade for trinkets at a counter. This is an irresistible concept for kids over 5 years old. I strongly suggest you budget an additional $3 to $5 per child to give them the pleasure of winning something. Kidsports conveniently offers gadgets you can get for only a few tickets.

NEARBY ATTRACTIONS
Pearson Int'l Airport (10-min.) ...... p. 190
Centennial Mini-Indy (5-min.) ...... p. 196

Kidsports
· Mississauga
(905) 624-9400
www.
kidsports.sites.toronto.com

**D-3
West
of Toronto
35-min.**

Schedule: Monday to Sunday, 10 am to 8 pm (closes at 9 pm on Fridays).

Admission: Around $9/children 3 years and up, $5/under 3 years, $2/under one year, $2/adults. Check their website for specials.

Directions: 4500 Dixie Road, Mississauga (south of Eglinton).

PLAY-A-SAURUS

Photo: Courtesy of Play-A-Saurus

Still pretty but noisier

I fell for the zany murals that cover all the walls. Here, huge dinosaurs relax on the couch. There, other dinosaurs seem as busy as the kids on the floor and in the large climbing structure. And on the floor, little dinosaurs enthralled my daughter.

Since my last visit, they've kept the murals but they have traded the spacious layout (which allowed parents to watch their brood without difficulty) for more action for the kids.

They've added a large climbing structure surrounding the ball pit, from which they slide into the balls (**Saurus Land**) and a large inflatable structure (noisier, but much appreciated by the little jumping beans).

Because of these additions, the playground, which used to be interesting for kids 7 and under, can now appeal to older kids as well.

Photo: Courtesy of Play-A-Saurus

TIPS (fun for 2 to 12 years)
• Socks are required at all times.
• They no longer offer special events for Halloween, Christmas and Easter.
• They sell snacks.
• **Erin Mills Town Centre** (www.erinmills.ca) is a 10-minute drive away (at Eglinton and Erin Mills Pkwy). It includes **Sears**, **Zellers**, **The Bay** and **Indigo**.

NEARBY ATTRACTIONS
Streetsville Memorial Park (15-min.) p. 303

Play-A-Saurus
• Mississauga
(905) 607-6060
www.playasaurus.ca

D-3
N-W
of Toronto
35-min.

Schedule: Open Tuesday to Friday, 9 am to 3:30 pm. Private parties on the weekends. Closed on Mondays.

Admission: $8/child, $4/sibling, FREE for adult and infant with older sibling.

Directions: 3355 The Collegeway (Units 30 & 31), Mississauga. From QEW West, take exit #124/Winston Churchill northbound. Turn west on The Collegeway. The playground is at the corner of Ridgeway Drive and Collegeway, on your right.

CHUCK E. CHEESE

While her brother is enthralled by the machines, my daughter climbs next to **Chuck E. Cheese** and dances along as the big plush mechanical mouse sings a lively tune with its musicians.

A video clip is shown on a couple of monitors by the stage and every song is followed by a five minute shut down of the mechanical band. Let's party!

Games on the menu

At first, the place looks like a well-staffed family restaurant (which it is). Then, the noise level reminds you this is an amusement centre above all!

As we get settled in a booth located by a huge maze structure of tubes and tunnels, we notice an army of kids free-roaming the site. Between the short, free-of-charge shows, the climbing structure (where adults are also welcome) and some 40 token games (many of them requiring only one token, and dispensing tickets to redeem for trinkets), the kids were so busy, I had the luxury of reading a few chapters of the book I had the good foresight to bring!

Food is ordered at the counter but waiters serve at your table.

TIPS (fun for 2 to 12 years)
• Socks are mandatory.
• I suggest you avoid these types of outings unless you are prepared to spend a few dollars on tokens. Even with dollars in hand, it seems you need loads of tickets to win anything remotely interesting (to you). As for my kids, all they really wanted was to win something... anything!
• We visited during Christmas time and the Chuck E. Cheese band's songs and clips were in the Christmas spirit.
• Pizza is Chuck E. Cheese's specialty. There is also a salad bar and hot sandwiches. Some value packages are real savers if you intend to buy tokens.

Chuck E. Cheese
www.chuckecheese.com

Schedule: Most locations are open daily, 9 am to 10 pm (closing at 11 pm on Fridays and Saturdays).

Admission: FREE (free refills on all soft drinks). See food coupons on website.

Directions: Willowdale: 2452 Sheppard Ave. East (just west of Victoria Park), 416-497-8855.

Newmarket: 17410 Yonge St. (south of Davis Dr.), 905-953-8664.

Whitby: 75 Consumer Dr., Building J (from Hwy 401, take exit #412/Thickson Rd. northbound, turn west on Consumer Dr.), 905-665-2142.

Mississauga: 4141 Dixie Rd., (south of Rathburn Rd.), 905-602-4090.

Vaughan: 3255 Rutherford Rd. (east of Hwy 400), 905-532-0241.

Mississauga West: 2945 Argentina Rd. (east of Winston Churchill Blvd., south of Hwy 401), 905-785-3593.

Cambridge: 42 Pine Bush Rd. (from Hwy 401, take exit #282/Hespeler Rd. southbound, turn east on Pine Bush), 519-621-7752.

Kingston: 768 Gardiner Rd. (from Hwy 401, exit at Gardiner Rd.), 613-634-7510.

PEANUT CLUB (NORTH YORK)

Monkey fun

The place is bright and colourful with house facades adorning the walls. The climbing structure is fit for little monkeys. An enclosure with a wall to wall castle interior holds all the toys to play house. It creates a feeling of intimacy quite appreciated by little homemakers.

Note there is a **Bowlerama** in the same building with a snack bar (www.bathurstbowlerama.com).

Peanut Club • North York (416) 782-8735 www.peanutclub.com	D-3 N-W of downtown 25-min.

 Schedule: Open for drop-in Monday to Friday, 9:30 am to 3 pm. (Closes at 2 pm during the summer. Closes at 5 pm on Tuesdays and Wednesdays from November through April.)

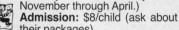 **Admission:** $8/child (ask about their packages).

 Directions: 2788 Bathurst Street, North York (south of Lawrence).

KIDS ZONE

In the zone

An original climbing structure with a pipe system allowing kids to talk from one tunnel to the next and a laser tag game can be found here.

Among other things, it includes an area with a giant ball and a suspended bridge. The place also offers a section for

 smaller children with kiddie rides and arcade, and a cafeteria with numerous tables. Their **Laser Tag** is a laser game for kids 8 to 16 years old (min. 48 inches high at the shoulder) and a stuff-your-own-bear activity.

Kids Zone Family Fun Centre • Whitby (905) 666-5437 www.kidszonedurham.com	C-4 East of Toronto 40-min.

Schedule: Normally open year-round on weekends, 10 am to 6:30 pm minimum, and Monday to Friday, 10 am to 4 pm minimum (extended seasonal hours). Check website for Laser and Teddy Bear hours.

 Admission: $8.50/2-12 years, $6/12-23 months, FREE for accompanying adults. Extra cost for **Laser Tag** and bear workshop.

Directions: 12 Stanley Court, Whitby. From Hwy 401, take exit #410/Brock St. northbound, turn east on Consumer Dr., north on Garden St., east again on Burns St.; Stanley Court is on the right.

THE BUSY GENIE

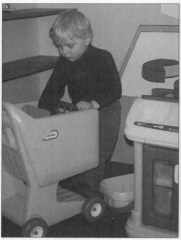

Life on a mini scale

When he was three years old, my little brother, seeing his mother suffering from a painful attack, hurried to get his medical kit to relieve her while the ambulance was coming. That's when I understood how seriously children take role-playing games. The Busy Genie (formerly Mary's Playland) knows this as a fact and offers us an indoor street, scaled perfectly to its miniature visitors.

ATTENTION! The **Busy Genie** was about to move at the time of print (see new address in the information box). The playground has once again changed administration since my last edition but they are keeping the great concept... and

moving it into a space twice as big.

I expect children will react the same when they enter the new place. They will fidget impatiently, sensing this is a different kind of playground.

The concept is simple, yet not an obvious one. Lovely displays that incorporate the best large plastic toys such as Little Tikes, are created to encourage creative play.

The new owner has assured me that you will find, side-by-side, a little house fully equipped with kitchen, dining room and living room on the second floor, a beauty salon that can accommodate a few clients, a garage (gas pump, tools and hardhat included), a grocery store (a real hit with my aspiring home economist) outfitted with food carts and produce displays. You will also find a basketball hoop and a multicoloured ball pit.

She's taking advantage of the bigger space to add a new soft foam play area for the little ones. The older kids will enjoy jumping in the new bounce castle and riding on cool plasma cars (ride-on toys).

TIPS (fun 8 years & under)
• Socks are mandatory.
• Snacks are available. They also sell many trinkets and small toys for parties and they have a popular consignment section selling clothing, toys, equipment.
• If you have errands in the neighbourhood, they offer a drop-off service: $15/one child per hour, reduced price for siblings. You need to call ahead to reserve a spot. Note that there's a **Mastermind Toys** store just one minute drive west of the playground (4242 Dundas West).

NEARBY ATTRACTIONS

The Busy Genie
• Etobicoke
(416) 236-5437
www.thebusygenie.com

D-3
N-W
of downtown
20-min.

Schedule: Monday to Friday, 9:30 am to 6 pm; Saturdays, 9:30 am to 1 pm (Sundays open for parties only).

Admission: $10/one child, $7/ sibling. Read TIPS about drop-off services. FREE parking.

Directions: 4133 Dundas Street West, Etobicoke (just east of Prince Edward Drive).

AMAZON DOWNTOWN

They're at that stage...

I watch my little butterfly flash by me and disappear into the climbing structure. A moment later, she reappears in the... eye of a huge monkey's head.

This place is special. It is one of the few I have visited that offers costumes to play dress-up and the only one with a small stage, complete with background curtains to fire up children's imaginations.

A puppet theatre comes as a bonus. This indoor playground also comes with the big climbing structure supporting the monkey head, ball pits, soft blocks and rider toys with some space to circulate.

I liked the large bay windows. Parents are allowed in the structure. Or they can rest on the large sofas.

TIPS (fun for 7 years & under)
- Socks are mandatory.
- They offer complimentary coffee and tea and sell candy.
- Check the ice cream shop **Dutch Dream** (10-minute walk away) on p. 476.

NEARBY ATTRACTIONS
Winston Churchill Park (5-min.) ... p. 362

Amazon Downtown
(416) 656-5832
www.
amazondowntown.com

D-3
N-W
of downtown
25-min.

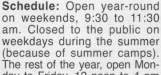

Schedule: Open year-round on weekends, 9:30 to 11:30 am. Closed to the public on weekdays during the summer (because of summer camps). The rest of the year, open Monday to Friday, 12 noon to 4 pm (open later some evenings, call to confirm).

Admission: $9/child over 10 months, FREE/10 months and under if with sibling (otherwise $6).

Directions: 21 Vaughan Road, Unit 108, Toronto (located on a v-shaped block south of St. Clair West). The playground is a 10-minute walk from **St. Clair West Subway Station**.

PLAYGROUNDS ON MY WISH LIST

For a change

I've never visited a small playground that wouldn't do the job if your main goal is to meet other parents/caregivers or give your child a chance to play with big toys you don't have at home. But if you want a change of scenery from your local playground, or if you happen to be in the vicinity of the following playgrounds, here are a few suggestions with a twist.

I have not had the chance to visit personally the indoor playgrounds listed below but based on my experience, these will be worth the drive.

Photo: Courtesy of The Funnery Play Park & Café

Mess for Fun
• North York
(30-min. north of downtown)
(416) 736-7101
www.messforfun.com
This playground with inflated structures, play structure and large toys is also a ceramic studio. Now, that's an interesting combination for siblings in different age groups! (The playground is designed for kids under 8 years old.)

Schedule: Tuesday, Wednesday, Saturday and Sunday, 10 am to 6 pm; Thursday and Friday, 12 noon to 6 pm. Closed on Mondays.
Admission: (For up to 2 hours) **Playground**: $8/child; **Ceramic Studio**: $7/adult and $5/14 years and under, plus the cost of the ceramic piece. **Paint & Play** combo: $11 plus the cost of the piece. Glaze is $1 per piece.
Directions: 73 Alness Street, Unit #3, North York (north of Finch, off Dufferin, turn west on Martin Ross Ave., then south on Alness).
Nearby: 10-min. drive from **Yorkdale Shopping Centre** (www.yorkdale.com).

Taima Zone
• Mississauga
(30-min. west of Toronto)
(905) 607-3861
www.taimazone.ca
Want to brush up on your Spanish? Go to this playground held by Venezuelans and offering Zumba sessions. Kids (who are potty trained) can play for $4 (in the two-storey structure or in the toddler area) while their mom takes a Zumba class. They have more events and classes offering families a chance to dance together.

Schedule: Monday to Friday, at least from 9:30 am to 7 pm. Weekends, at least 12 noon to 7 pm (call to verify that it's not closed for parties).
Admission: $9/2-14 years, $5/second sibling, FREE under 2 with siblings, $4/while parent is in class.
Directions: 3450 Ridgeway Drive, Unit #10, Mississauga. From QEW, take Winston Churchill north, then turn west on The Collegeway, and north on Ridgeway.

Photo: Courtesy of Zooz Indoor Playground

Zooz Indoor Playground
• Aurora
(35-min. north of Toronto)
(905) 713-1800
www.zoozindoorplayground.com
Great murals in this one! The large play structure is adorned with a giant toucan's head. They have climbing walls, video games, bouncing structure, costume section, small animals and a café-style section.

Schedule: Monday to Friday 9:30 am to 2:30 pm (closes at 7:30 pm on Wednesdays). Variable hours on weekends. Call!
Admission: $8/first child, $6/siblings, FREE/under 12 months (free regular coffee).
Directions: 73 Industrial Parkway North, Unit 2B, Aurora. From Hwy 404 (north of 401), take exit #45 (Wellington St.) westbound, turn north on Industrial Pkwy).
Nearby: Cineplex Odeon Aurora Cinemas (check www.cinemaclock.com).

Amazing Adventures Playland

• **Burlington**
(40-min. west of Toronto)
(905) 639-6544
www.amazingadventuresplayland.ca

The place includes a 17-foot-high play structure (adorned with a jet) with swirl slide, triple slide, trolley ride and more. There are two inflatable structures. They offer an enclosed area with motorized "motorcycles" for younger kids and a toddler section. That should help them blow off some steam! (They also have a **Build a Teddy** section.)

Schedule: Open daily from 9:30 am, closes at 3:30 pm Monday to Thursday, 8 pm on Fridays and 12 noon on weekends.
Admission: $8/2-12 years, $6/1-2 years, FREE under 1 year old with sibling.
Directions: 4325 Harvester Rd. Unit #5, Burlington. From QEW, take exit #107 (Appleby Line) southbound, then turn west on Harvester.

Photo: Courtesy of The Funnery Play Park & Café

The Funnery Play Park & Café

• **Newmarket**
(45-min. north of Toronto)
(905) 252-1619
www.funneryplaypark.com

This place seems like a good playground paying special attention to the comfort of the accompanying adults! French Press coffee, specialty teas, freshly baked squares, ambiance lighting, stools, chandelier... next to a gorgeous climbing structure with a tree-house and fun climbing ropes.

Schedule: Monday to Saturday, 9 am to 8 pm; Sunday, 9 am to 5 pm. Call ahead to make sure it's not closing earlier for a party.
Admission: $8/2-12 years, $6/1-2 years, FREE under 1 year old with sibling.
Directions: 611 Steven Court, Unit #3, Newmarket. From Hwy 404, take exit #49 (Mulock Dr.) and turn west on Mulock, then south on Steven Ct. (past Prospect St.).

Photo: Courtesy of In Play Inc.

In Play Inc.

• **Newmarket**
(45-min. north of Toronto)
(905) 953-8299
www.inplayinc.ca

Their spread of activities is impressive: huge playground, wide rock climbing wall, glow in the dark mini golf, arcade with redemption games, bear making, snack bar.

Schedule: Open daily from 9:30 am, closes at 3:30 pm Monday to Thursday, 8 pm on Fridays and 12 noon on weekends.
Admission: Each attraction is individually priced. Playground: $6/2-14 years old. Mini golf: $5/per round. Rock climbing: $7/unlimited. **Directions:** 18075 Leslie St., Newmarket. (There's another **In Play Inc.** in Barrie, see their website for details.)

Lil' Explorers Clubhouse

• **Markham**
(35-min. northeast of Toronto)
(905) 910-7529
www.lilexplorers.ca

This one caught my attention because it is one of the few that offers a climbing wall behind the raised play area adorned with a "helicopter". They also have fun climbing ropes. It doesn't seem really big but it includes an area for smaller kids. Check their events calendar about special characters and events days.

Schedule: Tuesday-Friday 10 am to 2:30 pm.
Admission: $7/first child, $5/additional siblings.
Directions: 190 Bullock Dr., Unit #10, Markham. From Hwy 404, exit at Hwy 7, turn east, then north on McCowan and east on Bullock.

PLAYGROUNDS WITH INFLATABLES

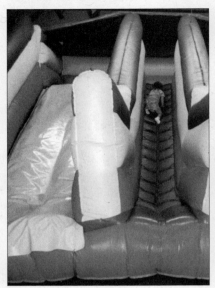

Slam-bam fun

These have to be the noisiest places, with all those air pumps at work.
Chances are your kids will accidentally
knock each other's heads (my kids did)
in the midst of such excitement! And yet,
bouncing and jumping on the inflated
structures remains a favourite of energetic children.

Such play centres can be a life-saver
during cold winter days, and a welcome
air-conditioned break during hot summer
days.

Under separate ownerships, the
two centres offer similar attractions
that include inflatable structures, token
machines and a large food area filled with
tables.

The Pickering one (the only one I
have visited) also offers a glow-in-the-
dark 9-hole mini golf room with dark
fluorescent mini golf lit under black light.
Beware, it could be in use for birthday
parties when you visit.

TIPS (fun for 4 to 12 years)
• Socks are mandatory.
• Parents are not allowed on the inflatable structures. These could be suitable
for kids under 4 years old if they are very
strong on their feet.
• Children have way more fun when
attending places like these with friends.

Air Zone Party & Play Centre
· Pickering
(905) 839-1047
www.airzoneparties.com

C-4
East
of Toronto
35-min.

Schedule: Open Monday to Saturday,
10 am to 8 pm; Sunday, 10 am to 6 pm.
Admission: $6/child on weekends, $1
less on weekdays, FREE for adults.
Extra fees/mini golf, arcade.
Directions: 1095 Kingston Rd., Pick-
ering (from Hwy 401, take exit #394/
Whites Rd. northbound, turn east on
Kingston Rd.).

Airzone Oshawa
· Oshawa
(905) 377-9663
www.airzoneoshawa.com

C-4
East
of Toronto
45-min.

Schedule: Tuesday to Friday, 10 am to
8 pm; weekends, 10 am to 6 pm (closes
at 7 pm on Saturdays in winter).
Admission: $6 per child on weekends,
$5 on weekdays, 2-for-1 on Tuesdays.
Directions: 385 Bloor Street, Oshawa
(from Hwy 401, take exit #416 towards
RR-54/Park Rd., then follow Bloor St.
East ramp toward RR-54 and turn east
on Bloor Street.

TORONTO'S KID-FEST

Unstoppable!

The concept is very simple. Fill a room with inflatable structures in all shapes and sizes and let the kids go wild. It's noisy. It's chaotic. It's pure fun. Plus, they get quite a workout at it, believe me. Bring lots of water.

In a fair, we get to climb up a few inflatable structures between two rides. Here, it's all about the inflatables. When we visited, I counted sixteen of them. Parents could climb on all of them.

There were simple ones with slides, suitable for young kids but others were elaborate, requiring a steep climb before you could go down a steeper slide. A really long one involved an obstacle course that raised their heartbeats. Another one invited kids to race against one another, starting with a jump head first through a giant doughnut.

Some, we had never seen or never had the chance to try. My 12-year-old companions could not get enough of the one with a large ball on a rope you push at your opponents to destabilize them and the one where you compete against your friend on an air-inflated arena with a padded jousting pole.

Their favourite was the bull rodeo. Hand-controlled by staff, it is suitable for any kid who can sit on a bull. The older the kids, the rougher it gets. They all end up being thrown off onto the soft mattress, which is a good show in itself.

When we visited, the event also included a birds of prey show, pony rides (for an extra $5) and many tables with vendors. The following year, they offered storytelling and magic shows.

TIPS (fun for 4 years +)

• If you go with a young child, you'll have to buy the all-day-ticket to accompany them. Many preschoolers need their parents' help to push their bum up steep climbs. In some inflatables with tunnels and labyrinth-like design, your child looses sight of you, which can be disturbing for toddlers.

• Older kids will be happy with you just waiting for them in the line-up of the next structure they'll go on (you only need to pay ground admission to play that dignified role). Bring a book!

• There's a small snack bar on site.

• The organization behind **Toronto Kids-Fest** also runs **Hamilton Kidfest** at the same time in Hamilton.

NEARBY ATTRACTIONS

Toronto's Kids-Fest	**D-3**
• Mississauga	**N-W**
www.kids-fest.ca	**of Toronto**
	35-min.

Schedule: Saturday to Monday on Family Day Weekend, from 10 am to 5 pm.

Admission: All Day Ride pass is $25/person (excludes a few rides). Individual tickets are $2 each if you buy 10 or more. Book online to save $3.

Directions: International Centre, 6900 Airport Rd., in Hall 3, Mississauga. From Hwy 427 northbound, take Dixon Road exit. Turn left at Dixon, it becomes Airport Road. The centre is on your right.

LITTLE NORWAY PARK

Who knew?

I never expected to find such a tall and beautiful totem in such a secluded little park. And there was much more to discover as we walked further in: a giant lion leaning on a slide, the small labyrinth, a little forest and the pier behind, overlooking the glittering water of Lake Ontario.

When you read the plaques by the entrance, you learn that this used to be a training camp for Norway's Air Force during World War II and that it was officially opened by the King of Nor-

way in 1987. I don't know when it fell into oblivion but this little park is a keeper.

There were many details to observe on the 12-metre totem, from the large whales at the bottom to the small people climbing stairs way up high. Then my little mountain goats explored the rock stairs under the small metal bridge.

The playground, located by the water, was hidden from our view so the huge concrete lion adorning it came as a great surprise.

A long pier is accessible through the little patch of evergreens (which are providing good shade for picnics). We walked on it towards the lake until we reached the open water of **Lake Ontario** sprinkled with tiny sailboats. Small planes landed on the runway on the island as a bonus. It made us forget where we were!

TIPS (fun for 2 to 10 years)

• There's no rail along the pier so you'll need to be extra careful with children. I don't recommend it with toddlers. The edges are too tempting…

• There's a wading pool in the playground. Bring bathing suits in case it should be open when you visit.

• The ferry ride to **Toronto City Centre Airport** is free and takes less than one minute to reach the island.

• **Harbourfront Community Centre** (627 Queen's Quay West, at Bathurst) offers $1 drop-in sessions to children 6 years and under, on Tuesdays and Thursdays. Call (416) 392-1509 or check www.harbourfrontcc.ca, go to *Programs & Services*, then *Family* and click on *Family Programs*.

• You'll find a great convenience store at the corner of Bathurst and Queen's Quay perfect for an impromptu picnic.

Little Norway Park
Dial 311 (new service)
www.toronto.ca/parks

D-3
Downtown
Toronto
5-min.

Schedule: Open year-round.
Admission: FREE.
Directions: Runs along Queen's Quay between Bathurst and Little Norway Crescent. There's public parking on the southwest corner of Bathurst Street.

McCleary Playground

Lets hope it's a new trend. The design is so cute I had to mention it in this guide. Plus, it might just give you an excuse to come and stroll in my hood: the up and coming Leslieville.

Every part that could possibly get reused from that fallen tree was used. The main part of the trunk, where the major branches usually split up, was installed upside-down to form a natural arch. Two park benches were made out of logs. That's not all! Two large Chesterfield chairs were carved out of the tree base, with matching coffee table. They even got a picnic table made out of three planks out of it.

Then they proceeded to create a slide using a natural ramp, and to fabricate a small climbing structure by attaching a net to huge rocks.

Who are "they"? They're the Bienenstock people under the umbrella of **Gardens for Living** (www.naturalplaygrounds.ca) with major funds and time given by ING DIRECT Canada, in partnership with the City of Toronto.

Cutting-edge design

Two summers ago when I came back from a holiday, I was saddened to discover the biggest tree in my local parkette by Queen Street lying down in pieces. Months later, I had the surprise to see that some ingenious designer had found a way to give it a second life.

TIPS (fun for 2 to 8 years)

• A sign on the premises says the equipment was designed for kids 5 to 12, probably for liability purposes. I don't see a problem for younger kids to use it and kids over 8 years will need bigger challenges. They'll find them in the big playground at the far end of **Jimmie Simpson Park**, across Queen Street. There's a double wading pool in this playground and the park includes an indoor pool.

• A favourite destination of local kids (and their parents) in the area is **Ed's Real Scoop** and its amazing homemade ice cream and gelato (920 Queen East, www.edsrealscoop.com).

• Other established treasures in the vicinity of the playground: **Bonjour Brioche**, one of the best croissant places in Toronto (812 Queen East, www.bonjourbrioche.com) and **Ambiance Chocolat**, chocolate offered at the best quality-price ratio in town (753-A Queen East, www.ambiancechocolat.ca).

McCleary Playground	D-3
Dial 311 (new service) www.toronto.ca/parks	**East** **of downtown** **15-min.**

Schedule: Open year-round.
Admission: FREE.
Directions: At the southwest corner of Queen East and Mc Gee Streets, Toronto. The park is across from the **Jimmie Simpson Community Centre**.

NEARBY ATTRACTIONS	
The Distillery (5-min.)	p. 380
Cherry Beach (5-min.)	p. 395

JAMIE BELL ADVENTURE PARK

A castle in the area

Guess how long it took High Park volunteers to build this playground from scratch? Ten days! OK, fine, there were about three thousand volunteers and planning had been a long-term affair. Even so, I admire the results of what people can achieve when they put their heart into it.

The masterpiece is shaped like a fortified castle. It occupies 10,000 sq. ft. A third of this area is dedicated to small children and is enclosed with a fence, for parents' peace of mind and there are a few picnic tables.

The staircase in the area for older

children gives a labyrinth-like impression (if you let small children go there, step up the supervision).

Kids line up to have a try at the old-fashioned swing made out of a large tire.

When they're done, kids will want to check the ducks' pond and the adjacent lane lined with animal paddocks, past the parking lot.

TIPS (fun for 2 to 12 years)
• BEWARE. From May 1 to October 1, on Sundays and holidays, the park can only be accessed from the Bloor Street entrance. You can park beside **Grenadier Restaurant** and walk 5 minutes to the playground.
• At other times, we prefer to enter the site through High Park Boulevard (accessible from Parkside Road) and turn left to park by the animal paddocks or at the end of Spring Drive. These parking lots are the closest to the castle.
• More about **High Park** on p. 454.

NEARBY ATTRACTIONS
Sunnyside Beach (5-min.) .... p. 403
Around High Park Station .... p. 455

High Park
Dial 311 (new service)
www.toronto.ca/parks

D-3
West of downtown 15-min.

Schedule: Open year-round.
Admission: FREE. (Read p. 454 about the small train rides.)

Directions: At the intersection of Bloor Street West and Parkside Drive, Toronto (Parkside Drive is accessible northbound from Lake Shore Blvd.). Read tips!

The playground is a 15-min. walk from **Keele Subway Station**.

DUFFERIN GROVE'S SANDPIT

Groovy!

It comes complete with running water, garden shovels and long logs. Imagine what small engineers can do here! They build labyrinths of water streams and bridges with their new friends. They dig holes. They create mini ponds...

It was so cute to see a bunch of preschoolers surrounding my 10-year-old boy scout, eager to help him as he undertook an ambitious bridge project.

Many had the astonished look kids have when they can't believe their luck: "At last! A place where I'm allowed to get dirty and play with the garden hose. Too good to be true; must hurry before someone stops me!"

I saw some resigned parents who watched their kids getting covered with mud in their Sunday clothes. Had they known, they would have brought a change of clothes.

The nearby playground is surrounded by a country-style split-rail fence and mature trees. It includes swings, climbing structures, a wading pool and a groovy little Smurfs-like house.

TIPS (fun for 2 to 12 years)
• Bring a change of clothes for your kids (or at least a towel for the car).
• There's a large wading pool right next to the playground. Bring bathing suits!
• More about **Dufferin Grove Park** on p. 456.

NEARBY ATTRACTIONS
Lansdowne Fence Streetscape ... p. 455

Dufferin Grove Park | D-3
(416) 392-0913 | **Downtown**
www.dufferinpark.ca | **Toronto**
| **15-min.**

 Schedule: Open year-round.
Admission: FREE access to the park.
 Directions: South of Bloor Street West, on the east side of Dufferin Street, Toronto (across from Dufferin Mall and a 5-min. walk south of **Dufferin Station**).

General tips about
Sports:

- Sunscreen, hats and enough bottles of water are a must during summer sports.
- A change of clothes is always a good idea when playing outside where there's a potential for mud (especially after a rainfall).
- Extra layers of clothes that you can add or take off could save the day during a winter outing. Bottles of water and snacks are also important since concessions are often closed for the season.

SPORTS

See **Ashbridge's Bay Skatepark** on p. 348.

ROGERS CENTRE

"Duck!"

The two boys were only 4 and 6 but already great baseball fans; the time was ripe to take them to their first game at the Rogers Centre. They brought their little baseball gloves. When their dad shouted: "It's coming!" they never doubted the authenticity of the ball as he picked up a brand new ball (that he had bought for the occasion) off the floor! It was the best day of their lives!

TIPS (fun for 5 years +)
• For the March Break 2011, they presented a **Disney on Ice show** (tickets from $15 to $39) and a **Spring Fling** (which seems to have been organized last minute, $20/all-day rides, $10/ground admission only). They offered a $10 saving if you did the two. Check their website for next year.
• Rogers Centre hosts the **Monster Jam** event on a weekend in January. My 10-year-old has begged me to go for years! Demolition derby, biggest trucks in the world on the biggest wheels; the works! Just never had the time to go. It costs around $15-$27. Check if they still offer their pit party ticket (extra cost) to have access to the floor to get closer to the trucks two hours before the show.
• Planning to attend a circus show at the Rogers Centre (or any other venue)? BEWARE! The cost of elephant rides and more is not included with the ticket and the intermissions are big commercials to promote $10 gadgets all kids want.

NEARBY ATTRACTIONS

I am not a baseball fan but when my dentist told me how he tricked his sons to create this magical moment, it made me want to rush to a baseball game, kids in tow.

My son doesn't know anything about baseball but he is into buildings, models and how things work, so we had a **Rogers Tour Experience**. We learned that the **Rogers Centre** required twice as much concrete as the CN Tower to build, enough concrete to stretch a sidewalk between Toronto and Montreal.

As we waited for the tour to begin, we watched a time-lapse film showing two years of building the former SkyDome into a two-minute clip made from a time-lapse camera. The tour began with a short movie in a small theatre, on the construction from the architects and the workers' points of view. (Note that these films are not automatically shown anymore but you can ask for them when you're buying the tour tickets. You've got nothing to lose.)

We looked at a model of the building. We had a peek at a giant baseball bat. Then, the first glimpse into the huge stadium (with a seating capacity of 50,600 during a baseball game) was impressive!

At the time, my 8-year-old son was not thrilled by the tour itself, but he loved visiting the **Hall of Fame** box with its trophies and photos of the Blue Jays as they were winning the World Series.

Rogers Centre	**D-3**
(416) 341-2770 (tours)	**Downtown**
(416) 341-1234 (Blue Jays)	**Toronto**
(416) 341-2746	**2-min. walk**
(Argonauts)	
www.rogerscentre.com	

 Schedule: Open year-round but schedule varies depending on special events. Call to confirm. The baseball season runs from early April to late September.

 Admission: Tour: $16/adults, $12/seniors and students, $10/5-11 years, FREE under 5.

 Game: Baseball starts at $10-$15, football starts at around $22.

Directions: At the corner of Front and Peter Streets, Toronto (entrance to the tour is between Gates # 1 and 2).

RAPTORS AT AIR CANADA CENTRE

"Thanks Dad!"

I had to see it to believe it: boys and girls, some barely five years old, eagerly following the game!

The truth is the enthusiasm of a roaring crowd is contagious and every minute when the teams are not competing is filled with action. When it's not the mascot **Raptor** fooling around with spectators by the aisles, it's the **Raptors Dance Pack** hitting the floor, or the half-time act. No wonder I heard a grateful boy exclaim, on the way back to their car: "Thanks Dad for taking me!"

A quick stop at the store to get some **Raptors** paraphernalia to show our support and another one to grab a mandatory hot dog and we were ready to find our seats. The Raptors and their visitors were already warming up and the mascot was stretching along with them. Then, a rain of metre-long balloons fell from the ceiling over the spectators in the **Lower Bowl Endzone** and **Baseline Prime** sections behind the visitors' basket. We later found out these were to be used by the Raptors fans to distract any opponent focusing on their free throws.

Foul play, rebounds, assists, running jump shots, one-handed jams... we saw it all. What we did not expect was the ever-present music and hilarious sound effects: sound of a bouncing spring when the ball would stray off the court, breaking glass noise when a player crashed into a panel.

We were lucky enough to be attending the game the Raptors won 84-76 against the Hornets during the 2004 season. Even for amateurs like us, it was a thing of beauty to watch Vince Carter do a half-court running jump-shot sinking into the basket as the buzzer announced the end of the third quarter.

That day, we saw the Raptors' 16-point lead melt down to six, two minutes before the end of the game. Talk about tension! And imagine the standing ovation when they won! But my guess is any Raptors game will always win the approval of young fans.

TIPS (fun for 5 years +)

• Parking beside **Air Canada Centre** during a game costs around $25! We found a spot under $10 in the parking lot on Windsor St., just north of Front St. and west of John St. (10-minute walk).

• We were in the first rows of the **Upper Bowl** seating area, at around $60 per ticket, and had a ball. But I checked it out and can assure you you'll see well wherever you sit in Air Canada Centre!

• Up to two hours before the game, ticket holders have free access to the BMO Fan Zone and its interactive basketball and hockey stations.

• On Sunday home games, kids used to be invited on the floor after the game to throw once into the basket. Let's hope they still are!

Air Canada Centre | D-3
(416) 815-5500 (info) | **Downtown**
(416) 872-5000 (sports) | **Toronto**
www.raptors.com | **10-min. walk**
www.mapleleafs.nhl.com
www.theaircanadacentre.com

Schedule: Basketball season runs from October to mid-April. Hockey goes from October to April. The tours are offered year-round, variable hours depending on the season.

Admission: Basketball tickets range from $12.50 to over $1,000! Individual hockey tickets are almost impossible to get. Try to call in September!

Directions: Between York and Bay Street, north of Lake Shore Blvd., Toronto. There's a covered passage to **Union Subway Station**, on Front Street.

LESLIE STREET SPIT

Urban wilderness

This is still an official dumping zone where people come to drop their brick, cement or asphalt from demolished buildings and other construction. This is also the best place to feel like you're biking by the ocean.

You can remain on the smooth trail for 3 kilometres, or take one of the sandier side trails to different lookout points all around the peninsula. We took an off the beaten track trail through a field and saw the most intriguing scene: a fully-blown white sail towering over the tall grass, the only indication that we were by the water.

In other parts of the park, we would have a full view of **Lake Ontario**'s glittering water taking turquoise shades under the summer sun.

Somewhere else, we saw rogue sculptures made out of metal rods and bricks found in the landfill.

We saw a lighthouse on top of a hill on one side of the path, and the CN Tower on top of the horizon on the oppo-

site side. We crossed a small bridge, we cycled by ponds, we even came across a bird sanctuary where cormorants nest in May.

It was past the time of the year when we're not allowed to enter the sanctuary and were in for a surprise (sensible souls beware): hundreds of dried bird skeletons were scattered all over the place. (We were later told by a park worker that many youngsters unfortunately fall off their crowded nests!)

It seems there are turtles, owls, frogs and rabbits along with the butterflies and over 300 species of birds amidst the 400 plant species found on **Leslie Spit**. Of course you won't see any of that if your main goal, when coming here, was to enjoy the feel of the wind through your hair and the sun on your face as you're swooshing by on your bike.

TIPS (fun for 5 years +)

• It will take you 45 minutes to bike on the looped trail of Leslie Spit at an average speed.
• Beware if you park in the parking lot adjacent to the entrance. It will be locked after the official hours! There's parking along Leslie Street and Unwin Avenue.
• There are normally chip trucks selling food and drinks by the entrance.

NEARBY ATTRACTIONS

Leslie Street Spit
www.friendsofthespit.ca
www.tommythompson-park.ca

D-3
East of downtown
15-min.

Schedule: Open 9 am to 6 pm, April to October, closes at 4:30 pm rest of the year. The bird sanctuary is closed from April to September 1.
Admission: FREE.

Directions: Leslie Street Spit (Tommy Thompson Park), Toronto. From Lakeshore Blvd., turn south on Leslie Street until you reach the park.

ASHBRIDGE'S BAY & THE BEACH

In the loop

Past the boulders and the boardwalk by Woodbine Beach, the paved path turns into a sinuous loop that goes up and down, surrounded by the bay and the lake. A real adventure for beginner bikers.

It only takes 15 minutes to bike around **Ashbridge's** loop but you can stop at the tip of the peninsula to take in a view of **Lake Ontario**. You can even access a pebble beach through the shrubbery.

On your way back, you can take the right branch of the fork leading you to **The Beach** area along the water, past the **Boardwalk Pub**.

The path offers a wide-open view of the beach. You can ride for 10 minutes to reach another loop amidst mature trees offering nice shade in the summer. There's a snack bar in this section and a playground further east.

The whole ride from the **Boardwalk Pub** to the eastern end takes approximately 15 minutes. Be careful! It is busy and pedestrians walking in couples tend to use the whole width of the path.

TIPS (fun for 5 years +)

• When I use a car to get to the bike trails and only intend to stay a couple of hours, I park in the parking lots of **Canadian Tire** or **Loblaws** (where I'll buy something, of course!), at the corner of Lake Shore Blvd. and Leslie Street. It is a 15-min. bike ride to **Ashbridge's Bay Park**, going eastbound on the trail along Lake Shore. **Leslie Spit** bike trail is only a 5-min. bike ride southbound down Leslie.

NEARBY ATTRACTIONS

Ashbridge's Bay Park & The Beach
D-3 East of downtown 20-min.
Dial 311 (new service)
www.toronto.ca/parks

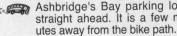

Schedule: Open year-round.
Admission: FREE. Parking fees at Ashbridge's Bay Park and Boardwalk Pub's parking lots.
Directions: From Gardiner Expressway eastbound, exit at Lake Shore Blvd. Turn south at Coxwell Avenue, Toronto. The Ashbridge's Bay parking lot is straight ahead. It is a few minutes away from the bike path.

KAY GARDNER BELTLINE PARK

Not in my backyard (unfortunately)

This has to be Toronto's best kept secret! A paved trail running east-west along the backyards of posh neighbourhoods. It is so discreet that it does not even show on Google satellite maps. Want to know where to find it?

Last summer, I ran into two trails called the **Kay Gardner Beltline**, in two different parts of town. I came to realize it was the same trail! The trail covers a bit less than 4.5 kms one way. It was part of a private railway line completed in 1892, which closed its passenger service just two years later. The freight function stopped in the 60's and the City of Toronto bought the land to make a park of it, thanks to the work of City Councillor Kay Gardner, hence the name.

This is heaven for joggers, bikers and walkers. The path is wide and lined with greenery all along, with trees forming natural arches over our heads at many spots.

You can easily access it at Mount Pleasant, Yonge, Avenue Road, Eglinton, Bathurst and Allen Road but there are more access points for locals along the route.

The first time I explored it, I strolled east until I reached its eastern end at Mount Pleasant Road. The following week, I walked with a friend to its western end and we hit the soundproof wall bordering Allen Road.

The 1-km stretch between Avenue Road and Eglinton Avenue West (where you'll pass under a bridge) is the one with the best glimpses into luxurious backyards. The pretty playground of lovely **Forest Hill Road Park** is waiting, just west of Avenue Road.

TIPS (fun for 5 years +)

• I recommend finding parking along the streets south of Eglinton Ave. West (east of Chaplin Crescent) to access the Beltline. There's an entrance to the park on Chaplin Crescent near Russell Hill Rd.

• There's also a public parking lot on Castle Knock Rd. just north of Eglinton, conveniently located near whimsical **Phipps Bakery Café** (420 Eglinton West, www.phippsbakerycafe.ca). It looks like a shop but there is a café in the back with colourful murals and a mosaic wall matching the scrumptious sweets in the display cases (they also serve lunch).

NEARBY ATTRACTIONS
Mt. Pleasant Cemetery (1-min. walk) p. 261
Around Davisville Station .... p. 471

Kay Gardner Beltline Park
Dial 311 (new service)
www.toronto.ca/parks

D-3
North
of downtown
25-min.

Schedule: Open year-round.
Admission: FREE.

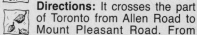
Directions: It crosses the part of Toronto from Allen Road to Mount Pleasant Road. From Allen Road to Bathurst, the Beltline runs south of Elm Ridge Drive, then it goes south of Chaplin Crescent, up to Yonge Street. East of Yonge, it continues to Mount Pleasant Road, north of the cemetery.

DOGSLED AT ROB ROY FARM

"Hike! Hike!"

Before seeing the farm's Siberian Huskies, we hear their high-pitched barking. They're smaller than I expected, and are harnessed to the sleds in groups of three. They let out febrile howls, excited by the anticipation of an outing. However, they rapidly calm down when my young trail blazer pets them.

We walk towards a large clearing, where I receive my first sled-driving lesson. Meanwhile, my son takes his place in the front of the dog handler's sled, on the only passenger seat.

I learn basic concepts. I have to place my feet on the sled's skates. In order to turn to one side, I need to lean my body the right way. When I want the dogs to move forward, I must yell "Hike!" And, most impor-

Photo: Courtesy of Rob Roy Farm

tantly, I must slam on the brakes immediately if my sled starts to pass its own dogs or if our team threatens to charge the sled ahead of us!

"Don't worry" says a member of the staff, "everyone falls..." How reassuring! In fact, I did fall once. I didn't hurt myself, and had plenty of time to hop back on.

An employee rides a snowmobile behind us. He's there to catch up with the sleds that have lost their drivers. My son is clinging to his sled and loudly encouraging the dogs to go faster.

When the sled slides without resistance, the speed is exhilarating and the dogs' joy is contagious. The ride lasts around 30 minutes. It's not very long, but in my case it was intense enough to leave me the following day with aches and pains in several arm muscles I didn't even know existed!

Meanwhile, my 21-month-old daughter stayed in Daddy's arms. They admired the farm animals: donkeys, pigs, guinea hens and barn cats. After the dogsled ride, we met at the barn and drank a hot chocolate.

TIPS (fun for 5 years +)

• Small passengers have to be old enough to be able to hang on to both sides of the dog handler's sled. Young children are not allowed to ride alone with inexperienced parents.

• The braking manoeuvre is a bit difficult for children to handle but the owner assured me many succeed and drive a sled. If they don't, they can always be passengers.

• Expect an igloo, weather permitting.

• They also rent snowshoes.

• They are located 30 minutes away from **Talisman Resort** (www.talisman.ca) and **Blue Mountain** (www.bluemountain.ca).

BURD'S FAMILY FISHING

The line is busy

You need fishing gear? They rent it out. The very idea of putting a desperate worm on a hook grosses you out? They'll do the dirty work for you. And most of all, you're afraid your pint-size fisherman (or woman) might return without a catch? Well, you can't come home empty-handed with the thousands of trout that inhabit the ponds at Burd's Trout Fishing. From now on, nothing stands between your child and the intriguing experience of fishing.

The tree-lined farm is a pretty sight with its two, one-acre ponds, each adorned with a lazy paddle wheel that gently stirs the water. A small brick path runs alongside the bigger pond, allowing for strollers and wheelchairs to circulate.

The bigger pond, for general public use, is stocked every week. The other pond is reserved for group use.

There's a laid-back country feeling to the place. But don't be fooled: no stone was left unturned in order to cater to our needs. The employees, dressed in sweatshirts printed with the farm's logo, offer courteous service. There is also a rain shelter, washrooms, the sale of beverages and snacks and, oh bliss, a small outdoor playground with sandbox (complete with toys!).

After weighing our catch, an employee killed, cut and cleaned our fish way too fast to trouble my little Nosey Parker, who was observing the whole scene with big... fish eyes.

Later on, we found out that the trout, being so fresh, were incredibly tasty. True, they weren't really a bargain compared to the market price, but watching my little guy frantically winding his reel to bring in the fighting fish was worth a million.

The proud look on his face while we were eating his catch wasn't bad either.

TIPS (fun for 4 years +)

• No permit required.
• One rod might actually be enough for two young children since one can bring the trout ashore with the rod while the other catches it with the net.
• Trout sells for around $1.99 per 100 grams so you could run a high bill. Lucky for us, we're allowed to catch a maximum of five trout per rod in use.
• The seven fish we caught measured between 18 and 25 cm and would now cost $31 altogether. The farm accepts payment by cash or credit card.

NEARBY ATTRACTIONS
Live Steamers (15-min.) .... p. 203
Bruce's Mill (10-min.) .... p. 243

Burd's Family Fishing
· Stouffville

C-3
N-E
of Toronto
30-min.

(905) 640-2928
www.burdsfamilyfishing.com

Schedule: Season runs daily from Victoria Day to Labour Day, weather permitting (weekends only from Easter to Victoria Day, and from Labour Day to Thanksgiving, 9 am to 6 pm (7 pm in the summer).
Admission: $5/visitor, FREE for 3 years and under, $5/rod rental and bait.
Directions: 13077 Hwy 48, Stouffville. From Hwy 404 North, take exit #37/Stouffville Road eastbound. Turn north on Hwy 48, look on the east side.

PRIMEROSE TROUT FARM

Simple pleasures

This one is off the beaten track so you don't really hear the cars from the highway. You're surrounded by nature. Everyone who's there is relaxed... except my kids when they catch their first fish!

Here, you won't find staff wearing the farm's logo on a sweatshirt and no one will clean the fish for you. But the owner who was observing my son in action from afar quietly came to offer some welcome fishing advice.

My daughter was more than happy to rely on her big brother to put the worm on the hook (the apple didn't fall too far from the tree for this one).

I thought it funny how she kept changing spots. At one point, she lost

patience and thought she would have a better chance to catch the fish with her net. Big brother was more patient and got a good one which she helped bring in.

They provide the fish cleaning facilities.

TIPS (fun for 4 years +)

We really enjoyed our lunch at **Superburger**, a hamburger joint in an air-conditioned streetcar located a few minutes from the trout farm on the northwest corner of Hwy 89 and Hwy 10.

NEARBY ATTRACTIONS
Walk of Tree Sculptures (20-min.) p. 110
Cheltenham Badlands (30-min.) p. 232

Primrose Trout Farm	C-2 N-W of Toronto 60-min.

Primrose Trout Farm
• Shelburne
(519) 925-3846
www.primrosetroutfarm.com

C-2
N-W
of Toronto
60-min.

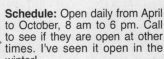

Schedule: Open daily from April to October, 8 am to 6 pm. Call to see if they are open at other times. I've seen it open in the winter!

Admission: $4/admission per person, FREE under 10 years old. Rod rental is $5. They sell ice and bait. The trout from the Family Pond is around $5.75 per lb.

Directions: R.R. #4, Shelburne. From Hwy 400 northbound, take exit to Hwy 89 westbound. Drive past Hwy 10, turn south on Blind Line.

ABOUT FISHING

Fun for shore!

In years of visiting the region inside out, I have noticed people fishing everywhere, at all times of the year. I've always wondered if they were allowed, how they knew which fish were edible, how they got their permit, etc.

Fishing regulations

The bottom line is that kids and youth under 18 years old don't need a fishing permit. If you just want to watch your kids fish, you don't need a permit either.

Only residents between 18 and 64 require a fishing licence. Licences are available from camps and lodges, summer camps, sporting goods stores or bait dealers. In smaller communities, they're often sold in general stores.

If you want to fish with your kids, you'll need to get at least the $12 **One-Day Fishing Licence**. If you intend to join them more than one day, you'll need to get the $25 **Conservation Fishing Licence** or the $37 **Sport Fishing Licence**, both good for one year.

The daily catch limit varies a lot depending on the species, the location, time of year and kind of licence you've got.

TIPS (fun for 4 years +)

• It appears that the best beginner's fishing gear to buy for a child should be a light reel on a 4 1/2 to 5 ft. lightweight rod with 6 to 12-lb. line which should be easily found for around $30.
• The picture on this page was taken at **Christie C.A.** (see p. 401).
• A conservation area I don't describe in my guide but which is probably the best for fishing is **Glen Haffy** at 19305 Airport Road, north of Caledon East, (905) 584-2922. It has two trout ponds regularly stocked and fishing equipment for rent. It even has two private ponds for groups to rent (www.thehillsofheadwaters.com).

MNR publications

Could not distinguish one from the other? No problem! Go to the **Ontario Ministry of Natural Resources (MNR)** website, in the *Publications* menu, under *F* and download their brochure *Fishing Regulations Summary* with a colour fish identification chart at the end.

My favourite brochure to download is their great *Take a Kid Fishing Guide* (under *T* in their *Publications* menu). It is filled with lovely pictures and very useful information for neophytes. It covers it all: tackle, hooks, sinkers, bobbers, bait, lures, etc. Illustrations will show you how to put together your tackle, how to make basic knots, how to cast. The last two pages include colour charts to identify your catch.

The pictures in their other publication, *Fish Ontario*, are even more beautiful. In it, I learned that the record lake trout caught in an Ontario lake was 63.12 lbs. (28.65 kg)... Really!

Around the city

If you want to know where the fishing spots are in and around the GTA, type *Urban Fishing Opportunities in Toronto & Surrounding Areas* on the Ministry website's search engine. It includes a list of the GTA fishing sites as well as the fish you're bound to find in them! Many of the sites listed in it are described in this guide.

Family Fishing Weekend

Ontario Family Fishing Weekend is an official three-day weekend of unlicenced fishing. This event allows adults to fish without a permit. It is locally driven. Some locations offer games for the children and prizes, others offer free use of equipment and bait. Many feature fly fishing demos and give fish identification tips.

Ministry of Natural Resources
1-800-667-1940 (info line)
1-800-387-7011 (Outdoors Cards)
www.mnr.gov.on.ca (select *Fish & Wildlife*)

Family Fishing Weekend
1-800-667-1940 (info line)
www.familyfishingweekend.com
Schedule: Usually on the first weekend of July (and recently during Family Day weekend in February).

FOOTBALL HALL OF FAME

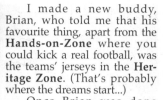

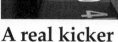

A real kicker

Judging by its website, I was seriously wondering if this attraction would be of any interest to children. It didn't seem interactive enough. Once on the premises, I realized I had underestimated the potential for such a place to fire-up little imaginations.

As I suspected, there were no females in sight in the place. Instead, fathers and sons roamed the museum, in the leisurely fashion they usually do when not under the wings of a watchful mother. Most of the little guys I saw were under 9. Just recognizing a team in the displays was a big event for them.

I made a new buddy, Brian, who told me that his favourite thing, apart from the **Hands-on-Zone** where you could kick a real football, was the teams' jerseys in the **Heritage Zone**. (That's probably where the dreams start...)

Once Brian was done kicking the football, patiently coached by his dad, a bunch of young friends took over, enthralled in a make-believe lively game.

I really liked the green carpet in the corridor, simulating the yards on a field, and the vintage equipment in the **Heritage Zone**. Of course, the **Grey Cup Championship** rings caught my attention. They're shiny!

I don't know anything about football, but I can imagine the appeal of the **Hall of Fame Members** collection of busts to a true fan. There's also a few screens with trivia and a small viewing section with seats showing clips of famous CFL plays (near a leg press station to test your strength).

TIPS (fun for 6 years +)

• This is the place where the **Grey Cup** comes to rest after touring with the winners of the current year, following the games. Don't expect to see it between November and February.

• The small store sells flags, jerseys, footballs and fact books from different teams.

• For cheaper parking and a chance to check out downtown Hamilton, park in municipal parking north of King St. West (at John St. North and King William St.); walk along King St. westbound to James St., then down south along James to Jackson St. (a 15-min. walk).

• Read tips about Hamilton restaurant **Connaught Fish & Chips** on p. 218.

Canadian Football Hall of Fame • Hamilton (905) 528-7566 www.cfhoff.ca	E-2 S-W of Toronto 55-min.

Schedule: Open year-round, Tuesday to Saturday, 9:30 am to 4:30 pm.

Admission: $7/adults, $3.50/seniors & students, $16/family of 4, FREE under 5 years.

Directions: 58 Jackson Street West, Hamilton. From QEW westbound, merge into Hwy 403 West. Exit at Main Street. Turn right at Macnab Street, then right at Jackson Street. There's City Hall parking lot at the end of the street but it's expensive. Read TIPS for cheaper option.

NEARBY ATTRACTIONS

HOCKEY HALL OF FAME

Shoot and score!

The Hockey Hall of Fame reflects the colourful palette of the world's many hockey teams and is as bright as any rink during playoffs. There is no need to be a serious fan to enjoy the many attractions displayed throughout the labyrinth-shaped path of discoveries.

The museum fills a large space in the underground of the eye-catching **Brookfield Place**. Devoted aficionados could easily spend an entire day reading the texts adjoining each gorgeous window display but there are also sufficient interactive displays to entertain children six years and older, particularly if they are hooked on the national sport.

My companions thoroughly enjoyed the **NHLPA Be A Player Zone**! In the glassed rooms of **Pepsi Shut Out**, they positioned themselves in front of a goal and tried to intercept soft pucks shot full blast by a virtual Marc Messier and Wayne Gretzky. Then, they'd stop shots fired by four virtual players (and watch themselves on the 8-by-10-foot screen.

On the other side, they waited anxiously for their turn at the **Source For Sports Shoot Out**, where they shot real pucks towards a virtual Eddie Belfour guarding the goal. Data such as their speed, precision and reaction time would show up on a screen.

A mezzanine area overlooks the game zone. It is part of the **TSN/RDS Broadcast Zone** and includes several broadcast pods where visitors can transform into sports commentators.

They watched clips of real games from a menu of classic moments as their comments are taped. (They found it challenging, except for yelling "He scores!") They could then compare with the actual comments from legendary broadcasters. Participants get a private access code to hear their play-by-play via www.hhof.com! (It stays on the web for a few days.)

Make sure to photograph your aspiring players in front of the gleaming **Stanley Cup**, located in the **Verizon Great Hall**. The room is capped by a dome 15 metres above, adorned with magnificent stained glass. The heavy doors of this ex-bank's vaults are an intriguing sight for children's active imaginations.

TIPS (fun for 6 years +)
• Parking at the Brookfield Place (off Wellington St. West) is expensive on weekdays but OK on weekends.
• Jerseys from most professional teams are available in small sizes in the big store.
• To stay in the Hockey spirit, have a bite at **Wayne Gretzky's** restaurant, a 5-min. drive west of the Hall of Fame. We loved its booths with lovely murals, good food, huge desserts and displays of Gretzky's memorabilia (99 Blue Jays Way, (416) 979-7825, www.gretzky.com/restaurant).

We can take our picture with the Stanley Cup or have our photo taken for $10 (for three 4-by-6-inch prints ready in a few minutes, with a website download).

Hockey Hall of Fame
(416) 360-7735
www.hhof.com

**D-3
Downtown
Toronto
5-min.**

 Schedule: From end of June to Labour Day, during Christmas and March Breaks, 9:30 am to 6 pm (opens at 10 am on Sundays). Fall/winter/spring: Monday to Friday, 10 am to 5 pm, Saturday, 9:30 am to 6 pm; Sunday, 10:30 am to 5 pm.

 Admission: $15/adults, $12/seniors, $10/4-13 years, FREE for children 3 years and under. (You can leave and re-enter.)

Directions: Brookfield Place, Concourse Level, Toronto (northwest corner of Yonge and Front Streets).

NEARBY ATTRACTIONS

BOBBY ORR HALL OF FAME

Parry Sound's son

As soon as we got out of our car in the large parking lot by the water, we saw boats coming in and out of the harbour, a float plane landing by the quay and a very long train rolling on the nearby railway bridge, along with a tall tower with a serious flight of stairs teasing us in the background. The Hall of Fame celebrating Bobby Orr's career was just a few minutes walk away in the modern Stockey Centre at the end of the road running along the harbour.

Past the impressive sculpture of Bobby Orr flying through the air (based on a famous picture taken right after he scored the winning goal for the 1970 **Stanley Cup**), the small museum has enough interactive activities to satisfy young hockey fans.

The goal of the game of skill **Top Shot** is to shoot and hit each of 9 panels as quickly as possible. **Real Hockey** allows you to choose a game and play along. **Be a Sports Caster** offers a selection of plays to comment on while you're being recorded.

Otherwise, amidst colourful displays, you can watch the clips of exceptional moments in hockey history. I'm not a real hockey fan but by watching some of them, even I could recognize that it was a thing of beauty to watch the Boston Bruins number 4 perform on the ice.

TIPS (fun for 6 years +)

• **Stockey Centre** includes a great deck overlooking **Georgian Bay** (by a tiny beach), where they offer free concerts in the summer. Check the line-up of shows presented in their 480-seat **Festival Performing Hall** on www.stockeycentre.com.

• **Bay Street Café** is the restaurant closest to the water (22 Bay Street). It is quite cute with decent food. We really enjoyed our table on the wrap-around balcony.

• We found and visited the structure we saw from the harbour. It belongs to the **West Parry Sound District Museum** unofficially known as the Museum on Tower Hill. (It's a 10-min. drive. Go north on Bay, turn east on Seguin and turn south on Great North Rd. just after the bridge, then take George St. up the hill to your left.) The tower was fun to climb and offered a great view of Parry Sound. The small museum had interesting displays. Check www.wpsdm.com for details.

Bobby Orr Hall of Fame
• Parry Sound
1-877-746-4466
www.bobbyorrhalloffame.com

Off the map North of Toronto 3 hrs

Schedule: From late June to Labour Day, open Tuesday to Sunday, 9 am to 5 pm. (Also closed Tuesdays and Sundays the rest of the year.)
Admission: $9/adults, $6/children, $25/family.
Directions: 2 Bay Street, Parry Sound. Take Hwy 400 northbound (it becomes Hwy 69 (Parry Sound/Sudbury). Take exit # 224 (Bowes Street/McDougall Road). Follow Bowes (it becomes Seguin), turn left at James Street. Continue onto Bay.

NEARBY ATTRACTIONS
Killbear P. P. (35-min.) .... p. 296

CLAIREVILLE RANCH

Conservation indeed

Some people have gone through all kinds of hoops to turn this huge piece of land into a golf course but, thanks to its Conservation Area status, it's been preserved, ensuring the survival of one of the last horseback riding ranches in the GTA at the same time.

I have tried to include horseback riding in my two previous editions but the ranches we visited would be gone before I would go to print. You could literally see the housing developments creeping close to those ranches.

Claireville Ranch has room to breath. Its one-hour trail rides guide you through woods and fields, and along a glittering river.

TIPS (fun for 10 years +)

• Kids must be 10 years old and most importantly, have a 27-inch minimum length of inseam. (Measure them from the crotch to the ground; my 10-year-old barely made it.) Closed shoes are a must.

• There are good old outhouses. The ranch normally sells some snacks and beverages but they might be out of stock. Better bring your own.

• Ask about their two-hour breakfast rides ($65 for this special experience).

• I recommend you come earlier to give your name and reserve a time slot. It would leave you time to have lunch in Brampton (just keep going west on Road 7, it becomes Queen Street, lined with the usual restaurant chains), then come back without waiting. We did not do that and had to wait 45 minutes for a spot.

When we were riding, a bird almost flew into my daughter and we admired two blue herons taking off from a turn in the stream. To think that we were just between Toronto and Brampton was mind-boggling!

I discovered my child was scared of trotting in the middle of our trail ride, when there's no way out! Fortunately, we were at the end of the line, so we could make our horses walk while the others trotted without being in the way. Of course, there's always the possibility that trail horses will just follow the horse in front at whatever speed they go.

Parents can lead their kids on a pony ride in an enclosed area in the field if they are too small or too scared.

Clairevile Ranch • Brampton (905) 794-0700 www.clairevilleranch.com	D-2 N-W of Toronto 35-min.

 Schedule: May to October (weekends by appointment only during wintertime). Call for exact hours (at least 11 am to 5 pm).
Admission: $30/1-hour ride (check their website for a discount coupon), $5 for a 10-min. pony ride, $5/helmet rental.
Directions: Claireville Conservation Area, Brampton. Drive northbound on Hwy 427 to the end, turn west on Hwy 7. Pass The Gore Rd., the small road leading to the ranch is on the south side, just across the road from McVean Drive.

NEARBY ATTRACTIONS
Chinguacousy Park (15-min.) ..... p. 286
Wild Water Kingdom (10-min.) .... p. 426

TORONTO CLIMBING ACADEMY

"There you go!"

"Is it the paparazzi corner?" teases a father. "Actually, we all work for the Globe!" I joke back. Truth is, if I am the only one writing about today's experience, I also have the least impressive equipment to catch the moment when my child conquers the 55-foot wall!

I did not expect all parents wanting to stay for the whole two-hour session.

Most of all, I did not expect them to cheer each climber in unison!

The young supervisor coaches each child during the climb, with step-by-step instructions punctuated by plenty of "Awesome!" or "There you go!" encouragements.

I read 5.4 at the bottom of the first wall. I am told 5 means "vertical", and 4, the degree of difficulty. Some impossible walls rate 5. 14! The other wall they climbed (a 5.5) was 55 feet tall; more than twice the height of the first one. Those who reach the top hit a button which turns on a red light. Thankfully, all the kids succeed.

The third climb was a corner wall. On his last climb, my son is bypassed by a spider woman on the "wall" above his head. She eventually falls, dangling safely at the end of her rope. "What happened?" asks a spectator. What did you expect? She was climbing on a... ceiling!

"Was it fun?" I later ask my little monkey when he comes down. "Yes!" "Does it hurt anywhere?" I inquire. "Everywhere!" is his reply. Go figure!

TIPS (fun for 6 years +)

• Shy children beware! Children climb with all eyes on them.
• I felt my tall 7-year-old's legs and arms were just long enough to reach the holds. A six-year-old in the group almost did not make it to the top. Bring good running shoes or rent climbing shoes for $5. The harness is included with the **Kids Love To Climb** package.
• For a fee of $35, parents who are beginners can be certified and learn how to supervise their child on their own.
• If you want to kill some time while the kids are doing their 2-hour session, there's a **Home Depot** nearby with **Second Cup** and **Harvey's**.
• **Joe Rockheads** at 29 Fraser Ave. offers the **Kids Climbs** program for $23/child, any time of the week (minimum three, 8 to 14-year-old kids). A good flexible birthday party solution! (416) 538-7670 or see www.joerockheads.com.

NEARBY ATTRACTIONS
East York Skatepark (5-min.) ...... p. 349

Toronto Climbing Academy (416) 406-5900 www. climbingacademy.com	**D-3 North of downtown 20-min.**

 Schedule: Monday to Friday, 12 noon to 11 pm; Saturday and Sunday, 10 am to 10 pm; Holidays, 10 am to 6 pm. **Kids Love To Climb** for 6-12 years: Saturday from 11 am to 1 pm.

 Admission: One Day pass $16/adults, $14/student, $10/10 years and under. Harness rental is $5. Kids Love to Climb is $25.

 Directions: 11 Curity Avenue, Toronto. From the Don Valley Pkwy, take Don Mills Road South. Turn left on O'Connor Drive, and left on Curity (north of St. Clair).

SCOOTER'S ROLLER PALACE

Hold on!

It was a hot summer night outside when we visited Scooter's so the light air-conditioning cooling the place was most welcome. A few minutes later, I was breaking a sweat just fitting my two kids into their skates. Still, it was nothing compared to what I felt the second I hit the rink!

Trying inline skates for the first time while holding the hand of my unsteady 6-year-old daughter on roller skates was a very bad idea! I held on to the boards and crawled back onto the carpet, went back to the rental counter and got myself good old four-wheel retro sturdy skates.

There were very few people on the family night we went. The good thing about it was that it meant fewer potential collisions with fellow skaters. The bad thing was that there was nowhere for me to hide to preserve my dignity.

There's a "disco" feeling to rollerskating. Add a ceiling punctuated with colour spotlights and a mirror ball reflecting on the shiny floor and you're back into the 70's... (or is it the 50's)! Add a couple of slow songs playing by the end of the evening and you might even get a flashback from your teenage years.

TIPS (fun for 6 years +)
• During the **Family** sessions, one non-skating adult is allowed to supervise a paying child.
• You can use a bike helmet. Knee and elbow pads are recommended.
• The more friends you take with you, the more fun your kids will have.
• They have a snack bar. You could also go to **Harvey's** next door.

NEARBY ATTRACTIONS
Rattray Marsh (5-min.) .... p. 274

The skate floor is huge. Some loops are printed on it, for the keeners who want to practise routines.

Scooter's Roller Palace actually offers affordable skating lessons for the young on Saturday mornings and for adults on Tuesday evenings. They also host late night skates (going from 8 pm to 3 am on the first Saturday of the month). They even have Christian Gospel skates some Sundays from midnight to 4 am, where the DJ plays contemporary Gospel music.

They have a disc jockey all the time. The place also includes two bowling lanes, pool tables and arcade games. They sell some glow trinkets which are really cool when skating in a dark room under black lights.

Scooter's Roller Palace
• Mississauga
(905) 823-4001
www.scooters.on.ca

**D-3
West
of Toronto
30-min.**

Schedule: Tuesday, 8-11 pm (16 years +); Wednesday, 6-9 pm (Family); Thursday, 8-11 pm (18 years +); Friday, 6-9 pm (Family) and 9-12 midnight (All ages); Saturday, 1-5 pm (Family) and 8-11 pm (All ages); Sunday, 1-5 pm (Family) and 8-11 pm (18 Years +). They are open for children on most holidays and P.D. days.
Admission: $7.25 to $13 depending on the session's day or length. **Rental**: $3.75/ roller skates or inline skates, $4.50/safety equipment.
Directions: 2105 Royal Windsor Drive, Mississauga. Take QEW, exit at Winston Churchill southbound, and turn east on Royal Windsor Drive (an extension of Lakeshore).

CJ SKATEBOARD PARK & SCHOOL

A dream comes true

The guys I'm accompanying can't believe their luck. There it is: a large foam pit at the bottom of a steep hill. What more can a teenage boy with a skateboard ask for? One after the other, they try all the crazy jumps they can think off without fear of getting hurt.

The foam pit alone would be reason enough to come to this indoor skatepark, but there's more. The whole room is superb, brightly lit and adorned with a great mural sided by a bumpy corridor of wavy blond wood going down hill. Their 12-foot half-pipe is gigantic and gorgeous.

There are also stairs, rails, quarter-pipe and more. In addition, they have a smaller room for beginners to practice without being in the way of the more experienced skaters.

Many screens in the lobby allow us to observe the kids in action. We can also watch them from the mezzanine on the second floor. The skatepark is open to inline skaters, BMX bike riders (and non-motorized scooters) as well.

TIPS (fun for 6 years +)

• They don't put an age limit, claiming their youngest student was 4 years old. I think you'll want to pay for some classes for your young daredevils before allowing them to venture on their own. Most boys I know were 8 or 9 when they started to tackle skateboarding. (Most moms I know would rather have them wait until they're 18, but that's another story.)

• Skaters under 18 must have a waiver signed by their parent or legal guardian in person on the site (or they can have it faxed). Consult their website to download the waiver and for more info.

• Participants under 16 must wear helmet, elbow, knee and wrist guards and running shoes. Helmet is still mandatory for those 16 years and over. They are quite strict about those rules and have staff walking around to enforce them.

• The skatepark includes a well stocked **Pro Shop**.

• Some food and snacks are sold on the premises.

CJ Skateboard Park & School
· Etobicoke
(416) 259-6888

D-3
West
of downtown
15-min.

www.cjskateboardpark.com

Schedule: Open Monday, 7 pm to 10 pm, Tuesday to Sunday, 12 noon to 10 pm. (Skateboards not allowed on Wednesday evenings. BMX/scooters only allowed on Wednesdays, 6:30 pm to 10 pm.)

Admission: $5/1st time visitor for annual ID card, $10/2-hour sessions. Rental: $5/skateboard or rollerblades, $2/pads, $1/helmet. FREE to watch from mezzanine.

Directions: 60 Horner Avenue, Etobicoke. From Gardiner Expy, take Islington exit, keep left side for Kipling. Go south (at the Evans Avenue sign). Turn east on Evans, then south on Horner.

NEARBY ATTRACTIONS

WALLACE EMERSON CENTRE

Hidden treasure

The area is busy with stores, I almost missed it, hidden in the back of the community centre.

Daredevils are riding their BMX bikes with skill; they've been at it for hours. Encouraged by the adult (me) observing them, they give their best shots.

Even though they're all with bikes (the park was created with them in mind), they confirm to me that kids also come with skateboards.

There's a great playground surrounded by trees and the centre includes an indoor pool, which younger siblings could enjoy while the oldest indulge in their extreme sport. Go to *Swimming & Pools* on their website, and click *Indoor Pools*, then pool's name and *Drop-In*.

Wallace Emerson Community Centre (416) 392-0039 www.toronto.ca/parks	D-3 N-W of downtown 20-min.

Schedule: Open year-round.
Admission: FREE.
Direction: 1260 Dufferin Street, Toronto (south of Dupont).

LEONARD LINTON PARK

Super bowl time

This skatepark is reminiscent of those days when pioneer skaters started to hone their skills in the empty pools of the suburbs.

Also known as **Vanderhoof Park**, this skatepark includes a great U-shaped bowl with an ambitious deep end and a separate section with ramps and stairs. A paved path links it all for a nice flow. And it is covered with graffiti.

Younger kids should try to go early. I know brave ones who show up at 7 am on the weekends, before the teenagers take over.

Last time we visited, there was an ice cream truck nearby, to add to the pleasure.

If you just want to drop your teenager and do some errands, the area is surrounded by big box stores: **Winners, Home Depot, Sobey's, LCBO, Best Buy, Starbucks**, etc, on Wicksteed Ave. (south of Research Rd.; **Pier 1 Imports, Canadian Tire, Pet Smart** and more on Eglinton (west of Brentcliffe).

Leonard Linton Park Dial 311 (new service) www.toronto.ca/parks	D-3 North of downtown 25-min.

Schedule: Open year-round.
Admission: FREE.
Directions: From Eglinton East, take Brentcliffe Road south, turn east on Research Road, Toronto. You can park by the skatepark.

ASHBRIDGE'S BAY SKATEPARK

"He popped the stairs!"

Don't know what this means? Neither did I, but a patient 13-year-old explained to me that this is when you strike the back of your skateboard against the ground so it will rise nose first into the air. Then there's the ollie, the kickflip, the heelflip... All of them equally painful to watch for a mother. Didn't know you were signing up for this, did you? Actually, you're not supposed to watch. You just drop them off with a bottle of water and plans to pick them up later, hoping for the best.

At first, I thought **Ashbridges's Bay** Skatepark didn't look that interesting. Without half-pipe or bumpy paths, it seemed quite flat. Then I learned from my friend's son that this is what they call a "street skatepark" which simulates the challenges a skater would find on a downtown street. Looking at it again, it all made sense: open space of a plaza, stairs, side of buildings, guardrails. Ashbridge's is an awesome street skatepark.

The challenges are demanding so most kids attending are teens 15 years and older. Experienced skaters definitely have more fun than the younger ones who prefer to tackle the periphery of the skatepark or stay in the small beginners' section on the east side of the park.

Some big kids put on quite a show so it is the perfect place for the beginners to see how it's done and what to expect after hundreds of hours of practise.

TIPS (fun for 6 years +)

• No kid over 13 was wearing a helmet when I was visiting. Check skate magazines and you'll understand why. It's not in the culture! The younger ones, who stayed in the small beginners area, had them on but as soon as they feel daring enough to explore the rest of the park, off goes the helmet. You may think that your child knows better but think again. The best way to be sure your child is skating in a safe way is to go to an indoor skatepark (where they ensure kids wear helmet and pads, for insurance purposes).

• There's a $2 parking lot at the corner of Woodbine and Eastern. You could drop off your teenager to skate while you go see a movie at **The Beach Cinema** just across Woodbine (for schedule, see www.cinemaclock.com). Or you could walk 10 minutes further east on Queen and stop at the great French bakery **Zane Patisserie**, for a bite (1852 Queen East).

Ashbridge's Bay Skatepark

D-3 East of downtown 20-min.

Dial 311 (new service)
www.toronto.ca/parks

Schedule: Open year-round.
Admission: FREE.
Directions: At the northwest corner of Lake Shore Blvd. East and Coxwell Avenue, Toronto.

NEARBY ATTRACTIONS

EAST YORK SKATEPARK

Go East, young man

There were kids of all ages when we visited. It seemed that they each could find something to do at their level in this skatepark. Advanced skaters and BMX bikers really enjoyed the large bowl covered in colourful graffiti.

Real amateurs say that the skatepark in **Stan Wadlow Park** has a great flow, is amazing for lines and has great ledges (whatever that means for a skater). I read a funny comment on a skate website that stated "it's just like street-skateboarding but without getting kicked out" (www.spectrum-sk8.com). I really like that they've allowed graffiti in this skatepark. When we visited, there was a gorgeous wave painted on one of the ledges, that looked like a Japanese print.

You can hit tennis balls against a wall erected for this purpose near the skatepark. Stan Wadlow Park has a great playground for younger siblings and an entrance to **Taylor Creek Park** in its northern part, perfect for bike rides along kilometres of paved path.

East York Skatepark Dial 311 (new service) www.toronto.ca/parks	D-3 N-E of downtown 30-min.

 Located in **Stan Wadlow Park**, Toronto. See p. 41 for directions.

CUMMER SKATEBOARD PARK

Action!

When we approach the side of the skatepark, a guy we had not noticed flies off from nowhere and flips back in a flash.

As we observed his routine, we realized that there was a slope, farther and higher in the back, which allowed him and other daredevils to gain an impressive speed before they threw themselves into what seemed like an empty pool and what I will learn to call a bowl.

This skatepark, adjacent to the **Cummer Community Centre** (which includes an indoor pool with giant slide and shallow area, and a snack bar), is small but packed with features with which the skaters seem to be very creative: stairs, ramps, concrete corridors, different levels and the deep bowl. We can see it all in a glimpse.

The strip of concrete surrounding the park is quite narrow so we have to be careful to stay out of the way of the skaters in action.

Cummer Community Centre • North York (416) 395-7803 www.toronto.ca/parks	D-3 North of downtown 35-min.

 Schedule: The outdoor park is open year-round. Go to *Swimming & Pools* on their website, and click *Indoor Pools*, then pool's name and *Drop-In Programs*.
Admission: FREE access to the skatepark. FREE/leisure swim.
Directions: 6000 Leslie Street, North York (north of Finch, just south of Cummer Avenue).

ICELAND SKATEPARK

Cool... but hot!

A sea of concrete waves is rippling before us. Iceland Skatepark seems bigger than the others!

Angles are not as accentuated as in other parks and slopes are not as high. As far as I can judge (from the humble point of view of a non-skater) the riders can't build as much speed here as in other parks but they can go for ever, not unlike a good back street lined with obstacles... without the cars (but we certainly hear them, the park is located along Highway 403, so it is noisy).

The municipal park includes a large kidney shaped bowl going 6 feet down, slopes and quarter-pipes.

In the midst of summer, in 30-degree heat, the sun is burning hot. Steamy skaters are ready to throw themselves face first into the nearby snow bank formed by the Zamboni's discharge from **Iceland**, the four indoor ice rinks in **Hershey Sportzone**. There's also a spray pad for younger siblings.

Iceland Skatepark	**D-3**
• Mississauga	**N-W**
(905) 615-4100	**of Toronto**
www.mississauga.ca	**35-min.**

Schedule: Open year-round.
Admission: FREE.
Directions: 705 Matheson Blvd. East, Mississauga. Take Hwy 403 West, exit at Eglinton westbound, turn right on Kennedy and right again on Matheson.

CHINGUACOUSY SKATEPARK

In the dirt

This skatepark is also BMX heaven, with parallel dirt paths, allowing healthy competitions between friends.

As we watched the skaters and riders in the skatepark, we saw MBX bikes in the background going up and down on the dirt paths. It sure looked tempting! I don't know of another place in the GTA where young riders can have this kind of fun in a city.

While younger siblings enjoy the rest of **Chinguacousy Park** (p. 286). Skaters will have a blast in this most impressive skatepark recently build.

Photo: City of Brampton

Chinguacousy Skatepark	**D-2**
• Brampton	**N-W**
(905) 458-6555	**of Toronto**
www.city.brampton.on.ca	**35-min.**

Schedule: Open year-round.
Admission: FREE.
Directions: Take Hwy 427 North to the end of the road, turn west on Hwy 7, then north on Bramalea Road. The skatepark is by the parking lot.

SHELL PARK

In a nutshell... loved it!

This is by far my favourite skate-park, strictly from an esthetic point of view. The place obviously belongs to the skaters.

I love the fact that the City of Oakville allowed colourful graffiti to blossom on the concrete instead of covering it with grey paint as soon as it appears. Let's hope nobody changes that! We've been to this park a couple of times and I could see that the graffiti is evolving!

The skatepark is contained in a large basin bordered by a large concrete side-walk. When standing on it, you glimpse

the whole park down below, with plenty of trees in the back-ground. It is nice-ly laid-out with slopes, quarter-pipes and ramps. The skate-park is located on the edge of a small forest with a trail and next to a playground and a lovely garden. It is a perfect spot for a picnic while you wait for your skater to throw in the towel.

If you feel confident enough to leave your capable skater behind, walk along Lakeshore 10-min. west to reach **Shelburne Park** (off a path just east of Shelburne Place) or 10-min. east to **South Shell Park** for a view of **Petro Canada Pier**.

TIPS (fun for 6 years +)

• After the skating session, I recommend you take a 2-minute drive back towards **Bronte Harbour**, at the foot of Twelve Mile Creek Lands, to check out the little **Bronte Beach Park**. Turn south on West River St. (which is on the west side of the creek); you'll find a public park-ing lot with access to the beach. We especially loved the western section of it, a tiny secluded sandy spot hidden by the trees. The small park on the east side of Bronte Harbour is also quite pretty.

• Read about nearby **Firehall** restaurant under Riverview Park on p. 354.

NEARBY ATTRACTIONS
Coronation Park (5-min.) .... p. 424

Shell Park
• Oakville
(905) 845-6601
www.oakville.ca/
skateboardpark.htm

D-2
West
of Toronto
35-min.

Schedule: Open year-round.
Admission: FREE.
Directions: From QEW, take exit #111/ Bronte Road southbound, turn west on Lakeshore. The park is on the north side.

MAJOR RINKS

Some object to skating in the crowded conditions on the weekend. However, you won't find that many skaters at all between 10 and 11 am. Moreover, given the rink's odd shape, there are some secluded spots to be enjoyed by those not too eager on speed skating.

In the square

Nathan Phillips Square (at the corner of Bay and Queen West, Toronto) and **Mel Lastman Square** (5100 Yonge St., North York) also boast large outdoor artificial ice rinks.

By the lake

From one side, it looks as if the rink extends all the way to Lake Ontario. From another, the sun shines on the imposing CN Tower.

The **Natrel Rink** at **Harbourfront Centre** (see p. 24 for directions) is decidedly a cool skating spot! From the **Lakeside EATS** outdoor terrace, visitors observe skaters while eating or sipping a hot chocolate (note it is closed on Mondays).

At Nathan Phillips Square, there's the **Café on the Square** and **Starbucks** and **Timothy's** at the corner of Bay and Queen West.

There's a food-court by **North York Station** exit by Mel Lastman Square, where you'll find hot chocolates.

It is here, at **Harbourfront Centre**, that we decided to introduce our little one to the trials and tribulations (and fun) of outdoor skating. He was quite surprised when his blades hit the slippery surface…

In the hour that followed, as we pulled him along between us, he would drop like a dead weight – a prisoner being brought to death row (but he was laughing)!

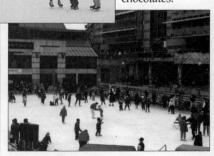

TIPS (fun for 5 years +)

- **Harbourfront** and **Nathan Phillips** offer blade sharpening service for $5.
- Don't count on cheering your dear one's arabesques, standing on the rink with your boots on. Only people with skates are permitted on the ice.
- The ice of these rinks is artificially maintained at freezing level, providing the external temperature does not exceed 8° C, and the sun doesn't shine too aggressively.
- More on **Cavalcade of Lights** at **Nathan Phillips Square** on p. 176.

Major rinks
(416) 304-1400 (Nathan Phillips)
(416) 973-4866 (Harbourfront)
www.cityrinks.ca

Schedule: Open from mid-November to mid-March, at least 10 am to 10 pm (weather permitting).

Admission: FREE. **Skate rental/Harbourfront:** $7/adults, $6/kids; **Nathan Phillips:** $10/adults, $5/seniors and children.

SPECIAL RINKS AND SKATING TRAILS

Brick Works Skating Trail

This cute rink opened in December 2010 at **Evergreen Brick Works** (see p. 273). The outdoor skating trail is within walls and turns into a garden in the spring. We can change in the great building nearby and get a hot chocolate in the **Belong Café** set to open in the spring 2011. The place is packed on Saturdays during the **Farmers' Market**.

They come in all shapes

Looking for something different to skate on? Skating trails and reflecting pools turned into rinks come to the rescue.

The following options have a few advantages over a natural pond. You don't have to be concerned about safety of the ice; you can count on ice at temperatures up to 8° C and you know Zambonies will make them nice and smooth.

Colonel Sam Smith Skating Trail

My favourite, this one opened in December 2010 (in **Colonel Samuel Smith Park** at the end of Kipling in Etobicoke). It took me 350 steps to walk around its figure-8 shape trail by an historic building with a tall chimney. For a hot chocolate, you can end the outing at **Tatsu's Bread**, the bakery just west of Kipling at 3180 Lake Shore (open at 8 am on Saturdays and 11 am on Sundays).

Barbara Ann Scott Rink

Unofficially called the **College Park Rink**, this rink turns into one of the biggest reflecting pools in Toronto in the spring. It is completely hidden from sight (in the backyard of the commercial complex at the southwest corner of College and Yonge, which includes **Winners**). There's a **Timothy's** by the entrance of the food-court adjacent to the rink. (See photo under **College Station** in p. 472.)

TIPS (fun for 5 years +)

• The ice of these rinks is artificially maintained at freezing level, providing the external temperature does not exceed 8° C, and the sun doesn't shine too aggressively.
• These places don't offer skate rental nor skate sharpening services.

Sherbourne Common Rink

This fenceless rink opened (east of Lower Jarvis on Queens Quay) in February 2011 in a park still under construction. In the summer, it will turn into a large wading pool. There will eventually be a café on site. Until then, you can stop for hot chocolate at the big **Loblaws** just west of Lower Jarvis and drink it on its mezzanine with a view of **Lake Ontario**.

Special rinks
www.cityrinks.ca
(the unofficial website of Toronto's outdoor skating rinks)

 Schedule: Search rinks by their name on City Rinks' website for exact schedule. Probably most will open early December to late February.
Admission: FREE.

POND SKATING

Bring on the shovel!

There's something about skating on natural ice... I think it is the mix of beauty and imperfection that gives us the feeling we're OK as we are and we fit into our environment. Plus, being surrounded by a wide surface of snow and trees certainly beats looking at hockey boards!

Riverview Park

This park is buzzing with action! It is the unofficial town meeting place for those who love to play outside. In addition to pond skating, visitors can enjoy a good tobogganing slope. The skating pond is located on the western side of the **Twelve Mile Creek** in front of **Riverview Park**, where a marsh has formed (an official fish sanctuary).

On the day we went local families had cleared a dozen rinks in different sizes and shapes. Hockey games were going on the bigger ones and parents were initiating their toddlers on the smaller ones. The ice was not bumpy at all, the result of a fast freeze overnight.

There was tobogganing going on by the entrance of the park. But if you really want more serious tobogganing check **Appleby College Hill** on p. 364, a 5-min. drive away.

I found one fun restaurant in the area to finish a nice outdoor outing: the **Firehall**. This one really plays the fire hall theme, with fire hydrants, firemen's gear, hoses, small fire truck ride and pictures of real fires on the walls.

The menu boasts tasty items such as extinguisher dip, fire crackers, three-alarm chicken fingers... They offer a kids' menu. They even sell kid-size fire-fighter hats for $6 (2441 Lakeshore Rd. West, 905-827-4445, www.thefirehall.ca).

A funny tradition in Oakville's **Coronation Park** (p. 424) is the annual **New Year's Day Polar Bear Dip** involving over 400 dippers and some 5,000 spectators to raise money for World Vision. For details, see www.polarbeardip.ca.

Mill Pond Park

The whole pond is cleared and managed by the Town of Richmond Hill. A sign indicates the ice conditions. You can call their **Parks & Recreation Department** to find out the conditions at (905) 884-8013.

There's an outdoor place to put on your skates and leave your boots as well as a small playground and some cages with geese and swans. There's even a parking lot and washrooms across the street from **Mill Pond Park**. A paved trail runs along the pond into a small forest. With gorgeous weeping willows brushing the pond, the place is a great picnic spot in the summer.

Check www.wintercarnival.net about **Richmond Hill's Winter Carnival** on the first weekend in February.

TIPS (fun for 5 years +)

• We need a couple of weeks with serious sub-zero temperatures in order for the pond's ice to be safe. As a rule of thumb, if dozens of people are already skating, it is safe. If you're first, scratch the ice to judge its state. If it is slushy, don't go there. Ice by the shore is always thinner.

• When you go pond skating, bring a shovel! If you're the first to show up, you'll need it! Or you can help widen an already existing rink and those who have cleaned the ice before you will be convinced of your good faith. If you are plain lazy (or have to hold a kid's hand instead of a shovel) I suggest you go on a Sunday. Chances are the other skaters will have worked for you the day before.

Saddington Park

The City of Mississauga used to manage this v-shaped pond. Now, it seems that locals still come and clear it off. It is set by **Lake Ontario** and surrounded by trees. Hockey players seem to stick to one branch of the "v" while leisure skaters hang around the other one. In the summer, the pond is lively with ducks, geese, a cute stream, a fountain and great willow trees almost brushing the water.

Pond skating

 Schedule: The ice is normally safe after two weeks of freezing weather. Our best bet is from mid-January to mid-February but it's all in Mother Nature's hands.

Admission: FREE.

Directions: Riverview Park/Oakville: Take the QEW, exit at Bronte Road southbound. Turn west on Lakeshore and north on Mississauga Street. The first street on your right is Riverview Street. It is a dead-end leading directly to the front of Riverview Park. People park along this street.

J.C. Saddington Park/Mississauga: See p. 303.

Mill Pond Park/Richmond Hill: Go west of Yonge, on Major Mackenzie Street. Turn north on Trench Street to Mill Street.

CEDARENA

Old-fashioned way

Interested in a small rustic ice rink, managed by volunteers for over eighty years and located in the back country, thirty minutes from Toronto? Then head for Cedarena.

At first sight, we were charmed by the tortuous path that leads down to the **Cedarena** ice rink, which sits nestled amidst cedar trees.

At the end of the path, there is a small woodstove-heated cabin, where many families sit tightly against each other, as they put on their skates. Outside, an even smaller porch can hardly contain the overflow of eager skaters ready to embark on the ice.

The boards surrounding the medium-sized rink make it look somewhat choked but the trees surrounding the rink make up for this.

When we visited, the ice was dented (hey! this is natural ice!) and the music rinky-dink. Yet, it did not keep skaters from having a jolly time. The intimate character of the place must have something to do with it. It has been a local tradition for over 80 years!

TIPS (fun for 5 years +)
• There are washrooms on site and a little snack bar that serves cider and hot chocolate.
• Check their website right after mild weather. In mid-February 2011, they had to closed the place due to flood threats from nearby **Rouge River**!

NEARBY ATTRACTIONS

Cedarena
• Markham
(905) 294-0038
(seasonal phone number)
www.cedarena.ca

C-3
N-E
of Toronto
35-min.

Schedule: The hours depend on volunteers' availability. Weather permitting, usually open Sundays, 1 pm to 4 pm and Thursday to Saturday, 7:30 pm to 10 pm (adults only on Tuesday evenings).
Admission: $5/adults, $2.50/15 years and under.
Directions: 7373 Reesor Road, Markham. From Hwy 401 East, take exit # 383/Markham northbound. Turn east on Steeles, then north on Reesor Road.

Skiing in Town?

The real thing!

From the «schlink» sound of the double chairlift, to the «swoosch» of skis scraping the slopes and the huge fireplace that sits in the ski chalet, Earl Bales looks like the real thing.

You won't see slopes running down to the **North York Ski Centre** as you would expect at a ski resort. That's because they run down the ravine behind the centre.

Hidden from view, you'll discover them when you walk over and stand at the top of the chairlift. There you'll find a gentle slope for beginners equipped with a Tow Rope. It is the best place to be introduced to this winter sport.

Don't expect great hills, but the highrises you spot on the horizon are there to remind you this is the middle of the city. This ski centre is a little miracle in itself!

Centennial Park Ski Hill

Centennial Park Ski Hill is the ski centre located in **Centennial Park**. It offers two shorter hills equipped with a T-bar and a Magic Carpet Lift, and a slope for tobogganing (more about it on p. 363).

TIPS (fun for 5 years +)

• Both ski centres have snowmaking equipment, night skiing and a snack bar. They also offer Alpine ski and snowboard lessons, and full sets of ski or snowboard equipment rentals as well.

• Another ski hill in the city can be found in Brampton's **Chinguacousy Park**. It has the ambitious name of **Mount Chinguacousy Ski Hill** but is just one small hill, really. Still, it comes with a carpet lift and a new ski chalet offering full service with snack bar. They rent all the equipment and provide lessons (905-458-6555 for details). What I really like about this little centre is that they also rent tubes for snow tubing! They call it "glorified tobogganing". You don't get the steep hills of the other tubing centres but I know a few dads who will think very highly of their carpet lift! I don't know about your family but in mine, it was Dad's job to bring the toboggan up the hill (with the kid on it). The carpet lift costs around $13/hour, $15.50/two hours (snow tube included, no toboggan allowed on carpet).

North York Ski Centre & Centennial Park Ski Hill (416) 338-6754 (info & snow conditions) www.toronto.ca/ski	**D-3 N-W** of downtown 35-min.

 Schedule: Usually from mid-December to mid-March. Open minimum from 10 am to 8 pm (closes at 6 pm on Sundays).

Admission: Prices are the same for both parks. Varying prices depending on age. No more than $28 for snow pass, no more than $25 for full rental ($9 for access to learning areas without lift).

Directions/North York Ski Centre: Earl Bales Park, 4169 Bathurst Street, North York (south of Sheppard Avenue). **Centennial Park Ski Hill:** 256 Centennial Park Road, Etobicoke (south of Eglinton Avenue West).

GLEN EDEN SNOW TUBING

When we visited, the February weather was so mild, one of the staff members was wearing shorts.

I thought the slopes a bit lame when I first saw them, but the ride down was quite fast. I was getting concerned by the acceleration that was building as I got really close to the end of the run when black rubber patches abruptly slowed me down. I recommend this tube park for parents of kids 5 to 8 years old.

Older kids know to visit the place in the evening, when the weather is colder and the chutes get icier. Younger kids will prefer daytime, when warmer temperatures create more friction under the tube.

Start here

Reluctant parents who've decided to give in and offer their enthusiastic kids the experience of snow tubing will love this one. It is the closest tube park to Toronto, and probably the one with the mildest slopes. (Not that you could not gain some speed on these slopes! On a good night, the staff have seen people fly by at 80 km/h on radar.)

The **Glen Eden Ski and Snowboard Centre** is located in the heart of **Kelso Conservation Area** in Milton. Its tube park includes four chutes and one tow lift.

TIPS (fun for 5 years +)

• Kids need to be a minimum of 42 inches (106 cm) tall to ride. Only one person per tube is allowed but you can hold another rider's tube handles to ride down in twos (or threes).

• The farthest parking spot is located 1/2 km from the ski chalet on the eastern part of the ski hills. It's a long way to walk back to the car with tired little skiers. Good news! A pedestrian walkway was built and now allows skiers to buy their ticket at the western chalet, by the parking lot.

• There's a snack bar inside the eastern chalet and exterior food counters at both lodges.

• See the **Halton Museum** on p. 378.

NEARBY ATTRACTIONS
Crawford Lake (15 min.) .... p. 384

Glen Eden Snow Tubing • Milton (905) 878-8455 www.gleneden.on.ca	D-2 West of Toronto 50-min.

Schedule: Call to confirm when the season starts, it depends on the weather. Always call to confirm tubing runs are open. They're confident the season can go until end of March Break. Glen Eden is open for night use but closes at around 4 pm in the spring. Check exact schedule.

Admission: Around $4/one ride, $20/six rides. Note that unused rides can be used anytime within the same season. Ask about special nights.

Directions: In **Kelso Conservation Area**, Milton. From Hwy 401 West, take exit #320/Hwy 25 northbound. Turn west on Sideroad #5 (Campbellville Rd.), then south on Tremaine Road and enter **Kelso C.A.**, west on Kelso Road.

SNOW VALLEY SNOW TUBING

Are you game?

The expanse of snow before us seems abruptly severed horizontally. Beyond this divide, long corridors stretch out, lined with a carpet of snow. Farther still, dark forests alternate with white fields. We need to walk right up to the edge of this imaginary line to discover a slope equivalent to a ten-storey descent.

My six-year-old friends stamp their feet with impatience as they await the attendant's signal… but not me! In a split second, I feel like I am on a free-falling, four-storey elevator ride.

Then I am showered with snow that rushes from under my tube (all the more surprising because my eyes were shut and my mouth was wide open). I speed up even more, and my tube starts revolving around itself. I grasp my handles, barely catching a glimpse of my two lads standing alongside the slope, laughing at my adventure. My pint-sized Olympic bobsledders are already asking for more!

The tubes are covered with a thick canvas, equipped with a strap that you tie to the lift, to be brought up the hill. But you must be careful, it's not the time to wipe your glasses. You get to the summit faster than you think! Both your hands are required to hang on to the tube when it is unhitched from the lift.

TIPS (fun for 5 years +)

• The first set of slopes is steeper. Tubers that choose the second group of gentler trails, located behind a row of trees, still come down at great speeds.
• On the day we visited, it took us ten minutes to go up, tube down and walk back to the lift. It was more advantageous to pay for a two-hour block of time. When there are long line-ups, it is recommended instead to buy a series of tickets, good for six descents.
• Minimum height to use the lift is 42". Smaller kids can walk up and slide down the **Kidz Play Area** (for $7 they get a kid-sized tube and one parent can access the park for free to help them out of the way).
• The **Chicken Chutes** in the **Kidz Village Area** (with 3 carpet lifts) are meant for small skiers and snowboarders.
• There are lockers and a cafeteria on site (and **Ski Snow Valley Barrie** next door offers 2-hour ski passes!).
• They have 7 kms of snowshoe trails. The cost of $14 includes snowshoe rental and the trail pass ($5 for trail pass only).

NEARBY ATTRACTIONS
Drysdale Tree Farm (35-min.) ..... p. 178

Snow Valley Snow Tubing Park
• Barrie
1-877-404-4744
www.skisnowvalley.com

B-2
North of Toronto 70-min.

Schedule: Open daily from mid-December to late March (weather permitting). Call for exact schedule.
Admission: $25/person for 4 hours or $20/6 rides ($16/weekdays except Christmas and March Breaks). One ride is $4. **Kidz Play Area**: $7 per child and free accompanying adult.
Directions: From Hwy 400 North, take exit Dunlop Street (#96B) westbound, turn north on George Johnson Road, then east on Snow Valley Road.

TORONTO SLOPES

Urban tobogganing

When snow finally graces our city, it's time to run to the slopes.

Glen Manor Drive

After a hearty brunch on Queen Street East in **The Beach**, I recommend you drive to Glen Manor Drive, and continue the day at **Glen Stewart Ravine** (p. 299). On the north side of Queen Street, Glen Manor divides in two at the beginning of the ravine.

There, a natural ice rink is maintained by the locals. A little further, the ravine deepens and the two facing slopes are sufficiently steep, despite their lack of length, to entertain kids of all ages.

From the top of the stairs at the entrance to the ravine, you can catch a lovely view of the area and the gorgeous residences and mature trees that overlook the slopes. Read about **Carolling in the Park** (and the **Pie Shack**) in the tips section on p. 299.

Riverdale Park East & West

On a different scale, Toronto's most challenging slope sits at **Riverdale Park East** (east of the Don Valley). It is quite broad, steep and long, and offers a stunning view of downtown Toronto's skyline.

And you can now have a great hot chocolate at nearby **Rooster Coffee House**, open at least 8 am to 5 pm (479 Broadview Ave.).

Hang on to your hats though if the slopes are even just slightly icy! In fact, it is best to avoid the area altogether when the shiny crust covers the slopes, as it becomes nearly impossible to climb back up.

The western face of Riverdale Park, across from the Don Valley Pkwy, is not as broad but is equally fun and challenging. Plus, it includes shorter sections, better for younger kids.

The **Riverdale Farm** is a 5-minute walk from this slope (see p. 60).

near the corner of Bloor and Crawford. The youngsters go down a gentle slope in front of the playground.

There are snack machines in the **Christie Pits Centre** and the rink might be open for free skating when you are visiting, so bring the skates.

Bickford Park

A few minutes walk south of Bloor on Christie, there's **Bickford Park**, a more secluded and gorgeous park with slopes of varying heights on both sides. It is conveniently located near **Linux Caffe** (325 Harbord St.), selling hot chocolates and more.

Lawrence Park Ravine

Pretty **Lawrence Park** (see above picture) is bowl-shaped, free of obstacles in the middle and surrounded by mature trees.

You can access the slope from all sides. The height varies so the site is suitable for different age groups. Bigger kids usually manage to create huge bumps to challenge themselves on the slope adjacent to Yonge Street.

Read about the steep hill in adjacent **Duplex Parquette** under **Lawrence Subway Station** on p. 469.

Christie Pits Park

Snow was pretty much gone on the steep slope next to the rink but I could still see the toboggan tracks. This hill must be a thrill for big kids, but beware of the poles 15 metres apart at the bottom of the hill. This is not where most people go.

Rather, they will use the wide slope

TIPS (fun for 4 years +)

• You will easily find parking on Glen Manor Drive along the park of the same name, as well as on Broadview Avenue along **Riverdale Park**.

• **Riverdale** and **Glen Manor Parks** have no washroom facilities. **Christie Pits** does. **Lawrence Park** visitors could use the **George H. Locke Library** branch (at the corner of Lawrence Ave. and Yonge St.) where kids could warm up as they choose some books to take back home.

Toronto slopes
Dial 311 (new service)
www.toronto.ca/parks

 Schedule: Open year-round.
Admission: FREE.
Directions:
Riverdale Park East: On Broadview Ave., between Danforth Ave. and Gerrard St.
Glen Manor Park: North of Queen St. East, between Glen Manor Dr. East and West, five blocks east of Kew Gardens.
Christie Pits Park: 779 Crawford St. The slope is just north of Bloor St., between Christie and Crawford Streets. Rink: (416) 392-0745.
Bickford Park: At the southeast corner of Grace and Harbord Streets. **Linux Caffe** is on the northeast corner of this intersection.
Lawrence Park Ravine: South of the public library at the southeast corner of Yonge Street and Lawrence Avenue.

SIR WINSTON CHURCHILL PARK

When I checked this slope, I did not have my young inspectors with me but I saw a whole class with their teacher joyfully walking from their local elementary school, armed with toboggans.

The upper part of the hill is blocked with fences. The lower section is shorter and less steep on the eastern side, more suitable for younger kids. From wherever you attack the slope, it is so long, the snow will slow you to a stop before you can hit anything. On the down side, kids will need to take a good walk back up the hill. Not for the lazy ones!

The small **Roycroft Wet Forest** lays at the bottom of the hill. In other seasons, it offers quite a change of scenery from the big city: a 5-minute walk amidst native shrubs and wildflowers and tall trees.

Prime location!

The snowy slope is endlessly winding down. When I looked at it from the bottom of the hill, I was impressed by the white panorama stretching high in front of me. That's a long and wide slope for the energetic ones.

TIPS (fun for 5 years +)

• A hot chocolate in the café of the **Forest Hill Market**, the Loblaws on St. Clair just west of Spadina, is the perfect way to start or finish this tobogganing outing. The grocery store offers plenty of parking (to its loyal customers) and you can catch a 5-minute trail leading to the park in front of it.

Under the bridge taking Spadina over the ravine, I discovered stone stairs leading to Russell Hill Drive. When my daughter was exploring them, in the middle of the summer when it was invaded by plants, it looked like she was climbing the ruins of an ancient Mayan city.

• Also check the ice-cream parlour **Dutch Dream**, open year-round, in the description of what's around **St. Clair West Subway Station** on p. 476.

Sir Winston Churchill Park	D-3
Dial 311 (new service)	**North**
www.toronto.ca/parks	of downtown 25-min.

Schedule: Open year-round.
Admission: FREE.
Directions: At the southeast corner of St. Clair Avenue West and Spadina Road, Toronto. There's street parking on Ardwold Gate just south of the park.

NEARBY ATTRACTIONS
Casa Loma (5-min.) .... p. 128

CENTENNIAL PARK

Off the record

At Centennial Park, there's the designated tobogganing area, and then there's the unofficial one where a sign, at the bottom of the hill, reads: "No hang-gliding or parasailing permitted." You get the picture.

There used to be many people using the unofficial slope at their own risk. The hill is really steep, lasts a long stretch, and has a great panorama at the top.

In 2011, the ski hill administration has hired police officers to patrol the forbidden hill and prevent people from risking their necks. If you show up on the weekends, they will redirect you to the official tobogganing hill.

TIPS (fun for 3 years +)

• See skiing at **Centennial** on p. 357.
• There are three greenhouses in **Centennial Park Conservatory**, located by the parking lot closer to Rathburn Road (FREE, open daily 10 am to 5 pm). It offers a nice contrast to winter, with colourful flowers, cactus, fish and turtles in a pond. An exotic way to end the outing. In 2010, they offered a **Christmas Flower Show** with special activities on the second Sunday of December, 12 noon to 4 pm (with Victorian carollers, carriage rides, hot cider and cookies) and a few candlelight nights. Call (416) 394-8543 to see what's in store for the current year.

NEARBY ATTRACTIONS

Fantasy Fair (15-min.) .... p. 34

It is located next to the parking lot accessible from Eglinton Avenue. The slope is not very steep but it goes down forever (which means parents will feel they are climbing up the hill forever with their younger child's toboggan in tow). It is lots of fun for the young crowd with a good toboggan.

Centennial Park
• Etobicoke
Dial 311 (new service)
www.toronto.ca/parks

D-3
N-W
of downtown
30-min.

Schedule: Open year-round.
Admission: FREE.
Directions: 56 Centennial Park Rd., Etobicoke. Take Hwy 427 North, exit Rathburn Rd. westbound, turn north on Centennial Park Rd. The official hill is at the southeast corner of Centennial Park Rd. and Eglinton Avenue.

RICHMOND HILL LIBRARY

One for the books

The slope by the Richmond Hill Library is long, moderately steep and... facing Atkinson Street.

Daredevils can't resist the part of the hill where big bumps give enough speed to require them to "put on the brakes" before they reach the street.

You will want the younger ones to use the safer slope closer to the parking lot. Inside the Library, a café sells great hot chocolate and coffee to warm up. There are washrooms.

See **The Wave Pool** on p. 417.

Richmond Hill Central Library • Richmond Hill (905) 884-9288 (library) www.richmondhill.ca	C-3 North of Toronto 35-min.

 Schedule: Open year-round.
Admission: FREE.
Directions: 1 Atkinson Street, Richmond Hill. From Hwy 404 North, take exit #31/Major Mackenzie Dr. westbound. The hill is south of the Library (at the corner of Yonge).

APPLEBY COLLEGE HILL

This hill gets an A+

When we saw this slope as we were driving by on Lakeshore, we just had to join the fun. It was wide and long. Trees were surrounding it and we could admire the blue lake on the horizon.

This gorgeous spot certainly is a favourite in Oakville, judging by the dozens of local families with kids of all ages enjoying it. But it's wide enough that everybody spreads out nicely. There's a large visitor's parking lot on the college's grounds. During the weekend, we could even park closer to the hill, on the western part of the school.

A one-minute drive away to the east, on the prettiest strip of Lakeshore Road in Old Oakville, there are lots of nice cafés selling hot chocolate, to top off the outing.

Read about nearby **Firehall** restaurant under **Riverview Park** on p. 354.

Appleby College Hill • Oakville	D-2 West of Toronto 35-min.

 Schedule: Open year-round.
Admission: FREE.
Directions: 540 Lakeshore Road West, Oakville. Take QEW, exit at Dorval Drive southbound, turn west on Lakeshore Road West. Appleby College is on the south side of the road.

ROUGE PARK

Unofficial fun

"Now I understand why there are so many broken toboggans along the slope!" comments my 7-year-old, rubbing his bottom after his first try from the top of the very steep hill.

In the midst of winter, everybody walks over the frozen (shallow) river to get to the hill located next to the parking lot off Twyn Rivers Drive in **Rouge Park**.

Trees buffer the noise of the city. Two hills are separated by a line of trees. One has to be in good shape to walk up the steep slope.

From above, it is a real pleasure to admire the forest panorama and to hear the laughter of the families sliding down the unofficial slope (at their own risk, I might add). Many teenagers go down on their snowboards.

For the next two hours, my son and his friend will feel more comfortable sticking to the lower half of the hill.

TIPS (fun for 6 years +)

• More about the **Rouge Park** trails near Twyn Rivers Drive on p. 304.
• There are no washrooms on site.

NEARBY ATTRACTIONS
Toronto Zoo (5-min.) .... p. 61

Rouge Park • Scarborough Dial 311 (new service) www.toronto.ca/parks	**D-3** **East** of downtown **35-min.**

 Schedule: Open year-round.
Admission: FREE.
Directions: From Hwy 401 East, take exit #389/Meadowvale Road northbound (keep to the right lanes as soon as you reach Morningside to catch this exit), turn east on Sheppard Avenue and take the first fork to the left, Twyn Rivers Drive (easy to miss when you are driving eastbound on Sheppard). You'll see a parking lot on your right.

BRONTE CREEK PROVINCIAL PARK

Hill addiction

Each time we go tobogganing, it's the same story. At the top of the hill, our little adrenaline addict smiles with anticipation, then lets out a long happy shout as he toboggans down. At the end of the descent, he bursts out with the laugh of victory, only to be towed back up (thanks to the private chairlift he finds in his stamina-filled daddy), again and again, happy to relive the experience.

Bronte Creek Park is a great summer outing. In the wintertime however, our attention shifts from the big pool to the large, well-maintained ice rink.

The rink's natural surroundings are quite pleasing and they have a bonfire.

There is a wide path climbing to the top of a hill overlooking the park. Its two faces hold much to be enjoyed by young toboggan fans. The view is far-reaching from both sides of the hill, offering athletes an unusually rare panorama.

You can access these activities via parking lot D.

After the winter sports, I suggest you drive to parking lot C, and walk to the farm's playground in a barn and its area with various farm animals. I strongly recommend you dress warmly as the barn is not heated in winter time. Note that there's a heated room within the barn for the parents patiently waiting for their kids to be done.

Spruce Farmhouse, the visitor centre and animal barns are open in winter.

TIPS (fun for 3 years +)
• They rent skates.
• A washroom and small snack bar are available close to the rink. Washrooms are also available next to the visitor centre.
• Check the **Lakeside Festival of Lights** in **Spencer Smith Park**, Burlington (www.burlingtonfestivaloflights.com).
• Read about the **Firehall** restaurant in Oakville under **Riverview Park** on p. 354, for a great finish to an outing in the cold.
• More about **Bronte Creek** and their **New Year's Eve** fun on p. 287.

Bronte Creek Provincial Park
· Burlington
(905) 827-6911
www.brontcreek.org

E-2
West
of Toronto
35-min.

Schedule: Open year-round from 8 am to dusk. Most activities are offered on weekends only during the fall, winter and spring. The rink is open 9 am to 9:30 pm.
Admission: $16 per vehicle.
Directions: From QEW West, take exit #109/Burloak Road northbound and follow signs.

ALBION HILLS C.A.

Panoramic tobogganing

It took us 45 minutes to reach Albion Hills, where I had been assured we'd find great tobogganing hills. Indeed, a long and wonderful slope awaited us, sitting against a breathtaking panorama! It promised an even acceleration without being too risky, and I know my little appraiser would have loved it... had I been able to wake him up! Kiddies' naps and snow conditions are undoubtedly the two unpredictables for family outings!

Our son did not bat an eye for the two hours of our visit but we tested the site ourselves. The slope's incline was long enough to provide lots of excitement, and not too steep to make the climb back unpleasant.

TIPS (fun for 4 years +)
• When Toronto's snow begins to melt, call **Albion Hills** to enquire about snow conditions, as the tobogganing season is often prolonged for another few weeks in that region.
• You can park your car not far from the centre's admission booth, close to a sign indicating "tobogganing". The slope is located on the left. Then drive to the ski chalet (follow the signs), where you will find washrooms, a snack bar, and ski rentals. They rent toboggans for around $7!
• More about **Albion Hills Conservation Area** during the summer on p. 398.

The day we visited, while Toronto's tobogganing hills were icy at best, those at Albion Hills boasted a lovely coat of fresh snow, completely enjoyable for sliding aficionados, perfect for cross-country skiers, many of whom passed us with beaming smiles!

They clear a section of the lake for ice skating, from mid-January to end of February, weather permitting.

Albion Hills Conservation Area • Caledon (416) 661-6600, ext. 5203 or (905) 880-0227 www.trca.on.ca	C-2 N-W of Toronto 50-min.

 Schedule: Open year-round from 9 am to dusk.
Admission: $6.50/adults, $5.50/ seniors, FREE for 15 years and under with their family (around $18/adults if you want to use the cross-country trails).
Directions: From Hwy 400 North, take exit #55/Hwy 9 westbound. Turn south on Hwy 50 and follow the signs.

NEARBY ATTRACTIONS
Kortright Centre (25-min.) .... p. 241

General tips about Time Travel:

- Most of these places normally involve staff members or volunteers dressed in period costumes to play the part.
- You too can dress up! It will add to the experience and you'll get a good reaction from the staff, volunteers and other visitors.
- Most of these attractions rely on volunteers, which explains why activities may vary a lot, one year to the next. It all depends on who's available, and when.

TIME TRAVEL

See **Sainte Marie among the Hurons** on p. 388.

MEDIEVAL TIMES

Over the sand-covered arena, powerful spotlights projected an entertaining ballet of coloured lights on a smoke screen. This captivated us until the show began.

We saw an act featuring well-trained horses. Then, the handsome long-haired equestrian warriors were introduced.

Guests in each section were greeting their knight as noisily as possible. Everyone burst out

Good times!

"Is that real metal?" asked my son, pointing towards the spear held by the knight greeting us. With just enough authority, the guard scraped the blade on the stone wall. Gritting our teeth, we concluded that the metal was definitely genuine. "Mi'lady, may I help you?" asked the ticket office attendant, before showing us the way to the table where we would all be crowned.

We found ourselves inside the "castle" antechamber, in front of a camera, alongside a count and countess (we were then pushed gently towards the next activities). During the meal, the photo they took was presented to us, which we are free to purchase. It did appeal to us, with its medieval-style frame and our hosts' superb costumes!

Inside, the 110,000 sq. ft. space has been turned into a dark, 11th Century castle, complete with coats of arms and murals depicting scenes of chivalry.

To the right of the grand hall, the stables are equipped with windows allowing us to admire the stallions with braided manes. On the other side, royal thrones are surrounded by suits of armour.

The master of ceremonies, to the sound of genuine resounding trumpets, invited us to enter the 1350-seat banquet hall. Wearing yellow crowns, the colour of the knight that we would be rooting for, we headed for the tables bearing the same colour.

laughing when the master of ceremonies described the people greeting the green knight as "scum" from the bad part of town, invited only thanks to the king's great generosity.

In the cheering department, we could not manage to outdo the blue section, completely filled by a group of friends, who encouraged each other to produce a happy clamour. The knights confronted each other at games of skill, and the queen rewarded the best with a flower, which they promptly threw at a beauty sitting in the audience.

Later, costumed waiters invaded the field, armed with chicken-covered trays. "You will love the taste of baby dragon!" our waiter confided to my incredulous son. We were also served spareribs, followed by coffee and dessert.

Then, the champion was needed to fight the revengeful son of an enemy killed by the king. Last time I checked, it was the king himself seeking revenge for his brother's death.

The story line has changed since my last visit but it remains the justification for games, joust and a tournament to choose a new champion.

When the knights fought each other in mortal combats (what a waste!) to determine the champion, my son very nearly climbed on his chair to better cheer for our yellow knight.

"Is he really dead?" anxiously inquired my young humanist when our knight collapses on the floor after a fatal blow.

In the darkness, real sparks were flying from swords clashing together. The fights resembled a choreography, which had to be well orchestrated! It is obvious that the well trained actors could easily suffer serious injuries while manipulating the really heavy weapons.

When the final confrontation took place between the champion and his enemy, *Carmina Burana* was thundering as a musical background. I was told the musical score of the new version is even more dramatic. Expect a grande finale!

When we returned to the hall, we got down on the dance floor to the beat of non-medieval music!

TIPS (fun for 6 years +)

• I recommend avoiding the small dungeon with an exhibit of reproductions of medieval torture instruments. Accompanied by graphic drawings, these apparatus bear witness to horrors very difficult to explain to children. After a fabulous show, visiting this little museum left a bitter taste in my mouth.

• The gift shop area is chock-full of varied "medieval" goods, from small accessories for children under $10 (ribbon crowns and plastic arms, to metal swords going for more than $500.

• With great pomp, short knighting ceremonies are performed on those who reserved in advance (extra fee of $25).

• They normally offer interesting promotions during **March Break**, Mother or Father's Day and other such occasions. See their website to find out about these.

• The meal is served with soft drinks or water and we eat with our fingers. Portions are generous, but do not expect a gastronomic feast. (Alcoholic drinks are also available for an additional cost.)

NEARBY ATTRACTIONS

Despite the fact that **Medieval Times** is an expensive outing (even more so with all the extras that can be purchased), the experience is worth the trip, thanks to dynamic actors and a very entertaining show.

Photos: Courtesy of Medieval Times

Medieval Times 1-888-935-6878 www.medievaltimes.com	**D-3** **Downtown Toronto** **10-min.**

Schedule: Open daily in June, July & August (fewer days the rest of the year), usually at 5 pm and 7:30 pm on Saturdays, 4 pm on Sundays, and 1 pm and/or 7:30 pm the other days. Open daily during March Break. Check their website for exact hours.

Admission: (tax not included) Show is $64/adults, $41/3-12 years. FREE/under 3 years on parent's lap, no meal. Parking fees apply. You can upgrade your ticket for $10 to get preferred seating, cheering banner and commemorative program and DVD.

Directions: Exhibition Place, Toronto. Take Lake Shore Blvd., go north on Strachan Avenue. Turn west into the grounds of Exhibition Place. Follow Princes Blvd. to Saskatchewan Road. There is a parking lot right next to the Medieval building.

FORT YORK

Kids hold the fort

Little soldiers learn how to hold the wooden rifle, to walk in step, to present arms and to fire at the order of a lenient officer. Giggles are guaranteed; bring out your cameras!

When they discover the historical and archaeological wealth of **Fort York**, Torontonians are surprised, as they've been passing by for years without noticing it. Nestled between buildings and highways, we forget this location has history.

On this site, the City of Toronto, initially named Fort York, was founded in 1793, following the demise of the French Fort Rouillé around 1750.

The historic site really comes to life in July and August with its daily historic military demonstrations of music, drill and artillery (cannon firing twice a day and firing of muskets), all performed by costumed employees. You're also treated to a historic tasting in the kitchens.

You can explore the basement of the **Officers' Brick Barracks**, built in 1815. More than 12,000 artefacts were found during the archaeological digs performed there from 1987 to 1990.

The **Centre Block House** is home to the military museum full of arms and uniforms from different times.

TIPS (fun for 4 years +)

• Fort York's favourite activity for children, the drill, is only offered during special events. Dates to remember: **Victoria Day**, **Canada Day** and **Simcoe Day,** when they usually offer special activities.
• During the **March Break**, they offer the **March Through Time** drop-in event for children 10 years and under (also including a kid's drill).
• Ask about their intriguing **Ghosts Walk Night** events a few nights in October, involving some strolling around the site (pre-registration, usually around $10/adults, $5/12 years and under).
• Fort York has had battle re-enactments in the past. Not lately. Check our index under **Battle re-enactments** for a list of places offering them (also see **Battle of Stoney Creek** on p. 375).

Fort York
(416) 392-6907
or (416) 338-3888 (events)
www.toronto.ca/museums

D-3
Downtown Toronto
10-min.

Schedule: Open year-round, 10 am to 5 pm (closes at 4 pm on weekdays after Labour Day until Victoria Day). Closed mid-December to January 1. Check the website for March Break hours.

Admission: Around $8/adults, $4/seniors and students, $3/6-12 years, FREE 5 years and under. Parking included with admission.

Directions: At the end of Garrison Road, Toronto. Take Lake Shore Blvd., go north on Strachan Avenue, east on Fleet Street.

COLBORNE LODGE

Easter traditions

Last spring when we visited High Park, several geese were walking over the pond ice and kids warmed up in the gorgeous nearby playground. The year before, the sun had been warm enough to melt the little chocolate eggs fallen from the kids' baskets on their way back from the egg hunt. Easter time is a tricky time of the year but one sure thing during this period is the Easter fun at Colborne Lodge.

Colborne Lodge was built in 1837 and still contains many of the original artefacts, but the adults better appreciate this. The best time to visit the historic museum is around Easter, for their traditional Easter activities.

First, there's the **Spring Egg Fun Day** usually on Palm Sunday (one week prior to Easter). The event's activities vary from one year to the next, depending on the volunteers involved. You can always count on egg dyeing in the lodge's kitchen, for a small fee, and chocolate egg hunts divided by age group in and around the **Children's Garden** by the lodge.

The **Easter Traditions** activities are usually offered on a few consecutive weekends around Easter time. The event includes a house tour, egg dyeing in the historic kitchen, using vegetable dye, and a game to spot hidden eggs around the house.

TIPS (fun for 4 years +)

• During **Easter** time, you can enter the park from High Park Blvd. off Parkside Rd. and park by the animal pens. An unofficial trail leads up the hill to Colborne Lodge. You can also park by **Grenadier** restaurant and take a 5-min. walk.
• You can usually pre-register for Christmas activities. They offer March Break activities, and a FREE outdoor **Harvest Festival** on the first Sunday in October.
• They offer **Haunted High Park**, involving tales and legends about the park in the candle lit house (a few nights at the end of October, pre-registration required).
• See **High Park** on p. 454.

NEARBY ATTRACTIONS

Colborne Lodge
(416) 392-6916
www.
toronto.ca/museums

| D-3 |
| **West** |
| of downtown |
| 15-min. |

Schedule: Open Tuesday to Sunday, from May to end of August (noon to 5 pm) and from October through December (noon to 4 pm). Open Friday to Sunday, from mid-January to April (noon to 4 pm). Also open on Thursdays in March and all week long during the March Break. **Spring Egg Fun Day** is always on the Sunday before Easter, usually noon to 3 pm).
Admission: Around $6/adults, around $3/seniors, students and children (a bit more during Christmas time). **Spring Egg Fun Day** is around $2/person.
Directions: 11 Colborne Lodge Drive, Toronto (in the south end of High Park. (See this park's directions on p. 454.)

SPADINA MUSEUM GARDEN PARTY

Garden party

It feels like the whole family has been invited to the garden party of very rich relatives. After behaving nicely when visiting the elegant Spadina House, children run wild under the shade of the huge trees to burn off energy under the indulgent gaze of proper ladies. They have all donned their fancy hats for the occasion.

Spadina Museum is a gorgeous 19th-century home set on an enormous property, by Toronto standards, with adjoining gardens. Back in 1900, only a few hundred very privileged guests could enjoy the site when the Austin family was holding its annual private strawberry social.

The house has recently undergone major renovations which have brought it back to what it was in the 1920's and 1930's. As a result, the museum is reinventing its line-up of activities.

For years, Spadina Museum has treated us with a strawberry social. Now, we are offered a garden party in the spirit of the 1920's. I was told we can still expect some strawberries and cream (and many other tasty options) but no shortcakes. We can also count on garden party activities for all ages. This should be one great garden party!

TIPS (fun for 5 years +)

• I recommend you buy your food or refreshment tickets as soon as you get in. There's a line-up to buy tickets and another one to actually get the food. Consider bringing a blanket to sit on the grass for the picnic.

• Ask about their Christmas events with a twist, 1920s style (2011: November 22 to December 31, Tuesday to Friday, 12 noon to 4 pm; weekends, 12 noon to 5 pm).

NEARBY ATTRACTIONS
Casa Loma (1-min. walk) .... p. 128
Sir W. Churchill Park (5-min. walk) p. 362

Spadina Museum
(416) 392-6910
www.
toronto.ca/museums

| D-3 |
| **North** |
| of downtown |
| **20-min.** |

Schedule: The **Garden Party** will be held on the third or last Sunday of June, from 12 noon to 4 pm (2011: June 26). The museum is open year-round on weekends, and also Tuesday to Sunday from April to Labour Day, from 12 noon to 5 pm (closes at 4 pm on weekdays from September to January).

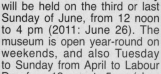

Admission: Around $8/adults, $5/seniors and students, $4/6-12 years old (a bit more during Christmas time). FREE under 6. **Garden Party:** $3/person plus cost of food.

Directions: 285 Spadina Road, Toronto (located just east of Casa Loma).

BATTLE OF STONEY CREEK

The muskets were good for one shot for each charge. Still, there is lots of firing and many artillery shots during the re-enactment. The noise creates quite an atmosphere with, of course, many soldiers "dying" on the battlefield.

Don't expect any hand-to-hand combat however, as soldiers of the time moved slowly and in straight lines towards the enemy, stopping to shoot or recharge as they went.

Time travel at its best!

Upon your arrival, you'll notice the military encampment, with its small white tents facing the Battlefield Museum. Women under their umbrellas, gather around campfires with their long dresses, while soldiers practise formations. Costumed children play with antique toys, and Native Warriors, in full make-up regalia, add a touch of authenticity. We find ourselves deep in 1813.

Next to the battlefield is an amusing section with old-fashioned games: fishing pond, wooden muskets firing rubber bands and wooden frames to entrap prisoners' heads and hands (for a small fee). Other attractions include the high monument to climb, the museum with costumed staff handing out cookies from the kitchen, horse and wagon rides and shooting demonstrations.

For the sole pleasure of acting, volunteers from all over Canada (some flying from the States) join in and don their costumes, put up their tents, prepare their authentic food and most of all, get ready to re-enact the **Battle of Stoney Creek**, which involved about 3000 Americans and 700 British troops in 1813.

As a general rule, tents with open doors mean you can sneak in and admire the historic furniture, made without nails, and different objects for daily use these passionate people have gathered.

The powder bullets, used with historic muskets, explode in a muffled sound as they are shot during the military drills.

TIPS (fun for 5 years +)
• There's no parking on site. Free parking and bus shuttle service are available at the **St. David's School**, on Centennial Parkway between Queenston Rd. and Randall Avenue.
• Check their calendar of events for activities on March Break and Christmas.

NEARBY ATTRACTIONS
Welland Canals (15-min.) .... p. 212
Albion Falls (10-min.) .... p. 252

Battlefield Museum • Stoney Creek (905) 662-8458 www.battlefieldhouse.ca
E-2 S-W of Toronto 65-min.

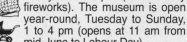

Schedule: The re-enactments take place the first weekend of June, with activities going on from Friday to Sunday (2011: June 4-5, 2012, June 1-3, 2013: May 31 to June 2). The battles are re-enacted on both afternoons at 3:30 pm, plus Saturday at 8:30 pm (followed by fireworks). The museum is open year-round, Tuesday to Sunday, 1 to 4 pm (opens at 11 am from mid-June to Labour Day).
Admission: Museum: Around $6.50/adults, $5.50/seniors & students, $4.50/6-16 years, $16.50/family, FREE under 6. **Battle re-enactment**: $8/adults, $2/5-16 years. FREE under 5 years old.
Directions: 77 King Street West, Stoney Creek. From QEW towards Niagara, take exit #88 (Centennial Pkwy/Hwy 20) southbound. From Centennial, turn left on King Street (museum is on your right).

MONTGOMERY'S INN

Tea is served

Some events are more interactive than others at Montgomery's Inn, but you can always count on their tearoom experience to complement your visit to this old Inn, dating from the 1830's.

Most historical buildings that can be visited in the region used to be private houses. The Montgomery family lived and made a living at Montgomery's Inn. The rooms' settings are therefore different than historical houses.

There is a worn-out floor in front of the bar counter, with tables and checkerboards. There's a small ballroom, and guest rooms with many beds. In those days, you rented a place in a bed, not a room. Can you imagine?

We visited during a special program requiring pre-registration during Christmas, when crafts and games were organized for young visitors. These might change from year to year, but the spirit remains the same.

TIPS (fun for 4 years +)

• See the *Songs & Stories* on their website for dates of storytelling usually offered during Halloween and Christmas time (advanced registration required, fees apply, call to confirm).
• In the tearoom, they serve tea and snacks for $5 per person. On special occasions, they serve fancier teas for $10 (**St. Patrick's**, **Victoria Day**, **Canada Day**...).

NEARBY ATTRACTIONS

When we visited, the kids made New Year's crackers. They created a game from the old days, made out of a button and a string, to take home.

They tried their hand at old-fashioned games: cup-a-ball, marbles and "traumatropes". They ground spices, grated lemon and cinnamon and rolled dough in the kitchen, supervised by a cook in costume.

The tearoom was our obvious next stop. The small pastries were delicious. I rediscovered the pleasure of pouring myself some good tea from a teapot. My 3-year-old was thrilled when I transferred her lemonade into my China tea cup and plate for her to taste. Fancy!

In July and August, enjoy **Shakespeare in the Park** (bring your own chair). Their **Farmer's Market** runs on Wednesdays, 3 pm to 7 pm, starting end of May.

Montgomery's Inn
• Etobicoke
(416) 394-8113
www.
montgomerysinn.com

**D-3
West
of downtown
35-min.**

Schedule: Open year-round, Tuesday to Sunday, 1 to 5 pm. Closed on Mondays. Tea served from 2 to 4 pm.

Admission: Around $6/adults, $3/ seniors and students, $2/12 and under. Tea with pastry is $5/visitor. Extra fees for special events.

Directions: 4709 Dundas Street West, Etobicoke (east of Islington Avenue, on the south side of Dundas).

GIBSON HOUSE MUSEUM

Hands-on history

The Gibson House Museum is the historic house offering the most hands-on activities. In the minds of young visitors, the museum's great discovery room for children makes the actual visit to the 1851 house look like a mere bonus.

Our costumed guide has all the patience in the world for the children's questions. The **Gibson House's** staff members and volunteers are used to dealing with young visitors.

During the Holiday season when we visit, we are allowed to touch a few old-fashioned toys, peek into a few bedrooms and stop at the kitchen for a taste of hot cider and a cookie.

Usually, in most other historic houses, once visitors have no more questions for the guide, the visit is over. Here, we head towards the modern-looking **Discovery Gallery**, where the real fun starts for children.

Some fifteen boxes, each bearing a label describing its contents, await us on the shelves. In the "Sheep" box, we find real wool kids can glue on a drawing of a sheep and take back home! I loved the quilt puzzles with wooden triangles and quilt designs to reproduce. Then there was the weaving box with materials to create our weaving device from scratch, great drawings to colour and more. (The boxes will vary from one year to the next.)

Clothing and accessories for boys and girls are available next to full mirrors. Beside a beautiful mural are two heavy buckets with a yoke. Once your children have tried to carry this apparatus, tell them that on a regular day, the Gibson children had to carry 15 buckets for cooking, many more for laundry or baths, and as drinking water for people or animals. The little chores you ask of them will become more bearable!

TIPS (fun for 4 years +)
- It is Pay What You Can on **Victoria Day**, **Canada Day**, **Simcoe Day** and **Family Day**.
- There are also more drop-in activities during March Break and Christmas time (usually on the first three Sundays). Check their website for details.
- On special occasions, you could have the chance to see a cooking demonstration in the historic kitchen (included with regular admission).

NEARBY ATTRACTIONS
Dempsey Park (5-min. walk) .... p. 283

Gibson House Museum
· North York
(416) 395-7432
www.toronto.ca/museums

**D-3
North
of downtown
35-min.**

  Schedule: Closed in September, open the rest of the year Tuesday to Sunday, noon to 5 pm (also open on Holiday Mondays).
Admission: Around $6/adults, $3/seniors, students and children (a bit more during Christmas or March Break).
 Directions: 5172 Yonge Street, North York. Major construction around the museum. Entrance now from Yonge, only when arriving from the north. Limited $5 parking spaces (big free parking lot is gone, read p. 281 for parking tips).

HALTON REGION MUSEUM

... and surroundings

On my way back from the snowtubing park located in the Kelso Conservation Area, I decided to check out the museum on site. When I entered the large red barn bearing the museum's name in big letters, I almost turned back right away. Although it seemed like a beautiful banquet room to rent, it didn't look like much to visit. It's a good thing an attentive staff member insisted on showing me the place.

TIPS (fun for 6 years +)

• The third floor is maintained at a cool temperature to better preserve the artefacts. It offers a great break for the kids to cool down after some time under the sun at the beach. It is open upon request during the museum hours, don't be shy!
• This whole park encompasses 16 km of overlapping trails for hiking and/or mountain biking with three levels of difficulty. You can get a map at the park's entrance or at the **Visitor's Centre**.
• When I asked about the trail to the top of the cliff, I was told that in a 20-minute walk on the way to the top of a rock plateau (and at the base of the quarry), we could see lots of **fossils** shaped like screws. That would make it worth the trip for young paleontologists. The top is only minutes away from there on. You access the trail from the tunnel by the ski chalet.
• During **Thanksgiving** weekend, **Kelso Conservation Area** offers **Fall Colours**, an event allowing us to catch a ski lift ride up the escarpment to admire fall colours! More about it on p. 193.
• More on **Glen Eden's Snow Tubing Park** on p. 358.
• More on **Kelso C.A.** during the summer on p. 399.

NEARBY ATTRACTIONS
Country Heritage Park (5-min.) ... p. 383

We had been here a number of times to enjoy the lake. Each time, the kids were so involved in water fun that I never got to visit the museum or stroll along the trail leading to the top of the **Niagara Escarpment**.

Turns out that within the first room I entered, there was an interesting display of the turbine developed by the Alexander family in 1898 to generate water power and electricity, using water from a natural spring up on the escarpment. The museum is actually located on the former site of the Alexander family farm. This family settled in 1836 and farmed the land until 1961!

A few galleries featuring carriages, lamps and lanterns were found on the second level but the real fun was on the third floor. There awaited a casual showcase of some of the 35,000-artefact collection of the **Halton Region Museum**.

I noticed many antiques kids would like to see: wreaths made out of dried flowers and human hair, chairs made out of buffalo horns or branches, seats with a hole (adult-size potty chairs), ancient washing machines and antique toys, to name a few. All are stored by categories on shelves, in a warehouse fashion.

Ask for the museum's **Discovery Hunt** sheet (an interactive way to explore the site and collect a little prize).

Halton Region Museum
• Milton
(905) 875-2200
www.conservationhalton.on.ca

**D-2
West
of Toronto
50-min.**

Schedule: Open year-round Monday to Friday, noon to 5 pm (also open on weekends from noon to 5 pm from Victoria Day to Thanksgiving). The park is open year-round from 8:30 am until dusk.
Admission: FREE, with park's admission ($6.25/adults, $4.50/5-14 years old).
Directions: From Hwy 401 West, take exit #320/Hwy 25 northbound, turn west on Campbellville Rd., then south on Tremaine Rd., follow **Kelso C.A.** signs.

WHITEHERN HISTORIC HOUSE

A real soap opera!

The front door was locked but a sign invited me to ring the doorbell. A few seconds later, a solemn butler welcomed me in and asked me to join the tour which was about to begin on the second floor. A few visitors were already crouched like good students on small chairs in front of the wall covered with family photos. The compelling story of the McQuesten saga that started to

TIPS (fun for 6 years +)

• You can only visit this house through a tour. You can join the ongoing tours at any time but I recommend you ask to join in when they go through the family tree. Knowing all about the family's character and ordeal really adds to the experience.

• The emphasis of the displays changes depending on the time of the year: love stories, tea time, royal visit and Christmas. During the summer, they offer live music in the garden from noon to 2 pm on Wednesdays. Check their website for more activities throughout the year (special fees apply).

• While you're there, have a look at the **Irving Zucker Sculpture Garden**, just across the street from **City Hall** (the large building at the end of Jackson). You can't see the sculptures from the sidewalk but climb up the stairs and you'll see a dozen pieces including a funny giant stick man.

• For cheaper parking and a chance to check out downtown Hamilton, park in municipal parking north of King St. West (at John St. North and King William St.); walk along King St. westbound to James St., then south along James to Jackson St. (a 15-min. walk).

NEARBY ATTRACTIONS

unfold as the butler went through the family tree soon made us forget all about the formal setting.

Man! These Victorian people did not need television to entertain themselves! In three generations, they went through enough drama to sustain the longest running series. Fortunes made and lost, devilish stepmother, sacrificing daughter, redeeming son, young lovers separated by death, more love stories crushed by a matriarch. Never a boring moment...

The whole house is set in the 1930's, based on archive pictures but when I visited in December, they had recreated a Christmas from the 1880's in the lavish dining room and in the dark parlour graced with a traditional tree. At its base were displayed a roster of vintage toys which belonged to the family.

We learned that the little cannons could be filled with real cannon powder and fired against the lead soldiers. The tour is filled with such information on the way things were done from the 1880's up to now. Even the 10-year-old who attended the tour, eyes glued to his smart phone, couldn't resist the storytelling and put his cell away.

Whitehern Historic House & Garden
• Hamilton
(905) 546-2018
www.whitehern.ca

E-2
S-W
of Toronto
55-min.

Schedule: Closed Mondays. Open Tuesday to Sunday, 11 am to 4 pm, from July 1 to Labour Day (1 pm to 4 pm rest of the year).
Admission: $6.50/adults, $5.50/ seniors & students, $4.50/6-12 years, $16.50/family, FREE under 6.
Directions: 41 Jackson Street West, Hamilton. From QEW westbound, merge into Hwy 403 West. Exit at Main Street. Turn right at Macnab St., then right at Jackson. There's City Hall parking lot at the end of the street (but read the tips).

THE DISTILLERY

ing chandelier and the tables in the mezzanine. And they will enjoy the treats, home-made lemonade and old-fashion sodas.

The public spaces surrounded by the beautifully restored buildings are really welcoming, especially when their trees are adorned with hundreds of small white lights. They often host craft shows and markets.

The Distillery is especially appealing when there's an event going on, and

A pedestrian village

This national historic site set in downtown Toronto includes over forty red brick buildings proclaimed "the best preserved collection of Victorian industrial architecture in North America".

Kids won't care that this was once the largest distillery in the world but they certainly will notice the brick lined and carless streets with weird sculptures.

They won't think much of the freshly roasted coffee smell at **Balzac's Coffee** (last building at the end of Trinity Street) but they will be impressed by the amaz-

there's plenty of those year-round. We've seen a Wolf Howl, a Dance Festival, Nuit Blanche and lately, the **Toronto Christmas Market** (which added a Victorian ambiance).

My personal favourite stops on the site are: **Pikto**, a photo lab and gallery stocked with funky merchandise (Case Goods Lane), **Bergo Design** (with a huge assortment of merchandise in all prices and sizes) and **SOMA Chocolate & Gelato** where you can taste the most amazing spicy hot chocolate in a tiny cup (both on Tank House Lane).

Kids enjoy the **Cube Works Studio** where all art pieces were made with Rubik's Cubes (Trinity Lane, Bldg 54).

You'll notice many visitors on Segways. They're rentals from **Segway Ontario** on The Distillery Lane ($40/30 minutes, 10 years and older and 85 pounds min. weight www.segwayofontario.com). They also rent bikes!

TIPS (fun for 6 years +)
• Check www.soulpepper.ca for the **Soulpepper Theatre Company** program presented at the **Young Centre for the Performing Arts** (Tank House Lane). Every other year, they present a fantastic **Christmas Carol** (see p. 168).
• If you are involved in a parents school council, drop by **Prologue to the Performing Arts** (Suite 201, Bldg 74 on Case Goods Lane) to grab their catalogue of school shows (read p. 118 on Prologue).
• For a light bite on an outdoor patio to enjoy the historic site, there's **Café Uno** (Distillery Lane) and lovely **Brick Street Bakery** (Trinity Lane).

The Distillery
(416) 364-1177
www.
thedistillerydistrict.com

D-3
**Downtown
Toronto**
10-min.

Schedule: Open year-round.
Admission: FREE.
Directions: 55 Mill Street, Toronto (between Parliament and Cherry Streets, south of Front Street).

BLACK CREEK PIONEER VILLAGE

Sneak in!

Here, the blacksmith hammers hot red iron; there, a weaver hums as she works. Elsewhere, a homemaker in her long dress bustles about in front of her ovens, while the harness maker handcrafts leather articles. This is Black Creek Pioneer Village: a fascinating replica of a small cluster of some 35 houses and businesses of the 1860's.

In fact, **Black Creek Pioneer Village** satisfies the "voyeur" within each one of us. Here, you can enter anywhere without bothering to knock! (I make sure to point this out to children when we visit.) I found it captivating to watch my young explorer open doors by himself and discover new territories.

Many of the rooms inside the houses you'll visit, you'll just be able to watch from the doorway. Thankfully, there is generally an area inside these buildings where you may roam freely.

If you come with younger children (as I did with my then 3-year-old son), anticipate their attention span will not exceed 15 seconds for a woodworker silently planing down a plank in the making of a barrel, or a weaver calmly working at her loom. But they might enjoy watching the shoemaker or the broom-maker at work.

Other details however, will satisfy their curiosity. For instance, there are farm animals in various parts of the site, and after all, the blacksmith makes lots of noise as he hits the red hot iron!

Let's not forget the treats sold at the old post office! Every day, you can smell fresh bread baking in the kitchens of the village's **Half Way House** restaurant.

Dads will be happy to know that in 2009, Black Creek has recreated a working brewery from the 1800s! You can visit the **Historic Brewery** on your own or pay an extra $4 for a tour involving three samples of authentic period ales. (Just saying...)

TIPS (fun for 4 years +)

• There are more activities during the March Break.
• Black Creek Village offers the **Battle of Black Creek** (with re-enactment) on Father's Day weekend (3rd weekend in June), **Canada Day Celebration**, the **Pioneer Festival** on the second or third weekend of September (2011: September 17) and the **Howling Hootenanny**, usually on the weekend prior to Halloween. There's more! Go to *What's On* on their website for details.
• See Christmas activities and **Christmas by the Lamplight** on p. 174.

NEARBY ATTRACTIONS
Reptilia (15-min.) .... p. 72

Black Creek Pioneer Village
• North York
(416) 736-1733
www.blackcreek.ca

D-3 North of downtown 35-min.

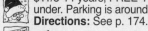

Schedule: Open May 1 to December prior to Christmas, at least from 11 am to 4:30 pm (extended hours during the summer and some weekends). Call to confirm. **Admission:** (tax not included) $15/adults, $14/ seniors, $11/5-14 years, FREE 4 years and under. Parking is around $7.
Directions: See p. 174.

MARKHAM MUSEUM

It takes a village...

Use this museum as an excuse to introduce yourself to Old Markham during one of its dynamic events when the Main Street is closed to traffic.

The **Markham Museum** is located at the end of Main Street and set in the original Mount Joy Public School built in 1907.

The surrounding historic village includes a blacksmith shop, Markham's oldest church, a sawmill, a general store and historic homes to visit. You can even climb into a railway car.

The buildings seem a bit lost on the site, for lack of a forest like at the Black Creek Pioneer Village, but the attraction offers an amazing list of events that greatly add to the ambiance.

Check their website for dates and details on special events such as **Applefest**, **Scaryfest** (to trick or treat through the village) and **Winterfest**.

During the main season, they offer a 9-hole mini golf allowing visitors to put through the past (included with admission, except on event days).

TIPS (fun for 4 years +)

• During winter, you'll find nice rinks without boards on the site (weather permitting). Bring your skates!

• Markham holds its **Santa Fest** (with **Markham Santa Claus Parade** on the last Saturday of November. The parade starts at Hwy 7 at 11 am, runs northbound along Main St. North and finishes at 12 noon at 16th Ave., near Markham Museum (check the parking map on www.markhamsantaclausparade.com). You could have lunch on Main St. (more restaurants around Wilson St.) then drive 5 minutes to Markham Museum for a visit and some skating.

• Among other Markham Main Street events, there's **Markham Village Music Festival** which includes a large kids' area with midway, petting zoo (always on the third weekend in June) and **Markham Auto Classic**, an opportunity to see over 300 vintage or custom cars (on the Sunday after Labour Day weekend).

NEARBY ATTRACTIONS
Lil' Explorers (10-min.) .... p. 321

Markham Museum
• Markham
(905) 294-4576
www.markham.ca
(click *Attractions*)
www.markhammainstreet.com

C-3
N-E
of Toronto
40-min.

Schedule: From Victoria Day to Labour Day weekend (closed on Labour Day), Monday to Friday, 10 am to 5 pm; weekends, 12 noon to 5 pm. The rest of the year, open Tuesday to Sunday, 12 noon to 5 pm (closed during Easter). Daily tours at 1 pm and 3 pm (except Mondays).

Admission: $6/adult, $5/student and seniors, $4/2-12 years, $15.50/family of 4. FREE under two years. Fees may vary during special events.

Directions: 9350 Hwy 48. From Hwy 401, take exit #383/ Markham Road northbound. Go past Hwy 407, where it becomes Main Street, then Hwy 48. The museum is just north of 16th Avenue on the west side.

COUNTRY HERITAGE PARK

A close shave!

A big sheep, held firmly in the grip of a farmer, sits (literally), on the cushion of her own wool, ready for "a close shave". As soon as she starts to bleat, the sheep in the pen walk towards her as if offering moral support.

TIPS (fun for 4 years +)

• Their calendar of events at the time of print included a few of their traditions: **The Teddy Bear's Picnic** (2011: June 18), an **Antique Tractor and Toy Show** (2011: July 15-17) and an **American Civil War** re-enactment. These are great! (2011: August 20-21).

• For a few years now, they've offered two SUPER (and affordable) events that will be a blast for the whole family (with many stages, large costumed cast, merchants and games): **Country Renaissance Festival** (1st weekend of June) and the **Pirate Festival** (weekend prior or including Simcoe Day, 2011: July 30 to August 1st).

• Ask about their **Parade of Lights** (2011: November 12-13 at 6 pm) with tractors decorated with lights, music in the barn and Santa's visit.

• I will have to go back to check out **On the way to Bethlehem**, a re-enactment of the nativity throughout the site, ending with Jesus in the log barn (2011: November 25-28, 6:30 pm to 9 pm).

• There's a snack bar and a small gift shop on the premises during the summer.

It was Sheep Day when we visited the **Country Heritage Park**. This special event has been dropped since, but you must have a look at their website to see the extent of the line-up of events, equally interesting, they have going on during the summer weekends.

We headed towards the nearby school where a teacher in a long skirt invited us to write with a grey stone on a black slate. We eventually sneaked out to catch a tractor ride around the farmstead. (You can hop on and off of the tractor ride as much as you want, which turns out to be really handy for the site is huge.)

There are some thirty buildings on site. Located in one area of the park, the **Dairy Industry Display**, the **All About Apples** barn and the **Steam Power** buildings offer the most interaction.

There, my little farmers "drove" a dairy delivery truck, and felt the suction of a milk pump (for cows, of course). They observed the workings of a steam machine, tested a hay bed, peeled and pressed apples the old-fashioned way and pet animals in the small pioneer farm. Since our last visit, they've acquired two cute miniature horses and they've added a very popular kids' playfarm.

Country Heritage Park	
Country Heritage Park • Milton 1-888-307-3276 or (905) 878-8151 www.countryheritagepark.com	**D-2 West of Toronto 45-min.**

 Schedule: The park is open to the public on weekends only, in July and August, 11 am to 4 pm (and year-round during special events, see their calendar.)

 Admission: (cash only) $8/ adults, $7/seniors, $5/6-12 years, FREE 5 years and under, $22/family of 5.

 Directions: 8560 Tremaine Road, Milton. From Hwy 401 West, take exit #320/Hwy 25 northbound. Turn west on Regional Rd. 9, then south on Tremaine.

NEARBY ATTRACTIONS

CRAWFORD LAKE C.A.

An Indian village

Walking into the fortified village through a corridor lined with 5-metre-high stakes is like entering another world. From the top of the palisade, my young warrior inspects his territory with a watchful eye. In such a setting, it's easy to imagine the life of native people who lived here centuries ago.

Inside the palisade is the **Crawford Lake Indian Village**, which was reconstructed using data collected during an extensive archaeological dig. The **Turtle Clan** longhouse stands close to the central square. With an austere exterior, it doesn't reveal the exoticism of its interior layout: roof openings to let the smoke out and the sunshine in, fur-covered sleeping areas, animal skins hung here and there, tools, clothing and jewelry.

Inside the second longhouse, the **Wolf House**, a short educational film was shown in a small theatre. A third of the Wolf House has regained its original look. To help visitors visualize the daily life of the Iroquois of yesteryear, big family clan

pictures are hidden behind large pelts. Children enjoy peeking through the holes to discover these worlds.

In the pretty **Visitor Centre** (which abounds in interactive information), we learned that the Village's presence was discovered after analyzing **Crawford Lake**'s bed. When corn pollen was identified in a sedimentation sample, it became evident that there had been agriculture close by. Research confirmed the hypothesis, and the remains of the village were then unearthed. A well marked trail leads to Crawford Lake. You can go around it by taking a wooden trail, relatively safe for young children. The walk lasts about half an hour. A couple of picnic tables are available by the lake.

Opposite to the lake trail, a stroller-accessible path leads to a belvedere offering a view of the **Niagara Escarpment** in about fifteen minutes. Another winding path offers a one-hour return hike into the forest, between roots and crevices, to the viewpoint.

TIPS (fun for 4 years +)
• Ask for a trail map at the **Visitor Centre** or download it from their website.
• During the weekends of the **Sweet Water Season** (March/April) and daily during the **March Break**, you can watch maple syrup being made from sap, sitting on a log around the fire. A staff member prepares and cooks corn flatbread to dip in syrup at the end of the presentation.

NEARBY ATTRACTIONS
Springridge Farm (15-min.) .... p. 144
Hilton Falls C.A. (10-min.) .... p. 250

Crawford Lake Conservation Area
• Milton
(905) 854-0234
www.conservationhalton.on.ca

D-2
West
of Toronto
45-min.

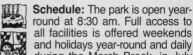

Schedule: The park is open year-round at 8:30 am. Full access to all facilities is offered weekends and holidays year-round and daily during the March Break, in July and August, from 10 am to 4 pm.
Admission: $7.25/adults, $6.25/seniors, $5/5-14 years, FREE 4 years and under.
Directions: From Hwy 401, take exit #312/Guelph Line southbound, in Milton, then follow the signs.

WESTFIELD HERITAGE VILLAGE

Wonderful events

If our visit on Anne of Green Gables Day (not offered anymore) reflects the quality of all events organized at the Westfield Heritage Village, my family could easily become addicted to the place.

At the fence, a trio of Anne of Green Gables look-alikes were greeting arriving friends, similarly clad. We looked around and saw dozens of young Annes. Later on, we were able to admire 45 of them, with genuine red hair or wigs and period dresses all lined up by the train station where they would be presented to the judges.

My son spent thirty minutes in the game zone, learning to walk on tin cans. I thought it was hilarious to watch a bunch of girls, sporting straw hats with red wool braids, compete in a tug-of-war game. Alongside the village bandstand, people lined up to dance to the fiddle. My daughter also shook it up, until a parade of antique cars started to race around the place.

The village includes 33 buildings. At the general store, we bought old-fashioned candy. At the Doctor's house, we took a look at the old-fashioned pill-making technique. My daughter was busy exploring the inside of... the coffin exhibited at the workshop door.

A fire burned near the log house, one of the buildings located off the beaten track. Next to it, the trading post was interesting, with pelts to touch and traps used by pioneers to catch animals. We walked across a covered bridge to return to the action.

TIPS (fun for 4 years +)

• Sundays in March as well as some weekdays during the March Break, it is maple syrup time with demonstrations of native, pioneer and modern methods. They serve pancakes at the restaurant and wagon rides to tour the village.

• For many years, they've offered the **American Civil War Experience**, with costumed actors, battle re-enactment and more (2011: Saturday June 25, 6 pm to 10 pm).

• There's something going on **Canada Day** and during the **Ice Cream Festival** (2011: July 31-August 1, 10 am to 4 pm).

• They offer **Haunted Halloween** nights in October (2011: October 28-29 6:30 pm to 9:30 pm).

• Check their **'Twas the Night Before Christmas** event with self-guided lantern tours, carol singers, toy makers and St. Nick's visit (three Saturdays before Christmas (2011: December 3, 10, 17, 5 pm to 9 pm).

• There is a restaurant on the premises offering full food services.

NEARBY ATTRACTIONS

Westfield Heritage Village
• Rockton
(519) 621-8851
www.westfieldheritage.ca

E-2
S-W
of Toronto
70-min.

  **Schedule:** The Village is open and alive with staff in period dress any Sunday and holidays from early April to late October, 12:30 to 4 pm (also on some days during the March Break and during special events, see *Special Events* on their website).

 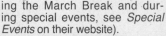 **Admission:** Regular Sundays are $8.50/adults, $7.50/ seniors, $5.50/6-12 years, FREE under 6 (a few dollars more during special events).

 Directions: 1049 Kirkwall Road, Rockton. Take QEW West to Hwy 403, then turn north on Hwy 6 to Hwy 5. Turn west on Hwy 5, then keep right on Hwy 8 to Kirkwall Road (formerly Regional Rd. 552) just past Rockton. The village is on the west side.

SIMCOE COUNTY MUSEUM

To explore inside out

Maybe I was just lucky but when I was there, the soft light of the fall sun bathing the historical small village made everything look picture perfect. It was the last week in the season to visit the buildings and there were hardly any other visitors. The carpet of red needles on the ground muffled my steps. The tall trees ruling the parkland hid the highway. For a moment, I thought I was back in the good old 1870's.

I was glad I made an impulse stop at this museum on my way back from another attraction in the area. I had noticed it several times over the years, being so close to Hwy 26, so it was now or never.

Imagine my surprise when I discovered a full-size Huron longhouse inside the main complex. Corn was drying in a corner and fur lay on furniture made out of branches. Nearby was a small activity centre with archaeological digging bins.

Around the corner awaited a strip of a Victorian street lined with shops. Through the window, I could see a Santa consulting a list of names. In another were antique toys. Further, a vast room was filled with antique furniture,

arranged to reconstruct whole Victorian rooms.

There was a display of musical instruments and old cameras. There was a model bridge and miniature trains.

After all this, the sixteen outdoor historical buildings felt like a bonus.

Right by the tiny school was a large bell one could ring. The train station was funny, with just a few metres of track in front of it. One could explore the **Spearin House**, which was home to Barrie's Spearin family for over five generations.

Simcoe County Museum
• Minesing
(705) 728-3721
www.museum.simcoe.ca

**B-2
North
of Toronto
70-min.**

Schedule: Open year-round Monday to Saturday, 9 am to 4:30 pm and Sunday, 1 pm to 4:30 pm. The outside buildings are open to the public from May 1 to the end of November.

Admission: $6/adults, $5/ students & seniors, $4/5-14 years old. FREE for 4 years and under.

Directions: 1151 Hwy 26, Minesing. Take Hwy 400 northbound to Barrie. From Barrie, follow Bayfield Street North and exit at Hwy 26. Look on south side.

TIPS (fun for 4 years +)
• They offer special activities throughout the March Break and one Victorian Christmas day usually around mid-December. Their Halloween evenings are offered on week days. Check their website for dates.
• On Sundays during the summer, they offer demonstrations, activities and guided tours with a costumed interpreter.

NEARBY ATTRACTIONS

DISCOVERY HARBOUR

Past and present in the same boat

My son had heard about feathers being used as pens, so he was intrigued by the real one on display in the office of the "Clerk-in-Charge". He could hardly believe his luck when the guide invited him to dip it into the inkwell and write his name in the official register. From then on, my child was hooked for the rest of the excellent summer tour.

In the **Sailor's Barracks**, the guide introduced us to sailors' sleeping habits as she hopped into one of the hammocks that hung one metre over my preschooler's head.

He tried a few times before settling into one. We then played a tossing game the sailors used to play. In the kitchen, attached to the **Commanding Officer's House**, my young cook pretended to mix one pound of this and one pound of that to make a pound cake.

In another barrack, he was absolutely thrilled to sit at a work-bench and work with old-fashioned tools, while my youngest one was seriously "re-arranging" the logs in the shed.

Trotting through the **Assistant Surgeon's House**, the **Home of the Clerk-in-Charge**, the **Naval Surveyor's House** and **Keating House** with its long table set for a family, we visited one intimate interior after another and observed a wide range of artefacts from the daily life of the 19th Century.

At the outer limits of **Discovery Harbour** (a full 30-minute walk from our starting point), we found the site's sole remaining original building: the impressive **Officer's Quarters**, built in the 1840's. The children loved to stroll along its many corridors.

After the tour, we explored two replica schooners, *Bee* and *Tecumseth*, moored at the **King's Wharf**, on our own. We explored the vessels' nooks and crannies, tackled the bells and examined more hammocks in the ships' holds.

TIPS (fun for 4 years +)

• When muddy, it is hard to push a stroller on the slightly sloped trails; a wagon would be a better option.

• They celebrate **Canada Day**, **Métis Day** with mocassin making, traditional celebrations, taxidermy (2011: August 6). They've offered a **Haunted Harbour** for the last few years (2011: October 26 to 28).

• There's the **King's Wharf Theatre** on site, presenting professionnal summer theatre (www.draytonentertainment.com, click on *Theatre*).

• Their restaurant serves lunches and snacks but you can stop at the **Dock Lunch**, in the port of Penetanguishene, for tasty fast food and ice cream at outdoor tables by the water, (705) 549-8111.

NEARBY ATTRACTIONS

Discovery Harbour
· Penetanguishene
(705) 549-8064
www.discoveryharbour.on.ca

A-2
North
of Toronto
90-min.

 Schedule: Open Monday to Friday, 10 am to 5 pm, from end of May to July 1 and seven days a week after that, until Labour Day. Last admission at 4:30 pm.

 Admission: Around $7/adults, $6.25/seniors and students, $5.25/6-12 years old, FREE 5 years and under.

 Directions: From Hwy 400, take exit #121/Hwy 93 to Penetanguishene, turn right at the water and follow ship logo.

SAINTE MARIE AMONG THE HURONS

Kids on a mission

Those who received a Catholic education might remember the stories in the history books of their youth. Father Brébeuf? The Jesuit mission? Well, it all happened in Midland (close by, actually) in 1649, at Sainte Marie among the Hurons.

This unique site is a vibrant testimony to the far-reaching impact of European cultural influence and the Christian religion. Judging by the multitude of languages heard during our visit, Europeans know about this and the word-of-mouth mill is going strong!

On the other side of the fence, we found costumed attendants busying themselves with chores reminiscent of the times. A native storyteller was talking with a few visitors while stirring the contents of a large pot.

Children loved to explore the buildings freely. We adopted their rhythm and therefore, did not see everything. Yet, we took time to view the river from above the bastion. The little ones were intrigued by the canoes built in the old tradition. We climbed up and down the stairs inside the Jesuits' residence, and tried their small beds.

Everything here was sculpted in wood, even the plates. We tried on clothing in the shoemaker's shop. Children loved the teepee and 3-metre-high sunflowers.

My young trapper was flabbergasted by the small fire an attendant quietly started in the hearth with sparks that flew from two stones he was hitting against one another.

At the end of our visit we enjoyed the **Sainte Marie Museum** and its refreshing coolness. It is decorated with great refinement, even in the texture of its wall coverings. The result of careful and extensive research, the museum harmoniously blends and juxtaposes expressions of 17th Century French culture, the frugal materialism of Canada's early settlers and the native culture (and it has been upgraded and digitized since our last visit. Even better!).

TIPS (fun for 4 years +)

• Get a map of the site at the entrance. Before you begin your visit, you may wish to view a 20-minute audio-visual presentation to get yourself in the mood.

• Various original craft activities are offered daily to kids in July and August.

• They do a **Thanksgiving Harvest Festival** with lots of hands-on activities and a **First Light** event with Christmas activities, end of November or early December.

• A **Powwow** is held in the park across from the attraction in September (2011: September 10-11).

• Ask about their **Aboriginal Festival** at the end of June (2011: June 25-26).

• The main building includes a cafeteria-style restaurant.

NEARBY ATTRACTIONS

Sainte Marie among the Hurons
• Midland
(705) 526-7838
www.saintemarieamongthehurons.on.ca

A-2
North of Toronto 90-min.

Schedule: Open daily mid-May to mid-October, 10 am to 5 pm. Open for self-guided tours only a few weeks prior and after the prime season, Monday to Friday. **Admission:** $12/adults, $10/ seniors, $10.50/students, $9.25/6-12 years old, FREE for 5 years and under (cheaper prior and after prime season).
Directions: From Hwy 400 North to Hwy 93 (Midland/Penetang), travel on Hwy 93 North to Midland, follow Hwy 12 eastbound to **Sainte Marie** (across from the **Martyrs' Shrine Church**).

Fanshawe Pioneer Village

Back to the past

Here, kids can actually scrub to their hearts content at the washboard. (And we all know how much fun doing the laundry can be, don't we?)

Many of the thirty buildings at **Fanshawe Village** are open to the public, displaying various antiques within reach.

The **Fanshawe School**, built in 1871, is charming with its rows of small wood-

en desks. Make sure to read the rules observed by the pupils of the time!

In a replica of the **Canadian Free Press Building**, a predecessor to the *London Free Press* founded in 1853, children can look at typesetting letters and engravings that were patiently set for the printing of the newspaper.

My little one enjoyed exploring the kitchen of London-born Canadian painter Paul Peel's childhood house, with its utensils and fridges of another era, and other curiosities. Last but not least, was a pedal-activated sewing machine.

The log house is a good example of the type of house built by the settlers who arrived in 1865. The **Pioneer Farm** shows the type of house they subsequently built, on wooden foundations this time, once they were better settled on their land. The **Jury's House**, which recently was fully restored, displays all the comforts available at the end of the 19th Century.

TIPS (fun for 4 years +)

• See their website for a description of all their special events. Among other things they usually plan a **Canada Day** event (which they call **Dominion Day**), **Haunted Village Hayrides** the last three weekends of October, and a **Visit to St. Nicholas** on December weekends.

• They usually present a great battle re-enactment: the **Fanshawe 1812 Grand Tactical** (2011: October 1-2).

• **Fanshawe Conservation Area** is located right next door by **Fanshawe Lake**. It includes a nice and long unsupervised beach and over 650 campsites. We really enjoyed it after our visit to the Village (www.fanshaweconservationarea.ca).

• The **Museum of Ontario Archaeology**, located at 1600 Attawandaron Rd, is a 15-min. drive away. It features indoor exhibits, a palisade, a longhouse and on-going excavation in the summer and reconstruction of 500-year-old **Lawson Iroquoian Village** (www.uwo.ca/museum).

NEARBY ATTRACTIONS
StoryBook Gardens (30-min.) .... p. 52
Children's Museum (20-min.) ...... p. 219

Fanshawe Pioneer Village
• London
(519) 457-1296
www.fanshawepioneervillage.ca

Off the map West of Toronto 2 1/4 hrs

Schedule: Open from Victoria Day weekend to Thanksgiving Day, Tuesday to Sunday and Holiday Mondays, 10 am to 4:30 pm (also open at other times for special events).

Admission: $7/person, FREE under 3 years (a bit more for special events).

Directions: 2609 Fanshawe Park Road East, London. From Hwy 401 West, take exit #194/ Veterans Memorial Hwy northbound. Turn west on Oxford St., then north on Clarke Road to Fanshawe Park Road.

General tips about
Water Fun

- This is the chapter to turn to when you want to enjoy some wet fun. It includes:
  - beaches
  - lakes
  - wading pools
  - spray pads
  - indoor and outdoor pools
  - water parks
  - water tubing
- Don't forget the bathing suits, towels, beach toys, good book, sunscreen, bottles of water, change for the lockers and cash for the ice cream cones.

WATER FUN

See water tubing at **Elora Gorge** on p. 432.

TORONTO ISLANDS

Centreville Amusement Park and the bicycle rentals. It is the most popular, crossing every 15 minutes on weekends (for most of the day). The **Hanlan's Point** ferry services the western end of Toronto Islands, while **Ward's Island** ferry reaches the eastern point. These two ferries cross every half-hour throughout the day.

Centre Island

In addition to the popular **Centreville Amusement Park** (p. 31), **Centre Island** offers two great wading pools on both sides of the path across the bridge.

If you walk on the path going left just before the bridge, you'll reach **Toronto Island Boat Rentals** where you can rent a paddle boat, canoe, rowboat or kayak to explore the channel.

If you walk instead further south past the bridge, you'll reach the **Island Bicycle Rental**, on the south shore of the island where you can rent bicycles, tandems, double-seaters or 4-seaters to ride along 20 kms of bike trails.

Islanders for a day

Did you know that an amusement park existed in the 1880's at the very same place today's Toronto City Centre Airport sits? In 1909, a baseball stadium was added to this park. Did you know that it's in this very stadium that Babe Ruth hit his first professional home run?

The **Toronto Islands** might have lost their identity as a recreation centre after the 1930's (when the stadium was closed, the amusement park demolished and the airport constructed) but they have since reclaimed the title with a vengeance, with over 1.2 million visitors a year.

Ferry ride

The adventure starts before you even reach the islands with a 15-minute ferry ride, the only way to get there.

My little sailor was tickled pink, unsure whether to check the panoramic view of the CN Tower and the tall buildings close to it, look at planes taking off from the airport, gaze at the white sailboats manoeuvering on **Lake Ontario**, or to simply explore the many bridges on the ferry itself.

Three ferry boats service the islands. The ferry that reaches **Centre Island** brings you closest to the

Nearby is **Gibraltar Beach** with a wide deck over the lake, that will make you feel you are by the ocean!

If you walk further east, you'll reach a boardwalk heading towards **Ward's Beach** and passing by the cute teahouse.

Ward's Island

The eastern part of Toronto Islands is where the year-round residents live. It is almost impossible to resist a nosy peek as you stroll by the little post-card cottages close to the boardwalk or within a short walk east from the **Ward's Island** ferry dock.

It is fun to see standard street signs indicating we're on Lakeshore Ave. or Third St. as we walk along the carless lanes between the houses.

Within a short walk south of the ferry dock, past the **Toronto Island Café**, you can reach the boardwalk and the intimate **Ward's Beach**.

The **Rectory Café** is accessible from the boardwalk, not too far west of the beach. They serve good food on the patio. When I sat there with a glass of wine after a great day at the beach, it felt like Toronto's best kept secret (www.therectorycafe.com).

North of the café is the little bridge to access **Algonquin Island**, the other residential section of Toronto Islands. If you follow the path west instead, and go past the fire station (!), you'll reach another bridge to uninhabited **Snake Island**.

It is a fun section of the islands to explore, with the channel on its south shore and a beach facing Toronto on the north. Last time we visited, there was rogue art on a tree stump by the beach.

Hanlan's Point

The **Hanlan's Point** ferry reaches the western end of Toronto Islands. It includes the small airport, tennis courts, a trout pond and **Hanlan Beach**, a 15-minute walk from the Hanlan's ferrry dock.

The entrance to the beach is near the tennis courts. Beyond the entrance, a number of smaller sandy trails, some looking like real tiny dunes, branch off from the main trail leading to the beach. BEWARE! You're entering Toronto's only nude beach!

It actually is an official "clothing optional area" where you don't have to undress... but many people do! This area has grown over the years to cover the whole beach. If you're uncomfortable with the situation, it is a 20-minute walk to reach Gibraltar Beach from Hanlan Beach (and another ten minutes to get to Centreville Amusement Park).

If you're cool with the nudist aspect, Hanlan Beach is one great sandy beach.

When we visited, on a weekday years ago, it was relatively deserted. The sand was burning our feet on our way to the lake where it was cooled by the breeze and so soft, the kids begged us to bury them in it.

At a glance, we took in the endless stretch of pristine water, with its swimmers frolicking against a backdrop of lazy white sailboats.

The CN Tower emerged behind the tree line. On the right hand side of the beach, we could watch small planes taking off from the airport, stretched out against the city landscape and reminding us we were still in the heart of Toronto.

The water along the south shore of the Toronto Islands (which includes Gibraltar Beach and Ward's Beach) is the cleanest water in the area, the islands acting as a filter. At Hanlan Beach, it remains shallow for a great distance, reaching no higher than an adult's waist for at least 50 metres. (Did I mention it's a nude beach?)

TIPS (fun for 3 years +)

• No cars are allowed on the ferry. The **Centre Island** ferry won't accept bikes aboard on summer weekends but the other two ferries always welcome them.

• Note that the line-up to the **Centre Island** ferry will be longer than usual during the **Dragon Boat Race Festival** on a weekend in June (2011: June 25-26). See www.dragonboats.com for details.

• Both **Shopsey Café**, near **Centre Island** ferry, and the **Carousel Café** in the amusement park overlooking the channel have a kids' menu. See their menus at www.centreisland.ca under *Restaurants*. In addition to the two restaurants mentioned in the Ward's Island section, there are also snack bars near Gibraltar Beach and near Hanlan's Point Beach.

NEARBY ATTRACTIONS
Harbourfront Centre (15-min. walk) p. 24

Toronto Islands	D-3
Dial 311 (new service)	**Toronto**
(416) 392-8193 (ferry)	**Islands**
(416) 203-0009 (bike rental)	**15-min.**
(416) 392-7161 (beach hotline)	
www.toronto.ca/parks/island	
www.torontoisland.org	

Schedule: Schedules vary depending on the season, and they're different for the weekends and the weekdays. See their website for exact times.

Admission: Return ferry fare is $6.50/adults, $4/seniors and students, $3/2-14 years, FREE under 2 years old.

Directions: Toronto Islands Ferry Terminal is located on Queen's Quay West, Toronto (at the foot of Bay Street).

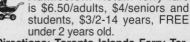

CHERRY BEACH

Cherry on top of the Sunday

Sorry for the easy pun but it was irresistible. It also describes very well our impression when we visited this beach on a hot summer Sunday when The Beach parking lots were full and we decided to come here instead.

Cherry Beach sits right in front of Tommy Thompson Park (where Leslie Street Spit is located) so it offers a different panorama than from The Beach area. You will see several small sailboats zigzagging between the two shores. When it's windy, it's paradise to kite surfers.

The sand is not as fine as on Woodbine Beach but there are many pebbles worth prospecting, according to my kids. On the eastern part of the beach, many tall trees offer shady spots for large families to picnic.

Another great advantage is the direct access to the bicycle trail leading towards

Leslie Spit, offering Toronto's least-crowded ride along the water (see p. 332).

Last summer, we had a lovely picnic with our neighbours on the western part of the park. The kids explored its trail leading to the point facing Toronto Islands.

TIPS (fun for all ages)

• It used to be that you could always count on Cherry Beach when The Beach was overcrowded. Last summer, on a perfect summer weekend, even Cherry Beach's parking lot was full (and many cars illegally parked along the road had parking tickets on their windows). Arrive before lunch and you should not have a problem.

• There's usually a chip truck by the parking lot or you can get something from the take-out counter of the huge Asian **T & T Supermarket** which opened at 222 Cherry Street (www.tnt-supermarket.com).

NEARBY ATTRACTIONS

Cherry Beach
(416) 392-7161
(beach hotline)
www.toronto.ca/parks

D-3
East
of downtown
10-min.

Schedule: Open year-round.
Admission: FREE.
Directions: Going eastbound on Lake Shore Blvd., turn south on Cherry Street, Toronto. You can not turn south on Cherry going westbound. You'll have to turn north on Cherry and find a way to U-turn back southbound.

ROUGE BEACH

Spread of Rouge

We climb up stairs, cross over a bridge and arrive at a boardwalk where we get a superb panorama of Lake Ontario, with a strip of sand pointing out from the shore of Rouge Beach, looking like the seashore during low tide.

The trail eventually takes off from the edge of the cliff, so we come down the path to get to the beach itself.

Rouge Beach is relatively long and wide, with great sand, and is equipped with changing rooms. When we were visiting, the kids had fun chasing tiny waves created by the wind.

Many people fish in the **Rouge Marsh** adjacent to the parking lot (accompanied by a large population of geese).

Some launch their canoes into **Little Rouge Creek**, visible from the shore. Others come from the lake, into the creek.

There's an undercurrent in that area but not at the beach.

TIPS (fun for all ages)

• Note that this beach is often not suitable for swimming due to the many geese visiting this site. Call the Beach hotline before you go.

• More about **Rouge River** on p. 304.

Rouge Beach
· Scarborough
(416) 392-7161
(beach hotline)
www.toronto.ca/parks

D-3
N-E
of downtown
30-min.

  Schedule: Open year-round.
Admission: FREE.
Directions: Take Hwy 401 East, follow Port Union signs, exit Port Union southbound. Turn east on Lawrence Ave., to the parking lot.

HEART LAKE C.A.

Dive into nature

Heart Lake's sandy beach is wide, and licensed fishermen can enjoy their sport looking for a few farmed trout, comfortably installed in the willows' shade. Beyond the area reserved for swimmers, boats criss-cross the heart-shaped pond, escorted by dragonflies.

The valley's picnic sites bordering the parking lot closest to the lake offer an inviting panorama. There, you feel the urge to roll on the grass. Big families are gathering for large picnics and the air is filled with the appetizing smells of meat sizzling on the barbecues. Unfortunately, you don't get a view of the lake from those sites.

The lake is stocked with rainbow trout every spring. You may fish from the shore or rent a boat to fish out on the water if you pay the daily angling fees ($5.75/adults, $2.85/5-14 years, FREE under 5 years old).

Half a kilometre from the parking lot by the lake, you'll find another parking lot that borders a lovely nature trail, past the **Hill & Dale** picnic lot. The whole family can stroll on it for 30 minutes, while enjoying the shade of 40-metre-high trees.

TIPS (fun for all ages)

• They now have an ambitious **Wild Wetland Splash Pad** located by **Birchview** picnic lot with a 550-person capacity.
• The snack bar is not always open on weekdays; better to bring a lunch.

Photo: Courtesy of Toronto and Region Conservation

Heart Lake Conservation Area
· **Brampton**
(905) 846-2494
(416) 667-6295 (reservations)
www.trca.on.ca

D-2
N-W
of Toronto
35-min.

Schedule: Open from late-April to Thanksgiving, 9 am until dusk (variable closing time for each month).

Admission: $6.50/adults, $5.50/seniors, FREE for 15 years and under with their family, **Splash pad:** $4.75/2-15 years, FREE for adults with kids. Row boat rental is $14 per hour or $35/half a day.

Directions: Take Hwy 410 North until it becomes Heart Lake Road, then go 2 kms north on Road #7.

NEARBY ATTRACTIONS
Chinguacousy Park (15-min.) ...... p. 286

ALBION HILLS C.A.

A quiet sandy hide-out

Albion Hills' beach is wide in certain areas, and sufficiently long to satisfy those seeking a quiet sandy hideout at its far end.

At the end of the more quiet sandy point, you can take a trail running up the hill bordering the water.

From the highest point, you will get a great view and be able to go down a sandy slope bringing you to the shores of the small lake.

If you cross the road by the entrance of the trail, you'll reach the narrow **Humber River**, complete with picnic areas along the way. It eventually leads to the

Photo: Courtesy of Toronto and Region Conservation

campground. You must take your car to access other hiking trails of 1.6 to 5.8 kilometre-long paths at **Elmview** or **Chalet Parking Lots**. You can rent a paddle boat or canoe to enjoy on the lake.

TIPS (fun for all ages)

• During a visit in May, we observed hundreds of tiny tadpoles in the water!

• Albion Hills' trails are open for mountain biking from the end of April to the end of October, weather permitting. All trails start at **Cedar Grove** parking lot.

• It offers around 260 campsites (quite close to one another) with a nice playground.

• The snack bar is mainly open during the weekends. You should bring your lunch on weekdays.

• They've added **Lakeview Splash**, the large wading pool with splash pad by the **Beach Parking Lot**.

• More about **Albion Hills** tobogganing in the winter on p. 367.

NEARBY ATTRACTIONS
South Simcoe Railway (15-min.)   p. 206

Albion Hills Conservation Area
· Caledon
(905) 880-0227
or (416) 667-6295 (reservations)
www.trca.on.ca

C-2
N-W
of Toronto
50-min.

Schedule: Open year-round from 9 am until dusk.

Admission: $6.50/adults, $5.50/ seniors, FREE for 15 years and under with their family, **Splash pad:** $3.75/person. Canoe or paddle boat rental is $14 per hour.

Directions: 16500 Hwy 50, Caledon. From Hwy 400 North, take exit #55/Hwy 9 westbound. Turn south on Hwy 50.

KELSO CONSERVATION AREA

Milton's water spot

For a successful outing in the Milton region, I recommend including a swim at Kelso Conservation Area.

Kelso Beach sits by a grassy park with lots of shade. The length of the beach used to be covered with transparent wires hung some ten metres above, to prevent bird visits. Needless to say the sand was clean! (But I don't know if they're still there.)

It is the ideal spot for a picnic but expect hordes of visitors after 1 pm. With children 7 years and older, you could hike all the way to the top of the escarpment. I have heard it takes more than 45 minutes to reach, but the panoramic view is amazing. Kelso is known in the region for its series of trails for serious mountain bikers. More on this conservation area and the **Halton Region Museum** on p. 378. See **Fall Colours Chairlift Ride** at Kelso on p. 193.

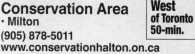

Kelso Conservation Area	D-2
· Milton	West of Toronto 50-min.
(905) 878-5011	
www.conservationhalton.on.ca	

 Schedule: Open year-round (summertime, from 8 am to 8 pm).
 Admission: Park admission: around $6.25/adults, $4.50/5-14, FREE under 5 years (includes bike pass). They used to rent canoes or double kayaks at around $16/hour and paddle boats at around $20/hour. Call to confirm.

Directions: From Hwy 401 West, take exit #320/Hwy 25 northbound, turn west on Campbellville Rd., then south on Tremaine Rd., follow signs.

ELORA QUARRY C.A.

Old-fashioned hole

With the passing years, a basin has formed at the bottom of Elora Quarry, abandoned since the 1930's. On hot summer days, you can dip into this water fed by pure springs.

We accessed the quarry through a small beach offering an excellent view of the 12-metre-high walls surrounding the body of water. Seen from the beach, the panorama is unique. On the other side of the quarry runs the **Grand River** where we saw some people fishing.

This intimate spot is quite different from nearby big **Elora Gorge Conservation Area** (see p. 432).

Elora Quarry Conservation Area	D-1
· Elora	West of Toronto 50-min.
(519) 846-5234	
www.grandriver.ca	

 Schedule: Open mid-June until Labour Day, from 10 am to 8 pm. **Admission:** $5.25/adults, $2.75/6-14 years, FREE 5 years and under.

 Directions: From Hwy 401 West, take exit #295/Hwy 6 northbound, then follow County Rd. 7 to Elora. Turn east on County Rd. 18 (also called Fergus-Elora Rd.). Elora Quarry is located between Elora and Fergus.

CENTENNIAL & JOHNSON BEACHES

While you're here

Last summer, I was looking for a few beach options near Barrie. There was the obvious Centennial Beach right downtown, at the heel of the bay, with a super playground by the water and the tall trademark fountain, but I wanted to know where the locals like to go. I was directed to secluded Johnson Beach, a five-minute drive east of the downtown.

It takes kids 10 minutes to walk across **Centennial Park**'s long and wide beach. From the many structures in its playground near the parking lot, you get a great view of **Lake Simcoe** and the tall fountain. Add to this ice cream from the snack bar in the park and a stop at **Barrie's Splash Pad** in **Heritage Park**, a 10-minute walk towards downtown along the water, and you get a great little summer outing. (You'll come across Ron Baird's giant sculpture *Spirit Catcher* on your way there. Impressive!)

Want more? I've not seen it myself but it seems there's **Duffer's by the Water**, a mini golf just a 3-minute walk south of Centennial Park's parking lot (at the head of Tiffin St.).

Even better, there's a 3.6-km paved bike path starting in **Allandale Station Park** (on the south side of the bay), going all around **Kempenfelt Bay** to Heritage Park (north of Centennial Beach). It leads into a flat 3.1 km finely crushed stone trail going past **Johnson Beach**.

The small Johnson Beach is just a 5-minute drive from Centennial Beach, on the north side of the bay. (Take Kempenfelt Drive to your right off Dunlop to see some pretty houses by the lake.)

A large wooden staircase leads to this cute and tiny beach (which includes changing rooms and bathrooms). From it, you can see Centennial Park to the far right. The trail passes right between the parking lot and this beach. It would be another great starting point for a bike ride.

TIPS (fun for all ages)

• At the corner of Dunlop St. East and Fred Grant St., you'll find a pretty part of old Barrie with restaurants, pubs and cafés, including a **Second Cup** (74 Dunlop East).

• The local theatre company **Theatre by the Bay** produces two summer shows every year throughout August: a Shakespeare play and a family show for children aged 3 and up. Check their website for details (55 Dunlop West, www.theatrebythebay.com).

NEARBY ATTRACTIONS

Centennial & Johnson Beaches
· Barrie
www.barrie.ca

B-2
North of Toronto
75-min.

Schedule: Open year-round.
Admission: FREE.
Directions: Centennial Beach: From Hwy 400 North, take Dunlop Street East exit. Turn south on Toronto Street (it becomes Lakeshore Drive). The parking lot is right after the marina. **Johnson Beach**: Stay on Dunlop Street East, drive through Barrie then take Kempenfelt Drive to your right (just because it's pretty); it will turn into Vancouver Street. Turn right on Shanty Bay Road, then right into the parking lot just before Johnson Street.

CHRISTIE LAKE C.A.

Check this out!

This sandy beach is 360 metres long and the happy bathers do lots of horsing around in the swimming area, never deeper than 5 feet.

It is perfect for parents to toss their ecstatic kids like potato sacks into the lake.

The swimming area used to be chlorinated but in 2010, they figured the quality of the water in the lake was equal or better to the treated area.

You can rent large inner tubes (for $8) to play on inside the boundaries, or rent paddle boats, canoes, kayaks, and rowboats to explore the rest of the lake.

We were not allowed to eat on the narrow beach to keep it clean but we had our picnic on the grass right next to it. One of the trails runs around the lake for 5.6 kms (get a map at the entrance).

Attention fishermen! **Christie** includes nine ponds (note that **Pond 8** is wheelchair accessible). They sell bait.

Christie Lake Conservation Area · Dundas (905) 628-3060 www.conservationhamilton.ca	E-2 S-W of Toronto 55-min.

 Schedule: Open year-round.
Admission: $9 per vehicle and driver, $4.50/add. passenger (cheaper off season). Watercraft rental is $15/hour on weekends ($10/hour on weekdays).
Directions: From QEW/403, take exit Hwy 6 North. Turn west on Hwy 5. Christie is on the south side.

SHADE'S MILLS C.A.

Paddle time

We were grateful for this nice swim almost right in town on our way back from other attractions in this region.

Despite its name, the beach is not in the shade but there are plenty of trees around the boat rental. Renting a canoe or a paddle boat was very tempting because of the shape of the reservoir, with a long arm of water to explore, stretching out one side. It would have taken the whole day to try everything. The conservation area's map showed a footbridge and 12 km of nature trails. They turn into cross-country ski trails in the winter. (Ask about their **ice fishing** and heated ice hut rentals.)

Shade's Mill Conservation Area · Cambridge (519) 621-3697 www.grandriver.ca	E-1 S-W of Toronto 75-min

 Schedule: Open year-round.
Admission: $5.25/adults, $2.75/6-14 years old, FREE 5 years and under. (For canoe or paddle boat rental, call to confirm.)
 Directions: 412 Avenue Road, Cambridge. From Hwy 401 West, take exit #282 at Hespeler Road South. Turn east on Avenue.

SANDY BEACH

A warmer side

After a few days of dipping my big toe into freezing Georgian Bay near Tobermory, I wanted to check if it was true that the water was warmer on the other side of the Bruce Peninsula. It is! Well, it was in the shallow waters of Myles Bay where we discovered Sandy Beach sitting on Lake Huron.

We showed up at this beach in **Black Creek Provincial Park** on a nice windy summer day, which made it a bit hard to keep the picnic sand-free. On the plus side, it created nice waves, which greatly

added to the pleasure of this great expanse of fine white sand.

The water being shallow over a long stretch, it is perfect for younger children. The beach is quite remote, which means there are no bells and whistles and there are not many people around. You're in for some classic beach fun, provided you brought a decent picnic.

I could not find any trail into the provincial park from the beach but there were changing rooms by the parking lot.

When we visited, a man had carefully uncovered an intriguing large rock covered with a naturally drawn pattern of circles. It looked like a giant dinosaur's egg. I'm wondering if it's still there! Maybe he buried it again.

TIPS (fun for all ages)

• We used our visit to **Sandy Beach** in the provincial park as an excuse to explore the countryside along Hwy 6 while we were spending a few days at Tobermory. We first stopped at Lion's Head, east of Hwy 6, at the end of Bruce Road 9 (a 45-minute drive from Tobermory) to replenish our picnic basket at the local grocery store **Helpers Food Market** on Webster Street. I found that country road to be much lovelier than the relatively boring Hwy 6 and it seemed to be the same for most east-west roads coming across the highway. **Lion's Head Beach** is pretty but we really wanted to check Sandy Beach. From Lion's Head, you return on Bruce Road and cross Hwy 6 and get to the other side of the peninsula to **Black Creek Provincial Park** (a 15-minute drive).

NEARBY ATTRACTIONS
Harvest Sculpture Gardens (30-min.) p. 111
Bruce Peninsula (60-min.) .... p. 276

Black Creek Provincial Park
• Strokes Bay
(519) 389-9056
www.ontarioparks.com

**Off the map
North
of Toronto
3 3/4 hrs**

Schedule: Open year-round.
Admission: FREE.
Directions: From Hwy 6, turn west at County Road 9. Then go north on Strokes Bay Road. Take the third road left (Myles Bay Shore Rd.), then the first road right (Sandy Beach Rd.) into **Black Creek Provincial Park**. (**Sandy Beach** is a 45-min. drive from Tobermory.)

SUNNYSIDE BEACH

That's the life!

I'm seated in Sunny-side Pavilion Café. Facing me, the blues of sky and water merge in an unending horizon. I gaze at two swans flying over the shoreline, hearing the rustle of their majestic white wings. My son is building a short-lived dam in the fine sand across the boardwalk. My little one is asleep in her stroller. A cappuccino in hand, I'm getting ready to relax.

Along Lake Shore Boulevard West, you've probably noticed a large, white building beside a long municipal pool. If you venture to the other side of this building, you'll discover a facade with arches and columns and a patio full of tables topped by umbrellas. The structure efficiently muffles the roar of motor vehicles circulating on the adjacent boulevard! Only the boardwalk separates the terrace from the beach.

Sunnyside Beach, the section of the waterfront in front of the pavilion, is now chlorinated (with a fabric shield separating it from the rest, a good thing because of all the birds frequenting the area).

TIPS (fun for all ages)
• The **Pavilion Café** offers an elaborate choice of hearty breakfasts. You can order coffee any way you like it. Salads are large and fresh. Gourmet pizzas are delicious. There's also the ice cream stand and snack bar on the west side of the café.
• The Pavilion's second floor was open to the public during a public art event last summer. It was the first time we got to see the great view from up there. Check their website to see if another one is offered.

NEARBY ATTRACTIONS
Humber Bay Park (5-min.) .... p. 269
High Park (5-min.) .... p. 454

East of the restaurant is the huge outdoor public **Gus Ryder/ Sunnyside Pool** (see p. 418). Past the pool, you'll find **Budapest Park** with playground, wading pool and a few dinosaurs to climb on!

Walk 10 min. west of the Sunnyside Café and you'll reach **Sir Casimir Gzowski Park**, with another wading pool and a playground with original climbing structures. Walk a bit more and you'll get to the bridge leading to **Humber Bay Park**.

Sunnyside Park
(416) 392-7161
(beach hotline)
(416) 531-2233 (café)
www.toronto.ca/parks
www.sunnysidepavilion.com

D-3
West
of downtown
15-min.

Schedule: Café: Usually open daily from May through September (weather permitting), with variable hours, usually from around 9:30 am to at least 11 pm during the summer. Call to confirm.

Admission: FREE admission to the beach. Municipal parking fee.
Directions: 1755 Lake Shore Blvd. West, Toronto. **From Lake Shore westbound:** Keep left to take Lake Shore exit and drive straight into the parking lot. **From Lake Shore eastbound:** Turn right at first parking lot east of Ellis Road.

THE BEACH NEIGHBOURHOOD

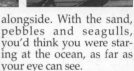

Life on the (water)front

Queen Street East, enlivened by small shops, cafés and great parks along the waterfront, indiscriminately attracts three categories of people: those being pulled by their dog, those following their stroller and finally, those who can enjoy a long brunch.

In our stroller days, we always began an outing to the **Beaches** by having breakfast at one of the district's restaurants around **Kew Gardens**.

We then explored the Kew Gardens playground. It offers a lovely castle-like climbing structure built around the central mature tree and a wading pool.

After playing hide and seek around the bandstand in the middle of the park, we would head for **Kew Beach**, 3 minutes away.

It's a renewed pleasure each time I look at the water. It sometimes appears turquoise beyond the boardwalk running

alongside. With the sand, pebbles and seagulls, you'd think you were staring at the ocean, as far as your eye can see.

A long bicycle trail runs along the boardwalk. Towards the east, it is lined with trees and there's a snack bar. Last time we visited, locals had created a labyrinth with rocks nearby.

The boardwalk ends 20 minutes farther, eastbound, at **Balmy Beach**. Along the way, you'll see another snack bar with some tables during the summer, near the private **Balmy Beach Club**. There's a playground in the adjacent little park.

Further east, you'll reach a secluded section of the beach, where you can sneak into the backyards of some great properties.

TIPS (fun for all ages)

• In the spring or the fall, bring an extra sweater. The breeze that sweeps across the beach makes it cooler than on Queen Street.

• Fireworks are usually offered at **Ashbridge's Bay Park** on **Victoria Day** and **Canada Day**. Call 311, the new phone service of the City of Toronto, to confirm.

• The Alliance **Beach Cinemas** are right behind Woodbine Park, at 1651 Queen St. East. It is our favourite theatre, with spacious seats, live music sometimes offered on Saturday nights, patio, café with lots of tables and checker games. And here, movies are hardly ever sold out. There's also **Fox**, the independent theatre in the eastern end of the Beach at 2236 Queen, where you pay $10/adults and $7/3-12 years. (Check listings for both on www.cinemaclock.com).

• Check **Dufflet's** slick zen decor in the restaurant section in the back of the store (1917 Queen E., www.dufflet. com). Our favourite family place to eat on Queen is **Green Eggplant** where the decor is colourful, the plates always look great and fresh and the prices are unbeatable for the quality (1968 Queen E., www. greeneggplant.com). We've enjoyed many all-day breakfasts at **Sunset Grill** (especially in the back under the skylights) (2006 Queen E., 416-690-9985, opens at 7 am). Now, I prefer a breakfast crepe wrap at **Juice & Java** (2102 Queen E.) or the amazing salty muffins and coffee of **Remarkable Bean** (2242 Queen E.). For a treat, I love the **Pie Shack** with the best country chic decor where you can relax and play boardgames (2305 Queen E.) and off the beaten track **Chocolate by Wickerhead Co.** selling exquisite artisanal chocolates at the best price (2375 Queen E.).

• More on **Ashbridge's Bay Park** and its bike path on p. 333.

• See the **Easter Parade** on p. 38.

If you walk ten minutes westbound from Kew Beach, there's a playground located by the beach as well as the huge **Donald D. Summerville** outdoor pool (416-392-0740). Along the way, if you're lucky, you'll see odd towers of rocks defying gravity, left by anonymous artists.

Beyond, the beach widens a lot and the sand becomes finer, you've reached **Woodbine Beach** from which we can see Ashbridge's **fireworks** during special events. This is where you'll see volleyball nets during the summer.

Another 10-minute walk and you'll see the playground located in front of the **Boardwalk Pub** and snack bar.

We really like the western part of the bay in that area. It offers huge stones on which older children love to leap about, tall trees and a scenic lookout of the bay and access to **Ashbridge's Bay Park** (see p. 333). Note that when you park near Ashbridge's Bay Park, it takes 10 minutes to walk to Woodbine Beach.

The Beach

D-3
East
of downtown
20-min.

Dial 311 (new service)
(416) 392-7161
(beach hotline)

www.beachestoronto.com

Schedule: Open year-round.
Admission: FREE (during the summer weekends and statutory holidays, there is a parking fee to park in the **Ashbridge's Bay** parking lot (the major lot located at the foot of Coxwell).

Directions: Between Coxwell and Victoria Park Avenues, Toronto (along the waterfront). From Gardiner Expwy. eastbound, exit at Lake Shore and drive to the end. Turn east at Queen Street.

NEARBY ATTRACTIONS
Woodbine Park (5-min. walk) ...... p. 270
Glen Stewart Ravine (5-min.) ..... p. 299

BLUFFER'S PARK

Cliffs from below

This beach, at first quite broad, narrows gradually. When dry, its sand is some of the finest I've seen in the area. My little lad threw himself down and made an angel with his arms and legs.

The beach spreads at the end of the fourth parking lot to the east. You reach it via a small road that borders the base of the cliffs which sit blazing in the summer light and look amazing during the fall.

A gravel path runs from the park-

ing lot along the cliff. There's an easy cut through the tall grass to access the middle of the beach, even with a stroller (but you won't be able to push your stroller into the sand).

As you walk further east along the beach, you'll discover another source of playful inspiration in the pieces of polished driftwood lying here and there. Last time we visited, people had built a solid whimsical shack out of these (see p. 134).

Further along, the beach narrows down and you're at the foot of the cliffs.

TIPS (fun for all ages)
• **Dogfish Bar and Grille** is a restaurant located at 7 Brimley Road South (in the **Bluffer's Park Marina**) offering a good view of the marina from its patio (see their menu on www.bluffersparkmarina.com).

• There's a **Lick's** hamburger joint a few minutes west of Midland on Kingston Rd. (2383 Kingston Rd., 416-267-3249, www.lickshomeburgers.com).
• More on the **Scarborough Bluffs** on p. 235.

Bluffer's Park
• Scarborough
Dial 311 (new service)
www.toronto.ca/parks

D-3
East
of downtown
25-min.

Schedule: Open year-round.
Admission: FREE.
Directions: Take Kingston Road eastbound. Turn south on Brimley Street (east of Midland). Go to the end of the fourth parking lot to the east.

BEACHWAY PARK

Sandbar is open

Beachway Park is part of the sandbar linking Burlington to Hamilton. It ends at the Burlington Canal, first opened in 1826 to provide Hamilton Harbour with navigable access to the Atlantic Ocean.

With Stelco and Dofasco as neighbours, the "Burlington Beach" hasn't had good press in the last decades. It was covered with black coal dust or light coloured ash in the 70's, it suffered bacteria warnings in the 80's, dead ducks in 1989, black paint-like water in 1995. To top it off, Hydro towers line along the beach. But, not knowing any of that, we arrived unbiased at the beach... and loved it!

TIPS (fun for all ages)
• **Spencer Smith Park**, a 5-min. drive east of the beach, has undergone a major renewal. Go to *Parks & Recreation*, then *The Waterfront* on their website to see the pictures of the new discovery centre, restaurant, water-jet playground and **Rotary Centennial Pond** (a huge reflecting pool which turns into a rink in the winter).
• You might want to finish the day with a movie at the independent movie theatre **Encore Upper Canada Place** (460 Brant St., north of Lakeshore, (905) 681-3456, see listing on www.cinemaclock.com).

NEARBY ATTRACTIONS
Royal Botanical (10-min.) .... p. 266
Bronte Creek P. P. (15-min.) ...... p. 287

The beach pavilion, with changing rooms, outdoor showers and arty wall adorned with a modern mosaic was very nice and was surrounded by tall grass and trees. Many families were already enjoying the water. The sun was hot and some trees were offering spots in the shade.

After some fries at the **Snack Shack**, we went for a dip. The water was quite shallow. The kids could run out over 20 metres without having water over the waist. A minus for serious swimmers, a major plus for kids who want to play tag.

If a lift bridge is something that could be a hit with your kids, don't for-

get to check the 380-foot-long **Burlington Canal Lift Bridge** at the western end of the beach. It will take you 20 minutes to walk from the beach pavilion to the canal or one minute to drive.

It lifts on demand for the large vessels and every hour and a half for leisure boats (approximately 4000 times in a year). Chances are you'll see it in action.

Beachway Park • Burlington (905) 825-6000 (ask for beach hotline) www.burlington.ca (click *Parks & Recreation*, then *Parks*)	E-2 S-W of Toronto 40-min.

 Schedule: Open year-round.
Admission: FREE.
Directions: From QEW, take exit #101/Brant Street southbound. Follow Brant. Turn west on Lakeshore Rd. You'll find free parking on the south side along the park.

WASAGA BEACH

"The world's longest freshwater beach"

All we see in the media is the portion of Wasaga Beach which resembles an American coastal city on March Break. This is only part of the reality. After all, Wasaga Beach is 14 kms long.

In some spots, the hot and soft sand is cooled by the shade from tall trees and it feels like paradise. Some other spots count bathers by the dozens instead of the hundreds. You'll even find a perfect playground if you go to the right place on the beach!

What makes **Wasaga Beach** so popular is that pretty much everywhere along the strip of beach, a 6-year-old can walk 100 metres into the water and still maintain her head above the water. In addition, being shallow, the water never gets as cold as the pristine water of **Georgian Bay** everywhere else.

The downside is if you want to have a good swim, you'll need to go quite far from the beach to have enough water to move in. But then, there's the threat of sea-doos and motorboats. On the bright side, those noisy vehicles make fun waves!

There was a big fire in 2007 but it did not destroy the buildings along Beach Drive (which borders only the western side of **Beach Area 1**). This is the hot spot with cars parked everywhere, traffic on the road as well as on the sidewalk, restaurants, ice cream parlours, beach shops, pierced navels, loud music, and annual **Corvette Beach Cruize** in late August.

As a rule of thumb, the further you go east and west of this area the less noisy and crowded it will be. You want to go there for a glimpse of the action but it's much better to move on in order to find a better beach spot to spend the day.

The **Beach Area 1** access is at the foot of Spruce Street, to the right just after the bridge taking Main Street across **Nottawasaga River**. When I saw the beautiful white sand overflowing from the beach to the parking lot, it reminded me of beach towns. Quite a change from Toronto!

There's no road past the parking lot along that eastern part of **Beach Area 1** so it's much prettier than its western neighbour in front of Beach Drive. It is noisy from all the boats motoring around between the lake and the river but the shops are far away.

Away from the boardwalk, you will find tall birch throwing their most appreciated shade. Come early if you want one of those for your family. There are no trees along Beach Drive.

Beach Area 2, accessible from 3rd Street, is quieter than the western part of **Beach Area 1**. Major development plans have been in the air for years for that section. Don't hold your breath.

Beach Area 3 is narrower on its eastern part. Trees are back but they are shorter. You see bushes near the entrance and more grass on the eastern part of that area. It is accessible from 22nd Street. You access **Beach Area 4** from 24th Street. From then on, the sand is not as soft, more packed.

Beach Area 5, which you access from 36th Street, might be your best bet with a young family. The children will split their time between the beach and its original playground amidst the trees (a wise way to cool down from the sun).

TIPS (fun for all ages)

• Even though the water is shallow, you need to keep a good eye on your younger children. When they fall, water does get over their heads! There is also the problem of an undertow that can take away inflatable toys (look for signs).

• Special events often take place at the **Beach Area 1**. We were there on **Labour Day** weekend and saw a dog show during the day and great fireworks on the Sunday evening. Activities vary from one year to the next. Check the *Events Calendar* under the *Visitor Menu* on their website.

• Note most shops are closed after Labour Day weekend.

• I never took the time to visit **Nancy Island Historic Site** (the small island in the middle of **Nottawasaga River**, which you can access from Mosley Street near 3rd St. North). I learned that this island was created by the deposit of silt and sand around the sunken hull of the Nancy during the War of 1812. They host a great battle re-enactment using the river (2011: July 22-24). Check the pictures on www.wasagundersiege1812.com!

• **Wasaga Waterworld**, the nearby water park, has been closed since 2008. There were promises of a large splash pad by the waterfront, which hasn't materialized. For the time being, it's just us and 14 kms of beach. (Not complaining!)

• If you are looking for a campground, it is a good idea to consider **Craigleith Provincial Park**, located 25 min. from Wasaga Beach (www.ontarioparks.com). It includes 165 campsites by a strip of slippery rocky shore on Georgian Bay. Your vehicle pass to that provincial park saves you the fee to access Wasaga Beach, also a provincial park. There's also the **Cedar Grove Park**, self-described as family camping with 1000 ft of sandy beach, (705-429-2134, 100 Cedar Grove Parkway).

Many large rocks were popping out from the water at **Beach Area 6**, accessible from 45th Street.

Overnight

Wasaga Beach is such a good getaway destination, it is worth staying overnight. (This said, the plain motel room we rented last minute was expensive and off the beach, like most of the area's accommodations. But I don't regret it.)

A good way to find an accommodation is through the website **www.wasagainfo.com**. Click on *Accommodations*, then use their search engine to look for a keyword (pool, kitchen, pets allowed, etc).

Unless you are choosing an accommodation located near the beach or offering rustic charm and some privacy, I strongly recommend at least selecting something with a pool. Note that hotels closer to the beach in the "hot" section in **Beach Area 1** risk being noisier at night.

Wasaga Beach Provincial Park	B-2 N-W of Toronto 1 3/4 hr
• Wasaga Beach (705) 429-2516 (park) 1-866-292-7242 (town) www.wasagebeachpark.com	

 Schedule: Open year-round (facilities available from mid-June to Thanksgiving).

Admission: Around $15/day per vehicle, good for all the parking lots (less after Labour Day).

Directions: Along Mosley Street in Wasaga Beach. From Hwy 400 North, take exit #98/Hwy 26/27 westbound, then follow Hwy 27 to Elmvale. Turn west on Hwy 92, it will lead you to Main Street and Mosley Street.

NEARBY ATTRACTIONS
Rounds Ranch (15-min.) .... p. 152
Scenic Caves (15-min.) .... p. 234

PROFESSOR'S LAKE

Spring-fed and urban

When I was told about this lake smack in the middle of a large suburban housing development, I envisioned... well, I just could not envision it! No wonder. The man-made lake is the first attempt of this kind in eastern Canada. It offers the best water in the region, a twisting water slide, a raft to jump from for the better swimmers and a large sandy beach. It is also surrounded by 750 housing units.

To access **Professor's Lake**, one has to go through a hallway in the recreation centre, which hides the lake from our view. When the beach revealed itself, I took in the panorama of the wide beach covered with pale sand, some 300 visitors (much less than I had expected for a great summer day) and the 65-acre mass of blue water. My kids ran like wild horses to

try the fun slide throwing happy children into the lake. My 5-year-old spent the next four hours on the slide while her 9-year-old brother kept jumping off the raft, more than 30 metres from shore (for confident swimmers).

Like many kids, mine could not care less about water attributes vital to me such as quality, temperature, colour or odour. Whatever water will do the job, as long as I allow them to swim in it. But I was really taken by the sensation of swimming in Professor's Lake, and so were the moms I introduced to this attraction. It felt... clean and refreshing!

There are many reasons for it. The former gravel pit is spring-fed. It offers a large shallow area but reaches 42 feet in its greatest depth. And unlike many lakes in the region, a storm drainage system was designed to bypass the lake so it is protected from water run-off from farms, houses and roads, following heavy rains.

Add lifeguards on the beach, at the raft and at both ends of the slide and you get a very relaxing outing for parents! Add plenty of canoes, kayaks paddle boats for rental at affordable prices to take advantage of the lake, and you get an outing suitable for all ages and genders.

TIPS (fun for all ages)

• The minimum height to use the slide is now 49 inches but it could change. Call for the last decision on that matter.
• A trail runs around the lake outside of the gated area.
• A snack bar sells hot dogs, snacks, popsicles and slush.
• A family movie would be a nice way to finish the day (the beach closes at 7 pm). There is **SilverCity Brampton** a 10-min. drive from the lake. (Take North Park Dr. west, turn north at Dixie Rd., west on Bovaird Dr., north on Great Lakes Drive and into **Trinity Common** to your left). See www.cinemaclock.com for listings.

NEARBY ATTRACTIONS
Chinguacousy Park (5-min.) .... p. 286

Professor's Lake
• Brampton
(905) 791-7751
www.brampton.ca

D-2
N-W
of Toronto
50-min.

Schedule: Open daily late June to Labour Day, 10 am to 7 pm.
Admission: Around $4/adults, $3/others. **Rental costs:** Around $9/30 min. for paddle boat, $6/1 hr for canoe, $8/1 hr for kayak.
Directions: From Hwy 401, take Hwy 427 northbound to the end, turn west on Hwy 7, then north on Torbram Road and west on North Park Drive.

CEDAR BEACH PARK

A private matter

The sign atop the stone gate with its gothic lettering, brings to mind the look of a summer camp from the 50's. The entrance's iron doors frame a blue square of water, and as we reach the top of steep stairs, the wide private beach reveals itself, promising an afternoon of fun.

The sand works well for elaborate "engineering" projects of bridges and tunnels. The shores of **Musselman's Lake** are comfortably shallow for a distance, and the deeper water is well marked with buoys.

The two parks near the parking lot include fun playgrounds, making a picnic even more enjoyable for the kids.

TIPS (fun for all ages)

• There's a slight algae smell to the water, typically in the midst of summer, though it was quite clear and refreshing when we visited. The water quality is monitored. You might want to call and check if their beach is open before you go.

• Kayaks, canoes and paddle boats can be rented by the day users at the campground. (During the weekdays, you might have to drive to the office to get a key to unlock the boat's padlock.) Ask at the office. Rental is $10/hour.

• They offer a **fireworks** display on **Labour Day**. Call for the exact date.

• The trailer park includes 41 tent campsites. The use of the pools and spray pad is for overnight campers ONLY.

• There's a snack bar on site. Picnic tables are lined up along the iron railing and we enjoyed eating there watching swimmers down below.

NEARBY ATTRACTIONS
York Durham Railway (15-min.) ... p. 204
Burd's Family Fishing (10-min.) ... p.336

 Cedar Beach Park
• Stouffville
(905) 642-1700
www.cedarbeach.com

C-3
N-E
of Toronto
50-min.

Schedule: The beach is open early April to late October, 8 am to dusk, weather permitting.
Admission: around $10/adults, $5/children ($8/adults and $4/kids on weekdays), FREE for babies.
Directions: 15014 9th Line, Musselmans Lake/Stouffville. From Hwy 404 North, take exit #45/Aurora Rd. eastbound, turn south on 9th Line (Regional Rd. 69).

EMERALD LAKE

A little gem!

This natural setting is utterly unique in the region. This is your chance to swim in the pristine green water of a spring-fed lake. This is your kids' opportunity to jump off a diving board into a real lake for some good old-fashioned fun.

The lakeshore consists of natural rock plates descending into the water like some man-made stairs. The water doesn't have the usual muddy texture of the small lakes with sandy bottoms. This one sits on pale bedrock, hence the emerald shade. Being spring-fed, it is cold!

Emerald Lake is a trailer resort and water park doing its job to entertain customers with: a 200-foot water slide with small receiving pool (48"+), a large kids pool with deck and water sprays, many volleyball courts and paddle boat and kayak rentals. Nothing too fancy. But when I swam in the farthest part of the

pollution-free lake, enclosed by overhanging boughs of trees, it felt like Eden…

From the water, I had a great spot to observe the daredevils, my 8-year-old included, jumping off the board atop the small cliff.

Later on, we rented a paddle boat and explored another section of the small lake with weeds and… big snails! My kids enjoyed jumping from the paddle-boat and were glad to rest on it for a while.

Since my visit, they've added a water trampoline and other water toys. They've also added a large splash pad near the kids' pool.

The rock plates on the lake's shore don't offer a gradual entrance into the water and they are slippery. It was a stressful section for parents of toddlers. The new spray pad is solving this problem. Young kids will be more than happy to stick to the water games area.

TIPS (fun for 2 years +)

• Life jacket is mandatory for anyone using the water toys (despite what you see on their website's photos; it's a new rule). You can bring your own or rent it there.

• The trailer resort also includes family campsites for tents. Call them one month in advance to reserve if you want a space during a long weekend. Camping's not your thing? They now have 6 cabins for rent.

• There's a snack bar and they have BBQ pits throughout the park. Bring your own charcoal.

NEARBY ATTRACTIONS

Emerald Lake
• Puslinch
1-800-679-1853
(905) 659-7923
www.emeraldlake.ca

**E-2
West
of Toronto
60-min.**

Schedule: Water park is open daily from Victoria Day weekend to Labour Day, 10 am to 8 pm.

Admission: $12/4 years and older, $6/seniors, FREE 3 years and under, $5/life jacket rental.

Directions: 4248 Gore Road, R.R. #2, Puslinch. From Hwy 401, take exit to Hwy 6 south. Turn west at West Flamborough Concession 11, for approx. 5 kms. The lake is on your right hand side.

COBOURG BEACH

Charge!

As soon as my little mermaid sees the wide and long beach at Victoria Park, she darts off, sure of her way, to a day of water fun.

The shallow water is pleasantly refreshing, yet it warms up quickly in the middle of summer. Swimmers walk through the waves some 50 metres ahead of us, while my daughter embarks on a digging engineering project in the water. She soon joins new friends for a game of wave catching and burying in the sand!

TIPS (fun for all ages)

• You'll find a nice ice cream parlour at the corner of Division and Charles Streets by the park before the beach entrance.

• The **Cobourg Waterfront Festival** returns every year during 3-4 consecutive days including **Canada Day**. It involves **fireworks** on July 1. There's also the **Sandcastle Festival** to look forward to on the last weekend in July or first in August (2011: July 30-31, competition on Saturday only). Both take place by the beach.

• Adjacent **Breakers on the Lake** has its own private beach and they rent nice cottages. That would make a really cool getaway! (see www.breakersonthelake.ca).

The spray pad by the boardwalk is lovely and colourful.

A two-minute drive away, there's a skatepark. We like to grab a take-out dinner (the ice cream place on Charles usually sells fast food) and sit by this skatepark to watch the skaters in action at the end of the day. (Take Queen or King Street east until you reach D'Arcy Street, then go towards the lake.)

Cobourg Beach
• Cobourg
1-888-262-6874
or (905) 372-5481
www.cobourgtourism.ca

C-5
East
of Toronto
75-min.

Schedule: Open year-round.
Admission: FREE.

Directions: Victoria Park, Cobourg. From Hwy 401 East, take exit #472/Regional Hwy 2 southbound. Turn east on King St., then south on Division Street.

COUCHICHING BEACH PARK

Summer treat

Ice cream, a playground by the beach, with a swing just a few metres from the water, soft sand. What more could a child want?

TIPS (fun for all ages)

• More about the **Mariposa Market** in the tips section of **McRae Provincial Park** on p. 290.

• During a girlfriends outing to see a show at the **Casino Rama** (10 minutes from Couchiching Beach), I was surprised to discover a splendid building which incorporated the Native culture into the architecture in a way I would expect to see in British Columbia, not in Ontario! There's no need to go to the casino to enjoy it. It includes an indoor waterfall near the gorgeous casual dining **Weirs** restaurant, a great ceiling projection and a wonderful store with native art for every budget (www.casinorama.com).

How about a miniature engine blowing its whistle in the park to invite the visitors on a one-km- long track?

How about a dynamic festival going on? Go to their *Festivals & Events* section on their website for the full listing of festivals.

In the summer, among others you can expect a big celebration on **Canada Day**, complete with fireworks at dusk. But there's also a very tempting **Scottish Festival** with a parade, the **Rotary-Lions Funfest** with a midway and the **Waterfront Festival** (with a cardboard boat race!).

The **Trans-Canada Trail** now includes a 9.5-km trail running through the City of Orillia. I've seen part of it east of Orillia and it was the perfect trail for a family bike outing.

Couchiching Beach Park
• Orillia
(705) 326-4424
www.orillia.com

A-3
North of Toronto
75-min

Schedule: Open year-round. The train runs weekends from Victoria Day to Canada Day, then daily until Labour Day, 11:30 am to 5:30 pm.
Admission: FREE park access. Train ride is around $3/person.
Directions: Take Hwy 11, exit eastbound on Coldwater Road. Turn right on Front Street, left on Mississauga Street, to the Port of Orillia and the beach.

NEARBY ATTRACTIONS

AGINCOURT LEISURE POOL

the fun, ship-wreck-shaped waterslide. Since my last visit, the coconut trees seen in the pictures have been replaced by palm trees, but they're still spraying water over our heads.

Behind the wading pool is the small, inter-mediate pool, perfect for introducing children to swimming.

Under the palm trees

We often crave turquoise water and palm trees. The Agincourt Recreation Centre pool offers an innovative alternative. It includes aqua-coloured water, water slides, an adjoining hot tub, a waterside restaurant and... spraying trees as a bonus!

As soon as we went in, the aquatic complex's originality, revealed by wide bay windows, caught my little one's admiring eye and made him walk towards the admission counter, wriggling with impatience.

It wasn't long before my son and other little pirates launched an attack on

Further to the right, swimmers 48 inches and over are going down the gigantic, spiral-shaped waterslide into a small pool lined with tall palm trees. They are greeted with a loud SPLASH!

To the left, adults can soak in the warm water of the Jacuzzi, reserved for bathers aged 13 years and up. Nearby, there's a sauna.

Tables are especially set up for swimmers in their bathing suits, over-looking palm trees and the pool area. They can order off the counter from the adjacent **Country Style** concession! When we visited, the illusion of being down South would have been perfect if observers hadn't been standing on the other side of the bay window, wearing their winter coats!

TIPS (fun for 2 years +)

• Bring your own lock if you wish to use the changing room lockers.
• The slide is open during the programs: **Leisure Swim**, **Family Swim**.
• The Parent and Tot program is reserved for adults accompanying children 6 years and under. It is usually less crowded.
• The **Country Style** is usually open on weekends, and some evenings.
• **Birchmount Pool** is similar with huge slide and tables by the pool. It is located at 93 Birchmount Road, call (416) 396-4311 or check website for details.

NEARBY ATTRACTIONS
Woodie Wood Chucks (15-min.)   p. 312
Chuck E. Cheese (20-min.) .... p. 316

Agincourt Leisure Pool
• Scarborough
(416) 396-4037 (centre)
www.toronto.ca/parks

D-3
N-E
of downtown
35-min.

   Schedule: Hours vary with the seaons (extended hours during Christmas and March Break). Call or check their website for details (go to *Swimming & Pools*, then *Indoor Pools*. Click on the name of the pool, then *Drop-In*, then *Swimming*). **Admission:** $2/adults, $1/ seniors, students and children, FREE under 19 months, $3/adults for lane swim.

Directions: 31 Glen Watford Drive, Scarborough. From Hwy 401 East, take exit #379/ Kennedy Road northbound (Glen Watford is north of Sheppard Avenue and east of Midland Avenue).

Douglas Snow Centre

Me Tarzan, me sad

It was the only pool in Toronto with a Tarzan rope and now it's gone! But there are still two great slides.

With or without the Tarzan rope, this is a beautiful pool! The huge pool offers a wide section with beach-like access, perfect for younger kids, and a profusion of water toys at your disposal in a separate room (you just need to ask the staff). They even have duck decoys!

Bigger kids will spend their time at the long, bumpy white slide and the huge flume slide with a few loops. Both land in the shallow section. Only those who pass a deep-end test will be allowed to use the flume slide. The slide is available during Leisure Swim.

The Tarzan rope fans will want to know that there is one at **Terry Fox Wave Pool** in **Mississauga Valley Community Centre** (1275 Mississauga Valley Blvd., 905-615-4670, www.mississauga.ca, $2.60/person, $7/family).

Douglas Snow **Aquatic Centre** • **North York** **(416) 395-7585** **www.toronto.ca/parks**	**D-3** **North** **of downtown** **40-min.**

Schedule: Hours vary over the seaons (extended hours during Christmas and March Break). Call or check their website for details (go to *Swimming & Pools*, then *Indoor Pools*. Click on the name of the pool, then *Drop-In*, then *Swimming*).

Admission: $2/adults, $1/seniors, students and children, $5/family, $3/ adults for lane swim.

Directions: 5100 Yonge Street, North York. Turn west on North York Blvd. The pool is at the corner of Beecroft Road.

River Grove Aquatics

Lighten up!

Nature is so nicely framed by the glass wall and the whole architecture of the pool that one would think they are swimming inside the McMichael Canadian Art Collection building!

Very high wooden ceiling, smooth arches and huge bay windows catch the daylight, beautifully filtered by the tall trees. Quite a setting for a community pool! Kids just love the triple loop red slide ending in shallow water and the blue one in the deeper end. Most of the pool is actually shallow. Balls, floats and life jackets are provided. A big whirlpool completes the experience. A large mezzanine on the second floor allows parents to watch their kids.

There are vending machines on site. The **Culham Trail** running along the **Credit River** is accessible from the back of the community centre (see p. 303).

River Grove **Community Centre** • **Mississauga** **(905) 615-4780 (pool)** **www.mississauga.ca**	**D-3** **N-W** **of Toronto** **35-min.**

Schedule: Hours vary with the seaons (extended hours during Christmas and March Break). Call or check their website for details (go to *Residents*, then *Recreation & Parks*. Click on *Swimming*, then *Drop-In*, then *Drop-in Schedules*).

Admission: $3.60/person, $9.34/family of 5.

Directions: 5800 River Grove Avenue, Mississauga. From the QEW, take exit #130/Mississauga North. Turn east on Main Street in Streetsville (it becomes Bristol Road). Turn north on River Grove.

THE WAVE POOL

Photo: Courtesy of The Wave Pool

Surf's up!

I had often heard of the Richmond Hill Wave Pool: a huge indoor pool with 4-foot-high waves. I was in no hurry to go there with my young son. Every time I thought of it, I imagined a heavy swell filled with excited kids who would menace my little tadpole.

How far I was from the truth! Not only is this aquatic complex very secure and exciting for little ones, it's as much fun for older kids.

The spacious **Wave Pool** aquatic complex forms a harmonious whole, bathed by natural light. Funny fish decorate the ceiling.

A few tables under umbrellas and lined with palm trees are aligned near the bay window. The centre supplies toys and life jackets.

With the irregular shape, the wave pool looks like a shallow bay you go into gradually, just like at the beach. Over a large 5,000 sq. ft. area, the water doesn't go higher than our knees. In this shallow section, the waves are calm, and have the perfect level of turbulence to entertain young children.

The big waves sweep across the rest of the pool in 15-min. sessions. The 160-foot-long water slide is reserved for users at least 48 inches high. What a surprise! Beside the wave pool is a superb whirlpool delighting young and old alike. It is 70 cms deep and it is kept at a temperature of 96 degrees F.

TIPS (fun for 2 years +)
• Services offered at the pool include a sauna, one changing room for families and lockers for 25¢ and $1.
• There's no snack bar. You can eat your own lunch upstairs in the gallery with tables and vending machines.
• There's another indoor wave pool in the **Mississauga Valley Community Centre** (1275 Mississauga Valley Blvd., 905-615-4670, www.mississauga.ca). It features 2-ft. waves during the Fun Wave swims in the 25-metre pool. Along with toys and basketball nets, they have a Tarzan rope!

NEARBY ATTRACTIONS
Putting Edge (5-min.) .... p. 36

The Wave Pool	**C-3**
• Richmond Hill	**North**
(905) 508-9283	**of Toronto**
www.wave.sites.toronto.	**40-min.**
com	

 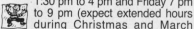

Schedule: Wave Swim sessions are offered year-round on weekends, 1:30 pm to 4 pm and 4:30 pm to 7 pm. From July to Labour Day, it is also open weekdays 1:30 pm to 4 pm and Friday 7 pm to 9 pm (expect extended hours during Christmas and March Break; and note it is sometimes closed for maintenance, better call to double check).

Admission: $8.50/16-54 years, $5.75/ seniors, $5.25/3-15 years, FREE for children 2 years and under (price for one period, you'll need to repay the admission fee if you're staying for the next session).

Directions: 5 Hopkins Street, Richmond Hill. From Yonge St., turn west on Major Mackenzie Drive, south on Arnold Crescent, then east on Hopkins Street.

SUNNYSIDE-GUS RYDER POOL

The playground in **Budapest Park**, just east of the pool features two dinosaurs! I've seen them change colour over the years but they're still standing. There's also a very large wading pool in the shade of tall trees, with the **Sunnyside Pavilion** by the lake in the background.

Cool size!

First, I noticed the tall Victorian arch of the white building while driving eastbound along Lakeshore Boulevard. Then, I saw the longest pool stretching right next to it. It turns out the arch marks the entrance of Toronto's biggest outdoor pool.

Big enough that kids in the large shallow end won't be in the way of those who want to do a serious lane swim workout. Everyone's happy.

Every time I've been to **Sunnyside-Gus Ryder Pool**, I've found the water too cold to my taste, but my kids don't mind. (I'm sure that after a good bike ride on the path running along the Lake Shore Boulevard, I'd be more than pleased with the water's temperature.)

During our last visit, on a windy day, we could see the colourful sails of the kite surfers over the pool's railing.

TIPS (fun for 4 years +)

• The parking lot closest to the pool is often full and then it's complicated to return. I recommend you park further west. (Read directions.)
• Bring quarters for the lockers. They don't provide change.
• There's a snack bar west of the building. For fancier food options offered in nearby **Sunnyside Pavilion Café** by **Sunnyside Beach**, see p. 403.

NEARBY ATTRACTIONS

Sunnyside-Gus Ryder Outdoor Pool

D-3
West
of downtown
35-min.

Dial 311 (new service)
www.toronto.ca/parks

Schedule: Usually open end of June to Labour Day (call closer to summer for hours).

Admission: I was told it's free but call closer to summer to confirm.

Directions: 1755 Lake Shore Blvd., Toronto. From Lake Shore westbound, turn left at Lake Shore East and drive straight ahead into the parking lot. If driving eastbound, enter into the parking lot just east of Ellis Avenue.

PETTICOAT CREEK C.A.

Not a petty pool!

The Petticoat Creek wading pool is huge and nicely surrounded by green lawn and small trees! It took me over 350 full steps to circumnavigate the edge of this blue wading pool.

We found ourselves a spot in the shade of a coniferous tree and we watched our kids run wildly into the shallow water. Some lines drawn at the bottom of the pool marked the vast shallow area. There was enough water to allow bigger kids to swim in the centre of the pool (where I had water below the shoulders).

ATTENTION! The pool was under construction at the time of print and they did not know exactly when they would open for the summer 2011. Call ahead!

The new pool will occupy the same space as the old one, with the most welcome addition of a large splash pad with interactive water features!

Petticoat Creek is located on a cliff by the shores of Lake Ontario. Outside the fenced pool area are picnic tables and a trail running along the bluffs. The view from above is great, however, the shoreline is unappealing, which explains why there's no stairs leading to it.

TIPS (fun for 2 years +)
• The old pool's water wasn't heated. Good news, the new one will use sustainable technologies to heat the water. (The water temperature is always warmer in the afternoon thanks to the sun's action.)
• Last time I checked, there were no railings at the edge of the cliff facing Lake Ontario along the **Waterfront Trail**.
• There are changing rooms and a snack bar on the premises.
• There are similar football field sized pools in **Bronte Creek** (p. 287) and **Earl Rowe** (p. 291) **Provincial Parks**.

NEARBY ATTRACTIONS
Toronto Zoo (5-min.) .... p. 61
Rouge Beach (5-min.) .... p. 396

Petticoat Creek Conservation Area
· Pickering
(905) 509-1534
www.trca.on.ca
(click attraction in *Places to Visit*)

C-4
East
of Toronto
35-min.

Schedule: Park is open from mid-May to Labour Day, 9 am to dusk. Pool opens early June to Labour Day, 10 am to 7 pm.
Admission: $6.50/adults, $5.50/ seniors, FREE 15 years and under with family (pool admission is an extra $4.75/2 years and over).
Directions: From Hwy 401 East, take exit #394 (Whites Rd.) southbound. From Hwy 401 West, take exit #397 south, follow Bayly St. west, turn south on Whites Road.

CANADA'S SUGAR BEACH

Sweet!

First came the yellow umbrellas of HtO Park west of Harbourfront Centre. Now, there's Sugar Beach with its pink umbrellas and beach chairs. Granted, you can't swim at this urban beach but it's got white sand; it's by the water and there's a spray pad! So take off those sandals and run that soft sand through your toes.

I've always liked to take the kids for a snack (and a coffee for their mom) by

TIPS (fun for 2 years +)

• **Loblaws'** customers can stay up to two hours in the free parking lot. I suggest you park there, go inside to buy some drinks and snacks for the kids (keeping your receipt to show your good faith), and don't go beyond the two-hour limit. There are security guards enforcing the time limit by marking down the plate numbers.

• You'll find parking lots within a 10-min. walk east and west of Sugar Beach.

• **Sherbourne Common**, just east of **Corus Entertainment**, opened in February 2011 with a nice rink (see p. 353) which will turn into a vast wading pool in the summer. The park spreads north and south of Queens Quay. It will feature some play structures but more importantly, it boasts an ultraviolet facility for the treatment of the storm water which will be filtered and released into an esthetic water channel leading to the lake, thanks to three tall artistic structures.

the windows on the second floor of the **Loblaws** by Queens Quay East. It's a vantage point to admire the turquoise mural of whales on the triangular facade of the Redpath's warehouse across the street and shimmering **Lake Ontario** in the background. Now we also get to admire the cute sandy patch adorned with 36 pink umbrellas by the new **Corus Entertainment** building.

The promenade which runs along the water in front of the large building is paved with cobblestones baring a maple leaf pattern and lined with trees and designer benches.

Don't get too excited about the three grass mounds that are so much fun to climb on. There's a sign warning us that they're temporary.

Make sure you get a good look inside Corus' building through their waterfront bay windows. Check the 4-storey-high flume slide (for their employees only) and the school of fish suspended from their ceiling. Very Pixar-ish, isn't it?

Canada's Sugar Beach www.waterfronttoronto.ca	D-3 Downtown Toronto 5-min.

 Schedule: Park open year-round. Sprays are usually active from end of May to late September, weather permitting.

Admission: FREE.

Directions: At the foot of Lower Jarvis Street, Toronto (south of Lake Shore Blvd.). The park is on the south side of Queen's Quay Blvd., just east of the **Corus** building.

CANOE LANDING

Big bobbers, beaver and boat

They think big around Bremner Boulevard! On the east side of Spadina Avenue are the Rogers Centre, with sculptures of giant people in their balconies, and the CN Tower. The park itself, west of Spadina, is surrounded by modern high-rise condos. It sits next to the 8-lane Gardiner Expressway. In it await huge bobbers and a giant canoe overlooking the highway.

The red canoe is large enough for drivers to notice from the Gardiner. I tried many times to get to it but just couldn't figure out how, but I finally got to the bottom of this problem. A new stretch of Fort York Blvd. (the western continuation of Bremner) is being built.

Canoe Landing Park was still towered by construction cranes at the time of print, and the road was not even finished but the park was already open to the public. I came for the canoe. I fell in awe of the colourful fishing bobbers standing in front of me by the entrance.

They were so whimsical, especially with all the serious buildings and CN Tower in the background. Next to them, there was a curious structure in white. It turns out this is a representation of a beaver dam from the same artist who did the bobbers and the canoe, artist-author Douglas Copland (the guy who coined the Generation X).

I was heading towards the red canoe when I heard the sound of running water. Looking back, I saw a dozen sprays of water shooting out of the ground between the fishing floats. The whole thing turns into a spray pad! (You've got to push a round button inlaid in the concrete floor near the installation.)

The little dog for whom a woman had activated the mechanism was ecstatic. It's not hard to imagine what a success this will be with kids. The vast park also includes the **Terry Fox Miracle Mile**, a running circuit they encourage you to do twice to complete a mile. It is marked by art pieces (also by Coupland).

TIPS (fun for 2 years +)
• There's a **Sobeys Urban Fresh** with indoor parking lot east of the park on Fort York. I recommend you take advantage of the $3 off their parking fee when you make a minimum purchase of $10 (maybe snacks and drinks for the kids). Leave half the parking ticket in your car and take the other half to be stamped at the store.

NEARBY ATTRACTIONS

Canoe Landing Park	D-3
Dial 311 (new service)	**Downtown**
www.toronto.ca/parks	**Toronto**
	10-min.

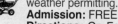

Schedule: Open year-round. Sprays are usually active from end of May to late September, weather permitting.
Admission: FREE.
Directions: On Fort York Blvd., Toronto. Turn west on Spadina Avenue (one block north of Lake Shore Blvd.). The park is just past Brunel Court.

SHOPS AT DON MILLS

Shopping spray

The Shops at Don Mills features a lovely plaza with the best pond-like fountain. Kids won't be able to resist its call. Bring a change of clothes, they might get wet. You never know when or where those sprays will pop out from the ground.

The spray choreography is fun to watch. Sprays can spurt from twenty different points. Then there's the larger fountain spurting even higher and unexpectedly. The beach-like access is an invitation for kids to step on the cobblestones and skip from one little raised bump to the next between two spraying sessions.

The whole complex has the feeling of a small fancy village with plenty of shops and restaurants. It includes a parkette with a vast **Skating Oval** in the winter and many special events throughout the year (see their *Events Calendar*).

Shops at Don Mills	**D-3**
• North York	**North**
(416) 447-0618	**of downtown**
www.shopsatdonmills.ca	**20-min.**

Schedule: The shops are open Monday to Friday, 10 am to 9 pm; Saturday, 9:30 am to 6 pm; Sunday, 11 am to 6 pm. The fountain runs from late spring to early fall.
Admission: FREE.
Directions: 1090 Don Mills Road, Toronto (2 kms north of the **Science Centre**), just south of Lawrence Avenue East.

HENDON PARK

Under the palm trees

After all these years, the palm trees are still standing. Hendon Park remains one of the cutest spray pads in town.

They've changed the park's playground since my last visit and I think it is not as spectacular visually, but it offers many challenges young ones will like. There are washrooms, picnic tables all around the splash pad, and a covered

section with benches (if the sun gets too hot). Many condos have been erected in the last few years, making it a nicer walk from **Finch Station** to the park than I remembered.

Hendon Park	**D-3**
• North York	**North**
Dial 311 (new service)	**of downtown**
www.toronto.ca/parks	**30-min.**

Schedule: Park open year-round. Sprays are usually active from end of May to late September, weather permitting.
Admission: FREE.
Directions: On Hendon Avenue, North York (one street north of Finch, west of Yonge). The park is four blocks down to your right, less than a 10-min walk from **Finch Subway Station**.

KIDSTOWN WATER PLAYGROUND

A real bargain!

When you accompany young children, you can't expect a better free activity than Kidstown Water Playground in Scarborough.

It used to be $1 per child but now it is free.

With water spurting whales, a water slide that ends in a wading pool, a large pirate boat armed with water pistols and corridor of spraying rings to navigate, this water park will thrill children 8 years old and younger. The older ones will be excited too, if they don't have high expectations from previous visits to larger commercial water parks. They'll love the large tipping bucket periodically spilling water on happy kids' heads.

The overall site covers approximately 2000 sq. feet and is surrounded by a grassy area with benches and picnic tables.

Beyond the fence, there is a colourful playground and a lovely grassy hill down which my little stuntman and his new pals happily rolled.

Kidstown is adjacent to L'Amoreaux Park and operated by the City of Toronto (see p. 285).

TIPS (fun for 8 years & under)

• There are change rooms and the park is entirely framed by a fence. However, the entrance gate is always opened by incoming and outgoing visitors. It is therefore safer to keep a watchful eye on children.
• There is a food vendor on the site.

NEARBY ATTRACTIONS

A 15-minute walk across McNicoll Avenue will bring you to the large pond of L'Amoreaux Park where I have frequently seen cranes. Nearby, a small forest and many trails prove nice for family exploration (see p. 285).

Kidstown Water Playground • Scarborough (416) 396-8325 (seasonal)	D-3 N-E of downtown 35-min.

Schedule: Open daily, usually from end of June to Labour Day, 10:30 am to 7:30 pm, weather permitting.
Admission: FREE.
Directions: 3159 Birchmount Road, Scarborough. From Hwy 401 East, take exit # 379/Kennedy Road northbound. Turn west on Finch Avenue and north on Birchmount Road.

CORONATION PARK

Water fun by the lake

The water sprays spurting out of the ground and out of posts planted in the pavement, wet the children. Facing them, there's a pebble beach with Lake Ontario in the background, as far as the eye can see. No wonder a wise Mom had recommended this Oakville park to me!

Note that since my last visit (when these pictures were taken) the park was completely renovated. They still offer the same kind of activities, in a different layout. The ambitious splash pad follows a castle theme with a giant crown dropping a curtain of water on the kids.

I was seduced by the site's features. The spray pad was surrounded by a lawn and beautiful, tall trees with peculiar knots. The children spent as much time refreshing themselves under the water sprays as they did inventing games with the thousands of plump pebbles in the shade of wide trees.

A paved trail leads to the pebble beach. The large toy truck we brought along worked well. A stone skipping contest kept us busy (I won. Mine skipped five times!).

A very dynamic (dry) playground is located on the premises. It includes two stimulating structures, one of them wooden with a hanging bridge and a tunnel-shaped slide, and three small climbing walls, perfect for small kids.

Photo: Courtesy of City of Oakville

TIPS (fun for 2 years +)
• A funny tradition in Coronation Park is the annual **New Year's Day Polar Bear Dip** involving over hundreds of dippers and some 5,000 spectators to raise money for World Vision. Always on January first. Fun starts at 12:30 pm, dip is at 2 pm. For details, see www.polarbeardip.ca.
• Read about nearby **Firehall** restaurant under **Riverview Park** on p. 354.

NEARBY ATTRACTIONS
Rattray Marsh (5-min.) .... p. 274
Shell Skate Park (5-min.) .... p. 351

Coronation Park
· Oakville
(905) 845-6601
www.oakville.ca

D-2
West
of Toronto
35-min.

Schedule: Open year-round.
Admission: FREE.
Directions: From QEW West, take exit #116/Dorval Dr. southbound, turn west on Lakeshore Rd.

ONTARIO PLACE

Photo: Courtesy of Ontario Place

waterslides (48" min. or 42"+ accompanied), plunging them into the darkness with their enclosed flumes.

There is also the 50 km/h ride down a gigantic funnel in **Hydrofuge** (48"+), ending with a 12-foot drop into the water. I passed on that one!

Biggest spray pad!

It used to be impossible for an adult to stay dry while accompanying a child to the water play area of Ontario Place. Grown-ups were the kids favourite targets to aim at with the fortress' water guns. These are gone, but you still can get really soaked... voluntarily.

Ontario Place has opted for a "zero depth" **Water Play Area**. They've dried up the small basins but have added lots of spray. The water play section involves 100,000 litres of active water with geysers and spouts shooting water. They've also added one of those tipping buckets dumping a massive amount of water on anticipating visitors.

The site is well adapted for young children due to its shallow depth.

It's also very entertaining for big kids, thanks to the other activities in **Soak City**. Older kids will go for more intense water games such as the **Rush River**, the raft ride which spans 873 feet (48" min. or 40"+ accompanied), or the **Pink Twister** (48"+) and the **Purple Pipeline**

TIPS (fun for 2 years +)
• The zero depth waterplay area is included with the ground admission. You need a pass (or ticket) to ride the slides.
• You can rent a locker for a loonie in the water park.
• Eating is forbidden in the waterplay area. Those exiting the area can get their hand stamped and return after eating. The snack bar by the lake offers a few tables with a view under the shade of umbrellas.
• More on **Ontario Place** on page 16.

Ontario Place's Soak City
(416) 314-9900
www.ontarioplace.com

D-3 Downtown Toronto 10-min.

Consult **Ontario Place** information box on p. 17 for schedule, costs, directions and nearby attractions.

WILD WATER KINGDOM

Wild indeed!

Waist-deep in the salt water pool, hordes of swimmers dance away with the encouragement of the weekend DJ and his music. My 6-year-old couldn't resist the invitation and jumps in (chest-deep), dancing the Macarena with his friends. There's no lack of ambiance at the Carribean Cove Pool.

Wild Water Kingdom is nearly half the price of Canada's Wonderland. If you plan to play in the water all day, this is certainly your best bet, especially with children 48" and over!

Sixteen body and tube slides, including two 7-storey speed slides along with a wave pool, a lazy river and the entertaining pool, are enough to satisfy the legions of teenagers invading the site daily.

All slides have a 48" minimum height requirement, except the **Cork Screw**, **Side Winder** and **Little Twister**,

which are accessible to children from 42" in height.

Younger children will thoroughly enjoy the large **Dolphin Bay** water playground. It offers beach-like access, small water slides passing through a mushroom, a fish and a frog, a splashing structure with sprays and a tube slide plus wading spots link it all. Then there's the **Big Tipper** with two large buckets emptying tons of water over the willing visitors. A playground is located right next to it.

By the water park are two mini golf courses, bumper boats and batting cages.

There's also a rock climbing wall under a waterfall in that section and I was told it is included in the admission price!

They opened the **WWK Drive-in** theatre in 2010.

TIPS (fun for 2 years +)
• No coolers are allowed on the site (exception is made for parents with babies). We had to take our cooler back to our car. You will find on-site lockers, many food stands, snack bars and a shop.
• Managed by Toronto Region Conservation Authority, **Indian Line Campground** offers 240 sites and is located along the **Claireville Reservoir**, right next to the water park. Call 1-800-304-9728 or check www.trca.on.ca.

NEARBY ATTRACTIONS
Swaminarayan Mandir (5-min.) .... p. 133
Pearson Airport (10-min.) .... p. 190

Wild Water Kingdom
• Brampton
(416) 369-9453
www.wildwaterkingdom.com

D-2
N-W
of Toronto
40-min.

Schedule: Open on weekends from early June, 10 am to 6 pm; then daily from end of June to Labour Day, 10 am to 7 pm (closes at 6 pm from late August).

Admission: (tax not included) Around $30/10 years and over, $23/4-9 years, FREE 3 years and under, $18/after 3 pm. **Drive-in:** Admission + movie combo is $35/adults, $25.50/4-9 years and seniors. Parking is $10.

Directions: 7855 Finch Avenue, Brampton. Take Hwy 427 North, turn west on Finch Avenue, follow the signs.

CANADA'S WONDERLAND

Splash!

It was not with a light heart that I watched my assertive little boy drag his huge tire for the first time, way up to the launching board of the Whirl Winds. He was so thrilled with his ride that he could not wait to get back in line to do it again! If your child is tall enough and already shows some daredevil inclinations at the local pool, you might want to let her try it too.

Some of **Splash Works**' water slides are 8 storeys tall! The **Riptide Racer**, for little kamikazes 40" and taller, allows them to race against others down the 8-lane splashway, head first and on their bellies.

Barracuda Blaster, **Body Blast** and **Black Hole** rides require 48" and taller but equally fun **Whirl Winds**, **Super Soaker** and **The Plunge** accept adventurers measuring 40-48" if they're wearing a life jacket.

The **Barracuda Blaster** ends up with a twist around the vertical walls of a giant

bowl before being flushed into the **Lazy River** (on which an adult and child can float on the same tube).

All the kids like the **Pump House**. It features a large coloured structure full of surprising water sprays, topped by a gigantic pail that gradually fills with 1,000 litres of water. Every five minutes, the pail's contents flow forcefully on the heads of delighted kids.

The large wave pool is equipped with lounge chairs.

For the little ones, there's **Splash Island**, an entertaining wading pool with sprays and mini water slides.

TIPS (fun for 2 years +)

• Kids under 48" tall must now wear a life jacket while swimming in the wave pool **Whitewater Bay**, the **Splash Island Pool Area** and the **Lazy River**. Children's life jackets are available for free. Lockers, beach shop and snack bar are found within the water park as well.

• More on **Canada's Wonderland** on page 18.

Canada's Wonderland	**C-3**
• Vaughan	**North**
(905) 832-8131	**of Toronto**
www.canadaswonderland.com	**40-min.**

Consult **Canada's Wonderland** information box on p. 19 for schedule, costs, directions and nearby attractions. **Splash Works** is open on weekends in June, 11 am to 6 pm; then daily until Labour Day, 11 am to 7 pm.

WILD WATERWORKS

Works for me!

You can observe children in almost all directions from the ground by the wave pool which sits in the heart of the action.

From the bounty of water activities offered and the new huge slides accessible to children of all ages, to the immense wave pool, you will find **Wild Waterworks** leaves nothing to be desired.

The **Eazy River** (a sinuous water path on which you can flow down atop an inner tube), is the only one I know of that comes equipped with side showers, fountains and nooks and crannies. My son and his father chose a double ring to float on and bump me!

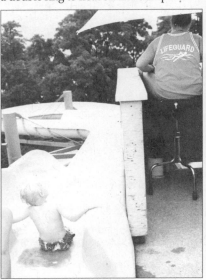

Little Squirt Works, the large wading pool for young bathers is quite fun with its unusual shape framed by stairs. The water doesn't go higher than the knees. It is full of small fountains that squirt intermittently and little roofs streaming with water.

The **Corkscrew** and **Kamikaze** body slides are some six storeys high, much to the delight of swimmers (42" and taller). I tried them both and found them surprisingly smooth, a little like a gentle toboggan ride. The giant tube slides **Night Rider** and **Blue Demon** offer a 480-foot-long drop, solo or with a friend (minimum 47" or successful swim test).

Since my last visit, they've added two more tube slides **Vertigo** and **Slide Winder** (minimum 42").

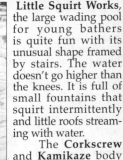

Photo: Courtesy of Baranga's on the Beach

Confederation Park

Just north of the water park after the road bend is **Adventure Village** (589 Van Wagners Beach Rd., www.adventure-village. com). We're always too tired after a day at the water park to visit. They have crammed as many activities as can be in this attraction: climbing wall, outdoor laser tag, bumper cars, gemstone mining, mini golf, arcade, batting cages and a Bungee trampoline on which you can jump four storeys high.

Instead of grabbing a bite at the water park's snack bar at the end of the day, we prefer to go to **Hutch's**, further north (280 Van Wagner's Beach Rd., www. hutchsonthebeach.com).

Hutch's is a true-to-form greasy-spoon. I love the 50's feeling, love the booths by the large bay windows overlooking the lake, and love the fries.

You order, wait a lot while you play music from the jukebox or watch the seagulls teasing people on the beach. Then your number gets called and you retrieve your steamy food. Yummy and affordable! There's also a dairy bar.

Once, we went for the fancier option and had dinner at **Baranga's on the Beach** south of Hutch's (380 Van Wagner's Beach Rd., www.barangas.ca).

Baranga's has got to be the best waterfront patio by **Lake Ontario**. They offer a wide choice on their menu, not the cheapest but with many affordable options and they have a kids' menu. Expect fancy Greek food, salad combinations, pasta, finger food, copious brunches and more.

When we arrived at the restaurant after a day of water fun, exotic music was playing, candles were already lighting the vast patio and the lake in the background was coloured in blue and yellow hues from the sunset. The overall impression was that of a restaurant by the ocean.

Finally, north of Hutch's is outdoor **Lakeland Go-Kart**.

TIPS (fun for 2 years +)
• Take advantage of the reduced admission fee after 4 pm. We visited on a warm but cloudy Saturday afternoon and found the place enjoyably quiet. We never waited more than 5 minutes for a ride on the slides. Plus there was no traffic when we left Toronto in the middle of the afternoon!
• Order online to save on regular price.
• If with younger kids who want to try the slides, go down first so you can assist them when they reach the bottom.
• There are snack bars on site.
• Note that the campground in **Confederation Park** has closed permanently.
• There's an 8-km waterfront bike path running from the Confederation Park to the **Burlington Lift Bridge**, passing in front of **Baranga's** and **Hutch's**.

Wild Waterworks

Wild Waterworks	E-2
• Hamilton	S-W
1-800-555-8775, ext. 5007	of Toronto
or (905) 547-6141	50-min.
www.conservationhamilton.ca	

 Schedule: Open weekends from early June and daily from mid-June to Labour Day. (Variable hours in June). From July to mid-August, 10 am to 8 pm. Mid-August to Labour Day, 10 am to 6 pm. All weather permitting.
Admission: $23.50/adults, $19.50/seniors, $15.40/4-10 years, FREE 3 years and under, around $12.50/visitor after 4 pm (or after 3 pm when park closes at 6 pm). $5 to rent tube for wave pool ($4 after 4 pm). Vehicle entrance to Confederation Park is $9.50.
Directions : From QEW West, take exit #88/Centennial Pkwy.-Hwy 20. Turn north towards the lake, follow signs to **Confederation Park**.

CEDAR PARK RESORT

Refreshing combo

Being the place with the biggest water games in the Bowmanville area, Cedar Park is a great complement to a visit to one of the local attractions, for a full-day outing in the region.

There are three giant water slides (48"+), a good playground on a large patch of sand, a water play area with dunking buckets, a huge pool and even a mini golf. The water park is attached to a trailer park and includes a snack bar.

NEARBY ATTRACTIONS
Bowmanville Zoo (15-min.) .... p. 65
Jungle Cat World (15-min.) .... p. 73

Cedar Park Resort
• Bowmanville
(905) 263-8109
www.cedarparkresort.ca

C-4
East
of Toronto
60-min.

Schedule: Park open daily mid-June to Labour Day from 10 am. Varying closing times in June. From July, closes at 8 pm Friday to Sunday, and at 7 pm Monday to Thursday. Pool closes an hour earlier.
Admission: (cash only) Ground admission and pool access is $9/adults, $8/3-12 years, FREE 2 and under. Mini golf is an extra $4.50, water slides are an extra $7 per visitor (min. height of 48").
Directions: 6296 Cedar Park Rd., Bowmanville. From Hwy 401 East, take exit #431/Regional Rd. 57 north. Turn east on 6th Concession, then north on Cedar Park.

WILD WATER & WHEELS

Curious?

Water is for the 210-foot-long double spiral flume (42" min.) and the bumper boat ride (48" min.). Wheels is for the go-kart circuit.

When we visited, there was also a merry-go-round, a giant carpet slide (145 feet long and 35 feet high with five huge bumps) which was equally fun for the whole family, batting cages and a mini

golf. The real surprise was the **Pipeline Express Coaster**! It is a metal toboggan rolling on tracks on a structure five storeys high and 850 feet long. The view from the top is amazing… and the drop at the beginning of the ride is breathtaking!

NEARBY ATTRACTIONS
Riverview Park & Zoo (10-min.) .... p. 69

Wild Water & Wheels
• Peterborough
(705) 876-9292 (seasonal)

B-5
N-E
of Toronto
2 hrs

Schedule: Open early April until last Sunday in September, 10 am to 9 pm from the end of June to Labour Day, and at least from 12 noon to 6 pm before and after that. Call to confirm.
Admission: Approximately $6 for each ride and $15 for the water slides.
Directions: 1650 Chemong Road, Peterborough. From Hwy 401 East, take exit #436 (Hwy 35/115) northbound. Follow Hwy 115 to Hwy 28 northbound. At Fowlers Corners, turn eastbound (right), then right again on Chemong.

FALLSVIEW WATERPARK

Action!

As soon as they smell a hint of chlorine, my four companions run wildly through the glassed skypass and instantly split into two age-related teams. It will take me 20 minutes to find them in order to put their wristbands on.

The place is quite a sight! Tropical climate, palm trees, blue dome simulating the sky and, down below, tons of kids screaming with delight.

This impressive water park includes 16 slides, some 6 storeys high, some fit for the younger crowd hanging around the **Beach**

House section with the 1,000 gallon tipping bucket.

After a few hours of action, the gang is ready for lunch at the **Planet Hollywood** snack bar by the pool. As we eat, the friends are retelling their best exploits. The yellow slide is unanimously declared the scariest. I wouldn't know. Didn't get near the thing!

Later in the day, we took our ice cream to the mezzanine to lay on the lounge chairs while taking in the overall view of the water park. We were also able to admire the falls from the large bay windows in the south-west corner. A must!

Fallsview Waterpark offers an outdoor heated all-season pool with basketball nets at varying heights. We stayed at the **Skyline Inn**, the one with the elevated walkway offering a more dramatic access to the waterpark. Its rooms all open into pretty indoor courtyards where kids can run free.

Crowne Plaza Niagara-Fallsview and **Sheraton on the Falls**, two other hotels offering the package, are fancier and include indoor pools. Both have indoor access to the water park.

TIPS (fun for 2 years +)

• You may enter the water park anytime on the day your package begins, until 3 pm the day it ends. We checked out early, left our luggage in the car and stayed at the water park to the last minute.

• Gorgeous 100,000 sq. foot **Great Wolf Lodge** (www.greatwolf.com) offers 13 slides, 4 pools and a 4-storey-high tree-house fort. It is a bit more expensive but everyone I know who has been there loved it. The downside is that it is 4 km north of the Falls while the **Skyline Inn** where I stayed was right in the action.

• More about **Niagara Falls** on p. 253.

NEARBY ATTRACTIONS

Fallsview Waterpark • Niagara Falls **1-888-234-8408** www. fallsviewwaterpark.com	**E-4** **Niagara** **Region** **90-min.**

Schedule: Closed in January and a few Tuesdays and Wednesday from February to mid-June. Open the rest of the time from at least 10 am to 8 pm.

Admission: (one hotel night for a family of 4 and 4 water park passes) **Skyline Inn**: around $160 in low season and $250 in high season, $20 one extra kid. (Rates varie throughout the year.)

Directions: 5685 Falls Ave., Niagara Falls. The water park is between Victoria and Falls Avenues, east of Clifton Hill.

ELORA GORGE C.A.

For your inner child

For years I have noticed people floating down the river on inner tubes as I watched from the trail above at Elora Gorge. I always thought they were just random people, looking for adventure and braving the natural elements on their own. I was wrong... There is actually a whole crowd of them, seeking thrills, with the full consent of the conservation authority's administration.

Which explained the sign "Tubing Sold Out" at the gate when we got to **Elora Gorge** at 1 pm on a Saturday, planning to try out tubing ourselves. (As I found out later on, there was a way out of this disappointing situation. Read tips.)

First, let's say that tubing down this river is not as adventurous as it seems from above (in periods of dry weather). My 9-year-old thought the one-hour-long descent did not offer enough action as real whirlpools formed only in three spots (expect more action earlier in the season). Still, it beats floating down the lazy river in any water park.

Adults really enjoy the relaxing sight-seeing, offering a different view of the cliffs.

Children must be at least 42 inches tall and accompanied by a legal guardian who can sign a waiver in order to be allowed to ride. I have seen parents on their tube with a child on their lap (not recommended in fast flowing water).

The equipment consists of a helmet (hockey style), a vest and a tube. You can bring your own, but it can be rented at the beach house. Unfortunately, the activity is quite popular on hot summer weekends when tubes can be sold out by 9 am!

We waited over an hour before some tubes became available but it wasn't all that bad. My patient husband spent the time in the line-up, a good book in one hand and a sandwich in the other, while the rest of us swam in the small lake by the beach house.

water is cold but the current is slower at this point so it offers a great spot to swim for those who are just accompanying... Unless they want to rush back to the trail to take a picture when their friends' tubes pass under the bridge where the cliffs reach a height of 70 feet.

Once you have your equipment, you can catch the school bus serving as a shuttle from the beach house to the launching area. Instead, we chose to drive following the tubing signs along the park's road. We easily found a parking spot and the opening through the bush to the trail leading down the river (also indicated by a little sign). It was hilarious to follow the line of gigantic black tubes through the woods.

The section of **Grand River** where everyone gets in the water is simply gorgeous! High walls of rocks with splashes of greenery closely frame the river. The

TIPS (fun for 5 years +)

• BEWARE! During periods of high water flow, water tubing could be cancelled. Call for the "current" conditions.

• Some farms in the vicinity announce tubes for sale, knowing about the limited number of tubes for rent at the park. Tubes generally sell for $15, with $5 back if you return them. When we were visiting, the beach house allowed people to use their air pump to put air into their own tubes.

• The tubes are huge! Kids under 9 will hardly fit on top of them. We could only fit one in our trunk and I had to wear the other one around my waist inside our 4 X 4. Bring bungee cords to creatively tie them on to the roof.

• Wear shoes while tubing, to prevent your feet from scratching against the rocks. The segment of trail leading to the river is lined with slippery rocks. Flip-flops beware!

• Bring a waterproof camera (with a strap) for great pictures as you go down.

• This conservation area includes 550 campsites, some nicely secluded.

• There's a snack bar at the beach house.

NEARBY ATTRACTIONS

Elora Gorge Conservation Area

D-1 West of Toronto 65-min.

• Elora
(519) 846-9742
1-877-558-4722 (camp reservations)
www.grandriver.ca

Schedule: Park: open year-round from 8 am to dusk. **Registration shop**: open 9 am to 7 pm, weekends only in May, June and September and daily from last week of June to Labour Day. Shuttle bus on weekends until 6 pm, in July and August only.

Admission: $5.25/adults, $2.75/6-14 years, FREE 5 years and under. Tubing wristband is $2.75. Full equipment rental is around $25 (or $15/tube, $10/helmet, $10/life jacket), plus deposit.

Directions: From Hwy 401 West, take exit #295/Hwy 6 northbound, then follow County Rd. 7 to Elora. Turn left at the first light on County Rd. 21. Elora Gorge is on the right.

ALPHABETICAL INDEX

LOCATION INDEX (TORONTO)

LOCATION INDEX (OTHER CITIES)

AROUND THE SUBWAY

Carless outings!

Find out what's interesting for kids, within a 10-minute walk of every Toronto subway station.

General tips about subway rides

- To estimate the duration of a ride, count two minutes per station.
- Not all the stations have elevators and the escalators are often one way only. Expect to carry your stroller and dare to ask for help! You'll be surprised.
- Not all entrances to one station are staffed. Bring the exact change if you're not sure what to expect.
- There could be 200 metres between two exits of one station. Read the exit signs carefully to exit the street closest to your destination.
- Streetcars and buses don't sell the **TTC** day pass. It is sold at the staffed stations. (See www.ttc.ca.)

Subway and Rapid Transit Route Map

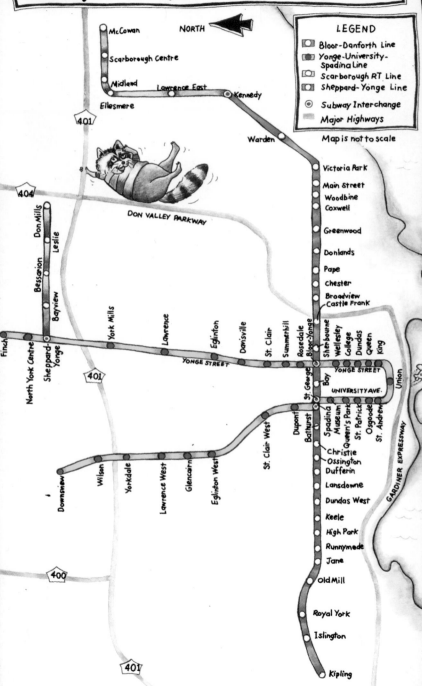

TOM RILEY PARK

White noise

Listen carefully, past the noise of the trains rolling on the tracks, past the cars whooshing by all around the urban setting... This sound you hear doesn't come from the subway's air vent. It's Mimico Creek!

You'll notice a lovely community garden by the southern entrance to the park off Bloor Street. Kids will enjoy watching the TTC trains flash by over the nearby viaduct. A sight we normally don't see up close!

Different dirt trails have been worn by previous visitors to reach the creek. Young explorers are bound to find one that suits their capabilities.

Walking northbound on the winding paved trail running through the long and wide park, you'll reach a playground nicely set by tall trees.

A bit further on the east side, you'll see a small bridge, the perfect spot to see the wild ducks. Adventurers who stroll along the dirt trail following the

creek upstream will discover funky graffiti under another viaduct. This path will lead you over a second bridge, to the northern entrance of the park. It will take you less than 15 minutes to walk back to the southern entrance.

TIPS (fun for 4 years +)

• There's a municipal parking lot on Bloor, by the southern entrance of the park. Beware, the parking lot by the northern entrance seems to require a permit.

• The paved path is less than 1 km long and winding, great for young cyclists.

NEARBY ATTRACTIONS
Islington Mural (15-min. walk) .... p. 109
Montgomery's Inn (10-min. walk) ... p. 376

Thomas Riley Park	D-3
• Etobicoke	**West**
Dial 311 (new service)	**of downtown**
www.toronto.ca/parks	**20-min.**

Schedule: Open year-round.
Admission: FREE.
Directions: 3216 Bloor Street West, Toronto. There are three accesses. From the north side of Bloor St. (east of Islington), from Aberfoyle Crescent (off Islington, just north of **Islington Subway Station**) or from Islington Ave. (north of Cordova Ave.).

GREEN LINE (BLOOR-DANFORTH)

KIPLING

Walk a few minutes up Aukland Rd. to reach Dundas West, then spot the cows (1) on top of **Medium Rare** butcher shop. The poor bovines are surrounded by burger shops!

Walk a few minutes westbound on Dundas to get to **Bowlerama** (2) (5429 Dundas, www.bowlerama.com). You'll find lots of fast food chains west of this. Across the street, visit **Wild Birds Unlimited** offering the biggest selection of bird feeders (5468 Dundas, www.wbu.com/toronto).

McCall's, which has to be biggest cake supply store in town, is less than 10-min. walk from Aukland (walk east on Dundas, past the **Starbucks**, to Kipling, go north to 3810 Bloor, www.mccalls-cakes.com).

ISLINGTON

The **Clarica Shopping Centre** at this station offers a fancy food court.

If you go west on Bloor West, past the intriguing underpass, and take the stairs up, you'll reach the outdoor playground and impressive gazebo of **Michael Power Place** (3) along Dundas West.

East of that playground on Dundas, you've got to see some of the amazing murals (4) (5) which are part of the **Village of Islington Murals** project (see p. 109). They cover many buildings within a 10-min. walk along Dundas. Wow!

When you exit the station, go north on Islington and east on Aberfoyle Ct. past the tennis courts and you'll reach a path leading to gorgeous **Thomas Riley Park** (see p. 451).

Walk north through the park for 15 minutes to its exit off Islington, near Dundas West. If you want to walk a few extra minutes east on Dundas, you'll reach **Montgomery Inn** (see p. 376).

On the 10-min. walk southbound back to the station, check out the white mermaid on a horse sculpture (6) on Cordova Avenue east of Islington.

ROYAL YORK

Go west on Bloor West and north on Brentwood Rd. to reach the fun ceramic studio **All Fired Up** (8 Brentwood, www.afu-ceramics.com, 416-233-5512). They have a fun selection of pieces interesting to kids. Nearby **Brentwood Public Library** (36 Brentwood) is under renovations until 2012.

West of the station is also the **Kingsway** indepedendant movie theatre (3030 Bloor, www.kingswaytheatre.com).

OLD MILL

Take Old Mill Trail north and turn east on Old Mill Rd. to reach **Old Mill Inn**, a fabulous place for a brunch buffet with the family, (www.oldmilltoronto.ca).

Across the bridge is the entrance to **Étienne Brûlé Park** with a paved trail along the **Humber River** (see p. 453).

JANE

Nothing special for kids.

RUNNYMEDE

Lots of fun stores for moms along this stretch of Bloor! For kids, there's **Groom Pet Shop** with small pets.

Runnymede Public Library (2178 Bloor) and **Melonhead** for kids' haircuts (2100 Bloor, 416-762-0800) are east of the station.

(1) Kipling

(2) Kipling

(3) Islington

(4) Islington

(5) Islington

(6) Islington

ÉTIENNE BRÛLÉ PARK

Dam if you don't

Six low dams, spread along its course between Old Mill Road and Dundas Street, control Humber River's flow, hence the lovely sound of cascades we hear as we walk.

The best way to appreciate the **Humber River** is to park by **Étienne Brûlé Park** right by the stream.

Two parallel trails follow the river, one for bicycles and one for pedestrians. They are bordered by tall trees and even cliffs towered by luxurious homes on both sides of the river at some points, creating a unique intimate scenery.

With kids, it will take 30 minutes to walk from the parking lot to the Dundas overpass (with a small playground in between). The trail actually exits on Lundy Lane where you turn west (left)

on Old Dundas Street. The trail then runs down along the river bank to continue north of the overpass.

Ten more minutes and you'll reach the **Dundas Pedestrian Bridge**, with the train track way over your head. Across Humber River, it becomes **Lambton Woods** (see p. 263).

Humber Marshes Park

Many choose to park near **Humber Marshes Park** as a starting point, for a longer bike ride. The initial scenery is not particularly interesting near the marshes but 5 minutes into your stroll, you reach some gorgeous spots overlooking the river.

From there, it will take some 15 minutes to walk to the Old Mill bridge. There's nothing as striking about the trail going through **Kings Mill Park** (across the street from Étienne Brûlé's parking lot) but kids will find it intriguing to walk under the bridge.

TIPS (fun for 4 years +)
• **Toronto Adventures** offers an **Intro to Kayaking or Canoeing & Humber River Guided Tour** that goes down and back up the river, ending at the starting location. ($50/person, equipment and life jackets included). Check www.torontoadventures.ca or call 416-536-2067 for details. Children under 8 must be with an adult.
• The **Old Mill Inn** (very popular for its fancy Sunday brunches and lunch buffets) is located near Étienne Brûlé Park (21 Old Mill Rd., www.oldmilltoronto.com).
• Just east of **Étienne Brûlé Park**'s parking lot, you can access Humber Blvd. on bike (it's a one-way, you won't be able to drive northbound on it). The lovely narrow road (closed in the winter) runs along the west shore of Humber River and is quite secluded. It reaches Dundas.

NEARBY ATTRACTIONS
Around Runnymede Station .... p. 452

Humber River	I-9
• Etobicoke	**West**
(416) 392-1111	**of downtown**
www.toronto.ca/parks	**25-min.**

Schedule: Open year-round.
Admission: FREE.

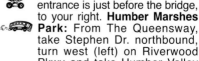

Directions: Étienne Brûlé Park: From Bloor St. West (east of Royal York Rd.) take Old Mill Rd. northbound. The parking lot's entrance is just after the bridge (10-min. walk from **Old Mill Subway Station**). **Kings Mill Park**'s entrance is just before the bridge, to your right. **Humber Marshes Park:** From The Queensway, take Stephen Dr. northbound, turn west (left) on Riverwood Pkwy and take Humber Valley Rd. to your right, then take the first right fork, into the parking lot.

HIGH PARK

Toronto's true nature

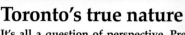

It's all a question of perspective. Previously, I associated High Park with romantic walks along Grenadier Pond and Shakespeare at the fascinating outdoor theatre. Now, when I think of High Park, I see animals and a castle, and I hear the little train's bell joyfully ringing through the park's 161 hectares...

There's a trackless little train operating on a nine-station circuit around the park from spring to autumn. You can get on the train at the station of your choice, get off where you want to, and stay as long as you wish before hopping back on. You have the privilege of getting back on at the same station or at the next one, to complete the circuit to your starting point.

The **High Park** train's flexibility

allows visitors to build an itinerary suited to their schedule, to take advantage of the various pleasures offered at the park. For us, it starts with the playground.

Jamie Bell Adventure Park is simply the most original playground in town (more about it on p. 326). It is located next to the big duck pond, the animal pens which house bison, goats, llamas and sheep, a snack bar as well

as one of the train's stops. When the children have played all they want, let the little train take you to **Grenadier Pond**, a few stations further (a 15-min. ride for young conductors).

After exploring this area of the park, you can hop back on the train to come back, ten minutes later, to your starting point. From there, you can visit Deer Pen Road's animals.

TIPS (fun for 2 years +)
• To get to the parking lot closest to the castle playground, take the entrance south of Bloor, on the west side of Parkside Dr. (High Park Blvd.). WARNING! This entrance is closed on Sundays and Holidays from May 1 to October 1.
• High Park includes bike trails, an dog off-leash area (near the restaurant), snack bars (near the big playground and by the Bloor entrance), a large outdoor pool as well as a wading pool, closer to the Bloor Street entrance, near **High Park Station**. Check their website for a map.
• There's also **Grenadier Restaurant** with dining room and take-out counter.
• More about Shakespeare's **Dream in High Park** on p. 117 (in the Tips section).
• More about **Colborne Lodge** and **Easter** activities at High Park on p. 373.
• For a different way to explore the park, see p. 455 under **High Park Station**.

NEARBY ATTRACTIONS
Sunnyside Pavilion Café .... p. 403

High Park
Dial 311 (new service)
www.highparktoronto.com

D-3
West of downtown
15-min.

 Schedule: Open year-round. **Train:** operates daily from May 1 to Labour Day, from 10:30 am to dusk (weekends only in April and after Labour Day until October 31, weather permitting.

 Admission: FREE. **Train:** (sold by train operator, cash only): $4/16 years and older, $3/ seniors and children under 16.

Directions: The main entrance is on the south side of Bloor St. West (west of Parkside Dr.) Toronto. It is a 5-min. walk from both **Keele** and **High Park Subway Stations**. Read tips!

HIGH PARK

A few minutes east on Bloor is the main entrance to **High Park** (see p. 454). For a more off the beaten track adventure to access the park, go west instead. Grab coffee and snacks at the cool **Café Novo** (7), at the corner of Parkview Gardens, and cross to the south side of Bloor to access the staircase before Ellis Park Road (8). You'll reach **Wendigo Pond** with a small playground, in a lovely setting by a bridge (9) leading into High Park. If you take the path to the right across the bridge, you'll be able to walk along **Grenadier Pond** and reach **Colborne Lodge** in 30 minutes.

KEELE

This station is a brisk 15-minute walk from **High Park**'s amazing castle playground (off Parkdale, south of Bloor) but it is really worth it (see p. 326)! **Lithuania Park** offers a pretty playground and wading pool, north on Keele.

DUNDAS WEST

Check the giant yellow boxing gloves of the club on Dundas, just south of Bloor! With little adventurers, walk north on Dundas and try the pathway going over the train tracks (10) on the east side. A few minutes on the other side of the track, you'll reach **Yasi's** (11), the funky all-day breakfast place (299 Wallace, www.yasisplace.ca). A few minutes more, south on Lansdowne, is the art project described lower.

LANSDOWNE

Less than 5 minutes north of the station, you can admire the really cool **Lansdowne Fence Streetscape** project (12) (13) set around a large piece of property along Lansdowne.

(7) High Park

(8) High Park

(9) High Park

(10) Dundas West

(11) Dundas West

(12) Lansdowne

(13) Lansdowne

DUFFERIN GROVE PARK

Community spirit

I was surfing the website of Project for Public Spaces, a non-profit organization dedicated to promoting great community places. Guess what is listed in their *Great Public Spaces* section? Our own Dufferin Grove Park!

This park might have been a seedy one back in the 90's but those days are over! **The Friends of the Grove**, a neighbourhood association, turned it around.

First time we entered the park, families were busy fixing individual pizzas to cook in one of the two outdoor

wood ovens. Isn't it the most clever idea to bring a community together? Some people had brought their own toppings they offered to share with us.

Further, a large playground surrounded by a split-rail fence (much prettier than wire fence) was filled with a laughing crowd. Nearby, we discovered the best feature I have seen in a public park: a unique gigantic sandpit (more about it on p. 327).

You've got to admire the details on the funny house they built to offer sinks for the public (an artistic answer to the City's sanitary requirements). Totally in sync with the place's mentality.

This is one of the few parks where we can get permission to make a fire. (See their website about campfires.)

TIPS (fun for 2 years +)

• You'll find free parking at **Dufferin Mall** across the street. By the way, this mall includes **Walmart**, **Toys 'R Us** and **Winners!**
• Weather permitting, from May to September, the **Pizza Days** usually take place on Wednesdays, 12 noon to 2 pm, and Sundays, 1 to 3 pm. A piece of dough, tomato sauce and cheese are included in the $2.50 fee. Check their website for more info about **Friday Night Suppers.**
• The **Zamboni Café** sells light meals during the skating season. There's even more food options on Thursdays during the **Farmers' Market** from 3 to 7 pm.
• The **Clay and Paper Theatre** has been involved with the park for years. Among other things they do, read about their **Night of Dread Parade** around October 31 and related workshops on p. 46.
• The **Native Child and Family Services** usually organize a great little **Pow Wow** for families on the last Saturday of September, noon to 5 pm. Check the park's website closer to the date.
• More about the playground on p. 327.

NEARBY ATTRACTIONS
Lansdowne Fence Streetscape ... p. 455

Dufferin Grove Park | D-3
(416) 392-0913 | West of
www.dufferinpark.ca | downtown 15-min.

 Schedule: Open year-round.
 Admission: FREE access to the park.
 Directions: South of Bloor Street West, on the east side of Dufferin St., Toronto (across from Dufferin Mall and a 5-min. walk south of **Dufferin Subway Station**).

DUFFERIN

A 5-minute walk south of Bloor on Dufferin, you'll find Toronto's biggest sandpit in the groovy playground of **Dufferin Grove Park (14)** (see p. 456). This park is also well know for its outdoor skating rink **(15)** and home-made bread slices in the winter.

It is located across from **Dufferin Mall** (including **Toys R Us**, **Winners** and **Walmart** under the same roof).

Bloor Gladstone Public Library is just east of the station (1101 Bloor).

OSSINGTON

This area offers a mix of multicultural businesses of no interest for kids, but my teenager is a big fan of the Portuguese BBQ chicken at take-out counter **Sardinha O Rei Dos Frangos**, at the corner of Delaware Ave. and Bloor West. And you'll find one of the best places for Portuguese custard pies a bit further west at **Courense Bakery (16)** (1014 Bloor).

Musicians will want to know that **Long & McQuade** is just around the corner (925 Bloor).

CHRISTIE

Christie Park across from the station offers a great outdoor pool with twisting slide **(17)**, a good playground with wading pool and more **(18) (19)**.

A few minutes south of Bloor West on Grace St., you'll find **Bickford Park**'s good slopes (see p. 361). Funky **Linux Café** across the street **(20)** serves yummy food such as French toast with hot chocolate (perfect after some tobogganing).

Bloor St., east of Christie up to Bathurst St., is **Koreatown (21)** with Korean signs and Korean food. A good time to try bubble tea.

(14) Dufferin

(15) Dufferin

(16) Ossington

(17) Christie

(18) Christie

(19) Christie

(20) Christie

(21) Christie

(22) Bathurst

(23) Bathurst

(24) Bathurst

(25) Spadina

(26) St. George

BATHURST

You can't miss Toronto's landmark **Honest Eds (22)** near the station. This huge store, filled with funny old signs to read, sold cheap stuff way before the dollar stores started popping up.

Mirvish Village (23), just west of Honest Eds, is worth the visit, with **The Beguiling** holding an extraordinary selection of adults and kids comic books (601 Markham, www.beguiling.com), and **Vintage Video**, selling DVD versions of classics from the 70's and older (604 Markham, www.vintagevideocanada.com).

West of the station, check **Snake & Lattes** (600 Bloor), a café with a really cool concept: you pay $5 (less for kids) for the right to play all day (no in and out privilege) with their collection of over 1,000 games **(24)**! **Palmerston Public Library** is nearby (560 Palmerston Ave., north of Bloor).

South of Bloor, west side of Bathurst, is old-fashioned **Kidstuff Toy Store** (738 Bathurst, 416-535-2212).

Nearby, the **Bathurst Street Theatre** often presents affordable musicals (736 Bathurst, go to www.ticketmaster.ca, and enter the name of the theatre to find out the current production).

The excellent **Parentbooks** specializing in parenting books is located south of Bloor, east of Bathurst (201 Harbord, www.parentbooks.ca).

East of the station, you'll find **Bloor Cinema** (506 Bloor, www.bloorcinema.com) and many second-hand stores for DVDs, CDs or books.

SPADINA

(interchange to YELLOW)
Beware! This one can be tricky. There are actually two **Spadina Stations**. The attractions listed here are closer to the Spadina Station on the **GREEN** Line along Bloor with an exit to Bloor Street. There's a corridor (which used to be a moving walkway) linking it to the Spadina Station on the **YELLOW** Line a few blocks north on Spadina (with an exit to Spadina near Kendal Avenue). When I need to change lines, I find it easier to do so at St. George Station.

On the corner of Bloor and Spadina is the **Miles Nadal Jewish Community Centre** where you can buy a day pass to access their saltwater public pool (www.milesnadaljcc.ca). The complex hosts a venue featuring musicals, plays and movies (www.algreentheatre.com).

West of Spadina along Bloor Street is the truly cool neighbourhood of **The Annex**. Running between Bathurst and Spadina, it bursts with restaurants, food stores and shops of all kinds. One of the favourites is the large **Future Bakery (25)** with vast patio, serving copious all-day breakfast, cakes and pastries (483 Bloor, 416-922-5875). It is located across from **Tutti Fruitti** candy store.

Check out the small gift shop **Outer Layers** for cool gadgets (430 Bloor, www.outerlayer.com).

The **Tafelmusik** is performing at **Trinity-St. Paul's** (427 Bloor, www.tafelmusik.org).

ST. GEORGE

(interchange to YELLOW)
Cross to the south side of Bloor and you're at the great **Bata Shoe Museum (26)** (see p. 225).

Just north of the station's exit on Bedford, **Taddle Creek Park** is undergoing renovations which will include a new playground.

BAY

As you exit the station, **Yorkville Park (27)** offers a patchwork of small gardens along Cumberland Street, starting with a 650-ton mound of granite any child will want to conquer. The north side of Cumberland is lined with great shops (28).

Cumberland cinema (29), is at the heart of trendy Yorkville (159 Cumberland, see www.cinemaclock.com for listings).

Kidding Awound (30) is our favourite store in the area. It is packed with gift ideas for everyone (91 Cumberland, www.kiddingawound.com). **Rolo** is smaller but it also sells a wide spread of fun gadgets (24 Bellair Street, north of Cumberland, www.rolostore.com).

The old **Yorkville Fire Station 312 (31)** is adjacent to the **Yorkville Public Library** (34 Yorkville Ave., one street north of Cumberland).

For a visual treat as well as a tasty one, get a chocolate lollipop in the shop of **MoRoCo** (99 Yorkville, www.morocochocolat.com), check its modern glam lounge with chandeliers, black floor and purple furniture and make plans to come back with girlfriends!

The fancy shopping centre **Hazelton Lanes** is located north of Yorkville on Hazelton. The mall is of no interest to kids (too many "boring" clothing stores) but there are a few sculptures along Hazelton that should intrigue them (32) (33).

There's a **Winners** nearby, on Bloor Street, next to **Starbucks**. The **ROM** (see p. 222) and the **Gardiner Museum** (see p. 90) are only a few minutes away.

Varsity Cineplex is just south of Bloor on Bay (www.cinemaclock.com) next to an **Indigo** bookstore.

(27) Bay

(28) Bay

(29) Bay

(31) Bay

(30) Bay

(32) Bay

(33) Bay

(34) Bloor/Yonge

(35) Sherbourne

(36) Sherbourne

(37) Sherbourne

(38) Castle Frank

BLOOR/YONGE
(interchange to YELLOW)

From Avenue Road to Yonge along Bloor Street West are many high-end stores mixed with big name chains. The recent street renovations and tree planting will pay off during the summer!

Going north, past the **Toronto Reference Library**, stop at **Crêpes à Gogo** for a yummy $5 folded crêpe (18 Yorkville Ave. at Yonge, www.crepesagogo.com). Then reach Collier St. across Yonge St. and follow that lovely street past Church, to the dead-end section where you'll find stairs (34) leading down to **Rosedale Valley Road** path (for a glimpse of this unique road set in a ravine between tall trees).

SHERBOURNE

There's lots of surprises around this one, starting with the lined tunnel with murals going under Bloor (exit at Glen Road to see it).

The passageway leads to a boardwalk running over Rosedale Valley Road (35) and the impressive houses of Rosedale neighbourhood.

From the Glen Road exit, turn west on Howard St. and you'll see **St. James Town West Park** including an unexpected playground.

Walk southbound on Sherbourne for another intriguing sight: the **Shrine of Our Lady of Lourdes Church** (36) with its bronze statue of Mary's apparition to a girl. So many people have touched it, it's shinier on certain spots! Enter into the church; it is gorgeous and bigger than it looks from outside. **St. James Town Public Library** is just a bit further south (495 Sherbourne).

From the station, go west on Bloor, past Mt. Pleasant Rd. and down the stairs leading to **Rosedale Valley Road**, for a different perspective of the area!

West of Jarvis is the recently renovated **St. Paul's Church**. (Don't miss the vintage coloured-glass windows in the washrooms!)

Across the street is the whimsical sculpture *Community* (37) featuring twenty people of different ages in action. In the background, on the grounds of **Manulife Towers**, is a cute paved trail leading to St. Paul's Square.

Finish the tour by going underneath the monoliths at the north-east corner of Bloor and Church, and check the bears crest on the wall of the north-west building.

CASTLE FRANK

Kids won't appreciate the amazing houses north of the station but you will!

Go up Castle Frank Rd. to reach the discrete entrance of **Graigleigh Gardens** (see p. 280). An opening in the middle of its northern side will give you access to the ravine (38) going down the majestic ravine. It's the best outing for young explorers but not for strollers!

At the fork in the trails, one can follow the signs for **Moore Park** (see p. 300) passing by the **Evergreen Brickworks Park** (see p. 273) or **David A. Balfour Park** (see p. 470), both roughly 2 kms away.

BROADVIEW

It is quite impressive to walk over the Don Valley Parkway on the **Prince Edward Viaduct** (39). The panorama is spectacular and below are the speeding cars and the lazy river. You'll find a telescope aiming at the **CN Tower**, halfway along the viaduct, which you can use for free.

A 5-min. walk south of Danforth, on Broadview Ave., is outdoor **Riverdale Pool** with twisting slide (40). **Riverdale Park** includes a playground and a most ambitious tobogganing slope (see p. 360).

It's also where you'll get the best panorama of Toronto from the top of its hill (41). And to add to the pleasure, across from the park, there's **Rooster Coffee House** (42) (43), open 7 am to 7 pm, selling hot chocolate and supplying blankets in the late fall for those who want to admire the sunset from its outdoor patio (479 Broadview, www.rooster-coffeehouse.com).

Thorncliffe Public Library is a 10-min. walk north on Broadview (turn west on Pretora, north on Cambridge, then west to 48 Thorncliffe).

A few blocks east of the station is the **Music Hall** venue (147 Danforth, www.themusichall.ca) where you may sometimes catch a family show.

East of it, the **Children's After Hours Clinic** is one of the few drop-in clinics for children (235 Danforth, 416-461-3000, www.kidsafterhourscare.ca).

CHESTER

You are in the heart of posh Riverdale. Turn west to access **The Big Carrot** (44), the large natural food market (358 Danforth, www.thebigcarrot.ca), and **Book City**. Further is **Melonhead** Hair Care (294 Danforth). Eastbound, up to Pape, Danforth is filled with restaurants and shops (home decor stores, shoes and Greek food). **It's My Party** sits next to **Wimpy's Diner** (45), straight from the 50's (443 Danforth). Across the street, a favourite is the colourful candy store **Sucker's** (46) (450 Danforth).

(39) Broadview

(40) Broadview

(41) Broadview

(42) Broadview

(43) Broadview

(44) Chester

(45) Chester

(46) Chester

WITHROW PARK

closer to a large wading pool and the tennis courts and the other, on top of the mound, with a view of the path running down along Logan Avenue. Walk just a block further south and you'll reach a local favourite, the **Riverdale Perks Café** (633 Logan) serving yummy treats, light lunches and good coffee.

Location, location

Just south of busy Danforth with all its restaurants, treat shops and nice stores, Withrow Park sits between two lovely streets amidst one of the great neighbourhoods in Toronto.

There's enough space here going up and down the hill to stretch any visitors' legs (there's a big off-leash section in the middle of the park for the four-legged ones). It is the best location to watch **Dusk Dance** (see p. 84) and offers great outdoor Shakespeare (see p. 117).

There are two playgrounds. One

Withrow Park
Dial 311 (new service)
www.toronto.ca/parks

D-3
East
of downtown
15-min.

 Schedule: Open year-round.
Admission: FREE.
 Directions: A 5-min. walk from **Pape Subway Station**, Toronto. South of Danforth (between Carlaw Ave. and Logan Ave.).

MONARCH PARK

Park with a twist

Luscious Monarch Park is far from the flat grassy patch we often see in small parks. Its landscape is rolling and is filled with mature trees.

Its playground is great but the park's best feature is the outdoor pool with a twisting slide. (If the slide is closed when

you visit, ask when it will be reopened. Sometimes, they're just waiting to have enough staff to open it on that same day.)

As a bonus for little adventurers, you'll find a tunnel adorned with murals at the south-east end of the park, a good opportunity to test for echo. On the other side of this short tunnel, walk down Woodfield to Walpole and you'll see a variety store (time to stock up on snacks and drinks before heading back for more water fun).

Monarch Park
Dial 311 (new service)
www.toronto.ca/parks

D-3
East
of downtown
20-min.

 Schedule: Open year-round.
Admission: FREE.
 Directions: A 10-min. walk from **Greenwood Subway Station**, Toronto. Walk south on Greenwood or Lamb until you reach Felstead.

PAPE
Pape/Danforth Public Library is just south of the station (701 Pape).

Grab a bag of honey balls at **Athens Pastry** (509 Danforth), then walk west along Danforth to reach Logan, for a real feel of **Greektown** (47). On the way, there's **Treasure Island Toy Store** (581 Danforth).

South on Logan, there are two great playgrounds and one large wading pool in the beautiful **Withrow Park** (see. p. 462).

DONLANDS
West of Donlands Avenue, is a funky café aptly named **The One in the Only Café** (48), serving great coffee, snacks and light lunch from 10 am to 3 pm (972 Danforth, www.theonlycafe.com).

GREENWOOD
At the corner of Danforth and Lamb (the first street east of Greenwood) is **Comics & More** (1325 Danforth, check www.shop.comicsnmore.ca).

Walk further south on Lamb to Felstead and you'll reach the luscious **Monarch Park**, with outdoor pool (see p. 462).

If you feel like Timbits, check the unique **Tim Hortons** in the refurbished **Roxy/Allenby Theatre** (49), a couple of minutes west of the station (1213 Danforth).

COXWELL
The small bowling place **Danforth Bowl** is just west of Coxwell (1554 Danforth, www.danforthbowl.com).

Just east of Coxwell is the **Bus Terminal**, an original kitschy greasy spoon (50) with LP covers and movie star pictures all over the wall (1606 Danforth, 416-463-4680). Look for a dragon head! **Danforth/Coxwell Public Library** is across the street (1675 Danforth).

WOODBINE
West of Woodbine is the great art supply store **DeSerres** (2056 Danforth, www.deserres.ca). Across the street the lovely little **Cake Town Café** has opened.

A bit further west lies **East Lynn Park** with a wading pool down the slope, and gorgeous playground **Rusty's Reach** (51). In the winter, they maintain a natural ice rink (52).

Further west, are **Wheels & Wings Hobbies** for amateurs of model planes (1880 Danforth, www.wheelswingshobbies.com) and **John's Hobbies**, for miniature trains (2188 Danforth, www.johnshobbies.ca), east of Woodbine.

MAIN STREET
There's a small playground with wading pool in **Coleman Park**, north of Danforth, just east of the station. **Main Street Public Library** is a 10-min. walk south (137 Main).

VICTORIA PARK
Mini golf is a rarity in Toronto but you'll find a very pretty course in the **Beach Fairway Golf Range** (53) (411 Victoria Park Ave., see p. 35).

It sits a 10-min. walk south of the station, on the east side of Victoria Park like a little green oasis, just north of a **McDonald's**.

Less than 10 minutes north of the station, you'll find an entrance to **Taylor Creek Park** on the west side of Victoria Park.

WARDEN
I didn't expect to find a river amidst the concrete high-rises and 6-lane wide avenues at Warden and St. Clair! But there it is, in **Warden Woods Park** (see p. 464).

KENNEDY
(interchange to BLUE)
See p. 465.

(47) Pape

(48) Donlands

(49) Greenwood

(50) Coxwell

(51) Woodbine

(52) Woodbine

(53) Victoria Park

WARDEN WOODS PARK

Woods in the hood

After a short walk along the TTC's grey parking lots by the 6-lane-wide Warden Avenue, the last thing I expected was the sight of a willow tree brushing the water of a bouncing creek strutting over large rocks at the bottom of a curvy valley.

Just a few minutes from **Warden Station** a 2-km trail starts running south of St. Clair East down to Pharmacy Road near a parking lot.

The paved trail is a little uneven but wide: the perfect place to bike with older kids when they're sturdier on their wheels. It is sinuous, goes up and down through a mature forest and runs along the **Massey Creek**. The works!

If you access the park from St. Clair, the creek will reveal itself to your right after the country-style fence. It is easy to get to the riverside in this section of the stream. If you decide to do so, make sure your young explorers see the "secret vault" by the willow tree (a cement structure which is actually a storm sewer outlet, to stay away from during or after a heavy rain).

Halfway from either entrance, you'll

find some stairs formed by beams encased among the roots on the hill. They lead to a great park with a small playground. Note that the climb up is quite steep and not stroller accessible!

Nearby, if you hear the wooshing sound of water, it doesn't come from the creek but from the waste water running underground. A little reminder that we are still in the city. On a more poetic note, I heard the song of birds I don't normally hear in my neighbourhood.

Further, you'll see a pretty bridge crossing over the river. It leads to a series of other dirt trails. If you remain on the main trail (also called the **Gus Harris Trail**), you'll reach the parking lot adjacent to Pharmacy Avenue in a few minutes.

TIPS (fun for 8 years +)

• There's a convenience store in the apartment building at the corner of Teesdale Place and Pharmacy, just south of the park.

• In the winter, people do cross-country skiing in the park.

NEARBY ATTRACTIONS
Beach Fairway Golf Range (10-min.) p. 35

Warden Woods Park
Dial 311 (new service)

www.toronto.ca/parks

D-3
N-E
of downtown
25-min.

 Schedule: Open year-round. Beware of the river if you visit after a rainstorm or a big melt.
Admission: FREE.
Directions: A 3-min. walk from **Warden Subway Station**, Toronto. West of Warden Ave. and south of St. Clair Ave. East. The 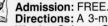 other entrance is on Pharmacy Ave., north of Danforth Avenue.

BLUE LINE
(SCARBOROUGH RT)

KENNEDY
(interchange to YELLOW)
There's a superb mural on the exterior wall of the exit closest to Eglinton. Impressive! (54) (55) (56) (57) (58)

Kennedy/Eglinton Public Library (2380 Eglinton) is less than a 10-min. walk west of the station.

LAWRENCE EAST
Between Lawrence and Ellesmere, Kennedy is lined with large stores selling furniture, appliances, etc. Useful to know but not for kids.

ELLESMERE
Nothing of interest for kids.

MIDLAND
This station is next to **Hamilton's Theatrical Supply**, a big costume rental store catering to adults and also selling items for kids (2065 Midland, www.hamiltonstheatrical.com). Go 10 mins. south on Midland, then east on Ellesmere Rd. to access **Birkdale Park** (see p. 284).

SCARBOROUGH
This station serves **Scarborough Town Centre** (www.scarboroughtowncentre.com). The mall includes a **Famous Players Coliseum** (www.cinemaclock.com).

This mall has a special asset: **Kornelia's Korner**, an indoor playground offering drop-off service with qualified staff ($5/hour, max. 3 hours). It is located in **Section R** near **The Children's Place** (416-296-0901).

There's **PJ's Pet Centre (59)** (down the escalator in the **Food Court** section), **Toys Toys Toys**, **Games Workshop**, **Mind Games**, **The Bay**, **Sears** and **Walmart**.

McCOWAN
Nothing special for kids.

(54) Kennedy

(55) Kennedy

(56) Kennedy

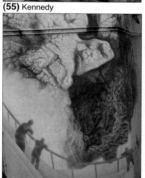

(57) Kennedy

(58) Kennedy

(59) Scarborough

(60) Leslie

(61) Leslie

(62) Leslie

(63) Leslie

(64) Leslie

(65) Bayview

PURPLE LINE
(SHEPPARD)

DON MILLS

Fairview Mall (www.fairviewmall.ca) is served by this station.

It includes **SilverCity Theatre** (www.cinemaclock.com) near the **Shoppers Drug Mart**, as well as **Toys Toys Toys** and **Disney Store** among others.

You'll find **Fairview Public Library** just north of the mall exit by the Shoppers Drug Mart. It hosts a theatre where a local company, currently in its 34th season, produces affordable plays and musicals (www.stagecentreproductions.com).

LESLIE

If you miss the shuttle, **Ikea** and its free indoor playground is only a 10-minute walk away (west on Sheppard and down Provost). Check the splendid murals (60) (61) (62) on the way and try to find the bee!

You can access **East Don Park** off the little street just west of the north-west corner of Sheppard and Leslie. There's a bridge (63) going over the **Don River** and a winding paved path (64) leading far up north.

BESSARION

Nothing special for kids.

BAYVIEW

This is at the door of posh **Bayview Village** mall (www.bayviewvillageshops.com) with high-end stores, many restaurants and a **Chapters**.

Go north on Bayview to reach **Bayview Village Park** (65) (see p. 282). You'll find **Bayview Public Library** on the way (2901 Bayview).

SHEPPARD/YONGE
(interchange to YELLOW)
See p. 467.

YELLOW LINE
(YONGE-UNIVERSITY-SPADINA)

(66) Finch

FINCH

Some 10 minutes north of the station, you'll find action at the **Bowlerama** (5837 Yonge, www.bowlerama.com) in the **Newtonbrook Plaza** (also home to a **Scholar's Choice** store and second-hand sport equipment **Play It Again**.

Walk less than 10-min. westbound on Hendon (just north of the station on the west side of Yonge) to reach the lovely spray pad of **Hendon Park** (66) (see p. 422).

NORTH YORK

This station opens into **Mel Lastman Square**, impressive with fountains, outdoor stage, outdoor ice rink (see p. 352), not to forget the majestic **North York Central Public Library** (with a Teen section including retro comfy couches and cool silenced juke boxes). The great **Douglas Snow Aquatic Centre** (67) with twisting slide is located west of it (see p. 416). Don't miss the sculpture of a giant mouth (68) just south of the entrance of nearby **Toronto Centre for the Arts** venue (www.tocentre.com).

Across from the square is the futuristic cinema **Empire Empress Walk** (5095 Yonge, www.cinemaclock.com).

Those who sew will appreciate knowing there's a **Fabricland** adjacent to the cinema.

North of the station, the **Rose Garden** leading to the **Gibson House** (see p. 377) was replaced by a high-rise under construction. Walk west along Park Home, past the sculpture of a cute colt, then north on Beecroft Rd. and you'll

soon reach **Dempsey Park** (see p. 283) with a truly original playground (69).

SHEPPARD/YONGE
(interchange to PURPLE)

At Sheppard, there's Cineplex **Sheppard Centre Grande** (4861 Yonge, www.cinemaclock.com).

If you walk northbound on Yonge, turn east on Hollywood Avenue, then south on Doris, in 10 minutes you'll see the crazy building of **Claude Watson School for the Arts** (130 Doris Avenue) with giant honeycombs plastered on the building. On the other side of the street awaits **Willowdale Park** (70).

The small theatre for younger kids **Solar Stage** is located in the **Madison Centre**, on the west side of Yonge a few blocks north of Sheppard (4950 Yonge, www.solarstage.on.ca, see p. 118).

YORK MILLS

With little adventurers, first explore the pathway covered with graffiti running under Yonge (using the outdoor stairs adjacent to the station along Yonge Street). Then, walk down the paved trail in the park just east of the station. It reaches Mill Street.

I suggest you turn west on Mill to access the southern entrance to **York Mills Valley Park** (see p. 468). This way, you'll get the best view of the lovely path along the river and nearby playground (71) with tall hill in the background. (Looks like the perfect spot for serious tobogganing!)

To your left, you'll see the little bridge on Donino Avenue. Near that bridge, you'll be able to get closer to the stream.

(67) North York

(68) North York

(69) North York

(70) Sheppard/Yonge

(71) York Mills

YORK MILLS VALLEY PARK

From Donino Ave., you can walk to the parking lot off Mill Street or take another paved path at the corner of Mills and Campbell Crescent, by the statue of C. W. Jefferys (an artist and historian who lived nearby).

This will lead you back to the subway station where you'll want to take the outdoor stairs going down along Yonge, to explore the graffiti in the long tunnel under Yonge and see the glistening water of the winding river.

Where am I?

The tall buildings at York Mills and Yonge are flanked with trees but there's still no country in sight. Walk south of Mill Street, and you're in another world altogether.

If you have a chance, drive through the quiet streets accessible from Donino Avenue. They all lead to gorgeous dead-ends lined with dream homes (especially Donwoods Drive leading to St. Margaret Drive).

You can easily reach the paved trail off Mill Street from the south of the park's parking lot. There, you'll see water running down the concrete slope by a white house that looks like a fancy cottage. The illusion of being in the country is perfect even though the stream, actually the **West Don River**, is flowing on concrete at this point.

Further, the path reaches a very nice playground with a great hill as a background. If you keep going, you'll get to the bridge. That's the best spot to see the water and view the cars driving over the viaduct (what can I say, little guys like that).

TIPS (fun for 5 years +)

• There's a parking lot with machines by the park, which you can access from Yonge or Mill Streets.
• There's a gas station with washrooms and a convenience store selling coffee in front of **York Mills Subway Station**.
• The hill by the playground seems perfect for some serious tobogganing on its south part. A more gentle slope on the north will cater to the younger crowd.

NEARBY ATTRACTIONS
Around Lawrence Station .... p. 469

York Mills Valley Park

	D-3
Dial 311 (new service)	**Downtown**
www.toronto.ca/parks	**Toronto**
	20-min.

Schedule: Open year-round.
Admission: FREE.

Directions: Just east of Yonge Street, on both sides of Mill Street, Toronto. It is adjacent to **York Mills Subway Station**, south of York Mills Road.

LAWRENCE

North of Lawrence is a roster of restaurants and shops along Yonge and up to Melrose Ave., where you'll find a **McDonald's** (3400 Yonge, 10-min. walk from Lawrence exit off Ranleigh Ave.).

Note that the station platforms exiting to Lawrence Ave. are located a few blocks south of the Ranleigh Avenue exit.

Check the lane behind the McDonald's to see the "Mural Walk project" (72), a series of cute murals from Melrose to Fairlawn, including the big one on **Mastermind Toys,** my favourite stop with kids, (3350 Yonge, www.mastermindtoys.com).

South at Fairlawn Ave. is **Patisserie Sebastien,** (French pastries anyone?) and just south of it, the indoor playground **Just Ducky Yonge Kids,** catering to kids 5 years and under (3300 Yonge, www.justducky.ca), with a fun little toy store attached. Across the street is **PJ's Pets** with small animals (3291 Yonge, www.pjspet.com).

If you walk one minute west on Woburn Ave., you'll find a small playground that did the job for my young kids, years ago.

Older kids will like **Paradise Comics** (3278 Yonge) and **Games Workshop** (3251 Yonge).

Just north of Lawrence Ave. is **Fire Station 131** (3135 Yonge on the east side). Dare to ask the firemen to visit. Nearby is **Melonhead** Children's Hair Care (3215 Yonge).

Next to the **Locke Public Library**, at Yonge and Lawrence, is a lovely playground down the hill of **Lawrence Park Ravine** (73). It continues south of Lympstone, offering a great slope for tobogganing (see p. 360).

Alexander Muir **Memorial Garden**, further south, leads to **Blythwood Ravine** (towards Mt. Pleasant Rd.) followed by **Sherwood Ravine** (see p. 301).

Duplex Parkette across Yonge, south of Chatsworth Dr., is a spot where local daredevils go tobogganning. It leads to **Chatsworth Ravine** (74) across from Duplex Avenue. (It has it all: steep access, dirt paths to explore and a small creek under a tiny bridge.)

EGLINTON

A few minutes west of Yonge on Eglinton is the great arts and craft supplier **DeSerres** (124 Eglinton W., www.deserres.ca).

A bit farther is the **North Toronto Memorial Community Centre** (75) with indoor and outdoor pools including big fun slides (200 Eglinton W., 416-392-6590). If you follow the trail in the back of that centre, you'll reach **Tommy Flynn Playground** (76).

The Cineplex **SilverCity Yonge & Eglinton** is just north of the station, near the **Indigo** (there's also a **Toys R Us** in that building) and **Northern District Public Library** is just further north (40 Orchard View Blvd.).

A great outing combo for movie buffs is to eat at the **Mandarin** buffet (2200 Yonge, south of Eglinton) then go to Cineplex **Canada Square**, up the stairs. (See listings at www.cinemaclock.com.)

A 10-min. walk south of the station, make a stop at scrumptious French bakery **La Bamboche** just east off Yonge (4 Manor Rd. east) or **Village Chill** ice cream shop in front.

The **Mysteriously Yours** theatre is just a bit further south (2026 Yonge, www.mysteriouslyyours.com, see p. 86).

(72) Lawrence

(73) Lawrence

(74) Lawrence

(75) Eglinton

(76) Eglinton

DAVID A. BALFOUR PARK

By the water...

Before you reach the Balfour Park, you've got to check out the cluster of reflecting pools on the western part of the adjacent Rosehill Reservoir. It is big enough to show on a city map!

I visited this spot in the fall, when the fountain had been shut down and the three blue reflecting pools emptied but it was nevertheless impressive, with its little bridges and molecule-shaped sculpture, framed by high-rises.

Small signs warned us that entering the pools is prohibited. Can't imagine how one would prevent kids from dipping their big toe... There's a wading pool in the southern part of the park but I'm not sure it is still functional.

Behind the slope east of the wading pool, you'll find a pretty playground which seems sheltered from the rest of the world and the entrance to the nature trail.

It is a real treat to go down this trail as you quickly see the ravine closing on you.

From the upper ramp, you see a small bridge way down there. Were you to go down that road, you'd be able to reach the trail running along the **Evergreen Brickworks Park**, then the **Moore** Park Ravine, roughly 3 kilometres away.

If you follow **David Balfour**'s trail northbound, it'll lead you in 10 minutes to the northern entrance of the park. On the way, you'll notice a little waterfall if you look carefully. This truly is an enclave in the midst of the city.

TIPS (fun for 5 years +)

• There's a **Sobey's** on Pleasant Blvd. (south of St. Clair, east of Yonge) offering 1 1/2 hr free parking with min. $15 purchase.

• More on **Moore Ravine** on p. 300.

NEARBY ATTRACTIONS

David A. Balfour Park | D-3 **Dowtown Toronto 15-min.**
Dial 311 (new service)
www.toronto.ca/parks

Schedule: Open year-round.
Admission: FREE.

Directions: A 10-min. walk south of **St. Clair Subway Station**, Toronto. East of Yonge, take Avoca Avenue south, it becomes Rosehill Avenue.

DAVISVILLE

To get to **Oriole Park**, walk a few minutes west on Chaplin Crescent (north of the station) and take the small passageway through the houses across from Colin Ave. The playground includes a wading pool and is been upgraded in 2011 (old shown on photo (77)). See p. 334 about the **Beltline** trail (78) which runs south of Oriole Park. South of the station (east side of Yonge) is a staircase leading to an entrance to **Mt. Pleasant Cemetery** (79) (see p. 261).

Ten minutes east on Davisville Ave. is **June Rowlands Park** with a nice playground. It is near the best stretch of Mt. Pleasant Rd. with two costume stores, a doll house shop next to **Mini Grid** (a model car store with a racing track you can check out during the kids' Sunday club at 608 Mt. Pleasant, www.mini-grid.com), two independent theatres **Regent** and **Mount Pleasant**, **Mastermind Toys** (639 Mt. Pleasant) and **Mabel's Fables** bookstore (662 Mt. Pleasant), all withing 10 mins. when walking northbound.

ST. CLAIR

Deer Park Public Library is just east of the station (40 St. Clair). From St. Clair Ave., east of the station, turn south on Avoca Ave. It will lead you to the **Rosehill Reservoir** (80) (81) and reflecting pools. There's a playground hidden in the back with access to **David Balfour Park** (see p. 470).

SUMMERHILL

South of the station, the viaduct looks straight from the 19th century (82). If you sit by **Timothy's** windows, you'll get a great view. The building sits in **Scrivener Square** (83) near a catchy modern fountain.

(77) Davisville

(78) Davisville

(79) Davisville

(80) St. Clair

(81) St. Clair

(82) Summerhill

(83) Summerhill

(84) Rosedale

(85) College

(86) Dundas

(87) Dundas

(88) Dundas

ROSEDALE

Between this station and **Summerhill Station**, you'll find high-end home decor stores alternating with restaurants and cafés.

Just across the street is **Ramsdel Park**. You can't see it from Yonge but this park includes a playground and wading pool in a very nice setting.

I enjoyed sitting by the open windows by the terrace and tall trees of **Café Doria** to catch the summer breeze... with a dessert (1094 Yonge, 416-920-5315).

The real French bakery **Patachou** is not to be missed. So many delicious treats to try (84)! It also has a patio in the summer (1120 Yonge, 416-927-1105).

BLOOR/YONGE/

(interchange to GREEN)
See p. 460.

WELLESLEY

The cool indoor skatepark **Shred Central** that was the only thing for kids around this station has sadly closed.

COLLEGE

The **Toronto Police Museum** is just west of Yonge (40 College, www.torontopolice.on.ca, see p. 220).

If you walk south, around the large building at the south-west corner of Yonge and College (which includes one of my favourite **Winners**), you'll reach **College Park** (officially known as **Barbara Ann Scott Park** (85). It features one of the biggest fountains with reflecting pool in the city and turns into an artificial ice rink in the winter!

There's a **Tutti Fruitti** candy store at the corner of Yonge and Carlton.

The movie theatre **Carlton** was saved from closure in 2010 (20 Carlton, www.cinemaclock.com). If you push a bit farther, east of Jarvis, there's **Allen Gardens** (see p. 260).

DUNDAS

Yonge-Dundas Square (86) is our own little Times Square (see p. 112). Last time we looked up, there were four screens, three electronic boards and twelve billboards competing for our attention on the buildings framing the square.

Consult their calendar of events for the spread of activities going on year-round (www.ydsquare.com).

Following all this action, it is amazing to find the pond of **Devonian Square** (87), usually turned into a rink during the winter, on Victoria (one street east of Yonge, north of Dundas). If you turn right and walk a bit further east into Gould Street around that square, go through the arch of South and West **Kerr Hall**. You'll discover an old building façade (88) in the middle of the park!

AMC Yonge & Dundas 24 is right across the square on Dundas (www.cinemaclock.com).

The station exits into the **Eaton Centre**. Cross the centre and take the door on the west side by the Sears to discover another oasis: **Trinity Square** (see p. 113).

QUEEN

This station also exits into the **Eaton Centre** where a tall fountain and glassed elevators reaching suspended geese are a hit (see p. 182).

The **Elgin Theatre** is across the street, and **Canon Theatre** and **Massey Hall** are nearby (consult www.ticketmaster.ca to see what's performing in these venues).

Eggspectation all-day breakfast is very popular with families (220 Yonge, www.eggspectation.ca).

KING

Go west on King, you'll see the impressive **Scotia Plaza** to your right (40 King). Walk inside to check the huge mural of falls inside the **Scotia Bank**. Then cross King and access **Commerce Court** through the fun-shaped arch right in front to see the... elephants (89)! And raise your nose to take in those high-rises surrounding the courtyard (90).

If you want to treat the kids, return under the arch and take the stairs down, near the **CIBC**. Follow the **West Commerce Court** signs, it will lead you to **Petit Four** (www.petit-four.ca), a take-out bakery selling the cutest little cakes in a glass (91) for $2.

Farther west on King is the **Toronto Dominion Centre**. Walk across its courtyard and go meet the cows (92) on the other side of Wellington! (It's their temporary location until they return to their pasture in the big courtyard.)

Walk south on Yonge to **Brookfield Place** to admire the architecture. Even kids will react to the mighty arches (93).

This is the home of the **Marché Restaurant**, one of the best places to dine with a family. Kids can stroll around the different food stations and there's something for every taste (www.marche.moevenpick.com, write *Brookfield* in the *Quicksearch*).

You will find the **Hockey Hall of Fame** in the lower level of the building (see p. 340).

If you walk north of **King Station** and turn east on Adelaide, just west of Victoria on the south side, you'll see a beautiful courtyard with a labyrinth of chiseled glass walls (94) (95) and a few sculptures with fountain.

(89) King

(91) King

(93) King or Union

(90) King

(92) King

(94) King

(95) King

(96) Union

(97) Union

(98) Union

(99) Union/Queens Quay

(100) Union/Queens Quay

(101) Union/Queens Quay

(102) Union/Queens Quay

UNION

There's an indoor corridor linking **Union Station** to **Air Canada Centre**, south of the station (see p. 331). All around that building, you'll see many scenes carved into the walls. Walk through the centre to its western exit and you'll see giant poles adorned with stars reaching the sky **(96)**.

The **Sony Centre**, where we can often see family shows, is located on the south-east corner of Yonge and Front (www.sonycentre.ca), and the **St. Lawrence Centre** is further east on Front (www.stlc.com). That stretch of Front includes the impressive trompe-l'oeil (which incidentally reproduces the **Winners** building on Front) of the **Flatiron** building **(97)** in **Berczy Park**. There really is a European feeling **(98)** to it.

West of Union Station, I noticed **Game Trek**, a great toy store for adults and kids (100 Front West, www.gametrek.ca) in the lower level of the **Fairmount Royal York**.

The **CN Tower** (see p. 124) is a 10-min. walk further west along Front.

Note that you can catch an underground streetcar to the **Queens Quay** stop with your transfer (just follow the signs to **Harbourfront** inside the station). It passes by Harbourfront (see p. 24).

Just north of Queens Quay stop on Bay St. is **Waterpark Promenade** with a food court by a huge sort of boat skeleton hanging in the air **(99)**.

East of Bay is a giant sculpture my kids called "the peanut" **(100)**. Further east, past the big mural of whales **(101)**, you'll find the new **Canada's Sugar Beach** with splash pad **(102)** (see p. 420).

ST. ANDREWS

If you happen to be around on Wednesdays, Thursdays (and sometimes Fridays), you'll be able to visit the **48th Highlanders Museum** (103) in the basement of **St. Andrew's Church** (entrance on King, east of Simcoe, www.48thhighlanders. com).

The volunteers in this small museum have an encyclopedic memory and can walk you through the war memorabilia. The kids will be allowed to try the Highland Regiment's ceremony hat topped with black ostrich feathers. Bring the camera!

Beyond **Roy Thomson Hall** is the great courtyard by **City Hall** and **CBC** buildings, with fountain and sculptures to explore (see p. 126).

OSGOODE

Many don't realize that gorgeous **Osgoode Hall** behind the fancy iron fences (104) is open to the public! You've got to see this place (130 Queen West, at the north-east corner of University and Queen, www.osgoodehall.com). You'll like the architectural details. Kids will fancy the imposing judge chairs scattered all over.

When you look up, at the north-west corner of the Queen-University intersection, you see the **Canada Life** weather beacon (105). Depending on the weather, its light will change, running up if the temperature is getting warmer. If you go inside the building (330 University), you can get a card summarizing the codes of the beacon and see a miniature model of the tower.

The **Nathan Phillips Square** is just a few minutes east of the station (see p. 114).

ST. PATRICK

The **Textile Museum** is but a few minutes east from this station and one of the best little museums in Toronto. Go east on Dundas and turn south on Centre Ave. (55 Centre, www.textilemuseum.ca, see p. 221).

A few minutes west on Dundas and you'll see the funky shape of the **OCAD** on McCaul. Walk around it and you'll discover the playground of **Grange Park** with a large wading pool overlooked by the modern **AGO** (see p. 88).

There are many art supply stores around the OCAD but my favourite is **Aboveground** (74 McCaul, www.abovegroundartsupplies.com).

QUEEN'S PARK

Check the firefighters monument at the north-east corner at this station (106) and what looks like a giant hot air balloon inside the building at the north-west corner (hosting a **Second Cup**).

This station is just south of the large **Queen's Park** hosting yearly **Word on the Street** book fair (see p. 93).

Lillian H. Smith Public Library, west on College, offers the best collection of kids' books of all the Library branches (239 College).

MUSEUM

The **Gardiner Museum** is right there (111 Queen's Park, www.gardinermuseum.on.ca, see p. 90) as well as the **Royal Ontario Museum** (www.rom.on.ca, see p. 222).

University of Toronto's courtyards are fun to explore. I recommend that you take the **Philosopher's Walk**, just west of the ROM. Walk through to Hoskin Ave. then turn west and enter the **Trinity College** to access its inner courtyard (107). Simply breathtaking!

(103) St. Andrews

(104) Osgoode

(105) Osgoode

(106) Queen's Park

(107) Museum

(108) Dupont

(109) Dupont

(110) St. Clair West

(111) St. Clair West

(112) St. Clair West

(113) St. Clair West

ST. GEORGE
(interchange to GREEN)
See p. 458.

SPADINA
(interchange to GREEN)
Beware! This station can be confusing (read p. 458). No attractions of interest to kids north of it. For a description of the attractions a few minutes south of it, see the GREEN Line **Spadina Station** on p. 458.

DUPONT
It will take you less than 10 minutes to reach **Casa Loma (108) (109)** and enjoy one of their fun special events and shows (www.casaloma. org, see p. 128). Go north on Spadina, then west on Davenport to access the staircase leading to the castle's entrance on Austin Terrace. The **Spadina Museum** is just east of it (285 Spadina, 416-392-6910, see p. 374).

ST. CLAIR WEST
Walk 10 minutes west on St. Clair (going north on Vaughan Rd.) and you reach whimsical year-round ice cream parlour **Dutch Dream (110)** (78 Vaughan, 416-656-6959). **Wychwood Public Library** is south of St. Clair (1431 Bathurst). Ten minutes east of the station is **Sir Winston Churchill Park** (see p. 362).

An entrance to **Cedarvale Park** (see p. 281) is just north of the Heath Street exit (112). If you go east on Heath and north on Spadina, it will take you 5 min. to get to cool **Hope Street Café (111)** east of Lonsdale in **Forest Hill**. A few minutes further on Spadina, past **Suydam Park**, go west on Strathearn to admire a gorgeous statue of kids (113).

Suydam Park leads to **Relmar Gardens (114)** and a cosy playground, from which you can also access Cedarvale Park.

EGLINTON WEST

Walk 10 minutes south of Eglinton on the west side of Strathearn Road and you'll meet the huge **Cedarvale Park** (115) (see p. 281).

GLENCAIRN

There's a nice playground in **Viewmount Park** (east of the station, follow the first path southbound along Allen Road). Remain on that path and you'll reach **Beltline Trail** (116) within 10 minutes (see p. 334).

LAWRENCE WEST

Lawrence Square mall is just off this station. It includes a **Zellers** (www. shoplawrencesquare.com).

YORKDALE

This station serves **Yorkdale Mall** (www.yorkdale. com), a huge centre with great light display during Christmas (see p. 182). Animal lovers will go crazy for the themed-restaurant **Rainforest Café** (117) (www.rainforestcafe.com) and they will enjoy **PJ's Pets** (118) near the food court (www.pjspet.com).

Across Dufferin (facing the Sears), you'll notice the giant telescope on the roof of the cool science store **Efton's** (119) (3350 Dufferin, www. escience.ca).

Surprisingly, there's a nice playground by Highway 401! Simply follow the paved path east of the station to access **Baycrest Park** (120).

WILSON

There's a new **Michaels** craft store one block south of the station (30 Billy Bishop Way, www.michaels.com) and a **Second Cup** across the parking lot to the west.

DOWNSVIEW

Downsview Park and **Canadian Air & Space Museum** located in this area are more than 2 kms away.

(114) St. Clair West

(115) Eglinton West

(116) Glencairn

(117) Yorkdale

(118) Yorkdale

(119) Yorkdale

(120) Yorkdale

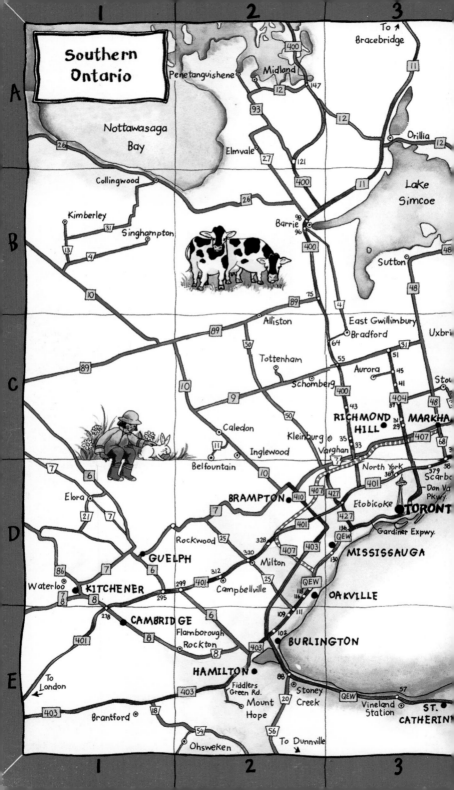

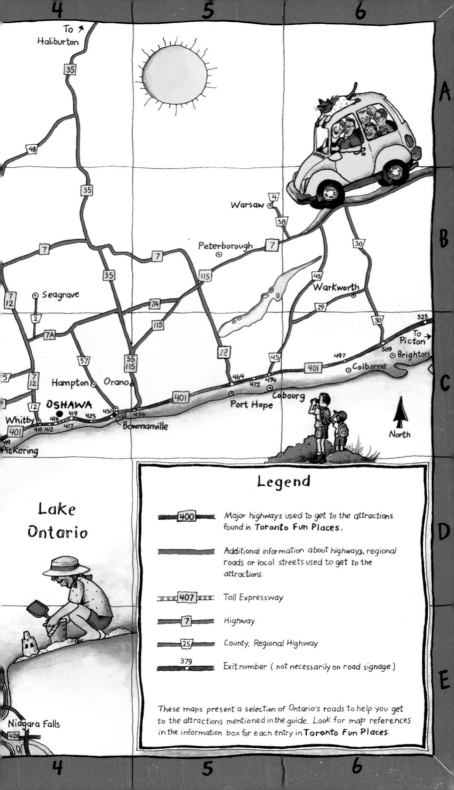

4   5   6

To Haliburton

35

A

48

35

Warsaw

38

B

Peterborough

7

30

115

45

Warkworth

Seagrave

7
12

7A

29

2

30

525

115

To Picton

7A

22

509

Brighton

57

35
115

45

497

5

7
12

Hampton   Orano

464   401   Colborne

Cobourg

12

401

Whitby   419 425 431

417   432 436   Port Hope

C

401 410 412 417

OSHAWA

Bowmanville

599

Pickering

North

Lake
Ontario

Legend

D

400   Major highways used to get to the attractions
found in **Toronto Fun Places**.

Additional information about highways, regional
roads or local streets used to get to the
attractions.

407   Toll Expressway

7   Highway

25   County, Regional Highway

379   Exit number (not necessarily on road signage)

E

Niagara Falls

These maps present a selection of Ontario's roads to help you get
to the attractions mentioned in the guide. Look for map references
in the information box for each entry in **Toronto Fun Places**.

420

4   5   6

Been there?
Add your comments!

Other parents would love to read your comments, anecdotes or tips about the attractions in **Toronto FUN Places**.

Toronto FUN Places' new website is just around the corner. It will allow you to share your outing experiences with the rest of us.

torontofunplaces.com